'Shipman's account of Dubois' story is fascinating; much of it is set in an exotic location, and it is important for the insights it gives into the development of anthropology and the study of human evolution...The ultimate pathos and tragedy of Dubois' story is painfully well portrayed by Shipman'
Douglas Palmer, *Nature*

'[Pat Shipman] is one of the new breed of excellent science journalists who have the knack of making the obscure clear and the complicated plain' Fay Weldon, *Daily Mail*

'In *The Man Who Found the Missing Link*, Pat Shipman provides us with a detailed biography of someone who fits perfectly the image of the modern-day human-fossil hunter... well-documented account of Dubois' life...Shipman succeeds in showing Dubois as a psychologically complicated and deeply conflicted individual, as well as shedding a different light on his work' Jeffrey H. Schwartz, *TLS*

'Shipman's final assessment of Dubois is short, sharp and interesting...it is refreshing to be given Dubois's story in purely contemporary terms...As the sole biography of Dubois it will at least be of value to those who are fascinated by human evolution' Michael Taylor, *New Scientist*

'Shipman skilfully uses contemporary archives to tell the moving story of this driven scientist, his friendships, enmities and achievements' *Sunday Times*

Pat Shipman, an anthropologist at Pennsylvania State University, is the author of *The Wisdom of Bones* (with Alan Walker, which won the 1997 Rhone-Poulenc Science Prize, and *Taking Wing* which won the Phi Beta Kappa Prize in Science. Her other books include *The Evolution of Racism*, *Life History of a Fossil* and *The Neandertals* (with Erik Trinkaus). She has written for *Discover, Natural History* and *New Scientist*.

The Man Who Found the Missing Link

The Extraordinary Life of Eugene Dubois

PAT SHIPMAN

PHOENIX

A PHOENIX PAPERBACK

First published in Great Britain in 2001
by Weidenfeld & Nicolson
This paperback edition published in 2002
by Phoenix,
an imprint of Orion Books Ltd,
Orion House, 5 Upper St Martin's Lane,
London WC2H 9EA

First published in the United States
by Simon & Schuster, New York

A CIP catalogue record for this book
is available from the British Library.

ISBN 0 75381 341 6

Printed in Great Britain by
The Guernsey Press Co. Ltd, Guernsey, C.I.

Contents

Author's Note

After Dubois's death, his daughter Eugenie spent days burning materials that she did not want to go into the Dubois Archives (letter, Eugenie to Brongersma, 21 January 1941). Extensive documentary evidence remains intact, and is cited in the endnotes; sources have been edited lightly for clarity, if at all. Translations from the Dutch and German are almost all the work of my invaluable research assistant, Dr Paul Storm. The endnotes indicate where I have filled in intriguing omissions resulting from Eugenie's actions.

I have followed Dutch conventions for the capitalization of surnames.

For M. E. F. T. D., of course

We live by admiration, love, and hope.

WORDSWORTH

Words copied by Dubois on to the frontispiece of the field notebook he began in September 1893.

CHAPTER I

An Echo of the Past

The letter came by the last post on a sunny afternoon in February 1937. Looking out of the window, Dubois searched for the slightest hint of green buds that he knew would come first to the willow trees at De Bedelaar. It was still very brisk out, not yet warm. The promise of renewal seemed cruel when any real hope of it was still far away.

He was slow to realize what had come, it was so unexpected. His mind was not so quick as it once had been, now that he was in his eightieth year, but he had not become as vague as Anna had. The servant girl brought the post in as usual; he sat down at the desk, put on his glasses, and took up his letter-opener. He carefully inserted the blade into the corner of the flap and slit each envelope neatly. It was his habit to read his letters in order, placing them in a tidy pile before he paused to compose his answers. While he skimmed the letters, Anna prattled on, unaware that anything of significance was happening. Most of the post was ordinary – bills, a few letters of inquiry from colleagues or students. When he picked up the last letter, unsuspecting, he was momentarily confused by the two styles of handwriting on the envelope. The hand that had written his name was crabbed and somehow familiar, but he could not place it immediately; the other, the one that had written the address, was completely unknown to him. When he opened that envelope and saw the tissue-thin paper inside, something stirred in his memory. As soon as he read the salutation, he *knew*, as if he had been expecting this letter for years.

He decided that he could not read it in front of Anna and rang for the servant. 'Take your mistress to sit in the back garden for a while,' he said to her. He waited until they had left and the room was quiet to unfold the translucent, crinkling pages. He didn't need to turn over the last page to look for the signature. There was only one person from whom it could have come, only one person in Kediri, in faraway Java, who would have written to him.

'My dear doctor,' the letter began. He always addressed Dubois so, even when they saw each other daily. How long had it been since Dubois had heard from him? It must have been forty years. Forty years since his friend called him 'my dear doctor'. From anyone else, these words might have been only a courtesy, an acknowledgement of his professorial status and medical degree. From Prentice they were a term of endearment, an evocation of the intimacy and friendship they had shared so long ago.

Kediri, 7 February 1936

An echo of the Past!
'Dost thou recall?'
My dear doctor,

You will hardly expect a letter from *me*! It is long, so very long since last we saw each other.

The philosopher, Renan, in addressing the shade of his departed sister who while in life had accompanied him in his sojourn in the Holy Land, said: –

'Dost thou recall from the bosom of God where thou reposest' –
and I might say now: –

Dost thou recall from the quietness of your peaceful study in the homeland – the days now long, long flown which we passed together in the peaceful atmosphere of dear old Mr. Boyd's Koffeeland Mringin, – the good old man's dwelling Ngrodjo, Willisea the block house he put up for you at Jonojang, my own quiet abode at remote Tempoersarie?

Do you remember the many pleasant meetings we had at Ngrodjo when the old gentleman & I listened with so much interest to your enlightening & informative conversation? Indeed we learned *much* from you, and our minds ever reverted with satisfaction to the many agreeable meetings we three had together. Do you recall our excursion to Trinil the scene of your labours (where the famous *Pithecanthropus erectus* was found), when contrary to your wont you regaled us at dinner in the evening with a *bottle of wine* saying it 'aided digestion'.

Do you remember our bathing next day in the river, our pleasant walk in the afternoon to the station along the country road where a snake swallowed a frog and you at once ran to the rescue forcing the snake to disgorge the frog which, still quite alive, first looked *to the right* & *to the left*, and then lightheartedly plunged into the stream by the roadside? Do you remember the beautiful flowers at the station which we looked at while waiting for the train? One had a delicate light blue tint and you said *that* was well nigh your *favourite* colour!

Do you remember the long walks you & I had through the wide spread coffee gardens at Mringin?...

Do you remember the two corporals of the engineers who looked after your team of convicts, at the excavation work? Their mode of life ever amused you – living like kings at the *beginning* of each month when money was plentiful, and ever on *very* short rations towards the *end* of the month when the money was *all spent*! Through your favourable report they got promoted in time to the rank of Sergeant. Then you photographed them & noticed how they were manoeuvring to bring full into the picture their arm shewing the new sergeant's *stripes!* ... And Mr. Mulder, P. T. Sanvraar, & Mr. Turner, controller, at Toeloeng Agoeng. Do you remember our age – you, Mr. Mulder & I – was 34 years. Ah, yes, the golden days of youth! Perhaps we had our troubles, too, but we had *youth*, *health*, *home*, and *length of days* before us! Dost thou recall?

As oft as I look back, the recollection of that happy time is a green spot in my memory, and will endure as long as life lasts!

Good old Mr. Boyd died in 1902 at Kediri under Van Buren's care from *cancer of the throat*, aged 74, & was buried at Toeloeng Agoeng. We were all present, and the Asst. Resident, Regent & etc & etc attended also. It may be the kind old man smoked too heavily?

While he still lived we often spoke of you after your departure from Java, very, very, often, & always with esteem & affection. Yes, we both loved you, and never could forget you! Like a sun that had come into our orbit you brought us light and happiness – it was just a chance in life never likely to recur, for *when* does it happen that a man of learning ever comes to live on a coffee estate *for any length of time*?

Later on coffee prices fell by 50% and all profit was gone. After Mr. Boyd's death Mringin was sold. Eventually it was given back to government & is now *Bosch Reserve*, no Ngrodjo, Willisea, Tempoersarie are all *forest* now, with not a soul living there any more, and only you & I remain today to muse over the past! Who would have foretold *that*, 40 years ago, when you & I were young!

My own coffee place near Mringin (Djaean was the name) suffered from the crisis in coffee & after 5 years I left it to be manager of the tapioca fabriek – the plantation called Brangganan at Ngadiloewek, 8 miles from Kediri on the high road to Kras – which an intimate friend of mine had taken over. Djaean we kept on, & sold later to rubber tree people in Lombok, who still work the estate. So it is *not* closed like good old Mringin. There I remained about 20 years. Much money was made & eventually my friend sold it for a fancy price & my work there ended. I was then 60 years of age. Since that time I have been interested in other things. I made enough money, but owing to the terrible slump of the past 6 years (malaise) nearly everybody in Java is about bankrupt! Like the majority I have lost cruelly. At least ⅔ of what I had are gone. Today I have to live frugally to manage. I am still dependent on coffee for part of my income & coffee alas is down to f8–9.70 per picol – (formerly f55 to f60), simply ruinous; but there it is, & nothing can be done for no one is to blame – it is just a long spell of *bad times* with all values desperately *low* – no profit possible, and –

> 'What can't be cured
> Must be endured!'

One has just to make the best of things. The depression has been world-wide, & all have suffered. In Java those who had anything, have lost ¼, or ¾, or all…Last year (1935) only ± 16% of the sugar mills of Java worked. The rest were closed & the staff discharged. A terrible loss to the Treasury, & to the country.…

However nothing can be done save to live on quietly in hope, or wait on better days coming soon. So I shall leave this gloomy theme & not depress you with a tale of woe!

I saw in the papers that you retired when 70 years old in 1928. Of course Mr. Boyd & I *fully expected* you to become *Professor*; it could not have been otherwise for your whole mind was ever bent on the acquisition of knowledge. I hope your life at home has been agreeable & satisfactory – that you have but *few* regrets & have experienced *no* heavy losses of whatever sort.

I must now say goodbye. I trust you are in good health. With all good wishes to you & yours,

Believe me as always,

Sincerely yours,

Adam Prentice

P.S. My own health is fairly good. I never had any very serious sickness to speak about – a little dysentery once or twice, years ago; and I have still pleasure in existence. But we are getting up in years & haven't the vigour of former days. I will be 78 years old in a few months. You will be about the same, and I fear not many of our friends remain today!

N.B. This letter will be forwarded to you by Mr. C. Van den Koppel, a state official of Batavia now travelling to Holland via Australia &

America. He will find out your address at present in Holland.
Again goodbye – 'Fare thee well.'

Dubois folded the letter and placed it in his lap for a moment.
When was the last time someone had told him that they loved him?
When was the last time that he had brought light and happiness
into someone's life? He was close to weeping as the memories
flooded his mind.

To know that Prentice remembered, too – that the past echoed
for him, too – was sweet, but the pleasure was tinged with sad
mockery. He and Prentice were no longer the handsome young
men they once had been, when they were together in Java. Thirty-
four years old! What an age: so young, so hopeful, so naive. Now
Dubois felt old and fat and cold and tired.

Apparently Prentice had never made enough money to return to
Europe, as he'd once wished. But maybe he had become used to the
way of living there in Java, with the warmth and the sunshine and
the servants. He'd had a beautiful *nyai*, a sweet and quiet native
mistress, who looked after him in the years after his wife died. Was
the *nyai* still there, aged but graceful, caring for him even now?
Those who came back to Europe weren't able to live like that, with
servants and large houses with fine gardens. Java could never have
been Dubois's home. Even if he had adapted enough to be considered Indische, he would always have been an outsider born in
Europe, and his work was here. He was glad to spend his days at
his beautiful De Bedelaar, his own Dutch corner of nature, near
Haelen.

Dubois catalogued his possessions in his mind, systematically.
He had his house and his garden, his lake, his woods, his birds, his
library, his specimens. He did not have youth, or hope, or even
much ambition any more. He did not have Prentice, or anyone who
loved him. Prentice had been a true companion. They had been
young together, and so sure, so certain – and now, no one else
remembered but Prentice.

He heard the outer door open and close and knew that Anna had
come back into the house. He wasn't ready to see her, or anyone
else. It was impossible, with so much in his heart and on his face,
too, no doubt. How could he explain why the letter had affected
him so? He could not let her read it; it would be a desecration. He
took off his glasses and carefully placed them in his breast pocket;
the letter, too, went there for safekeeping. Then he got up, went into
the hallway, and put on his felt hat and a loose coat, not bothering

to button it properly. He went out of the front door, walking slowly toward the bench by the lake. He often sat there in the afternoons; it was a good time to watch the birds and note which ones had returned from their winter farther south. No one would think it strange of him to sit alone there, thinking, for some hours. He lived a solitary life anyway, even though Anna still visited occasionally.

The earth along the path through the beechwood was springy and soft, from centuries of accumulation of fallen leaves and moss. The ground was no longer hard and bare; with his scientist's eye, he noticed the few brave plants that were poking their green noses up through the leaf litter. But there were not many yet; it was too early, too cold still for them, he thought. Nature always had time; she did not hurry. The woods knew that life returned, that nothing was ever gone for ever. It was a luxury of the young and of plants, to be so certain.

He reached the bench and used his sleeve to wipe away a faint skim of frost, leaving a shadow of moisture and dirt on the wool. He sat down heavily and removed the letter from his pocket. He unfolded it carefully and simply held the pages in his large, soft, liver-spotted hand. His hands had once been so skilled; they dissected the finest anatomical structures, drew close likenesses, and even sculpted a figure once or twice; these hands had painstakingly removed rock matrix from priceless fossil specimens. Once he had been envied for his fine manual skills as well as his brains; too many scholars, even physicians, were ham-handed and clumsy, needing others to carry out the detailed work. Not him, not then. And now his hands lay gnarled and crooked-fingered in his lap, holding a letter from his past.

To have Prentice suddenly reappear like that, sounding as full of joy and life as always, understanding Dubois's mind better than he ever did himself, was almost too much to bear. Dubois could not think clearly. Indeed, he could hardly breathe for the shock of it. It was like having an attack of asthma; his chest was tight. He took off his hat, crumpling the letter a little in the process. With the other hand, he rubbed his bald head, disarranging the fringe of snow-white hair over his ears. It was a gesture he made often when he was thinking now; it gave him an oddly wild look, like a merganser chick: untamed, startled, perhaps about to try to take flight. After a moment, he put his hat back upon his head for warmth, but carelessly, not setting it straight. He was an old man. He was not concerned with his appearance.

He felt the texture of the letter in his hand and sat very still, looking at the lake, watching for coots and ducks. He was remembering those years in Java and that companionship. There had never been another time like it.

Dubois had achieved everything he set out to, even though all about him scoffed. It was in Java that he had become the man who found the missing link: him, Marie Eugène François Thomas Dubois. In Java, he began his true life. The missing link had been the most important thing in his life, as he knew it would be. It was everything.

But now he realized what he had left behind in Java, something he had not known was of such value. For there had never been another friend like Prentice, never another companion of his heart and mind like him. It was improbable, that friendship between the Dutch scientist and the Scottish planter. Their backgrounds were different, their training had little overlap, but they both shared a burning curiosity, physical vigour, and an urgent need to show what they could do when they were freed from the petty restrictions of small-minded European society.

He turned the facts over and over in his mind, musing. He hadn't known then how rarely such a friendship comes into a man's life; he hadn't known it was his only chance. Then, he had only thought about finding the missing link and achieving something important in science. He had known Prentice's companionship was a great comfort, for the Scotsman had understood the significance of what Dubois was doing. They had in common the need to do something grand. How could a man bear to live without trying to make his mark in the world? He should have valued Prentice more highly, though; he had been too preoccupied with fossils. He hadn't known how cold and lonely the years after the discovery would be. The years of his greatest professional accomplishments, the years in which his name and discoveries became famous around the world, had left him living here in solitude. He stared at the thin light playing on the water. Sometimes a ripple caught the sunshine, reflecting the light brightly enough to make his pale-blue eyes water.

The light had been different in Java: hotter, more merciless, sometimes incapacitating. Sometimes there was so much light that he couldn't bear to be outside and then he had sought the shade, any meagre, pale scrap of shade.

In the forests, the light was dappled, filtered through a thousand tones of green and yellow, and the air was tangible with humidity, like a wall that pushed against him at every step. Sometimes it was so quiet that the song of an unseen bird would split the air, like a gunshot, making him jump. And there were those interminable insects, the ones that creaked and popped and whirred like a madman's confounded invention, deep in the forest where no inventors ever strayed, where no houses were built, no books were read, no music was played. There was just forest and green and leaves and more green. The locusts carried on and on and on with their rasping noise until it became embedded in his brain, echoing in the beating of his heart and the rhythm of his breathing. And then they'd stop, leaving a silence so profound that it could wake him out of a sound sleep. Or it might be a pair of long-armed gibbons sitting on a branch bellowing their gurgling, echoing call through the forest, the call that he thought must be heard all the way to Sumatra.

Forest: what a word for it. It was nothing like this beechwood at De Bedelaar. It was another thing entirely, a jungle, a creature in and of itself. In some places, he walked in a cathedral of trees, forest giants that soared above his head blocking out most of the light. In other places, he could not walk because there was so much vegetation. He'd fought his way up the hillsides, sweating and straining up the steep slopes, leading his weary horse, urging the men on, slashing at the alang-alang grass that shredded their clothes. Tiny pieces of alang-alang worked their way into the skin, leaving itching, red rashes that took days to heal.

Every night, the routine had been the same, Dubois saw to that. Stopped, made camp, talked to each man – not just the engineers – to find out if any of them had seen anything useful. Then cleaned the new wounds and blisters and lesions, bandaged the worst of them, hoping no infections would grow tomorrow. Salved the rashes and insect bites, cleaned and treated yesterday's sores that were still swollen and red, dosed those men with fever. While he attended to the health of the coolies, he'd have one of the engineers assess the supplies while the other sent sound men to get water and firewood. The cook, the *kokkie*, would be setting up the kitchen and he'd remind her, every night, to boil the drinking water thoroughly before using it. Then Dubois would have a long drink of water, or juice if there was any, and a bath in his portable canvas tub. While he waited for dinner, he'd make notes and consult the map and plan the next day's survey.

Even with the engineers and all the coolies to do the carrying and the heavy labour, these expeditions weren't easy. Sometimes he'd thought they only made more people to look after, until he remembered what it was like to work on his own, packing and unpacking his horse, making the fire, buying the food and cooking it too. Still, he had had to do so much himself, all the medical work, all the thinking, all the decisions. No one else knew anything about fossils and even the engineers didn't know much useful geology. But they went on, they always went on – looking for caves, looking for fossils, looking for fame and glory, not knowing what he had already found.

Dubois sat on the bench until the sun started to go down and he grew cold. It was time to go back to the large white house and return to the present. He read the letter one more time, and then rose and turned to go. The breeze came up and he realized that his face was wet. Tears had plunged down the deep crevasses beside his nose and mouth, leaving damp streaks in their wake. He couldn't go into the house like that; he couldn't let anyone see. He rummaged impatiently in his pockets for a handkerchief, turning out rocks and feathers, a few small bones, a dried bit of fern. He found only one crumpled, soiled square of linen. Why didn't he have a fresh one? Why … oh, it didn't matter, not really. He wiped his face as best he could. He had last used the handkerchief a few days ago, to wrap up some tiny seedlings he was transplanting, and he wasn't certain that the effect would be all that could be desired. It would have to do. Anna would not notice a few fragments of dried leaf or soil caught in the white stubble on his chin.

She never really looked at him these days anyway. Most of what she saw was long ago and far away. For that night, perhaps, maybe the two of them would be the same. All that mattered to him, too, was long ago and far away now.

And he smiled a little and stumped back toward the house, a solitary, solid man, a little less alone in the last light of the evening than he had been the day before.

CHAPTER 2

The Beginning

In the days that followed, Dubois was held hostage by the events of his past. He was absent-minded, searching for the pattern of his life: how had he come to this in old age? What signs marked his path, for good or ill? Where were the turning points?

The beginning of the story was long ago, perhaps even before his birth, for no scientist was ever born in isolation. Dubois had been born on 28 January 1858, an interesting between-time in science. It had been some six months after the first Neanderthal skeleton was found in Germany and a little more than a year before Charles Darwin published *The Origin of Species* in England. The former had been the first tangible proof of Man's evolution, the latter the theory that placed the find in a context and gave it meaning. He saw now that those momentous events stood like gateposts through which he had passed as he started down the path to his future.

Eijsden, where Dubois had grown up, was a small village in South Limburg, the little piece of Holland that stretches southward between Belgium and Germany. Limburgers, with their strong regional accent, were often caricatured as provincial or countrified by other Hollanders. Many families in Limburg were Catholic, as the Dubois family was, and conservative. Save Maastricht, there were no large cities in Limburg, only the river and the beautiful, peaceful countryside. There Dubois had returned in his old age, seeking that peace and calm at De Bedelaar, where he could rest and reflect.

His father, Jean Joseph Balthasar Dubois, was an apothecary and sometime mayor of the village, one of its most educated men. Mayor Dubois was a large, sturdy man, with a certain portliness and a wide, florid face that bespoke a good life and few anxieties. He was blond and blue-eyed and projected an air of authority, of certainty, and great dignity. He was by nature deliberate, unexcitable, and thorough. The Dubois family consisted of Jean Joseph, his wife, Trinette (née Marie Catherine Floriberta Agnes Roebroeck) and their four children. Trinette was a small, plump,

Eugène Dubois was born in Eijsden and educated in Roermond and
Amsterdam; he lived in The Hague, in Amsterdam and finally at De
Bedelaar near Haelen. He is buried in Venlo.

The family Dubois, photographed in 1886. Front row, seated, left to right: Eugène's sister Marie (Mère Marie-Angélique) and his mother, Trinette. Back row, standing, left to right: Eugène Dubois; his sister Gérardine; his brother, Victor; and his father, Jean Joseph.

good-hearted woman, who suffered from a certain amount of social ambition. They were an important family in Eijsden, highly respectable, and she intended that her children should do them proud. She was well contented with her life, her house – one of the grandest, a good solid brick house that took up a full block of the village – and her handsome family.

The family motto was *Recte et fortiter*, 'Straight and strong', and young Eugène took seriously the charge of maintaining the family honour. Indeed, his usual posture was so square-shouldered and erect that people often remarked on it. Combined with his energy and his habit of looking at people directly with his pale, blue eyes, this posture gave Dubois a striking appearance, even as a youth. Eugène was a strong child, like his father, but much quicker and far more impatient. He would grow up to be a tall, handsome, irrepressibly curious man, with a temperament so restless that it was impossible for him not to think, impossible for him to be still in his mind.

His brother Victor, younger by one year, was a different sort of being entirely. Victor was solid of build, like their father, with their mother's colouring. He was slow in speech and lax in thought, unable to fix his attention on anything difficult for long. Eugène was fair, tall, and relatively slender, all ambition and fire; his brother dark, broad-faced, phlegmatic and slow. The girls, Marie Antoinette and Gérardine Jeanette, repeated the dichotomy. Marie, two years younger than Victor, had Dubois's colouring and was full of curiosity. She and Dubois were natural allies within a family dominated by slower, more cautious people. The baby, Gérardine, was five years younger than Dubois, only seven years old when he went away to school. She had her mother's dark eyes, dark hair, and sallow complexion, like Victor, and much of his complacency, too.

In school, Dubois worked hard. Learning and stimulation of his mind pleased him more than almost anything else, although he was also a powerful swimmer. He was cleverer than the other pupils; he knew this without being told. Still, he did not let himself drift along, for he burned to know more than anyone else, he was hungry for knowledge. He wanted to ensure that he was at the top of his classes; he needed, for his own satisfaction, to be the best. He never believed his quick wits alone would suffice. He saw that many of his classmates were stupid or lazy or both. It made him a little self-satisfied, but his assessment was valid. He was a brilliant student, especially in the natural sciences, and hoped to discover a truth, a fact as solid and important as a brick, one that would last for ever. The name of Eugène Dubois would be known in science.

The first time anything important happened to Dubois was in 1868, when he was only ten years old. There were notices in the newspapers that the renowned German biologist Karl Vogt was coming to Limburg to lecture to the public on evolutionary theory. Dubois's science master had spoken of Karl Vogt and Dubois begged to attend the event, but his father did not think it appropriate fare for a youngster, even a precocious child interested in science. All Dubois could do was follow the reports in the newspaper of the event and its aftermath. They were exciting enough; it was the first step in his awakening.

The morning after the lecture, Dubois waited until his father read and discarded the newspaper and then snatched it up to take into the large walled garden behind the house to look for an account of Vogt's lecture. Dubois's favourite tree was huge and full, its trunk surrounded by a circular bench, and he took the paper there to study it. He often sat there to read his precious books, or to watch and draw the birds, insects, and plants of the garden; it was where he pondered discoveries and theories and dreamt up experiments. Under his tree, he felt protected, *safe*, and invisible, even though his mother could glance through the sheer curtains and see him if she chose. As long as she saw his blond head shining in the sun, his eyes fixed on some text or creature, she did not worry. As he had a certain tendency to sneak off for a swim in the river when he ought to be at church or doing his schoolwork, he needed to be watched.

The newspaper account of Vogt's lecture suggested it was almost a literal call to arms, the beginning of a tremendous battle of beliefs. Vogt's presentation of the evidence for evolutionary theory touched everyone: students, teachers, doctors, lawyers, bankers, newspaper editors, clergymen, educated people from many walks of life, and even some of the poorly educated but inquisitive working class. Dubois knew something of the principles of evolutionary theory – natural selection and survival of the fittest – from his science master and his reading. In his science class, he was captivated by the way these few simple ideas explained the entire natural world and the organisms in it. What he did not know beforehand, for he was still very young and naive, was that Vogt's well-delivered speech could turn the normally placid Dutch audience into combatants in a war over the truth.

What was at stake was a view of the world, of the very essence of reality. Most people in Europe believed life – particularly human life – was largely preordained and the order of society was static. Those with power and wealth guided the workings of the world because they were inherently superior. That inherent superiority, the privilege of the privileged classes, derived from God, who had created all creatures in their appropriate and perfect place. As snakes and worms were meant to crawl on the ground, so the poor were best suited to menial tasks and were most vulnerable to disease and vice. As the birds and higher beasts of the land rose above those lowly, crawling creatures, so, too, were the wealthy more able, more wise, and more suited to rule over other creatures and over other, less able men. Though individual effort and abilities counted for something, dramatic changes in status or life were not to be expected. That was the stuff of fairy tales, in which the prince was mistaken for a pauper or the ash-sweeping stepchild married a prince. In the real world, those who lived proper, God-fearing lives succeeded and those who did not suffered and perished.

But this smug, orderly world was not the one pictured by evolutionists. The watchword of evolution was change, descent with modification over time. Evolution thus re-created the world as a different sort of place, one of process and flux, of struggle marked by the success (in terms of survival or greater numbers of offspring) of those who were most fit. Evolution was revolution, asserting that positions in the grand scheme of things changed, and always would change, because it was in their nature to change. The history of life was dynamic, a story marked by conflict and competition, not by stodgy pre-existing sameness. Many found this a deeply menacing view of the world.

Vogt demonstrated the enormous body of evidence concerning the likenesses between humans and other organisms. He argued that all creatures were constructed to such a detailed, common plan that they must surely have shared one ancestry. The creatures of the present had evolved by imperceptible changes from that common ancestor, as had Man. Humans were a part of the natural world, the animal world, he asserted, not utterly apart from it. He gave special attention to delineating the links between the apes and Man, for if Man was but a cousin to the savage and bestial apes, then all creatures on the earth were united in a common existence, a common descent, and a common history of upheaval, struggle, and change.

For the first time, reading about the reactions to Vogt's lectures, Dubois began to intuit the intimate link between ideas and society, between science and the people. What became evident was that acceptance of a theory was not a matter of science alone but also of human nature and human emotions. The lecture in Limburg provoked a scandalous mêlée. The newspaper accounts were guarded, but it was clear to Dubois's sharp mind that the occasion was much more sensational than anyone dared admit directly.

There, sitting on that bench, *his* bench, poring over the newspaper accounts of Vogt's lecture, Dubois longed to be a man of science, a man to whom everyone listened, a man with great ideas who would discover the truth. He opened the back door of the house to return the newspaper to its place, in case his father wanted to see it again. The sunlight streamed across the black and white marble floor, reaching toward the large front door. The house was lovely and welcoming, with generous-sized rooms with high ceilings and elegant woodwork. In the hallway was a fine, large spiral staircase with a curved wooden banister that led up to the first floor.

It was afternoon now and only a few customers had stepped past the large windows and entered the apothecary's shop through its tall, double wooden door with a clear transom window above. The people in the village approved of Mayor Dubois's house; there was no ostentation about it, save its sheer size and the separate, arched entrance where carriages could drive directly from the street into the courtyard. The public face of the house was austere and unadorned, utterly respectable, and inexpressibly Dutch.

The apothecary was in one of the large front rooms looking out over the street. Dubois entered through a door from the interior of the house, quietly so as not to attract attention. It was a grand and very sombre room, decorated in dark green and deep red and black, with dark woodwork. It was one of his favourite places in the entire house. The lace curtains draping the large front windows strained the light – it was like the pale-green sea passing through a fisherman's net – and ensured a certain privacy for the customers. Important business was conducted in that room: his father listened to ailments and complaints and issued prescriptions to make people well again. In the whole village, only he and the doctor knew the right mixtures and the right doses to heal the sick.

Dubois especially liked the rows and rows of jars and bottles full of medicines that glinted when the sunlight struck them. He stood in front of them, reading the names to himself like an incantation: alum and antimony, ammonia, arsenic, benzoin, bismuth, calomel, camphor, castor oil, carbonate of soda, camomile, compound of chalk, henbane, ipecacuanha, laudanum, lime water, madder, magnesia, morphia, nitre, opium, peppermint, prussic acid, quinine, rhubarb, sal volatile, squill, tincture of iodine, zinc oxide. The names were like a secret scientific spell to banish sickness and evil. Better even than the jars of mysterious mixtures were the shelves full of thick-backed leather books – solid books stuffed full of long words and important facts. The room was like a church or a temple to Dubois. Nothing was hurried in the pharmacy, nothing was urgent; all was known and all would be cured in time. His father was a precise and knowledgeable man.

Standing there quietly, Dubois overheard some of the customers discussing Vogt's lecture. He was amazed to learn that the audience challenged Vogt's ideas, his interpretations, his very evidence, despite his reputation as a great scholar. Dubois had been taught all his life to treat authorities with due respect for their position and wisdom. How could anyone doubt the word and knowledge of such a renowned man of science? Could Vogt have been mistaken, even deceptive? How could the people of Limburg have been so rude, so insulting to a famous visitor?

And yet, apparently, it was true. An elderly lady, Mevrouw Schilling, was waiting with her companion for a tonic. Thin and sharp, she was still quick-tongued and lively despite the age that gave her white hair and a wrinkled face. She had attended Vogt's lecture and described how a member of the audience had stood up to ask a question in German, interrupting Vogt. That small fact puzzled Dubois: what had been the purpose of asking the question in German, not Dutch? Not everyone in the audience spoke German, although many did. Had the speaker been attempting to demonstrate his own high level of education? Or had he been perhaps trying to ensure that the German-speaking Vogt under-stood him perfectly? Whatever the point of the choice of language, the query itself struck Dubois as very peculiar.

'What the man said was this,' repeated Mevrouw Schilling, now curling her mouth oddly to mimic a pedantic expression and tone of voice: ' "Dr. Vogt, tell me this: do apes have churches? Do they have libraries?" ' She cocked her head in a questioning attitude.

The boy wondered what the man had meant by that. Was build-ing churches and libraries, then, the test of humanness? Where was the logic in that? He did not want to eavesdrop, which was rude, but he thought it acceptable since Mevrouw Schilling's bell-like tones could be heard throughout the pharmacy.

'After the questions,' she declared, 'I heard some of the students laugh. Then one of them said that neither the illiterate peasants of Russia nor the savages of darkest Africa have libraries or churches, yet they are still human. Well, they may be human, I suppose, but they are certainly benighted and unenlightened, that's all I have to say!' She shook her head so firmly that some of her silver locks, until now confined to an orderly and well-behaved bun at the nape of her neck, quivered and fell free.

'They didn't say such a thing!' exclaimed her companion. Dubois vaguely recognized her; she was, he thought, a married daughter, but he could not recall her name. She was a middle-aged, maternal woman. Her buxom figure was encased in a dark brown bombazine dress with matching cape that rustled majestically as she walked. She was the personification of conservative rectitude, from the fine leather on her buttoned shoes to the discreet feather in her modest hat.

'They did. But what did he mean?' Mevrouw Schilling persisted, her voice growing querulous with confusion. 'I don't understand these clever young people any more. I mean, of course apes don't have libraries or churches. That is an utterly ridiculous idea. So what does it all have to do with this new theory everyone is so angry about?'

'I think, my dear,' her daughter said comfortingly, her ample bosom jiggling slightly as she patted her mother's arm, 'the students thought that a lack of civilized institutions did not disqualify apes from being closely related to Man.'

'No!' replied the other, snorting slightly and peering through her glasses. She tapped the tip of her furled parasol in indignation. 'Related to apes? Is that what that dreadful German was speaking of? Apes? I most certainly am not related to one. But I don't see what a library has to do with it.' They collected the prescription, nodded goodbye to the apothecary and his well-brought-up young son, and swept out into the street, tut-tutting a staccato of disapproval as they went.

Dubois stood dumbfounded, pondering the extraordinary story he had overheard. 'Eugène,' his father called to him, 'don't just stand there staring into space. If you have no schoolwork to do, then come here and help me make up prescriptions. Mijnheer Buikstra will call later for his usual, and I need to make up some more stomach tablets and some headache powders. Bring over the magnesia, that's it, the large bottle, and then I need the camomile.' The rest of the afternoon, Dubois fetched and carried and wrapped for his father, all the while listening to the gossip about the lecture.

Most of the townspeople who came into the pharmacy that day were shocked by the content of the lecture and thought the students had behaved abominably. There was talk of hooting, like ape calls, and a rhythmical stamping of feet like the beat of primitive tom-toms in the jungle. Dubois could hardly credit such behaviour in a public lecture; who would have dared? He for one would have been soundly spanked and sent to bed without supper for such rudeness, he had no doubt.

'I don't know about you, Mayor,' confided Mijnheer De Pauly, the owner of one of the more prosperous shops in town, 'but I had to laugh when all of the noise started up and the ladies scurried out of the lecture hall like so many hens in a thunderstorm, leaving the men to argue and bluster.'

'I'm afraid I was not there,' replied Dubois's father politely, 'though my boy here is very interested in science.'

'Just as well,' agreed De Pauly, nodding sagely. He was a tall man whose well-cut grey frock coat announced the success of his business endeavours. 'You don't want to let him get mixed up with such things while he is still so young.'

Dubois himself was agape at what he had overheard. If the ladies had all run out, had the meeting been out of control, a riot? Dubois tried to imagine the scene. How could these ideas have provoked such a response? And wouldn't he, too, have laughed to see all the ladies bustling out, offended, and the gentlemen pointing their fingers at each other and raising their voices, crowing for supremacy?

'It was a shocking event, just shocking,' De Pauly went on. 'I don't know which was worse: the vehemence of some people's views or the general unwillingness to listen and evaluate evidence calmly. I had no idea so many of the town leaders were such old ladies that they are frightened of a new theory. Well, I must thank you for these pills, Mayor,' De Pauly said, taking the parcel and handing over payment. 'I'm sure they'll do the trick. Good day to you! Good day to you, young Eugène.'

Dubois bobbed his head politely to the man as he left. Afterward, he thought admiringly that a very powerful truth must lie within those deceptively simple ideas of Darwin's. Evolution was everything new, modern, and disturbing. It would change the old order and Dubois, impatient to grow up, would like that. He could hardly wait for his chance to change things in life, to right the wrongs, to improve upon the old ways. He did not yet know it, but part of the attraction he felt to evolutionary theory resulted from its ability to upset the old order. The other part was the sheer scientific power of the theory. He was drawn to it with an almost religious fervour.

Pondering the exciting events at Vogt's lecture, Dubois concluded that some people simply didn't want to learn about new ideas. They were too fixed in their thinking, too old, too boring. He must never make that mistake. He must remember always to listen to new ideas.

Jean Joseph approved of Dubois's growing interest in science, for he had always planned that his eldest son would become an apothecary, like him. As Dubois's twelfth birthday approached, the boy asked his father to send him to the State HBS, the technical high school, at Roermond. It was an unconventional choice of school, and Jean Joseph was deeply conventional, but he knew that the facilities for studying chemistry, zoology, mineralogy and botany at the HBS were like those of a small university, with laboratories full of the best equipment and superb teachers. The danger was that such teachers would teach his son ideas as well as facts, including that new evolutionary theory.

The elder Dubois did not consent immediately but took the matter into consideration. What fostered his son's cause was that some of the other Catholic families in Eijsden heard about the idea almost immediately. The furore caused by Vogt's lecture had not been forgotten, though it had been two years earlier, and the old biddies of the village were horrified that Jean Joseph considered sending his son to such a place. 'He'll lose his religion,' they predicted with conviction as they gossiped in the shops and on street corners. 'They'll teach him all those anti-Christian theories, and soon he'll believe them. He's a nice boy, a smart boy, but the mayor will be sorry if he sends his son to such a place!' In the end, they clucked and fussed so tiresomely that Jean Joseph decided to send Eugène to the HBS in part to defy them.

Eugène remained impeccably polite and studious, but attending the HBS accelerated the process of his breaking free of convention. By the end of his first year at Roermond, when he was thirteen, he was starting to question the teachings of the Church. He did not know how to focus this uneasiness, but he began to doubt everything, almost reflexively.

Much later he articulated these feelings. 'I always knew that if I could succeed in concentrating my thoughts well on a problem, then I will live my true life. Then I am absorbed by the problem. To achieve great things, one must cast aside the unimportant and the sentimental, one must follow truth.' And so I have, he thought, and so I have.

Dubois had no intention of becoming an apothecary like his father. He wanted to study the natural sciences and evolution, which meant attending medical school. Roermond was a good place to lay the foundation for such studies. It was also the crèche that nurtured evolutionary ideas and independent thinking. His new science master recognized the keenness of Dubois's mind and suggested he read some of the great books they discussed in class: Darwin's *Origin of Species*, his new book, *Descent of Man*, Huxley's *Man's Place in Nature*, and Haeckel's masterful *History of Creation*. Darwin's work was where it all began, where evolutionary theory was laid out for the first time, but Huxley's book was the more convincing. It was simple, short, full of facts, and impossible to refute; for anyone who read it, there could be no further doubt that man was simply a modified ape. Huxley persuaded that man differed less in his anatomy from the chimpanzee or the gorilla than those man-like apes did from the lowest apes.

Haeckel's book was the second great revelation of Dubois's young life. His prose was easier for the youngster to understand than the others'. Haeckel's style was sweeping, vivid, inspiring. Early in the book, Eugène came across a passage that left him gasping. It was as if Haeckel had plucked the half-formed thoughts from Dubois's own mind and crystallized them into written words.

As a consequence of the Theory of Descent or Transmutation, we are now in a position to establish scientifically the groundwork of a *non-miraculous history of the development of the human race* ... If any person feels the necessity of conceiving the coming into existence of this matter as the work of a supernatural creative power, of the creative force of something outside of matter, we have nothing to say against it. But we must remark that thereby not even the smallest advantage is gained for a scientific knowledge of nature. Such a conception of an immaterial force, which at first creates matter, is an article of faith which has nothing whatever to do with human science. *Where faith commences, science ends.*

Reading Haeckel's words was for Dubois like emerging from the dark confines of the chrysalis. He could feel his creeping wormlike self first exposed and then transformed by the light of knowledge. Religion was finished for Dubois now. Haeckel's words had burst the woolly cocoon of confused, everyday thought, revealing a theory of descent with modification that shone with truth.

Dubois made no conscious choice; it was an irresistible metamorphosis whose time had come. Belief without proof was blind faith, *blind* faith. It crippled the mind and the judgement, surely a sin greater than any forbidden in the Bible. From that moment on, Dubois adopted as his personal credo the need to question, to think things through for himself. He could accept nothing simply on the grounds of dutiful obedience; he read Haeckel's words and they resonated within his mind. He became an evolutionist, as indelibly as one who took holy orders became a priest. Though his mind was sharp, Dubois's tongue was not. He was still young, dependent, untried. Until he was grown, he would not tell anyone how he felt about religion, nor would he share his sense of revelation; it was better not to.

CHAPTER 3

The Game

At Roermond, Dubois invented a game in his mind, for he did not think any of his schoolfellows would play. It was a simple game. First, he asked himself, 'What is the most important thing yet to be discovered? What is the best proof of evolution? Where can the biggest contribution be made?' Then he tried to formulate an answer, carefully weighing the pros and cons of different discoveries, looking for the one he should devote his life to. He was determined to be a part of this revolution, for it was the greatest movement of his day. Science would change the world as surely as evolution changed bodies.

Some days Dubois followed Vogt in thinking that embryology would hold the most crucial answers. If he truly understood development, if he could find out the reason that a dog embryo one day stopped looking like a chicken embryo and became a dog, surely that information would reveal a great deal about the evolutionary relationships among living organisms. That would show *how* evolution proceeded, step by step. Other days he favoured Huxley's work, showing how feature after feature linked Man to apes and then to monkeys, demonstrating the unity of the living primates. This, too, was a strong, encyclopedic approach to the problem of evolution.

But sometimes he had a rather novel thought, one not much favoured by the men of science of the day. His inspiration came from Haeckel's *History of Creation*, which he read over and over, it was so full of wisdom. The pages were almost falling out of their binding from use. Haeckel outlined the general course of evolution clearly, tracing Man's descent by stages from the lowest life forms, through the one-celled protozoans to the worms, fishes, and lizards, and up through mammals. Like Huxley, he saw the closest group to Man as the Primates: the lemurs, monkeys, and apes. And Haeckel maintained that there was a link, a link as yet unknown, between apes and Man. He described this missing link in words that Dubois nearly memorized:

The Ape-like men, or Pithecanthropi, very probably existed towards the end of the Tertiary period. They originated out of the Man-like Apes, or Anthropoides, by becoming completely habituated to an upright walk...Although these Ape-like Men must...have been much more akin to real Men than the Man-like Apes could have been, yet they did not possess the real and chief characteristic of Man, namely, the articulate human language or words, the corresponding development of a higher consciousness, and the formation of ideas...

And:

Those processes of development which led to the origin of the most Ape-like Men out of the most Man-like Apes must be looked for in the two adaptational changes which, above all others, contributed to the making of Man, namely *upright walk* and *articulate speech*. The two *physiological* functions necessarily originated together with two corresponding *morphological* transmutations, with which they stand in closest correlation, namely, the differentiation of the two pairs of limbs and the differentiation of the larynx.

Haeckel even hypothesized that the evolution of the upright walk long preceded the evolution of speech. It was a theory that could be tested, Dubois realized, if only the fossils of that missing link, the *Pithecanthropus*, could be found. Finding the missing link would be like seeing the results of a brilliant experiment, only the experiment was conducted not by himself but by the forces of natural selection and survival of the fittest, in the distant past. Such a fossil would surely prove the evolution of man, in a tangible way. Finding it would be the greatest scientific discovery ever.

He did not know where to find such a fossil, or how. These points were yet of no concern. What matters was that he became convinced he was the one who would find the missing link. He was deaf to other arguments, unimpressed by other scientific questions. His eardrums vibrated to only one tune, the song of the problem he had to conquer: the missing link, the missing link, the missing link. In his years at Roermond, Dubois's ambition coalesced out of the intellectual milieu like a crystal precipitating out of solution. Of his fellow students, Dubois was the most passionate, the most committed to science. He was the one who never swerved from his own road, who never deviated from his conviction. For him, learning about evolution was much more interesting than any other part of natural science. He was not drawn by physics or chemistry, important though they might be. Medicine or an apothecary career, for example – simply doling out remedies to the sick – seemed mundane. It was learning that had already been discovered; it presented no challenge except that of acquiring competency. In evolution, he could make new knowledge. Evolution revealed how the universe was organized, how life itself was formed. Evolution promised someday to divulge the secrets of how man became human. Here was the strength of a unifying principle for all of the natural sciences and for Dubois's life.

As the old ladies of Eijsden had predicted, Dubois's education at the HBS transformed him. He was no longer a bright boy who was interested in the sciences; he was a dedicated evolutionist. And here he parted company with his father intellectually. He could not follow in his father's footsteps; he had not the character for it. He was incapable of following anyone's path but his own. He wished to please his father – earning his father's praise was one of Dubois's fondest desires – but he could not strive for love and approval on his father's terms. He had grown up; he was now himself, inflexibly, stubbornly, and thoroughly himself. He could not be his father's son any longer.

Before he went home for the Christmas holidays in his last year at the HBS, Dubois worried how to explain to his father that he wanted to attend medical school, not become an apothecary. He knew his father had performed invaluable service as an apothecary, and he honoured that, but he sought something more. He hoped, knowing it was probably in vain, that his father would be proud of him for choosing his own path. Anyway, Dubois had no choice. He could not do something so small as becoming an apothecary and a mayor like his father. It was too confining. He was meant for bigger things.

The planned confrontation with his father was forestalled by unexpected news that awaited him at Eijsden. Marie – his favourite sister, his special ally in the family – had decided to enter a convent. She would become a nun and devote her life to God. His parents were very pleased with Marie's decision, so proud of her that they could not wait to spread the news to all their acquaintances.

It was a tragedy. Marie? The one who giggled and played pranks with him? The one who could make him laugh in the midst of a solemn occasion just by the look in her eyes? A nun? Dubois felt almost physically ill at the news. Unbeknownst to him, Marie had already spent some weeks with the Ursuline Sisters, to make certain of her choice. Those who would be novices had to learn difficult lessons of obedience, silence, propriety, and Marie had fared well. She was learning to walk, not run, to speak softly when spoken to and to hold her tongue otherwise, to keep her blue eyes downcast and her lively opinions to herself

Marie was making a terrible, terrible mistake, Dubois thought. Oh please, let her give this up. There was no truth in religion, she would waste her precious life on custom and propriety! He could not voice these thoughts to Marie lest he wounded her; he knew she was a believer. He was as gentle as he could manage to be with her.

'Marie, you cannot do this,' he pleaded with her earnestly once they were alone. 'You can't join the convent. Please. You don't have to give up your life to be a good Catholic; there are other ways.'

'Ja, Eugène,' she replied serenely, 'ja, I can join. The Mother Superior has already told me I will be accepted as a novice after Christmas if it is still my wish. And it will be.' She smiled a little, quietly, as befitted a nun.

He looked at her sadly. He did not like the new way she had restrained her hair instead of letting the curls dangle over her shoulder. 'But Marie,' Dubois agonized, his face contorted, 'it is the end of everything. You cannot be yourself, you cannot be clever or go to school, you cannot even marry and have children!' He tried every argument he could think of that would hold weight with her, withholding the one that truly mattered: religion was false, was unproven, unprovable.

'I know,' she replied gently, looking up at her dear brother in his torment. She took his hand, as she had done so often when she was a little girl and needed his protection or guidance. 'I know. And I shall have to leave you and my home, too. But I will be the bride of Christ, Eugène. You cannot imagine the peace of the convent. It is so holy and so calm. I shall be very happy there.'

'Calm?' Dubois repeated miserably. 'You would give everything up for calm?' He turned his face away for fear she would see the thoughts in his mind.

'Listen, Eugène. Look at me. I have already chosen the name I will take upon my ordination, I think. How would you feel about Mère Marie-Angélique?'

'Are you then to be someone else?' Dubois asked softly.

'I must be. Entering the convent will make me a new person.'

He hated the very idea of becoming someone else. In his life, he had struggled so hard to become who he was. 'They are all so solemn and so holy, those nuns. How can you bear it? Don't you ever want to laugh and shout and disrupt the service?'

'No...' Marie started to say, and then became more honest. 'Well, maybe ja, a little,' she giggled, 'sometimes. But nuns can still laugh. God welcomes laughter and joy. Obedience and joy balance each other out, you know.'

'Obedience,' repeated Dubois dully. To him the word sounded like a sentence of death. 'Obedience. I do not think it is a virtue. What about thinking for yourself, finding your own way?'

'That is a man's road, Eugène,' Marie pointed out. 'You may do it, I believe you will do it. But it is not a way for me. I could never do it. My road leads to the convent, with God's will.'

There was no changing her mind. Dubois's heart ached at the loss of his cherished sister. She was gone for ever, his Marie Antoinette Hélène Dubois, and Mère Marie-Angélique, who would take her place, could never be his friend. She would be devoted to the Church, and he was bound over to Truth and Science.

CHAPTER 4

Ambition

In 1877, at the age of nineteen, Dubois left Roermond to study medicine at the University of Amsterdam. Amsterdam was a large city, a part of the world arena in science, art, and music. The buildings were old and grey, dignified, some very beautiful and ornate. He had never seen such grand architecture before. Some of the lecture halls where he listened to his professors were magnificent, oak-panelled chambers with black horsehair chairs, elaborately carved and decorated ceilings, and steeply stepped floors, so that every student could see the professor's actions and demonstrations clearly. True, he could not study under Darwin or Huxley or Haeckel, but his professors were renowned leaders of science. There was J. D. van der Waals, who was unravelling the intricate laws of physics and motion; the botanist and evolutionist Hugo De Vries, studying inheritance of traits in plants; Thomas Place, the brilliant physiologist; and the renowned anatomist Max Fürbringer, who had trained in Jena in Germany under Ernst Haeckel himself.

Under their tutelage, Dubois's mind began to blossom. By the end of the first year – a year filled with long days and nights of reading and study – Dubois felt he had found his place in life. His brilliance was soon widely recognized, for he came top of every class. His dissections were the finest, his drawings the most detailed and meticulous, and his experiments seemed always to work. His fellows sometimes teased him about his 'golden hands' and his flawless memory, but it was affectionate teasing, based on admiration. They did not often tease him about being a provincial Limburger, for he was soon as cosmopolitan as any of them.

To Dubois's irritation, in the second year he was followed by his easygoing younger brother, Victor. And for Victor there would be no long nights of study, no hours bent over a microscope, no dissections that required every ounce of skill and dexterity he could muster. As ever, Victor got by with a minimum of work and a maximum of personal charm. The family assumed they would share rooms – of course they would, they were brothers – but it was not a happy arrangement. As he matured, Dubois walked more and more along an idiosyncratic path of his own devising. He made a point of following his own convictions; he openly flouted beliefs or behaviours he deemed worthless. His intent was to achieve a certain transparency, to live his convictions throughout his entire character and soul. He had no respect for those who put on conventional beliefs like a fashionable coat, to be removed and replaced when another style came along.

By the time his younger brother arrived in Amsterdam, Dubois had abandoned all the trappings of Catholicism. He no longer attended mass on Sundays or confession during the week; he neither crossed himself nor muttered Hail Marys at appropriate moments; he systematically excised all habits of observance from his behaviour. Victor, less bold and lacking firm convictions in any case, was annoyed and embarrassed by his elder brother's open rejection of religion, as perhaps Dubois intended him to be. Living in such close proximity, the contrasts between them rubbed the two brothers' sensibilities raw. Each became more fixed in his ways, less flexible, less tolerant of the other's choices.

The final conflagration started to smoulder when Victor, goaded by his brother's behaviour, accused Dubois of failing to be a good Catholic. 'You bring shame on our family,' Victor chastised him. 'We have been good Catholics for more than three hundred years and you decide the faith is no longer enough for you! You only think of yourself, never of your effect on others.'

These were bitter words to a man like Dubois. Worse yet, Victor spoke to Dubois like a parent, when he was merely the younger brother. Stung by his brother's scolding, Dubois disparaged his brother's petty orthodoxy. 'Better to be a thinking agnostic,' he replied bitterly, using the term coined by Huxley, 'better to be one who searches his conscience and admits he does not know about God and religion, than to be a submissive Catholic. You never think about anything, not God, not your family, not even yourself. You just do what is expected. I would not be like you.'

'Nor I you!' came the angry reply.

After that, they avoided each other for some weeks. In time, there came a hesitant truce, accompanied by tentative kindnesses or small shows of consideration on both their parts. Victor obtained some especially nice tea, and shared it with Dubois. Dubois brought home a newspaper with an article in it his brother might find interesting. Slowly, they began to take meals together again. They did not discuss their differences, but nor did they fire glances of anger and irritation at each other every time they crossed paths.

At the end of a difficult exam week, they planned to go out to dinner together, a rare occurrence, and it was perhaps in both brothers' minds to seal the peace with the other. Academic pressures had shortened their tempers but had also distracted them from their differences; they were united for once in striving to do their best. They chose a favourite restaurant, a place popular with students for its filling and inexpensive meals. But the fragile reconciliation was threatened almost immediately. As soon as they ordered, the problem was painfully apparent. It was Friday, and Dubois requested beef while Victor, the observant Catholic, asked for haddock.

Every bite of gravy-laden beef that Dubois savoured seemed a personal affront to Victor, who dutifully swallowed his dry and overcooked fish. Victor was uncharacteristically enraged. Dubois was himself so annoyed with Victor's mindless adherence to custom that he flaunted his enjoyment of the excellent beef. What began as a friendly evening deteriorated into silent hostility. Surrounded by a cheerful crowd of their fellow students, exuberant at their temporary release from academic obligations, the brothers sat sullenly and ate without speaking to each other.

When they attained the privacy of their rooms, Victor exploded. 'How can you embarrass me in public like that? Why is it you must insult God by eating meat on Fridays? Everyone knows we are Catholics. What do you suppose they think?' He was so angry that he did not dare to look at his infuriating brother, who busied himself hanging up their coats and hats.

'Everyone does *not* know we are Catholics,' retorted Dubois hotly, turning from the hall stand. He wondered how Victor could be so stupid. 'Or if they do, they are sadly mistaken, for I am no longer a Catholic.'

Victor stopped pacing and caught his breath audibly, stunned by such blasphemy. Like Victor, Dubois had been born, christened, and confirmed a Catholic. Members of the Dubois family had always been Catholics, back to their oldest known relative, Bastin de Try, in 1500. Each brother had pledged himself to God at confirmation and Victor was unable to imagine breaking such a promise – not, of course, that he had any intention of abandoning the pleasures of life, not like Marie, but still ... Victor asked himself if his brother could actually mean to refute the faith that had been part of their identities since birth. He opened his mouth to speak, but Dubois's next words came first. They were strong and clear, and cut through Victor's confusion like a scalpel peeling back flesh in the anatomy laboratory.

'I am no longer a Catholic,' Dubois repeated. 'I am a scientist.' He stood firm and still and upright, looking straight at his brother, daring him to object.

Even Victor could not mistake Dubois's meaning any longer. Dubois had cast aside the religion that Victor had always accepted and followed, somewhat passively to be sure, but it was as much a part of him as breathing. Dubois had examined one of the implicit tenets of Victor's existence and found it wanting. Victor had never examined anything critically; it was too much trouble to think so hard. Victor was stunned into silence. Finally, he turned to his brother, his elder brother, and begged for compromise. 'Can't you just soften a little for appearances' sake?' pleaded Victor, reaching out a hand but not quite daring to touch his brother's arm. 'Just in public? Why must you make such an issue of your scientific beliefs? Why must you reject everything else and throw it in my face?' There was no answer from Dubois, who looked back at him with a calm and open gaze. Victor dropped his hand, rejected.

Then he continued, 'Think of Marie, our sister.' Dubois closed his eyes in pain. Victor could never have comprehended that Marie's taking the veil was a tragic and misguided waste of life in Dubois's eyes. Victor thought it a fine thing, a heroic move. 'Would it be so terrible for you to eat fish on Fridays as a sign of respect for her beliefs, whatever you think?'

'Oh, no,' replied Dubois, very quietly, as if he was explaining the obvious to a child. 'I can eat fish on Fridays. I *shall* eat fish on Fridays. But I shall do it because fish is what I wish to eat – not because it is what the Pope wants me to eat. I think for myself.'

And that was the end of it. After such blasphemy and disrespect from Dubois, after such unconsidered and blind obedience from Victor, there was no retreat from their entrenched positions. No compromise was possible; indeed, no real contact between them was possible any longer. Within a few days, the brothers made other living arrangements. To be fair, few would have found Dubois an easy man to live with; wisely, he took rooms on his own.

Now that he could organize things to suit only himself, Dubois's days were much the same. He arose early, at three or four in the morning, to study. He took only a cup of tea, which he brewed up himself, and some toast browned over the gas ring, before starting. At seven, he stopped for an egg and more tea. Lectures and demonstrations began at nine; he never missed one. He was always up to date with his reading and he completed his assignments on time; it was a point of pride with Dubois. Afterwards, he ate a simple meal prepared by his landlady and then studied again, putting in perhaps fourteen hours of work a day. Between three a.m. and five p.m., he would not tolerate frivolity or interruptions from others. His friends and colleagues soon learned not to disturb him during the day, for he did not want to come out to sit in a café, gossiping and drinking coffee. He never had time to discuss the day's news or the latest music, or to make plans for an outing to see the new production at the theatre. He had things to learn: facts, principles, theories. He was ambitious, serious, and terribly clever.

In the evening, he reverted to being a young man like any other. At the stroke of five, he called a halt to his work and began to enjoy his social life. A different man emerged from Dubois's rooms than the quiet, studious one who awoke so early to get ahead in his work. This Dubois was young and handsome and fond of the company of pretty women. He had a mellow baritone voice and a light, athletic step on the dance floor. The ladies admired his strong physique and blond, blue-eyed good looks. Dubois enjoyed his effect on the young ladies of Amsterdam, and he sensed the approval of their parents. Being a most eligible bachelor with an oft-predicted brilliant future ahead of him was a most pleasant circumstance. He attended concerts and parties; at the weekends he indulged in elaborate Sunday afternoon teas, or picnics when the weather was fair. He rarely lacked for feminine attention. His evenings were as unserious and sociable as his days were intense and solitary.

Some of his fellow students were surprised to see the charming side of his nature; others took it simply as the balance to his focused ambition and determination. Without self-discipline, Dubois knew he might have been as aimlessly happy as his brother. But Victor would never come up with a startling new idea or a clever new approach. Victor was content to drift passively, passing exams but not excelling, learning facts but not too many. His laxity filled Dubois with a kind of horror for the easy road that led to naught of significance.

In 1881, Dubois was offered the assistantship in anatomy under

Dr Fürbringer, a coveted position. He accepted with delight. The very day after Dubois accepted Fürbringer's position, Thomas Place offered him an assistantship in physiology. No one in memory had ever been offered two such positions at the University of Amsterdam, Dubois proudly wrote to his parents. This was not empty bragging; it was true.

Ironically, the second offer posed an unparalleled problem. Had the offers come simultaneously, Dubois would have preferred to take up Place's assistantship, as both the man and the field seemed more naturally congenial to him than Fürbringer and anatomy. But Dubois had accepted Fürbringer's position promptly; he could not now withdraw without dishonour. Mild regret tinged Dubois's real enthusiasm for anatomy as he entered cheerfully into his new position with Fürbringer. He did not foresee the bitter struggles that would develop between them over the ownership of ideas and research. He could not have imagined that a man of Fürbringer's reputation would want to take credit for his junior's work. Why would he think such a thing? And yet, in a few years' time, Dubois would come to feel that Fürbringer was doing just that. Dubois became hypersensitive, like a once-scalded hand that could not bear the slightest heat. In time, his sense of injustice forced him to leave his academic career. Later he could see the irony of his situation, for the conflict with Fürbringer would be the engine that propelled Dubois into greatness. Dubois even wondered if the accident of timing that led him to work with Fürbringer was preordained. Why had Fürbringer found him first, Place second? Was he meant to work with Fürbringer, so he would be driven out of Amsterdam? Had he been born to find the missing link?

These were disconcertingly mystical questions for one so thoroughly scientific, yet he could not quiet them. They nagged at him, begging for explanation, for rational cause and effect. But they had no answers. Events followed the course they took for reasons that could not be discerned scientifically. When he thought on it, Dubois was amused that there appeared to be such a strong direction to his life: his birth at the right time; his schooling in Roermond, which had exposed him to the thinking of Darwin, Huxley, Haeckel, and Vogt; his medical training at Amsterdam, where he had learnt so much and then been turned away from normal academic life, toward the missing link. He contented himself with the thought that trends and patterns were always more visible in retrospect than in prospect.

As he started his new job, Dubois was too busy developing his talents as an anatomist to be introspective or to worry about the distant future. In 1884, he qualified as a physician; his promotion to prosector in anatomy followed in the same year with breathtaking rapidity. He was in charge not only of the human anatomy course for medical students at Amsterdam but also of another course for the State School of Applied Art. He conceived a programme of research on the embryological formation and development of the larynx, not forgetting Haeckel's words about the importance of the origin of articulate speech. If be became the man who understood the larynx, he would be the man with something to say about the evolution of human speech.

CHAPTER 5

Lightning Rod

For some time, Dubois called on Mia Cuypers. Their acquaintance began with Dubois's friendship with her father, Petrus, Holland's leading architect and a well-known man. His beautiful design for the new Rijksmuseum, begun in 1877 and nearing completion, was already being hailed as a brilliant example of Gothic Revival architecture. It represented a new way of thinking about buildings, about public spaces. Cuypers was the centre of an informal circle of Catholic intellectuals and artists in Amsterdam, who welcomed Dubois into their fellowship. The Cuyperses were also an 'Indies family', one with many members who had lived and worked in the Dutch East Indies. Dubois could not keep track of all of the Cuyperses' Indies connections. There seemed to be myriad photographs of brothers and uncles posed under potted palms or lounging in rattan chairs, of aunts and cousins sitting in smart carriages under huge tropical trees. Perhaps this collective experience in the colonies made the Cuyperses a little unconventional in their thinking and behaviour; perhaps the cause was simple creativity. At any rate, their home was furnished with exotic oriental carpets, and the watercolours featured sharp-edged volcanoes and placid rice paddies. Instead of a good Paisley shawl, they had an intricate, floral-patterned fabric, woven with threads of gold, draped over the piano; they call it *songket* cloth. The Cuyperses enjoyed people from an unusual range of backgrounds. In their company, the talk was of ideas and music, principles of art and design, trends and principles to guide the future. Dubois was captivated by it all.

As Dubois became a more regular caller, and Mia a more constant participant in his visits, the Cuyperses began to fancy Dubois as a possible son-in-law. Subtly, they made it known to him that the thought pleased them. He was an eminently suitable young man, outspoken yet thoughtful, and they knew their daughter to be neither dependably demure nor consistently sensible. She was far too opinionated and much too intelligent for most people's taste. Her parents, perhaps unwisely, had allowed her to develop some rather modern ideas and had educated her more than was common for a young woman of her class. She even looked unusual, being taller and more athletic than most young women, and cared less about fashions and hairdos than about theories and ideas. She had a disarmingly direct gaze in her large brown eyes and, upon occasion, a sharp tongue for the pompous, the self-important, or the hypocritical. She was not fashionably submissive, nor did she wish to be. In fact, she was even regarded as unwomanly by some. Others predicted that a good, solid husband and a few children were just what Mia needed to settle her down and drive all those silly ideas from her head.

Dubois fulfilled the hypothetical requirements for Mia's prospective husband nicely. He came from a respectable Catholic family, even if he did not seem terribly observant, and he was intelligent enough to suit Mia well, or so her parents thought. Dubois was flattered by the Cuyperses' tacit approval and the sparkling company in their home, and he rather liked their spirited daughter. She was neither tediously unoriginal nor brainless, as were many of the young ladies of his acquaintance. Her opinions were usually backed by knowledge and thought.

'Doctor, do you think,' she challenged him on one occasion, 'that women ought to take up medicine?' Her dark straight brows emphasized her eyes, not unflatteringly.

'But my dear,' Dubois replied, 'there are already many women who work as nurses. And some of the best midwives I have ever known are female; they have a good touch with their patients, tremendous fortitude, good skills. Of course women are highly suitable for such work! There can be no doubt about it.'

'No, no, you misunderstand me, Doctor. What I mean is, should women be admitted into medical practice as physicians? Ought they to attend medical school, working alongside the men?' Mia explained earnestly. 'Don't you think they might have an advantage in treating female patients, a greater ease of communication, perhaps, about ladies' troubles? And examinations, you know, physical examinations of patients. Surely this is a delicate matter.'

Startled, Dubois answered without thinking carefully first. 'You have a point there, Miss Cuypers,' he conceded. 'Not that any medical man would overstep the bounds of … of … propriety with his female patients, of course not. We are trained professionals. But it might indeed be easier for a woman to divulge … um … intimate problems to another woman.

'As for becoming physicians, I am not sure. You know, the training in medical school is not for the fainthearted. Some of the things students are exposed to are not very salubrious, rather shocking even, and difficult to bear. Dissections of cadavers, some of the terrible diseases of the poor and ignorant... The squalor in which some patients live is dreadful, most unsuitable for the finer sex. I'm really not sure a woman should be confronted with such things.'

'Oh, Doctor.' Mia laughed. 'Who do you think has birthed all the babies since time immemorial? Who do you think has dressed the soldiers' wounds in battle, boiled the lice off their clothes, wiped up the messes in the sickrooms, and changed the bloody sheets? Have you not heard of Florence Nightingale in England and the school she founded to train nurses? She worked on the battlefield in the Crimea, in the thick of things. We women are not such fragile creatures as you take us for! I agree, many women would prefer to be cosseted, protected, and spared the ugly realities of poverty and disease; many men, too, I suspect, if given the choice. But every place that men are, women are also, and we are usually doing the looking-after. And if women can be nurses, why not doctors as well?'

'You're right, Miss Cuypers,' Dubois said, joining her in laughter at his own expense. 'I should have thought more carefully before I spoke. Though the demands of the medical profession would be impossible to combine with the role of wife and mother, I can see no reason why an intelligent woman should not choose to become a physician. Healing, caring for the sick, helping others is a natural talent for many women. Denying them the knowledge to do it better is foolish.'

Dubois had never before met a young woman with serious views. It was a novel and slightly disquieting experience, but one that he enjoyed. He began to consider the possibility of a future with Mia at his side. It might be an asset to have a clever wife, especially one from a prominent family. When he was a full professor, she could be counted on to preside over a tea table and converse brightly at a dinner table with erudite men. Whereas some wives were always at risk of appearing uneducated fools, with Mia the problem might be to teach her not to correct their guests' errors so bluntly as she was inclined to. Mia did not conceal her wit with feminine wiles, he knew that, but nor was she unattractive. She both spoke and dressed well, if a trifle plainly. Having such a wife would show how forward-thinking and modern Dubois was.

He decided to spend an afternoon alone with Mia in some suitable setting to consider every aspect of their possible future together. He should be able to read her feelings for him from her behaviour. It was a delicate agenda not easily accomplished in others' company. Dubois did not care to ask for her hand if he had to risk rejection. No, he would rather seek some subtle sign of a favourable answer before he posed the question. He thought it was rather like conducting a few more experiments to gain a better knowledge of the situation, before publicly advancing a new theory. He certainly wanted to be on solid ground before he said anything to her or her father.

He saw a notice of a concert in the park on the following Sunday afternoon. That would be the perfect occasion for his experiment in congeniality, if the weather was fair. The public gardens were at their peak and the programme promised to be a pleasant entertainment. He called in at the Cuyperses' house briefly that evening to ask whether Mia would accompany him to this concert. The Cuypers approved of the arrangement, of course; nothing could be more circumspect than a daytime outing in public, even if Mia and Dubois would be unchaperoned. As for Mia, she agreed with a nod and a smile of genuine pleasure. 'I should like that very much. I so enjoy good music.'

As he walked briskly home, he was contented at how compatible they seemed in their tastes. He believed she was more tractable than people thought, less unruly. She was simply high-spirited and quick-witted, like his sister Marie when she had been young, and resented being hemmed in by convention. If she could turn her energies to making a comfortable and serene home for a husband and children of her own, she might be a very pleasant wife indeed.

On Sunday, the weather dawned fine and warm. Mia looked very pretty in her pale muslin gown. The flattering little hat perched atop her piled-up hair showed off her fine eyes. Dubois was proud to have her on his arm in public. He, too, had taken extra care in his dress for the occasion, donning a top hat, pale-grey gloves, and his new, very fashionable, double-breasted blue coat. They settled into good seats just before the programme began.

The first part of the concert was lighthearted and lively and the crowd was cheerful. From time to time, Dubois and Mia exchanged glances of enjoyment that seemed to speak of shared tastes. At the intermission, they got up to stroll around and mingle with the other concertgoers, so the ladies could display their elegant gowns and the gentlemen could tip their hats to friends and acquaintances. And then, to Dubois's astonishment, Mia smiled and nodded to an Oriental man as he walked past. He was well-dressed, though his striped trousers were a little colourful, and he was behaving properly, but Dubois was taken aback nonetheless. He wondered what Mia was thinking of, greeting a person like that. Before he could speak or act, the man approached them.

Raising his hat, he inquired, 'It is Miss Cuypers? What a great pleasure it is to see you again.'

She smiled graciously in return and turned to Dubois, who was struck dumb by the fact that she actually knew such a person. Before he could think how to rescue her from this unwise encounter, Mia introduced him to the other man. He was a Chinese government official, the Honourable Mr F. G. Taen-Err-Toung, who bowed in respect to Dubois at the introduction. Mia's action had put Dubois in a quandary. He had been formally introduced to Taen-Err-Toung; he could not turn away and depart with Mia without being unutterably rude. To linger was unseemly, bound to encourage familiarity with a foreigner, but he had to engage in conversation at least briefly. He took refuge in a few comments about the concert and the musicians.

To Dubois's relief, Taen-Err-Toung was a music lover and asked if they thought the tempo of the second selection, the Mozart, hadn't been a little too hurried. Polite remarks flowed easily and the entire situation was less awkward than Dubois had feared at first. Nonetheless, the man was a foreigner – Chinese, not even European – and clearly not someone with whom they should engage in lengthy discourse. Dubois prompted Mia to move away once or twice, with slight pressure on her elbow, but she stood her ground, prolonging the encounter. Dubois recognized, surprised, that Mia was being stubborn, even wilful. She was intentionally ignoring his wishes, even though they were in her best interest. He was startled and a little irritated, yet his curiosity was awakened. Why was she deliberately engaging in conversation with this man? What was he to her? The scientist in him emerged; he stopped reacting and began observing.

Mia was much more animated in Taen-Err-Toung's presence than she had been before. She smiled and laughed and caught the Chinese man's eye, as if they were close acquaintances of long standing. She clearly enjoyed Taen-Err-Toung's company – much more, if he were honest with himself, than she seemed to enjoy his own. Could Taen-Err-Toung be a friend of Mia's father? Perhaps an Indies connection? In the Indies, he supposed, Europeans might socialize with prominent Chinese officials. This was, after all, an educated man, not a coolie; perhaps that was the explanation. Dubois worked a reference to the colonies into the conversation, but Taen-Err-Toung did not respond as one linked to the Cuyperses by mutual colonial acquaintances. After a few minutes, Dubois reached the shocking but obvious conclusion: the primary connection between the Chinese man and the Cuypers family lay with Mia herself. The intermission drew to a close; they had spoken with no one else, and Dubois had much to ponder during the rest of the concert.

The music finished about an hour later, but Dubois was inattentive. After the last note had died and the applause appreciatively rendered to the musicians, Dubois sat staring fixedly into the distance, thinking, until Mia placed her hand on his arm familiarly and asked, 'Shall we go now?'

'Ja, ja,' Dubois replied, retrieving his attention from his reveries. 'Of course. Let us go.'

Much of the crowd had dispersed, but Mia again walked toward Mr Taen-Err-Toung to speak with him. Now Dubois could see the situation plainly: Mia fancied not himself, the young Dutch lecturer, but this Chinese official. Perhaps she had even known in advance that Taen-Err-Toung was likely to attend such a concert and finagled an invitation from Dubois! There were very few places where a young lady could respectably meet with a man, much less a man of another race.

Dubois thought indignantly for a moment that she had used him as a decoy, a dupe. Then, his mild jealousy expended, he softened and let his good sense come to the fore. After all, he had suffered no indignity or embarrassment. She had behaved in a perfectly correct fashion, greeting an acquaintance and introducing him, as respectability demanded, even if it was distinctly unusual to know such a person. Somehow she had arranged to meet him here. What a thing to do! He decided that she was really a very odd girl, much more peculiar than he had taken her for.

He looked at Mia with new eyes, wondering in what other ways he had misjudged her. She looked to him as she always did, attractive with a broad brow and pleasant countenance, intelligence shining from her eyes rather than flirtation, her mien serious rather than coy. Yet she was vastly different in his estimation. She was now a young woman who had sought out the companionship of a Chinese man, as a friend, perhaps even as a suitor. That, at any rate, was how she was behaving and how he must judge her.

They bade goodbye to Mr Taen-Err-Toung and started to walk back across the park, Dubois still examining his own feelings closely. He was surprised at her actions and his pride was wounded slightly. He had been on the verge of letting himself develop deeper feelings for her. How little he had understood then of her true nature! Of course, there had really been nothing between them, no understanding at all, only a friendly acquaintance with the daughter of a prominent man whom he admired. No one could say otherwise. Dubois's behaviour had been impeccable. What he had once thought and had not expressed was no one's business but his own. The thought gave scant comfort, for it was not entirely honest. He had been close to speaking to her father – and he might well have been refused in favour of a Chinese suitor.

His mind moved swiftly, exploring the possible scenarios and the consequences of her attachment to a Chinese man. The conclusion was always the same. However well-bred and highly placed, Taen-Err-Toung was still Chinese, as foreign and un-Dutch as anyone could be.

They walked on, Mia and Dubois, until she interrupted his thoughts with a question. As soon as she voiced it, he knew his deductions were correct. He was not imagining an attraction where none existed, for the topic of her conversation was the very Chinese gentleman they had just left.

'How do you find Mr Taen-Err-Toung?' she asked earnestly, as if she savoured the mention of his very name. 'Is he not unusual?'

'Yes,' answered Dubois slowly. 'I am surprised to find a Chinese man so cultured, so knowledgeable about our music. I have not met his like before.'

'Yes,' – Mia smiled – 'I think so, too. He is a fine man.' They strolled on, ostensibly admiring the gardens, each preoccupied with private thoughts. When she broke the rather companionable silence again, it was to say a little shyly, 'My parents would not approve of my friendship with Mr Taen-Err-Toung.'

'No,' agreed Dubois, gravely and a little stiffly. 'I suppose not.'

'But he is a gentleman,' she continued, 'most interesting and educated. His views are … different, not Dutch. He has lived in so many places, you see, among many different peoples. He has seen parts of the world so different from our little life here in

Amsterdam. Perhaps...' She hesitated at her own boldness, and after a moment, resumed speaking. 'Perhaps we shall encounter him again another day.'

Their footsteps echoed on the pathway as they proceeded in silence for a moment or two. Dubois nodded, his eyes on her face. 'Perhaps we might.' She turned her gaze away from him, toward the fine display of tulips. Brilliant tulips, solid reds, demure pinks, and shining yellows – some even striped or frilled at the edges – filled the bed behind a border of glowing white tulips. Close inspection of the white blooms revealed their centres to be a deep purple-black, the darkness highlighting their paleness in contrast. In the sunlight, the mosaic of colours and shapes was so dazzling that it almost hurt the eye.

Mia spoke again, quietly. 'I should dearly love to know what he will think of the public lecture this Wednesday evening at the town hall, the one about the new style of painting in France. Wouldn't you?' She held her breath for a moment, waiting to see if Dubois had taken her meaning.

He caught her glance and returned it with a small, kindly smile. She could not read his thoughts. Did he understand? Or was his mind opaque? Abruptly he stopped walking and turned to face her, making a slight, formal bow from the waist. 'Miss Cuypers,' he said, on impulse, 'I shall be delighted if you would care to accompany me to that lecture. Should we happen to encounter the Honourable Mr Taen-Err-Toung on that occasion, then we may discover his opinion for ourselves.'

'Oh, ja,' she said ambiguously, 'I should like that.'

They walked on again in silence, past the ornamental fishponds. And then Dubois added mischievously, 'I have been told, you know, that I am quite tall and slender enough to serve as a lightning rod.'

Now it was Mia who stopped walking and turned to look at her companion sharply. She detected the glint of good humour in his eyes and smiled broadly in response. 'Indeed,' she said softly. 'You will serve well to draw the fire away. Thank you.'

And so the arrangement was set. In the weeks that followed, Dubois acted as the lightning rod, diverting the Cuyperses' attention while Mia and the Chinese man deepened their friendship. Before long, however, she and Dubois had been seen together so often that people began to murmur of an announcement in the offing, an engagement. If scandal was to be avoided – if Dubois was not to appear a cad – he had either to propose or to cease his attentions to Mia. The latter seemed the only wise choice, as he knew better than anyone else of her affection for another.

Lightning struck quickly once the lightning rod was gone. Her parents accidentally saw Mia in Taen-Err-Toung's company, talking so earnestly that their intimacy was obvious.

'You must break it off,' her father said sternly. 'It is all very well to be tolerant and to treat people of inferior races politely; they may even be very interesting acquaintances, but a permanent attachment is out of the question.'

The Cuyperses' opposition was matched only by Mia's determination. 'You misjudge him,' Mia replied passionately. 'It is not an "attachment". He is a fine man and I shall marry him.'

Her father was startled by her bold words. He had hoped things had not gone this far, that the man had not deceived his daughter so seriously. 'I am not aware,' replied her father, a little ponderously, 'that Mr Taen-Err-Toung has asked for your hand. I am still your father, and your future husband must receive my approval and blessing.' Mia turned and left the room.

Within twenty-four hours, Taen-Err-Toung called formally upon the Cuyperses. They asked the maid to admit him at once, rather than leave him standing on the doorstep in full view of the neighbours. The maid showed him into the parlour, where Mia's parents sat, stiffly, eyeing this alien person with more than a little suspicion. Within a surprisingly short time, the Chinese man openly declared his intention to make Mia his wife and asked for their approval.

'I know you have not anticipated a husband like me for your daughter,' Taen-Err-Toung said directly and calmly, 'but it is my wish, and hers. Please ask me what you like about my job, my family, my prospects. I beg you to give me a chance, to become acquainted with my character before making your decision about your daughter's future. You do not owe me this, I know, for I have been meeting your daughter without your knowledge. It was wrong of me, but it was not an intentional deception. We first met by accident in a public place. Once I discovered what pleasure I take in her company, I could not think how to make your acquaintance so that I might call on her properly, according to your custom.'

The Cuyperses' horror at the prospect of an interracial marriage diminished as the afternoon proceeded. The man's manner was civilized, he was obviously respectable and well educated, and he seemed genuinely fond of their difficult daughter. But their opposition to the match was too deeply rooted to be torn out so lightly. They might be tolerant of other ways and other races, but to marry a Chinese man would be exceedingly unwise. They tried every stratagem at their disposal to break off the relationship: anger, extracted promises, enforced separations. There seemed to be no way to prevent Mia from meeting Taen-Err-Toung, so wilful was she, except by making her a prisoner in her own home. It was a distasteful tactic, soon abandoned.

After a month of conflict, Mia's parents consented to an engagement of at least two years' duration. There were to be no furtive, concealed meetings. The engagement would be carried out openly and as respectably as a mixed-race engagement could be conducted. The Cuyperses were beginning to like their daughter's intended; he might well make her a good husband. His honesty and kindness were more important than his place of origin and they would say so by their behaviour. If others chose to dwell on his race, then they would reap the bitter fruit of their own small-mindedness.

The couple married in 1886, with the Cuyperses' blessing. Familiarity had done much to erase their sense of Taen-Err-Toung's foreignness and racial inferiority. He was an extraordinary Chinese man, as their daughter was an unusual young Dutch woman. Speculation about the strange married life that awaited Mia flowed in Amsterdam society like water in the canals. The gossips were confounded when nothing dramatic occurred. Mia did not grow pale and complain of his 'dreadful foreign ways', nor did she come running home to her parents in disgrace.

Dubois watched from a distance. He was pleased that he had not been more deeply involved with Mia, but he was also a little envious. He had never experienced the sort of passionate commitment shown by this pair of determined lovers. He had yet to meet any young lady, however charming or pretty, who could inspire him to rash actions. Oh, he had enjoyed the flirtations of his student days – enjoyed them very much – but his concentration and emotion were ultimately reserved for his work. It was science that stirred his passions, not romance.

CHAPTER 6

Love and Conflict

Although at first Dubois thought the affair with Mia Cuypers had cured him of romance, it was not long before he was attracted to one of the students who enrolled in his anatomy class at the art school in 1885. Her name was Anna Geertruida Lojenga. She was not one of the better students, for her artistic talent was limited and her memory for anatomical facts appalling. Still, Dubois had seen the danger of getting involved with a too-intelligent, opinionated young woman, so Anna's character came as something of a relief to him. She was lively and bright-eyed, with long, dark-chestnut hair wound becomingly up on her head. And while she was not clever, she was popular among the students, laughing at her own errors and making light of theirs. Anna's charm depended upon neither immodesty nor boldness; it derived from her naive ability to see the best in whatever happened. She did possess a certain facility in drawing and watercolours, a gentle talent becoming in a young lady. She also had a sweet singing voice and a fair gift for playing the piano, as Dubois discovered when he began to call on her. And she welcomed the attentions of her handsome young professor.

As their acquaintance deepened, Dubois found he liked the way her frivolity lightened his own natural gravity. He knew he was sometimes accused of being too serious, too sombre, and Anna teased him out of his solemnity. He enjoyed her laughter, her songs, and her merriment over simple pleasures, even if she sometimes made much of very little. He thought of her as being like a butterfly or a flower: charming, decorative, but not weighty. He flattered himself that his temperament balanced her natural lightness. And he was certain there was no chance he would be cast aside for a secret Chinese lover.

On 24 August 1885, a sultry afternoon, he asked permission from her father to speak to Anna about marriage. Before the day was out, the couple were officially engaged. Anna was alight with joy at the proposal and Dubois himself felt an unaccustomed brightness. Anna's parents thought Dubois amiable and recognized

Dubois marries Anna Lojenga, shown here, on 4 August 1886.

the value of a son-in-law with a promising future. They might have preferred an upstanding young man of their own faith, but no Lutheran suitor had presented himself. Dubois was a good match.

Both sets of parents saw Dubois as unalterably a Catholic, even as he was indelibly a Limburger, and they expected him to resume Catholic observance as he matured, misjudging Dubois completely. They feared that the religious differences might cause conflicts. Dubois's parents asked that Anna agree to raise the children in the Catholic faith; she dutifully pledged to do so. But no one saw that Dubois, the father of these future children, was not a Catholic himself but a scientist. Anna's parents insisted upon a year-long engagement, which was announced in Amsterdam, Eijsden, and Elburg, the Lojengas' home town. Dubois was amused at the parallel with the Cuyperses' reaction to Mr Taen-Err-Toung. Perhaps being born a Catholic Limburger made Dubois half as foreign as a Chinaman! But a year-long engagement would give him more time to get ahead in his career and would give Anna time to plan the wedding.

Late in 1885, Dubois was offered a lectureship, only one step below a full professorship, in anatomy at the University of Utrecht. It was a highly desirable position and so he discussed it with

Fürbringer, his chairman at the University of Amsterdam, out of courtesy.

'You really ought to stay here, Dubois,' Fürbringer advised him gravely. 'I know Utrecht seems a step up, but if you are patient and stay here at Amsterdam, it is you who will succeed me as professor when I retire in a few years' time. They aren't going to bring in someone from outside when I go; they'd rather promote a man from within, and you're the best one. So if you want to go to the top, staying put and continuing on the course you have set is the thing.' Flattered by the older man's interest, ambitious for the promised chair, Dubois turned the offer down. Turning down this opportunity awakened all ill-defined unease in Dubois's mind.

Through much of 1885, Dubois buried himself in the study of the comparative anatomy of the organ of speech and sound production. He dissected a series of different species of animals, making detailed drawings of all their structures, comparing each species with the others, tracing the development of the larynx both in embryos as they grew and in animals according to their evolutionary relationships with one another. In the back of his mind was always the question of the evolution of speech in humans.

Anna saw Dubois's single-minded devotion to his research but never entertained any doubts about the marriage. That was the sort of thing men did, became obsessed with their professions: it was to be expected and it had nothing to do with her life, except for the promise of financial security. Dubois offered her everything a young woman could dream of. He was handsome, young, loyal, and much admired. The pragmatic realities of day-to-day living with a man in love with his work did not cross her mind.

In 1886, Dubois was promoted to lecturer at the University of Amsterdam, the very rank he had turned down at Utrecht. When he told her the news, Anna was thrilled. Two promotions – first prosector, now lecturer – in the space of two years! He was surely the cleverest man on the faculty of the University of Amsterdam. Maybe, Anna thought, they would be able to afford a piano for the parlour, and in time, a horse and carriage. In every idle moment, Anna dreamt of their delightful future. She would be the lovely wife of the youngest and handsomest professor in Amsterdam. They would have beautiful children and a nursemaid to attend them. She would throw splendid dinner parties for his colleagues and visiting scholars; invitations would be sought eagerly as a sign of Dr Dubois's favour. She would have the most expensive china, the finest silver, the whitest linens, and the best flowers for her table.

Dubois was not as sanguine as Anna about the significance of his promotion. He was being rewarded, ostensibly, for his excellent research on the larynx which had been published in *Anatomische Anzeiger* early in 1886. Preparing and publishing that research had been difficult.

Back in the fall of 1885, Dubois had discerned a complex pattern in the morphology of the larynx in different animals. He checked his logic, reviewed his drawings and notes, consulted all the anatomical literature on the subject. Finally he wrote a draft of his first real manuscript. His main conclusion was that the larynx in mammals is derived from the fourth and fifth branchial arches in the embryo. This sounded like an esoteric point, of interest to only a few specialists. But the derivation of the mammalian larynx from the branchial arches implied that the human voice box evolved from the gill cartilage of fishes. The structure that had once filtered water to extract oxygen now 'filtered' air and made sound. It was a totally new finding and Dubois was proud of his work. It was yet another piece of evidence that showed an evolutionary link, a transition between two forms that appeared to be quite distinct, such as fishes and mammals.

With some trepidation, he had taken the manuscript to Fürbringer, asking for his advice and comments before submitting it to a scientific journal. He had hoped to have his first publication accepted before his wedding, if possible. Fürbringer understood the gravity of Dubois's maiden voyage into real scholarship and promised to give the manuscript his immediate attention. If Dubois came to his office the next afternoon, they could discuss the manuscript in detail. Dubois had awaited the interview anxiously. At the appointed hour, he presented himself in Fürbringer's august room, lined with bookcases packed with important-looking reference texts. A few specimens – an odd skull here, a pathological tibia, a curious tortoise shell there – interrupted the orderly ranks of scholarly books. The room was carpeted, comfortable, and very dignified, as befitted a full professor.

'Come in, my boy,' Fürbringer said heartily, turning from his large desk and gesturing Dubois into a heavy, padded chair. He picked up the manuscript. 'This is well done, Dubois, very well done. There are just a few points we should go over that need a bit of revision.' He leafed through the pages of the manuscript one by

Max Fürbringer, the renowned professor of anatomy at the University of Amsterdam, overshadowed Dubois.

one, applauding this illustration, suggesting minor changes in others, and pointing out passages and descriptions that might benefit from greater clarity. As the minutes passed, Dubois slowly relaxed. None of Fürbringer's criticisms were serious; none detracted from or jeopardized Dubois's main conclusion. The work was good. Fürbringer's small changes would improve the manuscript and would not take much time or effort on Dubois's part. He was greatly relieved. Then, just as Dubois prepared to excuse himself with thanks, Fürbringer brought up a final point.

'You know, Dubois,' he said, tapping the manuscript with his glasses, 'this work is very important. It completely confirms what I have been saying since about 1880: that the thyroid cartilage of the human larynx is derived from the fourth branchial arch. Of course, you have heard me mention this idea in lectures. I think that you ought to add a few sentences acknowledging my work on that matter, as it is so closely related to your topic. It will strengthen your claim about the derivation of the mammalian larynx in general.'

Dubois had been surprised into temporary speechlessness. Credit

Fürbringer for the idea? He had never heard Fürbringer say that the thyroid cartilage was derived from the fourth branchial arch. What could the man be talking about? Was he trying to claim credit for part of Dubois's discovery? Were Dubois's months of work in the dissecting room nothing but an elaboration of Fürbringer's previous idea? He was appalled. He wanted to ask Fürbringer where he had been while Dubois was working everything out, hour after hour, dissecting species after species, revealing and drawing the anatomical structures from every aspect. Why had he been all alone in the laboratory if this was really Fürbringer's work? The thoughts in his mind were so loud that he wondered why Fürbringer did not hear them.

Stammering with the sheer effort of controlling his words, he asked, 'D-do you really think so, sir? That I should cite your ideas about the thyroid cartilage? I wouldn't want to slight someone else's work, especially yours, of course not, only...' He berated himself for sounding like an unsure schoolboy instead of like a professional who had completed an important piece of research. No wonder Fürbringer did not believe he had done this on his own.

Fürbringer was patient and kindly; he had seen this reaction from young scholars before. The young always thought they had discovered the key to the universe all by themselves, when in reality they built on the work of those who went before. Because Dubois controlled himself well, Fürbringer badly misjudged the depth of the younger man's emotion. 'It's always a better idea, you know,' Fürbringer replied genially, not meaning to patronize his junior but nonetheless enraging Dubois further. 'Citing other people's previous work never detracts from your own.' Dubois's face barely concealed his disappointment, so Fürbringer added, to reassure him, "You'll see. You'll see I'm right in this in time." Then Fürbringer stood up to signal that the interview was over. He did not realize that he had sowed, watered, and fertilized the seeds of resentment in Dubois. The younger man had dutifully added a mention of Fürbringer's ideas to the manuscript, but he had felt as if he had been swindled. And now the rapid promotion to lecturer seemed like a pay-off for agreeing to let Fürbringer claim some of his work. He tried to explain to Anna why he was so ambivalent about his promotion and publication, but he barely understood his feelings himself.

The year's engagement afforded Dubois more than a few glimpses of Anna's silliness and frivolity. Sometimes he was amazed that she thought of his promotion and his career only in terms of furnishings for a house that they hadn't even found yet and couldn't afford. She was utterly absorbed by choosing her trousseau and wedding gifts. For Dubois, these things ranked little higher in importance than a fairy tale. He found it unsettling that there seemed not to be a serious thought in Anna's head, that she cared nothing for his work and understood even less. Why, she couldn't even remember if the larynx led to the stomach or was the voice box! The only speech she thought about was the one that would be made at her first dinner party. And then, softened by his fondness for her, he amended his criticisms. Anna was only twenty-one years old; it was surely just youth, just the tail-end of her natural girlish foolishness.

As the wedding date approached, Dubois hoped the change in his life would resolve the restlessness he had felt of late. Having a wife and a home of his own would be a sign of maturity, of having moved from the status of a student to that of a grown man with serious responsibilities. Yet sometimes the things Anna said gave him pause. He began to see how far beneath him she was mentally; intellectually, she stood not so high, like a little girl who barely came up to one's waist. But still, she was his little Anna, his little pet, and it was enough for now that she was young and pretty. Her skin was so soft, the lustre of her hair so attractive.

He ignored his occasional qualms and carried on out of a kind of romantic chivalry. Marie Eugène François Thomas Dubois had asked for the hand of Anna Geertruida Lojenga in marriage and they should be married. He would not prove their parents' doubts valid. They thought the problem between Dubois and Anna would be religious, as if religion were important. Pah! That was nothing.

They were wed on 4 August 1886, a strikingly attractive couple who were in many ways opposites. She was as dark as he was fair, as slender as he was barrel-chested, as laughing as he was grave. In the first flush of married life, they were happy and contented in their new roles, their differences adding spice, their affection smoothing over any difficulties. Anna loved playing at being a wife, furnishing their new home as she might a doll's house, seeking just the right lace for the curtains and the right fabric for the chairs for the living room. Selecting her tea set was a task over which she spent weeks, prolonging the decision because she found it all so enjoyable.

After the wedding, Dubois's more settled personal life gave him the courage to try to resolve the tension between Fürbringer and himself. In the fall of 1886, he sent Fürbringer a polite note, asking that he not attend Dubois's first lecture of the year. Teaching was for Dubois a nightmare; he had, in his five years as an anatomist, developed a deep aversion to this bread-and-butter task of his profession. He feared the students responded better to other men, even those less knowledgeable than he. He did not know why the students did not flock to him. He was cleverer than the others. He could have taught the students how to conduct an experiment or make an important observation, how to construct a good theory. But they did not love him. Perhaps he was too formal with them; he did not care for their boisterous jokes and pranks. Science was not an appropriate subject of jest. And perhaps, he thought, he expected too much of them, because he held the students to his own standards. But he didn't know any other way to be. He could not compromise science, any more than he could choose not to breathe.

Dubois's request thus had a dual function. He did not want to expose his shortcomings as a teacher to Fürbringer's critical gaze and he wanted to be sure that other professors who attended would see him as a fully independent scholar. With but one publication to his name, Dubois was extremely sensitive to the possibility that he would be seen as Fürbringer's 'boy', his protégé, whose every move was orchestrated by his mentor. Unfortunately, Fürbringer did not understand, or did not take seriously, the younger man's request. He replied to Dubois's request with a light-hearted note: 'So the question arises whether I am at least permitted to attend the lecture with a muzzle, or whether you are afraid that even this might damage your independent status?' Dubois's plea for understanding and protection from the older man had been completely misread. He felt mocked, and vowed never to forget these hurtful words.

His feelings of humiliation were offset, somewhat, by praise for his larynx work from a colleague, Max Weber. Only six years Dubois's senior, Weber belonged to the famed German school of biology, having been educated in Bonn and Berlin. He was already one of the foremost scholars in Europe. In 1879, Weber had joined the University of Amsterdam as Fürbringer's prosector in anatomy, the position that Dubois had recently occupied. In 1878, Weber had been lured away to the University of Utrecht to become a lecturer, as Dubois, too, might have been. Three years later, on the verge of being promoted to full professor at Utrecht, Weber had been tempted back to Amsterdam by an offer of a professorship of zoology, comparative anatomy, and comparative physiology. The deciding factor had been that Amsterdam also offered access to whatever rare animals died at the Royal Zoological Society Natura Artis Magistra, one of the finest zoological gardens in Europe. It was a great research opportunity.

Weber was known in Amsterdam as a bit of a potentate. He was never seen, even in the dissecting room, in anything less formal than a frock coat and starched collar. His beard was always meticulously shaped, his luxuriant dark moustaches waxed and upturned, his speech precise and measured. He was an influential

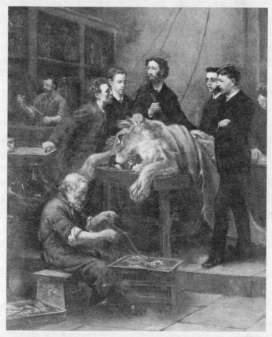

In this 1886 painting by Louis Straké, Professor Dr Max Weber
(centre, with beard and moustache) dissects a lion. From left to
right, standing: laboratory assistant Sleking; Jacobus Janse;
Johannes Oudemans; Weber; Frederich Went; the musician De Josselin
de Jong; and Sleking's son. In foreground, 'the last whaler,' probably a
member of the crew of the *Willem Barents*, in which Weber
sailed in 1881.

and excellent scientist, so it was an honour when Weber asked Dubois to contribute a section on the larynx in whales for the first volume of his enormous work on cetaceans. To everyone except Dubois, the parallel between Weber's meteoric trajectory and Dubois's was obvious. But Dubois saw only that Fürbringer blocked his path more and more. He vowed his research on the whale larynx would owe nothing to Fürbringer's influence. And he laid plans to compile all his larynx work into one comprehensive publication, as soon as the cetacean work was finished. Then no one would ever again doubt that the work was his own.

The topic Dubois had settled upon – a thorough comparative review of the anatomy and evolution of the larynx – was so enormous that it was flatly unwieldy. He had too many observations and too much information to organize and present clearly. As 1886 turned into 1887, he struggled with the manuscript on his own, day after day, writing passages, striking them out, moving paragraphs here and there in an attempt to bring logic and order to the information.

Fürbringer was eager to help and asked frequently – too frequently for Dubois's comfort – about the progress of the manuscript. Dubois suspected that Fürbringer's offers of assistance were nothing but thinly disguised efforts to find out what he had discovered. Why else would he repeatedly have urged Dubois to show him the manuscript? He resented the way Fürbringer was always passing along articles he thought Dubois might not have read, as if he had been too careless to follow the literature carefully.

The more Fürbringer tried to help, the more furtive Dubois grew. Soon he was reluctant to discuss his ideas or work with any of his colleagues. He became withdrawn, touchy, almost feverish, as if he were being literally poisoned with suspicion. Soon Dubois and Fürbringer were barely speaking – or rather, Fürbringer was speaking too much and Dubois too little. Dubois fretted he would never free himself from Fürbringer's influence, yet he could not see how to extricate himself from this sticky situation. If he stayed, if Fürbringer gave his endorsement as promised, he would become professor of anatomy. Would it be given, if Dubois remained staunchly independent? Would people see the promotion as his due? The problem spun around and around in his brain, like a child's top, careening wildly off balance. Unlike the toy, Dubois's worries never ran out of momentum and fell into blissful stillness.

CHAPTER 7

Turning Point

On 4 April 1887, a mere eight months after the wedding, Anna gave birth to Dubois's first child, Marie Eugenie. Dubois was proud to be the father of such a pretty child, and the husband of such a lovely wife; he was a real family man now. Still, Eugenie caused inevitable disruption in the household. They hired a nursemaid who looked after the baby well, but they had not anticipated the social consequences of the child's early arrival. When the birth was announced, eyebrows were raised in Amsterdam society and months were counted discreetly on fingers. Anna resumed entertaining as soon after the birth as was decent, inviting friends and Amsterdam relatives for tea in her new home. She made sure that the nursemaid was ready to bring the baby in, exquisitely dressed, to be shown off. To her surprise, there were rather many comments on Eugenie's robust size and obvious health.

'How big she is,' said a stout grey-haired matron, Mevrouw Hielkema, the wife of a prominent lawyer. She tickled Eugenie under her chubby chin and stroked her sweet head. 'And what lovely thick curls!' She smiled smugly.

'Oh, let me look at her, the darling,' cooed Mevrouw Van Boven, only a few years older than Anna. As the young wife of a prosperous banker, she had undertaken to raise the children left motherless by the death of his first wife, as well as to produce more heirs at regular intervals. 'Oh, ja' – she echoed the matron's sentiments slyly – 'isn't she plump and delicious? And so big. Mine were just so small at first.' And then she addressed Anna: 'I don't know how you did it.'

Anna's head came up suddenly: was this a comment on the health and size of her infant, or a subtle insult based on the apparent maturity of a child born so shortly after the wedding? She blushed and looked away, unable to think of a reply that would refute the lurking implication of impropriety.

'So often,' clucked another visitor, Mevrouw Hessing, who was a friend of Anna's mother, 'early babies are thin and weak. How fortunate you are, Anna, that she is so strong.' Turning to the baby and patting a plump hand, she added, 'Ja, and what a lovely girl you are.' Eugenie gurgled appreciatively at the attention and soft voice.

Eugenie *is* a lovely baby, Anna thought fiercely, her dark eyes flashing, and she had *not* been conceived before the wedding. Anna could not voice the thought, for it would have acknowledged an accusation of wrongdoing that had not quite been made. Eugenie grew a little restive and Anna gestured for the nursemaid to come and take the child. As they left, Eugenie cheerful and secure in her nursemaid's arms, one more pointed remark was offered.

'What a good thing it is that you and Dr Dubois married,' clucked Mejuffrouw de Perron, a bony, large-nosed spinster, squinting after the baby. She had ruined her eyesight with too much reading and was now notoriously shortsighted. She had put her cup down in the butter dish at more than one tea party, but she refused to wear the spectacles she so badly needed for fear they would make her look old. She still hoped vainly for a proposal of marriage. Normally, the *mejuffrouw* was a figure of fun to pretty young women, but Anna had been kinder to her than most. Now Anna looked at the homely woman, wondering how the *mejuffrouw* could so thoroughly misjudge her own attractiveness and how *she* could have so badly misjudged the woman's character. She had not thought catty remarks to be the *mejuffrouw*'s style.

'Oh, ja,' she replied sweetly, glad to have the chance to make her point. 'Otherwise we should not have that darling child.' She smiled blissfully at her tormentor and then, meaningfully, turned the smile on the others.

'Well, indeed...' sputtered one of the ladies.

'I mean... of course not,' added the *mejuffrouw* in confusion. Mevrouw van Boven, the sharpest of them all, shook her head as if agreeing it had been a silly misunderstanding, all the while thinking that Anna was a little more clever than she had taken her for. It was, as Shakespeare said, a 'palpable hit'.

'Will you have more tea?' Anna asked politely. 'Or perhaps' – she turned to Mevrouw van Boven, by far the plumpest of those present – 'a few more tea cakes? You seem to enjoy them so.'

'Ah, thank you, delicious,' she answered swiftly, unable to fend off the unflattering implication of greediness. 'Not another. I couldn't.'

Soon afterwards, the visiting ladies made their excuses and left.

Now Anna had time to replay in her mind the ambiguous compliments and double-edged praise she had received. No, she was not imagining insults where none existed. Apparently everyone believed that this blessedly healthy child had been born nine months after her conception, which must therefore have been a full month before the wedding.

By the time a few days had passed, Anna was more than a little disturbed about what people were saying and thinking. She had rarely faced malice before; her charm and sweet nature had armoured her heretofore against spite and jealousy. She was inexperienced in the ritual combat of society and did not know what to do. She knew, everyone knew, that early babies were usually small and sickly. No one could have called Eugenie, with her fat pink cheeks and chuckling smiles, either sickly or small. Therefore she was not an early child but an illegitimate one, evidence of a sin only partially concealed by a hasty wedding. In the weeks that followed the birth, Anna became fretful and despondent, while Eugenie thrived. Anna's characteristic sunny temperament deserted her for the first time in her life, leaving instead an anxious mother who doted unhealthily on her daughter. She interfered too often with the nursemaid, changing her mind and countermanding her own orders hourly. The nursemaid was an experienced woman who knew her place, but she had limited patience with Anna's incessant fussing. She wished, quite frankly, that this busybody of a mother would go away and leave her to raise Eugenie to be a placid, obedient child.

When Anna was not in the nursery interfering with the baby's routine, she was distracted and obsessed with the gossip she imagined was being traded at her darling child's expense. She worked and reworked the exact interpretation of every greeting she received, every remark made about Eugenie in her hearing, as if toiling over recalcitrant pieces of embroidery. Slowly, she began to lose control of the household. Meals were served early, or late, or were simply ill-planned; laundry was not attended to; mail sometimes got lost or went unanswered; and the weekly household accounts were not examined with the usual care. Anna lost weight – rapidly, unbecomingly – while Eugenie grew plump.

One morning at a breakfast marred by burnt toast and overdone eggs, Anna fidgeted ceaselessly, adjusting the silverware, rearranging the cups, placing and replacing her prized teapot at the end of the table until Dubois's nerves were almost as raw as hers. He had tried to ignore her anxiety, hoping his calm would quiet her. It was no use; her mind was so tortured that she could not be stilled. Finally she wondered querulously, for the dozenth time, what they could say or do to dispel the rumours of Eugenie's early conception.

At this, Dubois lost his temper and put his cup down so firmly in the saucer that it threatened to break. 'I will hear no more of such nonsense,' he thundered. 'Why do you listen to silly chatter and idle gossip?' He thumped the top of the table with the flat of his hand for emphasis. The china and silverware rattled. 'Can we conceal our child's age or birthdate? Can we lie about the date of our marriage? No, we cannot.'

Anna cringed at his raised voice and did not dare to look at him. He had never been so displeased with her, so angry. Eyes downcast, she busied herself mopping up the spilled tea with her napkin rather than ringing for the girl. Dubois got up noisily from the table and walked quickly over to the window, shaking his head impatiently. He paused, ostensibly to look at the weather but really because he needed a moment to clear his mind.

Anna turned in her chair to watch him. She started to speak in a small, trembling voice, knowing with one part of her mind that she was saying the wrong thing but unable to stop herself 'It is only that people say such cruel things about Eugenie…'

Dubois moved over to stand next to her where she was still seated at the table. The expression on his face stopped her voice in mid-sentence. He was standing very still, all his attention focused on her. His pale-blue eyes seemed to examine her most private thoughts. Her eyes filled with tears of shame and fear and confusion. Dubois was through raising his voice to Anna. He did not wish to bully her but she had pushed him past endurance. Now he spoke to her quietly, as if they were in church. 'Do…you… suppose…' he asked gravely, holding her face in his hands and looking directly into her eyes, 'do you suppose that anyone would think I did not behave honourably toward you during our engagement?'

The tears spilled down her pale, thin cheeks, loosed by the gentleness in his voice. She could not look away, his eyes were so compelling. 'No,' she answered miserably, 'they could not think such a thing of you. No.'

'Then,' concluded Dubois, exercising his logic relentlessly, 'there can be no cause for gossip, can there?'

'No,' Anna replied shakily. There was nothing more she could say. She knew and feared the power of gossip, the effect that even senseless rumours could have on social position. There was no opposing Dubois, however, because Dubois was a scientist who dealt only in facts. He was older, he was bigger, he was cleverer, and he was her husband. He was the unquestioned head of their young family. He was right.

Dubois patted her hair affectionately, as one might a naughty but now repentant child's, and then moved quietly across the room to the door. Before leaving, he stopped and turned to speak to her once again. Standing straight and tall, the very image of *Recte et fortiter*, he issued one simple command to his young wife. 'Anna,' he said seriously, 'you must calm yourself, pull yourself together.' He noted the untidy strands of hair coming loose; she had never before been slovenly.

'You are a wife, Anna, a mother; you have a daughter to look after now. If we have a welcome home, a healthy child, and a happy marriage, there will be no more talk. Making that home is your job. You must not trouble me with such foolishness. My job is to settle matters of great scientific importance. I cannot worry about you or the child or the running of the house.'

He left the room; in a moment, she heard the front door open and close. He had left the world she inhabited with her child and the servants to go to the university where his research awaited him.

Anna might be foolish, but she was no fool. Indeed, Dubois's outburst seemed to have given her some perspective on her troubles. His certainty and strength helped her regain her own; she had nothing to be ashamed of, and so she would not be ashamed. She would buy a new hat, arrange her hair in the new style, and hold her head up when she went out. When Dubois came home at the end of the day, she was more cheerful than she had been in weeks. Soon her appetite was better and she began to regain the weight she had lost. She seemed to have found a modicum of peace. In the evenings, she was able to sit quietly with her embroidery while Dubois read or tried to explain the discoveries he had made that day. She did not comprehend the matters that consumed him and found them, frankly, a little disgusting. She tried to make jokes about her own ignorance of anatomy – 'Perhaps I should have had a better teacher!' – but she rarely paid enough attention to understand him. From time to time, he still noticed a high colour in her cheeks when she was out with the baby and acquaintances stopped to speak to her, but that was all. Her terrors had been vanquished by his own immunity to them.

After a month or two had passed, the household was calm and cosy once again and Anna seemed to be her old self. Dubois thought back on the incident and was pleased at the effect of his words. Anna was learning, he thought with satisfaction. She might worry over silly things if she liked, but she must not trouble him with them. In time, with his guidance, he believed she would develop the maturity and wisdom not to worry over such things at all. All would be well.

Sitting in the prettily furnished living room, well fed and comfortable, Dubois reflected on the changes of the last year or two. From being an eligible bachelor, he had become a respectable family man. He was no longer an assistant with prospects, living in dingy rented rooms, but a lecturer with a lovely wife and a charming home. Anna went upstairs and he could hear her singing softly to their beautiful daughter. He was truly content. He would soon be the professor of anatomy at the University of Amsterdam, one of the youngest ever. He would discover great scientific facts, for he had already started on his research programme. It was a time of life to savour.

Dubois's sense of peace did not last long. His suspicions of Fürbringer and their awkward, even hostile, interactions continued almost daily. Then a momentous discovery swept aside Dubois's obsession with priority, as if it had been a mere spider's web across a much-travelled pathway.

In July 1887, Max Lohest, a Belgian geologist, and a colleague at the University of Liège, anatomist Julien Fraipont, published a monograph that seized the imagination of every person in Europe who was interested in science and natural history. The summer before, Lohest and a lawyer-cum-amateur-prehistorian, Marcel de Puydt, had found strange human fossils in a cave called Betche-aux-Rotches in Spy, Belgium. They had recovered not one but two Neanderthal skeletons, as well as many finely worked stone tools and the remains of extinct animals. The newly published monograph described and analysed the Neanderthal fossils from Spy, which were only the third discovery of any Neanderthal bones ever.

The first heavily mineralized skeleton had been found in 1856, in the Neander Valley of Germany, 'born' into the world about a year and a half before Dubois himself. Perhaps the Neanderthal was truly my older brother, he mused whimsically. The significance of that first skeleton and what it said about human ancestry were much debated at the time of its discovery. Then a much more complete skull, lacking any of the rest of the skeleton, that had been found years earlier on Gibraltar, was recognized as also being Neanderthal. With the Spy finds, there were now three partial skeletons, enough evidence to resolve at least some of the debates.

Dubois took down a favourite book, Huxley's *Man's Place in Nature*, to look again at the illustrations of the first Neanderthal to be found. He remembered the skull's jutting browridges, which many found shockingly apelike when the find was first announced by Johannes Fuhlrott, a schoolteacher, and anatomist Hermann Schaaffhausen of the University of Bonn. After analysing the fossils, Fuhlrott and Schaaffhausen had declared the Neanderthal to be an example of an ancient, primitive race from which modern Man had evolved.

Thus the pair acquired a powerful and formidable opponent, the brilliant German pathologist Rudolf Virchow. Virchow had once boasted that he *was* German science, there being no need to add

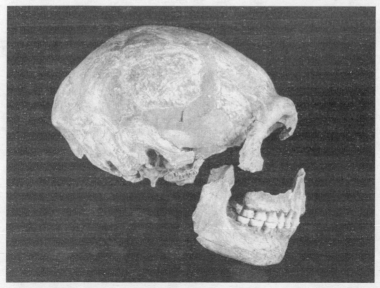

The discovery of this Neanderthal skull from Spy, Belgium, rekindles Dubois's interest in human evolution.

that German science was the best in the world. Sometimes called the Pope or the Pasha of Science behind his back, Virchow was rigidly autocratic and formal. He was also deeply and openly antagonistic to the idea of evolution. When Fuhlrott and Schaaffhausen called the Neanderthal fossils evidence of human evolution, Virchow and his acolytes replied promptly that these were nothing other than the bones of an old, deformed human, probably a man with a bad case of rickets. Since Virchow was the world's greatest authority on rickets, few dared challenge him. As for evolutionary theory itself, Virchow pronounced it little more than unsupported speculation, entirely lacking in proof. Now, after thirty years of Virchow's unrelenting scepticism, similar fossils had been discovered at Spy and scientific opinion had reversed itself, according to the newspaper clipping Dubois pasted into a book he labelled 'Nota Paleontologica'.

The supposition of Virchow…becomes untenable because the Spy skulls so closely resemble the Neanderthal skull and were found under such similar circumstances. We must…accustom ourselves to the idea that the ancestors of mankind also physically showed many resemblances with the anthropomorphic monkeys and apes.

And since the Spy skeletons were found in the same geologic layer as the fossilized bones of extinct rhinoceros, mammoth, reindeer, horse, and cave bear – the typical animals of the ancient Ice Ages in Europe – any learned man would be forced to conclude that Neanderthals had been contemporary with those creatures.

Reading of these finds diverted Dubois's attention forcibly from his quarrels with Fürbringer over the larynx research. He was excited, exhilarated: evolution was being proved true, in his life-time. These fossil discoveries confirmed the fact of human evolution in a new and tangible way. His boyhood game – 'what would be the most important discovery?' – rang again in his mind. He had once believed passionately that fossils were the key to understanding evolution, though none of the great books ever placed much emphasis on fossils. With a blinding stroke of clarity, Dubois realized that anatomy and embryology might offer indications of evolution's working, but only fossils could prove what had actually occurred, what had once lived, once evolved. Perhaps he had been wasting his research efforts, chasing the wrong sort of information.

Dubois's thoughts were tinged with jealousy: others had found a compelling proof of human evolution when he himself had not.

And he was the one who, from boyhood, had intended to find the missing link. Why had he let himself be diverted? These new finds reawakened his love of paleontology and drew his focus almost bodily away from his resentments and obsessions. He remembered once again the larger issues of human evolution that had started him on the pathway of science in the first place. One way out of his dilemma would be to find a fossil that would set him up as an expert in human evolution rather than just an anatomist.

As he pondered the new discoveries, Dubois returned to his bible of evolution, Haeckel's *History of Creation*. Here was what was central, important, worth finding. Study the larynx, unravel its mysteries, and you would understand speech. Speech was what made us human. Dubois had done that. He now knew more than any other man about the development and evolution of the larynx. He could see the continuity that stretched from the lowly fishes, with their breathing organs, to man himself and his most wondrous endowment, speech. Reading Haeckel was soothing to Dubois for a special reason, for Haeckel had managed to step out of the shadow of his renowned professor, Rudolf Virchow. Once the symbol of German scientific acumen, Virchow was now being left behind because of his unwillingness to consider new ideas and new developments; ironically, Haeckel, Virchow's former student, was leading the avant-garde.

The only fact that could possibly convince Virchow and his ilk would be the finding of the missing link. If Dubois could find it, the speechless *Pithecanthropus* that Haeckel wrote of, surely even Virchow could not deny it. Neanderthals were not enough, for they were only a low sort of human, a very primitive race. Only the fossil remains of the transitional form between ape and man could prove evolution irrefutably. There could be no denying evolution, with such a fossil in hand. To find the right fossil, the one with anatomy that was half-man, half-ape...What a grand thing it would be, to be the man who found the missing link! Dubois's boyhood ambition returned, more powerful than before.

No one knew exactly what this long-lost ancestor had looked like; no one really knew who had first called it the missing link. There was an old idea, the Great Chain of Being, that compared the creatures of the earth to links on a chain, each connected to the next, from lowest to highest. But the phrase itself had come into popular currency more recently. In 1877, when Darwin had gone to Cambridge University to receive an honorary degree, the

students had played a joke based on the phrase. Before the ceremony had begun, they had strung a cord from gallery to gallery
across the Senate House. Then, as Darwin was called up on to the
stage, they had released a monkey marionette that slowly slid along
the string, provoking titters and chuckles. The monkey had been
followed by a hoop decorated with ribbons, an object that had
been greeted with so much laughter as to cause Darwin to look up
from his shy reverie. He had seemed bewildered until he had realized it was none other than the missing link itself. Then his solemn
face had broken with delight.

Dubois especially liked the boldness of Haeckel's hypotheses: the
missing link first evolved upright posture, then the capacity for
speech. Dubois was fascinated anew with this idea. Gill structures
turned into larynxes, larynxes evolved into speech organs. Did
words make men human? If so, then Haeckel – with his flair for
writing and speaking so clearly – was perhaps more human than
some of the rest of us, Dubois thought ruefully.

Dubois knew what he would do now. The difficulties with
Fürbringer might fluctuate in seriousness, but they would never dis-
appear, so Dubois had to leave the university. The difference now
was that he conceived of leaving his position not only to escape
Fürbringer's overbearing influence but also to go in search of
greater scientific glory. He would find a way to look for the missing
link.

It was a breathtakingly bold and simple idea. No other man had
ever set out to find the fossil record of human evolution. Antiquarians and prehistorians were always poking around in caves
and rock shelters, to be sure, looking for bones and tools and signs
of ancient habitation. And paleontologists and geologists were
always wandering over exposures, rock hammers in hand, hoping
for fossils. Still, aiming at a particular target – drawing a bead on
the missing link himself – was an utterly novel idea that no one else
had ever acted upon. If Dubois found his quarry, he would never
again have to worry about being recognized as an independent
scientist. Prestige, positions, professorships: all would surely come
his way without effort, if only he could find the missing link.

He resolved to do it.

CHAPTER 8

To Find the Missing Link

Dubois was nothing if not logical. Now that he had decided on his goal, it remained only to think things through and decide how best to achieve success. Dubois attacked this research project methodically, even though it was still half a fantasy. First, he had to synthesize into a cohesive whole every bit of information he could wring from the scientific literature; then he needed to develop a strategy for his own work. He needed a sound and workable plan of action, for the stakes were high. For weeks stretching into months, he was preoccupied with thoughts and calculations. If he went to search for the missing link, he would be risking much. How was he to succeed where no one else had?

The first possibilities that occurred to him were that the others had not looked systematically and that they had not looked in the right place. The Neanderthal remains were too advanced, too nearly human to be the missing link. Despite their hulking browridges and crude, heavy bones, Neanderthals were so similar to modern humans that Virchow could dismiss them as pathological and Huxley considered them merely the most primitive of human races. Dubois's opinion was that Huxley was right. What Dubois sought was something markedly more apelike, more primitive than a Neanderthal.

Where would he find it? All the other ancient human remains that had ever been found (of which the Neanderthals were clearly the oldest and most primitive yet) had been discovered in Europe. Maybe Europe was the wrong place to look; maybe by the time human ancestors arrived in Europe they had been already too human. So where had they come *from*?

Logically, the roots of the human family tree must be sunk into the soil of the tropics, where apes lived today. Was the fundamental flaw in the work done to date that paleontologists and antiquarians had searched in Europe because that is where *they* were, where *they* lived – not where apes lived, and not where ape-men had lived? He began to work out his reasoning step by step; later, in

1888, he would submit for publication the arguments that he was now expanding and shaping in his mind, working like a skilled glassblower creating a fragile and complicated vessel.

Where exactly was he to look? Darwin, in *The Descent of Man*, proposed that man had originated in Africa, on the grounds that the African chimpanzees and gorillas were the apes most closely related to humans. Dubois was not so sure. Male chimpanzees and gorillas were so exaggerated in their anatomy, with enormous brows, protruding faces, and large, sharp canine teeth; sometimes they weighed twice as much as the females. No human race was like that. On the other hand, Haeckel argued that gibbons were the apes most akin to humans, because they were in many ways so generalized. They lived in faithful couples and sat upright on branches with their spouses. Males and females were about equal in size, though both sexes had long, sharp canines. Gibbons even walked upright on the ground, albeit with their greatly elongated arms held up on either side in a ludicrous fashion, a little like a tightrope walker. This behaviour might be a precursor to true bipedality. If so, then it would be best to go to the homeland of gibbons to search for the missing link. Both the various species of gibbon and the great red ape, the orang-utan, were Asian animals.

Dubois dissected the facts and arguments in his mind like the anatomist he was; for weeks, he read and reread every observation that might bear on the subject. After perusing some reports from the English paleontologist Richard Lydekker about fossil mammals from the Siwalik Hills of the northern frontier of British India, he wondered if *that* would be the best hunting ground. Lydekker named one of his new fossils *Troglodytes sivalensis*, the Siwalik chimpanzee, though he later revised the name to *Anthropopithecus sivalensis* to emphasize its differences from the living chimpanzee. In any case, those fossils proved that apes lived in Asia in the distant past, as they did now. There were precious few scraps of fossil ape from anywhere and it would not be wise to ignore such evidence. Dubois studied maps and Lydekker's drawings of the fossil. Indeed, Lydekker's finds were very suggestive.

Going to British India, however, posed a serious logistical problem. India was a long way from the Netherlands and, as a British colony, was a somewhat difficult place for Dubois to go. He didn't suppose that finding the missing link would be an easy task, quickly achieved, so he had to take Anna and Eugenie with him. How could he support them there, in a foreign land run by a rival nation? These tangled and difficult problems evaporated if he shifted his focus farther east, to the East Indies, which had been a Dutch colony for two hundred-odd years. He could take his family to the Indies; people spoke Dutch there; all the educated people and rulers would be Dutch in fact, except the native regents and princes. He knew several families like the Cuyperses, many of whose relatives had been in the Indies and prospered. All those Indies families would surely know something about the landscape and geography of the Indies; planters always did. The real question was: was the missing link in the Indies? No point going to look for it where it wasn't.

One evening, he went to his study to set down the meagre facts available to him. Of course, in one night he could not lay out everything he knew and didn't know. He went back to the task, day after day, trying to pin his thoughts down in orderly rows like beetles in a natural history cabinet. He wrote, crossed out, began again, revised. Finally his ideas began to take a definitive shape.

Point one: The missing link was a more apelike ancestor than those found in Europe. More apelike and more ancient fossils were likely to be found in the tropics, where the apes lived today. Fossils of great apes had recently been found in British India.

Point two: Fossils had also been found in the Dutch East Indies on the island of Java. They had been collected by the Javanese nobleman Raden Saleh, and also by the eccentric German physician-naturalist Franz Junghuhn.

Junghuhn's story was especially interesting. He had gone to Java in 1835 as a medical officer in the Royal Dutch East Indies Army, though somehow he had served for less than four years. From 1835 to 1848, Junghuhn had marched from one end of Java to the other, mostly as an employee of the Commission for Natural Sciences, learning languages, drawing and describing plants and geological formations, collecting fossils, and making the best maps available of Java. If Dubois could get a post as a naturalist in the Indies... He dragged his mind back to the task at hand.

Point three: Logic and geological principles suggested that Sumatra, another island in the Indies, would also contain many fossils. Sumatra was said to be riddled with limestone caves, and all of the best fossil sites in Europe were in caves.

The problem was that the Indies fossils might not be of the right age; for example, Europe had many fossils, but they seemed to be too recent. It was a crucial point. Here the construction of Dubois's cabinet of facts came to an abrupt halt. He needed more raw

Wallace's line divided the Far East into two zoogeographic regions,
one Asian and one Australian in nature. Since an Asian fossil
chimpanzee had been found, Dubois believed the transitional form
linking this ape to *Homo sapiens* would be found in the western part
of the East Indies.

materials, more information. It was not enough; it was not certain.
He could not risk everything for nothing.

His notebook sat closed and untouched – reproachful – on his
desk for days. Then he read some new and crucial reports about the
Indies fossils found by Raden Saleh, written by the geologist Karl
Martin. Martin's work was a revelation, providing just the information that Dubois needed. Martin had compared Raden Saleh's
Javan fossils with those from the Siwaliks, where Lydekker's
ancient chimpanzee came from, and had concluded that the two
groups of animals – the fossil faunas – were very similar and almost
certainly contemporaneous. It was exactly as Dubois had hoped.
He wanted to find the ancestors of Man who would have been of
about that age, not long after Man and ape had begun to evolve
separately. And Martin's work suggested that those ancestors were
in the Indies as well as in India.

Dubois reopened his notebook, fingered through the scribbled, crossed-over leaves, and started a new page. Upon it he wrote, happily:

'Point four: The known fossils from the Dutch East Indies are both Pleistocene in age and Asian in character. It is this period and this fauna in which we expect to find the missing link.'

Martin offered something more, an idea of great importance to Dubois's thinking. The similarities between the Siwalik and Javan fossils demonstrated the truth of one of Alfred Russel Wallace's great ideas, said Martin. Wallace was the natural historian who had conceived of natural selection simultaneously with Darwin. Their world-shaking papers – the ones that first put forward the theory of evolution and natural selection – had been read one after the other at a legendary meeting of the Linnaean Society in London, in July 1858. Little more than a year later, Darwin's *Origin of Species* appeared and rapidly became the standard explication of evolutionary theory. Wallace's greatest book came almost twenty years later. Published in 1876, it was called *The Geographical Distribution of Animals*.

On his trips through the Indies, Australia, and the Malay archipelago, collecting specimens for museums and private individuals, Wallace had noticed that there was a sort of invisible line falling to the east of Java. Between the islands of Bali and Lombok was a barrier – Wallace's line, as it became known – that divided the entire region into two natural parts.

To the west of Wallace's line were the large islands of the Indies: Java, Kalimantan, and Sumatra. They were inhabited by animals and birds that were closely related to those in South-East Asia, especially the Malay peninsula, India, and Ceylon. Wallace regarded these island faunas as fundamentally Asian in character and asked: how did this distinction come about? The answer was a geographic one. Java, Kalimantan, and Sumatra are surrounded by relatively shallow seas; they are, in fact, nothing more than the highest points on the huge continental shelf called Sunda, which extends outward from the South-East Asian mainland. Wallace speculated that, at one time, sea levels had been low and the Sunda Shelf had been solid ground. Asian animals could have spread from place to place on this extended mainland. When sea levels rose later, low-lying areas were flooded and the high points became islands, where the animals were cut off from those on the new mainland. Thus the entire Sunda Shelf had once been part of Asia, geographically and faunistically.

On the other side of Wallace's line, to the east of Bali, lie Lombok, Celebes, New Guinea, and the Moluccas, with very different faunas. Wallace saw the birds and animals indigenous to these eastern islands as fundamentally Australian in nature. Here he found marsupial species that kept their young in pouches, such as bandicoots and phalangers, and Australian birds, such as cockatoos and birds of paradise. The explanation for this pattern of distribution was similar. Just as the western islands sat on the submerged Sunda Shelf, which was attached to Asia, so these eastern islands sat in shallow waters on the submerged Sahul Shelf, what might be called greater Australia. At times of low sea levels, all the eastern islands would have been connected to the Australian mainland and shared an Australian fauna.

The issue was not only what was present where, but what was missing. The western islands of the Indies have no marsupial mammals, only Asian, placental mammals. The eastern islands, for their part, lack many of the typical Asian mammals: wild cats, wild dogs, and deer.

The invisible line between Lombok and Bali coincided with a formidable geographical gap, concealed beneath the ocean, known as the Lombok Strait. This enormous submarine trench separated the two great continental shelves, Sunda and Sahul. This deep strait was the rugged seam that stitched together the two great biogeographic regions, but the join was so treacherous and difficult to cross that it functioned as a geographic barrier. Both the continental shelves and the impassable strait between them had isolated Sunda from Sahul, keeping marsupials out of the Asian-Sunda mainland while preventing the Asian mammals from crossing into the Australian-Sahul. Martin observed that the similarities between the Siwalik and Indies fossil faunas proved that this biogeographic pattern had also existed in the distant past, for both the Indies and India were inhabited by mainland Asian species.

Point five: Geology, topography, climate, and geography all predicted that there would be fossils of Pleistocene age in the untouched caves of Sumatra. If Man's earliest apelike ancestors had evolved in Asia, then their fossilized remains ought to be part of that ancient Sumatran fauna. They had not yet been found because no one had yet looked in the right place.

Dubois sat up, pleased with his work, and rubbed his eyes. This was such a clear and compelling set of arguments, such a solid plan, that it must succeed. The fossils of the missing link must be in the Indies; it was overwhelmingly probable. The logic rang in Dubois's mind like the peals of an enormous church bell. He could not ignore them, nor could he understand why no one else had come to the same conclusion.

The sheer feasibility of going to the Indies weighed heavily with Dubois. Many Dutch sons had taken up opportunities in the Indies as merchants or planters, importers or exporters, government administrators or military men. The East Indies might be a long way from Holland, but they were psychologically a great deal closer than British India. The Indies were a little bit Dutch. Not many women and children had gone to the colonies; Dubois had heard that there were two European men for every white woman in the Indies. But some women went, some children went, and he couldn't possibly leave Anna here with little Eugenie all by herself. Anna was young and strong. They would go together. Disease was the greatest danger, but he would always be there to see to his family's health. And then, after he made his name, they could come home, like those who had made their fortunes in coffee or nutmeg and then retired to The Hague.

He felt as if he had discovered a continent, so tangible was his new conviction. He tried out his arguments the next day on Max Weber. To his surprise, Weber discouraged him; indeed he treated Dubois as if he had taken leave of his senses.

'Your plan is not practical, Dubois, don't you see that? Oh, it all sounds very pretty, as you say it, very nice, but very theoretical. You can't ruin your life for an idea patched together out of this and that, one fact here and another there. This doesn't sound like you at all. This is ... foolish.'

Dubois was stunned, but the scepticism hardened his attitude. Didn't Weber understand the brilliance of this synthesis? Didn't he see there was no way the plan could fail? Dubois even wondered, in passing, whether Weber wanted to put him off the idea so he could find the missing link himself. Later, having examined his plan once again, he went back to his colleague. He explained it all again, as if Weber has misunderstood, as if Dubois's first explanation had not been clear enough.

Weber was not swayed at all. 'Don't throw away all you have for a figment of your imagination, like the foolish boy in the Grimms' fairy tale,' he said to Dubois, kindly. 'This is real life. I know you are restless. I know you long for recognition of your hard work and intelligence. But it will come, it will come in time. Can't you be a little more patient, a little more prudent?'

He cautioned Dubois against making a hasty decision. 'I know you are very excited by the finds in Belgium, at Spy,' Weber said, 'we all are. The Neanderthals are fascinating evidence of the path of human evolution. But think how few fossils anyone has found of human ancestors. Almost nothing! Just those two skeletons from Spy, and the one from the Neander Valley, and that skull from Gibraltar. Every other fossil human ever found is anatomically modern. And mostly people find broken-up bits of fossil animals, not humans anyway. What good are animal bones for settling questions about human evolution?

'Oh, I agree with you,' Weber conceded. 'Martin is probably right that the Javan fossils are similar to the Siwalik ones. He is a good geologist. But how can you be sure you will find anything? And if you find fossils, why should they be anything other than more deer or pigs?'

Dubois had no answer for this, except that he knew in his heart he would find the missing link.

Weber continued: 'It is obvious that human ancestors don't fossilize very often, for no one ever finds them. Setting aside your career and prospects for this ... It is not a sound idea, Dubois. I urge you to think again.'

Dubois did not know how to respond, except to repeat his step-by-step logic once again, more passionately. He knew the fossils were there; they had to be there. The East Indies were the right place to find human ancestors; there were plenty of other fossils of the right age; there were lots of limestone caves to shelter and preserve fossils; they had to be there. The conclusion was so obvious to Dubois, but talking to Weber was like trying to describe sunlight to a blind man. Why couldn't he see for himself?

Weber listened again, patiently and attentively. Finally, he sighed and said to Dubois, 'For all that, you will not find the missing link, and you will give up your future.'

'But if I find the missing link ...' Dubois insisted.

'Ah,' said Weber, nodding and smiling. 'Then you are in one strike a famous man.'

It was the confirmation Dubois had been longing to hear, though Weber had not meant it as such. Dubois would go. He must.

CHAPTER 9

Logistics

The very next day, Dubois made an appointment to see the Secretary-General of the Colonial Office in The Hague, who would spare a few minutes late in the afternoon for Dr Dubois. All day he waited impatiently for the hours to pass, rehearsing his arguments in his mind. He intended to ask the Secretary-General to subsidize a research trip to the Indies to look for the missing link, so he had to present his ideas convincingly. Weber had been just practice.

The Secretary-General's office was very grand, large enough to hold a desk and chairs, several armchairs, a small sofa, and a number of tables, most covered in papers and those books that were not tucked tidily into immense walnut bookshelves. The furniture was large, ornate, meant to impress; the carpet was lush and thick. The room would have housed two full professors, Dubois thought, with ease. The Secretary-General was a very busy man, but he had heard of this rising young professor and was interested. Of course, he could not imagine what the man wanted with him. There were no medical schools or universities in the colonies; who would attend them? There were really no proper educational institutions at all. The colonists educated their children at home, by themselves or perhaps with a tutor or governess, or they sent the children back to boarding school. So Dubois could not be wanting to discuss education in the colonies or ask for a post. In fact, from what he had heard, Dr Dubois was widely predicted to become one of the top professors at Amsterdam, so why would he want to leave?

The professor was shown in, his steps echoing against the marble floor of the high-ceilinged corridor as he entered. The Secretary-General was more impressed by Dubois's handsome features, proud posture, and firm stride than he had expected to be. The Secretary-General stood and offered his hand, greeting Dubois cordially, and showed him to a comfortable chair away from the formality of his desk. He rang for tea to be brought in – a good sign, Dubois thought. Their opening conversation was polite but unfocused: the weather, mutual acquaintances, matters in the news. Finally the Secretary-General asked Dubois what he had come to see him about.

'I would like,' Dubois replied carefully, 'a government subsidy to go to the East Indies to find the missing link. You know, the missing link is the fossil form that connects apes to man, as in Darwin's great theory. Finding it would be a major advance of scientific knowledge.'

The Secretary-General's eyebrows rose and his pince-nez dropped from his nose to hang tethered to his waistcoat by a chain. Was this doubt, surprise, maybe shock? Dubois could not tell. He simply continued, as persuasively as he knew how.

'Now, this is not a mere pipe dream, sir; this is a well-supported scientific theory. There are many sound reasons why I believe this fossil will be found in the East Indies.' And then he began to build his logical edifice from the ground up.

But before Dubois had finished the preliminary sketch of his argument, the Secretary-General stopped him. 'I'm sorry, Dr Dubois,' he said firmly. Surely you know the Netherlands is in a serious economic depression just now. The Colonial Office cannot possibly subsidize a scientific research expedition in the East Indies at this time, particularly one that seems so risky. Many men die of malaria in the Indies, you know, or of cholera or typhoid. Much of the Indies is simply jungle, a few villages without roads, no proper maps. It can be very difficult to travel in the countryside, much more so to keep an expedition supplied and healthy. And the expense: prohibitive. And for what?' He gestured vaguely in the air, suggesting the lack of substance in these ideas, and then clicked his tongue.

'I'm sorry to be so discouraging,' the Secretary-General continued, 'but I think your chances of success are slight. Logic is all very well, but... well, let me just say that I think you have let yourself be carried away by that crazy book of Darwin's. There is little truth in it, you know, and much speculation. Evolution is not a fact, it is a theory. I regret, Dr Dubois, that there is nothing I can do to help you. I suggest you forget all about the missing link and concentrate on your career at the university. I have heard you are very well thought of there, with good prospects. Don't throw it all away over such foolishness: that's my recommendation.'

Nothing Dubois added would make the slightest change in the Secretary-General's opinion. In a daze of disappointment, Dubois thanked the official for seeing him and left before half an hour had passed. He felt … flattened, crushed like a top hat under the wheels of a brougham. All his hopes were soiled and lay ruined, in the gutter; all his clever synthesis was smashed and broken by the brisk tread of the Secretary-General's inflexible opinion. He had hoped for a more positive answer, had expected the logistical problems to be taken out of his hands and resolved by the bureaucracy of the Colonial Office. Instead, he had received nothing but discouragement.

Was he wrong in his reasoning? He reviewed his points, one by one, again and again, searching for flaws or weaknesses. No, the flaw lay not in his theory but in the man to whom he had proposed it, he decided on the way home. The Secretary-General was an administrator, a government man, not a man of science. He probably didn't understand Darwin's theory at all. He probably hadn't even read *The Origin of Species* or Haeckel's *History of Creation*. It was easy to call these ideas nonsense if you didn't know what they were. This man was judging the case simply by word of mouth. If he didn't believe in evolution – if he didn't know that there had been a missing link – how could he possibly have supported Dubois's expedition? That would have been truly foolish. Ah, ja, Dubois realized: 'truly foolish' was how the Secretary-General thought of him, too.

Even if he believed, as he didn't, that there was a missing link, the Secretary-General obviously did not see what Dubois knew. The link was there, in the Indies, waiting for him; he knew it. This was not mere speculation. He was an anatomist, a learned man, an expert in evolution. He had studied the natural sciences for years. He knew what was true and how to prove it. The problem was just that no one else saw the truth as clearly as he did. By the time he arrived home, he had recovered his optimism and doubled his determination. He must go to the Indies, because the most important discovery of the century awaited him there.

Besides, his conflicts with Fürbringer were growing unbearable. Dubois had not dared to speak with Fürbringer of his intention to search for the missing link, lest that, too, should somehow be usurped by the older man. Dubois bristled like a dog defending his territory from an interloper whenever Fürbringer appeared; he practically growled aloud and bared his teeth when Fürbringer offered advice or comment. The others could not help but see Dubois's sensitivity to Fürbringer. Weber, perhaps Dubois's closest friend at the university, tried to, but could, not erase Dubois's suspicions. Dubois was growing desperate, frantic to escape from Fürbringer's shadow. Finally, Weber wrote to Dubois, reluctantly giving his blessing to Dubois's plans to quit the university.

After thinking more about your plans it has become even clearer to me...that whether or not you go to the East Indies, you have lost your link with anatomy...From your point of view on teaching and its value and from your pessimistic ideas of science and from your outspoken dislike of teaching I think that, for you, happiness can never lie in the theoretical explanation. Posts of this kind are so hard to come by that they ought not be occupied by people who are not completely content in this working environment...You know the work demanded in anatomy and you didn't like it, unless it involved your own research; you like it so little that you want to choose another working environment. I think that you have already decided in this matter in your heart, have already made a decision, regardless of whether you go to the East Indies or establish yourself here as a doctor.

By now, the problem was not one of intent. Dubois knew what he must flee *from* and where he must go *to*, but not how to get there. His savings were woefully inadequate to pay the passage for himself, his wife, and his little daughter, much less to support them for months or even years. He did not like to ask his father for help, for Jean Joseph did not share his son's fascination with the missing link. The apothecary still wondered aloud sometimes if his son wouldn't have been better off to follow in his profession.

Dubois could think of only one way to go to the East Indies. Like Franz Junghuhn, Dubois had a skill that opened doors: he was a physician. He could sign on as a medical officer in the Koninklijk Nederlandsch-Indisch Leger, the Royal Dutch East Indies Army. And as time passed and Dubois's suspicions of Fürbringer flourished, the idea of enlisting seemed more and more attractive. He saw himself following in the footsteps of Junghuhn, a vision that took some of the bitterness out of the Colonial Office's refusal to fund him. Besides, going to the colonies to seek greater scope and opportunity was a long and honourable tradition in the Netherlands. He, too, sought a freer world, where discovery was not hampered by traditional thinking and narrow-minded, jealous men.

On 29 July he wrote inquiring about the possibility of enlisting as a military surgeon in the colonial army. Almost immediately, he received an answer: he would be accepted for an eight-year tour of duty if he passed a physical exam, scheduled for 4 August between nine and ten o'clock in the morning in Amsterdam. When he went home that night, he showed Anna the letter and explained to her what he had done. She listened to his complaints and even to his plans of going to the Indies, but she was startled to find it almost a fait accompli. Once he had passed his medical exam – and he surely would – then there would be two contracts to sign: one for him, agreeing to the terms of his eight-year enlistment; and one for her, pledging not to attempt to follow her husband on military campaigns in case of war. The sudden shift in the future was bewildering and even a little frightening to her, as Dubois could see from the expression on her face.

'Anna, you know I had no choice. You can see that. Fürbringer was taking credit for my work. You couldn't expect me to stay there in the face of that, could you?' She shook her head no, as Dubois tried to reassure her. 'Anna, you remember that I have told you of it, of my great idea. I will find the missing link in the East Indies; it will prove evolutionary theory to be true. It will make my name as a great scientist. I am certain that the missing link is in the Indies. There can be no doubt. So this is what we must do. We will go to the Indies, to make this discovery.'

Uncharacteristically, Anna held her tongue until she had sorted through the blur of thoughts in her mind. Until now, she had known where the future lay. She would be a professor's wife, living in a nice house in Amsterdam and raising children. Now she was on the verge of committing herself to go to the East Indies for eight years. Eight years seemed an eternity. By the time they returned to Holland, Anna would be thirty-two years old, baby Eugenie would be eight. She remembered having heard of Dutch schools set up for European children in the East Indies – perhaps in Batavia, in Java? – but her knowledge of the colonies' geography was vague. But, she thought rather complacently, if there were Dutch children in the Indies, there would be some way to educate them. And it must not be a terrible place to live, for all those ex-colonials in The Hague spoke of the Indies with such nostalgia.

Finally she spoke, an expression of almost mischievous glee on her face. 'Won't they all be surprised when we tell them?' she said, giggling a little at the thought. 'All those silly old women who make remarks about Eugenie – and those stuffy old men at the university who expect you to let them steal your work! Oh, I wish I could see their faces when you tell them. They aren't young enough or strong enough or clever enough to do something like this. I can't wait to tell Mama, and Papa, and your family. I am so proud.' Anna walked distractedly about the room as she talked, spilling over with excitement. Dubois listened and watched his wife in amazement.

'I always knew you would do something important, I knew it from the first time you walked into the classroom. I could see it in your eyes.' Her mind raced first in one direction and then in another. 'They say it is very sunny and warm and beautiful in the Indies, not grey and cold like Amsterdam in winter. Won't it be good to get away from these cold, raw winds and the bitterness of winter? The Indies always sound like a paradise when Indies families describe them, a tropical heaven where Dutch people live like royalty, with grand houses and lots of servants. Oh, won't it be an adventure!'

Anna and Dubois posed for this portrait shortly before they left for the East Indies.

Dubois had feared she would hate the idea, would dread leaving all that she knew. He had certainly underestimated her courage, her resilience. Anna turned to him abruptly, as if struck by the significance of the plan for their lives. Dubois waited for her words, waited for the fear or the protest to begin. Instead, Anna seemed suddenly practical and efficient. 'If this is what we must do to prove your brilliance to everyone, then I had better begin planning what we shall take with us. When would we sail?'

Dubois beamed with pleasure, taking her small, feminine hands in his large, capable ones, and kissing them affectionately. She had shown so much more character than he expected. 'We shall go, my little Anna, we shall go,' he repeated softly. 'I think we must sail before October is out. I shall check as soon as I have passed the medical exam. It will be a great adventure – just you, and me, and the baby.'

By the next Sunday, Dubois had passed his exam; by the end of August, they had received and signed their contracts with the army. Now they went to visit Dubois's parents to tell them of their plans. Dubois's father, adamantly opposed, responded as if his son could be talked out of this decision, as if an irrevocable step had not already been taken. As for Dubois's unhappiness at the university, that was the result of unworthy thoughts and ridiculous imaginings. Jean Joseph dismissed his son's problems with Fürbringer completely.

'You cannot believe,' the father blustered, his normally florid face turning choleric, 'that Fürbringer – that a man of his reputation – has any interest in stealing your ideas. What folly!' He shook his finger at his son, as if at a naughty child. 'You think you are cleverer than everyone else, but this is only sinful pride. Fürbringer is a great man, a brilliant man. Why would he need to take your ideas? If only you will put aside your absurd concerns, in a few years' time you can be the professor of anatomy, with a fine house overlooking the canal in Amsterdam. What could be better than that?'

Anna squirmed in her chair like a schoolgirl while her father-in-law scolded her husband. She hated it when they disagreed, as they clearly did now. She had hoped her in-laws might be pleased and excited for them, happy that Dubois was going to fulfil his dream at last. She did not know what to do except keep silent and pray for it to be over, Fortunately, Dubois made no reply. He simply stared at his father and waited. His very silence contrasted the virtues of a 'fine house overlooking the canal' with those of making a discovery of lasting importance to science. What a narrow vision his father had. If Jean Joseph Balthasar Dubois had ever known what it was to discover something new, he had forgotten how it felt.

The room was filled with disharmony as the two men looked at each other and weighed each other's character and determination.

'Will you have more tea, Father? Eugène? Anna?' Trinette asked nervously, to fill the void. The men did not show they had heard her question; Anna gratefully accepted more tea. Dubois's mother waved a plate vaguely, trying to smooth over the situation. 'Another cake? Just one more, Anna; they are your favourites. You must keep your strength up. You have a baby girl to look after.' The clatter of cups, the exercise of passing plates, the ordinary politeness seemed to ease the tension a little.

In a moment, Jean Joseph advanced another argument, seeing that his first had not changed his son's mind. 'Of course the professor puts his name on your papers, sometimes,' he said, thinking he was making a large concession to his touchy son by even admitting the practice. 'That is because Fürbringer is the professor, the supervisor of all those who work under him. He is like the father, who is the head of the family and responsible for all its members. Your name is Dubois, isn't it? Like my own? It shows the relationship between us. So of course your work should bear Fürbringer's name, too, from time to time. It is only fitting. If Fürbringer puts his name on your papers, it is like offering his imprimatur. It is the way things are done. There is nothing wrong with it, except to you because you are so proud and stubborn.'

The elder Dubois shifted in his chair, recalling with irritation almost thirty years of his son's stubbornness and idiosyncrasy. The memories prodded him like a knitting needle buried among the sofa cushions. 'You can never go someone else's way, Eugène, can you? You have no grace, no gratitude, no ability to compromise. It must always be your own way or not at all. Well, this attitude will not do, not in this world.'

'You raised me to be honest, Father,' Dubois replied stiffly. 'To claim another man's work as your own is surely a dishonesty. It is theft. Property of the mind is no different from material property. If a man takes your hat, and says it is his own, he is both stealing and lying: that is plain. If a man takes my ideas and passes them off as his own, that, too, is stealing and lying. Would you have me compromise my honesty? Besides, I have already signed the contract.'

His father made a noise of disgust but said nothing in reply. It was no use talking to his son; he was so unyielding. Jean Joseph would not accept his son's point of view, nor would the son heed his father's pragmatic advice. Fürbringer's actions aside, there was the missing link to be found. Dubois was not only leaving the university, he was also going to the East Indies. There was push and pull.

Dubois was filled with sadness as he and Anna left his parents' home to journey back to their own. Before coming, he had hoped to make them understand what a fine thing he was attempting; he had hoped for his father's praise and encouragement in this bold undertaking. Now he knew they understood nothing, did not share his vision at all. One day, he would return to Eijsden with the missing link, in triumph. Then Jean Joseph would see what it meant to the world of science. The name of Marie Eugène François Thomas Dubois would be on everyone's lips; his missing link would be in all the newspapers and journals and books. Then Jean Joseph would see that he had been right to pursue his vision. Then his father would be proud. Maybe his father was just too old and too tired to understand, to think the goal worth the risk.

As for Anna's parents, they were distraught when they learned of the plan to go to the East Indies. Her mother broke down and sobbed at the thought of her daughter and baby granddaughter being taken so far away for so long. 'The East Indies?' she cried in horror, pressing her crumpled handkerchief to her eyes. 'The Indies are full of tropical diseases and black men. Who knows what might befall you? There are snakes and tigers and poisonous plants, a thousand things to hurt you. Even good Dutchmen lose their morals there and go native, I have heard the stories many times. And what of Eugenie? She is just a baby. You can't take her to such a place. It is too dangerous. Oh no, no, you can't go.'

While Anna patted her mother's trembling hand and dried her tears – the daughter and mother reversing roles – Dubois tried to calm his mother-in-law's fears with logic. Thousands of Hollanders had lived in the Indies over the last two centuries. Truly, two out of three used to die of tropical diseases but not any more, not now. The new treatments were wonderfully effective.

'Besides,' Dubois said reassuringly, 'I am a doctor. Anna and Eugenie will be with me and I will look after them. You know I will. As for what happens to Europeans in the colonies, going native, that is all nonsense based on a few people who had no morals when they lived in Europe either. You have seen pictures in the homes of Indies families. They don't live in grass huts, running around naked except for a few beads and trinkets, like savages. We shall live in a proper house, with servants and a garden. We shall wear proper clothes, and Anna will see that the house is kept clean and sanitary. I am a professional man; this is my family. I will see that they are safe. After all, I am not some young rake shipped off to the colonies to escape his creditors or a woman he has wronged. No harm will come to us, I assure you.'

Anna's mother took little consolation in these words; she could think only of the separation, eight long years. Her father said little but sat close to his wife, as if his physical nearness might give comfort. That he, too, had doubts was obvious from the expression on his face, though he did not voice them as a woman would. He liked Dubois – thought him a good man, a sound man – and Anna was his wife. She had to go with him, if he was going.

Dubois tried to smile and restore a pleasant atmosphere of optimism. In response, Anna's mother made a visible effort to stop her tears and asked after Eugenie. With relief, they spoke about the baby for some minutes. Eugenie was their only granddaughter, so every event in her young life seemed important. Soon after, Dubois and Anna excused themselves, saying they mustn't be late returning home.

With the parental trials over, there was only one more group to be told the news. In some ways, this was the interview that Dubois dreaded most. He chose a moment when most of his colleagues were together to announce his intentions, so he would not have to face Fürbringer in a private interview. There was much consternation at his words. Clearly Fürbringer did not understand what Dubois had done and why, and he only reluctantly accepted Dubois's formal resignation. 'I advise against this, you know,' the professor said heavily, putting a hand on Dubois's shoulders. 'You have a great future ahead of you here. I have always planned that you will succeed me when I retire; surely you know that. You are already so well thought of. You must not throw the chance away.'

Dubois was implacable. 'I shall go,' he replied. 'I shall go and I shall find the missing link. Staying here, carrying on my dissections, publishing articles in scientific journals, moving up the academic ladder cannot compare with finding the missing link. I must go.'

Fürbringer sighed and offered his hand; Dubois hesitated for an awkward moment, and then took it firmly. The man had been good to him, but he had left Dubois no room to breathe. Opportunities would be broader in the Indies. Weber and De Vries were there too, wishing him luck, expressing their sorrow at losing a good friend and colleague. Perhaps they thought Dubois crazy, risking everything for one of Haeckel's ideas. No matter; they were his friends, they had worked with him for years, they would miss him.

'I was afraid you'd do this,' Weber admitted, 'you've been talking about your ideas so long and so ardently.' Fürbringer, surprised to hear that Weber had known of Dubois's plan in advance, shot a sharp look first at Weber, then at Dubois. 'Well, I wish you the best of luck,' Weber continued innocently, not realizing that he had said something startling. 'May you find your missing link! If anyone can do it, you can, that's for sure. If you need something sent to you – books, maybe, or instruments – let me know. But you'd better take most of what you need, you know. The mail ships may come twice a week, but they don't travel very fast.'

On one of his last days at the university, Dubois gave a final lecture, explaining his resignation and his research plans in the Indies. It was one of his best lectures, full of passionate conviction and brilliance. The students seemed awed, some envious, others shocked. Dubois was very pleased with himself when it was over.

A few days later, he received a letter from Fürbringer that left him incredulous. Fürbringer wrote as if he were trying to salvage Dubois's career, which was about to be ruined. He offered to edit the huge larynx manuscript and see to its publication; Dubois was dumbfounded at the man's audacity. Did Fürbringer think this, too, was his work, not Dubois's? Or did he think Dubois was a dead man, about to succumb to typhoid or malaria? Dubois had no intention of dying. He was going to live his true life. He would take that manuscript with him and work on it in the evenings. He would never turn it over to Fürbringer; better to leave the work unpublished than to publish it with Fürbringer's name on it. Dubois did not answer the letter, not even to tell Fürbringer when he and his family would sail. He did not want Fürbringer's face to be one of the last sights he saw as he left Holland. He needed to look forward, not back.

But as the steamship SS *Prinses Amalia* pulled out of Amsterdam harbour on 29 October 1887, Dubois regretted his pettiness. Hastily he wrote a farewell letter to his former mentor and dispatched it from the first port of call. Better to leave on a friendly note, he thought, than to take small-minded revenge.

Anna (seated, bottom right), Dubois (with beard, standing, second row), and baby Eugenie (not shown) leave for the Indies on October 29, 1887, on the SS *Prinses Amalia*.

The ship carried mail, parcels, other officers headed for Sumatra and Java, a few colonials returning from home leave, and a large group of nuns going to work in a mission. For weeks, these people were the entire world. Before leaving Amsterdam, Dubois had decided to grow a beard to symbolize the change in his identity. He was no longer an academic professor but a medical man and fossil-hunter. Now that the beard was past the short and prickly stage, Anna thought her husband looked very distinguished. She also admired his second lieutenant's uniform, with its smart tunic with brass buttons up the front and a high collar. How handsome he was! He was fit and strong and young, on the verge of a great adventure. She was glad to be married to him and not to one of the others.

Baby Eugenie was a pretty thing, just over six months old, and she was a great favourite on the ship. The nuns clucked and fussed over her endlessly. In this company, no one compared Eugenie's birthdate with her parents' wedding date. All they saw was her thick curly hair, fair Dutch complexion, and sunny disposition.

The voyage was long and sometimes rough. Anna was with child again, a few months gone, and she suffered from nausea whenever the sea was less than glassy calm. She was naturally cheerful, but she could not remember ever before feeling so poorly. She spent many days as close as possible to a convenient basin or bucket. Since Eugenie would not sit quietly for long, even to listen to her mother singing, it was a blessing to have the nuns as substitute mothers. They were always happy to walk the child around the deck or to play simple games with her. When Anna's nausea persisted, Dubois insisted on giving her a full medical examination, for he feared something might be going awry with the pregnancy. To his relief, he could find nothing but the wretched combination of seasickness and morning sickness. He advised her to rest, to sip water and nibble dry biscuits when she could. She suffered miserably for the first few weeks of the voyage, but sometimes in the afternoons she seemed her old gay self.

Fortunately, Dubois was robust as always, with a sound stomach and a good appetite. Only the roughest of seas upset his constitution. Since Anna often needed to lie quietly in the darkened cabin, her husband spent a good deal of time with his fellow officers, learning Malay, which they told him would be invaluable in dealing with servants and other natives. It was a challenge Dubois enjoyed, for he was gifted at languages. He already had a command of English and French, considerable knowledge of Latin and Greek, and a good deal of German. Basic Malay, simplified into a trading language by the seafaring natives and the colonists, was not very difficult for him.

The old Indies hands taught the first-timers with good-natured humour. In Malay, how something was said might be as important as what words were said. The subtlety of a yes that meant agreement, a yes that acknowledged the other's point without agreeing, and a yes that meant 'I seriously doubt what you say' could be crucial. Still, Malay was far simpler than High Javanese, the language used in the courts of the regents, sultans, and native princes; it had intricate rules of address and manner, based on the relative status of the speaker and the listener and the circumstances under which they conversed. Fortunately, Dubois would have little need of High Javanese.

When the men's Malay-language classes had progressed far enough, they started making jokes with one another. They practised simple conversations, gave mock orders, and competed with each other to think up silly things to ask for: 'Boy, bring me a baked coconut with elephant gravy, on the best china.' 'Have you planted the piano in the garden, as I told you to? Did you water it well?' The sense of boyish fun made the learning pleasant and polished the participants' fluency. Dubois tried to help Anna learn Malay, too, for their servants would speak little Dutch and she would be in charge of the household while he was at work or away searching for fossils. Perhaps he hoped too that the mental exercise would distract her from her nausea. He gave her lessons in the afternoon, when she was stronger and felt better, but Anna found it hard to concentrate. Moreover, Eugenie often demanded her mother's attention in the middle of a lesson.

Taught in isolation, with only her terribly clever husband present, Anna was very shy about speaking Malay. She feared she would mispronounce the words or that she would say something indelicate. The old-timers told cruel stories of the misguided and garbled commands of newcomers to the Indies and some stories got back to Anna. She imagined gruff voices making fun of her as she struggled to learn Malay. 'And she said to the houseboy,' one story (too vulgar to be told to a lady that Anna learned of nonetheless) went, 'taking him from door to door that night, "Make water here! Make water there!" instead of telling him to lock up!' Another tale featured the young mother who told the *babu* 'The baby is rotting,' like bad meat, instead of telling her the child was spoiled. 'Can you imagine?' the old Indies hands cackled in glee. 'No wonder the babu ran away; she probably thought the child had leprosy.' Anna feared becoming another humorous tale. Instead of babbling glibly as thoughts occurred to her, she developed the habit of thinking a sentence out carefully before she spoke it. The jolly camaraderie of the lounge was very different: Dubois and the other men boldly plunged into sentences, making all sorts of grammatical and pronunciation errors with unshakeable confidence. They could laugh at themselves; the natives would figure out what they meant, they had no fears. They were Dutch, they were male, they were superior.

As the ship travelled south and east, the healthy, brisk sea air of the European coast gave way to the much sultrier climate near the equator. Anna's fashionable long-sleeved, high-necked dresses were first warm and then downright stifling. She relied on a parasol or sought the shade when she appeared on deck, which was more frequently as the trip progressed. Likewise, Dubois's woollen military uniform was exceedingly uncomfortable. The high collar became soaked with sweat and rubbed against the skin of his neck, already tender with sunburn. When the ladies were not around, the military men unbuttoned their tunics or even removed them to get more air, but they could not, of course, appear in company in such a state of undress. If some of the soldiers lacked natural delicacy, the scandalized expressions of the nuns were enough to refine the coarsest temperament. They all looked forward to passing through the Suez Canal and arriving at Port Said, where traditionally the tropics began. There, Europeans on their way to the colonies usually flocked ashore to the Simons Artz Emporium to have lightweight tropical garments made up.

Dubois spent as much time as possible on deck, in the open air and breeze, despite the burning sun. He marvelled that Europeans could live and work in a tropical climate for long, and envied the young unmarried men, who moved their mattresses up on to the deck at night to sleep. The unabated heat sapped his vigour and blurred his concentration. He mopped the sweat from his face constantly, turning clean, crisp handkerchiefs into sodden messes at an astonishing rate. He began to understand all the stories about colonials who gave in to the seductive languor of the tropics – who 'went native' and lost their Dutchness. In this heat, moving or even thinking energetically required a tremendous effort. The effect was immensely irritating to Dubois, who prided himself on his character, sharpness of mind, and physical vigour.

He would not go native, he pledged. He would adapt and accustom himself to the heat, dressing in lighter clothing, working earlier in the mornings. He would do whatever he had to in order to be able to work hard. No one would work harder than he. He would not lower his standards.

He wondered whether, before leaving Amsterdam, he should have asked more questions about life in the Indies, but what difference would it have made? Knowing more would not change the weather. At the time he had been too busy packing up books and taking meticulous, detailed notes on every scientific article he had thought would be of use during his sojourn. The only library he would have in the Indies was what he brought with him, and books were heavy and costly to transport. If he was lucky, he would find a few colleagues who had brought out their own scientific libraries, and he might be able to borrow books from them now and again. But on the whole, he would be truly independent, at last. He used much of the time on the ship to fill the gaps in his knowledge about life in the Indies. He listened endlessly to those who had been out before about the best way to manage in the colonies, and asked every question his fertile brain gave birth to.

Anna simply lay in her cabin or in a deckchair, reclining in whatever shade or breeze she could find. She was miserably hot and uncomfortable, no longer so sick to her stomach, but far from her usual self. She felt like some spineless sea creature exposed by the low tide: soft, shapeless, hardly able to support the weight of her own body. The nuns brought cool cloths to place on her forehead and sat with her through the sweltering afternoons, sometimes reading aloud to her from soothing books. They urged her to swallow cooling drinks and to try to eat a little bland food, especially in the evenings when it was less hot. She must keep up her strength; as the wife and mother, she was the mainstay of the family and it was up to her to keep them safe and virtuous.

She thought to herself gratefully that their sympathetic attentions were probably as much help as any of their remedies. What, after all, would a group of ageing nuns know about the trials of pregnancy? She could not mention it, of course, but she felt as if the baby inside her was generating as much heat as the relentless sun overhead. It was as if there were some mystical connection between the sun and the child that grew within. This would be a tropical baby, conceived in the cold of Europe but carried and born and raised in the sun.

CHAPTER 10

Padang

At long last, on 11 December 1887, the ship arrived in Padang, Sumatra. The Dubois family had been on board for forty-four days and half a world of distance.

Padang – for this day, it was all of Sumatra to them – was the most astonishingly different place they had ever seen. Even the places they had passed coming through the Suez Canal, with natives in long, loose shirts strolling among palm trees and camels, were not as foreign as this. Despite the Dutch buildings – or perhaps because of them, they looked so out of place – no one could have mistaken this port for any place in the Netherlands, or for anywhere in Europe, not for a moment. The air was hot and damp and full of strange scents. Leaving the ship, walking down the docks, Dubois was suddenly enveloped in an invisible cloud of cinnamon, and then it was gone, replaced by the rich smell of some flowering plant he could not identify.

Gazing down the unpaved streets that surrounded the harbour, Dubois saw they were broad, tree-lined and pleasant. But the trees themselves were wrong, bizarre umbrella-shaped creations with leaves blue-green or silvery, not the deep green of Dutch trees. The people, the smells, the sounds, the vegetation – even the air itself was foreign. Nothing was tidy, constrained, neat; nothing was *Dutch*. Here in Padang there were comparatively many Europeans and quite a number of proper European buildings, but it all looked wrong. The lush, overblown tropical plants and trees looked somehow indecent next to the European buildings. The native dwellings looked more suitable, but utterly strange: long houses of bamboo with matting walls and upward-curving thatched roofs mimicking the line of a pair of bull's horns. And the heat and the closeness of all of those natives were daunting.

He and Anna were surrounded by brown-skinned natives: uniformed but barefoot servants in crisp white, awaiting their masters; minor officials carrying out their Byzantine duties; sailors, labourers, porters, and who-knows-what. Traders offered their

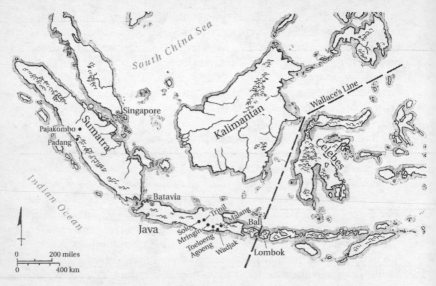

The Duboises lived in Padang and Pajakombo on Sumatra before
Dubois moved his operations to Java, where they lived at Toeloeng
Agoeng. Other major towns (Batavia, Solo, Malang) and fossil sites
(Wadjak, Trinil) are also shown.

wares, whatever those might be, calling out from the small, thatch-
roofed stalls that lined the roadside. Dubois called to mind the
Malay word for those small shops, *warung*s, with satisfaction. All
around them were sweating coolies, dark-skinned, dark-eyed, with
exotic headwraps, naked chests, and plaid sarongs tied round their
waists. These men carried all the crates and packages off the ship
and loaded smaller piles into two-wheeled carts, *dokar*s. Bigger
items went into the larger, four-wheeled vehicles, a new design
called a *delman*. Even the small, wiry ponies that pulled the carriages looked exotic. They seemed to come in every colour, from
dun to bay to a glossy chestnut. Most were decorated with horse
brasses, with colourful tassels of red and green or yellow tied to
their forelocks. The largest, heaviest goods were transported in
enormous crude wooden oxcarts, pulled slowly by huge, pale-
skinned, wet-nosed cattle with massive humps on their necks. They
must have weighed well over a thousand pounds, Dubois judged.

The natives, men and women both, were small and graceful, and
nearly all wore ankle-length sarongs. Somehow, the garment

imparted to the most muscular of men a strangely flowing movement, almost feminine. The natives seemed less solid than the
Europeans; they were certainly slighter and shorter and, of course,
much darker. Amid the crush of workers, colonials, and arrivals,
Dubois stood out as a striking figure: a big man, strong and self-
confident. He was five feet nine in his stocking feet, a full head
taller than most of the natives. In his hat and uniform – for, of
course, he was properly dressed for arrival – he was over six feet
tall, taller too than most of the Europeans. And he was muscular,
perhaps 175 pounds in weight with a barrel chest and big arms. His
impressive solidity was set off by his colouring. Both his beard and
his thick wavy hair were a golden reddish-blond; his eyes were
palest blue, a rare shade even in Holland. He was about as unnative
and as thoroughly Dutch in appearance as any person that could be
imagined.

Dubois was intrigued by the natives' exaggerated, high cheek-
bones and strong jaws. These features were especially pronounced
in the elderly, whose skin seemed translucent, as if he could see
straight through to the bones beneath. He admired their skulls
greatly, for he had never seen such a shape before. He thought he
should obtain some for study. He must make a few notes on them,
in any case. He was less attracted by the betel-stained, blackened
teeth and red gums that so many natives had and he was sickened
by their filthy habit of spitting a mixture of saliva and betel juice on
the ground. He wondered why anyone would chew betel when the
results were so disgusting.

He slowly became aware that he was the object of much attention. Some stared overtly, others more discreetly, for the natives
were naturally polite. To them, Dubois exuded power and wealth
and authority. These attributes, as much as his unusual physical
characteristics, meant that dark eyes would follow his actions
wherever he went in the Indies, for the entire eight years. The
surveillance was never-ending. He was examined as if he were a
fierce exotic bird, one that had sharp talons and a powerful beak,
one of which it was wise to be careful.

The heavy air was filled with a cacophony of languages: High
and Low Javanese, Madurese, Malay, Acehnese, Minangkabau,
Buginese, and endless dialects. But their voices were generally soft
and their faces friendly. Dubois could spot few signs of argument
or conflict as brown hands gestured gracefully, postures changed,
heads tilted at peculiar angles as if the necks that supported them

were made of rubber. Dubois was riveted by the scene in front of him, hardly knowing where to look first. There was more colour and activity here than in the busiest market day at home.

He became aware of small islands of Dutch and English language amidst the noise. The long-time European residents of the Indies, the Indische, had a strong accent and an unusual pattern of speech; they dropped the 'I's out of their sentences and elided some of the consonants, shortening and softening the words. This seemed to be part of the tropical languor, as if it was just too much trouble – or maybe too hot – to speak correctly.

Anna was at first a little giddy and then a touch frightened by the strangeness of the activity surrounding them. A wave of lightheadedness swept over her and she clung to Dubois's arm for support. 'Eugène,' she whispered urgently to him, 'are these strange brown people to be our servants, in our home? However will I speak to them?' She clutched a hot and squirming Eugenie closer to her side. 'How can I turn Eugenie over to a native nursemaid? Shall those brown hands touch her soft pink skin, wash her hair? Eugène, where have you brought me? What shall we do?' She was close to fainting.

'It is all right, Anna,' Dubois replied quietly. He held her arm firmly, encouraging her to stand still. His calm, solid presence reassured Anna and quieted Eugenie, too. 'We shall find an experienced babu at the military base.'

'Babu? A babu?' replied Anna, her eyes rolling a little hysterically.

'Yes, Anna, a babu, a nursemaid.' He kept his voice low and calm. 'You remember, Anna. We learned those words together. We shall hire a babu that someone Dutch has employed before, a woman with references. She will know just how to care for Eugenie. It will be perfectly safe,' he whispered comfortingly to her. 'You remember our plan. We shall need a babu for Eugenie, a kokkie to prepare the meals, a djongas or houseboy, a ladies' maid for you, and a garden boy – they call them tukang kebun, remember?'

These few words of Malay seemed somehow reassuring to Anna. She remembered them. She could not have summoned them up out of the confusion of her brain by herself, but she remembered them and they constituted a sort of plan. The words themselves repeated in her brain like a spell of protection: a *babu*, a *kokkie*, a *djongas*, another *babu* for me, and a *tukang kebun*; a *babu*, a *kokkie*, a *djongas*...

Before long, their piles of luggage were unloaded from the ship and a stocky uniformed man appeared at their side. 'Lieutenant Dr. Dubois?' he inquired, saluting.

'Yes,' replied Dubois. 'I am Dr Dubois. This is my wife, Anna, and my daughter.'

'Isn't she a beauty?' the man responded admiringly, patting Eugenie's disarranged curls. Then he remembered himself and his duty. 'Captain Hendrik Krull,' he said, bowing his head. 'Doctor, Mevrouw. Sent to collect you. This your luggage here?' He gestured toward the enormous pile of their belongings.

'Yes, that is it,' Dubois said, a little embarrassed.

'Certain you've got ever'thin'? No point leavin' barang-barang here, you know. Natives'll only steal it.'

'Yes, yes, that's all of it.'

'Ajo!' This was the first time they had heard this common Indies exclamation, an expression roughly equivalent to 'Let's get going!' The captain turned away from the Dubois and called to his men. 'Coolie! Adik! Here. That's their barang-barang. Careful now! Hati-hati! Don't break ever'thin'! Keep that trunk the right way up. Don't drop it.'

Krull was a wonder of efficiency. He somehow gathered up the Dubois and all their belongings and shepherded them effortlessly through the chaos. He handed them into a smart *delman* in a matter of moments. Anna sank gratefully into the feeling of being taken care of, while the coolies packed the luggage into a large oxcart that followed them down the broad, dusty street.

'Don't want to hang around here all day,' Krull confided. 'Need a rest, no doubt, and a meal before startin' to unpack. Quarters are ready for you. Sent my people over this mornin' to give it a bit of a clear-out.'

'Thank you,' said Anna vaguely; she hardly took in what he said, she was so distracted with looking around at the people and buildings and vegetation.

At the base, they were a little disappointed by the quarters assigned to them; the house was drab and small and poorly furnished. But it was clean, the walls were thick, and the roof looked sound. Still, Anna had expected something better for a second lieutenant's family. She had not yet seen the cramped, tin-roofed barracks where the enlisted men lived, or she would have known how good this accommodation was.

The officers' quarters were arranged in a long row, one after another, separated from the avenue by a low whitewashed cement wall. Each building was almost indistinguishable from the next but for differences in the plantings in the forecourts and gardens, if there were any. Where there were plantings, there was a European or Eurasian wife who tended them lovingly – or rather, who saw to it that the *tukang kebun*, the garden boy, tended them properly. No *njonja*, no married European lady, would have stooped to actual digging, planting, or weeding; that was natives' work. The *njonja* gave the orders, planned the garden, and oversaw the work, but she did not do it herself. But there were very few European or even Indo wives at the military base in Padang at all, although all the officers were Pures, people of European blood with no native admixture. The military discouraged marriage except among the senior men who had served honourably for years.

It was the rainy season when they arrived and every afternoon it rained for a few hours with a fury that the Dubois had never experienced. How could *rain* be foreign? wondered Anna. But it was. Water poured out of the sky. It was like standing in a waterfall. And everything was swimming in mud before the day was out. Mud got on everyone's boots, clothes, hands, and face; there was no way to avoid it. Mud spread itself insidiously throughout the house. A full staff of servants was an absolute necessity. Besides, as soon as they arrived at the base, there were dozens of would-be servants crouched in the yard in front of their house. Even the rain did not drive them away. They squatted on their heels and waited, silently, for the hiring to begin. Each hopeful employee bore his or her precious references, creased and crumpled pieces of paper that had been folded and refolded many times. As the natives were nearly all illiterate, and even the literate ones read no Dutch, they had no idea what the mysterious names on these aged pieces of paper said. But they knew they must have them if they were to gain employment from a *totok*, a newly arrived European.

Waking the next morning and seeing that the silent, dark-skinned, expectant crowd was still there, Anna knew she had to do something. She was nervous about dealing with natives, but they had been there all day and all night, and they showed no signs of leaving until she hired her staff. They simply waited and watched. She was unable to bear their collective inspection for another moment, although her dark hair spared her some of the incessant scrutiny meted out to Dubois.

Anna took a deep breath and began. She needed servants to

unpack, to clean, to cook, to look after Eugenie. The very idea of
having half a dozen people to look after the three of them delighted
her. What a fine lady she had become, all of a sudden! Trying to
project an aura of firm dignity, and failing utterly, Anna stepped
out on to the front veranda. She was only twenty-five years old, not
long a wife, and completely inexperienced in the way of things in
the Indies. She had almost no Malay at her command, so she gestured to one respectable-looking middle-aged man. She called him
forward in Dutch and, to her pleasure, he seemed to understand.
Slowly he stood up and walked forward, stopping respectfully a
few paces away from her. Anna smiled triumphantly. He understood her! She was elated; maybe she wouldn't have to learn Malay
after all. In this, she was completely mistaken.

The man held out his paper to her. 'Referentie,' he said, using
almost his only word of Dutch.

Anna took the paper solemnly and started to read. 'This is to
introduce Ahmad,' the writing said. 'He is an old rogue and will
steal from you regularly.' Anna was astonished. She read the sentence again; it had not changed. She composed her face as well as
she could and continued to read. 'When he is not stealing, he is as
lazy as the day is long. But he keeps the other servants from stealing
quite so much and he has a good appearance. He makes an acceptable djongas if you don't expect him to do much.' Anna could not
prevent a smile forming on her lips. Here, apparently, reference-
writing was a comic art. She struggled to maintain the dignity befit-
ting a *njonja*. Finally she just nodded and smiled tightly at Ahmad.
He stepped confidently to one side, turning proudly to face the
crowd of applicants. A number of the other waiting men sighed,
stood up, and walked away. They could see that Ahmad had been
hired, even if the *njonja* didn't know it yet.

Slowly, uncertainly, Anna proceeded to hire the others: first the
babu for Eugenie, then her ladies' maid, then the *kokkie*, and
finally the *tukang kebun*, thc garden boy. She still could not read
much on their faces, nor was she particularly concerned with their
feelings. Even the ladies' maid, who would be in intimate contact
with her, was unimaginably distant. The invisible barriers of race
and station meant that no European ever thought of his or her servants as fully human, though the aristocracy of the princes and
other noble Javanese families was recognized. Like everyone else in
her position, Anna never asked whether servants found it insulting
to be called by terms used for youngsters, such as *adik* – 'boy' – or

to have their names replaced by their occupations. Did a labourer dislike being called 'coolie'? Who knew? Who would think of such a question? European superiority was unquestioned. To be sure, there were many of mixed race in the Indies, but the 'whiter' someone appeared, the higher his or her status.

By the end of the afternoon, Anna had hired her household staff and the crowd of natives had dispersed. She felt relieved, lightened. How oppressive their dark, watchful presence had been to her! Of the new servants, the *babu* gave Anna the greatest sense of security. As promised by her excellent references, Sanikem was a quiet and graceful young woman, with a soft voice and a smile. Very quickly, Eugenie gave Sanikem her complete trust and devoted love; she was as happy and safe in her *babu*'s arms as in her mother's or father's. The ladies' maid, Lilik, also had a gentle way about her that made her easy company for Anna. She never intruded, never seemed in the way, but never strayed very far from her mistress, lest she need something. The *djongas* Ahmad held himself with an air of superiority and, in his crisp white uniform and spotless headwrap, added a style to the new household that Anna – and even more Dubois – approved of. They did not forget his reputation as a rogue, but they enjoyed his elegance and agreed that he was one of nature's gentlemen.

The servants had to maintain a constant vigilance to keep the floors clean and polished in the rainy season, attending to them each time anyone came in or out. The rain seemed to bring every sort of creeping creature into the house, into the cupboards and beds, under the cushions on the chairs. Insects crawled behind and beneath the books, silverfish made themselves at home between the pages of Dubois's precious library. Cockroaches of nightmarish size hid in the crevices in the furniture and behind the sideboard, beneath every box or receptacle placed on the floor. Anna could not help crying out every time she lifted an innocent object only to find a miniature terror lurking beneath it; Dubois feared for the safety of his books.

Small, spotted, splay-toed geckos climbed up and down the walls, hiding behind pictures and mirrors. They unnerved Anna at first, but she learned to appreciate their insect-eating ways. The servants refused to chase the geckos away, for they were considered lucky. Damp and mildew were more potent enemies, relentless, ubiquitous. They spoiled everything: books, photographs, linens, papers, shoes, clothes that touched each other as they hung in the wardrobe, even the folds in the curtains. The only way to dry anything was to hang it next to a fire or to spread it out over the bushes on a rare sunny morning, in the breeze.

Each day, when the rain started, Anna rushed outside to revel in it, like a child. Babu and Eugenie usually followed her and they danced for joy as the blissfully cooling drops struck their skin. After a few minutes, perhaps even half an hour on a lucky day, the initial sprinkle turned into a blatant downpour. And then for two or three hours the rain pounded angrily, constantly on the roof, falling down in torrents that beat holes and tiny canyons into the ground. The incessant noise seemed to invade the brain. Rain assaulted the senses, bringing temporary deafness. Inside the house, Anna's ears were pounded by wave after wave of noise until she could hear nothing at all; the same happened to Dubois at the hospital, where he had to shout at patients to make himself understood. The doctors and aides fell into a sort of dumbshow, waving their hands and miming actions rather than trying to speak. Rain made people blind, too, for it was impossible to see across the avenue or to the end of the garden. All that was visible, all that was audible, was rain. The smell of rain, the constant wetness, got everywhere, creeping up the steps on to the veranda, forcing its way through the bamboo blinds and finally into the house itself, invading every drawer and box and piece of furniture. Sometimes Anna wondered if Indies people were so fond of hot spices and curries because they wanted something to break the sensory monotony of the monsoon rains.

And yet, and yet...the rain was not all bad. The air was much cooler and fresher afterwards, and the rain always stopped. In the late afternoons, there was often a period of almost pleasant weather, when the world seemed new and lovely. Dubois walked slowly home from the hospital through the puddles and mud and the fresh, sweet smell of wet flowers and plants. This was the time for the evening bath, taken in the tiled *mandi* room out behind the main building. There was something wonderfully sensuous about ladling the cool water out of the enormous jar and pouring it slowly over oneself, washing away the sweat and the grit and the cares of the day.

The second bath was an important event in the set pattern of the day, which began with early coffee and the first bath. A solid breakfast on the veranda readied Dubois to go off to the hospital. There was a full lunch at midday, rice and meat and vegetables, with hot spicy condiments on the side, followed by a welcome nap; 'writing a letter' was the Indies euphemism for a brief sleep in the afternoon. Later, he returned to the hospital, coming home as the sun sank rapidly, when it was time for the second bath and a change of clothes. Uniforms and formal wear were put away; looser, cooler clothing was adopted for evening. Dubois put on lightweight batik or silk pyjama pants with a white *tutup*, the high-necked, button-fronted jacket popular in the tropics; Anna wore a loose kimono or a long, lace-edged jacket called a *kabayah* over a blouse, with a sarong wrapped about her waist. They put soft slippers on their feet, and Anna loosened her hair. Drinks and dinner were taken in comfort on the back veranda, in privacy. After dinner, it was time to sit in the soft glow of the paraffin lamps, listening to the lonely cries of insects and the shriek of soft-winged bats. Intermittently, there came the cheerful 'chi-chak, chi-chak' of a gecko in search of prey or fiercely defending its territory: some nondescript section of wall. Smoke drifted in from the cooking fires of the kampong, mixing with the fragrance of night-blooming melati bushes and the scent of the peppers and spices used in the dinner. Somewhere soft Indonesian voices murmured indistinctly, perhaps a sleepy child laughed, something rustled in the trees. Some nights, the melodious gonging of the gamelan, the traditional orchestra of the Indies, rang softly across the darkened landscape for hours.

The Indies seemed a gentle and welcoming world at times like this. Dubois and Anna often passed the evening companionably side by side, she in her rocker, he in a long rattan chair, the *panjang kursi*. They listened to the night noises and talked of the day's events. Sometimes she embroidered while he read, until the insects got so bad it was impossible to sit near the lamps. From time to time, a strange barking cry rang out – some nocturnal animal, in one of the large trees that lined the avenue? Some nights Anna heard an eerie keening sound, full of sorrow and mystery, that made her shiver. Dubois asked around, but he never learned what creatures made these sounds. He and Anna came to accept them as part of the Indies. Sometimes the night was still, with only the rustling of leaves or the rhythmical patter of the last raindrops to disturb the velvet silence.

During the day, Anna was hot and uncomfortable in her European clothes, and the mildew and mould soon damaged them. She could not, at first, bring herself to abandon the clothes from her trousseau and her first year of married life in Amsterdam, but then she saw how most of the other Dutch women in the Indies dressed. Even Pure women – not just half-caste Indos – often wore a sarong and *kabayah* during the day as well as in the evening. The clothes looked a little strange to Anna at first, so loose and shapeless on the corsetless women, but they were admirably practical, so cool and light. She had been in the colonies only a few weeks, and already she wasn't even dressing properly. Her mother would be shocked. The elaborate European fashions were cut to emphasize a buxom hour-glass figure, which Anna hadn't got, and were much too hot. Though she tried to preserve at least some of her favourite dresses for more formal occasions, Indies clothes gave her a sense of bodily freedom that was rather exhilarating.

Anna could not help but wonder why there were plenty of children on the base although wives were in short supply. Often, the children's hair was even darker than Eugenie's and their complexions tellingly light, sometimes almost white. Piecing together what she saw with bits of gossip, Anna learned that many of the officers had native concubines, *nyai*s, who ran their houses and bore their children. There was a well-understood code of conduct. A man didn't parade his *nyai*; she was not introduced to the European wives, nor would she ever be seen at dinner with Europeans. The *nyai*'s world was inside the house; she was a silent, graceful shadow who did not appear in the public domain. A *nyai*'s presence was obvious nonetheless, once Anna knew what to look for. There was an unmistakable woman's touch about a house: better, well-served food; beautiful furnishings; flowers; and a man who was contented and meticulously turned out. A *nyai* might not be openly acknowledged, but nor was she concealed.

Anna was bewildered by the matter-of-fact acceptance of *nyai*s and mixed-blood Indo children. Was this what people meant when they spoke of immorality in the colonies? Anna finally worked up the courage to ask Clara, one of the few other wives on the base, about it. Clara's first response was to reveal that her own family was an old Indies one with many 'darker' branches. Anna blushed, feeling somehow she had accused her new friend of something.

'Oh, Anna,' Clara teased her, 'you are such a totok! To be shocked at the presence of nyais…' She clucked and shook her head in wonderment. 'Very common, you know, for a young man to take up with a "walking dictionary". There have never been many women out here among the Pures, not even many Indo women. So whom is a man to marry? Who is to look after him, to make his home? The best thing a young man can do for his career in the Indies is take a nyai, a pretty, clever girl to teach him the language and the local customs. She runs his household, makes him comfortable, gives him children. In return, she lives very well: a nice house, servants, maybe jewelry and beautiful clothes... Of course, there are always a lot of Indo babies. Sometimes the fathers acknowledge them, even pay for a European education, if the relationship is a long-standin' one.'

'They take their father's name?' Anna was incredulous. In Holland, she had heard whispers of bastard children, but such offspring were hidden away. There might be furtive payments to the mother, who was of course ruined for life. This open recognition was shocking.

'Ja,' replied Clara, as simply as if she was describing the flowers in her garden. 'Happens fairly often. Sometimes a nyai is with a young man for only a brief spell, a few months or a year. Y'know how young men are, fall in love with one woman in June and another in September. Kassian!' she sighed, using the common Indies expression of sympathy and drawing out each syllable. 'Men can be so fickle. In a situation like that he won't acknowledge the children, but if he is with her for years and years... Even then, taking them away from their mother so they can be raised properly and educated usually causes a real susa, a big fuss. Much more expensive than letting them run free in the kampongs! An Indo boy with a good education can hold a responsible job, do well. And a girl, if she's a beauty and not too dark, she can make a good marriage – maybe even marry a Pure.'

Unable to help herself, Anna blurted in wonderment, 'Things are very different here!'

Clara looked at the expression on Anna's face and collapsed into laughter. 'Oh Anna!' she said through her giggles. 'You are such a child.'

Anna laughed, too, but she had an unsettled feeling, as if she had looked at a familiar room through a kaleidoscope. Nothing held its shape here; everything shifted and transmogrified into something else. She did not know where she was in this alien world. 'But sometimes, surely,' Anna said, growing serious, 'a man later marries – I mean really marries – a woman he has met at home on leave, a totok like me. What happens when she comes out to the Indies and finds her husband's brown-skinned children?' Her face grew sombre as she imagined the sense of betrayal.

'You have to understand life in the Indies,' Clara answered. 'That is the way things are here. Young officers have nyais, and most of the administrators and the planters, too. Anyone who marries a man in the Indies expects there was a nyai before her. And the children, they are just children. All of them are precious, whatever colour they are; so many children die here. Oh, everyone wants a fair child, like your Eugenie, but it doesn't matter much once they're here. Some people even say that the Indo babies are healthier than the Pures. Sometimes a woman whose baby has died adopts a native baby and raises it as her own: an anak mas, a golden child, we call that one.'

Anna had a great deal to think about and adjust to in her new life. Having a nursemaid to look after Eugenie in Amsterdam had been one thing – and, she remembered suddenly, that nursemaid was an opinionated thing, always on the verge of getting above herself. Babu was another matter entirely. Eugenie played happily with children from the kampong, sitting in the garden with only flowers, pebbles, and twigs for toys. She was admired for her gay charm – her mother's legacy – and for the fair complexion she had inherited from her father. In time her hair darkened until it was almost the exact shade of her mother's, but she retained her father's complexion. The striking Dubois family was more often talked of in the kampongs and military bases of West Sumatra than they realized.

After a month or two, Anna began to feel at home in Padang. She was no longer frightened to step outside the house or even, for that matter, to walk around inside her own home and lift objects beneath which insects might lurk. Her Malay was much improved, though she did not speak like a native – never that, of course. The *kokkie* remained a bit of a problem to Anna, for she cooked whatever she wanted. Strange dishes appeared on the table, full of rice and unfamiliar fruits and hot spices. Some of them were quite alarming and left Dubois and Anna coughing and spluttering from hot peppers. Others were tasty and appealing, but Anna did not know what they were called and so she could not ask for them again until she learned their names from a friend. Sometimes she wondered who was the employer and who the servant.

While Anna settled slowly into her new world, Dubois was plunged into his. He was inundated with hospital work almost immediately, for there were a great many patients. Malaria, typhoid, and typhus were daily fare, along with suppurating tropical ulcers that would not heal, tuberculosis, cholera, and myriad nameless but deadly fevers. Dubois was perfectly efficient with the usual ailments: the broken bones and gunshot wounds, the septic blisters from bad boots, the rotting teeth, the stomach cramps, bilious livers, and heart conditions. At first he often had to ask other physicians for advice, because there were medical problems here that he had never seen before. He learned quickly how to manage them; he had to. Infections and fevers appeared, ravaged the patient, and killed within days. This was life-and-death medicine with an urgency that Dubois had never witnessed before.

Almost daily, he came home to warn Anna about something: the need for vigilant hygiene; the poisonous snakes and insects, to be avoided and removed from the garden by the garden boy; the horrifying diseases that came like a wind out of the west in the morning and killed a child before nightfall. Not all was a nightmare, though. Almost daily, he came home to tell her about something wonderful he had discovered, too: a new flower, like the melati, a sweet-smelling jasmine that perfumed the evenings; a fabulous bird he had seen, with violet wings and shiny green tail feathers; a strange new animal that one of the boys had caught up a tree. It was a new world, this colony, both frightening and inspiring.

The press of hospital work did not diminish with the passage of the wet season; the dry season was as bad or worse. The stream of patients was so continuous that Dubois soon realized his ambitions for fossil-hunting would be pushed aside for years, if not for ever, if he was not persistent. He had not come this far to practise medicine, he reminded himself. He could have set up a practice in Amsterdam if that had been his goal. He had more important things to do than treat fevers and sew up wounds. No, he had come to the East Indies to find the missing link, and he meant to do it.

Dubois offered to lecture to his fellow officers about the missing link. Much as he detested teaching, talking about his missing link would be a pleasure. Nearly everyone attended, to take the measure of this new doctor from Amsterdam. And there was a dearth of entertainment at the base; any novelty was treasured. Dubois hoped his lecture would be the first step in persuading the commanding officers that he should be released from some of his hospital duties to search for fossils. He wanted to find the best way to frame his arguments, the most persuasive path through his logic. Then he would compose an article on the subject for publication and stake his claim to the search for the missing link. Everyone would know what he was trying to do and why.

The reception of his lecture was mixed. Some of the officers were keenly interested and came up afterwards to ply him with questions. Dubois counted these as successes, for he could see he had awakened their curiosity and stirred their scientific instincts. Some left wordlessly after the lecture with an odd expression on their faces. Perhaps they thought he was just another eccentric who had sought refuge in the colonies, like some ne'er-do-well son of a prominent family. A few, exhausted by their duties, fell asleep and snored gently through the lecture, never hearing Dubois's inspired words.

When Dubois squeezed out a day here or there to explore the area immediately surrounding the base, he found it unpromising. Padang sat on a flat coastal plain with few hills and no caves. It took hot hours of travel toward the interior to find caves; even there, he found no fossils.

He tried to get the Minangkabau, the local tribe, to lead him to better places. 'I am looking for caves with bones,' he said, 'old, old bones that are like rocks. I want the bones of old animals that do not live here any more. Can you take me to such a place?' The brown faces looked back at him with guarded eyes. Had they failed to understand? He tried again, with no better success. Dubois thought sometimes the natives were being downright evasive. They were very polite, they called him 'Tuan Dokter' respectfully, but they didn't offer any help. Maybe they had never seen any fossils. Or maybe they thought he was asking about the graves of their ancestors. They must have had feeling for the dead, they were so superstitious about ghosts and spirits. They believed so strongly in the old stories that they even made their houses with curving roofs, upturned at the ends, to symbolize the horns of the bull buffalo that had long ago saved them from Javan domination. He wondered if they thought he sought the bones of that animal. Did they believe that if he found such bones, disaster would befall the Minangkabau?

Frustration lent a bitter flavour to Dubois's days. The old feeling of desperation returned. He had to find a way out. He could not waste his life here. He did not know what to do. Anna could offer no help. By now she was so heavily pregnant that she could not concentrate at all. She seemed to him like some dull, placid brood mare, content enough but unable to think or speak cogently. It was up to him to solve this problem. He had brought his family to Padang, so surely he could get them out again. But where should they go, and how? He turned to his colleagues for advice. It was not, he explained, that he wanted to go back to the Netherlands. No, what he wanted to find was an army post where the countryside was more promising, with more caves. He asked his colleagues what they knew about the various regions of Sumatra: where were the hospitals? What was the landscape like? How densely settled was this area, or that? He requested a transfer to an upcountry convalescent hospital near Pajakombo. The area was more remote, less settled, and there was no huge army barracks full of potential patients nearby.

In April, his frustration was broken by some good news. The article based on the lecture he had given to his colleagues had been accepted and published in the *Natuurkundig Tijdschrift voor Nederlandsch-Indië* (Journal of the Natural History of the Netherlands Indies). Now the colonial government could not afford to ignore his ideas. The body of the text presented all his arguments in logical order, cementing them into a veritable wall of reasons why the East Indies would yield up the fossils of the missing link. When he finally read his words in print, he thought he had made a masterpiece. It was the best thing he had written yet. He was especially pleased with his closing words.

It is obvious that scholars from other countries will soon realize the promise of the East Indies. They will come and search for important fossils here and will find them, unless the Dutch authorities do something more to support such scientific work. And will the Netherlands, which has done so much for the natural sciences of the East Indian Colonies, remain indifferent when such important questions are concerned, while the road to their solution has been signposted?

With these words, he issued his challenge. If the authorities ignored his pleas for help, men from other countries would move in to find the missing link on Dutch territory; the implicit threat played nicely on the long-standing rivalry between the Dutch and the English. The Dutch had never forgiven the English for taking control of Java between 1811 and 1816, and they remained jealous of the English settlements throughout South-East Asia. The Dutch would hate to be beaten to an important discovery by the English, who were very interested in fossils and evolution. Those words of his would put a weasel in the henhouse, he thought eagerly. Only fools, having been warned, could fail to respond now to his requests for a proper Dutch expedition to find the missing link.

CHAPTER II

Pajakombo

Dubois sent a copy of the article to the governor of the west coast of Sumatra, R. C. Kroesen, with a letter. Kroesen was a thoughtful man, who read the article carefully and understood Dubois's arguments. He could see the wisdom of helping this earnest young man in his endeavours. He could see, too, the danger of ignoring him and being blamed if someone else found the missing link first.

Kroesen took two actions. First, he let Dubois know that once he found a good site, he would, as governor, make forced labourers available for the work. This amounted to substantial assistance. By law, natives were required to pay taxes to the colonial government. A farmer with good land could pay with specified export crops (indigo, sugar, tea, or coffee) in an amount equal to one-fifth of his yield. This was not a popular alternative and the natives preferred to grow rice to feed their families. The other alternative was to spend a month or two a year labouring on public works, such as maintaining roads, digging wells, or clearing land. Some officials abused the system, using forced labourers to tend their extensive personal gardens, build new houses, or work fields for the officials' profit. Dutch administrators argued that their salaries were insufficient to live in the grand style that befitted a *tuan besar*, a big man. Since natives expected their rulers to be both rich and generous, living modestly would have caused a loss of face. Whether Dubois's scientific expeditions were a proper use of forced labourers was never asked. 'Proper use' was what the governor said it was.

But Kroesen did not stop there. He also let it be known to Dubois's military superiors that he, the governor of West Sumatra, was taking a personal interest in Dubois's search for the missing link. Kroesen's support smoothed the ruts from Dubois's road. Perhaps as a direct result – who could ever tell how these things came about? – Dubois's requested transfer to the hospital in the highlands at Pajakombo came through. He would be in charge of the entire small hospital, with no one to answer to except his own conscience, and there were not many patients.

The Dubois family left for Pajakombo in May. Moving was an elaborate process, complete with numerous bearers, packhorses, oxcarts piled high with possessions, a sedan chair for Eugenie and another for Anna, who was now almost completely incapacitated with pregnancy. Most of the servants, who had worked for the family for five months, decided to move to Pajakombo also, for Anna and Eugenie were much admired and Dubois was considered a good *tuan*, a dignified, learned man of impressive stature.

Anna passed the long, arduous trip pleasantly, lying in the sedan chair and playing with Eugenie from time to time when Babu brought her over for a brief visit, napping, looking at the new scenery, and enjoying the steady change from the steamy coast climate to the brisker highlands. Every step along the way seemed to bring cooler air and higher elevation, a true blessing in her condition. The servants did most of the unpacking and settling into the new house; Anna reclined in a long chair, her feet up, and feebly directed the placement of objects.

Anna gave birth to their first son, Jean Marie François Dubois, at home in Pajakombo, on 15 June 1888. She was attended in labour by her husband and her maid. There were experienced native orderlies in the hospital, but they were all male and it did not seem proper to have them present at the birth of a white child. Besides, Dubois was certain that he needed no other help. The baby boy was healthy and robust, dark-haired like Anna but fair-skinned and strong, like his father. That very evening, while his wife and new son slept after their exhausting day, Dubois penned a letter to his parents, to tell them of the safe arrival of their first grandson, named Jean after his grandfather and Marie after his grandmother.

Pajakombo was far from the sweltering coast and the busy port of Padang. The Dubois were more isolated in the highlands than before. The army outpost in Pajakombo was so small that the only real reason to keep a European physician there was to run the convalescent hospital. Dubois was the sole qualified physician on staff. Men recovering from serious illnesses or wounds were sent to this hill station, away from the coast's heat and its heightened danger of fever or festering infection. Despite the pleasantly cool climate and the light workload, the place was so lonely that most medical officers requested a transfer out almost as soon as they arrived at Pajakombo. Most of the other Europeans at Pajakombo were the patients themselves, some of whom stayed for weeks or months. Sometimes Anna yearned for her women friends in Padang, but

Babu and Lilik, her maid, were a comfort. Babu was pleased to have another beautiful white baby to look after. She called Jean her little *sinjo*, or master, providing him with loving care and attention without upsetting Eugenie.

Dubois was proud to have a son; he had always hoped for a boy like he had been, intelligent, active, and strong. He held Jean in his arms, looking with amazement at his miniature eyelashes and translucent eyelids, admiring his curly dark hair, the beauty of his tiny hands. He gazed proudly at his son, blessed with the peaceful sleep of the innocent, and imagined his future. If Dubois's search for the missing link was successful, then Jean would grow up the son of a famous man, a scientist respected worldwide for his fossil discoveries. As a boy, he would have a position even greater than Dubois had had as the son of Eijsden's mayor and pharmacist. Doors would open for Jean; opportunities would present themselves for education, work, learning, maybe even adventure... Dubois felt wonderfully optimistic. He had a wife, two fine children, and the governor's support. He was poised to make his great find, to reach his goal. His ambitions seemed markedly closer to becoming reality. He had much more time to explore the countryside for caves, and the highlands were full of caves. Some of them were bound to contain fossils.

In September, another physician arrived, Dr Pollak. He was not an addition to the staff; he was recuperating from a bad case of chronic malaria that had left him thin and weak. Repeated doses of quinine had finally defeated the fevers, but Pollak needed time to rebuild his strength and stamina. He was luckier than most; the graveyards were full of young men who had succumbed to malaria in their first year in the Indies. Still, he would remain in the hospital at Pajakombo for too long, feeling too well to do nothing but not yet strong enough to leave.

Dubois often stopped by to sit with Pollak for a while, telling him of his ambitions and his conviction that the missing link lay hidden in a cave nearby. As another scientifically trained professional, Pollak soon grasped the essence of Dubois's arguments. He was intrigued; he had known very little of the missing link before now. Dubois left him a copy of his article. He was gratified, the next day, to see his new friend poring over the pages and making notes in the margin. 'This is a fine piece of work, Doctor,' Pollak said to him, looking up. 'You have opened my mind. I do hope you'll stop by later when you have time and answer some of my questions.' The missing link became a regular topic of conversation between the two, who liked nothing better than to speculate where Dubois would find it, how he should search for it, and what anatomical features it would turn out to possess. In this isolated place, Dubois had found a friend who was willing to help him plan and evaluate and had not the least interest in usurping his ideas. Pollak was no Weber or De Vries, for he was not so knowledgeable about evolution as they, but nor was there any risk of his turning into an idea thief.

'You know,' Pollak offered thoughtfully one day, 'you could make small expeditions of several days at a time, if you turned some of your responsibilities over to me. I am quite well enough for light medical duties. There are hardly any serious cases in the hospital just now; nothing I couldn't handle with the native orderlies. Why don't you take a few days and go searching some of the caves nearby? I can always send a runner for you if something arises that is too much for me. But things are quiet here, very quiet, and the patients don't need much attention.'

Dubois was genuinely surprised. Ambitious as he was, he had not considered asking Pollak to assume his duties. 'That's a very handsome offer,' he replied to his friend, 'very kind of you. As I am in charge, there is no one to approve or disapprove. Are you sure you feel strong enough?'

Pollak nodded, eager to do something, anything useful, and happy to be of help; he had never met another man with such a fertile mind and such determination.

'Then,' continued Dubois, 'perhaps we could try it for a few days at the end of this week. I could get on with my bone-hunting, maybe locate a site worth excavating. Once I find the right place, the Governor will let me have those labourers, and then it will be much easier to keep everything going even if I can't be there in person. If all goes well while I am away from the hospital – don't work yourself into a relapse, now – then we might make it a regular thing.'

The plan was put into effect. Dubois began to search the Pajakombo region systematically, checking every cave and rock shelter, making small test excavations, searching for any small fragment of tooth or bone. Most of the caves were sadly empty of fossils, as was only to be expected. But some contained fossils and Dubois collected them all, carefully marking and annotating his map. For weeks he found nothing but miserable, broken scraps. As

Pollak grew stronger, Dubois's forays grew longer. Being back at work improved Pollak's spirits, and it pleased him to see Dubois come striding back from his trips, spilling bits and pieces of fossils out of bags and boxes and showing him the markings on his maps.

But Dubois's was difficult work, and lonely: plodding through the countryside, climbing up absurdly steep hills, cutting paths through the prickly, recalcitrant underbrush, searching for caves. He brought along the teenaged son of the *tukang kebun* to carry equipment, gather firewood, and provide general assistance, but the boy's presence could not alleviate his profound isolation of mind and spirit, painful but not enough to blunt the razor's edge of his perseverance.

CHAPTER 12

Fossils

Within a few weeks, Dubois had accumulated a sizeable pile of fossils. His map was full of marks recording what he had found where; his notebook was cluttered with notes, calculations, and drawings. Soon he began to draw new maps of his own, taking great pleasure in the exercise of making each one beautiful, lettering it carefully, colouring in the different areas. His maps were both science and art, a tangible symbol of his growing knowledge.

The fossils he gathered were not complete skeletons or even whole bones; they were simply teeth and splinters of bone. A good museum would have rejected all of them. However, they represented the first collection of fossils from Sumatra, an island with a completely unknown fossil history before Dubois had begun his work. And, incomplete though the specimens were, they conveyed much information to Dubois's learned eye.

Nearly all of his fossils were teeth that had long since fallen out of the jaws that had contained them. But even these isolated teeth were very informative. As an anatomist, Dubois could usually identify the type of animal and sometimes even its species from a single tooth, but some of these were in worse shape than most. They had been gnawed – determinedly, repeatedly – by porcupines, leaving ridged and gouged surfaces. The splinters of bone, when Dubois found any, were similarly scored with broad, squared-off grooves left by chisel-shaped teeth. There was not much of the original anatomy left for him to study.

Still, Dubois could already say something useful about the fauna of ancient Sumatra. He fingered the better specimens, cataloguing them in his mind. There had been elephants here once, that was certain: these great, brick-sized lumps of dentin and enamel could belong to nothing else. And rhinos, too, with that F-shaped pattern on the crowns of their teeth, maybe not so very different from the living Sumatran rhinoceros. Here were a few tiger's teeth, sharp and long and shiny, and a pile of molars from pigs and deer and wild cattle. And here, here was the culprit himself, Dubois thought, picking up a few teeth of a porcupine, the animal that had chewed and damaged nearly every other fossil he had collected. The right animals had lived here in Sumatra in ancient times, there could be no doubt.

Dubois started exploring the highlands the month after Jean's birth. In August 1888, he embarked on prolonged field explorations and finally met with success: the cave called Lida Adjer had a few fossilized bones – intact, complete bones of a good variety of Pleistocene fauna, not just teeth and scraps. For once, Dubois had got there first, before those wretched porcupines. Was this *his* cave, the cave of the missing link? Maybe. The thought lent urgency to his preliminary visit to the cave.

Dubois collected an impressive pile of fossil riches and headed back to Pajakombo for more supplies. When he got home, he ran up the stairs of the front veranda to share the news with Anna while the boy followed with the crates and bags.

'Anna? Anna, come quickly!' he called.

She was there in a moment, having heard the sound of his horse's hoofbeats. 'Are you back then, Eugène?' she greeted him, smiling. 'Ahmad, get the Tuan some cool lime juice.'

'I have found my cave, Anna,' he blurted in a rush, 'I think I have found it. This is a fine site. You should see it: there are rhinos and pigs and deer everywhere. I shall write to Governor Kroesen immediately to tell him of this important find. I am so close now, so close. This might be the right place.'

Still recovering from the trial of childbirth, Anna had to rally her strength to respond to his excitement. She duly admired his fossils – dusty, oddly shaped things, but she knew they were all the world to him – and asked a few questions, but mostly she just smiled as he told her of his hopes. She thought perhaps it was all coming true, just as Dubois had predicted. She sat and adjusted the loose pillow on the rattan rocking chair for comfort. Even dirty and tired, Dubois was a handsome, clever man and she was glad to be his wife. Babu heard the commotion and shyly brought the children out on to the veranda to greet their father. Dubois was so exuberant that he lifted Eugenie up and whirled her around until she giggled and giggled. Then he went over to little Jean, in Babu's arms, to softly stroke his new son's porcelain cheek.

'Your papa has found a great thing today,' he told them. They did not understand, of course, they were far too young, but they knew their father was joyful and their mother was sweetly contented. Babu took them to bathe and change so they would not be underfoot. The Dubois family settled in for a happy evening, there in remote Pajakombo, up in the Padang Highlands of Sumatra.

Dubois wrote to Kroesen, telling him of the wonderful fossils at Lida Adjer and asking for the promised labourers. The governor replied promptly.

September 8, 1888

We are really going to look forward to a hopeful future ... To start, I will place officially at your disposal six forced labourers ...

Reading Kroesen's encouraging words filled Dubois with energy. Now it begins, he thought. Now I will find the missing link.

It took him a few weeks to get everything organized, and he had to wait for the coolies to appear, but Dubois was on fire and could not slow down. His moment had come; he could feel it. When everything was ready, the procession set off for Lida Adjer. He rode on horseback at the head of the small column, the coolies in their conical hats following. Sometimes he trotted back to urge on the sluggards at the back.

They set up camp near the entrance to Lida Adjer. They had brought along a woman as the cook; Dubois appointed one of the more intelligent men to be foreman, or *mandur*, while others with more muscle and less brain would do the digging, gather firewood, and haul water. Lida Adjer was the first cave where systematic work had been justified, so Dubois was forced to improvise his procedures and train his workers in them at the same time. The men were peasant farmers; they knew how to dig the soil to plant crops and they knew how to dig irrigation ditches and wells. This was neither of those tasks, and they were confused. They could have understood if the Tuan Dokter had ordered, 'Dig here, plant this crop.' They could have understood if he had said, 'I need a well here,' – or a drainage canal, or a ditch for irrigating the field. But he wanted something different from them. He wanted digging done with care, like digging up sweet potatoes when there was no remnant of stem or leaves, but the ground was like rock and needed a pickaxe. How could they work gently with pickaxes? Normally they worked for a while and then took a rest to smoke a cigarette, chew betel, drink water, relieve themselves, exchange a little gossip. Working slowly was perfectly sensible, but they did not want to work ceaselessly.

Inside the cave it was so chilly that the coolies complained. The Tuan Dokter showed them some old bones – fossils, he called them – that were heavy like stones. He told them that was what he was looking for, but they knew he was lying. What good would old bones be to anyone? Why would a Hollander go to all this trouble for something worthless? The Tuan Dokter's strange ideas did not end there. He wanted them to keep the excavated area roughly level at the bottom and he wanted them to maintain a regular shape, with corners. He drew the shape on the ground with a stick. If they did not follow it, the Tuan Dokter shouted. They would rather have followed a pleasing curve or rounded an edge than make a straight-sided hole. What was the use of that? It was not even beautiful to dig a hole that way.

Dubois explained it all again to the *mandur*, and the *mandur* instructed the men. This was the way the Tuan Dokter wanted you to dig; like this, not like that; keep this corner square, keep the wall of the excavation vertical. *This* instruction was repeated many, many times over the subsequent days. Limited progress was made in turning the ragtag assembly of peasants into a competent, if not efficient, excavation team.

What helped was that they realized the Tuan Dokter was completely convinced of the way he wanted them to work and absolutely immovable in his convictions. He wanted the hole dug the way he told them, and he would make them do it again if it was not right. They did not understand his drive or his determination, but they began to respect this unusual *orang belanda*. Hollanders were not usually so hardworking, and he was physically impressive. They had never seen such a man, so tall, so straight, so strong, so fair-haired. Strangest of all were his pale, clear, blue eyes. Sumatrans, of course, all had brown eyes; so did nearly all Indos and most of the Europeans they saw. But not the Tuan Dokter. It was the subject of much discussion. Eventually they decided among themselves that his eyes were like those of Garuda, the eagle-god. He could probably see right into their souls with those eyes, they were so piercing, so sharp. Perhaps he could see even the future and the past. He always knew whether they were trying to shirk a difficult task or pretending to be sick when they were not. Anyway, in the presence of the Tuan Dokter, no one dared to steal food or to sneak off to the nearest village to drink rice wine and find a girl.

Unlike other Europeans they had worked for, this one did not wander off to take a nap or sit in the shade smoking while they worked. The coolies found his motivations incomprehensible. Some of the men supposed the work involved one of the secrets of the *orang belanda*, the Hollanders, that they would never understand. Others thought it was some special Garuda secret. Whatever its source, they recognized and respected his determination. He was very strong – in his body, obviously – but also in his mind and in his will.

Before long the men did start to find the strange, rocklike bones that the Tuan Dokter wanted. How had he known they were there? Every find was given to the *mandur*, who in turn took it to the Tuan Dokter. He examined each specimen by paraffin lamp or more often took it to the cave entrance, where there was more light. All work stopped as Dubois inspected each find. The men waited for the pronouncement: was it good? Was this what they had been seeking? Could they stop digging in this cold cave? The Tuan Dokter always told them what they had found: the tooth of an elephant, he said, or a fragment of an ancient deer antler; this one was the tooth of a tiger, that one a buffalo. There were parts of stranger animals too, ones they hardly ever saw, like the rhino and the tapir. Sometimes he drew a small picture to show them what they had found and they stared at it, amazed. Dubois was pleased with each find. Soon he had a good and diverse fauna; he could list the animals that had lived together in the Pleistocene of Sumatra.

Normally dignified and calm, Dubois could not contain his exultation when the men found some fossil apes, rare orang-utans and gibbons. These were new species. Nothing was known of the ancestry of modern Asian apes, nothing! Lydekker could have his Siwalik Hills chimpanzee, for Dubois had the orang-utan and the gibbon of the Padang Highlands. This proved that they were finding fossils from a tropical forest, a wet jungle like the ones that covered much of Sumatra. And where there were apes, there would be ape-men. He was buoyant, floating in the pure joy of vindication. He promised the men that he would go hunting that afternoon, to bring meat for a feast, for he was an excellent shot and an avid hunter.

That night after dinner, he sat in his rattan chair on the small oriental carpet in front of his tent, making notes on his accomplishments. He was proud. He had proved that fossils of the right age could be found in Sumatra. He congratulated himself, picking up each of the specimens from the small table at his elbow. Here were the ancient apes that had lived with the ape-man; here were the rhino, the tapir, the buffalo. No one had ever discovered so much about the prehistory of Sumatra before. He had done this completely on his own initiative, with no resources except the labourers the governor had kindly sent him. All this was his own work, his inspiration. Perhaps he should name one of the new species after the governor, maybe this fine antelope. Kroesen would like that, having a new animal named after him. It would be a good way to acknowledge his help. He would call the species *Tetraceros kroesenii*.

In a few days, the men had exhausted the fossil deposits in Lida Adjer. There was no missing link here. He had found all he was going to find, despite his intuition to the contrary. Back home in Pajakombo, he wasted no time in writing up a provisional report of his finds and sending it to the Dutch East Indies government. A special copy went to Governor Kroesen, with a letter pointing out the importance of the fossils and the immense assistance given by the labourers he had provided. He also sent a copy to another influential supporter, Willem Groeneveldt, the Director of the Department of Education, Religion, and Industry, who oversaw scientific research in the Indies.

Dubois was hungry for success. Lida Adjer had been surely the first bite of the meal; he was sure to find his transitional ape-man in the next cave, or the next after that. For a long time he had felt like Sisyphus, doomed to push a rock eternally uphill, and now his luck had changed. He corrected his thoughts. No, it had not simply changed: *he* had changed it. His work was gaining speed and mass as it rushed downhill to become a landslide, surging toward his destiny, the missing link.

At home in the Netherlands the political climate for scientific research was changing rapidly. Max Weber, recently returned from an extended voyage to Sumatra, Java, Celebes, and Flores to collect freshwater fishes, now understood for himself the enormous unexploited potential for research represented by the Indies. His new wife, the botanist Anna Antoinette de Bosse, had discovered many new species of marine algae on the voyage. Weber saw that Dubois's arguments about the urgency of scientific research in the Indies could be extended to include all kinds of natural-historical research. To support and encourage such studies, Weber and some colleagues persuaded the government to form a Committee for the Promotion of Research in the Natural Sciences in the Dutch Colonies.

One of the first proposals brought before the committee was Dubois's search for the missing link. Though Weber had once listened to Dubois's plans with a certain scepticism, now he was a wholehearted believer. The geologist Karl Martin was in favour of Dubois's research too. Having studied Raden Saleh's fossils, Martin was sure that many more treasures lay undiscovered in the Indies. With Dubois's report on Lida Adjer and his published article as fuel, Weber and Martin made a persuasive case. The fossils Dubois had already found showed that his theory about the home of Man's origin was probably correct. He had already produced Sumatran fossils about which there was no information before – had revealed new, tangible, scientific knowledge – though the man had had not one guilder of government support. Martin emphasized how difficult this must have been, what a triumph it represented. Now the government must provide material assistance to Dubois before it was too late. Dubois could no longer be dismissed as a lunatic follower of Darwin's 'crazy book'. He was a visionary natural historian carrying out significant and successful inquiries into the origin of Man, in one of the least studied regions of the world. The committee agreed.

This additional support was especially sweet to Dubois. He had been so long an outsider, so long a seer in the land of the blind speaking of things invisible to others. He received a still larger crew, sometimes labourers and sometimes convicts, plus Corporals Franke and Van den Nesse from the engineering corps, who acted as supervisors. Dubois pondered strategies for searching for new caves. How much should he rely on existing maps in deciding which areas to visit? There were no really thorough, accurate maps of the Padang Highlands of Sumatra. He had to rely on word of mouth, instinct, and his knowledge of geology. There was one clue, one precious clue that he clung to: the mountain range in the Padang Highlands was known as Boekit Ngalau Sariboe, the 'mountains of a thousand caves'.

In March, Dubois received the best reward of all for his dedication and perseverance.

REGISTER OF RESOLUTIONS OF THE
GOVERNORS-GENERAL OF THE DUTCH-INDIES

Buitenzorg (March 6, 1889)

Firstly.

The military surgeon of the 2nd class M.E.F.T. Dubois, provisionally for the period of one year, to receive a grant of f250– (two hundred and fifty guilders) a month above his income and to be placed at the disposal of the Director of Education, Religion, and Industry, in order to be charged with paleontological research in caves in the government of Sumatra's West Coast and contingently in Java; with the order to report on the results of his research in a timely fashion to the above-mentioned Director and to place the obtained fossils at the disposition of the government.

and with the regulation:

a. that for travelling related to carrying out this research, he will be allotted a free use of means of transport or compensation for the costs of transport according to the existing regulations:

b. that as long as he stays at the disposal of the Director of Education, Religion, and Industry, he will be relieved of his medical duties.

Secondly.

To authorize the Commandant of the Army and Chief of the Department of War in the Dutch-Indies for the benefit of the above indicated research to retain two workmen from the Engineers; with regulation that they will receive a grant of f25– (twenty-five guilders) every month.

Thirdly.

To invite the Governor of Sumatra's West Coast, by this article, with reference to the indicated researches as far as they take place within the region of his administrative control, to dispose of as many forced labourers as will be desired by the Master M.E.F.T. Dubois, provided the total is not more than fifty at the same time; with regulation that the control and supervision of these forced labourers, conforming to the prescriptions of the Regulation of order and discipline among the prisoners in the Dutch-Indies, will be practised as much as possible by the leaders of the local authorities at the places where they are put to work.

Fourthly.

An abstract of this document will be given to the military surgeon Dubois for his information.

Now he was officially searching for the missing link. The drudgery of hospital work was behind him. All he could see ahead of him, as he pierced the veil of the future with his keen Garuda eyes, was research, fame, and glory. Now he would explore not just the immediate vicinity of Pajakombo but every one of the thousand caves of the Padang Highlands.

Garuda

Dubois was sure that better, richer caves with more fossils and better specimens lay ahead. When the rains stopped, in April 1889, he started his explorations in a much grander and more comfortable style. But most of the caves and rock shelters proved empty. It was deeply frustrating to clamber up hillsides and mountains in the heat, fighting his way through the vegetation, badgering the coolies forward, to find only bat-droppings and dirt. Dubois was muscular and fit, yet he found the unrewarded climbs very taxing. The predictable emptiness of the caves was discouraging. Even worse, some were empty of fossils but inhabited by a tiger or a bear. More than once, delegations of locals begged Dubois to shoot marauding tigers that were killing valuable water buffaloes and beloved small children.

The tiger-hunting episodes made the coolies very reluctant to venture into new caves. Dubois saw their hesitation as cowardice, for he had both a rifle and a fearless nature. He would show them his courage, as an example, when the next occasion presented itself. He did not need to wait long. They came to a large cave on a steep hill, with a low and narrow entrance. It was impossible to see into the interior by the light of a candle or paraffin lamp; this suggested the passageway was narrow for some distance. Dubois gestured and then ordered them to enter the cave. The men stood chattering quietly and incomprehensibly among themselves with worried faces. No one would step forward to be the first inside.

Now was the time to show them how a European behaved, Dubois thought. 'Very well,' he said. 'I shall go.'

He kneeled down and crawled into the cave, leaving his rifle with the men. He carried a gas lamp in one hand, leaving the other free. He squirmed his way forward on his belly and elbows until the passageway enlarged. He was relieved when both the sides and the roof sloped away from him into a much larger and more comfortable space. He crawled the last few feet and then stood and looked around, holding the lamp aloft. Before his eyes could focus in the dim light, he recognized the fetid smell that assaulted his nostrils: the stench of cat urine combined with the indescribable odour of rotting meat. He was in a tiger's lair. It was littered with partially eaten bones and deer legs in varying stages of decay. Over there, in the shadows, Dubois could just make out a large dark shape. To his immense relief, when he lifted the lantern high, the shape proved to be a pile of large bones, perhaps those of a buffalo. It occurred to him forcibly that the tiger might return at any moment.

There was no bravery in sitting in a tiger's lair. Dubois flung himself to the floor and decided to crawl backward out of the chamber. If he met the tiger coming in, the tiger would be faced with his stout boots, not his naked face. The difficulty was that he could not see where he was going. Unable to see anything except where he had been, he tried to feel the way with his feet. In his anxiety, he failed to follow a turn of the passageway and became firmly wedged. He could not free himself. It was a frightening realization. Worse yet, he felt faintly ridiculous. He thought he was close to the entrance, so he called to his men, but his voice was muffled by the bulk of his own body. There was no answer.

'Boy!' he cried again. Then louder, 'Boy! Adik!' Soon he was bellowing like a wounded buffalo. Surely the labourers must have heard him. Why were they not waiting obediently by the entrance to the cave, as he had imagined they would be? Had they all wandered off, leaving him there in a tiger's lair?

'Mandur!' he shouted again, using all the power of his lungs to call the foreman. The dust and dried debris on the cave floor, stirred up by his exertions, clung to the sweat on his face, making him more uncomfortable than ever. He was embarrassed, enraged, frightened.

'Mandur, toeloeng! Toeloeng degan cepat!' 'Foreman, help me! Help me quickly,' he yelled. Was that a noise behind him? Yes, the *mandur* was answering.

'Tuan Doktcr?' the *mandur* asked politely, addressing his master's booted feet. 'I am here. What assistance can I give?'

'*Help* me,' Dubois replied crossly. 'Cepat! Hurry up. I am stuck in this passageway. Have the men pull on my legs. *Carefully!* Hati-hati!'

The *mandur* gestured to the men to do as the Tuan Dokter asked. Two lay down and reached into the passageway to grab his feet; two more seized the feet of the first. Together they heaved on his legs, freeing him suddenly, like a cork from a bottle. The men concealed their smiles at the sight of their great blond Tuan, so dishevelled, stuck headfirst in a tiger's den. They had known it was a tiger's den, but the Tuan Dokter insisted on going in. Who were they to tell him otherwise?

When Dubois returned home, none the worse for wear, he wrote to his family in the Netherlands, telling them of his reassignment. He had hoped to have news of a new fossil site to tell them; instead there was only that embarrassing story of the tiger's den. Well, the caves full of fossils would come in time.

Communicating from the Indies with people at home had an odd rhythm. Letters were dutifully sent to Holland, letters from home regularly arrived in the Indies, but the arrivals replied to missives dispatched months before. Writing from the colonies was a little like putting a letter into a bottle and flinging it out to sea. By the time an answer came, if it did, the moment had passed. An entire life could be expended in the gap between letters. More than one Indies family had received letters of congratulation on the birth of a new child, letters that arrived on the very ship that would carry back news of that child's death.

Dubois was impatient to hear from his parents. When the looked-for letter came, it was bitterly disappointing. They did not understand how significant his achievements were; they did not see that he had already succeeded where everyone had predicted failure. All they saw was that he had committed himself even more deeply to a foolish and useless quest. As he read their letter, devoid of the approval and praise he had hoped for, Dubois's despair rose uncontrollably, flooding over the banks of his reason. The endorsements of the Governor of West Sumatra and the Director of the Department of Education, Religion, and Industry seemed to mean nothing to his parents.

It was in this state that Anna found him, sitting on the back veranda staring into the garden at nothing, clutching his parents' letter in his hand. She could see from his demeanour that something was terribly wrong. She sat down on the arm of his chair and gently took the crumpled pages from his hand.

'Oh,' she said softly, after skimming them. 'It doesn't matter, Eugène. I know what you have done. Max Weber and Karl Martin and all the others know what you have done. Your parents just can't see it yet. Your mother is not very educated and your father, though he is a big man in Eijsden, is only a country apothecary. He doesn't understand about the missing link.' She stroked his

Dubois photographed the village of Giring-Giring, near Padang, after collecting fossils from nearby caves.

beautiful blond hair and laid her cheek against the top of his head. 'When we go home, and you are famous among all the great men of science, then your father will see.'

Anna was no better educated than her mother-in-law. But she knew a good man with an aching heart when she saw one, and she knew her husband had given up much to come here. So had she, for that matter. But it was all beginning to turn out right now. He was finding fossils, and their children were healthy, and the highlands were so much cooler than that awful swamp of a coastal army base... A nap and a bath and a good dinner would surely put him right.

CHAPTER 14

Fevers and Spells

The mood of despair marked the onset of Dubois's first battle with malaria. He fell prey to enervating, fluctuating fevers that recurred and recurred like an evil force. A few hours after reading his father's letter, he was taken over, body and soul. Sweat puddled beneath his body, soaking the sheets and the mattress and any number of towels. The servants lifted him, changed the mattress, remade the bed, repeated it all again a few hours later. Anna applied cool, wet cloths to his forehead and wiped his burning body. Servants brought cool drinks and bowls of broth, and stood fanning him for hours. None of these treatments brought any relief; malaria had its own schedule. The burning heat was followed by teeth-chattering chills, a sensation of deep and final cold that felt as if death had invaded Dubois's bones. He could not quite believe that his heart was still pumping, his blood still warm. Surely his blood had turned to slush, like the grey half-melted ice in the canals of Amsterdam in winter. The servants brought blankets and quilts to warm him, they moved his bed near the fire, but it was not enough. He shook uncontrollably, like a pitiful leaf in a thunderstorm, pelted and pounded, wrung this way and that. This, too, subsided with time, leaving Dubois weak and pale.

The relentless rise and fall of body temperature over the hours and days that followed was more exhausting than any physical task Dubois had ever known – not that he was fully aware of his own state, for he could not think clearly. Merely opening his eyes or per-mitting Anna to spoon liquid down his throat was almost more exertion than he could muster the strength for. Breathing seemed so difficult, sitting up a trial, eating beyond conception. In his more lucid moments, he knew he had to take sustenance, especially salty soups and broths, for he was losing quarts, maybe gallons, of salt water during the sweating episodes. But giving in to the illness, letting the malaria sweep him away, seemed so easy, so inviting. After two days, Anna had him carried to the hospital where she could be relieved by Pollak and the orderlies.

'You must,' she whispered to him fiercely, spooning broth into his slack mouth. 'You must. You have things to do. You cannot give in now. You have a wife and two children. You have a destiny. You will not give in.'

Close as he was to unconsciousness, her urgent whispers penetrated the disordered grey fog of illness and reawakened his character. He began to fight, to prod his own brain into working, to will his body into resisting. He took a turn for the better.

'I think his case will prove to be a mild one after all,' Pollak told Anna, relieved when he checked on the patient later. 'I thought for a while there ... but no matter, I may have misjudged him. The next few hours should tell us. You go and get some rest. The orderlies can look after him now.'

Too tired to show her gratitude properly, Anna simply rose and headed back to their house where she collapsed in her room. This was the first time she had wrestled hand-to-hand with death. Without Pollak's help, Dubois would probably have been dead already; she could not have carried on much longer. The orderlies were experienced at nursing but would not take responsibility or make decisions; she could do that, but she lacked knowledge. She did not know what to do for these tropical ailments, so wickedly virulent. Dubois had not been any help, for he had been delirious half the time and too weak to think the rest.

If they had been alone, on some coffee plantation on some remote mountain, and her husband had contracted malaria, what would Anna have done? Despite the heat, she shivered a little from fear as she saw for the first time the reality of life for most Indies families. She'd have known what was wrong, but she wouldn't have known what to do about it. There would have been no doctor nearby to turn to, no hospital, maybe no supplies of quinine. She couldn't have had him transported any distance, even by sedan chair, in that weakened state; it would probably have killed him outright. So it would have been just nursing and comforting, that would have been all she could do, while her husband or maybe her child weakened and shook and sweated and died.

People died here every day, she realized suddenly, horribly. Death was everywhere, malaria just one of his servants. And malaria was a genial illness, almost companionable, reluctant to leave prematurely. Malaria never hesitated to pay a second visit, or a third. Sometimes it killed rapidly, impatiently; other times it lingered, went, then returned again and again to wreak slow destruction upon its chosen.

This was a hard, hard place, the Indies. Now Anna understood what coming here might have meant, might yet mean. Dubois had known and faced this horror silently from their first few days here, but Anna had not. She was aghast.

However, Dubois's health continued to improve. There was no question he would recover fairly rapidly, for a malaria victim. Doubtless his robust constitution was an asset. Before long, he was sitting up in bed, cheerfully organizing another expedition, consulting his maps, ordering supplies and equipment, asking the governor for more labourers. As he gained strength, he made hospital rounds and checked on the patients, discussing treatments and plans with Pollak, who would once again take over for him when he left to fossil-hunt.

Dubois searched an ever-widening area of the Padang Highlands. Weeks accumulated into months without success. The new areas were thick with forest and very precipitous, sometimes nearly vertical. There were few established tracks and no roads. The thorns of acacias and the barbs of alang-alang grass clutched relentlessly at clothes and skin. The only recourse was to send a few men in advance, using machetes to clear a pathway and to cut steps. No one wanted to do this for long. Tigers lurked and wild pigs attacked viciously, charging out of the forest as if their young had been threatened. Dubois shot them, which improved his meals but not those of his workers, who were mostly Muslim. One coolie was badly wounded by a boar and Dubois sent him back to the hospital with gangrene. Pollak could not save him.

The highland people were suspicious of his expedition, as if he had been searching for valuables to steal, and he had to keep a tight rein on the men to ward off misbehaviour. Some of the coolies were considered ruffians even in their own villages, where the power of public opinion and rules of expected behaviour were strongest. Villagers rarely offered any useful information and sometimes refused to sell them supplies.

Even the caves seemed to reject them, being more and more difficult to find, more and more consistently devoid of specimens. Only a few yielded fossils and then they were not very good. Dubois's sense of futility and frustration became entrenched. He was alert for attacks from animals or snakes but bored with finding nothing, seeing nothing, learning nothing. His health began to suffer, or perhaps it was a return of malaria. He was short-tempered with the men, demanding of the engineers, merciless toward himself.

They would continue. They would work harder. They would explore more caves. They would find something. They had to be more diligent, that was all. The relentlessness would have sent the men to the edge of rebellion, if they had had enough energy left to make trouble. About a quarter of them ran away, sneaking off in the night and melting into the shadows. They returned to their villages, Dubois supposed, or took refuge with relatives. He didn't know; he didn't care. They were gone. Those that remained were more intelligent, more loyal, more dutiful, or simply more exhausted. As the days passed, Dubois drove his coolies harder, certain he could break the spell of bad luck. The men knew things were going badly. Sores refused to heal, every wound festered, food spoiled and made them sick, water sources were found inexplicably dry in this, one of the wettest of countries. Among themselves, the men said that the Tuan Dokter was losing his power, his vision. He was no longer seeing what would happen now. His Garuda eyes grew cloudy, or maybe he was bewitched by some powerful enemy. It was a dangerous time and they had to be careful, very careful. *Hati-hati*!

Then one day they found a deep and promising cave and the Tuan Dokter seemed to be his old self, full of enthusiasm and energy. 'Come,' he said to several of the men. 'It is a big cave. We will all go in with lamps and look for the bones like rocks.' They followed him willingly enough, for he sounded again like a man with power. It was an exercise in self-discipline for Dubois. He had summoned his enthusiasm and his faith in himself, putting on a good face for the men. They would just go a little farther in, bring a few more lights so they could see properly. Perhaps this cave merited a test excavation, he thought. Then he began to have an odd feeling about it. A slight noise, a small sound, penetrated his concentration because it was wrong.

'Quiet! Diam!' he called to the men imperiously. For once, they obeyed instantly; all talking ceased. There was no sound but breathing, not even the shuffling of feet. The men could hear nothing, so in a moment they started to move again, exploring, looking.

'No, wait, tunggu,' ordered Dubois, and they fell silent again, out of respect. The noise – a tiny weak thing, almost a stillborn infant of a noise – came again. It was a little rattle and then a dull thud, then silence again. Dubois knew what it signified, this unimportant little noise. 'Turn and walk out!' he commanded the men. 'Get out *now*! But walk. *Do not run*. Do not touch anything.'

They responded to the tone of his voice, to the sound of authority. They did not know all of the Dutch words he used, but they understood the urgency. They turned in fear and walked out in terror, borrowing what courage and dignity they could from Dubois's stony face and rigid bearing. It was like walking away from a tiger, moving slowly for fear of provoking an attack and yet longing to run. Dubois left last of all.

Almost as soon as the cave was cleared, there was a terrible roar and a resonating impact. Dust and small pebbles exploded out of the cave mouth, coating them all from head to toe. The ceiling of the cave had collapsed. The labourers began to shriek and gabble in terror as they realized what had happened. The cave's interior, the place in which they had stood moments before, was now a solid mass of rubble. Every one of them would have lain buried beneath that pile of rock, but for one thing: the vision of their *tuan*. Their Tuan Dokter had foreseen the danger. He had heard the noise – the first faint noise which no one else could hear, the noise that maybe had not been for the ears but for the spirit – and it told him that the stones would drop. The evil spell upon him was broken or perhaps he had defeated the enemy who worked against him. The Tuan had saved them all. They looked at him with new admiration, and with fear, thinking of the great power at his disposal. He could hear the future.

Dubois was more than a little shaken, though he tried to disguise the trembling of his knees. 'It is early, but we will return to camp now,' he said calmly, then turned to lead the way back. He had to concentrate to walk without stumbling, without collapsing in terror at what might have been. No one would ever have found their bodies. Anna would never have known what became of him; the children would never have known. He would have been...gone, that is all. He would have been the mad Dutchman who had gone off looking for the missing link in the Padang Highlands and had never been heard of again. He would have been nothing, just dust, more crushed bones, a meal for the insects. He said nothing more to the men.

The incident became an integral part of the elaborate mythology the coolies were building about the Tuan Dokter, how he was stronger than other men, more powerful, and fiercer. He worked the men very hard. But he saw things even other *totoks* could not. Maybe he had an amulet that protected him from harm. How else had he escaped the tiger's lair and the cave-in? Who else had even heard the noise he noticed?

Though the men were awed by his prescience, tentacles of fear and despair curled and wound their way through Dubois's thoughts. Unwelcome images of failure, humiliation, and death haunt him. It was a long and lonely night for him, a tiny speck of Dutch genius lost in the middle of Sumatra. By the next day, he was laid flat with fever.

There was something malevolent about it all. The thought spun around and around his disordered mind; he could not concentrate on anything. It was fever, malaria, that was all, he told himself. It was not a spirit or a curse. He had a fever. He had to treat himself, as he treated the men. Call Pollak. No, he was not at the hospital, not at home, no Pollak. He had to get to his medical supplies, had to take quinine. But he could not stand, could not even sit up. When his boy came in to see why he was late for breakfast, he gestured to the boy to bring the medicine chest over. 'Obat,' he croaked faintly. 'Medicine, I need obat.' Leaning over the side of the bed, Dubois unlocked the case slowly, fumbling with the key. He opened the chest and extracted the precious bottle of quinine. 'Bring coffee and bread,' he told the boy. Exhausted, he lay back down and waited. The boy returned and held him up, so that he could drink the coffee, chew the bread, and swallow the quinine. Without food in his stomach the bitterness of the quinine would make him vomit. 'There,' he whispered. 'Bring soup later, biscuits. Get me a fresh towel.' He gestured feebly at his sweat-soaked face and chest.

While the fever did its dance, Dubois lay in his tent and waited. Waiting was not difficult, for his mind drifted off into confused, cloudy fantasies. The boy was loyal to the Tuan Dokter, for he was a special man. The Tuan was exhausted from his struggle against evil forces yesterday, so now he was vulnerable. The boy guarded him. He sat quietly outside Dubois's tent, listening and waiting to be of use. He took the blankets off when the Tuan was restless and sweating; he put them on again when the chills came, and even lay on top of the Tuan, outside the blankets, to add his body's heat and weight. He brought coffee and soup and tea and helped the Tuan eat. Dubois's days collapsed into nights; his nights warped into formless nightmares. Even a strong, young man was helpless in the grip of malaria. He could not shake it off by an effort of will. Fortunately, the boy grasped the idea of keeping his master quiet, clean, and comfortable and he saw that the water was thoroughly boiled to make tea or soup. He held the basin for the Tuan to urinate into and emptied it far from the tent. He learnt how much quinine Dubois was to take, and when, and made him swallow it.

When the fever abated, the expedition continued. The coolies had been glad of the rest. It was almost mid-October; rains were threatening. Dubois was still weaker than he was willing to show the men, and he was discouraged. He had accomplished very little this season. Perhaps he had been unusually lucky to find Lida Adjer early on, a rich site and relatively easy to get to. He must report to those who had supported him, educate them as this season had educated him, about the realities of fossil-hunting in Sumatra. He wrote to F. A. Jentink, the Director of the National Museum of Natural History in Leiden and a member of the research committee:

17 October 1889

Everything here has gone against me, and even with the utmost effort on my part, I have not achieved a hundredth part of what I had visualized. Where the cave explorations are concerned, the reverses began right at the start, with my coming here in the poeaza (the period of fasting) when the Malays are as indolent as frogs in winter...A survey of the caves I was provided with seemed fitted only to put me off the scent because there were very few real caves among them, Yet these did exist, as I saw later, and people had simply concealed their existence from me...because they thought that the 'Company' would appropriate the gold and saltpetre the inlanders get out of these caves...After these experiences I went searching without guides and in this way I have found a few very useful caves, but still never the best one could wish for. What's more, it was necessary to live out in the forest for weeks on end, usually under an overhanging rock or in an improvised hut, and it turns out that in the long run I can't stand up to that, however well I was able to bear the fatigue at first. Having now come back, with my third bout of high fever, which nearly finished me for all searching for 'diluvialia', I have had to give it up for good...

The trouble with the personnel was even worse. To begin with, one of the two engineers assigned to me to supervise the forced labourers was totally useless, and after repeated warnings and exhortations to carry out his duties properly he was transferred at my request... Meanwhile the other engineer died of fever...The number of forced labourers I have placed at my disposal is 50. Of these, some (7) have run away or have been turned out because of misbehaviour; at present (in the rains) 50% are sick. There are also foremen and cooks among them so that at the moment – it is sad, but true – only 12–15 labourers are working. A third drawback lies in the site itself. That it is overgrown with forest would not be so bad in itself, if there were only roads or at least paths, and if the steep limestone mountains did not make communication with most points as good as impossible, and if there were not a total lack of water in many of the mountain places.

As he composed the letter, he mused about the difference between Sumatra as it was and Sumatra as he had envisioned it, sitting in Amsterdam. He had thought finding the missing link would be a relatively simple task: all he would have to do was look in the right place. He saw now that looking and finding were more gruelling than he had anticipated. He did not want to die of fever before he found the missing link. He jestingly called the fossils 'diluvialia' in his letter, as if they had been remnants of the biblical Flood. The only flood they were associated with was a flood of sweat: sweat from digging, sweat from fever, sweat from climbing up and down these wretched mountains.

He hoped Jentink and the others would understand. Dubois would not give up the search, no indeed, but his sponsors needed to

In 1887, two corporals from the Engineering Corps, Gerardus Kriele (left) and Anthonie de Winter (right), joined Dubois to supervise the day-to-day work of the forced labourers.

understand how very taxing it was. Fossil-hunting was not a stroll across a meadow to inspect the exposures, or even a vigorous day's hike, as in Holland. No, fossil-hunting here was tigers and fevers and close-mouthed villagers who did not know their own area or would not tell a *tuan* what they knew. It was having to teach the men the most elementary work habits. And the first pair of engineers had been worse than useless. Maybe the two who had come to replace them, Anthonie de Winter and Gerardus Kriele, would be better. He hoped so. Still, all of it was up to him: all the decisions, all the evaluations, all the procedures and strategies had to be created by Dubois alone. If the prize had not been so important, it would have been less urgent to seek it.

He needed a better plan.

CHAPTER 15

To Java

The expedition was halted by the rainy season, but Dubois was still preoccupied with his fossils. He wrote for advice to the geologist Rogier D. M. Verbeek, who knew the Indies well. Verbeek replied promptly and kindly, suggesting Dubois might have more luck in Java, where Raden Saleh's fossils came from. Verbeek had seen a lot of limestone there, which was good for preserving fossils, and Java was not so wild as Sumatra. There were more roads, more people, and more cultivated fields and villages. While villagers might be a nuisance, they could also be very helpful. And the existence of roads and well-travelled paths would lessen Dubois's transportation problems. The expedition could search more ground if the men were not always having to make roads and paths; the supplies could be hauled by oxcart rather than carried by the coolies.

Dubois weighed the advice. Was Java the answer? Ease of access would be a real advantage. He could start by trying to relocate Raden Saleh's find-spots. Also, Junghuhn's maps of Java were much better than the vague, inaccurate ones of Sumatra he had access to. Verbeek's suggestion pricked Dubois's memory, reminding him of a piece of valuable information that he had completely neglected. Almost a year ago exactly, on 24 October 1888, a mining engineer named B. D. van Rietschoten had been searching for marble outcrops near a Javan hamlet called Wadjak. He had found instead an old, petrified skull and picked it up as a curiosity. Eventually, he had dispatched the skull to Carl Philip Sluiter, Curator of the Royal East Indies Society of Natural Science in Batavia. After a brief correspondence, Sluiter had generously forwarded the skull to Dubois in Sumatra with a letter, which had arrived like an unexpected gift.

21 December 1888

I received your letter of 15 November already some days ago, but I waited to answer until I received the box with the skull from Mr. Van

Rietschoten from Kediri. I have received it and looked at the contents. This is, however, in a very sad state. The skull is broken in a number of pieces, and everything is embedded with a tremendous incrustation of limestone. Because an examination of this species is completely outside my usual work, I think it would be best if I send the complete collection, as it is, to you. I have tried to remove the limestone from a small piece with hydrochloric acid and this works excellently. Another question is, however, whether the skull is a fossil or not. I myself doubt it is, judging from the condition of the bone, but I am not knowledgeable about such matters. Also the situation of the cave makes the age perhaps somewhat doubtful. So you will be able to make your own judgement about these things, I enclose the letter of Mr. Van Rietschoten, although it is rather insufficient.

Dubois had been astonished that a man who wasn't even looking for fossils could stumble across a fossil skull, when he himself had spent months scrambling up mountains deliberately searching for fossils with modest results. What exactly had this mining engineer found? He had set the box down on a table in his study, extracting each fragment carefully from its wrappings and laying them out upon a pad of folded cloth. What a thing this specimen was! Though it was in pieces, he could see easily that it *was* a skull, a type of human skull. And it was certainly fossilized; it weighed several pounds or more. It was worth cleaning off and fitting back together, but he already knew it wasn't his missing link. The brain-case was much too large and the face too small. It had reminded him of some of those old natives, with not an ounce of fat left on their faces. But it was nothing like an ape, still not strong enough in the face, no big canine teeth, the brain much too big. There were browridges, but not massive ones like a Neanderthal's or a gorilla's. No, this Wadjak man was primitive – very interesting – but human.

Because of that judgement about the skull's humanity, Dubois had cleaned, glued, and examined the fossil for only a few days. He knew the typical shapes of the skulls of various races of mankind and this skull was surely neither European nor mainland Chinese. There was something a little...a little crude about it. He had sent Sluiter a prompt evaluation of the specimen.

In every respect...the skull differs so greatly from the type of the present-day inhabitants of the West-Malay islands that there can be absolutely no doubt that it has nothing to do with that present-day race … While I don't dare to make a definite statement before I have had the opportunity of classifying it precisely through close study and comparison, the skull seems to me to show the greatest similarities with the Papuan type, and I am virtually certain that the first representative of the primordial people of Java has now been discovered.

With the dispatch of this letter, Dubois had pushed the Wadjak skull to the back of his mind. He had kept it, of course, but he had placed the box on a shelf that was rather hard to reach, for his attention had then been focused on the fine fossils from Lida Adjer. Now, in October 1889, Verbeek's letter reminded Dubois that he had paid far too little attention to the only human fossil ever to come from Java, which sat on a shelf in his own study. What a fool he was!

During the rainy season of 1889–90, the Wadjak skull drew Dubois back again and again. It was a fine specimen. Of all the caves on Sumatra that he had explored, only Lida Adjer had yielded fossils as good as this. This Wadjak skull proved that the

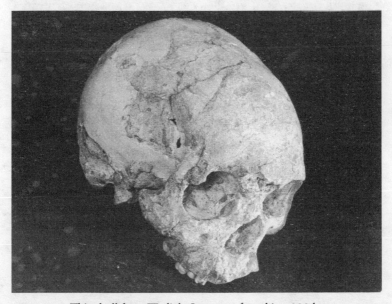

This skull from Wadjak, Java, was found in 1888 by
B. D. van Rietschoten, a mining engineer.

preservation of fossils was very good in at least one find-spot in Java. He looked up Wadjak in Junghuhn's map of the island of Java. The town was in East Java...Ah! near the volcano Mount Willis, very near the town of Toeloeng Agoeng, Kediri Residency. People said that East Java enjoyed a much healthier climate than Sumatra, much less malaria, so there would not be such a cruel risk to his health. There were Anna and the children to think of, too. Maybe he should start again in Java.

He broached the subject with Anna one quiet evening, after the children had been put to bed. The servants padded silently about, lighting the lamps, cleaning up after dinner, and the two of them sat side by side in long chairs. Feet up, comfortable, contented, Dubois looked over at his comely wife and thought that life was good.

'Anna,' he said softly, reaching out a hand to touch hers, 'do you like it here?'

She was surprised by the question; she had not considered whether she liked it here or not. They were here, she and her husband; her children were here; the servants were here; it was the Indies, not Amsterdam, and that was all. She was a good-tempered woman, happy in most circumstances. 'Why yes, I suppose so,' she replied, smiling. 'Why do you ask?'

'I thought that a move might be in order. I have not found a good cave since Lida Adjer, that July just after Jean was born. That was more than a year ago! I think that the caves of Sumatra are less promising than I once believed. Besides, there is so much fever here, so much; I didn't know how dangerous it would be. The children are still so small and helpless...'

'Have you noticed something?' Anna interrupted, alarmed. 'I thought Jean was a little fractious today, but just tired, in need of a nap. Do you think he was feverish? Or that redness on Eugenie's cheek. That is just an ordinary rash, isn't it? Do you think they...' She could not bring herself to finish the sentence, so awful was the prospect of her darling children coming down with some wicked tropical disease.

'No, no, not that,' he reassured her. 'They seem fine and healthy. I am sure they are well. But they might be safer somewhere else, somewhere where there would be better fossils, too, and where maybe I wouldn't have to be gone so much of the time. I shall propose to Groeneveldt that I move my expedition to East Java.'

'Java?' said Anna, vaguely. 'Will it take us long to get there? By boat, I suppose, from Padang. Show me on the map. Do we know anyone there? Would we be near Batavia? I hear there is quite a social life in Batavia.'

In the early spring of 1890, Dubois petitioned Governor Kroesen and Director Groeneveldt for permission to move his operations to East Java. Characteristically, he included a detailed, logical list of scientific reasons why the new plan was likely to meet with success. Permission was duly granted by government resolution on 14 April 1890. He would take Kriele and De Winter with him.

Once again, the Dubois family packed their belongings, which seemed to have grown hugely, fertilized perhaps by the rich tropical climate. They sailed from Padang for a new island, Java, and a new fossil-hunting ground. Before reaching Tanjung Priok, the harbour at Batavia, they passed the old harbour, Sunda Kelapa. Dubois spied a load of tropical lumber from Kalimantan being unloaded from a wooden Makassar schooner and pointed it out to his children. The swarthy Buginese sailors looked like pirates and perhaps they were. Small but muscular, they heaved massive loads of fresh red wood up on to their naked shoulders, two men to a load, using only a folded rag or two to protect their skin from the rough-cut planks. Then the pair walked slowly down the gangplank, a massive tree trunk rudely shaped with an adze to give a grip to horny bare feet. Thus the entire ship was unloaded, hundreds upon hundreds of pounds of lumber, until the hold was empty. The old harbour was packed with perhaps thirty of these wooden schooners, sleek and fast, painted in vibrant stripes of red and green, white, sunny yellow, and brilliant blue. Their dull, rust-coloured sails looked heavy, furled with stout ropes greasy with use. It was like encountering something from the eighteenth century, Dubois thought, when the Dutch ruled all the Spice Islands.

Before long, their steamer – it was also the mail boat – docked a little farther up the shore at Tanjung Priok. The Dubois were received by the European population of Batavia as eagerly as a package from home. Welcoming a new, handsome couple was an exciting prospect. And such an exotic thing Dr Dubois was here for: to find fossils! The more scientifically inclined among the men had some appreciation of what he was looking for, as did a few of the more educated women. No one had ever come to Java before to look for fossils except that eccentric German Junghuhn, who had bothered himself with all kinds of curiosities, and that had been years ago.

The Dubois were fêted and dined and introduced to all of the important people in the capital. They were caught up in a social whirl the like of which they had not seen since their courting days in Amsterdam. Dubois took the opportunity to explain his scientific aims to the men, seeking out Sluiter at the Natural History Museum in particular. The ladies showed Anna where to have new stylish dresses made up and clothes ordered for the family, too. She revelled in the opportunity to make women friends, to shop and talk of fashions at home. She had not realized how sorely she missed feminine company. There were so many goods available in the capital that she had not seen for a long time: china and fabric and furniture, paintings and books and music, imported foods from home that her mouth longed for. There were even potatoes, true Dutch potatoes, though they were in tins. Her head spun with the opulence of Batavia compared to their quiet, simple life in Pajakombo. For the first time in their short lives, the children played with other Dutch children, not natives.

The Dubois family enjoyed the sojourn in Batavia. Anna and Dubois promenaded in smart *delman*s along the Konigsplein, the broad avenue in the fashionable district, and went to receptions at the governor's house. They attended musical evenings, reviving some of the songs they used to sing together when they were courting, to general acclaim. Anna's clear soprano and even her out-of-practice skill at playing the piano were much praised. Of course, the pianos here were generally out of tune anyway; the impossible heat and constant humidity ruined musical instruments in a few months. But to play even an out-of-tune piano was a treat for Anna. Dubois's handsome features and proud stature drew the eyes of more than one colonial lady bored with her husband and the predictability of Batavia society. Dubois would do no more than flirt, and very mildly at that. He was not immune to the sidelong glances of the prettiest young matrons; he knew his novelty and athleticism made him a popular partner on the dance floor. But he was still more interested in science than in romance, as the ladies discovered to their regret.

Anna was a great success, a lovely *totok* wife not yet ruined in face or figure by the tropics and childbearing. She was gay, amusing, and new; no one had heard her stories before or grown weary of her personality. One eligible bachelor about ten years

Anna's senior, Willem, paid particular attention to her, bringing her cups of punch or tea, pulling the chair out for her to sit, fetching her fan when it was too warm, fluffing the pillows to ensure her comfort. It was Willem, not Dubois, who stood by her side through social occasions, asking with courtly attentiveness whether the lamp was too near or the evening too chilly. He seemingly asked no more than to be near Anna and to serve her. Dubois saw nothing wrong in this; it was a usual thing for a lady in the colonies to have a chaste admirer. He appreciated the compliment to his wife. Willem was a good chap, but why he had nothing better to do than listen to Anna's chatter and dance attendance on her, Dubois could not fathom. Anna glowed with the attention. After a month or two, Dubois declared it was time for them to go. He had to start up his expeditions again before the dry season was over. Or perhaps, just perhaps, he felt Willem's intentions were growing less innocent.

Dubois decided to settle in Toeloeng Agoeng, a town in East Java whose name meant 'Noble Help': a good omen, he thought. Located at the foot of majestic Mount Willis, Toeloeng Agoeng was close to Wadjak. But the real reason for moving there was that the house formerly occupied by the Dutch Assistant Resident, the second administrative official in Kediri province, could be leased at a very good price. There were few houses so fine in the eastern part of the island.

The family spent two long days on the train from Batavia to Toeloeng Agoeng, travelling with all of their belongings and no servants to help them. The Resident of Kediri province kindly sent a carriage and an oxcart to meet them at the station and take them to the house, which was elegant and spacious. It was a large one-storey building with a red-tile roof and generous verandas at both the front and rear. Substantial white pillars supported the roof over the veranda and a decorative wooden fretwork joined each pillar to its neighbour, except in the centre, where the broad stairs rose from the yard. It was a fine Indies house, both in the arrangement of its rooms and in its style of architecture.

The two deep, shady verandas, front and back, formed the foot and cap of a letter 'I', connected to each other by a long central hallway that was broad enough to be considered a room in its own right. Anna would arrange rows and rows of flowers, palms, and other plants in Chinese blue-and-white flowerpots right up the front steps and on to the veranda, as if to extend the garden into the house. Scrolled rattan furniture, rocking chairs and long chairs, were interspersed with conveniently placed small tables and small, ornate rugs. Anna took a critical took at the bamboo blinds of the front gallery, which had been spoiled by mildew and would need replacing.

From the front veranda, a central pair of large carved doors led to the inner gallery, a long narrow room that paralleled the verandas. The inner gallery was a more formal reception or entertaining area for guests, forming the transition between the public front gallery and the inner, more intimate rooms. Anna would hang large mirrors along the walls to reflect the light without lending heat; among the mirrors hung lithographs, and her prized collection of good delft plates. Maybe she would be able to get one of those colourful paintings by Dezentjé, the native artist who was all the rage in Batavia; they were so dramatic, full of pinky-orange sunsets and purple volcanoes. Potted palms, hibiscus and the like would soften the stiff arrangement of chairs and tables set against the walls.

If the verandas were the cap and foot of the letter 'I', then the central hallway was the vertical stem. It was reached by passing through a second wonderfully carved set of enormous doors. With the doors opened, Anna could see through the entire house from back to front. It was beautiful: cool and softly lit by the diffuse sunlight that reflected from the mirrors, the plates, and the gleaming marble floors. The interior was a vast, elegant expanse broken only by clusters of furniture and flowers. The smooth stone floors felt deliciously cool to bare feet. The children and servants sometimes lay flat upon the floors, to soak up the cool. Along each wall of the central hallway were doors that opened into smaller, rectangular rooms, four to a side. On one side were Dubois's study, a gentlemen's sitting room, a parlour, and a ladies' withdrawing room; on the other were the bedrooms for Anna and Dubois, Eugenie, and Jean, as well as the nursery proper. At the foot of the hallway, another set of doors opened on to the back veranda. It was a mirror image of the front veranda but it was a far more intimate and private space.

When they first arrived, they found a lovely mahogany sideboard with glass-fronted shelves in the central hallway; it was by far the nicest piece of furniture in the house. Anna thought she would display her fine tea set in it, and the best china, perhaps some crystal. But upon unpacking, she found her teapot – a prized wedding present – was broken beyond repair. It was to be expected, she thought a little sadly, when we move about so much. She soon learnt that the shops in Toeloeng Agoeng did not carry fine European china. Perhaps the Njonja might be able to find a comparable teapot in Batavia, she was told.

In the meantime, whimsically, she decided to buy a plain, ivory-coloured stoneware teapot from a Chinese merchant. The teapot had a humorous shape, like a plump Indies *njonja*, that appealed to Anna. It was well rounded and broad at the bottom, narrowing to a sort of waist just above the lower attachment of the handle, and swelling generously again at the top to receive the lid. The only decoration was a pair of incised parallel lines that demarcated a stripe around the widest part – that, and the clever angling of the handle, just where a thumb-rest was needed to balance the weight of a full pot. The spout was stout but rather elegantly curved, with angles that repeated the one on the handle. The overall effect was of a European teapot crossed with Javanese chinoiserie. Anna thought of it as 'Njonja Dubois's teapot'. She was becoming a little bit Indische.

The Toeloeng Agoeng house sat on a property that, like the house, was much deeper than wide. As she explored it, Anna was pleased by the layout of the house and the compound. Behind the main house lay the large and private garden, surrounded by a low wall of whitewashed stone. The garden had once been lovely, she could see, and would be an excellent place for the children to play. It was planted with flowering bushes – frangipani, melati, and tjempaka, a variety of magnolia – and fruit trees. There was a coconut tree, a few feathery casuarinas, some papayas, and a small group of mango trees, though everything was in need of a good deal of attention. She would set the new *tukang kebun* to pruning and fertilizing and ridding the garden of snakes and scorpions at once. Set off by itself was one very large waringin tree, the habitual roost of a small flock of cooing, brightly coloured doves. Anna thought she might have a circular bench built around it, to remind Dubois of the one in his parents' garden in Eijsden.

Behind the garden was a separate building with the *mandi* room for bathing, the toilets, the laundry room, the kitchen, and storage rooms. Opposite were the stables, with stalls for four horses. The servants' quarters made up a small kampong or village farther back on the property, where the noise of their children and chickens and the smoke from their cooking fires would not bother the Tuan Dokter or the Njonja. Like every Indies household, this one was a miniature of the colony itself, a hybrid born of the mingling of Javanese and Dutch cultures under tropical skies.

Anna had to hire new servants but she felt much more confident after living in the Indies for three years. She did rather well this time, she believed, especially with the four most important servants: the *djongas* Nassi, the *kokkie*, the children's *babu*, and her own *babu*. Dubois's pay had increased with his secondment to the Department of Education, Religion, and Industry, so Anna hired additional servants: a *syce*, who would look after Dubois's horse and would also help the head gardener, and a laundrywoman and seamstress. Anna felt very grand, having such a large staff and a fine, high-ceilinged house with large rooms and a marble floor. Soon after arriving in Toeloeng Agoeng, she realized she was with child again and her happiness was complete.

Toeloeng Agoeng was ideally placed for Dubois's explorations. He relished being free of interference. The closest military outpost was Fort Van Den Bosch in Ngawi, almost 150 miles away. At last Dubois was accountable to no one, no one but himself and his director, Willem Groeneveldt. What made him feel most free was the certainty that there would be no summons to come and help out at the hospital or to turn up for some military event or other. He could devote himself entirely to science.

Dubois returned home from his first brief expedition bearing not boxes and crates of fossils, as Anna expected, but a huge, grotesque bird in an enormous bamboo cage shaped like a minaret. It was a marabou stork, to be a pet. Anna could not imagine why he had brought this creature home. Like all its kind, the stork was ugly, almost five feet tall with long, knobbly legs. Its repulsive head was nearly bald, mottled pink and grey in colour. From its neck hung an obscenely naked, wrinkled, pink pouch like an old man's scrotum, not that Anna allowed herself to think of such things. For all its homeliness, the marabou was a formidable creature, with a wingspan of nearly nine feet and a long, heavy beak. Its beady eyes assessed constantly whether anything within its view was edible. Indeed, the loathsome bird soon exhibited a fondness for carrion and rotting meat, as well as a deadly tendency to attack anything smaller than itself. Lizards, geckos, snakes, mice, worms, insects, fruits, and even unwary chickens were fodder for this nightmarish apparition.

Still, something about its stately pacing around the yard amused Dubois; Anna could see the humour in it, when he pointed it out.

In the back garden at Toeloeng Agoeng, one of Dubois's servants was
to build a pen for the marabou stork named the Adjutant.

The bird walked slowly, peering down its long beak as if looking
down its nose at everything. Its angular, stiff-jointed walk was a
ghastly parody of a self-important military man's. 'Do you see?'
said Dubois to Anna, chuckling. 'It is the very image of that
pompous colonel in Batavia. Let us call him the Adjutant. That is
the nickname for these birds in Africa, I believe.' It pleased Dubois
to look out from his study window and see the Adjutant lurching
around the garden, unaware of its own ungainliness. Secretly, Anna
hated it and the children were terrified. The *kokkie* complained
that the Adjutant snatched food from her as she carried it from the
kitchen to the house, and Babu was certain it would eat the children's fingers or toes. One day Dubois saw her beating the stork
with a fallen branch, defending the children from its vicious beak.
After that he had a pen constructed to confine the stork to a corner
of the garden.

CHAPTER 16

Java Fossils

Dubois planned first to reconnoitre the caves and rock shelters near Wadjak, where Van Rietschoten had found the skull. As before, the greatest problem he faced was in training the labourers, but his assistants, Corporals Kriele and De Winter from the engineering corps, far surpassed their predecessors in their ability to understand the work, supervise the coolies, and map the excavations.

They met with almost immediate success at Wadjak. There were more extinct mammals there: fossils of antelope, rhino, pig, two sorts of monkey, and even Dubois's nemesis, a porcupine. After a few days' work, they discovered a second human skull, more fragmentary than Van Rietschoten's, but very similar in shape and size: confirmation that they had relocated the find-spot. Once the second skull was prepared and cleaned, Dubois was unsurprised to find it was of the same race as the first. Later work in the same area yielded a few fragments of a skeleton belonging to one of the skulls. As he explained to Groeneveldt in his first report, these remains were human: no missing link but scientifically important examples of an extinct Australian race at a higher level of evolutionary development than the Neanderthal fossils of Europe and thus undoubtedly fairly recent.

He decided to explore farther inland, along the entire range of the Kendeng Hills where Raden Saleh's fossils had come from. If the Kendeng Hills fauna was really like that of the Siwaliks of British India, Dubois might find something as good as Lydekker's *Anthropopithecus*. From June until the beginning of October 1890, Dubois's men surveyed the entire length of the range, tramping more than a hundred miles from near the town of Semarang on the central north coast almost to Soerabaja, the thriving port at the eastern end of Java. It was a demanding but profitable endeavour; they found numerous sites like Kedoeng Loeboe and Kedoeng Broebus, with mammalian fossils more abundant and more complete than those of Sumatra. Yet Dubois was still looking in the wrong places. Looking in caves and rock shelters was a poor strategy in Java. During the dry season the hills and slopes were carpeted in thick, leathery djati or teak leaves, each as big as a dinner plate and tough as a poorly cured hide. The djati leaves made walking awkward and almost completely obscured the ground and anything lying on its surface.

Frustrated, Dubois led the men away from the mountains and along the riverbanks, where movement was easier. Unexpectedly, they spied fossils in the exposed riverbeds. This was a completely new type of find-spot, out in the open air away from caves or natural overhangs. With a flash of insight, Dubois realized that he had been hampered by a European notion of where fossils would be found, a notion that did not apply here because the topography was different. Java had few lowland caves; most of the land was dead flat and covered with luxuriant vegetation or cultivated fields. The mountains – volcanoes really – constituted the only relief and they rose abruptly out of the plains, without foothills, like cups that a child had placed on a table top in play. Everything in Java was horizontal or vertical.

To find fossils, Dubois needed a glimpse of what lay entombed in the rock beneath the surface. Rivers were his best excavators, more valuable than a thousand coolies, for rivers had been cutting their way through the rocks and soil of Java for eons. In the dry season, when the water was low, the underlying sediments were exposed to anyone who had an eye to see what was there. Rivers were Dubois's window into the past. He would search where no one else had looked before and he would find what no one had found before. He explained his new strategy to Kriele and De Winter, who understood almost immediately and were grateful to be spared the endless climbing up and down mountains. From now on, they would search the rivers in the dry season, walking along the bluffs and looking down at the exposed sediments, being especially careful in searching point bars where sand and debris accumulated at the bends in the river.

Together, Dubois and the engineers laid out a plan of exploration focusing on one of East Java's major rivers, the Bengawan Solo. They would work west from the fort at Ngawi, where they could obtain provisions and supplies. Dubois would select likely spots for excavation, leaving the day-to-day work in the hands of Kriele and De Winter. They would make sketch maps, take precise notes on anything they found, and send frequent reports and crates

Dubois would sort his fossils on the veranda at Toeloeng Agoeng,
leaving a narrow walkway to the front door.

of fossils back to him at Toeloeng Agoeng. They were to label
fossils according to where they were found. If they found anything
exceptional, he would join them as soon as possible.

After starting the men off, Dubois settled into family life at
Toeloeng Agoeng. Whenever a crate of fossils arrived, he investigated it with enormous anticipation, unwrapping specimens one by
one from the djati leaves that cushioned them: who knew what lay
within? He laid out the fossils to make preliminary identifications.
The larger ones – a nine-foot-long elephant tusk, the two-foot-long
skull of an extinct buffalo with a six-foot spread of horns – simply
would not fit into his study. Before long he took over the front
veranda as a sorting space. There, he could work protected against
rain and sun, with a pleasant breeze to keep his head clear as he
arranged, cleaned, compared, and labelled specimens. Soon the
fossils usurped nearly the whole veranda, like a tiresome guest who
called at teatime, settled into a comfortable chair, and would not
leave. There was only an ever-narrowing bone-free path from the
front steps to the inside of the house. It was awkward, Dubois
could see that, and unconventional, but he was a man of science
and these specimens were his life.

Despite his intentions to stay at home more and guard his health,

Dubois was drawn to the sites like an ant to sugar. When exciting fossils began to appear, he had to go to see the place where they had been found for himself. And when Kriele or De Winter wrote that they were about to move camp, Dubois felt compelled to join them and pick the next spot himself. But as her third pregnancy advanced, Anna asked him to stay at home more. He agreed. He needed more time to prepare, identify, and study the fossils, for no one else in all of the Indies could be trusted to do this exacting work.

At the end of 1890, Dubois wrote, a trifle smugly, to tell Groeneveldt that he and his men had collected hundreds of fossils from several different sites in East Java. In his quarterly report, he described the fossils from the Kendeng Hills and those found along the banks of the Bengawan Solo. He could already prove that there were two different types of elephant (*Stegodon*, an extinct type, and a relative of the modern *Elephas*) in the ancient fauna, as well as extinct hippos, rhinos, hyenas, felines, and pigs. Some of the species or genera still existed, but not in the Indies. Clearly the Javan fossil fauna was derived from that of mainland Asia, in accordance with Wallace's brilliant notion.

Establishing the precise age of paleontological specimens was a tricky matter, but faunas could be correlated from one region to another and Dubois's conclusion was that the Javan fauna he was collecting now was a little older than Sumatra's and a little younger than Siwalik's. The Javan fossils were from the end of the Pliocene or even from the Pleistocene, the period when the missing link must have lived. Thus, these sites were the right age and had the right kind of Asian animals. He would surely find the missing link soon.

In his final report of the year, Dubois was able to boast of an exceptional find made on 24 November 1890.

Amidst the remains of typical representations of the fauna concerned, and in the same layer of sandstone-like andesitic [volcanic] tufa, a human fossil was found, the right side of the chin of a lower jaw with the sockets of the canine tooth and of the first and second premolar... When it came to me it still had on it a small piece of sandstone-like andesitic tufa, which is the chief sediment among the bones found.

At last he had found an ancient human fossil, older than the Wadjak remains. Admittedly, the specimen was a small and rather unimpressive fragment, only a bit of jaw with two teeth in it. Its incompleteness made it difficult to classify, leaving Dubois elated at

This mandible or lower jaw from Kedoeng Broebus was the first good find in Java. The dotted line indicated the placement of this fragment on a human jaw.

its discovery, frustrated at its ambiguity. About the most that he could say was that its chin was minimal, even less marked than in the Neanderthal's, and that it was distinctly human. He listed the specimen as *Homo spec. indet.*, paleontologist's jargon for an indeterminate or unknown species of the genus *Homo*. If only there were more of it!

Until now, Dubois's secondment to the Department of Education, Religion, and Industry had needed annual renewal. On the basis of the many fine fossils he had collected in Java in 1890, Dubois asked Groeneveldt for a three-year commitment. During 1891, 1892 and 1893, he proposed to focus on two areas, caves in the Kendeng Hills in the wet season and the exposed riverbanks of the Bengawan Solo in the dry. To Dubois's great pleasure, Groeneveldt heartily approved the proposed plans.

It had taken Dubois more than three long years of persuasion and exploration and fever, but the effort had been worth it. He now knew how to search effectively for fossils, and where. Groeneveldt was impressed, offering his support and congratulations. From afar, by letter, Dubois's father expressed only pessimism and doubt.

CHAPTER 17

Coolies

Dubois's decision to stay close to home during the end of 1890 and the beginning of 1891 had almost immediate repercussions. While the coolies, whether labourers or convicts, had great respect for the Tuan Dokter (the legend of his magical powers had followed him here), they did not honour Kriele and De Winter. With Dubois too long absent from the site, the coolies became surly, lazy, and insolent. The letters from the engineers rang with peal after peal of complaints.

Dubois tried separating the engineers from each other, thinking they might find it easier to manage smaller groups of men. He sent De Winter off to work in rock shelters and caves on the south coast of Java, while Kriele worked in the north. Nothing improved. By June, De Winter was so desperate to make his case to Dubois that he sent a letter of complaint addressed to Anna.

> Bessole, 28 June 1890
> Will you also be so kind as to say to the Doctor that I have sent away three forced labourers because of illness, but I suppose that it is laziness, because they have asked me three times to go back to Toeloeng Agoeng because the work here is too heavy.

The next month, De Winter wrote again: 'All the forced labourers ask me for clothes because they come back from the cave and they have been drilling and their clothes are full of drill-spatter.'
Kriele fared no better.

> Kedoeng Broebus, 11 July 1890
> Now I have here 25 forced labourers but they are such a strange people: 4 have already run away, 6 are ill, 1 is dead. It would not be a bad thing if you would send some belly-drink because they are all troubled with their bellies.

Soon the two engineers fell out with each other; Dubois did not know why. De Winter wrote, 'So it is also very hard for me without a mandur, therefore I ask you politely if I may have the mandur that works with Kriele because Kriele has only 8 men and I have 15.'

Dubois could not spare the time to go to the sites, for on 16 January 1891, Victor Marie Dubois greeted the world with a bellow, another healthy, vigorous baby boy safely delivered by his father. He was perfect, tiny, and Dubois was very proud. And yet, before long, Anna's complete absorption in the three children left Dubois feeling a little neglected. He was no longer the centre of the family. He was peripheral to that indissoluble unit of mother and children. Still, he could not leave and, despite the engineers' complaints, the work seemed to be going fairly well.

Dubois longed for someone to discuss the new fossils with. Maybe Sluiter, that fellow in Batavia who had sent him the Wadjak skull, would be interested. Dubois wrote, telling Sluiter of the progress of the digs and the finding of the fragmentary jaw at Kedoeng Broebus. He also asked Sluiter to send various books and articles he needed for analysis of the jaw. Sluiter replied cheerfully enough but, to Dubois's astonishment, demurred over sending the books, citing the 'perils' of trusting such items to the unreliable postal service.

Dubois was deeply offended; after all, some of the books he had requested were his very own, lent to Sluiter when he had been in Batavia. He could not help but imagine some ulterior motive on Sluiter's part. The edifice of their friendship, walls barely in place, was already developing serious cracks. Sluiter wrote again,

6 January 1891

I really would like to send you back the boxes by return of post, to prove to you that the black suspicions that you felt about me are completely groundless...Even if you need the books slightly for Heaven's sake write me then, then I would send back immediately what you want. It would be like a nail in my coffin if I suspected in the slightest that I had wheedled the books out of you through my clumsy writing.

A fine letter, but he did not send the books and Dubois was not pacified. How was he to work as a scientist in such society? Sluiter, a man he liked and trusted, now would not return Dubois's own books!

Sluiter wrote again at the end of January.

23 January 1891

Why are you so disconsolate in your letters? I believe that your isolation there in Toeloeng Agoeng makes you melancholy. It is certainly a pity that you cannot dash over to Batavia more often to convince yourself that the sympathy we developed for each other during your brief visit has certainly not lessened... Write me one day and tell me what is really the matter. I don't mean to be a busybody, but maybe I can contribute something from the sidelines that will improve the relationships among the small number of scientific men that the Indies can boast of.

Indeed, Dubois had sunk into a monsoon season gloom. He thought nostalgically about his colleagues at Padang and Pajakombo, especially Pollak – a good man, Pollak! But at Toeloeng Agoeng, there was no one, and Sluiter was a bitter disappointment. The government officials were preoccupied with miles of road mended, bridges built, crops taxed; the planters, when they came into town, were generally drinking too heavily to hold any sort of complex thought in their minds; the merchants were small-minded and pedestrian. Toeloeng Agoeng might be a major railroad stop and, compared to Pajakombo, a thriving metropolis, but Dubois felt utterly isolated.

Late in March 1891, the problems with the coolies took an alarming turn. De Winter, working in the north in Kantjilan, caught one of his labourers throwing fossils into the alang-alang grass, trying to conceal them and bring the burdensome work of excavation to a faster close. De Winter could not tell how long the sabotage had been going on. He only knew that the man had committed a grave offence, a scientific mutiny of the vilest sort. On March 29, he wrote to Dubois telling him that he had taken the miscreant directly to the head-*jaksa*, the native magistrate, who had caused the man to be flogged.

Dubois was appalled at the news, both of the man's iniquity and of his harsh punishment. What was he to do? The laws governing the treatment of forced labourers were clear. The sentence had been ordered by a native magistrate and was therefore legal, though De Winter was strictly forbidden to beat his coolies on his own authority. Dubois considered flogging an inhuman treatment, suitable only for stubborn mules or lazy oxen. There were other ways of maintaining firm discipline.

The coolies dug for fossils at the same unhurried pace that they planted crops, Dubois thought, working with pickaxes or short-handled hoes called *patjol*s. It was completely meaningless labour in the hot sun, as far as the coolies were concerned. Now that he considered it, Dubois was a little surprised that the men remained as good-natured as they did. But he had to find a way to get them to work better, more reliably. He did not understand the coolies at all. Before he had come to the Indies, Taen-Err-Toung had been the only Asian whom Dubois had ever met, and he was no peasant working off his tax burden or serving out his sentence.

Even Dubois's own workers, men he thought he knew, were capable of shocking barbarities. He learned this one day when a party of his coolies happened upon a village where only the women were at home. As if it were a perfectly normal response to the situation, his coolies began looting the village and assaulting the unprotected women. The women screamed and hammered on the village gong; Dubois heard it from a considerable distance and so did the men of the village, who rushed back to protect their homes and families. A huge mêlée ensued, locals against forced labourers. A number of men on both sides were seriously hurt.

The incident came to official attention and the Resident ordered a formal hearing to determine guilt. Of course Dubois attended, ashamed of his coolies' part in the affair. One of his crew was sentenced to fifty strokes with a cane.

'You shall have to keep more of an eye on the coolies,' he reprimanded Kriele and De Winter back in camp. 'We cannot permit such behaviour.'

The engineers protested loudly: the raid had not been carried out with their approval or their knowledge. They would never have allowed the men to do such a thing if they had known of it.

'Of course not, I know,' Dubois conceded. 'But it cannot happen again. We are in charge of these men. *You* are in charge of them. They will not break the law when they are under my authority, especially not in such a barbaric way. And why is that man, whatever his name is, not unhappy at his sentence? Fifty lashes is a severe beating.'

'Tuan Dokter,' Kriele explained, trying to be tactful, 'he does not expect to receive the sentence. The natives bribe the guards to let them off easily, with light strokes and fewer strokes. He has been convicted before and he knows he will not suffer much. That is the way things are done here. He was convicted only because he was so badly wounded that no one would believe he was somewhere else at the time, even if he bribed witnesses to say so.'

'Is this true?' demanded Dubois of the other engineer, De Winter. 'Yes, sir,' De Winter confirmed reluctantly, fingering his dark moustache uneasily, for he could sense Dubois's disapproval. 'Most of those convicted never receive their full sentence and some of them are not punished at all. It is the way in the Indies.'

'Well, that is not the way it is going to be in my camp,' Dubois insisted. 'This was an unprovoked, vicious crime. Men for whom I am responsible cannot go around thieving and assaulting unprotected women.'

Dubois insisted on supervising the caning personally. It was a horrible ordeal. Long before the fifty lashes were completed, the man's back was welted and bleeding, muscle and bone exposed. Nonetheless, Dubois saw to it that the man received his full sentence. Afterwards, Dubois treated the man with salves and released him from further work. He was repulsed by both crime and punishment.

A few days later, Dubois spied another worker, a venal, greasy man, sporting some new rings on his fat fingers: booty from the village, Dubois suspected. Something had to be done; he had to find out the truth. Apparently innocently, Dubois selected the man to go with him to explore a deep sinkhole in the limestone, where the villagers said fossils could sometimes be found. He had the men lower the two of them down on ropes to the floor of the pit, well below ground level. Of course, the pit was barren of fossils. Dubois was not disappointed, for he had wanted only a good place for a private confrontation. He turned to the man and began to question him about the rings, using his powerful physique and formidable presence to intimidate the man into telling the truth.

'Where did you get those rings?' he asked. There was no answer; the coolie squatted at his feet, eyes averted. 'If you do not tell me where you have obtained them,' Dubois threatened, looking down at the man, 'you will not leave this pit alive. There will be a terrible accident, most unfortunate.'

The coolie pleaded his innocence, his fat cheeks trembling, his eyes bulging in fear. 'No, Tuan Dokter, bok'n, bok'n, not stolen,' he stammered. But he did not meet Dubois's pale eyes with his dark ones.

'You did not have those rings before,' continued Dubois sternly, ignoring the protestations of innocence. 'You took them from that village, didn't you?'

'Bok'n Tuan Dokter, bok'n ...' the man repeated earnestly, sweat dribbling down his forehead and falling like raindrops on to the dusty ground.

'You are not listening.' Dubois took hold of the man's shoulder and shook him a little. The man's flesh seemed spongy, like the meat of an overripe papaya, and Dubois was disgusted at the feel of him. 'Look at me!' Reluctantly, the coolie lifted his eyes from the ground. 'Now, tell me where you got the rings. I want the truth. You know I can see the truth when others cannot. Where did those rings come from?'

The man confessed: he had stolen them during the raid on the village. He had not the moral fibre to resist Dubois's assertions or the piercing look in his Garuda eyes. 'But do not turn me over to the head-jaksa, please, Tuan Dokter,' the man begged, knowing now that any sentence of flogging would be carried out in full. 'I work for you; I am part of your gang of men. You are my tuan. You punish me, as you see fit. That is right.'

Dubois had seen enough of the harsh justice of the native magistrate to agree. He would not allow flogging, but the man had to be punished. Dubois returned the rings to the village headman. The next morning, he carried out the punishment he had conceived. He strapped an enormously heavy fossil, an elephant bone, on to the miscreant's back. It was a four-foot-long cylinder of solid stone. Dubois announced to all the workers that this man was being punished for theft. He would carry this burden all day long while he performed his normal daily work. He was not to be helped by others. Anyone who helped him would receive the elephant punishment himself. The natives were wide-eyed and serious-faced. They nodded their understanding of the punishment and the rules of behaviour. By the end of the day, the thief was bowed and utterly exhausted, but he made no protest and showed no resentment.

The incident increased Dubois's prestige further. He was surely supernatural. No one ever saw Dubois drinking liquor, like an ordinary man. If they clambered up a mountain, he clambered up faster than any of them. If he ordered them to carry firewood, it was less than he could carry himself. As a matter of principle, he never resorted to coarse language and he was never seen unkempt or dirty. He could see the truth when it was hidden and he knew what lay underneath the ground. He moved through life like a man on a holy mission, and the coolies revered him.

In contrast, Kriele and De Winter were physically less impressive, being thin-chested and long-limbed. They were naturally more dishevelled, their uniforms cheap and often rumpled, their moustaches poorly trimmed, their hair a little long. And their concentration wandered noticeably during long and unprofitable excavations. Sometimes, too, Dubois found altogether too many empty beer bottles when he visited the camp. The engineers were not bad men or stupid ones. They simply lacked Dubois's moral fibre and intensity of purpose. The natives thought the engineers perfectly ordinary *orang belanda*s. Like all Dutch, they were sometimes arrogant, usually unfair, frequently insulting, and often incomprehensible. They drank, they smoked, they shouted, and they were sometimes seen in the company of the prettiest of Javanese girls. The engineers they understood; they recognized the type.

But Dubois was something else, something extraordinary, the coolies concluded. He was a chosen man. Clearly he had been given a special role or *dharma* through a divine revelation: that was the only possible explanation. They accorded him a place in their pantheon and agreed that he operated above the strictures of law or customary behaviour. Dubois was destined for greatness.

CHAPTER 18

Discoveries at Trinil

Whatever the workers whispered among themselves, Dubois never mistook himself for a god. He was a dedicated man of science, cleverer and harder-working than the others, that was all. Yet sometimes he had an intuition that amounted to a stroke of genius, like coming to the Indies in the first place, like searching the river-banks instead of looking for caves. He had never believed in destiny, at least not before coming to Java. But things were different here, inexplicable; even a strong-minded Dutchman sometimes felt the workings of the supernatural.

Dubois's uncanny ability to reach beyond the readily observable manifested itself again in the choice of a new site for excavation. Working down the Bengawan Solo from the fort, looking for a glint of bone and a likely place to dig, they passed many bends in the large, slow, brown river. The point bar near the tiny village of

Dubois selected a site along the Bengawan Solo near the village of Trinil for a major excavation.

Trinil was undistinguished, except for a thumb-shaped piece of the bank that projected above the ground. Dubois looked at that shape and felt a strange enthusiasm creep over him. Why? He did not know. It was not rational; it was intuition, or ... something else. He had a strong feeling at this place; there was something mystical about it, though he could not say what. A religious man might even have called it God's providence, he supposed, but he was not a religious man.

'Let us dig here,' he said, and they did.

Almost at once, the men began to find fossils. Dubois left the crew there, working hard at the excavation, and returned to Toeloeng Agoeng. By the end of the month of August 1891, the team had found many species in the sandstones at Trinil: the remains of the axis deer, an extinct buffalo, the elephant *Stegodon*, and others. Dubois started calling the site his 'charnel house', believing that the skeletons were those of animals killed and preserved by the volcanic eruptions in this region. Not for nothing was the region of Ngawi known as the hellhole of Java. It was full of ancient lavas and lapilli, and some days it seemed as hot as the inside of an active volcano. The fossils were a kind of salvation.

In September 1891, the men made their next really important find on Java. It was the right third molar, the last cheek tooth, from the upper jaw of an apelike primate.

When the fossil arrived at Toeloeng Agoeng, wrapped in the usual djati leaf, Dubois was jubilant. The tooth was something very like Lydekker's chimpanzee from India, *Anthropopithecus sivalensis*. Dubois had only a single tooth, not a jaw, and he believed his specimen was not quite as ancient as Lydekker's. He knew now that he would have to travel to India to make detailed comparisons between the two.

Dubois's third quarterly report to Groeneveldt in 1891 celebrated the Trinil site and its fossil fauna. Specimens were abundant, largely complete, and often beautiful in their stony way. He was sure he was approaching the missing link. There was no doubt in his mind that his quarry was fossilized and waiting, here, on Java.

The most important find was a molar (the third molar of the upper right side) of a chimpanzee (*Anthropopithecus*). The genus of anthropoid apes, occurring only in West- and Central-equatorial Africa today, lived in British India in the Pliocene and, as we can see from this discovery, during the Pleistocene in Java.

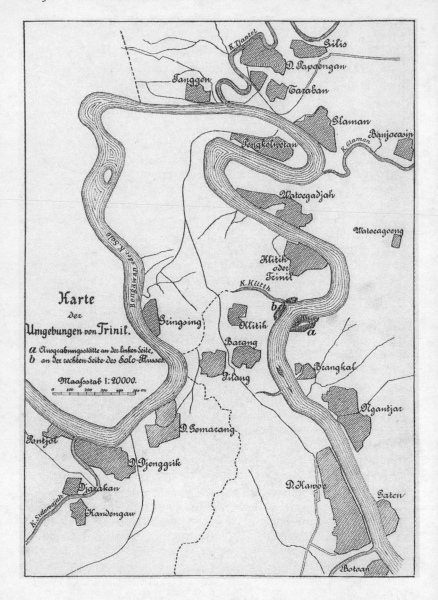

Dubois's hand-drawn map of the area shows the exact location of the
site at Trinil where he made his greatest discoveries.

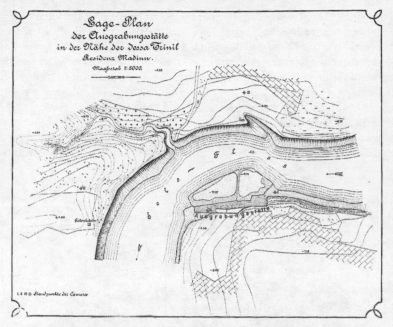

Lage-Plan
der Ausgrabungsstätte
in der Nähe der dessa Trinil
Residenz Madiun.
Maasstab 1:5000.

A second, more detailed map recorded additional information about
the excavation and the location of standpoints (Standpunt I, II, III)
from which Dubois photographed the dig.

This remarkable find was soon eclipsed. In October, the engineers turned up a strange bone; it was about the size of a large
coconut – not the green outer part, but the dense, hairy seed itself –
and it was similar in shape to half of a coconut that had been split
longitudinally, except that the fossil was more pear-shaped than
ovoid. At first, the corporals thought it might be the carapace of a
turtle. It was a dark rich chocolate brown in colour and thoroughly
fossilized, heavy with the stony matrix that encrusted many surfaces. The corporals did not dare try to clean off the matrix for fear
of damaging the specimen. They packed the fossil as it was in djati
leaves, with the others from the last few weeks' work, and sent it
off to Dubois.

The specimen was not a turtle carapace but the skullcap of a
higher primate, something big-brained. The face and the bottom of
the skull were broken away, but there could be no doubt of what it
was. The engineers' notes and letters indicated it came from the

same level as the *Anthropopithecus* tooth. There was only the one other primate fossil at Trinil, so Dubois thought the skullcap was probably from the same individual as the tooth. The skullcap had a sort of chimpanzee look to it, too, with a big browridge and, behind it, a pinched-in place, a postorbital constriction before the swelling of the braincase. It was a stunning fossil, showing the approximate size of the braincase and much of the shape of the skull. Dubois had nothing with which to compare the skullcap directly, for there was no such thing as a chimpanzee skull in all of the Indies. His last quarterly report of 1891 to Groeneveldt had a triumphal tone.

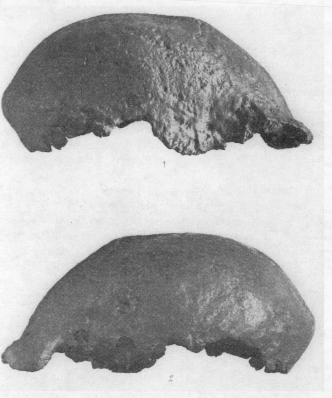

In October 1891, the skullcap of *Pithecanthropus* was found at Trinil. (Top, right side: bottom, left side.)

Near the place on the left bank of the river where the molar was found, a beautiful skull vault has been excavated that, undoubtedly (like the molar), has to be ascribed to the genus *Anthropopithecus (Troglodytes)* ...

As far as the species is concerned, the skull can be distinguished from the living chimpanzees: first because it is larger, second because of its higher vault... The height of the frontal part is not lower than the human skull from Neanderthal or the first skull from Spy; but the fossil chimpanzee deviates from these because its parietals are flatter and the occipital is less developed. With the Pliocene *Anthropopithecus sivalensis*, of which there is only an incomplete mandible known, only the molar can be compared directly. Probably there is a close affinity between them.

Following protocol, Dubois compared his find to the other known genera of fossil apes. His fossil was neither the 'Oak Ape' *Dryopithecus fontanii* from France, known mostly from jaws and teeth, nor the gibbonlike *Pliopithecus antiquus* from Europe. Those fossil apes were much smaller; this skull was too big. He could also see plainly that this was not a modern chimpanzee.

Besides, the most important fact was that the living chimpanzee, in his teeth, approaches humans more closely than does the gorilla or the orang-utan, which is found in the same region of Java, while this Pleistocene chimpanzee approaches the human more closely because of its skull.

He had found an exceptional fossil, more primitive than a Neanderthal, apelike in its teeth and yet most humanlike in its skull. He closed the report by observing proudly that, before this find, Lydekker's jaw of a Siwalik chimpanzee was 'all that we possessed in the way of fossil higher anthropoids, so it is clear from this what a gain for science the Javanese fossil is'.

Dubois was enormously tempted to assign a scientific name to the new find. Naming a new species of this importance would have established his place in the annals of science for ever, much more so than the other new fossil mammals he had already found. The obvious name, *Anthropopithecus javanensis*, rolled nicely off his tongue. This name would demonstrate the close evolutionary relationship between his fossil and Lydekker's Siwalik *Anthropopithecus*, while also indicating the place of origin as Java. But it was too premature, he decided; more study was needed before he formally named the fossil. On 30 December 1891, he sent a letter to Governor Kroesen in West Sumatra, informing him of the find. 'The creature to which this skullcap had once belonged,' he wrote, 'was truly a new and closer link in the largely buried chain connecting us to the "lower" mammals.'

The skullcap had been found, unfortunately, late in the dry season, in October when the heavy afternoon rains were already beginning. Excavation could not continue much longer, so Dubois ordered the men to work more intensively for a few weeks, to no avail. Whatever else lay beneath the waters of the Bengawan Solo, within those buried sediments, would have to wait until April or May when the next dry season commenced.

Dubois used the rainy season to study the new fossils carefully and to begin the nerve-racking task of picking away the stony matrix from inside the braincase. Using pins, sharpened bamboo sticks, pointed medical instruments, flattened nails, fine chisels, Anna's large embroidery needles – anything, in fact, that seemed vaguely suitable – Dubois worked a little every day to clean the skullcap, cradling it on a sand-filled muslin bag on his desk. He stopped from time to time, rubbing his hands to relieve the tension and peering at his progress through his large magnifying glass. Sometimes he simply stood, swinging his arms to relax his muscles, and looking out of the window at the pouring rain. It was close, concentrated work. One slip, one push with too much pressure, one tap too hard on a fine chisel, and the fossilized vault bones might shatter. It was a job requiring tremendous manual dexterity and infinite patience, the latter not being one of Dubois's usual virtues. The work also required a detailed knowledge of anatomy; he had to anticipate the curvature and shape of as-yet-invisible structures so as not to damage them. Every day he could see a little bit more; every day, he inspected the braincase anew and marvelled at its shape.

He was deeply frustrated by his lack of comparative material and literature, felt himself awash with specific anatomical questions that could not be answered with his resources. Dubois stared at the few images of chimpanzee skulls in his books, hoping to see more than was shown, until he thought he was going blind. He acquired three gibbon skulls and a few human ones, but they were not enough. He already knew his skull was neither human nor gibbon. He felt a terrible need to discuss his find, but there was no one.

CHAPTER 19

Gathering Resources

Early in 1892, Dubois wrote to Max Weber in Holland, pleading with him to send a chimpanzee skull. Surely with Weber's connections at the zoological gardens he could lay his hands on a chimpanzee skull! Weber understood Dubois's pressing need, but a chimpanzee skull was not easy to come by in Europe. He searched the catalogues of those who supplied curiosities to the public and specimens to the museums, wrote in vain to other anatomists and natural historians. All he had to report to Dubois was that neither Amsterdam nor Leiden possessed a chimpanzee skull that could be sent to Java. Months passed while Dubois waited anxiously in Toeloeng Agoeng for word from Weber: impatient at the delay, grateful for Weber's efforts, despairing of their success.

In July, Dubois and Anna were invited to a reception at the Resident's house in Kediri. Anna dearly wanted to go, and Dubois agreed. He was doing no one any good waiting at home for a skull that never arrived. They packed up their best clothes and departed for Kediri. It was one of the few trips out of Toeloeng Agoeng that they had made since settling there; Anna was as excited as a girl. Perhaps the reception, the society, would take Dubois's mind off his troubles. Besides, it was a good opportunity to speak to the Resident, the Assistant Resident, the Regent, and other important officials.

Dubois expected nothing of the reception until he spied two men he did not know: a pair of strangers in the stiflingly limited society of Kediri province. One was about his own age, one considerably older. His spirits lifted suddenly and inexplicably, like a schoolboy who saw some girl he had worshipped ardently from afar. The younger man had an odd look on his intelligent face; perhaps he was just as bored as Dubois by idle gossip and polite chit-chat. He stood next to the older, dignified man. Dubois found someone to introduce him to them.

The older man was Robert Boyd, a planter of Scots extraction born in Batavia, the son of another Robert Boyd. The elder Boyd had come to Java from Aberdeenshire during Stamford Raffles' brief rule and had stayed on after the colony reverted to Dutch rule in 1816. That Robert Boyd had established a successful trading business in the port towns of Semarang and Soerabaja, marrying a Javanese woman. The second of his seven children, the son born 20 February 1828, was the Robert Boyd who stood in front of Dubois at the reception. Now sixty-four years old, Boyd was a dignified patriarch, with an aquiline face accentuated by a pair of fine white drooping moustaches and a shock of snow-white hair. He was well read, despite or perhaps because of his isolated life on the plantation, and well travelled within Java. His intelligence was uncompromising, but there was great kindness in his manner. Dubois liked him immediately.

Boyd owned a large upland plantation not far from Toeloeng Agoeng, where the fertile soils of Mount Willis were excellent for coffee-growing. The plantation was named Mringin, after the Javanese name for the tall banyan trees that grew there in abundance. The main house was called Ngrodjo, Javanese for 'central headquarters'. In 1848, at twenty, Boyd had married an Indo woman, Embok Maas Warsina. When she had died after almost twenty years of marriage, he had still been in his prime. He had remarried at forty, this time choosing as his bride a real princess,

The 'Old Warrior,' Robert Boyd, became one of Dubois's
closest friends.

from one of the old, aristocratic Javanese families in Solo, Raden Roro Samira. She had been a beautiful woman, naturally elegant and refined as only a Solo princess could be. At their marriage, she had taken the Christian name Grace, to please Boyd. She had been ten years younger than he and yet she, too, had died well before him, only four years after the wedding. That had been in 1872, twenty years ago, and Ngrodjo had been largely a bachelor establishment ever since. Grace's daughter, Anna Grace Penelope, survived, and the household was enlivened by Boyd's *nyai* and their children, but he had not married again.

The younger man was Adam Prentice, a Scotsman of thirty-two years, Dubois's own age. He was a handsome man, fair and blue-eyed like Dubois, just an inch or so taller and leaner. Prentice's broad-shouldered build and physical self-confidence betrayed his years of living a demanding outdoor life on plantations. It was Prentice who walked or rode the entire plantation from end to end, following the rough roads once a month. He checked the trees and inspected them for coffee leaf disease and other pests; he listened to the *mandur*s' problems and suggested solutions; he settled minor and major disputes among workers; he planned the week-to-week work on different parts of the plantation. He was up every day before dawn, tending to a thousand diverse duties that kept the plantation running and the crop good. He had an uncanny skill at handling the men and, as time went on, Boyd had come to trust him with more and more responsibility.

By nature a confident man, Prentice had been shaken by a recent bereavement. Two years before meeting Dubois, Prentice had been working on another plantation; there he had received a promotion, which finally had given him a salary sufficient to marry. He had promptly proposed to his sweetheart, Jane de Clonie MacLennan, and had been accepted. The daughter of another planter in East Java, Jane had been a pretty woman with an enviably fair Scottish complexion and auburn-tinged, luxuriant hair. Her good looks had made her seem fragile, but she had been a strong and practical young woman. She could shoot a gun as well as any of her brothers, break a horse, and plant a flower garden; she could teach a child to read, write, calculate, and dance a credible waltz; she could dress a wound or make a dress. More than once she had helped with picking and sorting the beans on her father's plantation, and with keeping the books. She and Prentice had loved each other dearly.

Their wedding had been a gala weekend party on her father's plantation in Pasoeroean on 16 January 1890. All their friends and relations had attended, including Jane's eldest and favourite brother, Theo, and his wife, Isabella. Isabella's father, Robert Boyd, had been invited to the wedding too, in the open-handed colonial way. It had been their first meeting, but Boyd and Prentice had immediately taken to each other. Before the weekend was over, Boyd had impulsively offered Prentice the job of managing Mringin, as a sort of wedding present. There would be another rise in pay, and a brand-new house for the newlyweds at Tempoersarie, at the far end of the plantation.

Prentice had taken to the job at Mringin as if he had been born to it. He liked Boyd and the way he treated his workers. He was good to them, honest and firm, and they were fiercely loyal to the Tuan Boyd. The small house at Tempoersarie had seemed perfect to the young couple. Jane had been so proud to furnish and decorate her first home as a *njonja* and soon had a garden started. In August 1891, she had been delighted when a visit to the doctor in Kediri confirmed that she was pregnant. She and Prentice had been filled with hopes and plans for their family. They had both expected an easy pregnancy and birth, for Jane was wide-hipped and healthy. She had been born at home with only a midwife in attendance, and so had all her siblings. 'Easy as popping a banana out of its peel for women built like us,' her mother Doortje had always said.

Jane's labour had started on the morning of 20 May and nothing had gone as expected. The contractions had been severe, she had bled and bled, and still the baby had not come out. After twenty-four hours, the midwife could do nothing more to help. The baby was still alive, she thought, but it would not come out, and Jane was weak and pale. Prentice had sent a man with a swift horse for the doctor. Still the contractions continued; still the blood flowed, until Jane was barely conscious. By the time the doctor arrived, Jane was in a bad way.

'Mr Prentice,' the doctor had said gravely, after examining her, 'I do not think I can save your wife. She has lost too much blood. If you agree, I can try to save the child, but it will surely kill your wife.'

And so it had been. By the evening of the twenty-first, Prentice's world had been shattered. His beloved wife, his tender, funny, wonderful wife, was dead in childbirth. The baby, a boy, had survived, weakened and feeble, but breathing and crying. Prentice had been so overwhelmed by the unfairness of it all, by the tragedy that had so suddenly befallen him, he did not know what to do. From somewhere, someone had obtained a wet nurse, a Javanese woman whose full breasts offered plenty of milk for little Gerard. In his grief, Prentice had never really known where she had come from or who had found her; someone had, and she had saved the child. But nothing would bring back his Jane or his hopes for the future. Later, he had remembered little of the first week after Jane's death. Did he eat? Did he sleep? Did he bathe? He had no idea. All he could remember was the descent of a blackness so profound there seemed no possibility of light.

What pulled him out of his despair was the child. With good milk flowing into his rosebud mouth, Gerard strengthened and grew impossibly quickly. His laugh one day was Prentice's first new memory: a little gurgling chuckle, a sound of pure joy, that had penetrated his father's grief. Here was a reason to live: an enchanting, lovely child with Jane's eyes and a hint of reddish curls. Prentice's love for Gerard was not without pain, however. The baby was a living reminder of Jane, and of her death; he was the star that showed up the empty night of Prentice's existence. Worse yet, in weeks Prentice realized it was impossible for him to raise the child on his own. The wet nurse was good with Gerard, very good, and after nursing was finished, she would stay on as *babu*. But Prentice's job demanded that he travel throughout the plantation for weeks on end. He could not leave the baby alone with a wet nurse in remote Tempoersarie, with no Europeans for miles. Anything might have happened. And as the child grew, who would be there to teach him and look after him? He would not have his only son raised solely by a *babu*, however loving and devoted. That would not be right.

It took great courage, for the act was like cutting off his own hand, but Prentice arranged to send the child away, to Jane's father and stepmother in the East Javan hill station of Malang. They would raise him until Prentice's situation changed. The wet nurse would go with him. The journey down the mountain to Malang was one of terrible duty. Prentice took his son, the only person he had left to love, to the child's grandparents. His other task was to see to the placing of the stone on Jane's grave in Malang. There was no pleasure in either.

> Jane de Clonie MacLennan
> died 21 May 1892
> beloved wife of Adam Prentice
> Blessed are the pure in heart for
> they shall see God.

Malang was only half a day's travel away from Tempoersarie and was one of the prettiest towns in Java, every planter's retirement dream. There were white-pillared, gracious houses, with cool verandas and large gardens set off by neatly whitewashed walls. The avenues were long and broad, lined with trees and flowering bushes; the climate was pleasantly cool for Java. It would be a good place for the boy to grow up.

Boyd suggested that Prentice stay in Malang for a while: 'Help the baby settle in, y'know.' It was a kind suggestion; Boyd could see that Prentice was overwhelmed by his loss, and the plantation could survive without him for a while. Prentice could not focus his thoughts, could not muster enthusiasm for anything. Sometimes he felt indignant – angry – as if he had been robbed, but he could not identify a thief to loose his anger upon. Other times he was simply empty, lifeless and colourless as a dead rice stalk. He thought bitterly from time to time that the trouble was that he had mislaid his hopes, his dreams. Jane had always used to tease him about his carelessness; he would lose his boots, his watch, his record book repeatedly. When he asked her where the missing item had gone to, she would reply with a smile, 'Now think, where can you have left it?' Then they would both laugh and Jane would tell him where he had left whatever he had lost. This time he knew where he had left his dreams: in the graveyard, with her. Mostly it was brute determination and the routine of life that held him together. And there were reasons to try, to go on: the boy, the job, the gratitude he owed Boyd, his good friend and employer.

A month or so later, Boyd came down the mountain to attend the Resident's reception in Kediri, hoping that Prentice was sufficiently recovered to come back to Mringin with him. Though most Indies planters were hard-drinking, rough, uncivilized men, unused to citified ways, Boyd and Prentice were cast from a different mould. They were country gentlemen with a love of the land and a passion for natural history. They were both kind and clever, not a common combination, and these qualities made them welcome in any home in the colonies. The Resident's reception was a trying occasion for Prentice, one of his first ventures into society since his wife's death. He could not make trivial conversation any longer. He grew furious that others could, that people could waste their lives in such idle chatter. It took a profound effort of will to remain polite.

His new acquaintance, Dr Dubois, seemed different. He, too, had little use for empty pleasantries; he preferred to talk of something real, something important. He asked real questions, listened thoughtfully to their replies. Prentice did not say much at first, but there was a look in his eye that Dubois responded to. Gossip in the colonies spread news efficiently, so Boyd and Prentice knew that Dubois was a physician seconded to the Department of Education, Religion, and Industry from the army. What they had not heard before this evening was the true reason why Dubois was in Java. Dubois told them the story of his scientific quest; unable to disguise his passion, he would judge their worth by their reactions.

Boyd was full of suggestions of places he might search: an intelligent, knowledgeable man, Dubois thought. He understood what Dubois meant, and he immediately addressed himself to the problem.

Prentice's reaction was extraordinary for one in his circumstances. The idea of searching for an ancient, missing link so captured his imagination that he forgot his own grief and sorrow. He had so many questions to ask of the good doctor. He was stunned by the notion that there was this one thing, this one creature, that would weave together all of life into a unified whole. He was full of admiration for Dubois's vision and passion. Something in Dubois's life called to the part of Prentice that had been quiescent, shrouded in pain and mourning. Prentice lost track of what Dubois was saying for a moment, observing with surprise his own interest. He had thought that part of him had died with Jane, but he saw it was not true. There were people in the world worth knowing, worth being with, and he had just met one.

Prentice had no reason to trust Dubois with information so personal, but he did, instinctively. Almost telegraphically, Prentice shared the facts of his situation with his new friend, as if in apology.

'You will have heard, perhaps,' he said in a low, intimate voice, 'of my circumstances.' He looked quizzically at Dubois, who shook his head, no, and waited.

'I have recently lost my wife, Jane. She died giving birth to our only child, a son. It has left me ...' He turned his face away, unable to find the words to describe his condition. He paused for a painful moment before continuing. 'My son will live in Malang, with my in-laws, until I can care for him myself. I ... well, let me say I am not myself. I once had a deep interest in natural history, though, and your undertaking intrigues me. I should be pleased to learn more of it, to get to know you better. But you must forgive me if I seem from time to time a little ... rude, distracted. I am still in mourning.'

After a long moment of silence, Dubois spoke, his eyes full of sympathy. 'Of course; I see. It is a hard thing,' he said, lightly touching Prentice's elbow, 'a hard, hard thing. I cannot imagine ...' He fell silent and then continued, 'I suppose that you must persevere. It will take much courage, but you must do it, for the boy's sake. For your own.'

Prentice nodded tightly, not trusting himself to speak. Dubois had spoken straight to his heart. He and Dubois turned and walked out of the inner gallery on to the front veranda. They stood there in silence, looking out at the darkness. In age, temperament, and looks, they might have been brothers. Dubois had intuited more about how Prentice felt than anyone, despite their brief acquaintance. His kindness and sympathy were so painful and so welcome to Prentice that he feared he would weep. As they stood there companionably, quietly, Prentice became aware of an easing in his chest, as if a wire snare that had bound him to sorrow had been released.

A few minutes later, Boyd joined them on the veranda. He lighted a cigarette and sat with Prentice and Dubois without speaking. Outside were the night noises, the dark calls and hoots and the eerie creaking of bamboo that sounded like a soul in torment. The sweet smells of woodsmoke and spices drifted through the night air. Inside were the bright, tinkling chatter of an Indies reception, the clanking of glasses, a few snippets of music here and there, falsetto laughter. Out on the veranda, they inhabited a crepuscular zone, neither light nor dark. They were suspended between worlds in a region where the mysticism of Java met the practicality of Holland, weaving the disparate into a new whole.

Prentice took a deep breath. 'Tell us,' he said, 'how you came to be here, Doctor. How is it you made such a bold decision?'

Dubois answered with an account of his own past, giving more than the facts of his life this time: his promising start at

Amsterdam, his need to escape Fürbringer's influence, his hope of earning his father's approval by making a great discovery.

'I left all that – my position at the university, my parents, my country – to come here, because it is here that I will find the missing link. I know it must exist, for I have read the writings of Darwin and Haeckel and Huxley, all the true men of science. I know it must be here. So I have dedicated myself to finding the form that links apes and Man, that proves evolution once and for all,' Dubois explained simply. 'I only hope I shall not lose my life in the endeavour. The malaria has nearly killed me a few times, but not yet, not yet.'

'Dreadful disease,' agreed Boyd solemnly. 'Even with quinine, many a man dies of it in a few days. I suppose you carry a full medical kit with you on your expeditions?' Dubois nodded. 'Yes, you'd need to. No telling what troubles you might encounter. We have to do a lot of doctoring on the plantation. Everything from machete wounds to fevers and childbirth: the lot.'

These were dangerous topics for Prentice; they threatened to mire him once again in thoughts of death and dying. He deliberately turned away, allowing his intellect to draw him in another direction. 'But what about this missing link, Doctor? What exactly do you think it will be like? I am not so learned as you in these matters, but I have read a little about evolutionary theory. When I was a young man and we went back to England on leave, people were still arguing about Darwin's book. My father used to love to tell the story of Bishop Samuel Wilberforce being bested in debate by the anatomist, Thomas Huxley. ' "Tell me, sir," ' Prentice mimicked, putting on resonant, pompous tones and clutching his lapels as if they were a clergyman's vestments, ' "is it from your grandmother or your grandfather that you are descended from the apes?" That's the Bishop,' he clarified. 'And then Huxley says righteously, "I would rather have an ape for a grandfather, sir, than a man who uses his position to conceal the truth!" ' Boyd and Dubois shared a hearty laugh at his reenactment of the debate; even Prentice smiled wanly.

'Huxley said something like that, in any case,' Prentice continued. 'But even though that was thirty years ago, not everyone accepts the theory of evolution at home. I think it is the same in Holland? Then the man who finds the missing link will make a great contribution to science, possibly the greatest ever. He would prove Darwin's ideas true.'

Dubois's handsome face flushed with pleasure at Prentice's remarks. This was an educated man, a man like him. 'Ja,' he said warmly 'ja. I am here because there is nothing – nothing – more important in science to do.' There was a touch of embarrassment in his voice at admitting to the audacity of his goal.

'Then we are doubly honoured to make your acquaintance, Doctor,' said Boyd, with a slight bow of his head. He gestured in the air with the hand that held his cigarette, as if sketching a bright future with its glowing end. 'To meet a man of such vision, a dedicated man of science is a rare thing in the Indies.'

Boyd did not know how deeply true his words were. Dubois did. He had never been like anyone else, never met anyone who truly understood him. He had always been one of a kind, an outsider, different. It was not always a comfortable role to play, but he had never played another. He did not know how.

Friendship

Prentice and Boyd came to see Dubois's specimens the next morning at Dubois's invitation; he could explain better what he had been finding if he could show them the fossils. Perhaps they would care to take the midday meal with his family, as well. They were delighted to accept.

They arrived promptly for mid-morning coffee, planning to stay into the afternoon. The three fell quickly into happy companionship: inspecting the fossils; listening while Dubois pointed out this feature and that; comparing specimens to drawings in books; looking over the maps and diagrams from the excavations. The planters were not ignorant of anatomy, for they had butchered many an animal and were keenly interested in natural history. They had never before thought about anatomy analytically, as Dubois did. He showed them how an animal's anatomy revealed its purpose and function in the world.

'Now, this antelope tooth here, you see how those teeth are ridged? Those enamel ridges cut up the grass it eats. And these, now, these are a pig: quite different, ja? Little bumps on the teeth, like little volcanoes. Different food: not grass. The same sort of thing works for the limbs. The antelope has long, slender limbs, for fast running; that big bump of bone there is for the attachment of a powerful muscle, to move the leg. Not so the pig. You see how different it is?'

Dubois could read an animal's bones as if they were a written record of its ancestry and habits, whether he had ever seen the beast alive or not. Even long extinct creatures told him their secrets. Prentice and Boyd were stunned, fascinated. Before the morning was out, they began to acquire a little of the knowledge that let them do as Dubois did. It was like learning to read. They understood the principle but their vocabulary of shapes and bony bumps and depressions was still very limited. They were like children compared to Dubois. The hours passed so pleasantly that Anna had to call them three times to come to the meal before they heard her.

It was the beginning of a remarkable friendship. The relationships were not symmetrical, for Boyd was Prentice's superior, and a much older man than the others. He was less interested in physical challenges, less likely to propose a hike to the top of the mountain than a calm cigarette in a rocking chair on the shady veranda. His curiosity was tempered by his greater maturity; he lent a helpful balance and stability to their interactions. He offered fatherly advice to the younger men when he could do so without insult, for both Prentice and Dubois were proud and he would not break their spirits. He enjoyed listening to Dubois's ideas, according him an unquestioning respect for his learning that the younger man treasured. Boyd's mind had stayed flexible and he never lacked for passionate convictions. In private, the younger men called him the Old Warrior.

Prentice and Dubois were like a pair of boys playing a game, pushing each other to greater heights, faster accomplishments, bigger dreams. The immediate congeniality they had felt upon meeting deepened into real intimacy within weeks. In the tropics, acquaintance progressed to friendship with a speed that would have been remarkable in Europe. But here, distances were great and the infrequency of visits lent them greater import. Relationships sprouted, blossomed, fruited, and ripened – or spoiled – in a few weeks, like exotic tropical plants.

Of the two, Prentice was the practical one, the man who could organize a workforce or build a road, who knew where the best provisions could be obtained and the fastest horses bought. Dubois was strong and bold, Prentice's match in most physical endeavours, his superior in book knowledge, his inferior in knowledge of Javanese ways. They shared the same sort of independent mind and painful honesty. Dubois trusted Prentice completely, more than any man he had ever known. It was an odd friendship, for they had been raised in different cultures with vastly different educations, and yet they seemed to have everything that mattered in common. Prentice was soon closer to Dubois than his brother Victor had ever been. Dubois knew without asking that, with Prentice, there would never be any shirking or cheating, no drifting along thoughtlessly in that infuriating way of Victor's. Dubois saw that Prentice was honest all the way through: clear as a piece of glass, deep as the ocean. His character shone out of his eyes. It was what Prentice was, not so much what he said or did, that Dubois valued. He thought it was his great good fortune to meet such a man, here of all places.

When they were together, he and Prentice, Dubois noticed that something almost magical happened, something unprecedented. Dubois could not explain it. It was as if he could think faster and more clearly when Prentice was there. As the friendship deepened, they developed a style of communicating that seemed to operate as much through intuition as by words. They were united in a bond of understanding that Dubois had never before experienced.

The gift of Dubois's close friendship enabled Prentice to reduce his grief to manageable proportions; he learned to live again. In a few more months, he was yearning once more to achieve and accomplish, to make a difference to the world. His passion matched Dubois's own. It did not matter that one pursued a sort of holy grail of coffee – better strains, better treatment of diseased plants, better techniques for planting and tending the trees – and the other chased the missing link. What mattered was that they shared the intensity of purpose, the purity of desire.

Dubois soon became a regular visitor at Mringin, a haven of calm and civilization in the unsettled wilderness of Java. It was for him a centre of intellectual stimulation, for the genuine give-and-take that had been so lacking in his life. Half a day's ride on horse-back up the steep roads and trails took him to Ngrodjo. Boyd's house stood alone on the mountain in a clearing fringed by waringin trees and surrounded by hundreds of acres of coffee trees. The trees were equally spaced, each with its own irrigation ditch; each tree pruned short to facilitate picking. To Boyd and Prentice's already warm friendship, Dubois added the spice of his genius, his own way of seeing and questioning. It was a blessing. They had not been bored – there was always something to worry about or plan for on a plantation – but they had not been challenged like this before. Dubois led them into a world of the mind to which they had been strangers. As the weeks passed, he rode up the mountain to Ngrodjo more and more often. Anna actually came to expect him to pack up a small bag and go, whenever the fossils from Kriele and De Winter were especially interesting. Ngrodjo had been built to be the home that Boyd would share with Grace, his second wife, the Solo princess. Few of Grace's feminine touches had survived the decades since her death. Ngrodjo was a masculine place – functional, comfortable, expansive – with a natural, not a planned, beauty. It was still a family home, too, but the family itself was ever-changing. The first crop of Boyd children was gone, the three sons, William, Alexander, and Robert, working on other plantations, the first daughter, Janet, killed in a horseback-riding accident; and the last girl, Isabella, married to Jane's brother Theo. There had been only three children of Boyd's marriage to Grace: Erroll, who had died before he was three months old, and the two girls, Anna Grace, and another Janet. Their half-sister, Elena, the child of Boyd's *nyai*, was also at Ngrodjo. There always seemed to be more than three girl children around, however. Big-eyed, sweet-faced, dark or fair or in-between, they were Boyd's grandchildren or the offspring of servants or workers. There were even a few children of no particular parentage who had adopted Mringin as their home. No matter; they were welcome, whoever their parents were. Ngrodjo was the heart of Mringin, with a life and joy all its own, and the heart of Ngrodjo was her people.

As the dry season grew hotter, Dubois occasionally took his entire family up to Ngrodjo. It was an enormous trouble, a real *susa*, to take all of them and the appropriate servants up the mountain. Dubois rode ahead on his horse, his luggage strapped to the saddle, while Anna, Babu, and the children followed in sedan chairs carried by coolies with a rhythmic bounce. The *syce* came behind with pack animals and coolies carrying still more luggage. The steep sinuous road from Toeloeng Agoeng to Ngrodjo twisted and wriggled back upon itself again and again like an eel, gaining only a few feet with each pass across the mountain. It was slow going, but the oppressive heat lifted as they gained altitude step by step. Halfway up, a delicious coolness enveloped them, like a silken cloak. There was a freshness in the air that they had felt nowhere else in the Indies. The secret must have resided in the trees, in the mountain itself. Perhaps the sensation was a part of the spirit of the place; they did not know or care.

At night, they revelled in the luxury of needing light blankets on their beds. After dark, the leaves on the trees rustled in the breeze, the night birds called, the fruit bats flapped silently on golden wings. The locusts in the forest began to drone so loudly that the children complained they would never get to sleep, but they did of course, almost as soon as they put their heads down. The children knew they were as safe here as at home, for Mama was here, and Papa, and their faithful Babu lay on a mat across the doorway.

In the morning, the valleys were obscured by a thick, opaque cloud, as if the rest of the world, outside of Ngrodjo, had disappeared while they slept. Only the tops of a few tall trees were left behind, poking through the mist, to show where there had once been a forest. The gardens of Ngrodjo were indistinct and the mist turned familiar objects into fantasies – was that tree a minaret? that bush a dragon? After breakfast, the sun slowly burned off the cloud and children's laughter echoed as they explored the garden and the edges of the forest. The little ones played themselves into happy exhaustion, running with the dogs, riding ponies, chasing birds, catching geckos, watched over by their babus. On one visit, they romped with a marvellous tiger cub that Boyd had acquired as a pet, but it soon grew too large and fierce to be their playmate. Boyd kept it, though, training the animal to pull the cart that carried the monthly payroll up the winding road through the plantation to Mringin. The tiger did not particularly enjoy the task, but its slow, soft-pawed menace put a stop to all attempts to intercept the cart and steal the payroll. One day the tiger was found dead in its large enclosure in the garden, having eaten poisoned meat. The miscreant was never found.

Anna had no other women to talk to at Ngrodjo, but she didn't mind. She supposed there must be a *nyai* somewhere about, mother to some of those *café-au-lait* children, but she never caught sight of her and she never asked. What would she have talked to a *nyai* about, anyway, if they had met? Fashions at home? The latest

Robert Boyd (centre), surrounded by servants and children at his coffee plantation, Mringin. The tiger cub was later trained to pull the payroll cart.

magazines in the 'travelling library', the box from Europe that slowly made its way from home to home in the Indies? It seemed unlikely. Anna was able to enjoy being a guest in someone else's comfortable and well-run house, with no responsibilities.

Prentice loved to see Dubois's family. Anna and the children reminded him of what might have been, of the life he and Jane might have had, but it was no longer a painful vision. He found Anna charming, graceful, and soothing, as Jane had been. Eugenie and Jean were nice children, but Victor was Prentice's especial favourite. He was only six months older than Gerard, whom he missed badly. Being with Victor was a sort of substitute for being with his own child. Sometimes Prentice closed his eyes and thought, This is what my boy is like. Gerard would be as tall as this now, maybe able to throw a ball like Victor, running and laughing in the garden in Malang…It eased the pain of separation.

But Dubois enjoyed his stays at Ngrodjo better if he went alone. His family distracted him from what he came for, the companionship of Prentice and Boyd, the discussions, the exercise of brainpower. Soon Dubois came to realize that Ngrodjo was more his home than the house in Toeloeng Agoeng; Boyd and Prentice were closer to him than his own wife and children. It was a sobering thought, but true. Anna and the children did not need him and they never challenged him. He had always to move at their snail-like speed, with endless distractions; there was no getting anywhere if the children were involved. And Anna did not even really listen to him any more when he talked about ideas or theories. Maybe she never had; he could not be sure. But at Ngrodjo, he felt a sense of complete belonging, of fulfilment and even love. Sitting on the veranda with these two men, talking about ideas, looking out over the spectacular view and admiring the mottled bluey-green of acres and acres of coffee trees: it gave him such peace. He had never before felt so at home, so accepted for who and what he was.

The three lent one another books or articles cut from newspapers and discussed them through letters or at later meetings. How unlike Dubois's stilted friendship with Sluiter! Though his fossils were in Toeloeng Agoeng cluttering up the front veranda, he found an emotional and intellectual satisfaction at Ngrodjo that was unmatched. No tentative theory he formulated about the fossils, no observation, had any reality until he had discussed it thoroughly with Boyd and Prentice. These two men melted his isolation with the warmth of their friendship. In their company, he suffered no doubts about his eventual success, for *they* had no doubts. He would find the missing link – probably there at Trinil, the most promising site he had found yet. If the missing link was not there, it would be somewhere, soon. Their faith in Dubois renewed his courage, replenished his determination.

Trinil

In mid-May 1892, it was dry enough to resume work at Trinil. The coolies removed the soft silt deposited by the river during the rainy season and then waited for the sun to dry everything out so that it was possible to start digging. Kriele and De Winter had resolved their problems and used the drying time to make a new plot of the excavation, measuring the position of the squared-off hole and its depth. Dubois reminded them to keep the best records they could of the excavation; it was crucial to recognize the different geologic layers and to separate their contents.

Word soon reached Dubois in Toeloeng Agoeng that the coolies were again uncovering many excellent fossils. He decided to visit the site. He would stay for a while, to remind the labourers of the way they were to dig and to help the engineers establish a regular daily schedule. After two weeks, Dubois's enthusiasm for the site had vanished, and he wrote in his diary

> July 28, 1892. A few cool windy days seduced me into setting up my tent nearby the excavation. After a stay of 14 days I discover that there is no more unsuitable place available in Java, because of health and malaria, for the study of fossils than this hell (which I, being born Roman Catholic, had mistaken for purgatory).

It was relentlessly hot and airless at Trinil. Although the big, brown Bengawan Solo lapped lazily at the base of the point bar, only a few feet below the edge of the excavation, there was no breeze. Any movement of air was blocked by the high bluffs or was dissipated by the sinuous bends of the riverbed.

Dubois was again stricken with malaria. For some days, he believed he would die there at Trinil, adding his bones to the growing pile of fossils, his Charnel House. They could just lay his body in the excavation and cover him up, he thought miserably. He wondered idly how long it would take his skeleton to fossilize. Years? Millennia? And the cool, the lovely cool of the river... He wouldn't mind dying so much if he could only lie in that cool, cool

river for ever with all his fossils around him. He did not die, nor
did he linger at Trinil long after his recovery. He packed up the
fossils excavated to date and headed back to the shady house at
Toeloeng Agoeng to take more quinine and await further
shipments of specimens.

In August, the engineers made a discovery of tremendous significance, though it took some weeks to reach Toeloeng Agoeng. The
new specimen was a fine and nearly complete femur of a large and
long-legged animal. It was found by a coolie, hoeing with unusual
vigour after being told off by Kriele for laziness. The *ping* of the
metal blade of his *patjol* as it struck the fossilized bone was unmistakable, so the coolie stopped digging immediately and notified
Kriele. Thinking it might be something important, Kriele finished
excavating the specimen himself. His energy was rewarded; when
the femur was completely uncovered, he could see it was an
unusual specimen. He could also see it was no longer complete.
The initial *patjol* blow had broken some fragments off the end of
the bone – so he ordered all the coolies to cease excavating immediately. They were instead to search every inch of ground surrounding the find-spot. With their fingers, they were to sift every
handful, every crumb of sediment until they found the missing bits.
It was dark when they completed the task.

After dinner, Kriele showed De Winter the new femur. He agreed
with Kriele that they had not had anything like this before. Maybe
Dubois would be pleased with it; maybe it was his missing link.
Neither knew much anatomy, but they knew this was not the bone
of pig, an antelope, or a tiger. It had to be something new. Together
they planned how to glue the missing pieces back into place. This
was a delicate task, better done in daylight than in the wavering
half-light of a paraffin lamp. De Winter agreed to see to the repair
job in the morning while Kriele started the coolies digging.
Unfortunately, the luck that had led the coolie to the femur did not
hold, as Kriele explained to Dubois in a letter.

> 7 September 1892
> De Winter told me that those small pieces missing from the thigh
> bone were blown away by a strong wind while being glued together
> on a djati leaf, and could never be found again.

Dubois reprimanded the engineers for their carelessness. Still, he
could not be too severe with them for it was such a good find. The
femur surely came from a large, apelike primate and it had been

excavated from the same geologic layer as the tooth and the skull-cap. The bone was too large and strongly built to come from either a fossil orang-utan or a gibbon, like those he had found on Sumatra, so it had to be part of the Javan chimpanzee, *Anthro-popithecus*, just like the skullcap and tooth. Otherwise, Dubois thought, laughing to himself at the folly of such a proposition, we have to believe that two such rare apes died and were preserved within yards of each other, one leaving only its head and tooth, the other only its leg.

He was anxious to go up to Mringin to show the new fossil to Prentice and Boyd. Before then, though, he must understand the bone better. Its shape was fascinating. It was amazingly similar to a human femur, a bone Dubois knew as well as he knew his own thigh. He had seen dozens, nay hundreds, of femurs in the anatomy lab. He would never have predicted that the animal of the tooth and pear-shaped, ape-browed skullcap would have such a femur. Of course, he could be mistaken about the skullcap. There was still matrix to be removed. When that was done and the chimpanzee skull arrived – if it ever arrived – perhaps he would find the skull-cap less apelike and more human than he thought. If not, the creature must have been a chimera indeed.

The most obvious difference between the fossil and any other femur Dubois had seen was a large growth of pathological bone tissue on the inside of the thigh, up toward the hip joint. The growth was the aftermath of an old, healed injury, obviously, but what injury? He could not remember anything in the anatomical collections at Amsterdam with such a growth. The growth was very large, the size of a woman's fist, which suggested that walking had been very painful for a long time after this injury. How had the creature survived long enough for the new bone to form? He could not say. This bone was a curious record of the past.

He sketched the bone, using the exercise of drawing to make himself see in greater detail. Eventually, he would produce an exact drawing using the specialized instrument called a camera lucida, which projected an image of the specimen on to the page so that it could be traced with great precision. He had improved on the design of the camera lucida a little himself; he could turn out exquisitely accurate drawings. For now, he examined the specimen by drawing it roughly and analysed it by taking detailed measurements and notes. He found only a few features that struck him as more apelike than human; it was a very humanlike femur,

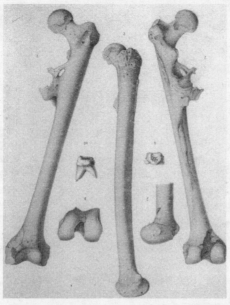

Dubois drew the upper third molar together with the left femur or thigh bone of *Pithecanthropus erectus* for his monograph. The femur is shown in (1) anterior, (2) lateral, (3) posterior, and (4) distal views; also shown is (5) the medial side of the distal or knee end. The molar is shown in distal (6a) and occlusal (6b) views.

certainly. However *Anthropopithecus* had lived, it had been adapted to walking upright like a man. That fact raised disturbing possibilities.

After a few days, he packed up his precious fossils in padded wooden boxes he had had made for them, strapped the boxes behind his saddle, and rode up to Mringin to share his good fortune with his friends.

'Halloooo!' he called as soon as Ngrodjo came into view. 'I've got something extraordinary.'

His timing was good; Prentice had finished a tour of the plantation and would be staying at Ngrodjo for some few days, consulting with Boyd over the plans for picking the beans. They set aside their work immediately: the Doctor was here, with a new discovery.

'Let me show it to you,' Dubois said proudly, unstrapping his boxes. He handed his wiry bay gelding to the waiting *syce*, who would give the horse a good brushing and see to its needs. Boyd and Prentice hastily cleared the table of cups and record books, making space for Dubois to open his boxes.

'Djongas,' Boyd called, waving a cigarette-laden hand above his head, 'bring cool lime juice for the Tuan Dokter, and more hot water for the tea.' But Dubois could not wait to quench his thirst before showing his treasures to his friends.

He began immediately. 'You know about the tooth,' Dubois said, opening a box and taking out a small tin soap dish. He opened the tin, within which the molar rested on a bed of cotton wool like a baby in a cradle. 'That was the first find, September of last year. It definitely belongs to an ape or something nearly human, I am certain of that. And then' – he moved to the next box, bigger, deeper, with more padding covered in velvet – 'then there is the skullcap. We found that last October.' He extracted the fragile specimen and handed it to Boyd, who held it gently and carefully.

'Isn't it a beauty?' Boyd said admiringly, while Prentice nodded in agreement. 'I'd forgotten how fine it is. And you've cleaned out much more of the matrix. Do these indentations on the inside tell you anything about its brain?'

'I think so,' replied Dubois, a little surprised at the Old Warrior's acumen. 'They would if it were a man. But I haven't got my chimpanzee skull yet, for comparison.'

'Ah, kassian,' said Prentice sympathetically, clucking his tongue. 'Not yet? Weber will find you one though, before long.'

'And now,' announced Dubois dramatically, opening the largest, longest box, 'now there is this. They found it a few weeks ago, in August, though it didn't reach me until early September.' He withdrew the long brown femur and displayed it across both of his palms with a flourish. Prentice put down the cigarette tin that held the tooth and stretched out a hand to take the femur. Then he stopped his movement and looked at Dubois, questioningly. 'No need for great care, Prentice, no need,' Dubois reassured him. 'The thing is as solid as an oak tree.'

'So it is,' Prentice agreed, examining the curious object. Then he pointed at the bone's upper end. 'This is the ball joint for the hip, isn't it? But Doctor, what is this here, this growth on the bone? Surely that is not normal.'

'You will not guess again!' cheered Dubois, using a Dutch expression. 'You are too clever. Ja, the creature had some sort of injury, a massive wound I think, that bled and clotted and eventually turned into this pathological bone. Very puzzling thing, that. What I can't get over is how like a man's femur it is. The ball of the hip joint is really spherical, with this pit for the attachment of ligamentum teres.' He remembered himself and added a hasty aside, gesturing. 'The ligamentum teres carries the blood supply to the head of the femur.' Boyd and Prentice nodded their understanding, so he continued. 'The shape of that ball is just like yours or mine. The strong, straight shaft is very human too, and the knee joint. Why, the condyles, these things like the rockers on a chair at the distal end, are practically the twin of every set I've ever seen in the anatomy room!'

His friends shared his evident delight in the specimen. Then Boyd asked the important question. 'Doctor, tell us, is this the same thing as your skullcap? The bones look alike to me, both that same shiny brown colour and very hard.'

'I think so,' said Dubois carefully, 'I think so. The tooth is that of an ape, definitely. The skullcap has browridges like a large ape's but too big a braincase for an ape, and the femur is undoubtedly from a large apelike animal that walked on two legs like a man. The specimens are just too complete for me to be wrong about this. The most telling thing is that the engineers say they all came from the same geologic stratum, within maybe twelve or fifteen metres of one another. I believe they must come from one individual. It is terribly important, that.'

They fell silent, awed at the wonderful thing that had befallen one of them. Three bones – the head, the tooth, and the leg – were from one animal, a completely unknown apelike beast with puzzlingly manlike features. What a triumph! Over the next few days, they examined the fossils again and again, Dubois pointing out anatomical details, Boyd and Prentice acting as sounding boards for his ideas and raising new possibilities. They could not offer Dubois scientific expertise in anatomy, for he far surpassed them in that regard. What they could and did offer him was their devoted attention and interest, their validation of his discovery.

'Doctor,' asked Prentice quietly the next afternoon, when they had run out of questions and observations to share, 'is this *it*? Is this your missing link? Have you found it at last?'

Dubois didn't answer right away. He didn't know what to say to this crucial question, asked by his dearest friend. 'I don't know, Prentice,' Dubois replied hesitantly. 'I just don't know yet. I must be sure before I say a thing like that. I must be *certain*. But this femur is a big surprise to me, and the size of that braincase...' His voice trailed off. He started again in a moment, trying to express his thoughts, 'And then the browridges... You see, I can't help thinking that there is a lot of ape in that skull, and a lot of man in that femur. Doesn't that sound like a transitional species, a link between apes and man?'

He looked at Prentice with his pale-blue eyes and Prentice looked back at him, believing in him utterly. Dubois didn't yet dare to declare that this was the missing link, that his long search was over. But they both could see the idea dancing at the edge of their consciousness, like a shy woodland creature that hesitated at the edge of a clearing.

CHAPTER 22

The Birth of *Pithecanthropus*

The rains started again before the workers could find any more primate fossils at Trinil, and Dubois closed down the excavation for the season. What a pity. But there it was: the river was rising. Whatever fossils hid in the sediments had waited a long time and would have to wait for next year.

In November, he was elated to hear that Weber had procured a chimpanzee skull for him in Berlin, only the month before. The skull should be arriving in Java soon. Dubois took to meeting the mail train from Batavia almost every day. The rest of the time he worked on framing the sentences of his third quarterly report of 1892, which would be sent to his supporters: Groeneveldt at the Department of Education, Religion, and Industry, Jentink in Holland, and Kroesen in Sumatra.

The most important find of the month of August is the left femur of *Anthropopithecus*, of which the existence was shown a year ago by a molar and a skullcap. This femur lay in the same geological level as the other two fossils, although it lay upstream from the others by about 15 metres along the course of the ancient river that had deposited the volcanic material. From the conditions under which they were found and from comparative research it appears that the three skeletal elements belonged to the same individual, probably a female, and were very ancient.

The next part of his report gave the interpretation and significance of the find. He wrote and rewrote this section many times before submitting it. He would not deny the implications of the femur's shape, nor did he wish to overstate them.

This being was in no way equipped to climb trees in the manner of the chimpanzee, the gorilla, and the orang-utan. On the contrary, it is obvious from the entire construction of the femur that this bone fulfilled the same mechanical role as in the human body. Taking this view of the thigh bone, one can say with absolute certainty that *Anthropopithecus* of Java stood upright and moved like a human.

Then he estimated the cranial capacity of the skullcap, following a key publication by Theodor Bischoff that he had recently obtained. Bischoff documented the mathematical relationship between various linear measurements of a chimpanzee skull and the volume of its braincase. If the relationship held true for this creature, then – while Bischoff's ape had a brain volume of 410 cc – the Trinil skullcap had an impressive 700 cc of brain in its skull. This volume was still much smaller than a human's, about 1250 cc in Europeans, less in other races usually thought to be inferior.

Dubois's concluding paragraph was bold. The femur proved he had a new species of ancient ape, not Lydekker's *Anthropopithecus sivalensis* but something of his own, an upright ape.

Because of this find a surprising and important fact has been brought to light. The Javanese *Anthropopithecus*, which in its skull is more human than any other known anthropoid ape, already had an upright, erect posture, which has always been considered to be the exclusive privilege of humans. Thus this ancient Pleistocene ape from our island is the first known transitional form linking Man more closely with his next of kin among the mammals. *Anthropopithecus erectus* Eug. Dubois, through each of its known skeletal elements, more closely approaches the human condition than any other anthropoid ape, especially in the femur – a fact that is totally in accord with what Lamarck proclaimed and which was explained later by Darwin and others: that the first step on the road to becoming human taken by our ancestors was acquiring upright posture. Consequently, the factual evidence is now in hand that, as some have already suspected, the East Indies was the cradle of mankind.

Dubois copied the report in a good hand and submitted it to Groeneveldt on 27 November.

Within a week he realized he had made a terrible mistake: he had misunderstood how Bischoff had measured his chimpanzee skull. If Dubois's measurements were taken differently, then his estimate of brain size was bound to be wrong. The very idea made his heart pound and his head ache. How could he have been so careless? He had been in too much of a hurry, too impatient. It was his worst fault. Hands shaking, he measured and remeasured the fossil skullcap several times, confirming his initial error. Each time he calculated the size of the braincase anew, using the corrected measurements, and its volume was even greater than he had initially estimated. In fact, it was enormous. After the fourth repetition, Dubois accepted that the skullcap had a cranial capacity of nearly 1000 cc.

This was an amazing value, more than twice the size of Bischoff's chimpanzee. No ape's brain was that large, he thought; it was not possible. This Javan skull was comparable in brain size to some human races, like the Andaman Islanders or the Australian Aborigines. It was an astounding discovery. Could it be true? Dubois measured yet again, repeated his calculations, arrived at the same figure. It was true.

He wrote to Groeneveldt immediately asking that the passage be corrected when the report was published. There was no way to disguise his stupid mistake. The key thing was to find out the truth and make it known.

4 December 1892

In calculating the relative volume of the brain of *Anthropopithecus erectus*, the results being mentioned in the report for the third quarter recently submitted, I made a regrettable mistake. The brain of this transitional form was considerably larger than one would gather from the report…nearly 1000 cc.

This fact tipped the balance of the creature from ape to…almost human. This had to be something very like the missing link: an upright-walking ape with a brain as big as some humans'. The thought that his search was over made Dubois's chest feel too small to contain his heart. His thoughts whirled in his skull like dust devils, fast, faster, so much to do…Both elated and apprehensive, he worked feverishly on the formal description of these new fossils. He scribbled a quick note and sent it up to Ngrodjo with a boy, to let Prentice and Boyd know what was happening: 'I have made a terrible mistake. Skullcap 1000 cc, not 700. You see what this means. Please excuse my temporary absence. I will visit and explain fully as soon as possible.'

And then, two weeks later – on 18 December – the chimpanzee skull finally arrived from Weber. 'Anna, it has come, it has come!' Dubois called joyfully as he bounded up the steps of the house. 'Here it is at last!' Anna and the children and most of the servants came running. It had been more than a year since Dubois had first written to Weber, with his request. The entire household had been tensely awaiting the arrival of the precious skull, which for some strange reason the Tuan Dokter needed so badly.

He opened the parcel carefully and unwrapped the skull. 'Look, Eugenie,' he said, bending down to show the prize to his daughter, 'look. This is the skull of a chimpanzee all the way from Africa!'

'Is it very 'portant, Father?' asked Eugenie dubiously, poking at the skull with a small, chubby finger. At five, she understood little of what this meant; Jean, at four, knew still less; and Victor, cuddled in Babu's arms, sensed only the happy tone of his father's voice.

'Ja,' said her father contentedly, turning the skull over in his hands. He pulled his magnifying glass from his pocket to stare at a minute anatomical detail. 'Ja, Eugenie. With this, I can understand my fossil skullcap from Trinil. With this, I can learn how close to the apes and how close to man he was. This is very important.'

Eugenie nodded and smiled at her tall, handsome father. She adored him and often won his praise with clever questions.

'That's good, Father,' offered little Jean seriously, pretending that he understood. Anna hugged the children and Babu hustled them into the garden while Dubois headed for his study. They were not to disturb their father; he had scientific work to do now. But even the little ones knew that the household would be a happy place for days to come. Dubois settled down to write a note of thanks to Weber.

19 December 1892

I received your letter of October 21st, saying that you had finally found me a chimpanzee skull, on the 28th of November. Yesterday the postal parcel, sent at the same time as your letter in October, finally arrived. Especially the *chimpanzee skull* I have awaited with desire and on the tiptoe of expectation.

With the chimp skull and the gibbon and human skulls he had collected previously, Dubois could make his own observations and be sure of them. He compared the gibbon to the human, the gibbon to the chimp, the chimp to the human, and all three species to the fossil. The anatomy of the Trinil skullcap was strikingly similar to that of the chimpanzee skull except that the fossil was so much larger-brained. The sheer brain size made the fossil resemble the human skull in shape, too, despite those apelike browridges. And then there was the femur from Trinil to be considered, so like a human thigh bone, so unlike a chimpanzee's.

Dubois worked in a frenzy over the next few days. He took his meals on a tray in the study and barely saw his wife, his children, or even the light of day. All he could see was his skulls. He started work at first light and stopped at night only when Anna came in and insisted that he needed his rest. There was so much to do, to learn; it was so imperative to get it right.

Christmas morning, Dubois arose very early. He carried his cup of coffee into the study in the pearly light of dawn; it was a special time of day, when he felt like the only person awake in the world. There the fossils sat, solid and brown and hard as rocks, on his desk, waiting for him.

'Good morning,' he said to them fancifully, bowing at the waist, 'and Merry Christmas to you.' The modern skulls, yellowish white and a little greasy to the touch, sat patiently on another table. He nodded politely in their direction and sat down at his desk. For the next few hours, he checked his measurements again and read through his pages of notes and comments. He reviewed his sketches of the fossil skullcap, comparing them with sketches of the modern skulls, blocking with his hand those parts that were broken away on the fossil. Right lateral view; posterior view; left lateral view; anterior view; superior view; inferior view: yes, the observations were all correct. Then he proceeded to the tooth and the femur. Point by point, he compared the anatomy of the fossils with modern teeth and femurs once again. His mind was absolutely calm. The conclusion was clear. When he had retired last night, he had been convinced. This morning, he had corroborated everything once again. Now he was completely certain.

He packed his specimens away carefully, each on its own cushioned velvet bed within its own wooden box, fastening its lid with a small brass clasp. He placed each box carefully on the shelf where it belonged and put away the modern skulls, too. Then he tidied his desk, putting away books and organizing his papers and notebooks until all was straight.

He walked out of the study, closing the door quietly behind him, and found Anna eating breakfast on the back veranda. 'It is done, Anna,' he said, contented but as weary as if he had been up all night. He seated himself at the table opposite her. 'I have found it. Those bones are the missing link. It is true, at last.' He smiled a slow, wise smile, not a boy's enthusiastic grin. He was in this moment a man who knew exactly where he stood.

Anna was uncertain; his mood was an enigma to her. 'You do not sound very pleased,' she offered, hesitantly. 'Are you sure?'

'Oh, ja, ja,' Dubois nodded, helping himself to tea and toast. The *djongas* had seen him come in and would bring his boiled egg and fruit shortly. 'It is certain, I shall spend today with you and the children. Tomorrow I will finalize my report. But I have it, Anna, I have found the missing link. Everyone will see now; everyone will understand I am not just a crazy man who ran off to the Indies in search of an idea.'

Anna stood up and came around the table to embrace him. 'I am very proud of you, Eugène,' she said fondly. 'I knew you would do this. I never doubted it. What a Christmas gift to us all!' It was a lovely morning, she thought, her eyes shining with pride.

Dubois had barely finished his breakfast when they heard the children awakening. 'Mama! Papa!' little voices called excitedly. 'Are you up? It is Christmas! Come on, Babu, it is Christmas! Don't be so slow!' The holiday was upon them.

The next day, Dubois returned to concentrated work on the fossils. That day, and all the next, working late into the night, he organized and polished his facts, getting the report ready to send to Groeneveldt. By the morning of the twenty-eighth, he was well satisfied with what he had done. He did not expect to make further revisions now. In the very act of writing the covering letter to Groeneveldt, he had an epiphany. He had intended to keep the name *Anthropopithecus erectus* with which he had endowed the fossils in his third quarterly report, written but a month earlier. But as he penned the letter 'A', for *Anthropopithecus*, the truth of the matter overwhelmed him. It was wrong. He lifted his pen from the paper. No, this was an injustice, he thought. These fossils were not Lydekker's chimpanzee from the Siwaliks, transported to Java; they were not a chimpanzee at all. They were something entirely new. They were the transitional form, the missing link that joined apes to Man, and he knew it. He could not call the fossils *Anthropopithecus* any longer.

There was only one name that could be given to this creature. He superimposed a 'P' over the 'A' and wrote *Pithecanthropus*, Ernst Haeckel's name for the hypothetical missing link. That name would make his position clear to any man of science. Now, what species name was he to attach to the genus *Pithecanthropus*? He could not use Haeckel's proposed name, *alalus* – 'speechless' – without some evidence that it was correct. Who could tell if this creature had been able to talk, from what was known of it? There was no face, no jaw, and even the inside of the braincase was not yet entirely cleaned of matrix. It would be wrong to name this fossil based on information he did not have. He would call it *erectus*, *Pithecanthropus erectus*, a name that would honour both the marvellously manlike femur and the capacious but strangely apelike skull. His missing link would be known as the ape-man who walked erect, *Pithecanthropus erectus*. The name had a good ring to it. And to himself, and a few friends, the creature would be known by its initials, *P.e.*

He wrote to Groeneveldt:

28 December 1892

I have, Your Excellency, the honour of offering the first instalment of the description of some of the fossils I have collected. This instalment deals with only one species, *Pithecanthropus erectus*.

It was five years, two weeks, and three days after Dubois's arrival in the Indies. He had abandoned his job in Amsterdam and sailed halfway around the world; he had kept his wife and daughter safe, and fathered two sons and brought them into the world; he had searched two islands for fossils; he had survived three terrible bouts of malaria, tigers' lairs, and cave-ins; he had begged and argued and persuaded until the government itself had provided help; and he had collected and cleaned and identified thousands of mammalian fossils. And he, Marie Eugène François Thomas Dubois, had found the missing link.

CHAPTER 23

1893

Dubois longed to visit Boyd and Prentice at Ngrodjo in the new year as soon as possible, to go over every scrap of evidence with them. Before he could, Prentice stopped in Toeloeng Agoeng unexpectedly on his way back from Malang. It had been a painful Christmas for Prentice, the first since Jane's death. His boy was well, thriving, but Prentice was able to spend little time with him. The boy instinctively turned to his grandfather, not to his father. That fact burned in Prentice's memory like a flame.

And so Prentice came to Toeloeng Agoeng seeking solace and companionship in the home of his best friend. How he envied Dubois the comfortable, familial air of his household! He treasured the echo of Eugenie's and Jean's voices as they played boisterous games in the garden, the sound of Anna's clear soprano singing lullabies to little Victor. And he saw the warmth of a woman's touch about the house: the flowers, the pretty tablecloth, the homey meals, the silver-framed photographs of Holland – how he missed all that! Anna's beauty and femininity rounded the sharp edges of reality, softened the harshness of life in the Indies. Prentice missed having a wife badly.

Talking with Dubois about the fossils and their new name took Prentice's mind off his losses. How fine *P.e.* was! Dubois's open enthusiasm was contagious. Prentice was proud to be among the first to know what this extraordinary man had done. Only much later did Prentice suspect that his friend had deliberately spent extra time explaining and displaying the fossils in order to lighten Prentice's melancholy mood. He was grateful that the doctor understood him so well and so kindly. And the doctor's medicine worked; his shared joy brought Prentice back to the here and now of life in Java, drawing him away from the sad might-have-beens. He was able to return to Mringin with renewed hope for the future. Dubois had succeeded against tremendous odds; so would Prentice. He might be able to start up a plantation of his own before too long. Then he could make a real home and a life for his son. Hard work and perseverance and strength were what it took.

Before Prentice left, Dubois asked him for advice about a problem he had just come to apprehend. Dubois had found the missing link. What was he now to do? It was Dubois's responsibility to write a monograph, to make the specimen known to the scientific community in Europe. Yet he was hampered by the paucity of comparative material. He had no osteological collection, only three gibbon skulls, a few humans, and a chimpanzee skull at his disposal – and that last had required heroic efforts on Weber's part. Compounding the difficulty was the lack of a good, up-to-date scientific library; not even in Batavia was there such a thing.

Could Dubois write a detailed scientific analysis of the fossils that would stand for all time under such conditions? Should he try? To turn out a work that was not thorough or up-to-date would be tragic, and his circumstances were certainly difficult. On the other hand, if he waited until his return to Holland to write, then publication would be sorely delayed. Dubois was obligated by the terms of his enlistment to stay in Java until late in 1895, almost three years hence.

Dubois and Prentice played devil's advocate with each other, marshalling the arguments for and against each course of action, switching roles, exploring all alternatives. Nothing was decided. Later, when Dubois travelled up to Ngrodjo, the two of them reviewed it all for Boyd.

'Doctor,' Boyd asked carefully, feeling his way toward the crux of the problem, 'what is it you have to do in this monograph? What is *in* books like this one?'

Dubois was taken aback; he had not considered this practical but central issue. 'Well, Boyd,' he began, 'you know, no one has really ever written one before, not like this. Fraipont and Lohest wrote a monograph on the Spy Neanderthals, that's the closest thing. Let's see. They talk about the site a bit; they describe the fossils, and then they compare the specimens to the various races of man to see which are the descendants of Neanderthals. But that's not what I'd have to do. Ja, I must describe the fossils, give all the measurements and figures and so on, and I have to explain what they mean. But the proper comparisons here are with apes, not with living humans. The question is not "which race is closest to *P.e.*?" but "Where in the evolutionary transition from ape to man does *P.e.* lie?"'

'Would you have to discuss many other fossil specimens to answer that question?' queried Boyd. 'Do you have to go and study fossils collected from other parts of the world to write your monograph?'

'No,' said Dubois, breaking into a broad grin as he realized the truth, 'I don't, because there isn't anything else like this. Even Lydckker's *Anthropopithecus* in India: I certainly ought to go and see it, but it is only a piece of upper jaw. How can I compare a fragment of upper jaw with my skullcap or my femur?'

'You ought to stand on your own two feet, then,' said Boyd forcefully, swallowing the last of his drink and thumping the empty glass on the table. 'Use your own experience and good judgement. You've got some skulls to compare it with; you know what femurs are like and could lay your hands on a few without much trouble. You've got a pretty good little library there in Toeloeng Agoeng in your own study. I don't see any real reason to wait. And there's every reason not to delay,' Boyd concluded sensibly.

'Good point,' agreed Prentice, nodding. 'The doctor has no road to follow. He is cutting his own path into new territory. He has something entirely new. *P.e.* lies between apes and man; it's not just some primitive sort of human. If I can see that with what the doctor has, then so can the men of science in Europe. Doctor, all you need to do is lay out the evidence of what you've found, honest and straight, without any fancy comparisons.'

Boyd raised another point in favour of writing now. 'It's not very likely,' he admitted, his voice deepening as the subject grew more serious, 'but delay might be a fatal mistake. What if some other fellow has read your article on the promise of the Indies and comes and finds a fossil for himself? Now that there's a committee in Holland to promote and support scientific research in the Indies, someone else could come looking – and finding.'

Dubois paled at his friend's words. He had not considered such a possibility, at least not since he had found his own fossils, but of course the danger was there. Martin the geologist, for one, was terribly interested in the Indies; so was Verbeek. They would probably have an easy time gaining support from the committee for an expedition now that Dubois had pointed the way. What if they found something like *P.e.* and published first?

'No, Dubois,' said Prentice firmly, 'you must do it now. It is your duty and your right. You have done all the work and you have succeeded with so little help. Now you deserve the glory.'

'Yes,' concurred Boyd. 'You owe it to science and to yourself to publish as soon as you can. Don't hurry now, you don't want to "marry in haste and repent at leisure", as the proverb says. But you must start now and do all that you can from here.'

'You both advise that course of action?' asked Dubois, looking at each man in turn. Prentice nodded; Boyd did too. 'Then I shall do it. I think you are right. And since this monograph is a new thing, I shall do it as I like. After all, I have carried out the entire project to my own design from the beginning.'

The next morning, Dubois rode back down the mountain to Toeloeng Agoeng and his fossils. It was a new year and a new phase in his life. He was now the man who had found the missing link. He had only to tell the world.

The task of writing the monograph proved far from simple. Replicating someone else's pattern of organization would have been far easier than inventing one. He struggled to order his observations and to describe the finds clearly and simply. He had to decide not only what needed to be illustrated but also how to convey the fossils' features accurately. Meanwhile, Kriele and De Winter and the labourers were still at work in the mountains. The endless litany of complaints about the coolies continued. The engineers had offered a small monetary reward for good specimens as a means of curbing the coolies' tendency to throw away or hide fossils. Boxes of fossils continued to arrive at Toeloeng Agoeng, but the offered reward went unclaimed.

In February, something extraordinary occurred. The first Dubois knew of it was when the Assistant Resident drove up to his house in Toeloeng Agoeng unexpectedly in a *delman*. 'Have you seen this yet, Dubois?' the man asked, waving a copy of the *Bataviaasch Nieuwsblad* as he picked his away up the bone-laden steps to the veranda.

The *Bataviaasch Nieuwsblad* was a new type of newspaper, an invention that could be laid squarely at the feet of its editor and publisher, P. A. Daum. It was an opposition press, a paper that was regularly and outspokenly critical of the government's colonial policies. Daum's sarcastic 'tropical style' was well known and had been the cause of his firing from every paper he had ever worked for, save those he owned himself. Still, Daum's great ability as a writer made him a force to be reckoned with in the Indies, and he said what no one else dared to. To boost sales and fill pages, Daum had begun to serialize scandalous novels about the Indies. They were enormously popular, for the characters were often based on recognizable colonial figures and revolved around situations closely resembling life. The novels were innovative, too, for they were written in a simple, conversational style – parlando, it was

Dubois's fossils covered the shaded veranda and the steps to
the garden.

called – very different from the formal language of the European
novel.

The little-known truth was that the novels, like almost everything else in the paper, from the editorials to the news reports and
the advertisements, were by Daum's own hand. He disguised his
role behind a constantly changing array of pseudonyms, but the
truth was that few other journalists would write for him. The issue
of the paper that the Assistant Resident brought to Dubois's door
was dated Monday, 6 February 1893.

'Come sit in a comfortable chair, in the shade,' said Dubois
genially to the Assistant Resident, indicating the only chair on the
veranda that could be reached without stepping over fossils. 'Can
the boy get you a cup of tea, or a cold juice perhaps?' Dubois beck-
oned for the *djongas*. Once the official was settled comfortably,
Dubois returned to the business at hand. 'Now what is it you think
I should read?'

'It is this, on the third page,' the Assistant Resident replied,
handing over the newspaper.

IN PURSUANCE OF PALEONTOLOGICAL
INVESTIGATIONS OF JAVA
(Report to the Mining Works, third quarter 1892)

It is well known that etymologists sometimes explain the origin of
words through most surprising derivations and on such occasions

produce results that are astounding to the uninitiated, but if we compare these attempts with what some paleontologists dare to do with reference to fossils, then their endeavour appears to be child's play.

This flashed across my mind as I read the article mentioned at the head of this piece.

For some time, the military surgeon Eug. Dubois busies himself with paleontological investigations and, because of his predilection for such studies, works with exceptional diligence and assiduity. He is totally absorbed by his work, so to speak. As a firm Darwinist, he dreams of making a discovery which the great master of evolution will greet with joy. Namely, the discovery of the until-recently missing link between the animal world and man.

Should this be taken amiss? I do not believe so. At present Darwinism is the backbone of the education of most high school graduates. The heavy facts that are brought up against Darwin's theory by the most competent authorities – these leave them cold. Examine their libraries and, ten to one, you will not find a single paper in which Darwin's theory is opposed. It is old-fashioned to think differently, their teachers have told them.

I fear, however, that this time the Darwinian outlook of the esteemed Mr. Dubois has played a trick on him, a danger that an impartial observer would have escaped.

What then is the case?

In the Kediri region, in volcanic beds, he found some time ago a skull-cap, not an undamaged skull, but a fragment, along with a loose molar.

In August 1892 he found, 15 metres from the place where the skull-cap and tooth had been lying, a thigh bone with a striking resemblance in measurements and shape to the bone of the leg that supports humans.

Instead of thinking of the remains of a human skeleton (Dubois had already demonstrated the presence of a primitive race here in Java, more like the Papuan race than the present population, in a previous report) he makes comparisons (the details of which are not known yet) with a more surprising result than the most abstruse etymologist has ever put forward!

Given: a molar and one skull fragment found together as well as a left femur, that has been found 15 metres further away.

Until now, Dubois had been skimming the article but he stopped when he reached these words and read them aloud. 'A "skull frag-ment"?' he repeated, outraged. 'A fragment? I have the better part of a skull, lacking only the face. I have as much of the skull as the original Neanderthal fossil, more than Lydekker's *Anthropopithecus*. This is no fragment! I have shown it to you, Assistant Resident, haven't I?'

'Ja, ja, two times,' the official replied a little anxiously. He feared Dubois would insist on showing him all of the thousands of fossils crowded on to the veranda.

'This author has set out to make me sound like a fool! What else does he say? Here, ja, here is the place.' Dubois read on aloud.

Question: What does this mean?
A non-Darwinist would scratch himself through his fur before he would propose a genetic link between the monkey skull and the monkey molar and the femur, which has a close speaking acquaintance with a human femur.
Not so the esteemed Mr. Dubois.

'His sarcasm is really too much,' protested Dubois, and the Assistant Resident nodded in agreement. ' "The *esteemed* Mr Dubois"! What a backhanded compliment. Now, what else does this scoundrel say?'

With the data mentioned above, he thinks that the theories of Darwin and Lamarck have been confirmed, that the first step on the road of the incarnation of our ancestors has been acquired with erect posture (page 11);
That molar, skull fragment, and left thigh bone were once part of an upright female apeman, named Anthropopithecus erectus Eug. Dubois (Page 11).
That this creature fed differently from the present-day anthropomorphic apes, despising tree-climbing and even carrying artificial weapons (page 14).
Finally, according to the esteemed Mr. Dubois, this is the actual evidence that the Indies were the cradle of the human genus (page 14).
Whew, that's it!
Why is this animal given such a beautiful name? Why wasn't he named Hanoman(*) communis of the family Hanomanaceae ... ? The historian would have gained something from the find, but Anthropopithecus erectus!
No, I am afraid that the esteemed Mr. Dubois, prejudiced because he has completely swallowed Darwinism, has gone too far, and has constructed a connection between the human femur and the monkey skull and molar where none has ever existed. If humans also lived, at the time

when the cataclysmic eruption buried so many dead animals in volcanic tuff, no one would be surprised that humans also would be killed and their skeletons or remains of severed body parts would be preserved in the tuff.

In the meantime, this publication of Dr. Dubois will create a furore, especially in the 'Land of Intellectuals', and it appears to me that the facts must be reviewed by an impartial committee of experts, before the government should endorse such a report.

'Oh, the man is sly, very sly indeed,' Dubois asserted. 'And who is he, anyway?' Dubois glanced down at the bottom of the page, to the signature, and read it, too, aloud.

Signed,
    Homo Erectus
    Batavia 3 February 1893
(*) Hanoman is a white monkey, according to the Javanese mythology of Dhewi Handjani, that is also called Dhoyopati or Boyosoeto.
                                    Note of the editorial staff.

'Ha!' exclaimed Dubois, stabbing at the page with his index finger. 'Ha! Homo Erectus! That's a good joke. So this Homo Erectus thinks my fossil species is nothing but a monkey, does he? Nearly one thousand cc in its brain and it is a monkey, like Hanoman? Oh, ja, ja, of course. Why should the Amsterdam anatomist know anything about anatomy?' Dubois laughed ironically and then continued. 'And of course I – who studied anatomy for years, who picked the spot for the excavation, who have examined every find from Sumatra and Java – I am too foolish to understand that these three pieces are from different animals. Somehow, this Homo Erectus thinks that three different primates, all the same size, mind you, have died and been buried within a few metres of each other at Trinil. When there is only a handful of fossil primates in all of Asia, I have the good fortune to find a site with three species, one of which has left only its head, one its leg, and one its tooth.' He placed his hand on his chest, dramatically to announce, 'I am a lucky man!' Then he turned to his visitor. 'Really, Assistant Resident, I don't know whether to laugh at this fellow or be outraged. What does he know about my fossils? He hasn't looked at them, not for five minutes, that much is sure. Is *he* an anatomist? I wasn't aware of there being another in Java. He can't be a trained man of science or he wouldn't be so sceptical about Darwinism.'

Unconsciously, Dubois rested his hand on one of his specimens and stroked it gently, comfortingly, as if it were a beloved pet.

'And this person, whoever he is, is already out of date: he's read my third quarterly report, but not the fourth. I wonder what he'd make of my calling the beast *Pithecanthropus erectus* to show that it is Haeckel's missing link. I dare say he won't like that one bit.'

'Funny thing, ja?' asked the Assistant Resident, a little relieved by Dubois's relatively moderate reaction. He had feared a tidal wave of outrage, a demand for prosecution for libel, or some such. 'He's awfully scathing for not knowing anything about the subject. I expect he's one of these opinionated colonial types, thinks he knows everything because he's got a big plantation or a prosperous business. Can't say I think much of a man who hides behind an assumed name, though, d'you? It's not the behaviour of a gentleman.'

'Exactly!' agreed Dubois. 'If he's got an opinion about my bones, why doesn't he say so and come here and look at them? You know me, Assistant Resident. Have I ever denied anyone a look at my fossils who wanted to see them?'

'Certainly not,' replied the Assistant Resident. He was not the only person in East Java who had been shown the fossils at length when they hadn't the least interest in them. 'It wouldn't be fitting behaviour for a scientist to hide the fossils away, and we all know, Doctor, that you're a scientist all the way through.' He paused and then added another point. 'You know, this *Bataviaasch Nieuwsblad* is a bit of a rag, not a respectable paper. Everyone reads it, but that editor, Daum, he's always going off on some tirade or other. Why, he's already been thrown in jail once for publicly criticizing the government, and he started this paper up as soon as he got out! He's just the sort of fellow who'd publish a scurrilous, anonymous letter like this.' His face showed a good deal of righteous indignation.

Dubois appreciated the display of loyalty. Suddenly his face changed and he broke into a mischievous grin as a new thought crossed his mind. 'Ah, Assistant Resident, this is good news after all. He has drawn attention to my find, made it important. One thing is for sure: my *Pithecanthropus erectus* won't be born into the world unnoticed after this!' At that, the two men burst into good-natured laughter.

'Will you answer him in the next issue, Doctor, show him up?' asked the Assistant Resident, curious.

Dubois considered. 'No, I don't think so. I've got a lot of scientific work to do, writing my monograph. There is no point in conversing with idiots who have no interest in the facts.' He decided to ignore Homo Erectus's absurd essay and get on with his writing.

Dubois worked his way methodically through the material as best he could, relying on his personal library, his notes of the published literature, and his own thorough knowledge of anatomy. How hard was this, compared with finding the fossils in the first place? Dubois put in an official request to be sent to British India to examine Lydekker's *Anthropopithecus* specimen, but it was not granted. Apparently the army felt it had done enough for him already.

Before excavation could start up again, *P.e.* was once again thrust into the spotlight. The *Tijdschrift van het Koninklijk Nederlandsch Aardrijkskundig Genootschap* (Journal of the Royal Dutch Geographical Society) reprinted Dubois's third quarterly report in its entirety, including the name *Anthropopithecus erectus*. That was perhaps agreeable, but the action of the Society's secretary, J. A. C. A. Timmerman, was not, for Timmerman added a note that Dubois's conclusion that the Indies were the cradle of the human race had been reached 'rather hastily'.

Dubois was confounded and insulted. What did Timmerman know of Dubois's labours and expertise? Did he know that Dubois had sacrificed a fat professorship in Amsterdam to come to the Indies to find the missing link? Did he know how Dubois had laboured, fighting against uninformed opinion, sceptical colleagues and family, reluctant coolies, difficult geography, and disease itself to find the missing link? Dubois had done all that; Timmerman had done nothing. Did he know that Dubois had been looking for the missing link since 1887, nearly six years? 'Hasty'? How could Timmerman call Dubois hasty? Timmerman sat in his comfortable chair and read one tiny report about the fossils, and he had the audacity to call Dubois hasty.

The bitter taste of these attacks lingered, making Dubois uneasy and unsettled. His mood fluctuated from optimism to despair and back again. Sometimes he had high hopes for 1893: Anna was with child again; his monograph was proceeding well; there might still be more bones from Trinil. Other times the entire endeavour seemed useless, if ignorant men could discount his conclusions before they had even seen his evidence. Prentice and Boyd were of enormous help to him. Their view was that these criticisms would evaporate as soon as Dubois presented the facts, so he had to ignore them and get on with the business of writing up his fossils. Dubois leaned heavily on their friendship and good sense.

The illustrations were of paramount importance, for they showed the anatomy of the fossils. Dubois worked carefully with the camera lucida and experimented endlessly with photographing the fossils, too. When his monograph was published, he hoped, his fossils would be so exquisitely documented that no one would be able to doubt his conclusions. The words had to be correct too: systematic, well organized, clear. Under the strain of all of this work, Dubois sometimes lost heart and became short-tempered, especially when the children were noisy and boisterous. And there was soon to be a fourth! He could not imagine how the chaos of four children would ever be subdued. Babu simply had to learn to keep them quiet and happy and out from underfoot.

Dubois became obsessed with the idea that the monograph itself was as important as the fossils. This would be the official announcement of his *Pithecanthropus erectus*; this would be the publication that justified all the risks and hardships he had endured; this would establish his reputation as a top man of science. The monograph had to be of the highest scientific quality, or Dubois would fail. To have found the missing link and still to be disbelieved – ah, that would be a painful punishment indeed!

CHAPTER 24

Disaster

One of the thoughts that sustained Dubois through the first half of 1893 was the hope that Trinil would yield even more fossils of *P.e.* Kriele and De Winter started the coolies excavating there again in April. There was a renewed urgency about the work, now that success was so close, but no more fossils of *P.e.* were found.

At the beginning of May, Dubois's world was shattered like a fossil struck by a *patjol*. He received a letter from his mother telling him that his father had died, on 11 April, at the age of fifty-nine. There had been no warning, no long illness, only unexpected finality. Nothing in Dubois's life had ever been so terrible as this blow – not the disappointments, the rejections, the fevers, the critics, the empty caves, the coolies' sabotage, the loneliness. Dubois had never imagined that his father might die before he could return home in triumph. It was impossible, unfair, untrue... no, it was true. Jean Joseph Balthasar Dubois would never see his son's great gamble pay off. He would never see the name of Marie Eugène François Thomas Dubois become famous in scientific circles throughout Europe. And he would never see Jean or Victor or this new baby, Dubois's fourth, the one that grew and waited to be born.

It was too cruel a fate. Dubois's devotion to science had separated him from his father. Now, as the moment of reconciliation had come within reach, his father had died. The rift between them would never be healed.

Dubois could not work, nor could he see anyone. He sent a brief note to Prentice but left it to Anna to explain to everyone else. He did not care what she said, to whom. His thoughts were only of his terrible, terrible loss. It was a black time; he could hardly bear the presence of anyone, even his family. Of all his friends and acquaintances, Prentice was the one who knew best the ways of grieving and the road to healing. And he silently returned the kindness and sympathy that Dubois had once showed to him.

Ngrodjo, Saturday morning

Dear Doctor,

We have been examining the forest these few days. I have not called to see you as we have a visitor and I understand from your letter that you are seeking privacy. I fear you have very bad news from Europe, though I would fain hope it were otherwise.

As to Lalie Djuvo, the cottage is at your disposal whenever you wish to go there. You take the train to Sorrong.

Dog cart to Kasrie	1/50
Dog cart Kasrie to Pringen	2/50
Horse Pringen to Trettes	–/50
Horse next morning Trettes to L.D.	5/00 (sometimes only
f4/00 for horse)	

You better stay the night at Trettes, either in the big house (if it not be let) or in the school room (if the big house be let). The mandoor Sarieman at Trettes has the keys of L.D. Tell him you come from Toeloeng Agoeng, are a friend of mine & wish to stay at L.D. Ask him to get a horse, coolies & rice & etc. for you to go there & to send Pak Termoh or some other trustworthy coolie (wages 75c or f1/00 per day but better pay only 75c which is quite enough to cook & watch the house, keys, & etc.) There is also an orang djager at L.D. & if you take a boy with you then you don't require to keep Pak Termoh or another coolie, but just as you like.

Sincerely yours,

Adam Prentice

If you take a boy with you give him money & tell him how much to pay. The coolies always ask more, but do not expect it!

The next day, 5 May, Dubois journeyed up to the Lalie Djuvo plateau where the bungalow sat. It was small but comfortable, beautifully sited with a breathtaking view: remote, peaceful, silent. He could be alone there with his thoughts and his grief in this lovely place. There were no bustle, no children, no callers, no noise. The boy saw to Dubois's meals, when the Tuan Dokter wished to eat, and stayed out of the way the rest of the time. Dubois walked, rode, sometimes read, but usually he could not concentrate enough to know what words passed before his eyes. Mostly he endured. He remembered his father, the things not said and the things he had wished unsaid. It could not be done. There was no hope.

He observed the sky, the birds, the trees; he watched the sun rise and set. The sun and moon seemed to move at a pace not unlike his own; he slowly began to heal. In time, the hills and the sky reminded Dubois there was something bigger than his loss. He remembered the endless, magnificent unrolling of evolution, a twisting path that led from time immemorial to time unimaginable. And on it, he was like a small rock or tiny frond of fern, just one insignificant being in the long course of human evolution.

After five days, Prentice came up to Lalie Djuvo, ostensibly to bring Dubois more supplies. He came prepared to leave again promptly if Dubois wished to be alone, but he could see that his mute companionship and devoted friendship were welcome. He did not jar Dubois's sensibilities, did not intrude in any way. He offered only himself, his kindness, his warmth. Prentice and Dubois spent many hours together, speaking little, doing much. Physical activity was healing somehow.

On the eleventh, they decided to trek up to the peak of Gunung Ardjoena, the mountain that loomed over the plateau. They packed water, a little bread and cheese, and some fruit, and began to climb just after dawn. It was an intimidating slope, but they were young and strong and used to exertion. It was cool when they set out. They climbed higher, paralleling the course of the sun itself. There was no way to escape the baking rays; they had to be simply accepted. By late morning they had reached the summit and the world lay at their feet. They found a shady spot to rest in, sitting back to back and looking down on the vista of green and trees and jungle and more green, as far as the eye could see. Here and there, dotted against the landscape were little villages, thatched roofs visible like tufts of dried grass against the green, a curl of smoke from a fire, a few square green rice paddies outlined against the wilderness.

'How trivial humans are,' said Dubois quietly.

'Yes,' said Prentice. 'Our lives are very small compared to all this.' He gestured with a sweep of his arm. 'And yet, we are part of it, part of it all.'

'Ja,' answered Dubois after a moment. 'Ja. We are a little bit, not much, but there.'

They sat a while longer, drinking their water, eating their food, each enjoying the physical closeness of the other and the harmony of their thoughts.

'It is a hard thing,' offered Prentice in a soft voice. 'I remember what you told me, when we met: it is a hard, hard thing.' Dubois did not answer. He did not need to. 'I think,' Prentice said slowly,

'I think I will mark our presence on this occasion.' He got up and went over to a large boulder. He selected a round, fist-sized stone to use as a hammer against his pocketknife, the improvised chisel. After half an hour or so of determined hammering, the letters of his name were visible: 'Adam Prentice'. His presence was inscribed in the rock.

Prentice walked back over to Dubois, who sat silently on his own, not having moved during Prentice's labours. Prentice stopped in front of his friend, mutely offering the tools with an outstretched hand. Dubois looked up, his eyes full of his sorrows but not so blind that he failed to see the answering warmth in his friend's eyes. Dubois took the stone in his right hand, reaching up his left to grasp Prentice's own strong, brown arm for assistance in rising. The two friends walked together the few paces back to the boulder. Prentice pointed to a place above his own name, looking at Dubois with questioning eyes.

'No,' said Dubois, almost inaudibly. 'Next to yours, *with* yours, my friend, not above.' And there he carved his name upon the boulder, a monument to stand for all time. Completing his task, he stood back to look at their work, satisfied. The two men brushed their fingers over the carvings, freeing small pieces of dirt and debris, and smiled. It was done.

Later they made their way back down the mountain, jolting their knees with every step, watching for loose rocks and soil that would send them careening down the slope. They were tired but enjoyed the stretch and bend of muscles and joints, the pleasures of youth and strength. It was a slow return from the heights to mere reality, but a pleasant one. They stopped to wash the sweat from their hands and faces in a clear stream halfway down. The water was so inviting that they threw off their clothes and swam in the shallow pool. It made them feel wonderful, alive and free. They reached the bungalow at Lalie Djuvo in the afternoon, in time for a nap and a bath and the evening meal on the veranda. The stars seemed especially brilliant, the sky unusually clear that night.

Prentice stayed about a week and then went back to Mringin, while Dubois travelled home to Toeloeng Agoeng and his family. He was ready to return, ready for the warm chaos of family life, ready to engage with his fossils and monograph once again. He threw himself back into his work with renewed energy. None of the crates that had come from Kriele and De Winter held any new treasures, but Dubois was not so disappointed. He did not need anything more. He was writing this monograph for his father, for himself, for the new child that grew in Anna's womb, and for *P.e.* He made swift progress now, as if the interval away from the work had enabled his ideas to mature and ripen without his being aware of the process.

He saw a great deal of Prentice and Boyd during that year, more than ever. And sometimes as he worked alone in his study he mused about the time at Lalie Djuvo. Prentice saved my life, he thought, smiling at the memory. He saved my life.

CHAPTER 25

Letters from a Friend

Mringin, 9 July 1893

Dear Doctor,

Herewith I have much pleasure in presenting you a volume entitled 'A Popular History of Science'. I also send you an ink bottle I obtained for you at Soerabaja. I do not flatter myself that it is exactly what you wanted, but I could not get a more suitable one here.

I further send you a photograph of my child taken last month when he had completed his first year.

By this opportunity I return with thanks Mr. Opzoomer's pamphlet 'De Vrucht der Godsdienst' [The Fruit of Religion]. I have read it carefully through and to a great extent would agree with his views, but from a Darwinian standpoint of evolution I should, I think, look at the matter in a different light. Therefore much of what Opzoomer writes seems to me to be overdrawn, still to a great extent I would be happy to endorse his views.

I still have yours of Tyndall's work entitled 'New Fragments'. I have not yet finished its perusal.

With my kind regards to all your household, hoping one and all are in good health and that your work is progressing to your satisfaction. Believe me to be

Very sincerely yours,

Adam Prentice

How very thoughtful of Prentice, to send the book and to buy him the ink bottle he needed, Dubois thought. And the photo of his child! Dubois looked at it closely. He could see Prentice in the boy's face, there was no doubt of it: something about the eyes and the set of the nose. Dubois was pleased with the photo, knowing how Prentice treasured Gerard. In his response, he asked Prentice to send one of himself, as well. He was a rare friend indeed. He and Dubois corresponded every few days now, unless they saw each other, so close had they become.

The monograph was coming along nicely. Dubois felt now that

he could see the shape of the whole, which made the information fall neatly into place. His experiments with the camera lucida were producing good results – high-quality illustrations of the third molar and the thigh bone – that, accompanied by some full-sized photographs, should make for a handsome volume. Dubois had decided to write it in German, the language of science in Europe. To publish in Dutch would limit his audience too much and the English morphologists were not yet as highly regarded as the Germans. The latter's supremacy, at least, owed much to Virchow and Haeckel and their influence. Writing in German was a struggle for Dubois because every word, every sentence, had to be absolutely correct. It all took a great deal of time. Perhaps, though, he would also publish a translation of the monograph, to make it more available to the English, who were often so poorly versed in other languages.

He outlined his plans in a letter to Prentice, to see what his reaction was. His first task in the monograph was to describe the defining characteristics of his new species, *Pithecanthropus erectus* Eug. Dubois. This description had to meet strict rules of nomenclature and must be sufficiently exacting so that a trained observer, faced with another fossil, could readily decide whether it was or was not the same thing as *Pithecanthropus erectus*. He had to do nothing less than characterize, justify, and make recognizable the essence of *P.e.*, as it was known from his specimens. Then he planned to recount the history of discovery – briefly, for this was not a geological treatise but a morphological and anatomical one. The meat of the monograph would be the description and interpretation of the three fossils themselves, in minute detail, with comparisons to bones of closely related species: the human, gibbon, and chimpanzee material. Since *P.e.* lacked the huge bony crests and muscle markings of gorillas or orang-utans, these more massive ape species need not be discussed at all. And since *P.e.* was certainly not human, there was no need to examine the variations within the races of mankind. He could close with a summary of his general conclusions about the evolutionary place and importance of *P.e.*

He expected the manuscript to be completed this year, in 1893, or early 1894 at the latest. He would take it to Batavia to be printed – that would take a few weeks or even a month, he supposed – and then he would mail it to everyone of importance in Europe. That way the monograph would reach the scientific community six months or so before his return to Europe at the end of his tour of duty. He might even, he thought, undertake that trip to British India to see Lydekker's fossils before sailing for home. After all, he was already halfway around the world from Europe. He was not likely ever to be closer to India than here.

Tempoersarie, 13 July 1893

My dear Doctor,

It was with great pleasure I received this morning your very kind letter of yesterday with the excellent work by Newcomb which I shall highly prize not merely for the interesting subject matter of the book, but yet more for the sake of the giver.

I am glad you are so pleased with the photograph of my child. His name is Gerard Alexander, and he has to bear the surname of Prentice-MacLennan. The portrait was taken when he was fully 12 months old. His birthday was 21 May 1892.

So you are to return to Europe in a year's time! I earnestly trust the conditions under which you return will be such as you could hope from Government. Your visit to Calcutta will interest you, I am sure, and now you are in the East it is an opportunity that won't again occur.

I am happy the publication of your book in English will soon be accomplished. I shall be very happy indeed to be favoured with a copy and shall regard it with peculiar affection on account of the associations connected with it. That affection will be still increased if, as I hope, the work will make a name in Europe for its author.

It will perhaps surprise you to learn that I am leaving Mringin. I shall be in Toeloeng Agoeng on the fourth of August and on the morning of the fifth. I proceed with the fast train to Semarang to administer the coffee estate of 'Geboegan' at Oenarang for one year as the owner is going to Europe to see his children. His name is P. J van der Leeuw. His wife died two months ago of measles, in Europe. We all have our troubles! When the year is finished I expect another administration. Thus you see there is no chance of my going to Europe soon, but the time will yet come, I hope. As I before informed you I am interested in making an application for undeveloped land on the Yang (Besoekie) & hoped ere now to hear something about it but, although fully two years ago, no reply to the land application has yet been received. Government are however now commencing the new railway in that direction & I daresay will give out grounds there in order to make traffic for the railway. If that application is given out, and I live, I shall expect to be in an independent position after 6 or 7 years as my friends have money to plant coffee & will give me the administration and a third share – very generous, indeed! The question however is, 'Will Gov't give out the grounds or refuse them?'

I have much pleasure in sending you my portrait taken just after our marriage – in happier moments, gone for evermore! You will favour me with one of your own when you have the opportunity?

Re Semarang – At first I disliked the idea of going out there and did not decide until the 7th of this month. I am now glad however that I am going, as Mr. V/d Leeuw is a man of energy & method, and I shall have the opportunity of learning much while in charge of his estate. In answer to my telegram accepting the situation, he wrote that I had taken a load off his heart, and he could now go to Europe & remain there with an easy mind.

At present, I have stopped all reading for a time (though not without a struggle), and am working hard at Javanese as it is imperative I speak that language fluently. Afterwards, however, I shall return with ardour to those fascinating subjects that engross my thoughts.

Hoping to have the pleasure of seeing you soon.

Believe me with kind regards to Mrs. Dubois and yourself,

Yours very sincerely,
Adam Prentice

Prentice was to leave Mringin! Dubois was deeply saddened. He had all but forgotten how lonely he had been before he met Prentice and Boyd. Mringin without Prentice would not be the same. Prentice had meant so much to him, especially during those days at Lalie Djuvo. He had expected to continue seeing Prentice often until he returned to Holland, maybe even to persuade Prentice to return to Europe at the same time. Prentice was a rare man and now he, too, would be taken from Dubois, or at least placed well out of easy reach. Still, he had to think of his friend and not of his own selfish desires. He could only wish Prentice well. It was a good opportunity, taking over Van der Leeuw's plantation. Prentice had suffered such a terrible loss, with such good grace and courage; perhaps it was his turn now for success.

Dubois conceived of the idea of taking Prentice and Boyd to Trinil for a few days. It was not long before Prentice would leave for Oenerang, so they had to make plans quickly. Dubois wanted very much to share the place of his discovery with these, his closest companions, his most ardent supporters. To be sure, Trinil was no highland bungalow or pretty hill station; it was hot and dreary and conditions were primitive. But a few days there should do them no harm, and they had often expressed an interest in seeing his excavations for themselves.

Who knew? Perhaps the engineers would have a surprise for him when they got to Trinil. He had one for them, in any case. Unbeknownst to Kriele and De Winter, Dubois had recommended them for promotion to sergeant for their stalwart work. He had just heard from the governor that their promotions had been granted, so he could take their new stripes with him. That should please them. Besides, it was time to see how the coolies were behaving – or rather, to see if they were behaving any worse than usual.

Tempoersarie, 16 July 1893

My dear Doctor,

My best thanks for your warm, hearty letter. I hope to merit by the fulfilment of my duties all the good wishes you entertain regarding me and I know and feel you sincerely mean all you write. Yes, I wish a happier, a much happier future for both of us than we have experienced during the past year, and if fate has not brighter days in store for us, we have at least sounded its depths of misery, and much worse than we have had in the past year – personal bereavements, anxiety of mind, uncertainty for the future – cannot be meted out to us. I think I shall now go on progressing (in a worldly sense) until I have obtained independency, but if reverses overtake me I shall endeavour to bear them philosophically. If you have been enabled in any way to profit by me during the days we spent here together, the debt is much much larger on my side, for I have borrowed from you besides a mass of actual facts, new ideas and a broader insight into the things of the universe – acquisitions above all mere worldly wealth; and that being so, you have no thanks to give me, but rather thanks to receive *from* me.

Now those days of fellowship are drawing to a close their value is enhanced. Like so many other advantages we esteem them more fully when they have passed away & are lost to us.

I shall be happy to accompany you to Trinil on Tuesday together with Mr. Boyd.* I shall set out for Toeloeng Agoeng tomorrow afternoon & reach there tomorrow evening.

I am in haste to close as I am pressed for time.

With kind regards to Mrs. Dubois and yourself
    Believe me to be
        Sincerely yours,
        Adam Prentice.

*It is perhaps the last opportunity we shall have – the three of us – of going together in company. A.P.

The excursion to Trinil was nearly perfect. Regrettably, there were no new remains of *P.e.* from the diggings, but there were plenty of good mammal fossils and the weather was relatively cool and cooperative. The engineers, Kriele and De Winter, were most pleased with their unexpected promotions and took their stripes immediately to their tents, to sew them on to their uniforms. An hour later, Kriele, the bolder of the two, approached Dubois.

'Sorry to bother you, Doctor, when you have your guests here,' he said a little hesitantly, 'but could I ask you something?'

'Ja, Sergeant, it is no trouble. What do you wish?' Dubois answered jovially.

'De Winter and I, we wondered if you might take our photographs. We would like to have a picture to send to our families. And it is such a rare occasion to have distinguished visitors at the site, we thought you might want to celebrate a little. I have taken the liberty of asking the kokkie for an especially fine dinner tonight.' Kriele smiled, a little embarrassed at his forwardness.

'An excellent idea!' Dubois responded. 'What do you think, Boyd, Prentice?' he asked jokingly. 'Shall we take a photograph of these fine fellows?'

'Yes indeed,' Prentice answered. 'They have surely been instrumental in your success here. A portrait is certainly called for!'

'You look pretty handsome in those uniforms, boys,' teased Boyd gruffly. 'Will you send the photos to your sweethearts?'

Kriele grinned, for that was exactly what he intended to do with the photograph. De Winter, who had no sweetheart, would send it only to his mother.

Dubois and his friends inspected the excavation and the new fossils until it was time for the evening bath and dinner. To everyone's surprise, Dubois produced a bottle of wine from his luggage. He had never before been observed to drink any sort of alcohol in the field, so determined was he to set an example for the coolies. But this was a special occasion, a celebration, as Kriele had indicated, and possibly the only time he would be in Trinil with the people he cared for most.

After the Old Warrior retired to bed, Prentice and Dubois sat up late into the night talking. No other person had ever been such easy company for Dubois. He feared he had no gift for friendship, but Prentice was as true a friend as a man could wish for. In return, Prentice saw no fault in Dubois, no shortcomings, only the good, perhaps merely the reflection of his own goodness, mirrored in Dubois's eyes. Around Prentice, Dubois felt free to be himself, to be exactly what he was: brilliant, quick, impatient, with a mind so finely focused that he sometimes appeared to be deeply selfish. Yet Dubois was a good and courageous man and Prentice loved him for it.

The trip to Trinil stayed in Dubois's memory as a brief moment of peace and happiness in a dreadful year. Soon after their return, Prentice left for Oenerang, some hours away. Dubois was rather lonely and Anna seemed unwell, not herself. Dubois passed it off as an adjustment to the lack of Prentice's welcome company, but soon he realized something more serious was wrong. Anna rushed back from her bath in the *mandi* room one day, badly frightened. She was bleeding from her womb; the water was stained pink. It was not yet time for the baby to be born; she had had no contractions,

Gerardus Kriele and Anthonie de Winter posed for these photographs on 19 July 1893, in their new sergeant's stripes.

and her waters had not burst. What was going on? Concerned, Dubois examined her thoroughly. He could detect nothing wrong, except the insidious bleeding which stopped, started again, stopped over the next few hours. They both hoped for the best, but it was the worst that came.

Early on the morning of 30 August 1893, Anna went into labour and was delivered of a stillborn foetus. Dubois received the tiny, lifeless corpse into his hands. It was a girl, a miniature, perfect child with blonde hair ... a child who did not breathe or cry or open her eyes. She was dead, and there was no reason why.

Anna was hysterical with grief and pain. 'How could you bring us to this cursed place?' she accused him. 'What are we doing here in this foreign land where children die as easily as leaves drop from the trees? And you, you run away, up the mountain to your friends at Mringin, abandoning me and the children. You know how badly I feel the heat when I am with child! How could you leave me?'

They were bitter words and Dubois had no answer for them. He did not know what had gone wrong or why the little girl died, but he was filled with guilt. It was true, he had devoted more time and attention to Prentice than to Anna in recent months. But he had not thought she needed him any longer, she was so consumed by the children and their needs. There seemed to be no room for him in the family at Toeloeng Agoeng, but he was welcome and needed at Ngrodjo.

Was it his fault she had lost the child? He did not know. He searched his memory for something, some small ailment of Anna's that he might have treated, some symptom ... He found nothing, only that the child was dead. They would have named her Anna Jeanette, in honour of Anna and Dubois's late father, had she lived. Perhaps it was no one's fault. Some things were incomprehensible in the Indies, and death was chief among them. Death struck rich and poor, loved and unloved, European and Indo alike, without mercy. What might that child have been? It was a cruel question, for now she was nothing but a searing wound to the heart. Anna felt she had been torn to pieces. Dubois was overwhelmed with grief and guilt. And sometimes he asked himself, in the deepest, most private portion of his mind: Would this one have been *my* child? Was this the one who would have been like me?

CHAPTER 26

Aftermath

The Indies were a cruel country. One day little Anna Jeanette died, the next Dubois had to see to her burial, before the ghastly rot set in. Funerals could not be postponed in this climate. Anna was still confined to bed, weak and weeping inconsolably, exhausted from venting her anger at God and Dubois and anyone else who might have decreed this bitter fate.

Babu approached Dubois, eyes downcast and very serious. 'Tuan Dokter,' she said quietly, 'I am sorry but you must come. The Njonja is crying. She will not let me take the dead baby from the room. She says the little one will awaken and call for her.'

'I will come, Babu,' replied Dubois, stifling his own sorrow. When he entered his wife's bedroom, he saw the pitcher lying shattered on the floor and water everywhere. 'What is this?' he asked.

'The Njonja threw it at me,' Babu whispered. 'She shouted at me for stealing the baby.'

'Oh,' said Dubois, shaken. This was not like Anna at all. She was even worse than he had thought. 'The Njonja is ill from the baby dying. She does not know what she is doing,' he explained. It was as close to an apology as a *tuan* could offer a *babu*. Babu understood. 'You may leave us now, Babu,' Dubois said. 'Clean up the mess later.'

He went over to the bedside and sat down, taking his wife's hand in his. 'Anna,' he said softly, 'Anna.' She awakened from her exhausted sleep, opening her red and swollen eyes, her lovely hair now greasy with sweat and snot and tears.

'Does the baby need me?' she asked, confused, trying to sit up.

'No Anna, no,' he replied. 'I am sorry, Anna. The baby is dead. She could not live, I don't know why. I must take her to the cemetery and bury her today.'

'No,' Anna whimpered. 'No, please.' She clutched at his hand restlessly.

'Ja, Anna, it must be. You know it. You know how things are

here. I am so sorry, Anna, so sorry.' He wiped her face with a damp cloth. He did not like to look at her directly, for fear she would burst into bitter accusations once again.

'No, Eugène,' Anna insisted, pounding the bed with a feeble fist. 'You cannot take her! You cannot leave her in that horrible old cemetery all alone. I will not let you.'

'I must, Anna. The weather is very hot. We cannot leave her here. These things must be…taken care of. We shall put up a lovely stone for her, our little girl. We can go visit it every day if you like.'

'No!' Anna screamed wildly, trying to get out of bed and go to her child. 'You cannot take her away! She is a baby. You cannot leave her alone. She must stay with me!'

'Anna, Anna.' Dubois held her, comfortingly. 'You are very tired. We are all upset.' He settled her gently back in bed, then got up to mix a powder into a glass of water. 'Anna, I will give you a little sedative. You need to sleep. Now drink this, there's a good girl.' He helped her to sit up and swallow the potion.

'Yes, Eugène, I am tired, so tired,' she replied slowly. She looked over at the still little form, lying in a cradle on the whitest linens. 'Anna Jeanette is dead, isn't she?'

Dubois nodded slowly, carefully. 'I am so sorry, Anna. There was nothing I could do. I am very, very sorry. She must be buried today.'

'If I let you take Anna Jeanette,' Anna offered, 'you must promise me something.'

'What is it?'

Anna looked at him steadily and said, 'You will bury her across the street, in that little Javanese cemetery behind the wall. She won't be alone there; there are other children and she can hear her brothers and sister playing.'

'Anna—' Dubois started to protest. And then he thought, Why not? Who would care but Anna and himself? 'Very well, Anna, I promise. I will keep her there, near us, where she won't be alone.'

And it was done, that very day. The Javanese were confused and frightened. They did not understand why the Tuan Dokter and the Njonja did not bury their baby in their own place, with all the other European babies. Why was she here, among their people? In the end, they decided it did not matter. A dead child was a dead child, loved and mourned whoever its mother. The grave was so tiny, not much more than a foot long, surrounded with thin

Javanese bricks. Dubois ordered a piece of marble to be carved as a gravestone.

> Here rests Anna Jeanette Dubois
> Daughter of Marie Eugène François Thomas Dubois
> and Anna Geertruida Lojenga Dubois
> August 30, 1893
> + Toeloeng Agoeng
> * Toeloeng Agoeng

In keeping with local custom, the place of birth was preceded by a '+' and the place of death by a '*'.

It was many weeks before Anna recovered in mind or body. She was, for a time, perhaps a little mad. The other children were bewildered. Babu still took care of them, loved them; Kokkie still cooked for them; but Mama cried and looked sad. She would not play with them or sing to them, like before, and she would not let them out of her sight. They did not know what to do to make things better.

Dubois too was bewildered, haunted by his own grief, confused by hers. He could not forget Anna's reproaches. In his mind, he knew that babies died inexplicably in Amsterdam as well as in Toeloeng Agoeng. In his mind, he was not responsible for the child's death. In his heart, he felt that perhaps he was. He had placed his science and his intellect above his family. That had been the path of betrayal, the one that had led him away from them. Somehow that choice had caused this tragedy. He could not bear to look at Anna's tear-stained eyes and ravaged face. They did not speak very often any more.

A week later, he decided he had to take decisive action. The grave was not enough, it was too impersonal. So that he would never forget the day on which Anna Jeanette had died, Dubois wrote in his pocket calendar: 'Anna abortus.' Every time he opened it, he saw the words, like a cold, factual public decree: 'Anna abortus.' There were no words written on any other day of that week. Later, he crossed the words out, using deep strokes of his pencil as if he could alter the reality by obscuring them. It changed nothing, neither the grief nor the guilt nor the anger. The next day, to force himself to face the truth, he wrote it again: 'Anna abortus.'

He laboured on, working on his monograph when he could concentrate. His father and child both lay dead in the ground, but he had resurrected *P.e.*, dead these many, many years. It seemed a hollow exchange. Sometimes he thought his work was very trivial, not worth the cost. But they might both have died anyway, and his soul too, had he stayed in Amsterdam. All he could do was turn to science, increase his devotion to the truth. He redoubled his efforts, like a nun saying extra novenas for the dead. He had to do even better now. He would continue to place science above everything, for the truths he discovered would last for ever, and people only died and left him alone.

He practised science as a priest practises religion. If he had been religious, he would have said his life was dedicated to the glory of God, as his sister Marie had said when she had joined the convent so many years ago. He searched for truth, for the essence of things. However burdened his heart was, it was his duty to carry on with his scientific work. In truth, there would be peace, there would be rest. There was none anywhere else.

CHAPTER 27

Perseverance

Dubois was deeply alone.

His father was dead. There was an awful finality about it. His father had never given his approval of Dubois's aims and never would. His mother, thinking to comfort her son, wrote that she was saying extra prayers and lighting candles for Dubois's soul. He presumed she prayed to lessen his punishment for the sins of pride and of failing to honour his father. Dubois could not decide which gave him greater pain: his mother's well-meaning violation of his deepest convictions, or his feeling of abandonment at his father's death. The child he would have named in his father's memory was dead too, a chapter closed before its first words had been written. Anna was dead to him now, too, of course. The youthful affection and goodwill that had fuelled the early days of this marriage of opposites had been expended. Whatever deeper ties grew in their place had withered under the parching burden of grief. The loss of this child had left between Anna and Dubois only a barren wasteland where nothing could grow.

Even Prentice was lost to Dubois. In this time of despair, letters were not enough. He needed his friend's presence, his solidity and sympathy. But Dubois could not travel as far as Oenarang now. It was his duty, and he always honoured his duty, to stay at home with the grieving stranger to whom he was married. He could not even go up to Ngrodjo, to seek solace from Boyd. Every time he conceived of going, Anna's angry words echoed in his mind: 'You run away, up the mountain…' and he knew he could not go.

Anna did not think of Dubois's state; she only wondered if she would survive this trial. Little Anna's death was the embodiment of a mother's greatest fear in the Indies. Anna supposed she had to survive, for who would look after the other children if she did not? But it was a long time before she laughed or sang again. She got out of bed in the morning as an act of sheer courage. She bathed and dressed properly when she was able to, which was not always. She walked across the road to sit by the pathetic little grave in the

Javanese cemetery for hours, one hand resting on the gravestone, turning into a stone herself. She did not know whether she wept or not, the difference between the two states being so trivial. Sometimes Dubois thought he heard her talking to the dead child, or even crooning a soft lullaby, but he did not dare go over to see what she was doing. What could he do for her? What comfort could he offer, what apology? There was none.

The Javanese who came to leave offerings at their own families' graves were a little frightened of Anna at first. This strange, pale *njonja* had no business being in their cemetery. And they could see that her soul was in danger of quitting her body. She did not speak to them; she might not even see them. They took care not to come to her notice.

Dubois had a bed made up in his study and started to sleep there every night. He told the servants it was so he would not disturb Anna, who needed rest to recover from the after-effects of the birth. No one was fooled, not even the children. It was just one more way in which he withdrew from Anna and retreated into his work. He restricted his world for a time to the two rooms, his study and what had been formerly the gentlemen's sitting room, coming out mostly to take meals. Yet the work seemed sterile. He waited for more crates of fossils to come from Kriele and De Winter at Trinil and received only complaints of cold, of sickness, bellyaches. Before the baby's death, he had had notes from Kriele and De Winter, both complaining. Kriele's had been written first.

Trinil, 8 August 1893

A very friendly request to separate me as soon as possible from De Winter; since we have had yesterday such a dreadful conflict.

De Winter's was next:

25 August 1893

The Resident from Solo has not been able to give me prisoners, as he is afraid they will run away here, and besides there are so few prisoners in Solo. Now they provide me with 10 free-men, without payment, who will be picked up with the supplies today. In my view this work can never go right with those free-people without payment, for every morning those people must come from different desas or villages, and every day others, and besides to order those people or to instruct or to keep them working the whole day just like prisoners will be difficult. I will try to work with the free-people and will send you later a message about that.

On 3 September, De Winter wrote again and things were no better.

Regarding the free people, their work leaves much to be desired. You can imagine yourself that those people come to work from villages hours away in the neighbourhood, and thus they find it impossible to be with me in the morning. When I want to start, around 7 o'clock in the morning, there is as usual no one, for example; someone comes at 7 o'clock, two at half past 7, three at 9 o'clock, etc: then at 11 o'clock I let them go to their homes to eat, and I tell them that they must be back at 1 o'clock, but then at 3 o'clock there is still no one. You will see how difficult this is.

The engineers would have to work out their difficulties without intervention from Dubois. He carried on with the tedious work of cleaning and examining specimens, on good days finding something he believed was a new species. Then he often made notes for an article about the species. He was proud that his was an outstanding collection of Javan fossil animals, even if they were so far mostly stored on his veranda. They were mute, beautiful in their dusty way. The fossils did not accuse him of wrongdoing, of neglect. They only spoke to him passionately of the past, of their adaptations and ways of living and ways of dying. The fossils were very forgiving. They were his most constant companions now.

He knew he should be working on his monograph, but it was hard to keep focused on the work when there were so many tangled emotions to obscure the facts. Sometimes he simply set that project aside, telling himself he would complete it once the dry season's excavations at Trinil were finished. More fossils of *P.e.* might turn up at any time, after all, and they would need to be incorporated into the work.

Other, less sensitive projects helped fill his time and distracted him from his problems. Last year, in 1892, he had published an article about ancient climates and environments in the *Natuurkundig Tijdschrift voor Nederlandsch-Indië* (Journal of the Natural Sciences of the Netherlands Indies). Now he expanded the work, elaborating his ideas, and submitted it as a small book to a publisher in Nijmegen. Checking and correcting the proofs in the last few weeks before publication was relatively mindless work, which he finished during the worst of his despair. There was something numbingly abstract, soothingly unemotional about looking over the pages, altering a word here or correcting a misspelling there. He also worked halfheartedly on the English translation, for Swan Sonnenschein & Co. had expressed interest in *The Climates of the Geological Past and Their Relation to the Evolution of the Sun*.

At the end of September, there was a letter from Prentice.

Geboegan, Oenarang, 27 September 1893

My dear Doctor,

How has time been dealing with you lately? With me it has been far from agreeable. You know how comfortable I was in a sense at Mringin and on what a friendly footing I stood with my employer Mr. Boyd, our mutual friend? Well, here everything turned out exactly the reverse. During the past 7 weeks I have had nothing but very hard work and little or no friendship. My master has been in very bad health and worse temper. My working hours have been from 4 a.m. till 6 p.m. I have never had a pleasant meal here till today. We did not eat our food, we merely gulped it down, & never, or hardly ever, was a word spoken at table. Mr. Boyd can tell you how he found it when he brought me here. Very few people could have stood it out, and many and many a time did I regret much ever having left the friendly shelter of Mringin for the inhospitable surroundings of Geboegan. Yesterday however I did get some relief as my chief left for Semarang and does not return here. On 3rd October I go down to Semarang to see him away. He sails for Europe per S. S. Gedeh on 5 October.

So far for myself and how is it with you and yours at Toeloeng Agoeng, and how is your work progressing at Trinil? I have often looked back with pleasure to the excursion we made there together, & to our bathing in the river & etc. & etc. Have you found anything further of the missing link or other interesting fossils? Are you going to Calcutta at the end of the year, or what plans have you got?

Needless to say I have read nothing since my arrival here – reading has been altogether out of the question, the matter of the precise colour and form of coffee beans, and the cost of cleaning 100 coffee trees, are of more importance to those here than the highest scientific investigation or discoveries. My time is all taken up in work, work, work.

It is warmer here than at Mringin. The parcel indeed runs up to 4000 feet, but the house is situated at 1200 feet elevation and has a large zinc roof.

How has your book on climates been received in Europe? (I have drank nothing [sic] since coming here.)

With best wishes to yourself and family, hoping you are well, & trusting to hear from you soon.
        Believe me to be,
            Sincerely yours,
            Adam Prentice

Ah, Prentice too was unhappy, isolated. Dubois would not have wished these feelings on his dearest friend. If only Van de Leeuw had been a genial man, a good man, like Boyd: it was too much to expect, Dubois supposed. How he wished he could join Prentice for a few days or a week, as Prentice had joined him at the house at Lalie Djuvo, when they had read and walked and ridden and climbed Gunung Ardjoena together. They would not have another such time for healing and companionship. It had been a luxury not to be repeated. Still, he would write and try to tell Prentice of little Anna's death and his wife's suffering, and his own.

With the dry season coming to an end, Dubois made a very short trip to Trinil to inspect the site one last time. No more fossils of *P.e.* had been forthcoming, though the rhinos and elephants and tigers and buffalo continued selflessly to donate their bones to his Indies museum. He did not believe that there was more of *P.e.* to be found at Trinil; the thing was done, over. He decided to erect a monu-

Dubois designed a monument, which was erected at Trinil on
5 September 1894, to mark permanently the location of the site.

ment at the site, something permanent. He designed a cement marker and told Kriele and De Winter to place it on the high bluff opposite the site itself in 1894. Attached to it would be a bronze plaque. In Dutch it read:

P.e.

◄— 175m ONO —►

1891/1893

There it stood, for all time: *P.e.* had been found, 175 metres east-north-east of *here*, with an arrow pointing to the bend in the river where the fossils had been found, between 1891 and 1893. Neither Dubois's name nor his initials appeared anywhere on the marker. This fact puzzled some later scientists: why had he not laid open claim to his wonderful find? But to think that was to misunderstand the purpose of the plinth. It was not a monument to vanity. It was not there to honour Marie Eugène François Thomas Dubois or to speak of the prospects he left in Amsterdam, the families grieved and separated, the bouts of malaria, and the deaths of his father and daughter. This was an eternal witness to the missing link, missing no longer: to *P.e.*

CHAPTER 28

The Monograph

The monograph was a different sort of monument to the work. The pages began to pile up now, taking their final form and needing no further revisions. The illustrations were done, and they were handsome. Dubois was proud of them. There would be both photographs and camera lucida drawings of the bones; tables of measurements and comparisons with the ape skulls; and a few diagrams.

The text began with a description of the geographic location of the find-spot along the Bengawan Solo and a brief mention of the important Pleistocene mammals excavated there. But the monograph was not the place for detailed descriptions or analyses of the fauna; those would come in later, more focused publications. He described the general geological setting and explained that the tooth and skullcap had been found within about one metre of each other, the femur being some fifteen metres farther upstream from those two but in the same layer. He had a great deal more information about the site itself and the plan of digging, but those details did not belong here. This monograph concerned the morphology of *P.e.*, not the geology of Java.

Dubois struggled to make clear the relationship among the three fossils of *P.e.*, to forestall specious arguments like those that had been raised by that fool who called himself Homo Erectus. Dubois wrote simply, 'It would be foolish to doubt the three relics belong together on the basis of this slight distance between their locations.' He used the German word *thöricht* for 'foolish'. The choice would come back to haunt him.

He offered the following evidence in support of his conclusion. First, the incomplete condition of the skeleton of *P.e.* was unremarkable, for no complete skeleton of any animal had been found throughout the entire excavation, although thousands of fossils had been recovered. Another proof was the condition of other species, in which skeletal elements from a single individual had been found separated by as much as twenty or thirty metres. Finally, since no other specimen had been found in all of Java that could possibly represent *P.e.* – with the possible exception of the very fragmentary jaw from Kedoeng Broebus – it seemed obvious that these three bones, buried so close to one another in the same sedimentary layer on the same point bar, were from one individual.

This introduction set the stage for the anatomical and morphological description of the fossils. Dubois began with the skullcap, undoubtedly the most important and impressive specimen. The outside of the skullcap was now completely clean of matrix, but some of the interior was still obscured with sediment. It was too dangerous to proceed further in cleaning the specimen without better conditions and tools. Nor could he measure the volume of the skullcap directly, either by pouring in seeds or water, as was commonly done. But the volume was obviously large and obviously important, so Dubois used the method he had invented in his third quarterly report of 1892 to estimate the volume of the skullcap from its linear measurements. It did not seem so difficult to him, with his talents in mathematics.

Clearly the volume that was enclosed by a shape was determined by the dimensions of that shape, whether it was a skullcap, a sphere, or a box. Because the skullcap of *P.e.* most closely resembled a chimpanzee's, Dubois first used the chimpanzee as a standard of comparison. The total external length of the skullcap of *P.e.* was 185 mm, 1.33 times the recorded length of Bischoff's chimpanzee skull. Similarly, the total breadth of the skullcap of *P.e.* was about 1.33 times greater than that of Bischoff's chimpanzee. All other things being equal, this implied that the volume of the skullcap was $1.33^3 \times 410$, the volume of Bischoff's chimpanzee skull, or 2.35×410, which equalled 963.5 cc.

The problem with this estimate was that 'all other things' were not equal, for the skullcap of *P.e.* had a much higher vault than that of a chimpanzee. How much difference did vault height make to skull volume? Dubois investigated the question by comparing the measurements of male and female chimpanzee skulls, and found that a higher vault increased the capacity of the braincase by at least one-seventh of the total. Adjusting his calculations for *P.e.* accordingly, Dubois arrived at a minimum volume estimate of 984 cc. When he repeated these calculations using a gibbon rather than a chimpanzee as the standard, the result was 991 cc. The two estimates were gratifyingly similar. There could be no doubt that the braincase of *P.e.* enclosed a volume close to 1000 cc, as big as the brains of some human races. No chimpanzee or gibbon had a cranial capacity approaching this value; the chimpanzee Dubois had in his possession, thanks to Weber, contained 365 cc; two gibbon skulls in his collection, both male, contained 135 and 140 cc, while a third – of a different species of gibbon – was 133 cc. Braincase volumes reported in the literature for other apes fell far short, never ranging higher than 465 cc, measured by Bischoff for a male gorilla. Thus for Dubois the truly impressive size of the braincase of *P.e.* was a strong link to humans, an indication that *P.e.* was well along the journey toward humanity, while yet not having arrived at its evolutionary destination.

Because its braincase was so large, Dubois suggested that the missing face of *P.e.* must also have been more human than apelike. And other aspects of the skullcap were reminiscent of human crania. The browridges over the bony orbits resembled those on the fossil Neanderthal skulls from Europe. Dubois, like Huxley, considered the Neanderthals to be a low and primitive race of human, so he did not compare *P.e.* with them in any detail. His interest was in placing *P.e.* along the continuum that linked apes and humans, not in ordering it within the range of human races. Besides, he did not have casts of the Neanderthal skulls to work with and he decided not even to attempt to procure them. It would take much too long and the comparison was irrelevant.

There was Virchow's vehement and influential opposition to Neanderthals to be considered, too. In his monograph, Dubois remarked that the Neanderthal skulls were perhaps deformed; their femurs certainly were, for the femur of *P.e.* was much more humanlike than the thigh bones of Neanderthals. There was no point in comparing a normal specimen with a diseased one, and *P.e.*'s femur was normal, except for that lump of pathological bone where an injury had healed.

While the skullcap had humanlike features, notably its size and volume and the remarkable height of its vault, it still also resembled a chimpanzee skull. Part of the resemblance could be attributed to the shape of the back of the skullcap. Partway down the posterior profile of the skullcap was a distinct protuberance called by anatomists the occipital torus. Below the torus, the skull slanted steeply inward, a combination of features common in gibbons and young chimpanzees. The torus and change of profile might be exaggerated in *P.e.*, Dubois suggested, because the species had had an upright posture (attested to by the shape of the femur). This humanlike posture placed the skull of *P.e.* atop its spine like

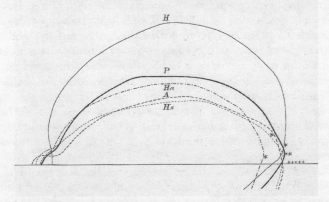

Dubois compared the skull profiles of (P) *Pithecanthropus*, (H) a modern human, (Ha) an agile gibbon, (A) a chimpanzee, and (Hs) a siamang, another type of gibbon. The human skull is the largest, but *Pithecanthropus*'s skull vault is bigger than the apes'.

an apple balancing on a pencil, a most un-apelike position for a rather apelike skull to be in.

Dubois also noted that the sutures between the different bones of the skullcap were so completely fused that they were no longer readily visible. This was a sign of physical maturity, even perhaps of old age. Moreover, the general gracility of the skullcap and the striking lack of bony crests suggested that this individual *P.e.* had probably been female. It was strangely satisfying to be able to deduce such fine details of his missing link's life!

When he arrived at this point in the writing, Dubois felt that he had accomplished a great deal. Describing the skull and presenting his subtle views of its mixed ape and human features were difficult. He strove always for clarity, for precision, for irrefutable logic. It was concentrated work and complex, sapping his fragile strength while it grounded him anew in his work.

One of Dubois's last cogent thoughts before he sank yet again into a malarial fever was that Anna seemed somewhat better and the children less fractious. When he emerged once again to consciousness, he found that Prentice had called at Toeloeng Agoeng. Prentice! And he had left again, without seeing Dubois, who lay sweating and delirious in his bed, not a hundred feet away. What a precious chance had been lost.

'He is a very nice man, your friend Prentice,' Anna said, smiling at the memory of the visit. 'He stayed all afternoon. He was so sympathetic and understanding about the loss of our daughter, he quite eased my pain with his kind way and gentle conversation. Too bad that you were too ill to see him. I know he was sorry to miss you. If only he were still at Mringin, as in the old days, we might see him more often.'

Dubois felt a stab of jealousy. It seemed grossly unfair that Anna had seen Prentice and he had not, that Anna had had the benefit of Prentice's kindness and he had not. He had to have some relief, some comfort.

Boyd's daughter, Anna Grace, was about to be married, to M. G. de Witte, a man in the sugar trade. They planned to settle in Blitar afterwards, near the sugar mill. The wedding itself was to be held in October, in Toeloeng Agoeng, with an enormous colonial party up at Mringin to follow. Dubois and Anna had of course planned to attend the wedding, but now Dubois proposed that they travel up to Ngrodjo early and stayed on for the celebration afterwards. Normally this was the sort of event Dubois detested, with far too much drink and far too many people behaving idiotically, but on this occasion it sounded more like a welcome escape. Most of the guests would drink and dance and flirt all night, then sleep late into the day before starting in again on picnics and excursions and games. As long as the servants continued to clean up the messes and produced more food and drink at frequent intervals, the party would bounce raucously along with little help from the host. Dubois was counting on that to enable him to steal some quiet time with Boyd. They could go off on horseback to inspect the coffee or something, just to get away from the party.

Anna hesitated at first, for attending would mean abandoning her daily vigil at little Anna's grave. But she agreed nonetheless. She had always enjoyed parties and the prospect of music and conversation and maybe a few handsome men to flirt with seemed to lift her black mood.

Before they set off, Dubois wrote to Prentice. When they returned from Mringin, the reply from his faithful friend was waiting for him.

Oenarang, 31 October 1893

Dear Doctor,

I was sorry not to have met you during my brief visit to Ngrodjo, but owing to your fever and my work outside examining ground we missed each other.

I hope however your general health is good and trust you will yet pay me a visit here ere going to Calcutta. It is rather a long way, to be sure, yet I hope time and circumstances will permit you to come to Geboegan. My own visit to Ngrodjo was wholly unexpected, or I should have advised you beforehand. I was suddenly called to Pasoerean on business of my father-in-law's, &, being in East Java, took advantage of the opportunity to call both at Malang and at Toeloeng Agoeng. My child enjoys perfect health and seems to me to be growing wonderfully. He can walk about the room already and understands whatever is said to him but can't speak yet, or won't speak. He is now 17 (seventeen) months of age.

What news have you now about your climate book? The critics have had time to peruse its pages. What opinions do they express respecting it? I trust it has been well received and has enhanced your reputation. Have you had it printed in English or not?

With my kindest regards to Mrs. Dubois and the family, trusting you are yet at Mringin enjoying a cool climate and open air bathing.

Believe me to be
    Sincerely yours,
    Adam Prentice

CHAPTER 29

Writing Up

The days at Ngrodjo gave Dubois a little peace to add to his small store. He was able to resume work on his monograph in November. The introduction was completed, and the section on the skullcap. The next section had to describe the molar tooth.

There was not much to say. In some aspects the tooth seemed humanlike; in others – especially in the wrinkling and folding of the shiny enamel – apelike. There was nothing remarkable about it and it showed little wear. Dubois had to admit that the tooth by itself could not be firmly identified. It was certainly from a higher primate, but nothing ruled out its belonging to a chimpanzee or an orang-utan or a human. Still, the tooth was clearly from an adult, a fact consistent with its belonging to the same individual as the skullcap and femur that had been found so close by.

The femur was another story entirely. In all its principal features, the thigh bone was human. Its size and shape would not have seemed out of place in the anatomy laboratory, though it was twice as heavy as a modern femur of similar size on account of being fossilized. And the shaft itself, so straight and strong, was appropriately angled to pass the body weight from the joint at the hip in toward midline to reach the knee, as in Man. The ball of the femur, where it met the hip bone, and the condyles, where it met the upper end of the tibia at the knee, were thoroughly human. In all its mechanical details, this femur was functionally identical to that of any modern, upright-walking human. With a bone like this, so thoroughly different from the thigh bone of apes, *P.e.* must have walked like a man.

Only in small details, like the somewhat poorly developed ridges where various muscles attached to the bone, was the femur somewhat more apelike than humanlike. Dubois did not want these differences to be overlooked:

The points suffice, however – as I would emphatically point out – to separate the species in question from Man, who always shows differences in this respect. On these points, minor ones from a mechanical point of view, the femur resembles that of the anthropoid apes.

Then there was the pathology on the femur to deal with. As a physician, Dubois had seen such growths – exostoses – before. It had to be the result of a ghastly wound to the thigh. How exactly had *P.e.* been injured? It was not an easy question to answer. The most likely alternatives, to Dubois's fertile mind, involved weapons or tools, perhaps a wooden arrow or the tip of a lance driven deep, penetrating the muscle and the bone of the thigh. This scenario implied that *P.e.* had used and made tools, which Dubois believed likely but, on available evidence, unprovable. In any case, the wound had occurred and had bled copiously. The huge, irregular clot that resulted had eventually ossified, turning into the strangely sculptured excrescence visible now on the femur. Ossification, though, was not a rapid process. How had an individual so badly wounded survived long enough for healing to occur? Had someone taken care of her? Who?

These questions were too theoretical and emotional for Dubois's taste. He moved on, instead, to deal with more concrete matters. He called the femur the 'pillar, girder, and siphon' of the body; it was the main support of the body weight, the main lever that thrust the body forward into movement. Thus the substantial size of the bone was very revealing. His first impulse, upon receiving the femur from Kriele and De Winter, had been to hold it in front of his own, for comparison. *P.e.*'s thigh bone was very nearly as long as Dubois's: a remarkable fact. A femur this size could have supported – was built to support – a large man. No one had ever before tried to determine the stature of an individual from the length of his femur, but it did not take Dubois long to work out a rough estimate. With a femur as long as this one, *P.e.* must have stood perhaps 1.7 metres (5 feet 7 inches) high, only a few inches shorter than Dubois himself.

For a creature of this size to move by swinging from its arms through the trees, like a gibbon, seemed ridiculous, especially with a femur shaped for upright walking as this one was. Even the angle of the shaft from condyle to hip joint was much closer to a human's than an ape's. Dubois measured the angle of the femur of *P.e.* as 125 degrees from the horizontal plane of the knee; he cited published reports on human femurs ranging from 112 to 135 degrees, while ape femurs were nearly vertical (180 degrees) in orientation.

Moreover, the torsion on the shaft of the femur indicated that the ape-man walked flat-footed, not on the outer edge of the foot like an orang-utan or a chimpanzee.

How long ago had this surprising creature attained such height? There was no precise means of dating the fossils or the beds from which they were extracted. The Siwalik fauna from India was considered to be Miocene, for it contained very archaic animals and none that survive today. Such faunas had to be older than the Trinil fauna, for the mammals at Trinil were not so archaic and even included a few species, like the gaur (a type of wild cattle), that still existed. Thus both the higher primates – *Anthropopithecus* from the Siwaliks and *Pithecanthropus* from Trinil – and the other mammals suggested the Javan fossils were more recent than the Siwalik ones. How recent? If the Siwalik fauna was late Miocene, Dubois guessed that the Trinil fossils came from the subsequent Pliocene period or perhaps even later still, from the early Pleistocene.

As for the place of *Pithecanthropus* along the evolutionary road from ape to human, Dubois had no doubt: it was an intermediate. 'An Anthropopithekos has become a Pithekanthropos... *Pithecanthropus erectus* is the transitional form which, according to the theory of evolution, must have existed between Man and the anthropoid apes: he is Man's ancestor.'

By its anatomy, *P.e.* demonstrated the proof of the proposition put forward by Darwin and the French scholar Lamarck. Clearly the femur, with its almost completely humanlike form, showed that upright walking evolved first, while the skullcap attested to the later development of the large brain that characterized humans.

If *Anthropopithecus* had evolved into *Pithecanthropus*, had *P.e.* in turn evolved into Man? It was a weighty question. Dubois believed she might have, although the evolution must have happened rapidly. By the time of the great ice ages, in the early Pleistocene, true but primitive humans like Neanderthals already inhabited Europe and survived by hunting new species such as the reindeer, horse, woolly rhino, and so on. Thus the preceding era, during which these new forms had evolved, must have been a time of rapidly changing conditions. Many archaic mammals had become extinct and a few new ones had arisen and evolved rapidly, like the clever and upright ape-man that was ancestral to man. As its brain and body improved, its selective advantages became ever greater. Man's ancestors had experienced a period of accelerating change, evolving *per saltum*, by leaps. Evolution, Dubois became convinced, was not a matter of *gradual* changes.

Ah, and what about the other apes? Where had they evolved from? Dubois sighed and thought again. He had to work out the answer to that problem separately. He tried to construct from the scant fossil record of ape evolution a series of evolutionary steps that seemed logical. Gibbons were the only living apes to regularly walk upright, although of course this was neither their habitual means of locomotion nor the gait to which they were most strongly adapted. Still – Dubois nodded to himself – it had to be taken into account; this fact was a clue to the past history of apes. If a gibbonlike form was ancestral to all of the apes, it could have imparted to its descendants some of the features of tooth and skull that were seen in *Anthropopithecus* and *Pithecanthropus*, as well as a limited ability to walk upright. But *Anthropopithecus* was a chimpanzee, an ape, and *Pithecanthropus* was just as clearly neither ape nor man. Perhaps *Anthropopithecus* had been the progenitor of both lineages: the dividing point, from which some descendants had evolved into apes and others into *P.e.* and humans. That would account for the gibbonlike features found in all three. Nothing was known of the ancestor of the Siwalik *Anthropopithecus* so, following Haeckel's lead, Dubois proposed it had been a gibbonlike form and named it *Prothylobates*, meaning 'forerunner of the gibbon *Hylobates*'.

The final question was to what zoological family *P.e.* belonged. Dubois could not justify putting the ape-man into the human family, the Hominidae, not with that apelike molar and ape-shaped skull. Nor could he accept that *P.e.* was simply an ape, an ancient member of the Simiidae. How could an ape have had a femur that so closely resembled a human's? What ape had a skull that housed nearly a thousand cubic centimetres of brain? No, *P.e.* was not an ape, either. There was only one logical place for *P.e.*

Although already quite advanced in the development of the human type... this Pleistocene form had not yet reached it. – It occupied a position between this type and the type of the great apes... Considering all these circumstances I feel compelled to place the species in a new genus – *Pithecanthropus* – but also in a new family – Pithecanthropidae – between the Hominidae and the Simiidae...

Dubois knew this bold move might cause a furore – not many men have had the opportunity to name a new species, much less to create a new genus and recognize a whole new family of mammals – but he believed the decision to be honest and correct. *P.e.* was neither ape nor human. It was so distinctive as to warrant a unique taxonomic position. He had found something totally new, and his classification had to reflect that. If the world was surprised ... well, let it be surprised. He had the fossils to prove his contention.

It was late in 1893 when he finished the manuscript. He had been as handicapped by Prentice's absence as by the lack of comparative osteological samples, but he had finished his work on his own and he was proud. Completing it gave him a feeling of peace and satisfaction that nothing else had ever offered. He had found it – found his missing link – and proved Darwin's theory correct when everyone around him had said the project was impossible and mad.

CHAPTER 30

Separation and Loss

Dubois was pleased with life again, happy to be able to tell Prentice in his Christmas letter that he would take the manuscript to Batavia to be printed in the new year. He would lengthen his trip, making a detour through Semarang on the way back if Prentice could come there to see him. It would let him share with his friend the satisfaction of having finished his job, even if they could only meet for a few hours.

As this awful year, punctuated by tragedies, came to a close, Anna seemed to improve, become more like her old self. Yet a shadow flickered in her eyes from time to time, attesting to a wound that would never heal completely. Once she had sat for hours on the back veranda after dinner, embroidering and listening to the night sounds while Dubois read. Now a new, disquieting sound invaded the night-time peace of their garden. It was a dreadful call, an unearthly groaning sound full of suffering. They had never heard its like before. As its first anguished notes split the night, Anna shivered despite the heat and gathered up her things and went to her room. She could not bear to be outside in the night with whatever it was that cried so pitifully.

Her *babu*, who had been squatting on the veranda a discreet distance away, arose and followed close behind her. 'Ah, Njonja,' said Babu approvingly, 'better to go in. Do not listen to pontianaks.'

'What do you mean, Babu?' Anna asked sharply. 'What is that noise?'

'Njonja, it is pontianaks, female demons, because of the death of the baby. Her soul is crying, up in the trees. You hear it; you know. But do not listen. Pontianaks only bring disaster and doom.'

The wailing started up again, penetrating even to the interior of the house. Anna began to cry and shake, whether from fear or sorrow she did not know. The call pierced her body, bringing forth an echoing cry of loss from her very marrow, a cry that no one else could hear. It was as if her dead baby was being wrenched from her body over and over again.

'Will they go away, Babu?' she pleaded helplessly. 'Will they always be there now?'

'Ah,' replied Babu evasively, 'no one can know. Mungkin, mungkin tidak.' She made a Javanese gesture of ambiguity with her eyebrows. The *njonja* did not seem to understand, so she repeated herself, using English this time. 'Perhaps yes; perhaps no.'

'Is there nothing we can do?' begged Anna. She knew she would die if this torture continued every night. Life in such pain could not be possible.

'If the Tuan Dokter gives a sedaka, an offering, to the pontianaks,' Babu suggested hesitantly. 'Perhaps then they go.'

In her state of agitation, Anna thought Dubois on the veranda was oblivious. She was mistaken. The terrible, anguished cry seemed to claw at his soul. As a matter of principle, he tried to ignore it, to explain it away. With the onset of each wail, his jaw clenched and his spine stiffened, as if he was physically resisting its power. He exerted a tremendous effort of will to concentrate on his book. He was a man of great fortitude and he would not be driven from his own veranda. *Recte et fortiter*, *Recte et fortiter*: he repeated the family motto to himself like a prayer. But no European prayer could banish this Javanese thing that screamed in the night.

Anna decided she could not go back out on the veranda to speak to Eugène. What was there to say, anyway? 'Do you hear that sound, the moaning of our dead daughter's soul in torment?' It was not the sort of question one asked Dr Dubois, even if one was his wife. Anna went to her room and tried to sleep with the doors and windows closed and a pillow over her head. It was stifling, airless, and still the cry sliced through her flimsy defences like a tiger's claws ripping through a mosquito net. She dozed briefly, to awake with a start, covered in sweat, her heart pounding in fear, her body curled in a self-protective foetal position. She did not know what to do or to believe. All that she knew was that her baby lay across the road in a shallow grave and some... *being*... in the garden was expressing her anguish.

In the morning, Anna told Dubois what Babu had said about the noise. He did not want to believe it. 'This is superstitious nonsense, Anna, just the silly tales of an uneducated babu,' he blustered to cover his own unease. It had taken a lot of willpower, a lot of his sheer Dutchness, to stay out on the veranda the night before after Anna had gone to bed, pretending not to notice the awful cries.

She turned her face away, so tired and anxious that she looked as if she had been physically pummeled. She did not argue with him; she had never argued with him. She did not expect sympathy but hoped for it. 'Babu says,' she remarked quietly, 'that perhaps if we got a dukun in, a native priest, to hold a special ceremony, the pontianaks would go away.' She could not bring herself to beg him openly but the tone of her voice was enough.

'Anna,' he said more tenderly, 'Anna. It will probably be gone tonight. It was just some animal, maybe a civet cat in heat. You will never hear it again.'

But it was not gone, whatever it might be. That night it repeated its heart-rending moans and wails, and the night after, and the night after that, until Dubois stopped counting. The question was not 'Will it cry tonight?' but only 'When will it begin?' The expectation, the waiting, was as demoralizing as the sound itself. Anna no longer sat with him in the evenings at all, though she could not escape the cries and she could not sleep once they had started. The only time she could rest was in the afternoons, when *it* was silent, and even then she had terrible dreams.

Dubois determined to hold his ground on the veranda. No one could tell him what made the noise, nor could he imagine a creature that could produce a sound of such longing and misery. But he realized that he had to do something, soon. Anna was deteriorating again, losing contact with reality, growing pale and fretful from lack of sleep. She never asked him again about getting in a *dukun* to perform a ceremony, but he could see the question in her frightened eyes, day after day.

Finally he gave in and asked the *djongas* Nassi to arrange it. There was a palpable air of relaxation in the household, as if all the inhabitants had been holding their breaths, hoping and praying for the Tuan Dokter to see sense. The servants knew well that the Dutch did not always – did not often – understand the importance of such things. It was a peculiarity of the Dutch – perhaps a failure in their upbringing? – that they were so often blind to the spirit world. This trait did not mean they were exempt from its punishments: see how many of them died, babies and strong young men alike! See how often their plantations and businesses collapsed in financial ruin! And no wonder. No Javanese would go through life without taking steps to protect against disaster. Still, it was difficult always to foresee what would be the right amulets, offerings, or ceremonies. Even a careful Javanese made mistakes.

The next day, an old, old man came to the garden. He was nearly toothless, his back bent into a C, his hair thin. There seemed to be no flesh on him at all, just a nearly transparent covering of tissue-thin, brown, wrinkled skin. He walked painfully, with a stilted, shuffling gait, as if his knees and ankles could not be trusted to change their position without breaking. Dubois thought he had never seen such an old man before in his life. What could his age be? Ninety? One hundred? More? Could this ancient wreck of a man have seen the decline and fall of the VOC, the Vereenigde Oost-Indische Companie or Dutch East India Company, at the close of the eighteenth century? However old the *dukun* might be, the servants treated him with the greatest respect – as if he were the Pope himself, Dubois thought ironically. Yet, for all his decrepitude, the old man had a certain presence that even Dubois could feel; there was a power about him, a strength that had nothing to do with his pitiful physical condition.

Dubois watched out of the window but could not see most of what the man did. For a long time, he seemed to wander aimlessly through the garden, mumbling and muttering in a high-pitched falsetto, scattering something – herbs? dried remains of something – here and there. Sometimes he lit small fires and added to them something that he had brought with him, carefully folded in a fragment of beautifully batiked cloth. Whatever it was made the fires

The djongas, Nassi, arranged for a dukun to drive away the demons
in the garden.

smoke, and then he puffed the smoke here and there with the pitiful remnants of his lung power. He extinguished each fire by pouring a thin liquid on to it from a little flask that he also extracted from his cloth sack, waiting until each spot was cold before addressing the next. For a long time afterwards, he sat rocking under the trees with his eyes closed, humming or perhaps singing to himself in a quavering voice. When the song was finished, he sat unmoving for such a long time that Dubois began to worry that he had gone to sleep, or died. What a susa *that* would be: the *dukun* dying in the middle of the ceremony, in their very own garden! The Dubois family would probably have had to leave this house, maybe leave Java, if such a thing had happened.

Eventually the old man slowly got up and shuffled to the foot of the stairs, up to the back veranda. In a moment, the *djongas* appeared, carrying his payment, as prescribed, on the palm of his hand, wrapped in a clean white linen cloth covered in red blossoms. As he came forward, the *djongas* bowed his head to avoid the old man's eyes. He took care not to touch the *dukun* as he handed over the parcel of linen. The flowers tumbled to the ground as the transfer was effected, and they were left where they fell. The old man spoke to the *djongas* in a whisper, warning him that no one was to disturb the remains of the fires for three days, no matter what. The *djongas* nodded his understanding. No one swept up the garden for a full week. The servants, when they could not avoid passing through it, scurried, eyes down, placing their feet very carefully. Babu would not allow the children to play there either.

The ceremony looked to Dubois like the rankest mumbo-jumbo, a combination of overacted mysteriousness and arbitrary improvisation that could have no possible effect on anything living in the garden. He did not interfere, for Anna's sake, but he was very sceptical.

Still, he had been here long enough to know that more than distance and culture separate Java from the Netherlands. A strange, indefinable quality flavoured the very air in Java; forces were at work here that could not be grasped or understood. In this place, even this tough-minded scientist, who denied that which could not be measured, had to acknowledge the possibility of spirits and magic. He did not know how this could be so. Something about Java defied logic. Maybe dead babies had a voice in Java. Maybe it *was* Anna Jeanette, calling to them from the little graveyard across the road. He did not know. His scientific techniques for deducing the truth did not apply to such things. What he knew was that the night cries stopped after the old *dukun*'s visit, and he was grateful.

In January 1894 he packed the long, handwritten pages, the precious photographs and drawings carefully for the train trip to the capital. His first duty upon arriving in Batavia was to go over each page in excruciating detail with the printers. They had to understand everything: the unfamiliar scientific terms, where this illustration went and that one, how the captions were to be printed. There was only one firm in Batavia whose work was of high enough quality, Dubois thought, and so he entrusted the work to them. As he walked away from their offices, he felt a terrible pang of regret. This had to be the way Prentice had felt, leaving Gerard with his in-laws for the first time, Dubois thought.

While in Batavia, he took time to report to his superiors in the army and to the governor on his progress. They were pleased that the monograph would soon be forthcoming although, he warned them, it dealt only with *P.e.* and not with the abundant fossil fauna he had collected. That would have to wait for later publications. His superiors suggested that he might consider reenlisting – his scientific work had gone so well, produced such impressive results – but he could not spend another tour of duty in Java. Another eight years might kill them all. He feared for Anna's sanity and, always, for the children's health. His own health was surely compromised, for he was plagued by intermittent fevers that made him as useless and limp as an empty snakeskin. Besides, he had already found what he had come for. No, his tour of duty would end in 1895 and he would go home. Once again, he asked for permission to travel to British India, to inspect the Siwalik fossils for himself and perhaps visit some of the sites where they came from. This time, he was successful. He might go at the end of 1894.

Dubois tended somewhat absentmindedly to some shopping Anna had asked him to do, an endless list. And then, laden with more luggage than he had come with, he reboarded the train, this time taking the line that travelled the northern route, through Cirebon to Semarang. He had only a few hours with Prentice in Semarang before he had to catch the late train that ran south across the island to Solo. There, he would rejoin the line that went through Magelang and Kediri before turning south to Toeloeng Agoeng.

Dubois found himself foolishly excited at seeing his friend again; it had been so long since they had seen each other often, but the goodwill was as strong as ever. Disembarking at Semarang, Dubois paused a moment on the step to look around at the confusion and chaos of the station. There were Dutch travellers in their dusty suits, weary and travel-stained as he himself must be; military men in sweat-soaked uniforms; a few pretty *njonja*s returning upcountry from a holiday in Batavia in their new outfits; hard-bitten, red-faced planters coming back to their plantations. Swarms of porters appeared with a wave of the stationmaster's arm, seizing everyone's luggage and *barang-barang* with enthusiasm. Dozens of vendors came forward as the passengers disembarked, calling out what drinks and snacks or newspapers they had to offer. Entire Javanese families squatted with their lumpy bundles of possessions on the platform, waiting for a train or perhaps simply settling in to beg for a living. Small brown-skinned boys dodged through the crowds, celebrating the sheer excitement of the hordes of people and the magnificent puff-puff-puff of the gleaming steam engines. The sheer activity and randomness of it all were pure Indies, Dubois thought.

Through the crowds and the colours and the noise came Prentice, that good honest face, those clear blue eyes, shining with sincerity. He strode along like the embodiment of some god, a blond Prince Ardjoena out of the Javanese sagas perhaps: strong and young and handsome. Dubois dropped his luggage and surged forward to greet his friend. Their handshake turned into a clasping bear-hug, so delighted was each with the other's presence.

'Let's get a boy to watch your luggage – just leave it there – and we'll get out of this and go have a decent meal,' Prentice proposed. They hired a trustworthy-looking boy and left the station, striding side by side out of the clamour to find a quiet restaurant where they could talk. They spoke from their hearts, of their worries and struggles and triumphs, with no hint of jealousy or misunderstanding to mar their accord. They were as close as ever, as close as they had been on Gunung Ardjoena, and they reminisced over that wonderful time, and the trip to Trinil, too. It was the blessing of their friendship that they could be silent together in perfect harmony, too. Soon it was time to return to the station and find the boy, who was dutifully waiting. Dubois hated to say goodbye to Prentice yet again. He boarded the train with a feeling of fullness tinged with regret; what wonderful days those had been, when he and Prentice had seen each other nearly every day. To be separated once again from Prentice was like leaving a part of himself behind.

No, Dubois corrected himself. Prentice was not a part of him. He was outside, a different man altogether, a better one. But he was what enabled Dubois to be himself, his true self. Somehow he freed Dubois, showed him the right way to go, to behave, to think. Everything was so clear in his presence. It was a rare gift to know such a man.

Intermission

As the dry season began, Dubois decided not to send Kriele and De Winter and their motley crew of labourers back to Trinil for a full season. He did not expect more specimens of *P.e.* to turn up; indeed, it would have been inconvenient to find more with the monograph already at the printers. But they would place the monument at Trinil before returning to various collection sites in order to take more detailed notes on the geology and improve their sketch maps. The engineers complained ceaselessly about the coolies, the coolies complained ceaselessly about the work, they all bemoaned the difficult living conditions. The troubles now seemed as timeless and cyclical as the rise and fall of the Bengawan Solo itself. Dubois was more concerned with making sure the mammalian fauna already in his possession was properly cleaned, packed, and crated for shipment, and that his notebooks were up to date. With a great sense of anticipation, he waited for the proofs from the printers in Batavia, for his first glimpse of his own, glorious, triumphal monograph.

With Dubois's scientific quest over, the tensions in the family eased. Anna grew better and better daily; she and Dubois resumed cordial and pleasant relations, if not the affectionate intimacy they had once enjoyed. The children grew calmer and more placid as their mother's hours at the cemetery diminished. Time was repairing the wounds left by the deaths, though the scars were permanent.

Dubois was focused on his monograph, compiling lists of those to whom he would send it for maximum effect, and planning his trip to India and the family's long-awaited return to Holland. After seven years in the Indies, the last year seemed to fly by unnaturally swiftly. He and Prentice resumed their intellectual dialogue via letters, as of old. Dubois was not so burdened with troubles as he once had been, and Prentice began to succeed handily at running the plantation now that the owner, Van der Leeuw, was no longer disagreeably underfoot. They corresponded about many topics, including John Tyndall's disproof of the idea that life could

By September 1894, the excavation at Trinil was huge but no more
Pithecanthropus remains were uncovered.

generate spontaneously from inanimate ingredients, a crucial
advance in biology. It was the sort of issue they would once have
argued on the veranda at Mringin.

Geboegan, Oenarang, 30 June 1894

My dear Doctor,

I was very agreeably surprised to receive the package you sent by
post today. Please accept my heartiest thanks for the books which I
doubly prize for the importance of their contents and for the goodwill
of the giver.

You need not fear I shall peruse them with any hostile feeling.
Having renounced my early beliefs – not without a hard struggle, and
reluctantly, yet decisively – and having come to regard in a more scientific and truer light the mysterious universe in which I live and the
problems bound up in it – this latter owing to my acquaintance with
you, to what I have learned from you in conversation, and what I
have gained by the perusal of the books you have already favoured
me with – my mind is now open, I trust, to receive any truth without
bias or prejudice.

Rest assured I shall carefully and attentively and profitably peruse
the books now so kindly given me. I too was pained by reading a
cold, unsympathetic criticism of Tyndall and his work. He was

indeed the apostle of science, and the quickening of your mind received from a perusal of what he wrote was no doubt felt by many, many more searchers after truth & knowledge. That a great mind like the physiologist Helmholtz should admire & esteem the eloquent & devoted priest of science is alone a sufficient reward for Tyndall's labours, and a mighty rebuke to the carpings of lesser critics.

I shall now draw to a close as I am wearied & my hand tremulous. I have been 7 hours on horseback in the sun today. We are getting more coffee than our taxation, and my work is appreciated both by the bank at Semarang and by the owner of this estate in Holland.

With best thanks & best wishes,
    Believe me,
        Sincerely yours,
        Adam Prentice
Compliments to Mrs. Dubois

At the beginning of August, the copies of the monograph were ready. The printers packed them up and sent them by fast train to Toeloeng Agoeng. Dubois could not keep his hands from shaking as he unwrapped them, even though he had corrected the proofs with the greatest of care and knew the result must be fine. The book looked to his eyes like a miracle. It was a handsome volume, oversized, and bound in a dignified buff-coloured board. As he paged through it, he pronounced the illustrations to be excellent, the paper good, the typeface strong. It was a work anyone might be proud of, especially one who had nearly died to accomplish it.

He showed the work off to his uncomprehending family – the children seemed more genuinely interested than Anna was – and to anyone else who had expressed the least interest in his work. He carried a copy up to Ngrodjo, to share it with Boyd. Then he carefully wrapped dozens of other copies to send back to Europe. These were his envoys, who would carry his ideas across the oceans back to the scholars of Europe. Soon they would all know what he had found. Soon the name of *P.e.* would be on everyone's lips as the link that was missing no longer from Darwin's chain of evolution.

Dubois was uncharacteristically relaxed, happier and more at peace than he had been for years. The major tasks before him were packing up his fossils, making sure their documentation was complete, and planning his trip to India. Best of all, Prentice's long year at Gcboegan was drawing to a close and he would soon be back at Ngrodjo, where Dubois could see him often. He, Boyd, and Prentice would be able to sit together again on the veranda and try to bring order to the universe. The prospect filled his heart with joy.

In late October, Prentice received word at long last that his application to develop wasteland as a plantation was likely to be granted. He would be given a piece of land south of Kediri, near the village of Ngawiluwih, not far from Mringin. He wrote to Dubois in a state of high excitement; his ambition to have his own plantation was at last coming to pass.

Mringin, 20 October 1894

My Dear Doctor,

Thanks for your kind letter of the 17th inst. Mr. Boyd is very sorry indeed that you should have misunderstood him especially as he had before asked you to take nothing amiss from him as he meant it all well with you and has always considered you a good friend. Nor can he even in the least recall the circumstances that seem to have made a painful impression in your mind. The weather, too, unfortunately for next year's coffee crop, is and has been miserably wet at Mringin and misty so that visitors cannot enjoy the climate much, but all the same any friend who does not mind these things is highly welcome to come, especially an old frequenter like yourself.

I am intending to begin a new estate close to here & the commission will be here shortly to inspect the pillars & etc. I can get no permission to begin planting until all these matters are arranged. Thanks for your hearty good wishes for my success in this new venture which I anticipate will turn out well.

The 'Climates' book remains long in suspense, but I trust the work will be published soon in English. What is the general impression now in Germany & among the learned respecting the views you express in this book?

Mr. Van Velthoven and Mr. Goernat are coming to Mringin tomorrow for one day. Messrs. Henderson & Budd, friends of mine, are coming here today to stay two days. They are going to inspect the forest here with me. I have cut a narrow footpath through it to facilitate inspection but I trust it won't be wet tomorrow, as it is today.

My child is in magnificent health in Malang.

When are you going to Calcutta?

Come up please to Mringin at any time that suits you, with Mrs. Dubois and the children, and receive the kind regards of Mr. Boyd and

    Yours Sincerely,
    Adam Prentice

P.S. I often look back with pleasure to our excursion to Trinil. Whenever I pass the turn-off to Trinil at Kedoeng Gale (I rather forget the name) my recollection dwells upon the rustic holiday you provided for us. Indeed, I would like to make another visit with you. A.P.

Dubois's answer to this letter was a silent gift, a copy of the monograph itself. There was no greater treasure he could have given anyone, nor no person in the world whom he valued more highly than Prentice. Because it came from Prentice, Dubois decided, too, to accept the secondhand apology from Boyd, who had shown an appalling lack of enthusiasm for the monograph when Dubois had taken it to him. How could he react so offhand-edly to receiving the greatest scientific work of the century? Perhaps, Dubois conceded grudgingly, the Old Warrior had been simply a bit under the weather or preoccupied. He would let the matter pass, now.

Prentice soon wrote again.

Toeloeng Agoeng, 3 November 1894

My Dear Doctor,

I was agreeably surprised this morning to be presented with a handsome volume relating full particulars of your wonderful discov-ery of the missing link (or one of them). I shall look through the volume with great interest.

I am going today at 12 o'clock to Blitar. Perhaps I may be back again on Tuesday and if so I shall endeavour to give you a call in the evening when I hope to find you in good health and spirits.

Meanwhile, with best thanks, and with kind regards to you all (in which Mr. Boyd who is down here changing money heartily joins).

  Believe me,
    Sincerely yours,
    Adam Prentice

But Prentice did not come. Dubois waited out Tuesday afternoon and evening in a pleasant state of expectation; Anna, too, was looking forward to the promised visit, for she had come to enjoy Prentice's good-humoured company greatly. The hours passed, but neither Prentice nor word from him arrived. When a second day and evening passed without word, Dubois became alarmed. He penned a hasty note and sent a boy to Prentice's lodgings, inquiring as to his well-being. Was his friend down with fever, perhaps, in need of Dubois's medical attention? He would willingly have dropped everything and gone to him. The truth was better than he feared.

Toeloeng Agoeng, 7 November 1894

My Dear Doctor,

I have been 3 days in house with a swollen throat inside, in consequence, I think, of going with wet shoes 2 days.

However, with taking care of myself, I am now almost better, and tomorrow I am going again up to Mringin. If you are receiving no visitors this evening and have nothing particular to do, I should be glad to call round at your house this evening at any hour that best suits your convenience.

When your messenger called last night, I had just retired to my room to escape the night air.

With kind regards,
Believe me,
Sincerely yours,
Adam Prentice

P.S. I write this letter on my knee to be out of all draught.

Dubois was relieved that Prentice was only mildly ill. As the time for his extended journey to India approached, he found himself worrying more obsessively about the health of those he held dear. Little Anna's death still haunted him and cast a pall over his relationship with his wife. He thought it would be an unbearable load of guilt if another of his loved ones fell ill and died for lack of his attention. And then he reminded himself, there had been nothing he could have done to save the baby's life. All his learning and skill and knowledge, all the medicines and scientific principles in his mental armoury, had been useless.

CHAPTER 32

To India

At last the end of the year approached and Dubois's longed-for trip to India was about to begin. It would be his last scientific gift to himself before leaving the Orient. His departure was fixed for two days after Christmas. He left in a state of elation, carrying with him a journal in which to record his observations and notes and a special parcel of letters from Prentice.

Mringin, 21 December 1894

My Dear Doctor,

Herewith the two letters of introduction (for Dr. Galloway & Mr. Lyon Sr.).

In addition, I shall write Mr. Lyon in the course of a day or two so that he knows in advance that you're coming. If you lodged with him or with Dr. Galloway it would be much pleasanter than in a hotel surrounded by strangers, but I do not know how either gentleman is at present situated as regards household arrangements. It is therefore better I write Mr. Lyon in advance.

I trust you will have a prosperous voyage, and profit greatly from your visit to Calcutta, so that you may always be able to look back upon it with pleasure.

The severance from your family is of course a great drawback, but it is only temporary, and it is unavoidable; and the time of your return will at length arrive.

Till then adieu, and believe me to be

Sincerely yours,

Adam Prentice

Prentice enclosed two nearly identical letters to Lyon and Galloway, introducing Dubois as a dear friend and asking them to show him every hospitality.

Dubois bade goodbye to his wife and family and departed by train for Batavia, arriving in Semarang early on the morning of the twenty-ninth. The steamer left for Singapore at nine on the morning of 4 January. The day was fine and the voyage seemed like a reward for his years of hard work. He started a journal, to record his impressions of the trip.

December 29, 1894. I met on board a very pleasant, though small, company: 1, Mijnheer Vermeulen, head of the customs in North Java, from the Noordbrabant province at home, thick and good-natured, witty and cheerful; 2, Harmsen, a globetrotter, making a trip around the world, at present coming from Siberia, who knows a lot of stories from his experiences there, in Japan, Africa, and America. 3, a midshipman, named Heus, who comes from the island of Lombok.

January 4, 1895. Till yesterday afternoon we had excellent weather. Then, however, we passed the north point of Bangka Island and we got heavy wind and swell from the Chinese sea, which made more or less all of us seasick. The motion of water and wind, and hence of our ship, kept on toward morning and it was difficult not to wake up again and again because of the way I rolled to and fro in the berth. Still I slept the sleep of the righteous despite the uncooperativeness of the elements. From Batavia thus far we have passed thousands of smaller islands, which are placed like dark-green bouquets in the light green sea of the straits of Bangka and Malakka. To the right is the mountainous Billiton Island and the larger but flatter Bangka Island, to the left is the long, low coastal strip of the Palembangsche region of southern Sumatra.

Toward morning, on our right side, we passed the islands of the Lingga Archipelago and then Riau, covered in forest and alang-alang grass in patches and small clusters of coconut trees. To the left was the splendid coast of eastern Sumatra – Siak and Djambi – with its richly indented bays and the land covered in original forest. It gave me inconceivable nostalgia for the pleasant times in Sumatra.

January 7 – Singapore. I arrived here toward 4 p.m. yesterday, still somewhat seasick, so perhaps the beautiful scene of the greatest and most gorgeous harbour of these regions had a diminished effect on me. But still I know that it was magnificent. First some small islands, then the coast of the large island on which Singapore is situated, mostly green but relieved with pink-brown rocks of granite and a cathedral and a great number of other large buildings and a forest of masts of ships and funnels of steamers and all sorts of other vessels. The rocky, capricious coastline tells me I am outside of the Dutch colonies, as we do not possess such a harbour either on Java or on Sumatra, nor on Kalimantan or any other island, for the surrounding land there in the Indies is always flat. The boat is hardly tied up than the Indians arrive on board and go ashore with their turbans and stately beards and their ridiculous thin statures. Going ashore myself and seeing the hackney carriages and bullock carts and rickshaws (which are pulled by the Chinese), I cannot help but realize that I am in an entirely different country than the Indies.

Having placed our luggage on a bullock cart under the supervision of a porter from the Hôtel de l'Europe, Mijnheer Vermeulen and I got into a hackney carriage and rode into the city. There are many large, new, or nearly new buildings in the monumental style, both private and public buildings, with excellently kept up roads and beautiful lawns (where I see at this very moment, from my window in the Hotel, a number of young Englishmen in white trousers and shirt-sleeves playing lawn tennis)...

Dinner does not differ a lot from the Dutch dinner, but it is followed by a sort of small rijstafel with many savoury dishes. Apart from that, another difference from our ways is the division of the day. In the morning at 7 o'clock a small teapot with its appurtenances and a thin slice of bread (with a little butter) is brought into the room by the Chinese room-boy (all the servants, even the waiters, are Chinese). After that, I have to wait until 9 o'clock when the 'brunch' starts. This is however a very substantial meal: fish with bread, omelette with bread, drumstick with bread, cheese with bread, then a cup of coffee...

We drove yesterday evening to the water-works, a reservoir that provides the city with water, and afterwards to the Botanical Garden. Because of the way it is situated, its outlooks and views, and because of its beautiful layout, the Botanical Garden here exceeds the one at Bogor in Java, though it has much less scientific value. In the garden are 3 mammals and 7 birds which pretend to be a zoo. The museum that I visited today is a beautiful building with a few badly-stuffed animals and other specimens, but also a large library of all sorts of works, including belles-lettres.

Dubois found the mixture of English, Malay, and Chinese cultures immensely interesting in comparison to the Dutch-Indies hybrid with which he was so familiar. The English were stiffer, more remote from the Chinese and Malays than was common in Java. There were no mixed marriages in evidence here, no crowds of pale-brown children with curly hair, no comely Chinese or Malay women dressed in European clothes standing demurely by their English husbands' sides. The English women – not that there were very many – maintained European dress.

Prentice's friends, Galloway and Lyon, adopted Dubois immediately as a friend. They showed him the sights of the town, took him to the museums and introduced him to curators and other scientific men, and generally made sure he was amused and welcomed. The few days in Singapore passed most pleasantly. On the ninth, Dubois set sail for Penang. It was an idyllic, comfortable voyage, he recorded in his journal.

> January 10, 1895 in the 'Pundua', in straits of Malakka between Singapore and Penang. Yesterday afternoon at half past four, the vessel – a big beautifully furnished ship of 2100 tons (3×as large as the packet service ferry), set sail. Luckily I received a cabin alone, one that is more spacious than the ones on the Dutch boats and furnished with a commodious sofa. The party of travellers is very mixed, there is even a Chinese; most of those travelling alone are the English, 1 English-speaking German (from Jena), further an Arabian Jew, an American, and a lady with her good-looking daughter...
>
> The island of Penang stands out clearly, with its mountain slopes dappled in dark green and yellow, the sky turning light blue with little white cloudlets floating above the land. A prau, an Indies outrigger, with 2 brown batwing sails drifts past our boat. The moon is at the pointing of sinking beneath the sea. A silver fish jumps out of the water and dives back in again several times. The sea is very calm and no wind blows.

The shipboard days passed in lazy comfort. For once, Dubois had no ambitions to pursue, no work to claim his attention: there was little to do except wait for the accolades of his European colleagues when they received his book. Dubois passed the time in writing in his journal and observing his fellow passengers. He told them amusing and exciting stories of his life in the Indies and hardly mentioned science or the missing link, which gave him a delightful sense of travelling incognito. At Penang, Dubois changed ships, taking the *Basnura* to Rangoon; from there he caught the *Abalda*, arriving in Calcutta on 20 January. This extended and ever-changing sea voyage was a rare and happy time in his life. There were even a few pretty women who were charmed by this handsome Dutchman, who told such interesting stories and spoke such good English. They did not guess what he was waiting for: the recognition that he had made the most important discovery of the century.

CHAPTER 33

Calcutta

As the ship docked, Dubois wondered whether Calcutta would live up to its nickname as the City of Palaces. Certainly the white spires and saffron-coloured domes of the government buildings he could see, set amidst the palm trees and banyans, gleamed attractively in the sunlight. He could just see the green of the enormous Maidan, a huge open park that stretched some two kilometres along the river's edge from the racecourse in the south to the Esplanade in the north.

He travelled into the city by carriage, observing, to his immense amusement, that the Maidan had a thriving population of marabou storks, just like the Adjutant they had kept in the garden at Toeloeng Agoeng for a while. Dominating the Maidan was Fort William, a large, solid octagonal construction built in the late 1700s to house all the town's European citizens in case of attack by the natives. Dubois could see that the British, like the Dutch in the Indies, had not always been welcome rulers. The Maidan owed its very existence to the fort; the space had been initially cleared of tracts of forest to give the soldiers a long, clear line of fire. Now it was a valuable public park, heavily used for entertainments and endless rounds of sports and games.

The Maidan's eastern edge would become familiar territory to Dubois, for it was traversed by the broad avenue known as Chowringhee, the home of the famous Indian Museum, where he would study the Siwalik collections. Said to be the largest museum in Asia, the Indian Museum boasted collections of zoological, archaeological, and geological objects, as well as an art gallery, all housed in a vast two-storey building completed in 1875. It was an impressive accomplishment, this elegant stone building with its double galleries decorated with stone arches. The whole embraced a central courtyard, with formal plantings and a fountain that cast a continuous spray into its octagonal pool. Dubois was a little embarrassed to compare this stately edifice with the shabby quarters allotted to the natural history museum in Batavia.

Farther still to the east, past the Indian Museum, was the wretched collection of huts and shacks of the bazaar, congested with the poor and full of every manner of food and merchandise, smelling of sweat and spices and fumes from cooking fires. It was still very like the native markets of the Indies, Dubois thought as he explored its margins. The people were still small and poor, dark-skinned and brightly clad – the women in saris, not sarongs, the men in loose pyjamas – and gabbled away in a hundred unintelligible languages. He ventured into the market only far enough to procure a fine turquoise-blue scarf for Anna, embroidered with gold thread in an intricate design. He did not suppose she would wear such a showy garment, but perhaps she would enjoy it. He purchased a few trinkets for the children as well. They were little different from what was available in Java, but they would show his family that he had been thinking of them even when he was far from home.

What preoccupied Dubois more than sightseeing and shopping was settling into the Grand Hotel, an impressive building with an elaborate whitewashed façade with balconies and balustrades everywhere. He had been told this was the best hotel in town; the room was certainly spacious after his neat cabin on the *Abalda*. But he was soon disenchanted with his accommodation and the other guests.

January 22, 1895. This morning it is again so really wintry and cold, with a draught on my face, that I am surprised that the shower is not as cold as ice; for that matter, it is cold enough. Still, it gives me a certain refreshment after the terrible all-night coughing of the man in the neighbouring room. In addition to that, he makes the most filthy sounds and swears under his breath and moves roughly, crashing into things; he always seems to be drunk from the large whiskies that I hear him prepare in the evening before going to bed. Accordingly I cannot stay here a night longer. Some way, somehow, I have to seek shelter here or in another hotel. To stay here for four weeks, without getting a decent rest – even for someone accustomed to travelling and marching like me – would be anything but refreshing.

At the museum, things went much better. The curators – Alcock, Finn, Holland, and Moll – were delighted to have a knowledgeable visitor. They were busy with their own work, of course, but they were hospitable and welcoming. Over tea and at lunch, he told them of his discoveries in the Indies. They were fascinated to learn of his work and looked forward to hearing his opinion of the resemblances between the Siwalik and Indies faunas. By the end of the day, he felt himself particularly drawn to Alcock, the friendly, intelligent head of the Department of Zoology and Archaeology, which housed Lydekker's fossils. Alcock generously solved Dubois's accommodation problem.

January 23, 1895. Alcock is a good fellow, though unfortunately for me he is interested in lower marine animals and therefore has few points of scientific contact with me. In the afternoon he invited me to take tea with him and proposed that I stay with him, which invitation I *hesitatingly* accepted.

It proved a good decision, for the two men got along congenially. Alcock's household was large and comfortable and well run, a bachelor establishment where Dubois soon felt content.

Most important of all were the fossils. Going through the collection was for him like walking blindfold across unknown terrain, never knowing whether he would sink into a sticky, smelly morass or stumble into a fragrant mass of orchids. Had Lydekker found something like his missing link? Was there some specimen here that

In 1895, Dubois's friends in India: Frank Finn (left, standing) and
A. Alcock (right, standing) both of the Indian Museum; and two Dutch
acquaintances, Carl Thieme (seated left) and Miss Thieme
(seated right).

would disprove all Dubois's ideas? He never knew what each new drawer and cabinet would reveal; until he had surveyed the entire collection, he could only wonder what specimens were there, what animals were represented in this sizeable fossil fauna from ancient India. He was soon reassured, however, and was able to write of his preliminary studies with satisfaction.

> January 23, 1895. Yesterday I studied in the museum some zoological and paleontological specimens, mainly the maxilla or upper jaw of *Anthropopithecus sivalensis*. According to me, Lydekker has described and pictured it wrongly, because he has inaccurately joined some of the fragments. The Siwalik fossil collection is in many respects much richer than mine, certainly so because a large part of it is in London and I cannot see it, but the condition and the preservation of the fossils disappoints me. In a number of aspects, my collection is richer. Buffalo, deer, and antelope – I have better and more beautiful ones, also many more elephant molars, and in general molars from all kinds of mammals. Nothing like my *P.e.* is to be found in the Siwalik collection...
>
> Taken all together, I believe now that my collection is even more significant than I assumed earlier. In *Nature* (January 3, p. 230) is a short note about my *Pithecanthropus* description, to which my friend and host Alcock drew my attention. It is not much more than an announcement, but it makes clear that my ape-man will not walk into the world unnoticed.

As Dubois did not have his own copy of *Nature*, and was reluctant to deface another's, he carefully copied the announcement out into his notebook.

> The significant name '*Pithecanthropus erectus*' is proposed by Dr. Eug. Dubois, of the Netherlands-Indies Army Service, for some fossil remains recently discovered in the andesitic tuffs of Java, as indicating the former existence in that island of an intermediate form between man and the anthropoid apes. The bones, which consist of an upper part of a skull, a very perfect femur, and an upper molar tooth, are elaborately described and figured in a quarto memoir recently published in Batavia.

It was not much, but it was a beginning. He liked the phrase 'elaborately described and figured'. It showed that someone appreciated the great care he had taken over the monograph.

Dubois found his colleagues at the Indian Museum extraordinarily congenial. The museum staff soon felt like a company of friends, exchanging ideas while at work and often meeting in their off-hours. They arranged a temporary membership for Dubois at their club, so he could join them for socializing and sport. They made a point of introducing him to C. L. Griesbach, the director of the Geological Survey of India, who knew the Siwalik Hills well and had much sound advice to offer. Dubois enjoyed himself. On the day before his thirty-seventh birthday, he wrote:

> January 27, 1895. This lady, the second one I talked to, was obviously a lovely and lively woman, different from what I had imagined English ladies to be: full of spirit and cheerful, and possessed of a calm charm that did me good, as if she were a pleasant scent or a beautiful flower.

Even the weekends offered Dubois new entertainments. An opportunity too good to miss arose when he learned that a group of natives from one of the remote islands east of the southern tip of India and south of Burma was to be exhibited nearby.

> February 2, 1895. Yesterday instead of going to the zoological garden, I went in the afternoon with Finn to see a troop of natives from the Andaman Islands – remarkable, small, black humans of an Australian type, of whom there are only 500 in existence. They are somewhat lighter in colour than negroes, but they are black enough, with faces that resemble those of Australian natives; their hair is crimped and plaited in bunches. The doctor (whose name I have forgotten) who collected them and will bring them to London asked me, as 'the discoverer of the missing link' – that is how I am generally known here on account of the note in *Nature* – if I took them for direct descendants of my missing link. English scientific men are so old-fashioned in their thinking! Meanwhile I am happy to have had a chance to see such a primitive and rare human race.

The English, Dubois realized, differ utterly from the Dutch in their exuberant emphasis on physical fitness and sports. As he had always prided himself on his strength and fitness, he found this national characteristic admirable.

> February 3, 1895. I see with great regret that we Dutch are so far behind our English counterparts. Among the officers there is not a single thick, impossible belly, no stiff physique without resilience, no drunken soldiers with wretched, mean faces. Even old officers (who, anyway, must retire from the army at 55) look supple and yet strong and still possess (as do the ladies) something youthful, something I

am not as a rule accustomed to finding among the Dutch... Their interest in sport and games is extraordinary; I realize now that this is where the strength and power of the English nation originates. Even ladies take part in the hunt, so that the daughter of the Inspector of Forestry actually shot a tiger some days ago, in the neighbourhood of Dehra Doon, where she is at present travelling...

Truly, it saddens me to think back on all those thick Dutch bellies in Java, as I must do whether I will or not. The great English public of ladies and gentlemen that surrounds me includes not one person (or perhaps only a single one) who resembles a degenerated lump of fat, as is so often the rule in Java. That some among us Dutch, like myself, differ in this regard is considered more a disadvantage than an advantage... Here, without exaggeration, everyone keeps his body strong and supple and healthy through moderate exercise and is in his work as good and as thorough. No heaviness of body and mind – as is with us nearly the rule – but also there are none who lack seriousness, no clowns or acrobats. Even the making of music by the moderately talented seems to me to be the outcome of the correct equilibrium of English society.

Dubois spent the last few days of his time in Calcutta trying to organize his trip upcountry, with a lot of help from Griesbach in particular, who wrote out pages of advice. Dubois felt it was essential to see Lydekker's sites for himself and to collect additional fossils from them if possible. It would have been foolish to come all this way and not return with a comparative collection of the Siwalik fauna. But the Siwaliks were a long way from Calcutta: he had to traverse some fifteen hundred kilometres of northern India. Although travelling on the Grand Trunk Road had an attractively romantic sound to it, Dubois could not imagine that voyaging on this ancient trade corridor stretching from Calcutta in the east to Peshawar in the North-West Frontier province, would be either comfortable or swift. He was far better off relying on the excellent railway system that spread across the Indian subcontinent like a spider's web. In a first-class compartment, he could depart from Calcutta on the night of 8 February and arrive, fresh and rested, in Ambala on the tenth.

Alcock kindly saw Dubois off at the station, even though the departure was late. The previous day, they had dispatched a large quantity of camping and collecting gear by goods train, to await Dubois's arrival at the other end. He carried with him only a small case with clothing, toiletries, a camera, notebooks, and writing instruments.

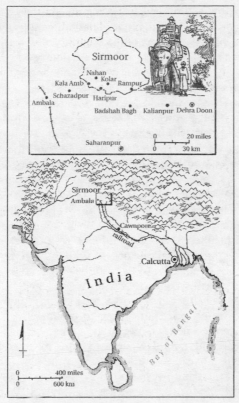

Dubois travelled from Calcutta by rail to Ambala and collected
fossils in the princely state of Sirmoor and neighbouring districts.

The station was an exercise in chaos. Travellers wended their
way through a maze of humanity to buy their tickets and arrive at
the correct platform. Boys and men carried luggage; children and
women sold newspapers, flowers, candies, hard-boiled eggs, and
every sort of food that could be eaten with the fingers; itinerant
magicians performed tricks to coax the unwary out of their rupees;
sadhus – holy men – meditated or held out their begging bowls;
Muslims spread their prayer mats and prayed to Mecca; Hindu
women squatted to tend small fires over which they cooked their
families' meagre meals. All this life and colour and squalor was
incongruously enclosed within the confines of the magnificent,

soaring railway station the British had built. It was a wedding cake of a building, large, echoing, cool, smelling of people and curry and steam, with a front façade so white it almost burnt the eyes. The whole scene was very like, and yet terribly unlike, the Indies, Dubois thought.

He found his comfortable first-class compartment, put his case under the seat, and threw open the window to shout his last goodbyes and thanks to Alcock, who was waiting on the platform.

'Have a good trip, Dubois!' Alcock shouted merrily. 'I'll see you when you get back. You can tell me all about your discoveries then. Have you got Gamble's address at the Forestry School in Dehra Doon? You must look him up, now.'

'Thank you, Alcock,' Dubois replied, waving. 'You've been a tremendous help. Say goodbye to the others at the museum for me. I'll make contact with Gamble at the Forestry School for sure.'

Like a mother hen, Alcock could not resist clucking over his visitor. 'Now, you've got all the other addresses and papers and the receipts for your goods that went yesterday?'

Dubois smiled; this concern was so like Alcock. 'Yes, yes,' he said pulling out a leather case in which he kept his papers: receipts, addresses, advice on prices and how to organize his trip and his men. 'Here are the ones for the small crates, and the one for the excavating gear, and…Ach! Where is the one for the tents?' As the train started to move, he shuffled through the chits and receipts. Leaning out of the window, he called back to his friend, 'Alcock, I haven't got the one for the tents after all. I must have left it in my pocket yesterday. Can you check in my things at your place?'

'Righty-ho, Dubois,' responded Alcock, trotting along beside the train. 'I'll check for it as soon as I get home. Don't worry! I'll send it along after you, to Ambala.'

Dubois settled back into his seat, disturbed. It was not like him to lose track of an important piece of paper; he was both embarrassed and concerned. All this travelling and packing and unpacking and depositing things here and there and the other place to be called for…it was all very complicated, especially in an unfamiliar culture.

He was pleased to find that the compartment was not fully booked. For the first leg of the trip, he was in company with two army officers making their way to a new posting. They made polite conversation for a while, but all turned in to sleep on the bunks (precisely made up with starched white sheets and a blanket and pillow) before long. Looking around the compartment, Dubois thoroughly approved of the good mahogany woodwork, the folding berths that could be tucked up and out of the way in the morning, and the neat little sink that folded down from the wall in the small toilet and washroom.

Alcock's cook had packed him up a tiffin box with some tea, fruit, bread and butter, a few hard-boiled eggs, and a teaspoonful of salt wrapped in a twist of paper, in case he got hungry before breakfast was served. For now, he was happy to read a little and then doze off, lulled by the rhythmic percussion of the train. In the morning he awakened early and was happy to watch the remarkable landscape out of the window as he sipped his tea. The tea was cold by now, of course, but it was better than nothing.

There was no mistaking this part of India for the Indies, Dubois decided. India was flat and hot and full of rivers from the swamps of Calcutta right across Bihar to the great River Ganges. But there were no cool green rice paddies, no groves of bananas and coconut trees, and no sheer, green-cloaked volcanoes suddenly arising out of the paddies, as in the Indies. Despite the rivers, this part of India seemed a much drier country, brown and dusty rather than lush like Java. Before long, the train arrived at Mokameh, along the banks of the Ganges, where breakfast was served. The system was most impressive. Meals took place at preordained stations at preordained times. Once the train pulled in, an elaborate restaurant service sprang into action. Each first-class compartment containing ongoing passengers was served by a particular cart, the responsibility of two restaurant-wallahs, as they were known in Anglo-Indian slang. The restaurant-wallahs positioned their cart outside 'their' first-class carriage, handing up silver-covered dishes of food, linen, cutlery, and drinks in a matter of moments. The meal was eaten and cleared away in less than half an hour, so the train could continue on schedule, as it invariably did. Dubois was amazed at the efficiency and predictability of it all. He dined well and peacefully and soon the train was clacking down the rails again, following the curving course of the Ganges for some miles.

Two hundred kilometres later, they arrived in Baxar, where lunch was served in the station waiting room while the compartments were brushed and cleaned. Another few hundred kilometres onward, they had tea in Allahabad, served again from carts manned by restaurant-wallahs, and at 18:25 precisely the train pulled into Cawnpore for dinner. Once again, the linen was spotless, starched and ironed; the trains ran exactly on time; the serving dishes were polished to a high gleam, and the food was plentiful. The British had accomplished so much in India, had almost civilized the place; it seemed so polished and well organized compared with Java.

At 8:04 on Sunday morning, two days after leaving Calcutta, Dubois arrived in Ambala. The city lay on the broad, fertile river plains north of Delhi. To the north he could see the impressive foothills and behind them the mountain ranges of the highlands, the Simla Hills, Mussoorrie Range, and the Siwaliks themselves. It was a dramatic landscape, enhanced by the high proportion of Sikhs who lived there. The Sikhs, Dubois had been told, were mainstays of the British Indian Army. Tall, well built, proud, and fiercely loyal warriors, the Sikh regiments were renowned for their courage, as well as for their magnificent beards and moustaches.

A letter from Alcock was waiting for Dubois at Lumley's Hotel in Ambala.

> Indian Museum, 9 February 1895
> I have been through all your papers and have also looked in the armoire among your clothes, but I cannot find the Railway Receipt for your tents.
> I cannot find it – my God!!
> I hope you have had a good journey, not too hot and not too cold.
> Mind you communicate with Mr. Gamble. I hear from Dr. King that Mr. Gamble is most pleased to hear that a geologist is at last coming to re-explore the Siwaliks, and that he will do all he can to help you. So mind you write to him, if you cannot call on him.

He didn't need the tents right away, but he could foresee that not having the receipts might be a problem. He sent a servant from the hotel over to try to collect them, along with the rest of his luggage. The other baggage and the small crates of equipment were all turned over cheerfully, but the luggage clerk obstinately refused to relinquish the tents. He waggled his head and shook his finger at the hotel servant, who dutifully repeated the entire performance for Dubois: 'Ah, no, you must tell the Sahib, I must have the correct chit, for I must file my papers and mark my forms properly or there will be complaints!' Here the luggage clerk had tapped his register book vigorously with his index finger, as if to emphasize how all-powerful the book was and the proper recording of all documents. 'Yes, I am deeply sorrowful,' he had continued, 'but I cannot give up the tents without the chit. Nothing may leave my domain without its passport,' he had chortled gleefully, 'no matter what the reason!' Dubois set the matter aside to deal with later, for he had a great many things to arrange while he was in Ambala and this seemed the least of them.

That night, relaxing in his room, Dubois unfolded Griesbach's sheets of scribbled advice and read them over once again. Running an expedition in India was a little different from running one in the Indies, he thought to himself. He would start tomorrow in trying to round up the permits, men, animals, and supplies he would need. He planned to be in the area fossil-hunting for over a month, perhaps six weeks all told, before heading back to Calcutta. Griesbach wrote:

Monday. Call on Deputy Commissioner at Katcherry. I have written to him about 10 camels, with 2 ordered to be ready on the 7th inst.

See that camel men have their ropes, they are obliged to supply one rope per camel, which is included in their wages. The wages (so much per camel per month) include also the services of the drivers, usually 1 for 3 or 4 camels. It is usually advantageous to carry ropes (hair-ropes) as reserve. Camel men expect to get at least 1/2 month's advances of wages.

Norton & Co. is a good shop for supply of stores etc. etc. Expensive but very good.

Get your servants; tell the hotel people, Norton & Co., or anybody else what men you require. Perhaps the Deputy Commissioner will know of men or give orders to his Tehsildar, the local tax-collector, to find suitable men.

You require:

wages about 12–15 rupees	1 cook or Khitmagar who knows a little cooking
7–8 rupees a month	1 Bhistie (water carrier)
6–7 rupees a month	1 Syce (for horse)
5 rupees a month	1 Grasscutter (for horse)
7 rupees a month each man	2 or 3 Khalassis or Chuprassis for general service in camp & pitching tents. For the latter not less than about 8–10 men are required, but your Khalassis will hunt up coolies for help. It would be better however to engage 4 Khalassis.

All these men will expect 'warm clothing'. I think they will be satisfied if you give them 6/- each man for that purpose. They also will want an advance of wages, generally a month's pay each man. The Cook will also want about 50/- advance for making arrangements about your food etc. He will have to buy all supplies at Ambala, such as rice, flour (Delhi flour in tins), salt, sugar, etc. etc.

Your man also will require all sorts of things such as 'charans' (cloth for cleaning dishes etc.), bootblacking, Momroggan & yellow soap for brown boots & saddle etc., etc. all which is only a few rupees.

It sounded a daunting task, finding three or four camel men, plus their camels and the ropes and other equipment, and then another eight to ten labourers to organize the camp, fetch water and firewood, and so on. The key seemed to be finding the right *khitmagar*, a combination of a butler and a *mandur* or foreman in the Indies. With the right *khitmagar*, all the rest would fall into place, so he would choose carefully. He wanted an intelligent man, with good English and good knowledge of the country, and an honest, practical sort of fellow good at commanding men. He would have to ask around.

Then there was the matter of his horse. Dubois had no intention of struggling up the Siwalik Hills and down again on foot when wiry native horses were readily available at reasonable prices. Griesbach had opinions about that, too.

For horse get about a manud (84 lbs) of grain; it is always good to keep some grain ready, as it cannot always be got in villages.

Tell the hotel servant that you want a horse, & get the dealers to bring round their animals to the hotel. You ought to find many ponies in Ambala at this time & ought not to have to pay more than from 100–180 rupees for one. The horse will require clothing (a so-called Jul), curry-comb & brush, bucket (for water), headstall and hair-ropes (also one or two cotton ropes). The syce will make all these arrangements and will cheat a little over it, but not much. It will cost about 12–15 rupees.

You might ask Capt. Mardall of the 17th Bengal Calvalry about purchase of a pony, if he is in Ambala. I give you a letter to Capt. Mardall of the 17th B.C. who is a friend of mine.

Also a letter to Major F. Drummond, in case he is in Ambala.

Call also on Mrs. Melliss, who is a great friend of mine, if she is in Umballa, where she generally lives during the winter. Wife of Colonel Melliss C.B. the Inspector-General of the Imperial Service Troops.

Appended here was a list of the regiments stationed in the Ambala Cantonment, which must be a large one, Dubois supposed, for there seemed to be a great many regiments: 18th Hussars, two batteries of the Royal Horse Artillery, two Mountain Batteries of the Royal Artillery, battalions from Norfolk, Somerset, and Derbyshire. There were, in addition, two native regiments commanded by British: the 17th Bengal Calvary and the Depot 32nd Pioneers. While the military men might be of great help to Dubois, he was intrigued by the mention of Mrs Melliss. From the notes, she seemed to be a closer friend to Griesbach than her husband was. Dubois could not help but wonder how close the friendship might be. Perhaps the stories about romances between lonely officers' wives and unmarried men upcountry were true. He had not previously suspected Griesbach of being a ladies' man, a – he searched his memory for the colourful English expression – a … poodle-faker, that was it! Perhaps he ought to call on this Mrs Melliss indeed, if she was such a charmer. Certainly the English women were very attractive and, from the sound of things, he might have some time to kill in Ambala before he was ready to set out in search of fossils.

Griesbach's notes were a fount of information. Dubois read on, trying to absorb the myriad pieces of advice. The most important concerned his permits and *purwanas*.

The Punjab Government has been informed about your travelling in the Punjab Siwaliks & also the Governor of the NorthWest Provinces, which begin on this side (east) of the Jumna River. You will get purwanas (sort of orders to local officials) from these Governments through the Deputy Commissioners of Ambala & perhaps Saharanpur. These purwanas are useful in case one gets into any difficulty about supplies or coolies & one gives usually one of the chuprassis the power to collect what one requires & armed with a stick and a purwana he manages generally to get what one requires. In the district you will get grain (for horse) perhaps, otherwise probably nothing but fowls, eggs, perhaps a sheep, milk now & then (best take a milchgoat with you) and practically nothing else.

Good heavens, Dubois thought: not only camels and ponies, but a goat! Whatever would Griesbach advise him to obtain next? Indeed, absurd as it sounded, Dubois had been advised to ask the Maharajah of Sirmoor to lend him an elephant for travel in the Siwaliks. Even after all his years in the Indies, British India seemed colourful and exotic.

Let me know when you get into difficulties, and always let me know your next address. Make a rough sort of plan of operations & find out from the postmaster [at] Ambala where your next postal stations will be. Have your things addressed there & keep a man going backwards & forwards. You must give the man a letter to the Postmaster, asking him to hand over your letters etc. to your man, otherwise you won't get them…

Do not forget to take with you a lot of wooden tent-pegs for your tent. Your men will get them made in Ambala. You will require a good lot more than is actually necessary, as they continually break & get lost. Of course you can renew them in bigger villages from time to time.

Griesbach seemed to have thought of everything, from Dubois's social life to the payment of his servants and the stockpiling of tent pegs. Dubois was amused by his concern for minutiae.

Two tasks occupied Dubois the next morning, 13 February. The first was applying to the Collector and Magistrate of the District of Saharanpur for a *purwana*. This was easily accomplished via the efficiency of the Raj postal system. Dubois wrote a suitably officious letter – how these English loved their administrative ceremonies! – and sent it off.

The second priority was rescuing his tents from the railway station, which he decided warranted a personal visit to the luggage clerk. Unfortunately nothing Dubois said made the slightest impact on the man, who was determined to follow the exact protocol he had been taught. Exasperated and not a little insulted that this native clerk should question his word, Dubois went directly to the stationmaster, a dignified Sikh with a massive beard and the largest turban Dubois had ever seen.

'Ah,' said the man gravely, nodding as he listened to Dubois's explanation. 'Wait here, Sahib. I will deal with this.' He disappeared into another office. Through the door, Dubois could hear raised voices in a language he did not understand. The Sikh stationmaster reappeared in a minute or two, flashing a fine set of white teeth in a smile. 'Now, Sahib, if you go outside, all of your things will be put into a bullock cart for you. There is a carriage waiting also. I have instructed the driver to take you and your belongings directly to the hotel.'

'Thank you very much,' said Dubois, wondering exactly what had transpired.

'Not at all,' came the answer, with a smile and an ambiguous shake of the head. Dubois slipped a coin into the man's hand and departed to his waiting transport.

Now what remained to be done while he waited for word from the Collector and Magistrate of Saharanpur was to put together his expedition: men, camels, ponies, and a vast quantity of supplies. Once this caravan was assembled, he would take off for Nahan, in the foothills of the Siwaliks, to meet with the Maharajah. Griesbach had warned him that the Maharajah was a prickly, awkward fellow, an old-fashioned absolute ruler with modern ideas and a heart full of pride. The Maharajah's princely state, Sirmoor, contained many of India's best fossil sites, so his permission and assistance were essential for working in the area. On the way to Nahan, Dubois could visit a few areas of which he had read in Lydekker's papers.

To Dubois's surprise, the arrangements seemed to be relatively simple, thanks to Griesbach's tips. By the afternoon of his first day in Ambala, he had contacted Captain Mardall, Griesbach's friend of the 17th Bengal Cavalry, who had in turn sent word to the horse dealer he did most business with to find Dr Dubois a good pony. And Norton & Company were organizing the *khitmagar* and the other men he needed, subject to his approval. What had seemed a daunting task had suddenly shrunk to manageable size. Inwardly, he blessed Griesbach and his wonderful advice several times over the course of the next few days. He anticipated this part of his travels with a certain glee: it would be like the old days in the Indies, hunting for fossils alone with some natives to look after him, but even better. For one thing, he need have no concern that he would be plagued by the enervating, sultry heat and threat of fever that had made his work so difficult in the Indies. Here in the highlands of the Siwalik Hills – really, the beginning of the mighty Himalayas – the temperatures at night were cool enough to leave hoar frost on the ground. During the day, the sun shone brightly and warmed the air enough to make for comfortable working conditions. No wonder that the entire British government moved to Simla, the prettiest hill station in the Siwaliks, to escape the stifling heat on the plains during April, May, and June. It seemed a healthy, pleasant climate after the exhausting business of hunting for fossils in the Indies.

This expedition had another enormous advantage over his previous endeavours. Now Dubois was not looking for sites; he was visiting fossil localities that had already been found. Of course he would do some new prospecting as he travelled; it would be foolish not to. But there would be no tedious scrabbling up mountainsides and slogging along swampy riverbanks to find nothing, as had so often happened in the Indies. With Lydekker's maps and local guides, he should be able to find fossils with relatively little trouble most of the time.

He wrote a quick letter to Griesbach to advise him of his safe arrival in Ambala, making an amusing story of the little inconvenience of reclaiming his tents. As he settled down to eat his second dinner at the Hotel Lumley, he thought that all was well, everything was going remarkably smoothly. Only one matter worried him: he still had heard nothing from Anna since arriving in India. He sent a projected itinerary to Alcock, who would forward his mail from Calcutta if any should arrive. At home, the end of the rainy season was nearing: a bad time for fever. In a day or two, a child could sicken and die; in a week or two, his whole family might have perished, one after another, in dreadful agony. After Anna Jeanette's death, it was easy to imagine the worst.

He could not understand why else Anna's letters had grown so infrequent. At the beginning of his trip, she had sent regular, twice-weekly missives. They were filled with trivialities and gossip, but at least they had reassured him of the continuing well-being of his family. This recent, inexplicable silence seemed ominous. What could she be thinking of? Had she perhaps relapsed into the despondency that had threatened to consume her after the baby's death? He looked back through her letters, reading each one carefully for a hint of oncoming catastrophe. All she said in her last letter was that Prentice had stopped in from time to time to visit and share a meal or to play with the boys. The sentences leapt off the page at him, filled with new meaning. Could it be...? No, Dubois could not believe such a thing, not of Prentice. There had to be something else, something terrible. Perhaps that thing in the garden, the *pontianak*, had started crying again. But she did not mention it.

By the time a few more days had passed, Dubois was deeply concerned about his wife and family. He added a note to his letter to Alcock, asking him to check with the Dutch consul, in case there was mail for him that had been put aside somehow or delayed. Should that yield nothing, would Alcock please send the following telegram immediately to Prentice: 'Sir, Please explain visits to my wife in my absence. – Dubois.'

CHAPTER 34

Sirmoor State

On the tenth, Dubois departed Ambala at the head of a long caravan of porters and camels, astride a nicely moving little chestnut mare with good strong legs. She was called Tez, which means 'bright' in Urdu. They were headed to Schazadpur some twenty or twenty-five miles to the north-east, across the Dangri Lake. They rested there overnight, Dubois's first experience of a *dak* bungalow. These small bungalows were sprinkled throughout the country, put up and maintained by locals for the use of visiting officials. By virtue of his association with the Indian Museum and the India Geological Survey, Dubois was fully entitled to use them – and he was grateful for it, too, as many areas had no European hotels at all. It was the first *dak* bungalow of many he would stay in: not elegant, but clean and sound and convenient. Dubois judged this amenity an excellent idea and made a note to himself to suggest it to the Resident when he returned to Java.

In the morning, he marched east and north with his men, crossing another lake and a river, arriving at the small village of Kala Amb in the afternoon. Now they were at the edge of Sirmoor State, with only nine miles to travel in a north-easterly direction to reach Nahan. Nahan proved to be a rather charming hill station, with well-maintained tree-lined streets laid out in a design based on a series of circles – a plan thought up, it was rumoured, by one of the previous maharajahs. Dubois had written in advance requesting an audience; when he arrived, he found a letter from the Maharajah's secretary, whose name was a spiky drizzle of ink like the mark madc by a spider that had fallen into an inkwell. The therefore anonymous secretary gave him an appointment to see the Maharajah at noon. It was the beginning of a prolonged wrangle to obtain the necessary permissions and *purwanas*.

Precisely at noon, Dubois presented himself at the palace. It was an extraordinary building, full of Moorish arches; courtyards enclosing fountains, pools, and gardens; statues, rugs, and intricate screens and decorations. The Maharajah received him in a room awash with carvings, gold leaf, and intricate designs. The decor was far too exotic and fussy for Dubois's taste – every square inch of every surface was carved or gilded or painted or inlaid with precious stones – but it certainly conveyed the Maharajah's wealth and power. The Maharajah himself, a small dark man with an enormous moustache, wore an *ackhan*, a long coat with high collar made of richly embroidered stuff, over tight-fitting trousers. On his head was a magnificent turban, fastened in front with a large, gaudy pearl surrounded by gems. His fingers were studded with jewels set in gold rings. Dubois's high-necked *tutup* jacket and crisply ironed trousers were nondescript by comparison, but he fingered his own luxuriant, ginger-coloured moustache with a certain satisfaction.

The Maharajah was dignified and educated, with a good command of English. Dubois had been warned not to come to the point too rapidly lest the Maharajah think him rude. The Maharajah knew very well the point of Dubois's visit; it remained his responsibility to turn the conversation in that direction. The Maharajah was apparently interested in the rajahs and princes of Java. Were their palaces like this one, so small and ordinary? he asked with a deprecating gesture that begged Dubois to praise the extravagant surroundings. Dubois answered tactfully that he had seen nothing to compare with the Maharajah's palace in the Indies, though there were many fine palaces there also, especially in the region of Solo.

Pleased, the Maharajah began to speak to Dubois of his great scheme for modernizing his people. He had set up a school to provide higher education in English for intelligent young men of good families in Sirmoor State. They would acquire the knowledge and customs that had made the European nations great and would be his state's ambassadors to the outside world. The Maharajah asked whether there were facilities in Java for the higher education of the noble families in English. Truthfully, Dubois could not boast that there were. There were few schools of any kind for natives, although the odd princeling might be sent to Batavia for an education or might even be privately schooled by a Dutch tutor. No, the only Javanese favoured with a truly European education were the legally recognized children of Dutch fathers and Javanese mothers, and most of them were sent home to Europe for the purpose. He was duly admiring of the Maharajah's farsighted plans, while silently wondering if education alone could possibly transform the ignorant, illiterate peasants he saw along the roadside into the equals of educated Europeans.

'Ah,' said the Maharajah shaking his head sagely. 'But I have forgotten. Your princes are no longer heads of state in their own country, so they can do nothing for their people. They are merely – what is the phrase? – *younger brothers*, to be commanded and led by their Dutch elders. Hmm.' He paused here and looked at Dubois accusingly, as if he were to blame for the difficulties of colonial rule. 'So it is a very awkward situation. No prince wants to be ordered about in his own home,' he said firmly. 'No one does.'

Dubois did not know how to reply and so said nothing.

The Maharajah left the room soon after that, rather abruptly. Dubois was bewildered. Had he insulted the Maharajah? He did not think so. Surely he had said nothing but the most polite platitudes. After some uncomfortable minutes alone in the room, Dubois was relieved when an aide entered and introduced himself. He questioned the aide strongly, pressing him for a clarification of the situation. Had the Maharajah refused his request by leaving without discussing the matter? No, no, Sahib, certainly not. The Maharajah was a busy man, you know; things to attend to. Be flattered that he agreed to see you himself. Was he certain that the Maharajah had not somehow forgotten the very reason for Dubois's call? Oh no, Sahib, came the reply. The Maharajah was the most intelligent of men. He never forgot a thing. No, he had a formidable memory, as befitted a ruler. Then had the Maharajah's assistance been tacitly granted? The aide could not say; such things were the Maharajah's business and he had not been instructed.

The aide would make a note of the things that Dubois would need while travelling in Sirmoor. Perhaps Dubois could draw up a list, and an itinerary? He could present it to the Maharajah tomorrow, perhaps, or the next day. In the meantime, a guesthouse would be put at Dubois's disposal. Perhaps the doctor would care to buy a fine pony, to make his own journey more comfortable? The Maharajah's Keeper of the Horse could find some prospects for him. Ah, the doctor had already purchased a pony. A pity, that; the horses were so much better here than in Ambala. And men; surely Dubois would need men. If he would simply let the aide know how many were required, he would send along some men needing employment. Because of the Maharajah's education scheme, it was possible to hire men with very good English indeed. No? Dubois had already hired all the men he needed for his entire expedition? Ah, what a shame. Yes, it would have been better to take some local men; they had more experience in the Siwaliks. Just as the Doctor wished, then.

Dubois spent the rest of the day walking around Nahan and resisting all urging to buy more equipment, hire more men, and purchase additional ponies. The next day, gratifyingly, he received a letter from the Collector and Magistrate of Saharanpur granting him the desired *purwana* for Saharanpur District. That decided him. If the Collector and Magistrate of Saharanpur could issue a *purwana* so easily, so could the Maharajah. Clearly the Maharajah was delaying, perhaps resenting the orders from the Raj to cooperate. The inactivity made Dubois restless, the Byzantine politics impatient. When the silence from the palace continued the next day, Dubois decided to set out from Sirmoor, so that he could get something done while the Maharajah procrastinated. Soon he was trotting Tez along briskly in the early morning light, heading toward Kolar, fifteen kilometres to the east. From there, he sent a telegram to Griesbach complaining of the Maharajah's behaviour. The man had been cordial, to be sure, but he had been in no way helpful. Could Griesbach somehow prod the Maharajah into action?

Dubois and his men travelled eastward and then turned north, staying at the tiny village of Rampur on the Jumna River before ascending into the Siwalik Hills proper. Unbeknownst to Dubois, Griesbach had cranked the vast machinery of the Raj into action. Letters were written and notes filed, a flurry of telegrams was sent, until finally a telegram was dispatched to the government of the Punjab repeating the request to order the Maharajah to give Dr Dubois every assistance. In the meantime, Dubois and his expedition marched on, arriving at Kalianpur on the twenty-second. There they would spend a few days collecting fossils. At last a letter from Alcock came by runner, sent on from Nahan.

> Indian Museum, 17 February 1895
>
> I was glad to hear of your safe arrival and I hope you are now unearthing the bones of Pleistocene ladies and gentlemen in plenty.
>
> The Dutch consul sent me a very thick envelope, which I took to be a letter from your wife: I therefore registered it and sent it on. I hope it reaches you safely. I have not sent the telegram yet, and shall not do so until I hear again from you. It is a great mistake – a mistake which I often make myself – to translate one's imagination into action: the imagination upsets no one but oneself, the action may upset other people.

Dubois was livid. What audacity, not to send Dubois's telegram, and he had taken Alcock for a friend, a colleague. He had believed Alcock when he had said how welcome Dubois was, what a pleasure it was to meet a fellow scientist doing such interesting work. Yes, but not enough of a pleasure to carry out a simple request of the utmost importance to Dubois. Really, the man was unspeakably rude and presumptuous. And as for Anna – well, time would tell what the envelope held and what story she had concocted to explain her actions.

All that day, and the next, Dubois drove himself and the men up and down the gullies and hills in a sort of frenzy. At least it was cool enough. Some of the men knew something about collecting, so Dubois did not have to teach them everything. They could recognize fossils and he asked them simply to call for him when they found a good or relatively complete old bone. They were not to touch it themselves until he had seen it, decided whether it was worth collecting, and made a note of its location *in situ*. By the end of two days, the accumulation of fossils was substantial and his anger had begun to wane. They left for Dehra Doon and the Forestry School station, where Gamble and the envelope sent via the Dutch consul awaited them.

Dehra Doon was a haven of civilization after camping in the remote settlement at Kalianpur. The Forestry School was well organized and had an impressive library of information about the area, from wildlife to geology to vegetation. A wiry, short man, little bigger than a native, with a tanned, weatherbeaten face, Gamble regaled Dubois with accounts of his work and studies: the relationship of the density of deodar trees to altitude; annual rainfall figures going back many years; surveys of the forest animals and their habitats. He had annotated copies of all the topographic maps from which Lydekker had worked when he was there. While not everyone would have found these matters entertaining, Gamble's enthusiasm and intensity were contagious. Besides he, like Dubois, was something of a scientific polymath, interested in almost everything in this tiny corner of the world. Only after Dubois had had a cool drink, a bath, a tour of the station, and a hot supper did Gamble produce the long-awaited envelope, saying rather casually, 'Oh, some things came for you from Cal the other day; a telegram and this envelope. It looks as if it must be from the Indies. Letters from home, eh, Doctor?'

Dubois could hardly prevent himself from snatching the packet out of Gamble's hands. Of course, the man had no way of knowing how important this might be, Dubois thought generously. 'Ah, thank you,' he said a little stiffly. 'I'm rather tired and I have been awaiting this package for some time. I think I will retire now and look it over. I'll see you in the morning, then?'

'Yes.' Gamble nodded. 'If you need something before then, just ring for the boy. Mohammed will see to anything you want.' He gestured to the slender young man in a spotless white uniform standing discreetly at the other side of the room.

Comfortably ensconced in his room, Dubois tore open the packet forwarded by the consul. It contained two letters from Anna, but no explanation. It was as if she were completely unaware of the anxiety she had caused him by her silence. She wrote of the weather, the children's games and health – 'you will be glad to see how well Eugenie is doing on her pony, and Jean seems to grow taller every day, you will hardly recognize him when you return.' Then there was a small problem with the servants, described in boring detail, and an account of the friends she had seen and the gossip she had heard. Oh, and that charming Mr Prentice had been by again on his way back from Malang. He had brought some of the most lovely potted plants that he had bought there – a really brilliant hibiscus that stood on the front veranda and a huge, fragrant frangipani that she had had the *tukang kebun* plant near the wall, in the far corner. The *tukang kebun* did not remember to water unless she nagged him, she suspected, but so far it seemed to be taking well because the small rains still came every other day or so.

The next letter was much the same, reassuring in that Anna sounded ordinary, as she always did. There was no word of illness or fever, no hint of hysteria in her tone. But Dubois noticed that Prentice had visited yet again – how many times was that since he had been gone? – and he wondered. Of course, Prentice was a charming man, and handsome: who should know that better than Dubois, his closest friend? And he had not remarried, though he had taken up with a lovely *nyai* from a nearby village. He must still be a little lonely for civilized company, especially with Dubois gone.

In the back of his mind, Dubois could feel the irritating wriggle of that small worm of suspicion, jealousy, and doubt. He thought that Prentice ought not to call on Anna so often. It was probably just friendly concern – Prentice knew how worried Dubois was at leaving Anna alone – and yet, and yet…The tropics moved respectable people to disreputable impulses. He knew this was true; he had seen it many, many times. No threat of scandal, no possible disruption of the family's peace was enough to prevent it. And in the Indies, where attitudes were more lax, the sinners need not even fear social ostracism, except for a brief period. All was forgivable in the Indies.

He determined to write Anna tonight, and Prentice. He would ask Anna to explain the sudden dearth of letters, to see what she said, and he would simply write Prentice an ordinary letter, telling him of his travels and discoveries. He needed only mention at the end that he understood Prentice had been calling on Anna rather often in his absence. Just a hint, nothing more: that was all it would take.

CHAPTER 35

Siwalik Adventures

For the next week, Dubois spent most of his days travelling and hunting for fossils, with considerable success. His itinerary sounded like a travelogue of the Saharanpur District: Dehra Doon, Khagnaur, Kalawala Pass, Kerwapani, Badshah Bagh, Kalesar, and Kolar. What he most wanted to do was spend a few weeks camping at the remote village of Haripur, in Sirmoor, where the best fossil sites were reputed to be. But he could not work there without the Maharajah's permission, and so far there had been no word from the palace. The man's obstinacy was infuriating! Before leaving Dehra Doon, Dubois sent another telegram asking once again for the *purwana*s, guide, and elephant he needed. A reassuring reply came the next day, but no guide, no elephant, and no *purwanas* appeared.

Dubois travelled on, exploring the areas where he was permitted to work. The scenery was spectacular, like nothing in the Indies. The plains and foothills were brown, dusty, dry; then, as he climbed up into the hills themselves, there were magnificent vistas of deodar trees, pine-covered slopes, much more vegetation of all sorts. His Indian pony Tez proved herself a sure-footed, tireless, good-tempered beast; he slowly winnowed his entourage of coolies, porters, and guides and trained them into a fairly effective force. The daily routine of setting up the camp, producing hot meals, settling in for the night, and then eating and packing up again in the morning was now well polished. Dubois had been fortunate in his choice of *khitmagar*.

When still more days passed with neither the guide nor further communication from the Maharajah, Dubois again telegraphed Griesbach, complaining in even stronger language about the lack of cooperation. Griesbach investigated, and identified what seemed to be the heart of the problem: 'Obstruction by Rajah Nahan owing it is stated to orders having been issued to Rajah through Extra Assistant Commissioner Ambala.' There was another round of official orders, which seemed to do nothing.

Events conspired to worsen Dubois's mood. Fossils seemed scarce. Runners sent back and forth to various postmasters found no letters from Anna. Dubois's conviction that Prentice was responsible grew daily more certain. Of course, she would have come to admire and respect his friend even more in Dubois's own absence. Of course; of course. Prentice wound perceptibly through her infrequent letters. Early in March, he heard from Alcock in Calcutta once again.

> Indian Museum, 3 March 1895
>
> I am glad to learn that you are safely started at last and I hope you will have good luck. I got your box of photographic apparatus landed, and sent it off by post last week. I fancy it will have reached you by this time. No letters have come for you for some time.
>
> I am sorry that you misunderstood my remarks about bottling up one's anxieties and apprehensions. I did not mean that I was annoyed because you asked me to send the telegram; but I meant to suggest that your own friends might be needlessly alarmed by a telegram.

He set the letter aside – what did Alcock know of this, anyway? – and tried to concentrate on his work. At least the English he had met so far found his work interesting, and there had already been a brief notice in *Nature* about his monograph. Soon there would be more, he thought: additional comments, reviews perhaps, or accounts of scientific meetings. If only he had not been at the ends of the earth, where news travelled so slowly. He had never been a patient man, and he was doubly frustrated now. When the box of photographic equipment arrived, he opened it immediately. To his surprise, the box also contained a copy of an article in the German journal *Naturwissenschaftlijke Wochenschrift* (Natural Science Weekly) about his monograph. How kind of Alcock to send it along, knowing he would want to see it as soon as possible.

As Dubois skimmed quickly through the article, his pleasant mood evaporated in seconds. The piece was written by Paul Matschie, a zoologist, and his opinion of the monograph was scathing. Dubois had utterly failed to persuade Matschie of the most fundamental fact: that the tooth, skullcap, and femur belonged to one individual animal. Without that basis, the rest of the work was a futile exercise in analysis of something that did not exist. 'My God!' exclaimed Dubois under his breath, as he read. He was a man who rarely used bad language, but this was shocking, shocking. 'Am I never to be freed of this absurdity? Is the idiotic opinion of that fool in Batavia, Homo Erectus, to follow me the rest of my days?' He threw the article down on to the table impatiently, angrily.

'Sahib?' asked one of his men softly. 'You need something, Sahib?'

'Yes, yes,' he replied irritably, snatching up the article again and reading the damning words over once more. 'Bring me some tea, some strong tea.'

'Yes, Sahib, right away, Sahib,' the man replied, making the respectful gesture of *namaste* – two hands pressed together, raised in front of the face, as in the Indies – before leaving swiftly and silently.

Dubois had already written Gamble, asking for news of the reception of his monograph, and now he wrote again. Matschie could not be the only one to have noticed his work. There would be other, more intelligent assessments, surely. He awaited the arrival of the post morosely, the triumphant mood he had enjoyed for weeks now turned dismal. There was no word from Java, from Europe, or from the Maharajah. He sent yet another letter to the latter, hoping it would produce the desired assistance. Perhaps telegrams were too terse, too curt; perhaps the Maharajah needed sweetness, coaxing. His letter of 4 March 1895, was answered the same day by one asking him to pay for the coolies he had requested and for fodder for the elephant. At last! So the problem was that the Maharajah wanted his people to be paid, not simply conscripted as in the Dutch East Indies. Dubois replied immediately, agreeing to the projected costs. By letter the next morning, the Maharajah confirmed that a guide and elephants were on their way to meet Dubois at Haripur.

The guide was Sukh Chain Sinha, the son of one of the Maharajah's *tehsildars*. He was an educated young man – a product of the Maharajah's own schools, he proudly informed Dubois – with good English. Dubois found him a little oily and officious in his presence, yet arrogant with the coolies. Heretofore the *khitmagar* had handled his responsibilities ably without fuss and the expedition had run smoothly. Now Sukh Chain Sinha was here and there were conflicting orders, disagreements, and resentments. Dubois realized he was burdened with this young fool, the Maharajah's chosen one (perhaps his spy?), for the duration of his stay in Sirmoor. He could not dismiss the youth, for his employment was clearly part of the price Dubois had to pay for the

Maharajah's cooperation, in addition to the ridiculous two rupees a day for the elephant's fodder and the four rupees a day for coolies. How could a man with a gold- and gem-encrusted palace niggle over two rupees a day for elephant fodder?

But the elephant was as helpful as it was exotic, for the thickly-vegetated terrain was difficult to navigate on foot or horseback. The view from the elephant's back proved excellent for spotting areas where there were exposures; Dubois's keen eyes could even pick out individual fossils sometimes. Dubois and the expedition settled into a good campsite in Haripur and began finding fine mammal specimens, similar to those that made up Lydekker's fauna. Dubois discovered that the Maharajah had even ordered his representative in Haripur to hand over to him 'some 5 fossil bones' in their possession. Five bones! To add to his hundreds... He must remember to express his thanks to the Maharajah.

Dubois was further cheered when he received a letter from Prentice a few days later. Now he could put his suspicions to rest, he thought; now he could see if there was anything between his best friend and his wife. It was unthinkable, impossible, a completely unfair suspicion. No, Prentice could not have... But the suspicion squirmed and grew in his mind, try as he might to kill it. This new letter would settle things. He had had so many from Prentice, they had corresponded so often, surely he would know instantly if anything was amiss.

Dubois borrowed this elephant from the Maharajah of Sirmoor to use in his explorations.

Toeloeng Agoeng, 7 March 1895

My dear Doctor,

I would have written you long ago but have been very busy at my work with the new coffee estate on the Willis and generally very wearied after my day's work or not much disposed for letter writing.

Things are going on after a fashion, but not very briskly. I have rather few workers and bad weather with difficult muddy roads & etc. & etc. Today I am down in town with Mr. Boyd as I require to see the Resident & controllers in connection with my coffee estate. I thus profit by the opportunity to write you a few lines but you will excuse brevity on my part as I have not much time and less news. Indeed there is nothing here worthy of mention. Everything is going along in its customary course. Dr. Van Buren of Djombang is come to Kediri on 1st April & Dr. v/d Veldt is going to Europe. Mr. Van der Woude is not in the best of health & is at present with the doctor at Blitar, I hear.

I suppose you have not seen much of northern British India? I trust you met with a kindly reception there and are pleased with your visit. You will no doubt have acquired fluency in speaking English and I sincerely hope your visit to Calcutta has been a profitable one for you from a scientific standpoint.

The time is nearing when your return to Java may be looked for as not far distant, & I trust you will find everything here in the best order and have no reason to regret the journey you undertook to British India.

When you return to Toeloeng Agoeng we shall be sure to meet you once more and hear of your travels.

Wishing you a safe return to Java, believe me to be, with kind regards in which Mr. Boyd heartily joins me,

Yours Sincerely,
Adam Prentice

The letter sounded just like Prentice, no different from any previous letter. The man was honest to the core, Dubois thought; he should never have doubted him. The bad weather must be making it difficult for Prentice to plant his coffee trees and build his roads and warehouses. And the lack of able workers: this was a problem Dubois knew well indeed. But Prentice was very good with the natives, very fair; he would manage.

... Odd that Prentice should write from Toeloeng Agoeng and make no mention of seeing Anna or the children. Wasn't it? If he were innocent?

Some nights later, he was again in the grip of a black mood. All his troubles over the last few years crowded in on him: the deaths; the endless difficulties of trying to find *P.e.*; the fevers that threatened his life and sanity; the lazy, insolent labourers who cheated at every opportunity; the villagers who would not tell him where fossils or caves were; the days of scrambling up mountains in that awful, awful heat. Now most of these tortures were repeated all over again in an Indian fashion, with that obstinate Maharajah, his odious guide, and the endless troubles with food for the ponies, goats, camels, and the elephant. And the review by that useless German scoundrel Matschie, who knew nothing about those fossils, nothing! Dubois should be hailed for his success at finding *P.e.*, honoured by every natural historian in Europe, not criticized. Somehow his courage seemed a little weak tonight. Perhaps he had a touch of fever coming on. Uncharacteristically, he tried to share his mood in a letter to Anna: 'The case of my missing link evokes more general interest than I had thought. If I possess enough cheerful fortitude to introduce her in Europe personally, I do not doubt she will be wonderfully victorious. That would shed a little light on my poor life, which has been so marked by sadness in the last years.'

A warm and sympathetic letter from Gamble in Dehra Doon arrived the next day, 15 March. Of the attacks by Matschie and others on Dubois's monograph, Gamble wrote, 'I hope you will succeed in bringing them all round eventually & possibly in making them stronger believers even than if they had accepted your demonstrations straight off. I suppose it is only human nature when a new thing is brought out, for the authorities to try to find all the arguments they can against it.'

Another missive came, this time from Griesbach, with a troubling remark about a review of Dubois's monograph. 'Did you read Lydekker's critique of your essay in *Nature*?' Griesbach asked. 'He is convinced that *Pithecanthropus* is no transitional form!'

These words haunted Dubois. What, exactly, had Lydekker said? What objection could he have voiced to *P.e.*'s transitional status? How could any anatomist have considered *P.e.* otherwise, with its apelike skull and humanlike femur? Where had he failed to convince?

In the meantime, the fossil-collecting in Haripur went well – very well, and Dubois would have an excellent collection to ship home to Holland – but there was nothing to compare to *P.e.* She was truly the greatest find of the nineteenth century, Dubois thought, never mind what Lydekker said or Matschie or anyone. On the twenty-fourth, he called an end to his adventures and set out for Barara, where he would catch the train back to Ambala and then back toward Calcutta. Though he tried to suppress them, his concerns coloured his next letter to Anna, written from Delhi.

> Griesbach writes about the critique of Lydekker in *Nature*. I regret that I have not yet read this critique; but I conclude it must be of little merit because Lydekker suffers from impossibly anti-Darwinian tendencies. After becoming better acquainted with his writings of the last few years during my visit here, I see him as a productive writer but a scientific man of only moderate value. He is an Indian scientist. Meanwhile, I desire very much to make the acquaintance of the piece in question.

He could not help pressing the pen more strongly into the page for that last sentence. Soon he would be back in Calcutta, catching a steamer to Rangoon, then on to Toeloeng Agoeng in late April or early May. His thoughts cycled over and over again, like a maddening tune that would not quit the brain. He convinced himself of the worst, of the ruin of both his career and his marriage. There was nothing he could do from this distance about Anna, but he sent a desperate telegram to Griesbach pleading for more information. No letters came to ease his mind, no copies of articles, no hopeful reviews from Europe: simply silence. It was worse than hearing bad news, this endless, mysterious, infuriating silence.

On the way back to Calcutta, he visited the Taj Mahal. Who could be in India and not see this exquisite tribute of Shah Jahan to his late, beloved wife, Arjumand Banu Begam? The visit left him colder than ever. He could see the elegance in the building's design, its rounded minaret, its tranquil reflecting pools, its beautifully kept formal gardens. He especially admired the warmth of the rosy marble chosen and carefully transported from Makrana in Rajasthan. But the experience raised only bitterness in his soul, by forcing the comparison with his own fate. Where were the admiring crowds for his monument to science and evolution? Where were the praise, the glory, the appreciation of the magnificent intellectual edifice *he* had constructed? And where, where indeed, was the loving, faithful wife who should be waiting for him? The train journey to Calcutta seemed much longer and more arduous than the trip out. What had once charmed now irritated; what had fascinated, bored.

Leaving India

Calcutta seemed dirty, ugly and noisy to him now, after the cool green quiet of the hill country. He wondered if his eyes had been deceived when he first saw Howrah Station, thinking it colourful and cheerful. His huge piles of luggage had been joined by crates of fossils from the Siwaliks that would need to be dispatched to Holland. At least he found a warm welcome at Alcock's house, and he had forgotten his irritation with Alcock.

'Doctor!' cried Alcock happily, coming out of the front door when he saw the carriage pull up. 'So you are back at last! And was your trip successful? Have you found many fine fossils? You must tell me all about it! And what are these – boxes of fossils, eh? Jolly good, jolly good.' Dubois could hardly get a word in edgewise, so effusive was his friend at his return. Perhaps it was for the best, for Dubois was feeling travel-stained and exhausted.

'Come in, come in,' urged Alcock, while the servants took care of the mountains of luggage. 'You must be in need of a wash-up and a cool drink. Go on up to your old room, I'll send Mohammed up to you.' Dubois was a good deal refreshed by his bath and his tumbler of cool lime juice. By the time he came down to greet Alcock properly, it was nearly time for lunch. He could see Alcock had laid on a special meal for him. Such a thoughtful friend, Alcock. They relaxed with cool drinks in the drawing room for half an hour or so while the preparations for the meal were completed.

'Thank you, Alcock, for making me welcome once more. The trip was exhausting, I don't mind telling you. I did get a lot of good fossils, though I never found any more of Lydekker's *Anthropopithecus*,' said Dubois.

'Ah, what a shame! Still, the beast must be very rare, I suppose,' replied Alcock. 'Griesbach has sent over a copy of that *Nature* note by Lydekker – unfortunate, that, really a little tough on you, but I suppose he has a right to his opinion. And some mail has just come for you, too.'

Dubois could not keep his weary eyes from skimming the *Nature* article, despite Alcock's and Griesbach's warnings. Lydekker's article started nicely enough, but only, Dubois thought, to make his later criticisms more pointed.

Review of Dubois's *Pithecanthropus erectus*, eine menschenaehnliche Uebergangsform aus Java.

Java, from its geographical situation, being just one of those countries where the remains of a connecting form between man & the higher apes would be extremely likely to occur ...

'Ha!' exclaimed Dubois aloud and Alcock looked up from his newspaper, sympathetically curious. 'At least the man has understood my fundamental reasoning about why the missing link would be found in the Indies,' Dubois explained to Alcock. 'I spelled it all out in my 1888 article and it is clear that Lydekker accepts my argument. How widely disbelieved that notion once was – "Don't be misled by Darwin's crazy book," they said to me – and now it is nothing more than a commonplace observation in an article in a learned journal by one of England's best-known paleontologists.'

'Ah yes,' murmured Alcock, knowing there was worse to come.

Dubois returned to his reading.

... zoologists have naturally been attracted to the title of the work before as it proclaims in no uncertain terms that such a missing link has actually been discovered. A feeling of disappointment will, however, probably come over the student, when he finds how imperfect are the remains on the evidence of which this startling announcement is made and when he has submitted them to a critical examination he will probably have little difficulty in concluding *that they do not belong to a wild animal at all.*

What audacity! That Lydekker, who had named *Anthropopithecus sivalensis* on the basis of a scrappy jaw fragment, should criticize Dubois for working with 'imperfect remains'. Indignation burned hotly in his mind. It was small consolation that Lydekker announced himself 'content' to accept Dubois's assertion that all three fossil specimens were derived from a single animal, for he found that animal to be human. The size of the braincase – huge for an ape, deficient for a man – he attributed to the skull owner's being 'a microcephalic idiot, of an unusually elongated type'. It was the same old jibe that had been made about the Neanderthal skullcap: can't be primitive or old, must be pathological. Lydekker's prejudice against Darwinism showed clearly in this, Dubois thought, just as Virchow's had when he had tried to discredit the Neanderthal remains.

Lydekker's conclusions were flatly dismissive:

Haeckel's '*Pithecanthropus*' may, therefore, be relegated to the position of an hypothetical unknown creature for which it was originally proposed; while the specific name '*erectus*' must become a synonym of the frequently misapplied '*sapiens*'.

The piece left a bitter taste in Dubois's mouth and a conviction that Lydekker was neither anatomist nor scientist at heart.

Dubois had never anticipated a problem of acceptance once the fossils had been found. To have failed in his great quest would have been difficult to bear, for so much had been at risk. But now he saw that the pain of outright failure would have been much less than the anguish caused by success achieved but unjustly ignored. He had found the missing link, and still it was not enough. What he reaped for his years of backbreaking, mind-wrenching, courageous work was bitter betrayal and criticism from armchair experts. Pah! He had no respect for these men, but their knives were sharp and cut deeply. And he bled and bled, with no one to staunch his wounds.

He turned to the second envelope Alcock had handed him, seeing at once that it was neither from Anna nor from Prentice as he had hoped and feared. It contained a begging letter from the Maharajah's spy, Sukh Chain Sinha, asking for a testimonial letter. It was as oleaginous as the man himself, and Dubois had no intention of recommending the youth to another innocent European. He folded the letter tightly and put it away. After a pause, Dubois asked Alcock hesitantly, 'I don't suppose that there were any other letters for me, letters from Java?'

'No,' Alcock shook his head sadly, reading Dubois's eagerness. 'Nothing has come. I've checked with the Dutch consul, too. Perhaps your wife feared to miss you, that you'd already got on the ship for Rangoon.'

'Ja,' remarked Dubois, dubiously, sadly. 'That must be it.' He knew full well how scatterbrained his wife was. Would she have even considered that the letter might miss him?

'Oh, but there *was* an envelope from America, though, came some time ago,' Alcock remembered suddenly. 'Mohammed!' The servant came running. 'Mohammed, where did we put the doctor's letter from America?'

'In the desk drawer, Sahib, in your office,' Mohammed answered. 'I will get it.'

In a moment, the envelope was in Dubois's hands. 'Maybe it's about your monograph,' Alcock guessed.

And so it proved to be. It was from the paleontologist Othniel Marsh, one of the few Americans to whom Dubois had sent his monograph. Dubois looked through the article quickly, and was pleased. 'Here, now Alcock, at least someone appreciates my work!' he said cheerfully, brandishing the article. 'This is from Marsh, at Yale you know, in the States. He's written a piece about my monograph in the *American Journal of Science*. He calls the unearthing of *P.e.* one of the most important discoveries since the finding of Neanderthal man. And listen to this: "It is only justice to Dr Dubois and his admirable memoir to say here, that he has proved to science the existence of a new prehistoric anthropoid form, not human indeed, but in size, brainpower and erect posture, much nearer Man than any animal hitherto discovered, living or extinct." '

Alcock listened attentively and then burst out, 'Jolly good! That's more like it. I think we ought to celebrate that. Shall we have some beer at lunch?' The two went in to eat happily gossiping and exchanging news.

The next day Dubois called on Griesbach, who had helped him so much, to discuss his findings and the various articles about *P.e.* Of all he had yet received, only Marsh's article had so far supported him. He was dismayed to learn that Marsh's reputation was somewhat tarnished.

'Y'know, Dubois,' Griesbach said confidingly, 'that Marsh chap seems a damned fine paleontologist, but there is talk about some bad business between him and Matthew Cope. I don't remember all the details – something about stealing fossils, or what the Americans quaintly call claim-jumping, I think. They're both after those dinosaur bones that the American West seems to be full of, and there's been some dirty dealing there. But Marsh still has a good reputation as a paleontologist, so his endorsement should help you out.'

Dubois visited the Indian Museum to see his other friends and to show them his fossils, taking some hours to compare his new specimens carefully with Lydekker's in the museum's collections. Now that the man had come out against him, Dubois would have hated to make a mistake in identifying a Siwalik species and leave himself vulnerable to Lydekker's further scorn. For the first time Dubois noticed undercurrents of disagreement, quarrel, and jealousy among his colleagues at the museum. Had he been blind to them before? Or had he simply been too much a stranger for them to talk frankly in front of him? Whichever the case, he was sadly disconcerted by the pettiness and edgy atmosphere he found among the curators. They seemed self-absorbed, all-consumed by their own territorial squabbles. He had hoped for more concern for his successes and interest in his opinions.

That evening Dubois wrote to Anna, mostly focusing on his worries about the reception his precious monograph and fossil were receiving abroad. Lydekker and Matschie were definitely on the 'con' side; only Marsh had so far enlisted pro-*P.e.* If it was to be a battle, he was as yet outnumbered. 'Marsh sent me a reprint from an American magazine about *P.e.*, in which figures are reproduced, pointing out its great importance,' he wrote Anna. 'He praised my work. But he has done a lot that has given him a bad name despite all his fame, because he has been involved in some American humbug.'

In the days that followed, there was no mail from Anna, nor from Prentice. Dubois's patience, limited at the best of times, snapped. There was no longer any doubt in his mind what had occurred. By their silence, his wife and his dearest friend had told him more plainly than any words that they did not care for him. Their pledges of constancy were rendered as cold and worthless as the ashes from a fire that had once warmed and lighted the darkness. It was a bitter, sour-faced man who crated up his Siwalik fossils a few days later to ship them off to Holland. With each passing day, he was more and more discouraged, more irritated by the eccentric ways of the British in India and by the squabbles that buzzed around the Indian Museum like a vicious swarm of insects.

On 14 April, he was more relieved than saddened to bid farewell to the India, the Raj, and her people. He sailed for home on the SS *Lindula*, calling first at Rangoon. With every passing mile, his anger grew blacker and his imagined reproaches more savage. He had spent four months and a great deal of money on this trip, and what had he to show for it? A few crates of fossils, miles upon miles of dusty, uncomfortable travel with useless, lazy natives, a few scenic views from the famous Siwalik Hills, and the public ruin of his private life. He had no doubt that the affair between Anna and Prentice was the talk of Java. Servants always knew these things, and they spread the word farther and faster than even the highly efficient European gossips did. In return for his eight long, hard years of work and perseverance, he had been served up dishes of acidic criticism by stay-at-home strangers and bitter faithlessness by those closest to him. The scientific scepticism burned like the hottest Indies pepper, the betrayal repelled him like the noxious smell of the durian fruit so beloved of Javanese natives. He could not imagine any combination of events that could have pained him more acutely than these. He wrote to Anna,

> 14 April 1895
> So I have now left the ground of India, and I am happy to have done so because, taking everything together, nothing – not the stay here, not the travelling, nor the country itself – has pleased me. Even the friendships that I have enjoyed here are spoiled because those who gave me friendship hated each other... The amount I have profited scientifically has certainly not been worth the labour and cost.

He was delayed in Rangoon several days, on account of some confusion at the booking office, but set off again by steamer for Penang on the twenty-third. With a good connection between ships there, it took him just a few more days to go from Penang to Singapore, where he called in on Prentice's friends Galloway and Lyon. Welcoming as they were, they had no news from the Indies to report. No letters, no explanations; nothing at all from Anna or Prentice. It was true, it was all true. He knew it by the almost tangible pain in his stomach, as if he had been poisoned. But there was no doctor's medicine that could heal him, no art that would diminish his anguish.

He arrived at Tanjung Priok in Batavia on 2 May. The exhausted and nearly broken man who returned was in shocking contrast to the hale, optimistic Dubois who had left months before. His acquaintances in Batavia wondered what had happened to him in India, whether he had caught another fever perhaps. Rather than struggle to be sociable, he pleaded travel fatigue and declined all invitations to dine that night or to stay on a few days. The next day, he set forth by train to Toeloeng Agoeng. It was a two-day journey that seemed much longer. Each passing mile brought him closer and closer to the ruin of his personal life and the confrontation with those who had been faithless. There was no avoiding it. He would have to survive whatever occurred and leave for Europe as soon as possible. He did not know how he could bear to live with Anna any longer. For that matter, if his missing link was totally rejected by the scientific world, he did not even know how he would find the courage to live at all.

Toeloeng Agoeng

As Dubois stepped off the train in Toeloeng Agoeng, he saw that everyone had come to meet him. Anna was standing there, in her prettiest European hat and dress, pale blue trimmed with a darker border that showed off her lustrous hair and fair skin to advantage. And Prentice was there, too, standing by her side, tall and sun-browned and handsome as ever. When he first spied Prentice, his heart leapt up with the anticipated joy of sharing with his friend all his discoveries and experiences in India – and then fell, as he remembered those damning letters. Prentice. Prentice and Anna. He had not anticipated the confrontation with them coming so soon, or so publicly. His face darkened with choler as he appreciated their cunning bravado. Oh *ja*, come to the train together to meet him, all innocent and above board! He looked around involuntarily, as if seeking an escape route, and instead saw the children and Babu waiting in a *delman*, all dressed in their best finery as if for a celebration. 'Papa, Papa!' the children cried waving frantically at the father they had not seen in more than four months. Babu lowered her eyes respectfully and waved shyly also. Behind their *delman* stood another, presumably to carry Anna, Dubois, and Prentice back home, and behind that, an ox cart waited to receive his luggage. How horribly well organized it all was, this nightmare.

Dubois had not succeeded where everyone else had failed by avoiding the difficult. *Recte et fortiter*, he thought to himself, squaring his shoulders and putting on his hat; *Recte et fortiter*. He would not be shamed or defeated, not here in public on the platform in full view of all of Toeloeng Agoeng. He walked forward boldly, carrying only his small case and leaving the rest for the coolies to fetch. 'Anna, my dear,' he said upon reaching the couple, his wife and his best friend. She took a step forward, holding up her arms for an embrace. He deflected this, kissing her a little coldly on the cheek. He could see in her eyes that she was puzzled, a little hurt.

'Dubois, my dear doctor!' exclaimed Prentice. There was no

avoiding his firm hug of welcome, though Dubois stiffened in his arms. He could bring himself neither to wholeheartedly return his friend's affection nor to openly reject it.

'Prentice,' he murmured over his friend's shoulder. 'I had not thought to see you here.'

'No,' said Prentice, stepping back and grabbing his hand for a warm shake, 'Mrs Dubois and I planned it as a surprise for you. We knew you'd think she'd be waiting at home, just as usual, but we found out what train you were on. Welcome home, old friend, welcome home!'

Dubois was overwhelmed by the apparent genuineness of the man's affection. Could his awful suspicions have been wrong? Could he have hardened his heart against Prentice for nothing? His thoughts flipped back and forth wildly, like a leaf in a high wind. No one could have feigned such fondness for Dubois had he been seducing Dubois's wife, no one. Surely...But there were those letters, and those weeks and weeks of no letters, and all the visits to Anna...What a terrible blackguard the man must be, to practise such deception while seeming open and honest. Prentice must have been truly a snake in disguise, a viper that had wound its way into his heart while intending only to impart the poisonous bite. Dubois did not know how to react, and so grew stiff and taciturn.

'And here are the children, Eugène,' Anna said gently as Babu brought them over. Dubois kneeled down to greet his brood, tidy and neat for once and behaving properly. He enveloped them, all three at once, in a bear hug, and kissed their heads.

'And how have you been, my little ones? Eugenie? Jean? Victor? Are you all well? Have you obeyed your mama and been good children?' They nodded solemnly, round-eyed at so much attention from their father, who seemed like a stranger to them.

'Papa, I have been learning how to ride my pony,' said Eugenie proudly, hoping for his approval. 'I could go out for rides with you. We can look for fossils.' Dubois chuckled and patted her curly head.

'And Papa, Papa, I can read lots of new words, now, and books, big books from home,' bragged Jean, pulling on his father's sleeve. He did not like to be outdone by his big sister. He expanded in his father's smile like a flower in the sun.

'I know my letters, Papa,' whispered Victor, a little anxiously. 'And the cat, the little tabby that lives in the kampong, has kittens and Mama says I can have one. Can I, Papa? Please?'

'Yes, Victor, all right, we will pick out a kitten for you,' said Dubois gently. He looked at Anna over the children's heads, while he talked to them. 'That's very good about your lessons, Jean. You shall read to me when we get home. And you can show me how well you can ride, Eugenie.' Anna could not interpret the meaningful glance Dubois had cast at her; she had no idea of his suspicions. She saw he was behaving oddly, but she did not understand why.

'You must be very weary, Dubois,' surmised Prentice, looking at Dubois's masklike expression, 'after such a long journey. We'll get you home quickly.' As he hustled Dubois's family down the platform toward the waiting *delman*s, he tried to fill the stony silence with conversation. He could not imagine what was wrong with Dubois; he seemed not to be himself. 'And was the journey successful, then? Did you find lots of fossils in the Siwaliks? Mrs Dubois showed me some of your letters; she used to send me a note up at Mringin when one arrived, so that I could come down and learn the latest news,' Prentice continued.

'Ja, ja,' said Dubois, nodding. 'It was a difficult journey in many ways, but I learned a great deal.' He paused and then continued, heavily, meaningfully, 'I even learned some things I never expected to. Sometimes you only understand the true nature of a thing when you are far from it.' With these words, he stared directly at Prentice, his eyes cold and penetrating.

Prentice had no idea what to make of this remark. He could feel the hostility emanating from Dubois, but he could think of nothing he had done to warrant it. Was Dubois perhaps angry that Prentice had joined in a family event? But he had always been so welcome at Dubois's house, so often a part of family occasions. All he could say by way of reply was, 'Ah, yes, Doctor. Well, you must tell me all about it when you have had time to rest. I am most anxious to hear about your discoveries and adventures.'

Both Prentice and Anna fell into an uneasy silence on the brief ride back to the house, cowed by Dubois's manner. Something had gone very wrong with their welcoming party. When they got back to the house, Anna shooed the children and Babu into the back garden and led the men onto the back veranda for cool drinks and a light meal she had had Kokkie prepare. Dubois excused himself to go and wash his face and change into more comfortable clothes while the others waited on the veranda.

'He is very tired, Mrs Dubois,' Prentice offered, settling into a rocking chair and rocking to and fro in it. 'That must be it.'

'Of course,' she agreed uncertainly, taking the seat closest to him. She placed her hand on his arm, pleadingly, hoping for understanding. 'But I thought it would please him so, to have us all there, you, me, the children. I thought it would show him how much he was missed while he was away. Why was he not pleased?'

'I don't know, Mrs Dubois,' replied Prentice, patting her hand comfortingly. 'I don't know. He seems almost angry about something. Perhaps...'

Dubois came back to the low murmur of their voices and the intimacy of their posture. He lost his temper in a flash. He strode over to them, keeping his voice down with effort, his face distorted with fury. 'Can't you even stay apart from each other for a few moments while I leave the room?' he hissed. 'Am I to have this going on under my very nose?'

Anna sprang back, hearing at first only the anger and not the specific accusation. Dubois turned to Prentice, who had stopped his rocking and sat, utterly still, staring at Dubois in shock. 'And *you*, my dear friend,' Dubois said bitterly, '*you* have so kindly looked in on my wife while I am gone, time after time, visit after visit, staying so long and so often that everyone in Toeloeng Agoeng must be talking of it. What *kind* concern for the well-being of my family,' he continued sarcastically, 'what an exhibition of true friendship. How could you treat me so?'

'Just what do you think I have been doing?' asked Prentice in a quiet, deadly tone of voice. He stood up to look his dear friend directly in the eye, for they were almost the same height. 'What exactly do you mean by those remarks?'

'Eugène –' Anna broke in breathlessly, pulling at Dubois's arm. 'Oh, no, no, you don't think—' She was so stunned that she was almost gabbling. The men were too absorbed in their confrontation with each other to pay much attention to anything she was saying. 'But, I mean, what do you think— Do you think— With the *children* here? My children?'

'Prentice,' answered Dubois in a voice full of the sadness of all eternity. 'You know exactly what I mean.' He tried to control the quaver in his voice, but he could not, and carried on regardless. 'You have been seducing my wife while I was in India. It is perfectly clear from the correspondence I received. I am only appalled that you have the treachery in your heart to come with her to the station to greet me.'

'*I did not!*' roared Prentice, flailing with his strong right arm as if to sweep away the accusation, and instead knocking over a table and potted palm. 'I have done no such thing!' He reached out with both hands and gripped Dubois on the shoulders, the two of them only a foot apart and looking like two versions of the same man. 'I did not,' he repeated in a stony whisper, staring into his beloved friend's eyes.

The servants had been squatting in the shadow of the veranda. Now they scurried over to right the table and sweep up the mess from the plant pot. As soon as possible, they backed away, crouching and averting their faces from the scene in front of them. They returned to their stations, deaf and mute to the unfolding conflict. They wanted only to be unseen, unnoticed, forgotten. They did not want the Tuan and Njonja to be angry with them later for what they had witnessed.

Dubois and Prentice stood like a tableau, face to face. There was hurt on both sides and anger: the measure of the deep bond of affection and understanding that they had shared. Either their intimacy would break under the strain of this accusation or it would survive for ever. They needed, both of them, to become sure of what they saw in each other's eyes, each other's hearts.

Anna interrupted, fussing and trying to smooth over the awkward situation. 'Mr Prentice,' she said a little shrilly, like a parody of an imperious *njonja*. 'Please *do* sit down again. I shall have the boy bring you another drink. Adik!' she called over one shoulder.

'Yes, Njonja?' inquired the *djongas* softly, not daring to look up or to approach too closely.

'Another drink for Tuan Prentice,' she said, never looking at the servant, who sidled silently into the house on bare feet. 'Now Eugène, we'll have no more of this,' she continued in an artificial voice, as if scolding a fractious child. 'You are tired and hungry and it makes you bad-tempered. Prolonged trips are always a strain on your constitution, and the last few months have been difficult for us all. After you've had your lunch and a rest, I'm sure you'll think better of this.'

Something had resolved itself between the two men, who had been ignoring Anna completely. Prentice released Dubois from his grasp – his embrace? – but not from his gaze. Dubois sat down in his chair, first looking at the floor thoughtfully and then lifting his head to return Prentice's look.

'And Mr Prentice,' she said, turning to the visitor and eyeing him down into his rocking chair, 'I'm sure no one is more grateful than the doctor for the thoughtful way you called in on me and the children from time to time, to hear the news of the doctor's success in India and to inquire after our well-being. It was most...civil of you, most kind. The children missed their father so much, I'm sure it was good for them when you had time to talk with them a little.' Some of this was lies, little social white lies, but she did not stop to think of that. Her objective was to re-establish normal social behaviour, and in that she succeeded. Abruptly, she ran out of courage and inventiveness and fell silent herself. At least she had prevented anything worse happening. There were no blows, no further shouting, only the echo of that terrible, terrible suspicion in Eugène's voice. She was still shocked at his words. How could he have thought...? Whatever had given him the idea that she...that she and Mr Prentice...that...She could not even formulate the words in her mind, for she was still a prim little *totok* from Amsterdam at heart.

Prentice made his excuses and rose to leave a few minutes later. Dubois stood up to see him out while Anna waited, frozen in fear, on the back veranda. She prayed that nothing would happen between them, not at the front, in the open, where everyone would see. She could hear no raised voices, so perhaps everything was all right.

Prentice turned to go down the steps to his horse and then turned back to face his friend. He could not leave without a last word. 'Doctor,' he said quietly, so no one else could hear, 'my dear doctor.' He gripped Dubois's hand firmly in both of his. 'You misjudge me. I am your true friend. You have had a bad time of it in India, I can see, or you would never think such a thing of me. Please come up to Mringin, as in the old days. You can tell me of your discoveries in India. Please.' His face was intense with sincerity and affection, as he thrust aside his own indignation in order to reach his friend's heart.

'I...' Dubois started to reply, but he could not control his voice. He placed a hand over Prentice's, but he was not sure yet what he thought, now that he had seen his friend. The entire confrontation had gone differently from the scene he had anticipated. His suspicions had been dislodged from the rock-hard certainties to which they had once clung limpetlike. He could not look at this man and think evil of him. He found it hard to speak. 'I...perhaps, Prentice, perhaps. I shall come if I can,' he finally stammered.

Prentice nodded, pressed Dubois's hand once again, and walked across the yard to mount his horse. The *syce* stood silently holding it, trying to be invisible. 'Mringin,' Prentice called in farewell, raising one arm in salute.

'Mringin,' replied Dubois softly, as if he were repeating a sacred pledge.

Prentice wheeled his horse and rode off, up the mountain, never to see Dubois again.

Departure

The remaining weeks of May and early June were spent in arranging transportation to the Netherlands for the fossils and the family. The Dubois would sail on a French mail-steamer departing on 27 June from Batavia for Marseilles, where they would catch a train to Paris and then another on to Amsterdam. In the meantime, there were possessions to be sorted – these to be sent home; these to be auctioned to clear the last of their debts and provide a cushion of money to see them through the first few months at home. The servants were given notice and Anna approached her friends and acquaintances to find positions for the better ones, the ones who had been really loyal and faithful. Each servant was given a written reference, which Anna knew would be produced proudly for the next newly arrived *totok*.

Dubois tried to put in order all of his notes and maps and scientific writings, making as sure as he could that every last detail that needed checking in Java had been verified. He organized the correspondence and field reports from De Winter and Kriele, placing the most extremely important papers in waterproof boxes in case of disaster on the voyage home. He remembered the trials of Alfred Russel Wallace, the great naturalist, who had lost almost his entire collection of specimens and his notes – indeed, and nearly his life, too – when the ship on which he had been returning from the Amazon had sunk within sight of land.

Dubois had a sort of suitcase made to hold the two lovely wooden boxes that housed the precious *P.e.* fossils, so that he would have only one case to look after as he brought them home, to Europe and their acceptance. He postponed the half-promised trip to Mringin to see Prentice, distracting himself with the many tasks that had to be completed before leaving. 'Next week I shall go up,' he promised himself, 'next week.' But in the end, he could not muster the courage to go and see Prentice again. What could he have said to this man, the man who had kept him from going mad when his father had died, who had gone to Trinil with him? What could he possibly have said to him now?

The criticisms from Europe continued to pile up mercilessly. The Dutch anthropologist Herman ten Kate joined the attack, writing in the *Nederlandsch koloniaal centraalblad* (Colonial Dutch Journal) that he too doubted the association of the skullcap, femur and tooth. In a cruel word play on Dubois's assertion that it would be foolish (*thöricht*) to presume that the specimens came from different individuals, Ten Kate remarked he would rather be regarded as *thöricht* than leap to such an unsupported conclusion. He regarded Dubois's method of calculating the cranial capacity from measurements of the skullcap as unproven in its accuracy.

And Rudolf Martin, the Swiss anthropologist, expressed his serious reservations, too, in an article in *Globus*. He too refused to accept the association of the three fossils and was sceptical of Dubois's estimated cranial capacity for *P.e.* Most of all, he faulted Dubois for failing to compare his fossil with the Neanderthal fossils, a point that particularly annoyed Dubois.

It was not as if I were sitting in Europe, Dubois fumed, needing only to stretch out my hand to obtain a cast of a Neanderthal skull. Besides, Neanderthals were much younger and really human. The *point* of my monograph was to compare *P.e.* to apes and humans, not to place it within the spectrum of the races of Man. *P.e.* was no human, that much was certain. Dubois began to feel like a sinner tied to the stake, the flames licking at his feet. Instead of praise for his astonishing achievement, he received only accusations of foolishness and incompetency. What crime had he committed? Finding the missing link, when no one else could? That was, perhaps, the truth. He was the Man Who Found the Missing Link, and now they resented him for it.

The next was Daniel Cunningham, a self-important anatomist in Dublin who made snide remarks in *Nature* and then had the audacity to give a lecture on *P.e.* on 23 February that was published in the *Journal of Anatomy and Physiology*. Dubois was outraged. What did this man know of *P.e.*? He could only have just read the monograph before giving his lecture. Cunningham, too, chastised Dubois for omitting comparisons to Neanderthals. Cunningham maintained that, since Neanderthals had cranial capacities of about 1200 cc, they had to lie on the direct lineage between *P.e.* and man: 'By a series of easy and nearly equal gradations we are led from the fossil form up through the Neanderthal and Spy forms to the modern cranial arch.' Feeling brain size was the more important issue, Cunningham denied the apelike shape of the *P.e.* cranium and concluded, magisterially,

The fossil cranium described by Dubois is unquestionably to be regarded as human. It is the lowest human cranium which has yet been described...The so-called *Pithecanthropus* is in the direct human line, although it occupies a place on this considerably lower than any human form at present known.

Dubois snorted incredulously as he read these words. But of course, how convenient for Cunningham and the others, how simple. If the skullcap was a primitive human, coupling it with the humanlike femur of *P.e.* eliminated all the awkwardness of assessing a transitional form. All evolution, in fact, neatly disappeared, and there was no need for Cunningham to grapple with the uncomfortable truth that there was, and had been, a missing link between apes and man.

Dubois kept his tally, dividing those who favoured his views from those who opposed them, noting also who believed the fossils derived from two or three separate animals, who thought the skull and femur human, who thought the skull apelike and the femur human, and so on. Opinions were so varied it was difficult to keep track. He would go back to Europe and show his specimens to every important man of science; surely that would convince them all. For some reason they did not understand his monograph properly. Perhaps, at thirty-nine pages, the work was too brief, but it was the best he could do in the Indies. Or perhaps the ideas were simply too new for them to be readily accepted. Darwin, he reminded himself, had been hotly criticized too.

The nearly endless details of packing and leave-taking finished, the Dubois family left Toeloeng Agoeng forever on 23 June, accompanied by Janet Boyd, the ten-year-old granddaughter of the Old Warrior. Janet would help with the Dubois children on the trip and then attend school in the Netherlands. Anna and Dubois made one last pilgrimage to the tiny grave in the Javanese cemetery across the road, laying flowers there and planting a frangipani. They instructed the servants to look after the grave and water the young tree, but they had little faith their wishes would be carried out for long. One more dead *totok* baby was nothing special to the Javanese. They had seen so many Europeans come and die that they were stoic. Anna wept at the thought of leaving that poor baby behind and all alone in the vastness of Java. Little Anna Jeanette would have been almost two years old by now if she had lived. There was nothing to be done, they had to go home again, and Anna accepted that, with difficulty. The grave of Anna Jeanette who might have been would be shaded by the frangipani as it grew, protected from the torrential rains and the burning sun. Perhaps in time the tree would drop its fragrant, thick-petalled, translucent flowers on her grave. While Babu sat with the children in the *delman*, they walked around their house once more, admiring its fine spacious proportions and cool marble floors, its lush garden and cool verandas. They would never have such a grand house again. Then they closed the doors for the last time and went off to the station with Janet, and the children, and the mountains of luggage.

When they arrived in Batavia, a letter from Prentice was waiting for Dubois.

Mringin, 23 June 1895

My Dear Doctor,

You will now be sitting in the train on the way to Batavia. I should indeed have liked to see you at your departure. Your promise of old, however, was to come up to Mringin for a day or two before you left. As you did not find time to do so, and I heard of your stay at Toeloeng Agoeng, I thought it better, even for your own sake, not to go down to take farewell of you & your family, & I therefore commissioned Mr. Boyd to bid you adieu for me.

The reason is this – You know you have taken me up wrongly on more than one occasion. You know what you once suspected me of in connection with Mrs. Dubois – a wholly groundless suspicion of course. Well, since I heard nothing from or about you just before your departure, I considered it best to keep away. An unguarded word, or even look, however innocent in itself, might revive some torturing suspicion in your mind & cast a cloud over your happiness. That is really why I kept away (as well as being very busy here) and I think it was better to keep away. At all events it obviated the smallest chance of any misunderstanding or wrong impression arising by any possibility in your mind.

However, from the bottom of my heart I wish you & yours a safe voyage, & good arrival in Europe, as well as health, happiness, & prosperity there. I hope to hear from you afterwards, and if I am ever rich enough to return to Europe I shall be sure to look you up in Holland.

Meanwhile believe me to be
   Very Sincerely Yours
      Adam Prentice

In haste (I predict you will appreciate Java more once you are settled in Europe?)
A.P.

Dubois read it through twice, slowly, as if memorizing the words. Then he folded the letter carefully and placed it inside the wooden suitcase that held the *P.e.* fossils for safekeeping. It seemed only right that Prentice should keep company with the missing link. They were the best of Java, Dubois thought.

CHAPTER 39

Europe

The ship to Marseilles became a little society, a tiny world unto itself, and the Dubois settled into a lazy rhythm of eating, reading in deckchairs, gossiping with fellow passengers, and napping. Restive from anxiety and lack of exercise, Dubois embarked on a regular programme of brisk striding around the deck, increasing the number of circuits every morning and evening like clockwork. He had Janet see to it that his children participated. They should not grow fat and lazy and sluglike, now or ever. He had no hope of overcoming Anna's basic nature or the indolence that had become ingrained in her during their eight years in the Indies.

Dubois and Anna had never really reconciled after the death of the baby and the matter of Prentice had only made relations more difficult. Dubois had not raised the latter subject with Anna since his homecoming and she did not dare disturb the tense civility between them by probing. She did not know if he had ever resolved his suspicions. She thought perhaps he had, for there was that letter awaiting them in Batavia, but of course he did not disclose its contents to her. The growing distance between them offered Anna a shield from Dubois's rigid, demanding nature. She grew more frivolous still, less systematic, less orderly, in a kind of instinctive, passive rebellion against his hardening nature. She never guessed that he was beset with worries all the way home, battling a terrible presentiment of failure. He could not admit the possibility to her. After eight years of work – eight years of death and fever and despair – he had actually found his fossils. Was he now to be denied the honour and acknowledgement he had earned? The cold fear settled deeper into his soul with every passing mile. The closer they came to Europe, and to judgement, the more Dubois armoured himself against hurt and rejection.

Somewhere in the long crossing of the Indian Ocean, Nature chose to reflect Dubois's inner turmoil by producing a ferocious storm. It began with a sudden blackening of the sky at midday and a tearing, rising wind. Before an hour passed, the waves had been whipped into a frenzy and the steamer tossed and heaved badly. A cold, grey, pelting rain drove the passengers into their cabins, where seasickness inevitably awaited them. At first the captain hoped to ride out the storm, but it was stronger and more extensive than he had estimated. The ship was pounded, dragged off course, covered in spume and rain that at least cleansed the decks of the vomit left by passengers trying, and failing, to make it to the rail before becoming sick. There seemed to be no end to the surging waves and wind. The rain struck like a hail of bullets.

Finally, fearing for the safety of the ship, the captain ordered everyone to leave the cabins and get into the lifeboats. He had not yet decided to abandon ship, but he wanted his passengers organized and ready, just in case. Ill, cold, wet, and frightened, the passengers huddled miserably in the small boats, not daring to look at the tumultuous dull green sea beneath them. The men fell silent; the women wept helplessly or clenched their teeth and straightened their backs, according to their dispositions; the children wailed and snivelled miserably. The Dubois party was no different from the rest, though Anna showed surprising courage lest she frighten the children further. She whispered to them, 'Papa will keep us safe, you'll see.' Overhearing this fairy tale, Dubois wondered what exactly he was supposed to do. Banish the storm? Chastise the waves for being too boisterous? For all his physical courage and strength, Dubois was daunted by the look of those tossing seas. These little, overcrowded boats could not last long if they were put to sea in such a storm, he feared. But if Anna's reassurance quietened the children, he supposed the story was a good one. Things would not be helped by hysteria.

And then he remembered the worst. He had left *P.e.* back in the cabin. If the ship went down, the fossils would be lost for ever. If he escaped drowning, he would arrive in Europe empty-handed, with no proof to show for his years of work. More than the fear of his own death, this fear of being mocked galvanized him. 'Anna,' he said, climbing out of the lifeboat, 'stay here. I will be right back.' And he ran across the heaving decks, slippery with rain, back to the cabin. In minutes that seemed like hours to his frightened family, Dubois returned, the precious wooden suitcase strapped to his chest and protected by one large, muscular arm. He clambered back into the lifeboat.

'Anna, listen to me,' he said firmly. 'If something happens, you must look after the children.' She nodded dutifully as she tried to anchor the bedraggled strands of hair that had fallen loose. She could not imagine what he was talking about. 'Anna, you take care of the children, ja? If the lifeboat is lowered, you see to the little ones, for I shall have to look after this' – Dubois placed his hand across the flat surface of the suitcase.

His meaning dawned on Anna and she turned her face away from him, so that he did not see her expression. *Ja, ja*, she thought resentfully, wiping the water from her children's faces with a sodden handkerchief. *Ja*, he will look after the fossils and I am to save the children, all three of mine and Janet too. The fossils have always been more precious to him than we were. Always. That was why he was always leaving us. The great swimmer, Dr Dubois, will save his fossils from the waves, not his children.

There was no more energy to waste in talk; the shivering family sat in the lifeboat, passively awaiting their fate. Their terror did not wane but exhausted itself; the children fell into a soggy, miserable sleep, for which Anna was grateful. After an interminable time, the storm began to wane. It felt like a miracle. Soon the captain ordered the passengers out of the lifeboats, back to their cabins. The ship had done it, she had ridden out the terrible storm, and they were safe. As they slowly climbed out of the boats, stretching cramped limbs and frozen hands, they could see the sky was lightening, the rain lessening, the waves calming. Dry clothes, warm blankets, and hot-water bottles awaited them in their cabins. The captain ordered the cook to serve up hot soup and bread as soon as possible to passengers and crew alike. Later that night at dinner, when everyone had recovered from the ordeal, there was a frantically gay atmosphere and plenty of wine. Dubois, with the others, raised his glass to toast their captain for his skill, but under his chair was the wooden suitcase. From now on, only when he was exercising would he let it far out of his grasp. He had almost lost everything and he would not be caught unawares again.

After the colourful and exotic harbours he had seen in the East, Dubois was not much impressed with Marseilles. It seemed dirty, rough, and dingy; the sailors looked like scoundrels and the only women who presented themselves to the eyes of the arrivals were less than respectable. Getting the family and the luggage through French customs and on to the boat-train seemed to take for ever, but at last they settled into a comfortable sleeping compartment, the ever-present wooden suitcase tucked neatly under Dubois's seat. By the next day they were in Paris, looking at the fashionable

European people and places that they had not seen in eight long years. The children were agog at the strangeness of it all. 'Where are all the natives, Mama?' Eugenie asked, querulously looking around the hotel. 'Why don't we have proper servants? Where is Babu?'

'Shhhh,' said her mother. 'We are in Paris now, in France. It is a different country from the Indies and natives don't live here. We won't have a babu anymore.'

'But we always have a babu, Mama,' Eugenie persisted, logically. 'Can Janet be our babu? And Mama, why do all the houses look funny, and the gardens? Why doesn't anyone wear sarongs and pretty clothes here? And it is so cold, Mama, like in the mountains at Mringin.'

Anna bent down to hold a quiet conversation with her daughter, this child who remembered only the sunlight and colours and dark-skinned natives of the Indies. The boys were quieter, but just as confused as their big sister. They had never seen a place like Paris before, and they were not sure they liked it. There was something indefinably... wrong... about Europe. They had been told all their lives that Europe was 'home', but it did not seem like home to them. Home was warm and sunny and full of flowers and loving *babus*; home smelled of incense and spices and woodsmoke. This cold, grey place, with its large stone buildings, gilded imperial statues, and ugly cement pavements was not home. This was some dreadful, dull, cold place. All the rest of their lives, the three Dubois children would remember Java as a paradise from which they had been taken without explanation.

They lunched in a café near the station before catching the next train for Amsterdam, where they would change to get the branch line that would take them to Eijsden, to 'Groetma's house'. They had deposited most of the luggage in the station. Only the wooden case still accompanied them, tucked securely under the table, where Dubois could feel it with his ankle. The children did not like the food and begged for *nasi goreng*, the fried-rice dish of the Indies, and fruit. Oblivious to their complaints, Dubois stared fixedly at one of the waiters, while Anna tried to coax the children into eating.

'Eugène,' she said finally, in a soft tone of voice, 'could you please explain to the children why they cannot have Indies food here?'

'What?' replied Dubois, startled. 'Oh, ja, of course. Now,

children, we are in Paris, in Europe. We are not in Java any more. And so here we eat the food that Parisians eat, and in Eijsden we will eat good Dutch food. We cannot get Indies food here; the people do not know how to cook it.' His explanation, or perhaps simply his greater moral authority, quietened the children and they began to eat, after first dubiously examining every mouthful.

'What *are* you staring at, Eugène?' Anna asked him.

'The waiter, Anna,' Dubois replied, as if it were obvious. The man had a high, prominent forehead, an aquiline nose, and a lantern jaw. 'Look at that skull! What I would give to have one like it for my collection!'

'Ja, I should have guessed,' Anna said with a sigh. 'Always your skulls and your bones. Don't you ever think about people?' But her husband did not hear her, and did not answer.

They sent a telegram to Dubois's mother; late the next night, they finally arrived at Eijsden. It was early August; the trip home had taken them just over six weeks. Dubois's mother had sent some carriages to the station to collect them, and various relatives had turned out to greet the long-absent Dubois family. It was a good thing so many had come, for there was so much luggage, and the children were so weary that they had to be carried. It was nearly midnight by the time they arrived in the Breuestraat in Eijsden, where a whole crowd of villagers had turned out to catch a glimpse of the professor they remembered as a young boy. 'He's made some great discovery,' they said to one another. A neighbour stood by the doorway, holding a lighted lantern aloft, while others unloaded the cases, trunks, boxes, and crates from the carriages. Someone carried the sleeping children in and Anna put them straight to bed upstairs, while Dubois stayed below to supervise the unloading of the mountains of luggage. Only a few noticed the heavy, wooden case that he handed over so reluctantly, saying, 'Take care with that! Don't drop it! It is the ape-man!'

Once all the things were safely stowed inside the house, and each helper had been thanked, the crowd dispersed. Anna and Dubois settled gratefully down to share a cup of tea and a slice of bread and butter with Dubois's mother. They felt disoriented, what with the lateness of the hour, the length of the journey, and the confusion of all of those people, most only half-remembered. It was a real pleasure to sit quietly and eat and drink a little.

After a while, Dubois felt somewhat recovered and decided it was time to make his announcement. It was no surprise, of course,

When the Dubois family returned to the Netherlands, they stayed with
Trinette (seated, left) in Eijsden. Anna (seated, right) helped Jean
(standing), Victor (seated, left), and Eugenie (seated, right) adjust to
their new life while Dubois worked harder than ever.

but his sense of occasion demanded that this be done formally.
'Thank you, Mama, for all the help, and for welcoming us so late at
night,' he began.

'Of course, of course,' his mother said, wearily but with a smile.
'My son and his family are always welcome here. I am only sorry
your father is not with us to see you, it would have pleased him so.'

'Ja, Mama,' Dubois replied, saddened. 'I miss him, too.' Bright-
ening a little, and squaring his broad shoulders, Dubois stood and
walked into the next room, extracting the precious case from the
chaotic pile of luggage. Taking out the skull box, he walked back
into the room where his mother and his wife were seated. 'But here,
Mama, here it is. Let me show you. Here is the missing link, the thing
that took me so far from home and took so many years to find.' With
a flourish, he opened he box to reveal the brown, shiny skullcap,
nestled safely in its bed of velvet. He held it out for his mother to see.

'So this is it?' she said dubiously, prodding the strange object
with a gnarled forefinger.

Dubois nodded proudly, 'Ja, Mama, that is the skull. That is *Pithecanthropus erectus.*' His mother looked up at him and he saw how much she had aged in eight years. 'Ja, Mama, this is it,' he repeated softly, gently.

'But, boy' – she sighed heavily, looking bewildered at his treasure – 'what use is it?'

A terrible pain was visible on Dubois's face for only an instant before he arranged his face into a mask of neutrality. Not even Anna noticed; she was too tired herself to watch carefully, and she did not understand the enormous significance of the gesture of showing *P.e.* to Dubois's mother. This was to have been the moment of triumph, the justification for the years and the risk and the distance from home. Dubois's mother understood none of it.

Dubois did not answer his mother's question, could not answer. There was no answer. If even now she could not see the importance of his discovery – even now, with the fossil in front of her – how could he possibly explain its value? It *had* no value to her, none at all. All he had sacrificed, all he had endured, all the trials through which he had persevered by sheer determination and force of character: these were nothing to her. He had been so sure she and his father would finally understand when he came home in triumph. But now he was back, and his father was dead, and his mother saw nothing. The prodigal son had returned, but there was no fatted calf.

What use is it, boy? What use is it? The words might as well have been carved with a knifepoint into the beating muscle of his heart, so deeply was he wounded. No use, Mama, he thought painfully, no use at all to you. Papa is still dead. I was still gone for eight years. Your grandchildren are strangers to you, and one lies dead in Toeloeng Agoeng. So the fossil is of no use at all.

He said nothing. He closed the box carefully, precisely, securing its lid with the fine brass clasp, and walked quickly out of the room. He replaced it in its wooden suitcase and put the suitcase in a safe, out-of-the-way spot. He went back and suggested that he and his wife retire for the night. 'It is time we got to bed, Anna. We are all very, very tired.'

CHAPTER 40

The Battlefield

In the morning, Dubois determined to ignore his pain. As if he were wrapping a fragile fossil in teak leaves, he packed determination, perseverance and pride around his delicate dream of accomplishment. He knew this, he thought to himself, he had learnt that, he had found the missing link, he had, he had, he had been right all along. By an effort of will, he summoned up his natural confidence and acted upon it as if he had not been bitterly disappointed. Very well, neither his mother nor his late father would ever understand that he had made the greatest discovery of the century; very well. His mother was not a scientist, any more than Anna or the children. He must not mourn over those who could not understand; he must not let them undermine his convictions. All he had risked was worthwhile, for he *had* found what he had sought. It might be tragic to be unappreciated, but it was not fatal. Perhaps in time he could resurrect his hope.

Dubois settled his family in a house in The Hague, where ex-colonials clustered nostalgically to talk of the *tempo doeloe*, the good old days in the Indies. Then he embarked on an almost holy crusade that lasted for the next few years of his life. He planned a campaign to convince not his family – he had given up on them – but those who mattered: his scientific colleagues. He had to catch up on all the journals, visit De Vries, Place, Fürbringer, and the others, find out what the talk was in scientific circles. He had to prepare himself for conferences and lectures. He had to publish more. The world might be sceptical now – it *was*, he reminded himself sternly, thinking of the articles he had seen – but it would soon come to agree with him. Once the men of science had seen his beautiful *P.e.*, they would agree that there was nothing to compare with her anywhere. He would introduce her to scientific society, he thought whimsically, as if she were a debutante at a coming-out ball. She would dazzle them with her sheer beauty; she would win the day, if only he could make them *look* at her.

And somehow, he had to secure a position suitable for one of his learning and accomplishments, where he could settle and study his fossils. True, he was still technically a military surgeon, albeit on the unattached list with no active duties, so the Ministry for the Colonies paid him a paltry salary. The Ministry for the Interior was responsible for the costs of housing his collections and arranging for assistants, but they were not generous. Dubois's first priority was to make people pay attention to his fossils, to his missing link, but after that, he had to attend to mundane financial matters, too.

His first salvo was fired in Leiden, at the Third International Congress of Zoology, held over five days (the sixteenth to the twenty-first) in September. It was a golden opportunity, for many of the elite of science were there: W. H. Flower, director of the British Museum of Natural History; A. Milne Edwards; Othniel Marsh, from Yale; and none other than the elderly pasha of German science himself, Rudolf Virchow. If he could change Virchow's mind, Dubois knew he would have won the battle of

Rudolf Virchow, the pathologist from Berlin, fiercely criticized Dubois's interpretation of *P.e.* This cartoon appeared in *Vanity Fair* on 25 May 1893.

scientific opinion. Virchow was his fiercest opponent, and Virchow had not mellowed with age. His passionate rejection of Darwin's evolutionary theory and of all claims for human evolution had only grown stronger and louder. His opinions had petrified over time, like bones turning into fossils. Virchow's control over German science had been only marginally diminished by his public battles with Ernst Haeckel over matters of evolution. Yes, Virchow was the enemy, the target, the one whose stubborn convictions had to be overturned if Dubois's wonderful find was to gain acceptance.

Virchow had already expressed himself unfavourably on the subject of *P.e.*, in a discussion following a sceptical lecture given by Wilhelm Krause on 19 January and in a later lecture of his own, both in Berlin. Like so many others, Virchow had argued that Dubois's cursory description of the conditions under which he had found the three fossil fragments was simply insufficient to support the claim that these were three pieces of a single individual. Cruelly echoing Dubois's assertion, Virchow had declared it would be truly 'foolish' – *thöricht* indeed – to fail to make a critical inquiry into this unproven point. The skullcap he had regarded as coming from a giant gibbon of some kind. As for the femur, it was human. Who but a human, helped by others, could have survived such a terrible injury to the thigh long enough for the clot to ossify? At best, he had conceded, such a femur could just possibly have come from a bipedal gibbonoid form. The molar he had completely ignored. His summary of Dubois's interpretation of *P.e.* had been devastating: 'Here the fantasy passes beyond all experience.'

Dubois was of two minds when he found out that his presentation of *P.e.* would be presided over by Virchow himself. On the one hand, Virchow's presence and attention were assured; on the other, Dubois might be exposed to harsh criticism in a most public forum. Well, so be it. Dubois had the fossils and he knew what they were. He was certain of his conclusions. He vowed to confront the old tiger in his lair, risking a painful clawing if that was what it would take to change Virchow's mind. He even invited Virchow and a select group of scientists to view the fossils before the public presentation, so they could examine and handle the specimens for themselves. It was a courageous move that cleared doubt from several minds but did not sway Virchow.

Having heard the criticisms of his monograph, Dubois took this opportunity to counter them. He squared his shoulders, stood up even straighter than usual, and prepared to fight for the minds of

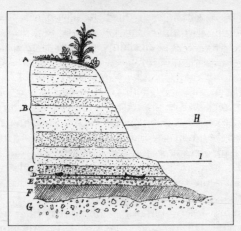

At the Third International Congress of Zoology in 1895, Dubois
showed the find-spots of the *P.e.* specimens on this geological section
of the deposits at Trinil. 'H' indicates the level of the river in the rainy
season; 'I' shows its level in the dry season.

those who listened to him. His anxiety made him stiffer, more
formal than ever; he knew it was not a good thing, but he could not
relax when so much was at stake. Now, for the first time, he presented the details of the discovery. He displayed diagrams of the
excavations and showed a schematic section of the geological formation at Trinil, including the all-important layer from which the
fossils had come. He indicated where in the geological sequence
the fossils had been found; he asserted that the layer was intact and
the fossils showed no signs of having been transported from anywhere else, as anyone present could verify for himself. The striking
chocolate-brown colour of the specimens and their patently
obvious heaviness, showing that they were thoroughly fossilized,
bespoke identical geological histories for the skullcap and femur.
Also, for the first time, he spoke about the fauna, the abundant
remains of other fossilized mammal bones and the detailed and
meticulous comparisons that had led him to conclude the entire
collection was of late Pliocene or early Pleistocene age.

Then he turned to the fossils themselves. If the femur was so
similar to that of a human, it could not also possibly belong to a
giant gibbon, as Virchow and others had previously suggested. Yet,
Dubois argued, if bipedal walking evolved at the very beginning of

human evolution – contrary to the predominant belief among the scientific community – then just such a strongly human femur, with a few apelike characteristics, would be expected. The skullcap, too, revealed its transitional nature even in the criticisms offered of his interpretation. Why did one scholar consider it fundamentally apelike while another claimed it was human? *Because it was in truth transitional, between ape and man*, Dubois told them. Only that interpretation accounted for the diverse anatomical features of the skullcap they saw before them.

It was painful, humiliating even, to have to restate publicly the criticisms of his monograph, but he could not dwell on that. The others had simply misunderstood, out of ignorance and surprise. He had to show them how to reach the conclusions that he had struggled so long and hard to reach, for he was right. He had to be patient. He had to be clear. This was not the time to express his feelings.

Next, he addressed the complaints about his estimate of cranial capacity. There was no accepted technique for making such estimates and, indeed, only one other scientist had tried to estimate *P.e.*'s cranial capacity for himself: Léonce-Pierre Manouvrier. Since 1885, this dapper Frenchman had been the Professor of Physical Anthropology at the prestigious École d'Anthropologie in Paris; more to the point, he was a leading authority in the new 'measuring school' of anthropology. Measuring, calculating, quantifying, and comparing anatomical features in consistent, reproducible ways were Manouvrier's passions. He was well respected as a meticulous scientist, a man not given to fanciful interpretations. What was stunning was that Manouvrier's wholly independent estimate of the cranial capacity of *P.e.* matched Dubois's own: 1000 cc. This was more than a telling coincidence! It was verification. While microcephalics and members of some races of humans had brains as small as this, Dubois conceded, these unusually small-brained types also had small bodies, which *P.e.* demonstrably did not. Thus, these estimates supported the idea that the braincase was small for a human, but very large for any known ape: transitional, in fact.

Dubois found himself breathing slightly rapidly from the effort of speaking in English; he was nearly fluent, but the finer points of meaning and usage sometimes escaped him. And he had to get his words right now. Trying to decipher and rebut every criticism in a foreign language was a formidable task. It would have been better

Léonce-Pierre Manouvrier of the École d'Anthropologie in Paris
defended Dubois and collaborated with him on a study of the variation
in human femurs.

if people had simply read and understood his monograph, much
better, for in print he could write and polish his words carefully.
He paused for a moment and looked around the room, gauging the
effect of his words on this learned audience. He could see some
nods of agreement, some eyebrows raised in surprise and concession. But he knew in his heart that his delivery was still too stilted,
too reserved; it was the old problem his anatomy students always
complained about. He did not capture the imagination. Even
though he passionately believed every word he spoke, the issues
were so important that he froze when he spoke of them. He could
not help holding himself aloof. It was a deeply ingrained reaction
from a man too often misunderstood, who had been too often
deeply wounded by the rejection of his novel ideas.

And Virchow, the worst of them all, sat there looking more like
an ancient tortoise than an ageing tiger. Even a tortoise could
administer a deadly bite, however. He was the master of the sarcastic rejoinder, the subtle twist of words that left his enemies bleeding. He was wrinkled and wizened, thin-haired and old: a small,
bent man who was physically unimpressive, especially in contrast

to Dubois's own square, muscular physique. Virchow was seventy-four, Dubois still a handsome thirty-seven. Dubois had youth and energy and the future on his side, not to mention an intellectual power probably the equal of Virchow's own. But behind his gold-rimmed oval glasses, Virchow's eyes were like black bullets, revealing the essential nature of the man: cold, proud, unyielding. Dubois had not yet reached Virchow, he could see that. Virchow's eyes showed only deep contempt for this obdurate young Dutchman.

Dubois took a deep breath and started on one of his last two points. He disliked public speaking and resented having to defend his ideas so vigorously, but it had to be done. In his monograph, he had not compared *P.e.* with the Neanderthal skulls from Europe; this had been an error. Now it was time to do so. He pointed out some similarities in shape between the Neanderthal skulls and the skullcap from Trinil, like the strong browridges and the elongated cranium. But, he emphasized, there were also important differences between the skulls. The Neanderthal skull was much more human-like than the skullcap of *P.e.*, for the former had a much higher and more domed cranial vault. The important difference was that, in overall capacity, Neanderthal skulls were enormous. The estimated cranial capacity of the original Neanderthal skull was 1230 cc, and the Spy skulls were comparably capacious – as big as many modern European skulls – while *P.e.* at about 1000 cc matched only the smallest-brained human races or microcephalics. Still the brain size of *P.e.* greatly exceeded that of modern apes, which never surpassed 600 cc. At this point, Dubois was happy to see some signs of agreement. He was filled with hope, for a moment; perhaps no one would any more say his beautiful *P.e.* was just another Neanderthal.

There, he thought to himself, that's a tricky point made. Now for the finale, the closing. If I can hold their attention to the very end, perhaps I can change some minds.

And with that, he moved on to discuss the molar and, stunningly, to produce a new find. There was another molar, he told his surprised listeners, also uncovered in October 1892, that had unfortunately escaped his attention until recently. It had been among a large number of other mammalian teeth found only three metres from the skullcap. The new tooth was more worn than the original one, he pointed out, which was to be expected since the original was a third or last molar and the new one occupied the position just in front of it. Since second molars erupted through the gum and came into wear well before third molars did, a discrepancy between teeth from one individual was normal.

In conclusion, despite many questions and criticisms raised in response to his brief monograph on *P.e.*, Dubois could see no reason whatsoever to revise his original interpretations and opinions. *Pithecanthropus erectus* was a transitional form, a missing link between apes and man, and he had found her. Now that they had been properly introduced to her, the distinguished members of the audience could surely see the wisdom of this judgement. As soon as he had expressed the sentiment, he realized it sounded pompous when he had meant to be light-hearted.

Dubois left the podium to mixed applause and murmurs of confusion and disagreement. Virchow opened the discussion, as merciless as ever. He was unconvinced that Dubois had found anything more than the remains of a giant gibbon – very nice, but no missing link – and reiterated his earlier criticisms. It was clear that the elderly pasha of German science had prepared his remarks in advance; there had never been any chance of changing his mind. Dubois was grateful when the American Marsh came forward to defend him. Marsh had observed many similar healed injuries in the femurs of apes' skeletons, he told the listeners, so Virchow's assertion that only a human could survive such a severe injury could not be correct. The healed injury itself was no grounds for assigning this femur to the human species, rather than to an ape-man. This was another telling point in Dubois's favour. Other speakers mentioned the illuminating presentation of the geology of Trinil. Showing the stratigraphic section and describing the layers had been an excellent strategy, and Dubois vowed to keep repeating this information wherever he spoke on the subject.

Now that opinion seemed to be turning his way, Dubois stood up to publicly invite the chemist J. M. van Bemmelen to carry out age tests on several of the mammal bones from the same layers as the *P.e.* fossils. It had been accepted for some time that the fluorine content in fossilized bones increased in proportion to their antiquity, though this technique could not provide an exact age for fossils. (Although some believed that Virchow had scored a complete victory over the foolish Dutchman, Van Bemmelen's findings, which he published later, supported Dubois's suggestion that these fossils were from the Pleistocene.)

Dubois returned home from the congress, pleased with the reception of his paper and determined to fight on until he had completely won over all the most influential scientists of the day. But almost immediately, Virchow started making trouble. Though Dubois had allowed this arch-sceptic special access to the fossils at the meeting in Leiden, Virchow had modified his criticisms not one whit as a result. And now Virchow complained to F. A. Jentink, the director of the National Museum of Natural History in Leiden, that he could not continue with a more detailed examination of the fossils. Jentink informed Dubois of this via postcard:

> 17 September 1895
> Professor Virchow complains that your pieces of evidence of *P. erectus* that were exhibited in Leiden are not here to look at, possibly to be studied by him or other scientists.

Really, Dubois thought to himself, this is outrageous. The man had an hour to look at the specimens in Leiden, yet wrote complaining to Jentink the very next day. Virchow received a copy of the monograph and he heard my illustrated talk. What more does he want to know, before I have finished publishing my analyses of my fossils myself? It is obvious that there is much, much more to do, now that I am back in Europe with proper libraries and museum resources. Does he want me to hand my baby over to him, lifting her out of her very cradle? Shall I entrust her to *him*, the man who above all others has doubted my word and impugned my scholarship? Virchow is too used to having his own way in everything in Germany, that is what is wrong with him. He can be rude and insulting to German scholars and they still kowtow to him and defer to his opinion. Well, I am under no such obligation to him, and I shall not do it.

Dubois formulated his reply immediately.

> 17 September 1895
> Judging from your recent postcard, it seems Professor Virchow does not know that the parts of *Pithecanthropus erectus* have not yet been fully described by me in such a manner that I can place them at the disposal of others as museum objects. The description that I have given already is, self-evidently, tentative and incomplete, because in Java I lacked the necessary comparative material and sufficient literature ... Meanwhile, it is obvious that the tentative description I have already published is so incomplete that there has been much misunderstanding ...

In October, he travelled to Brussels to speak before a meeting of the Société Belge de Géologie. Next on his itinerary was Liège, where he studied the Neanderthal fossils from Spy for himself, for the first time. It was a revelation. He was surprised by their appearance, for all that he had read the descriptions and studied the published photographs closely. There was indeed a similarity in overall skull shape to his *P.e.*, a compelling one. And he could now see, quite clearly, that Virchow's dismissal of these specimens as pathological had been entirely incorrect. Dubois was indefatigable. In the next few weeks, he travelled to Paris to the École d'Anthropologie, striking up a close collaboration with Manouvrier. At their first meeting, they examined together some four hundred human femurs, many of which Manouvrier had already checked at Dubois's request. They compiled a case for the distinctions between this large sample of human femurs and the femur of *P.e.* The information they gathered was complex and voluminous; they worked late into the night and adjourned to a nearby café to dine, talking all the while of the meaning and significance of their observations. With pencils and notebooks spread on the table next to their plates, the two men scribbled notes and sketched anatomical details of femurs they had measured, comparing and sharpening their conclusions. The by now battered suitcase, the one that had carried *P.e.* from Java to Holland and now halfway across Europe, sat beneath the table at their feet, like a naughty child who had crept in to eavesdrop on the adults' dinner conversation. So engrossed were the scientists in their discussion that the restaurant emptied without their noticing; finally a waiter came and asked them to leave, as the restaurant was closing. They folded up their notebooks, tucked them and their pencils away, and rose to walk back to Dubois's hotel.

But they never stopped talking, arguing, reasoning. Deep in the scientific intricacies of the form and function of the femur, neither man noticed that the abandoned suitcase still sat beneath the table where they had dined. They walked some blocks before Dubois sensed the emptiness of his left hand.

'Mon dieu, Manouvrier!' he cried out. 'Où est *Pithécanthropus?*' – 'My God, Manouvrier! Where is *Pithecanthropus?*' And with that, he dashed across the street, running panic-stricken back to the café. Manouvrier, older and less fit, followed at a more dignified pace, but one that reflected no less concern. They arrived at the restaurant as the proprietor was locking the doors.

'Où est *Pithécanthropus?*' Dubois blurted out, in an appallingly bad accent. He was flushed and breathing heavily, he was frightened, and his command of French deserted him. '*Pithécanthropus!*' he shouted at the uncomprehending man. '*Pithécanthropus! Les fossiles!*' He grabbed the man by the shoulders and shook him, trying to make him understand. Manouvrier hurried up, suave as ever, to extract the proprietor from Dubois's frantic grasp. He soon smoothed over the situation. He explained that the professor had left some valuable specimens in a suitcase under a table at the restaurant – that one over there, by the window, surely the good proprietor remembered how long they had sat there talking. The proprietor was puzzled; he remembered them, *oui, bien sûr*, but not any suitcase.

Then their waiter approached, drawn no doubt by the shouting and excitement. 'Ah, oui,' he admitted agreeably. 'J'ai trouvé une valise; j'ai cru que vous retournieriez pour elle.' (I found a suitcase; I thought you would return for it.) The words were like a blessing to Dubois. He closed his eyes a moment in silent thanks. The waiter took the keys from the proprietor, unlocked the door, and led them inside, to the cupboard where he had placed the suitcase, 'Voilà!' the waiter cried cheerfully, producing it like a magician extracting a rabbit from a hat. 'C'est à vous?' – 'It's yours?' He gestured toward Dubois.

'Ah, oui, oui, merci mille fois,' Dubois replied in a tremulous voice, opening the case to check that his fossils were there and then closing it with shaking hands. He clasped the suitcase to his chest. 'Merci; vous êtes très gentil; merci,' he muttered fervently, bowing and offering his hand for the waiter to shake. (Thank you; you are very kind; thank you.) Then he pressed a bill into the waiter's palm, not looking to check its denomination. Whatever it was, it was worth less than *P.e.* Manouvrier also had a few words with the man and then they left, walking back toward Dubois's hotel.

Dubois was completely distracted now, unable to carry on their conversation. A terrible disaster has been averted, he thought. If I cannot persuade my sceptics with the fossils in my hand, how much harder would it be if I had lost them, through carelessness? What would I have done? What would I have done? He could not hear Manouvrier's words, the question echoed so loudly in his head. What would I have done? The words were repeated in the hopeless sound his feet made on the pavement: what would I have done? What would I have done?

After a short while, Manouvrier realized his friend was not responding to his attempts at conversation and fell silent. Outside the hotel, Manouvrier bade Dubois good night, promising to call for him in the morning so they could continue their work. With a twinkle in his eye, he suggested Dubois sleep with the case under his pillow. If it had only been possible to sleep thus, Dubois would have done just that.

Some months later, Manouvrier published their comparisons and observations, and, with Dubois's full permission, also published his own reconstruction of the entire skull of *P.e.*, including the missing face and jaw, which graphically revealed his view of the skull as intermediate between apes and man. Dubois returned to Paris the next year in June, to attend the Quatorzième Conférence Annuelle Transformiste of the Société d'Anthropologie. His presentation there and previously at the École d'Anthropologie, combined with Manouvrier's influential endorsement, soon won over other French scientists. The anatomist August Pettit, the well-known prehistorian Gabriel de Mortillet, and the leading anthropologist René Verneau all openly accepted Dubois's interpretation. He felt triumphant.

In mid-November 1895, Dubois travelled to Edinburgh to lecture. Edinburgh was the home of the eminent anatomist and sceptic Sir William Turner, who had discussed and rejected Dubois's interpretation soon after receiving the original monograph. Edinburgh was also the home of the archaeologist Robert Munro, currently President of the British Association for the Advancement of Science. Munro declared himself more favourably inclined toward Dubois's theories. But then, as he said himself in a letter, 'Of course, not being a special anatomist my views have little weight. But I hold that your discovery is a practical illustration of theories propounded previously and of course this should be a strong argument in favour of the correctness of your opinion of *Pithecanthropus erectus*.' Hoping to bring Turner over to his point of view, and believing that Turner's support would be crucial, Dubois made sure that he had a cast of the skullcap and molars. After seeing the fossils and listening to Dubois's lecture, even the rather pompous Turner had to openly admit that the skullcap was more apelike than Dubois's exquisitely illustrated monograph had led him to think, though he confessed to some lingering reservations. Still, he conceded, *if* the deposits in which the bones had been found could be shown to be contemporaneous with the Quaternary deposits in Great Britain, then Dubois's discovery was very ancient and 'the most important hitherto recorded'.

Dubois was pleased. Ja, he thought, Turner is beginning to see the truth. Now we have only a short distance to travel to our rightful home, *P.e.* and I.

But Turner would not budge on the matter of the femur, which he persisted in thinking fully human. At a later meeting of the Royal Society, Munro argued against Turner. Of course the femur of an animal that had achieved an erect stance would resemble a human femur, for the two species' bones shared the same function. This was a subtle argument that Dubois liked; he made a mental note of it, for future presentations. Munro went one step further: 'After the erect position was attained, another evolution commenced, viz. the development of the brain and this was facilitated by the setting free of the upper limbs.'

Dubois spoke the next week at an evening meeting of the Royal Dublin Society. Once again, he was facing critics, for this was the very group before which, some ten months before, the anatomist Daniel Cunningham had openly criticized Dubois's monograph. Cunningham had felt that Dubois's failure to compare his skullcap with the Neanderthal skulls had been a fatal error. He had argued for an anatomical continuum from *P.e.*, through the Neanderthals, to modern humans, and had come to the bizarre conclusion that *P.e.* was merely the 'lowest human cranium yet to be described', a view he had later defended in an address to the Anatomical Society of Great Britain and Ireland.

Knowing the predisposition of his audience, Dubois was handsomely honest from the outset. He acknowledged that his interpretation of his finds was controversial: 'Professors Sir W. Turner, Cunningham, A. Keith, Lydekker, Paul Matschie, Rudolf Martin, and A. Pettit held that the thigh bone and calvaria were human. Only Professor Manouvrier of Paris, and Professor Marsh in America, admit to the *possibility* of the remains belonging to a transitional form between Man and the Apes,' he conceded in his talk. And he confessed openly to having had mistaken views of Neanderthals, which had led to his erroneous omission of them from his monograph. 'I am now wholly convinced,' he allowed, 'that they are not at all pathological, and was much struck by the great resemblance with the cranium of *Pithecanthropus*.' He repeated his geological information, presented his arguments about the anatomical features, and explained how only a transitional status would accommodate such a creature.

The question in Dubois's mind was, How would the discussion

go? He felt the talk had gone well, that he had changed some minds, but he kept his expression guarded until he was sure how things were going. Several of the most important men present – Sir William Flower, John Lubbock, Professors Thomson and Thane, Dr Garson, and Sir William Turner – united in congratulating Dubois upon his remarkable and interesting discovery and expressed their gratitude at being able to examine the specimens firsthand.

Flower had a particularly graceful way of expressing his opinion. 'It is unfortunate that the fragmentary condition of the remains of *Pithecanthropus* is such as to leave much of its real nature open to conjecture.' Undecided, thought Dubois, or unwilling to commit to a position publicly.

When Turner stood up to speak, Dubois prepared himself for a lengthy discourse, for he knew by now that Turner was enamoured of his own opinions. As expected, Turner did not discuss, he proclaimed.

The opportunity which Dr. Dubois has given us of seeing his very interesting specimens and the fuller description of the conditions under which they were found, have enabled us to realize their characters and antiquity much more clearly than was possible from a perusal of his memoir published last year...

As regards the thigh bone, the opportunity of carefully examining it, both last week in Edinburgh, and now at this meeting, does not lead me to alter the opinion which I expressed in my published criticism of the original memoir, that there is nothing in its form and appearance which would lead one to say that it possessed characters specifically or generically distinct from those of a human thigh bone...

As regards the skull, now that one has seen it, there is more difficulty in coming to a conclusion. If, however, the thigh bone and the calvaria belong to the same skeleton, and Dr. Dubois, from his personal examination of the locality, has no doubt on this point, the establishment of the human character of the femur would require us to regard the calvaria as also human... The calvaria is less distinctively human than the Neanderthal skullcap which everyone now admits to be human. In the latter there is a forehead with rounded frontal eminences, but in the Java specimen the frontal bone is flattened and slopes abruptly backwards in a manner such as approximates it much more to the shape in the ape than to a human skull, even as low as the Neanderthal...

In conclusion, may I express the thanks of the anthropologists in this country to Dr. Dubois for his courtesy in bringing the specimens for our inspection, and the further hope that the government of the Netherlands may continue the search for additional remains in the same locality.

Wanted more evidence, surmised Dubois, but was coming around. He saw the dual nature of the skullcap, that much was certain, even if he wouldn't accept the femur as being from an ape-man. It was an absurd proposition, for what creature had an ape-man's head and a man's thigh?

Next was Dr John George Garson, who, like Turner, emphasized the value of seeing the specimens for himself. Said Garson,

I have studied Dr. Dubois's memoir on *Pithecanthropus erectus* very carefully, and also the various criticisms of it which have been published. I am therefore extremely glad to see the specimens themselves, as they showed many morphological features of which the plates and diagrams gave but an imperfect idea; the paper which Dr. Dubois has read this evening sheds further light on the specimens. In the first instance, I was very uncertain as to the geological epoch to which they should be referred, but from additional information Dr. Dubois has just given regarding the mammalian fauna found in the same formation with them, I am satisfied as to their being Pliocene.

Dubois nodded unconsciously, satisfied that his discussion of the geology and fauna had been useful. He should have put more geology in the monograph. Garson continued, and some of the elaborate phrases simply washed over Dubois like a voiceless wind.

The femur is extremely human-like, and if taken alone would undoubtedly be said to be that of *Homo*...The calvaria, on the other hand, is very different and much more gibbon-like than one would imagine from the drawings of it... The characters of the calvaria... if taken alone, might be ascribed to a large extinct *Hylobates*, although it should be remembered that in these large extinct forms the brain is proportionately smaller than in the recent, whereas in this specimen the capacity of the calvaria indicates ... proportionately larger brains ... Considering the strong opinion Dr. Dubois has formed from examination of the strata and other mammalian remains therein contained, it is most reasonable to conclude that the specimens are probably parts of the skeleton of one animal, and that it belonged to one of those extinct species of primates more or less related to *Homo sapiens*...

Professor John Arthur Thomson, speaking later, echoed Garson's remarks. 'Yes,' Thomson observed,

What strikes me most forcibly is the very different complexion put upon the case, now that I have had an opportunity of examining the specimens. This only went to prove how difficult it is to form any correct opinion on such a matter by mere perusal of a monograph, however good. For my part, I feel justified in saying that the calvaria is undoubtedly ape-like in all its characters, except in regards to capacity: on the other hand the femur displays all the features of a well-developed human thigh bone.

Aha! rejoiced Dubois to himself at this juncture. They are beginning to see it, as I do. Neither ape nor human; both together; transitional. That was it; ja, that was it.

After some further pronouncements, Thomson concluded,

As to whether or no the calvaria and thigh bone belonged to the same individual is a matter of vital importance. Unfortunately, the evidence advanced is not conclusive, and the only course left open at present is to reserve one's judgement. This, however, does not detract from the remarkable value of the discovery of this skull, which I regard as by far the most important contribution to our knowledge of an intermediate form between man and the known apes.

The only scientist to come close to wholeheartedly endorsing Dubois's interpretation was a young surgeon, Arthur Keith, then newly appointed senior demonstrator in anatomy at the London Hospital. An ambitious man at the start of his academic career, Keith found the opportunity ripe for expressing an intelligent opinion in front of this august body of scientists. He was a little hesitant to engage in public debate, on account of his strong Scottish accent and a minor speech impediment that made him self-conscious in formal settings. But speaking in public, declaiming on evidence presented, was an essential skill for a British academic, and Keith aimed to be one of note. Although at first Keith had been sceptical of Dubois's assertion that the three original specimens were derived from a single species, he now generously reversed himself, while confessing to doubts about whether only a single individual was represented.

'The chief question to be settled,' Keith declared, 'is whether the skull is human or not. What is the criterion of a human skull? What is the criterion of an ape's skull? How are they to be distinguished?'

Arthur Keith, a young London anatomist, deftly summarized the problem about *P.e.*: 'The chief question to be settled is whether the skull is human or not.'

How indeed, Dubois thought. This young man had stated the problem admirably, neatly, for all that he was not a polished speaker.

To my mind there are only two differences between the skulls of men and apes, and they are differences, not in kind, but in degree. The first difference is the large excess of cranial capacity of the human skull: in the extent of its cranial capacity, the skull before us this evening merits to be called human. The second difference between the skulls of apes and men lies in the large development of muscular ridges and processes for the fixation of the masticatory apparatus, for chewing; the development is extensive in apes; it is slight in men. In the extent of this development, also, the calvaria in question is distinctly human.

Keith made clear that he agreed 'thoroughly' with Dr Dubois as to the genealogical position of his fossils; they represented the human race during the late Tertiary period. He would have preferred to call them Pliocene Man rather than *Pithecanthropus erectus*, but this was merely a matter of nomenclature.

In all, Dubois's heart was lightened by the numbers of scientists who began to echo his observations. First they had to observe, then they would conclude, he thought to himself contentedly. At the close of the meeting, by popular acclaim, the participants elected Dr Eugène Dubois an honorary fellow of the Anthropological Institute of Great Britain and Ireland, in grateful recognition of his important and interesting discoveries. The report of the meeting in the journal *Nature*, some weeks later, was largely favourable.

A friend sent Dubois a copy of the *Evening Telegraph* from Dublin, which took a still lighter view of the debate.

BONES OF CONTENTION

Saturday November 23, 1895

The lecture of Professor Dubois in Dublin on the *Pithecanthropus erectus* is a matter of extreme interest to intellectual people. There is nothing I revel more in than being translated into the dim ages when our forebears made large use of their toe-nails for climbing purposes, and of their teeth and foreclaws in order to vanquish their enemies. It is necessary to counteract the swelling pride and importance of people that they should be reminded occasionally by a Dubois or a Virchow from what very nasty creatures we have descended. The modern professor exists apparently to degrade his species as much as he can for fear it would think too much of itself and in order to show it that it cannot think too much of the professor. The *Pithecanthropus erectus* is one of the effects of the craze for distinction in this way...

These fossils in the opinion of the Professor constitute the Darwinian missing link. The skull must have been bigger than that of an ape, while the thigh-bone is bigger than a man's, and the tooth is something between the two. From the shape of the thigh bone it must have been upright – hence the word *Erectus*; from the shape of the same bone, Professor Cunningham thinks the owner must not have learned the art of sitting down. Hence we arrive at a point when we can say that we have the fossil remains of an animal who could stand but who couldn't squat. Fill up the rest of the animal from your imagination and you have the *Pithecanthropus erectus*, who some time between the end of the tertiary and the beginning of the quaternary period went about like a roaring lion seeking who pretended to better femoral development than him in order that he might kick him. Now, was the P.E. aforesaid a man or was he an ape? Judging from the femur, as man walks erect, so did the P.E.; ergo, he was a man. But then a man has evidently some more brains than P.E., and an ape has less; and the question is whether the

P.E. is to belong to either class, and if so, which. Neither upon the thigh-bone nor upon the question of brains can the professors agree, and some of them even contend that the thigh-bone has nothing to do with the skull, and that the tooth is not connected with either. In fact these osseous fragments are regular bones of contention between the professorial pundits. Virchow says one thing and Dubois says another. Dubois thinks that Virchow did not examine things enough, and if Virchow's opinion of Dubois were put in plain language, it would probably express itself as tête du bois...

Now for my opinion of this find. This world is full of irregularities... Now physically this *Pithecanthropus erectus* was in my opinion either a fool of a man with a big leg or an ape with a big head, or we might have in these three specimens the leg of a man, the head of an ape, and the tooth of the tiger that ate them both. The really important thing for mankind, however, seems to be that it does not matter which is the real state of the case.

The article, signed 'O'Mulligan', closed with numerous stanzas of doggerel.

Dubois had no time to savour his apparent fame, for he was due to speak in Berlin shortly. This battle was in deadly earnest, for all that Irish journalists might find it comical. He fought for his reputation, for *P.e.*, for the missing link itself. Berlin was Virchow's stronghold, so he could expect few converts there. Rudolf Martin, once a ferocious critic of Dubois, markedly softened his point of view, but Virchow and his followers Wilhelm Krause, A. A. W. Hubrecht, Herman Klaatsch, Johannes Bemuller and others held fast to the belief that *P.e.* was nothing but a giant gibbon. 'According to all the rules of classification,' Virchow intoned seriously, 'this creature was an animal, to wit, an ape,' and he would not be moved.

By the time of his lecture in Berlin, Dubois had managed to remove nearly all of the matrix from the inside of the skullcap. For this nerve-racking endeavour, he had invented a new technique using a heavy, foot-powered dental drill. Hours of experimentation on rocks, using different drill bits, led Dubois to decide that the most satisfactory bit was a diamond burr, with which he became quite proficient. He learned how to remove tiny bits of rock at a time, working with the utmost precision and delicacy. Only then did he cautiously apply this tool to the inside of his skullcap, skimming off the thin layer of matrix, in places only a tenth of a millimetre thick. It took weeks of concentrated work of the very sort to which Dubois's impatient temperament was poorly suited. But he was good with his hands and, besides, he would never have trusted another person to clean his precious *P.e.* During the process, he was noticeably short-tempered and irritable with his family and servants, so fearful was he of making an irreparable mistake. Every interruption was seen as a threat to *P.e.*'s physical integrity.

Now Dubois had freed the fossilized bone almost completely from its encasing matrix, revealing the impression of a river bed of blood vessels and irregular, rounded depressions into which the lobes of the brain had once fitted. He prepared an endocast, an impression that showed the inside of the skull and of the brain that had once nestled there. He hoped the new anatomical information about *P.e.*'s brain would prove persuasive, and he discussed it at length. As in humans, he told his sceptical German audience, the foramen magnum – the bony hole through which the spinal cord exited the skull – was far forward. This position was typical of animals with an upright posture. There was thus an anatomical consistency between femur and skullcap that reinforced the geological information suggesting the two came from a single animal. Also, some of the sulci and gyri – the ditches and hillocks – of the long-decayed brain were still evident on the inside of the skullcap, indicating a more human arrangement of brain tissue than in apes.

He even proposed a phylogenetic tree, a graphical description of *P.e.*'s evolutionary position, though he knew Virchow's deep resistance to evolutionary ideas.

'I am well aware,' he admitted modestly, 'of the exceptional mortality of such trees, but I also know that parts of them at least often survive, from which new life emerges. One has to try to visualize the kinship relations of the forms presently known, and I know of no better means to this end than the form of a phylogenetic tree.' The strategy failed utterly. Dubois's indicated willingness to modify his ideas in the future – the mark of a dedicated scientist – earned him no respect from the dogmatic Virchow, who was always certain of his opinion, his interpretations. The statement simply made Dubois appear weak in his eyes. Virchow was adamant: this skullcap was a gibbon and nothing more.

Yet by the end of 1895, a few significant cracks had appeared in the edifice of German scepticism. The paleontologists Wilhelm Branco and William Dames came forth with strong endorsements

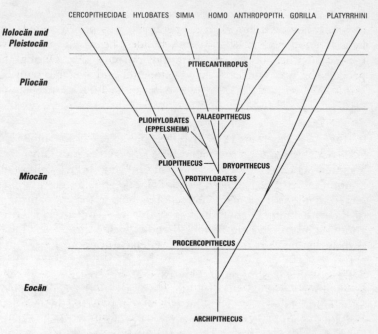

CERCOPITHECIDAE HYLOBATES SIMIA HOMO ANTHROPOPITH. GORILLA PLATYRRHINI

Holocän und
Pleistocän

PITHECANTHROPUS

Pliocän

PLIOHYLOBATES PALAEOPITHECUS
(EPPELSHEIM)

PLIOPITHECUS — DRYOPITHECUS
Miocän PROTHYLOBATES

PROCERCOPITHECUS

Eocän

ARCHIPITHECUS

During his lecture in Berlin, Dubois presented this phylogenetic tree
showing the place of *P.e.* in the human family, between *Paleopithecus*
(Lydekker's ancient *Anthropopithecus*) and man (*Homo*).

of Dubois's view, Branco even saying that no one familiar with
paleontological research could doubt that the three fossil specimens
of *P.e.* belonged together. Dubois's last engagement in 1895 was at
Jena, the home institution of Ernst Haeckel, a longtime foe of
Virchow's and one of Dubois's staunchest supporters. Haeckel
made sure Dubois was duly honoured during his visit.

It had been six months since Dubois arrived home with his precious *P.e.*, on that dark, disappointing night in Eijsden, and he was
exhausted, emotionally and physically. There was nowhere he
could unpack his enormous collection (414 crates' worth) and,
even if he had had the space, he was too weary with fighting. He
had done his best, he thought as he returned to The Hague for the
holidays. He had done what he had said he would do and now they
did not believe him. But he would make them believe him. Next
year, when he had rested: next year, he would fight again.

CHAPTER 41

More Skirmishes

In the early part of 1896, Dubois stayed at home more. In February, after much correspondence, Haeckel let him know that his attempts to persuade the University of Jena to give Dubois an honorary doctorate had been in vain. Haeckel had argued and presented opinions from many fine scholars but, in the end, anything to do with human evolution was simply too controversial. And although his lair was in Berlin, Virchow wielded too much influence in biology for the University of Jena to oppose him in this way.

Despite this frustration, in May 1896 Dubois received a friendly letter from Gustav Schwalbe, an anatomist at the University of Strasbourg. Like Haeckel, Schwalbe was one of Germany's few well-known and outspoken supporters of evolution. It was a fateful letter, for Schwalbe did Dubois an invaluable service.

12 May 1896

I delivered my lecture on your *P.e.* last Friday and expressed my conviction that, in any case, the skull cannot belong to a human and not to a monkey…Concerning the femur, I am convinced that you are right, when you think that it belongs to the skull and to the molar, and I have expressed my opinion…

Might you be interested to learn that we have here in the preparation room obtained a femur of an actor aged 52 years, with an exostosis resembling that on the *Pithecanthropus* femur?

Dubois most certainly was interested; what a wonderful thing it would be, to have a matching specimen of known history! In a few days' time, the actor's femur was on its way to him in The Hague. The resemblance was indeed striking; from that moment on, the actor's femur lived in the box with *P.e.*'s own femur, for handy comparison. It was especially useful for the actor was said not to be lame following the injury; he had made a full recovery, as had, presumably, *P.e.*

Though Dubois had already been in every European capital that mattered, he continued to press his case over the next few years. The scientific community *would* listen to him; his colleagues *would* look at his precious *P.e.* and see her for what she was. He thrust the fossils under their noses. By sheer force of personality and conviction, he refused to allow them to dismiss his ideas casually, without serious consideration. And all the while, he was constantly researching and revising, adding new information and new diagrams to his lectures, answering the criticisms of his talks and the resultant publications with an unceasing flow of argument and logic.

In June 1896, he returned to Paris, this time to be awarded the Prix Broca for outstanding achievements in anthropology. It was a moment to be savoured. He was surrounded, for once, by supporters: Manouvrier, Verneau, Pettit, De Mortillet, and others. He was fêted and praised and honoured at dinners. The only awkwardness was that Anna had begged to join him in Paris this time, especially to attend the elegant banquet held in Dubois's honour at the École d'Anthropologie, and he had agreed. Anna spent all afternoon constructing an elaborate hairdo, which did not suit her, and wore her most fashionable dress. She was determined to be charming, gay, and much admired by all these learned men. Her manner instead struck Dubois as boorish, uneducated, even lingeringly colonial. Anna had no conversation, no wit, no appreciation of the scientific accomplishments of the men who politely spoke with her. She laughed too shrilly and too loudly; she flirted like an unmarried coquette. In all, her behaviour was utterly unsuitable for the wife of a great scientific man, Dubois thought; it was an occasion he longed to forget.

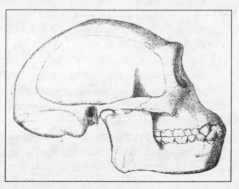

In 1896, Dubois reconstructed the shape of the complete skull of *P.e.*

From time to time, his old enemy resurfaced and he was flattened with fever again. He had done too much in 1895, he realized now: he had gone to India, climbed the Siwaliks and searched for fossils, returned home to the Indies and those awful suspicions about Anna and Prentice, sailed home to Holland, and barely settled in, left to lecture everywhere in Europe he could wangle an invitation. And all the time, every day, even now, he was thinking, learning, fending off criticisms, persuading sceptics, carrying out new research and new analysis until he was ready to drop. He vowed to guard his health a little more, to plan a less demanding schedule, even as he had learnt in the Indies that spending weeks camping and trekking through jungles was likely to kill him. The academy was a different sort of jungle, but the dangers were not to be underestimated. And things were not entirely happy at home, though he had little time and energy left over to deal with Anna and the children.

Dubois desperately needed a fixed academic post, an institution and a title to shelter him and his fossils. On 8 January 1897, the University of Amsterdam awarded him an honorary doctorate in botany and zoology, but not a professorship and not a salary. That same year, he was appointed curator of paleontology (and of the Dubois Collection) at the Teyler Museum in Haarlem, by an act of parliament. Dubois hoped it would finally be possible to unpack and arrange a suitable resting place for his large and important collection, which had so far been unceremoniously stored in unheated attics and cramped coach-houses. Though the curatorship carried only a modest salary, it was something. He moved his family from The Hague to Haarlem, taking a house convenient to the Teyler. Dubois felt that he was making progress in the battle for acceptance of *P.e.*, inch by inch, just as in excavating the sediments at Trinil. His missing link was coming into her own. He was finally beginning to assume the role of leading Dutch scientist that he had earned.

Early in 1898, the professorship of anatomy at the University of Amsterdam became vacant. It was the very position – Fürbringer's old professorship – that Dubois had turned his back on when he left Amsterdam to find the missing link. On 5 February Thomas Place, Dubois's old friend and mentor in physiology, wrote to ask Dubois if he would like to be nominated for the position. His competition was Otto Seydel, a German who had held the readership of anatomy, a position just below that of the chair, and the anatomist Louis Bolk, whom Dubois had never liked.

Dubois replied to Place's kind letter gratefully, but he stressed that the position was surely Seydel's by right; Seydel had doubtless worked hard for it. A few days later he received another letter about the matter, this time from Pierre Schrijnen, an apothecary, who knew Dubois's brother Victor. Victor was now a well-regarded physician, and Schrijnen was a man with some influence at the university. Like Place, Schrijnen was concerned that the best man be appointed to such a key position. His letter to Dubois was blunt and direct. 'Among the students,' he wrote, 'there is a rumour that you will not accept the position if you are nominated. Is this true?'

Dubois wrote to Place, hoping he could clear up the confusion with Schrijnen and the students.

18 February 1897

In my view, there is a regrettable agitation concerning the undertaking of this professorship in anatomy. This has given me the idea that perhaps my opinion concerning the nomination (that it should go to Seydel) should become more widely known or perhaps there is another way in which I can promote Dr. Seydel's nomination.

Place replied that the students disliked Seydel and were objecting to his possible appointment. He had only a slim chance of being accepted. But if Seydel was rejected and another candidate did not appear, the position would go to Dubois's old enemy Louis Bolk.

Oh, the students! Dubois sighed as he remembered his own trials with student popularity. They cared nothing for the quality of science or of intellect, only for the amusement a lecturer offered. Bolk might be popular, but his research was unsound; Dubois and Place agreed in this. Dubois would be a much better choice, as he was a much better anatomist and he was now a famous man in Europe, even if he had not been at the University of Amsterdam for many years. But Dubois's problem was twofold: the students did not know him personally, and what they did know of him was the ominous rumour that he would not accept the position if offered it. But that was a misunderstanding based on Dubois's noble effort to leave the field clear for Seydel. Dubois decided to give in to his friends' urging to put himself forward. Someone had to repair the damage done by the false rumour, however, if Dubois was to have a chance. In the meantime, these complex machinations had to remain confidential. Dubois sent Schrijnen a telegram via his brother Victor, for privacy's sake. He assured Schrijnen that he was willing to vie for the post, but he had to be assured that he would not be hemmed in by the position. He had to be free to carry on his research, whether in geology, fossils, brain weight and body size, or anything else that took his fancy. After all, a professor was a little king in a university and he had to have the right to move freely within his kingdom, as Fürbringer had always done. In the telegram, it amused Dubois to refer to Pierre Schrijnen as 'Piet', the Dutch equivalent of Pierre, and Place as 'Plaats', the Dutch translation of his name. As for himself, Dubois was 'Piet's friend'. It was like playing at espionage.

Dr. Victor Dubois, Venlo, 20 February 1898
Plaats wishes Piet's friend success which is not impossible if nobody believes him unwilling to accept the post. Will write to Plaats to do his best and communicate this confidentially to the examiners. Tell Piet that his friend always kept this possibility seriously in mind but in the first place his friend did not wish to be troublesome. His head and hands are full of other things which he will in no case give up. Maybe a combination is possible. Can Piet put this forward cleverly? If not, better to be silent. All this confidential.
　　Eugène

Dubois and his supporters had to sway opinion subtly for this plan to succeed. In Dubois's favour, he had been trained at Amsterdam and would have been likely to assume the professorship had he never left; he was also internationally recognized. His main handicap was that many at the university remembered how he had cast aside his brilliant future to go fossil-hunting, and no one liked to be rejected. Another problem was that Dubois had never been a skilled lecturer and the students were already up in arms. Also, Dubois's theories, though well known, were certainly controversial.

In the middle of the plotting and planning, Dubois received an infuriating letter from Victor. Somehow it was always Victor who stuck the knife in Dubois's side, reviving painfully Dubois's worst fears. Dubois thought Victor acted like the head of the family instead of the younger brother. In the letter, Victor chastised his brother for doggedly pursuing his research, come what may, reminding him that he had a family to support and an ageing mother who was sick with worry about her elder son's lack of a permanent position. Victor closed his letter with an admonition: 'I believe it is your duty still to do everything that is possible to be nominated for this position…It will need a lot of willpower to conquer your aversion to this, but (1) the final goal is not ignoble, and (2) it leads certainly to the goal.'

Dubois was enraged and deeply hurt. The goal? Who was Victor to speak to him of a goal, as if burrowing into a job, no matter what job at no matter what cost, ought to be Dubois's primary ambition? His lectures, his research, his writing were as compelling as they were exhausting. Didn't Victor know that in two and a half years Dubois had lectured in no fewer than nine European cities and institutions, refuting the criticisms of his monograph? He could not abandon *P.e.* now.

And had Victor overlooked Dubois's own publications? There had been two in 1895, the year after the monograph; another eleven in 1896; three in 1897; and perhaps another two would be out before the end of 1898. Some were brilliant, innovative; none was mundane. Dubois was working harder than he ever had as an anatomy professor, back in his early days. Simply because he was not very well paid, Victor – his younger brother Victor, the one who had never believed in working hard for any reason – thought he had the right to tell him what to do. It was insupportable, humiliating. Would his family never understand him? He wrote his reply in a fury, his pen nearly tearing into the page.

22 February 1898

Your letter of yesterday did not please me, because of the advice you gave me in it but above all because of the way in which you gave it…That you give me advice, certainly wrong advice that might even lead to my misfortune, is not your fault, because you do not know the situation well enough…

But what grieves me even more is that you place me in a position of inferiority, which you have no right to do. You must admit that with my 'impractical mind', which you ascribe to me as well as to our mother, I have managed to achieve a few things. Since I returned to the Netherlands, I have for example acquired two things: the opportunity to work and money for the publication of my description…

In the Indies, I achieved literally everything that I wanted. Abroad, my name is perhaps better known than that of any other living Dutchman. I have even been nominated for a professorship, even though I had explained explicitly that I did not desire it…

You cannot ascribe all this to luck, because I have desired and effected all of this…I have fixed my eyes upon a still further future.

What I really desire is a professorship not in anatomy...but in paleontology, and...I am confident of reaching that goal.

Have you ever considered that to execute a function well one must also be suitable? Otherwise, to accept such a position is to walk into misfortune...What life would await me if I accepted such a position and then did not, as I am afraid I would not, meet the expectations?...Certainly I could eventually find another post, but in the meantime it would be dreadful, especially under the current circumstances of agitation.

When, Dubois wondered, when were his trials to be over? Would he never stop needing to fight the sceptics? He was too proud to tell Victor that he was already doing everything he could to obtain the post. It would be too humiliating to admit he desired it, and then be rejected.

Indeed, the scheming and plotting of Place and Schrijnen on Dubois's behalf were all in vain. For whatever reason, the examiners awarded the post to Louis Bolk, a man Dubois had never liked before this and now liked even less. Dubois was deeply disappointed, even though he had once fled halfway around the world to avoid the prospect of taking up just such a job. Some days he looked back on his forty years of life and saw only a long line of nay-sayers: there had been Fürbringer, Weber, and De Vries; then the Secretary-General of the colonies; the entire military establishment whom he had had to badger for even a little free time; and worst of all, his family. They should have shown him respect and support, but they had been traitors, offering only scorn and condemnation. And now the university examiners preferred that idiot Bolk to him!

And yet, Dubois reminded himself, he had met with kindness, too. There had been Groeneveldt and Kroesen, supporting his expeditions in the Indies; De Winter and Kriele, faithfully supervising the coolies and never questioning Dubois's word; there had been Weber, come around at last and sending that chimpanzee skull; there had been Sluiter, who had sent the Wadjak skull and drawn him to Java; now there were Manouvrier and De Mortillet in France, Marsh and Osborn in America, Haeckel, Branco, and Dames in Germany, W. H. L. Duckworth and William Sollas in England. Yes, he had his supporters and defenders, and they were fine men. But above all, he realized, his greatest supporter, more important than any of these, had been Prentice, with his intelligent thoughtfulness, his understanding. It had been Prentice who had helped him through the most trying days, those days of discovery, and fever, and desperation. Even now that they were separated by so many miles, Prentice still wrote him from time to time, still applauded his triumphs, stoutly denied the legitimacy of his critics. Dubois smiled gently at his fond reminiscences of days spent with Prentice, of the man's honesty and loyalty.

Suddenly he was spurred out of his reverie into action. Where was that last letter Prentice had sent? He wanted to read it through again, to hear Prentice's voice once more. Dubois rummaged through his desk and found it, slowly opening the folded pages that brought back those happy days in Java once more. Was it his imagination, or was there a faint, spicy, indefinably tropical smell clinging to the pages?

Toeloeng Agoeng, 15 April 1896

My Dear Doctor,

Your pamphlets about the missing link reached us safely two days ago and both Mr. Boyd and I sat down diligently that evening to read the work through. I had just gone over to Mringin to see the Old Warrior. We were naturally greatly interested in your article and most pleased to see you were causing a stir in learned circles in Europe where you must now of necessity be well known. I shall not enter into any discussion on the matter of which you treat, after so many learned & qualified authorities having investigated the questions and being unable to come to any agreement as to the fossils being human or ape. It would be idle for a mere layman like myself to offer any opinion as the same must be a matter of pure guess as anything else. After reading your work however, and pondering over the views entertained by the many eminent men who have investigated the matter, it would seem to me that the bones are from one and the same being, that he must have been a very low man or a very high ape, thus probably between both, seeing no such highly developed ape has yet been found and no human remains have ever been found of such antiquity as you calculate for that of the formation in which you found the relics. If ape, then it is a species between any known ape and man, and if *Homo*, then it is of a race nearer the ape than any fossil *Homo* yet exhumed. Thus if not a missing link is discovered, you have at least discovered not only the lower but the most ancient type of man yet met with, and your discovery has in that case the merit of proving that man existed in an age in which it was till now deemed he had not been. I cannot help thinking what a pity it is that you were not allowed to prosecute your excavations further at Trinil. I did not then realize so fully as I do now the vast importance of your discovery there or I should have urged & urged, & urged you to continue & continue it. Of course your health prevented you greatly and your insecure position in gov't employment also unsettled your mind for continuous and laborious work of a mental kind. These things the world cannot know, but it is a pity all the same as further excavation on that lucky spot might have brought to light similar fossils. I notice from your pamphlet that it will take a year or two yet to complete your report on your collection. I hope you find it in every way agreeable and that both yourself and your family are all well and happy.

Mr. Boyd is as usual & is glad Janet is at such a nice school and under such nice teachers.

With me things are going along slowly. My plantation does not stand as well as I expected as my crop has not turned out well. This gives me much mental worry. I have been reading about nothing but coffee of late. I have lots to do & lots of little worries. I have not the leisure now that I had at Tempoersarie or Geboegan for scientific or learned reading, which I greatly regret. My boy is still at Malang & is growing well. With kindest regards & best wishes to you all.

Believe me,
    Ever Yours Sincerely,
    Adam Prentice

N.B. Mr. Boyd sends his thanks and kind wishes. A.P.

Yes, there was the man who understood him best, the true brother of his soul. There was the man, a true scientist by reading, not education, and yet a deep thinker. Prentice still believed in him; Prentice always had. Had it been nearly two years, then, since he had had a letter from Prentice? He had to make the time to write to Prentice, see how he was faring, learn the fate of his last crop. He would draw his strength from Prentice's faith.

CHAPTER 42

Using His Brains

Dubois's next big battle was in the summer of 1898, when he attended the Fourth International Congress of Zoology in Cambridge, England. It was an enormous affair, with all of the British and many international figures of science in attendance: John Lubbock (Lord Avebury), W. H. Flower, Adam Sedgwick, E. Ray Lankester, William Turner, D. J. Cunningham, Grafton Elliot Smith, John Evans, Arthur Keith, Richard Lydekker, John Forsyth Major, William Pycraft, D'Arcy Thompson, and Arthur Smith Woodward. The participants' list was also sprinkled liberally with military men, Fellows of the Royal Society, nobles, professors, and men of the cloth. Just before Dubois spoke, Ernst Haeckel himself addressed the assembly.

Dubois's ally Ernst Haeckel holds the skullcap of *Pithecanthropus* in this portrait, painted by Gabriel Max in 1896.

Haeckel's stirring presentation was masterful. He was a hand-some, vivacious man, now silver-haired and silver-bearded, but still vigorous and strong as ever. His resonant baritone literally shook the crystals on the chandeliers from time to time, when Haeckel emphasized a particularly telling point. He was mesmerizing. What a command of language Haeckel had! What marvellous clarity in explaining such vast topics! Watching Haeckel speak, Dubois thought to himself that it was good that his enemy was the dry and pedantic Virchow, with his slow and crackling speech, rather than Haeckel, with his ability to sway an audience.

Haeckel summarized the evidence for human evolution – indeed, for the evolution of all life on earth – brilliantly, alluding to the enormous body of evidence now amassed by comparative anato-mists in support of Darwin. Then Haeckel mounted a vigorous defence of Dubois's interpretation. As Dubois listened, admiringly, he realized he could not have asked for a more favourable summary of his own embattled ideas.

The next question now is, What has paleontology to say regarding these important results of comparative anatomy and their application to the system of the primates and to phylogeny? For it is the petrifactions that are the true 'footprints of the Creator', the immediate testimonials of the historical succession of the numerous groups of forms which have peopled this earthly ball for so many millions of years. Do petrifactions of the primates give us any determinate points of support? ... The most important and interesting of these petrifactions of the primates is the renowned *Pithecanthropus erectus*, which Eugène Dubois found in Java in 1894. As this Pliocene ape-man brought out a lively discussion at the last zoological congress held three years ago at Leiden, I may be permit-ted to say a few words in criticism of it.

From the proceedings of the congress at Leiden (at which I was not present), I learn that the most distinguished anatomists and zoologists expressed different views as to the nature of this remarkable *Pithecan-thropus*. Its remains, a skullcap, a femur, and some teeth, were so incomplete that it was not possible to arrive at a conclusive judgement regarding them. The final result of the long and spirited debate held on this subject was that among twelve distinguished authorities three declared the fossil remains to be those of a man, three that they were those of an ape. Six or more zoologists, on the contrary, stated what I believe to be the real fact, that they are the fossil remains of a form intermediate between ape and man ... The *Pithecanthropus erectus* of Dubois is in fact a relic of that extinct group intermediate between man and ape to which as long ago as 1886 I gave the name *Pithecanthropus*. He is the long-sought 'missing link' in the chain of the highest primates.

The able discoverer of *Pithecanthropus*, Eugène Dubois, has not only convincingly pointed out his high significance as a 'missing link', but has also shown in a very acute manner the relations which this intermediate form has on the one side to the lower races of mankind, on the other hand to the various known races of anthropoid apes...

For forming a correct judgement concerning this important *Pithecanthropus* and its immediate position between the anthropoids and man, two features are especially valuable: first, the close resemblance of the femur to that of man, and second, the relative size of the brain. Among the few anthropoid apes yet living the gibbons appear to be the lowest and oldest... they are also the most generalized and appear especially adapted to illustrate the 'transformation of apes into man'. The gibbons more than the other anthropoids have the habit of voluntarily assuming the upright position, whereby they walk upon the entire sole of the foot... The other modern apes... seek the upright position, and when they use it do not tread upon the entire sole but upon the outer edge of the foot... It is thus explained why it is that it is exactly the femur, in the gibbon *Hylobates* and *Pithecanthropus*, that is much more human in form than that of the gorilla, the orang, and the chimpanzee.

But also the skull, that 'mysterious vessel' of the organ of the soul, approaches nearest the human proportions both in *Pithecanthropus* and in the gibbon in important particulars – the rough, bony crests which the skulls of other anthropoids show are wanting... The capacity of the skull of *Pithecanthropus* is from 900 to 1000 cc, therefore about two-thirds of the capacity of an average human skull. On the other hand, the largest living anthropoids show a capacity half as high as this – 500 cc. So the capacity of the skull and consequently the size of the brain is in *Pithecanthropus* exactly midway between that of the anthropoid apes and the lower races of mankind...

The swell of Haeckel's rhetoric was spellbinding. Dubois listened as if he had never heard these arguments before, as if they were all fresh and new, instead of being his own offspring. How could anyone doubt such wisdom! And yet it *was* doubted, even scorned. But now, as the contradiction raised questions in the audience's mind, Haeckel moved skilfully on to demolish the opposition:

To this momentous interpretation, which is now accepted by nearly all naturalists, the renowned pathologist of Berlin, Rudolf Virchow, set up the most obstinate opposition. He went to Leiden for the special purpose of contradicting the idea that the *Pithecanthropus* is a transitional form, but met with little success. His contention that the skull and the femur of *Pithecanthropus* could not have belonged together, that the first belonged to an ape and the second to a man, was rejected at once by the expert paleontologists present, who declared unanimously that, in view of the extremely careful and conscientious account of the discovery 'there could not exist the slightest doubt that the remains belonged to one and the same individual'.

Dubois wished that Haeckel's felicitous reading of the events at that congress had been accurate. What trouble would have been saved if only everyone had accepted at once that the fossils belonged together! How many jibes and cruel jokes would he have been spared!

Haeckel continued,

Virchow further asserted that a pathological exostosis in the femur of *Pithecanthropus* likewise attested to its human characters, for only by the most careful attention by human hands can such disorders be cured. Immediately thereupon the famous paleontologist Marsh showed a number of similar exostoses upon the leg bones of wild apes, who had no 'nursing care' and yet recovered ... Finally, Virchow asserted that the deep notch between the orbital edges and the low skullcap of *Pithecanthropus* – a sign of a very deep conformation of the temporal fossa – were decisive for the ape-like character of the skull, and that such a formation never occurs in man. A few weeks later, Nehring ... showed that exactly the same formation was presented by a human skull from Santos in Brazil.

Virchow formerly had the same want of success with his 'pathological significance of the skulls of the lower races of man'. The famous skulls of Neanderthal, of Spy, of Moulin Quignon, of La Naulette, etc. – which taken together are the interesting isolated remains of an extinct lower race of man standing between *Pithecanthropus* and the races of the present day – these were all declared by Virchow to be pathological products; indeed the sagacious pathologist at last made the incredible assertion that 'all organic variations are pathological'; that they are produced only through disease. According to this all our noblest cultivated products, our hunting hounds and our horses, our noble grains and our fine table fruit, are, alas! diseased natural objects that have arisen by pathological change from the wild original forms that alone are 'healthy'.

...It must be remembered that for more than thirty years, Virchow has regarded it as his especial duty as a scientist to oppose the Darwinian theory and the doctrine of evolution necessarily connected with it... The most important conclusion from the latter, the 'descent of man from the ape', Virchow is well known to attack with zeal and energy. 'It is quite certain that man did not descend from the apes.' This assertion of the Berlin pathologist has been for twenty years past repeated innumerable times in religious and other periodicals – cited as the decisive judgement of the very highest authority – not caring in the least that now almost all experts of good judgement hold the opposite conviction. According to Virchow, the ape-man is a mere 'figment of a dream'; the petrified remains of *Pithecanthropus* are the palpable contradiction of such an unfounded theoretical assumption.

Haeckel's talk continued for some time, but Dubois could no longer absorb his words. Haeckel had so boldly supported him, so ably defended him that Dubois found himself in a sort of deaf halo of pleasure.

This was his best opportunity, he now realized. He knew many of the participants personally, having lectured at their institutions and sometimes stayed in their homes. His ideas had been endorsed by one of the great men of German science, and his worst doubter derided. And now he had to complete the job, persuade the audience, shatter their preconceived notions of what a transitional form would be like – because he had the goods, he had *P.e.*, and nothing else in the world could compete with her. He had once risked his life to find her, and he would not abandon her now. No, he would fight for her to the end, until she was seen for what she truly was: the missing link.

Dubois had invented an utterly new tactic for this conference. During the previous year, 1897, he had become fascinated with the idea that there might be a fixed and predictable relationship between brain size and body size among different types of animals. The idea of such a fixed ratio was not obvious, yet the concept was a magnificent one that revealed a crucial element in the design of being a mammal. Dubois and a few other anatomists – Manouvrier, Otto Snell, Fürbringer, and Lapicque – pursued this notion, which would eventually become a fundamental area of biological study.

Dubois's insight had been born long before the Cambridge congress. It had been evident to him for a long time that *P.e.*'s large braincase could not belong to an ape, for the body attached to such a brain would have been enormous in an apelike creature, while although the femur's possessor had been tall, the bone was not big enough to have supported a *huge* body. But what exactly *was* the size required for an apelike animal with a brain of 1000 cc? The question niggled at him and haunted him. He intuited that there was some consistent mathematical relationship between the two, brain and body, if only he could derive it. He believed that theoretically brain size was determined by two factors, the first being the animal's total body weight. But the relationship was not a simple one.

For example, anatomists had long noticed that small animals tended to have relatively bigger brains – more brain per unit of body weight – than large ones. The second factor at work was the developmental level of the animals' nervous system, its *cephalization*. Clearly some types of animals were more advanced or brainier than others. So there had to be some sort of sliding scale of brain size to body weight, with lower organisms having a lower ratio and higher ones (apes and man) having a higher ratio.

Fürbringer, Dubois's old mentor, had suggested that the explanation lay in the relatively larger body surface of small animals, which would cause them to lose body heat faster. Maybe, Fürbringer had postulated, the 'extra' brain in smaller animals was occupied by an extensive heat centre. And as early as 1892, Snell had proposed that the surface area of the body, which he symbolized by the letter 'P', was equal to the body weight taken to the ⅔ power, or $P^{0.66}$. To demonstrate this, Snell had considered pairs of closely related animals with similar degrees of nervous development, like a lion and a cat. Within such a pair, the brain weight was a simple function of body weight. Thus, the ratio of the lion's *body* weight (P_1) to the cat's body weight (P_2) would be identical to the ratio of the lion's *brain* weight ($P_1^{0.66}$) to the cat's brain weight ($P_2^{0.66}$).

Dubois admired Snell's attempt, but thought that he and Fürbringer had gone astray in attributing the constancy of the relationship to a metabolic function. For him, the issue was one of the structure and function of the nervous system. Dubois's starting point was the observation that the nervous system comprised two main types of structures: *sensory nerves*, which received information from the world through smell, taste, touch, vision, and hearing; and *motor nerves*, which produced actions by triggering muscle activity. Higher animals, Dubois thought, had more of each type of nerve and more complicated connections among them than lower animals did. And the relatively larger surface area of small animals meant that they would have relatively more sensory nerves per unit of body weight; they were more extensively innervated, in effect. If there were more sensory nerves, then there were more connections to the motor nerves and a higher overall cephalization. By analysing closely related pairs of species with similar cephalization, Dubois derived the exponent that expressed the relationship between surface area and body size. His result was 0.56, not Snell's 0.66.

'It is actually,' he had written in his first paper on the subject, in 1897, 'the size of the perceptive surface of the sense organs that determines the quantity of brains in animals of equally high organization.' In the same paper, he had ranked various species according to the extent to which their brain size deviated from that expected

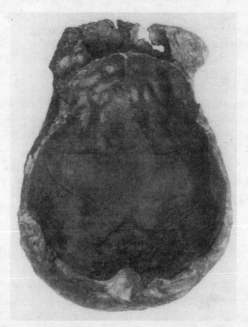

Dubois removed the last matrix from inside *P.e.*'s skullcap to reveal new information about its brain which he presented at the Fourth International Congress of Zoology in 1898.

for their body size. For each species, he had calculated a cephalization value, c. If $c = 1$, then the species had exactly the predicted
brain size for its body weight. If c was smaller than 1, the species
was relatively small-brained; if c was greater than 1, the species
was large-brained.

Although Dubois was very proud of this ingenious article, he
knew few of the scientists at the Cambridge congress would have
read it, for he wrote in Dutch. And now was the time to introduce
them to the ideas and their application to $P.e.$ If brain size had a
predictable relationship to body size, then this relationship proved
$P.e.$ to be the perfect transition between apes and man.

First, he explained his new method of estimating cranial capacity
for $P.e.$ The last traces of stony matrix had been removed from the
braincase, so he could estimate her cranial capacity more precisely
than ever. Since the incomplete skullcap had a volume of 570 cc, he
told his audience, the total brain had obviously been much larger.
If the relationship between the volume of the skullcap (enclosing
the upper part of the brain) and of an entire brain matched that in
humans, then the cranial capacity of $P.e.$ was approximately 798
cc. If the appropriate ratio was that found in apes, which have a
greater part of their brain housed in the missing lower section of
skull, then the cranial capacity of $P.e.$ was 861 cc. As a compromise
value, he accepted 855 cc as the correct value.

Next, he showed that the cephalization coefficient – the amount
of 'extra brain' – varied little in modern humans, since even the
smallest human brains were about 90 per cent the size of the
largest. If $P.e.$ had been as cephalized as a human, a brain size of
about 800 cc would have accompanied a body weight of 19 kilograms, or 41.8 pounds. This was a patently absurd weight for a
creature standing about 5 feet 7 inches tall with a strong and robust
femur. Dubois himself was two inches taller and weighed much
more than 42 pounds. If $P.e.$ had been as cephalized as an ape, then
the resultant weight would have been 230 kilograms, or just over
500 pounds: another ludicrous result. These calculations demonstrated how much the ratio of brain size to body weight varied in
different types of animals. As both answers yielded absurd body
weights, it was obvious that $Pithecanthropus$ was neither an ape
nor a man.

Rather than estimating body size from brain size, Dubois preferred to estimate each, independently, directly from the bones
themselves. The brain he had already shown to be about 855 cc;

the femur was constructed to carry an animal weighing about 70 to 75 kilograms, or 154 to 165 pounds. These values gave *P.e.* an entirely novel ratio of brain size to body weight, *intermediate* between apes and man. And that, Dubois emphasized triumphantly, revealed clearly the true phylogenetic position of *Pithecanthropus*. His was an elegant mathematical argument, based firmly on anatomical structures and biological laws.

His conclusion was, he hoped, irrefutable. 'From all these considerations,' he declared boldly, 'it follows that *Pithecanthropus erectus* undoubtedly is an intermediate form between Man and the Apes.' He did not need to add, 'as I have said all along'. His meaning was as brilliant and hard as a diamond. Yet once again, the august body before which he spoke failed to completely embrace his gems of wisdom.

It was ridiculous, Dubois thought. What better evidence could they expect? Were these men fools? Were they so jealous of his success that they would ignore the truth? He shook his head in disbelief. What poor vision so many of these scientists had, that they could not see the facts he laid before them so plainly. Almost as an aside, a minor point in what he felt had been his most compelling lecture on *P.e.*, he revealed that the Dutch Indies government had undertaken another dry season of excavation at Trinil, pursuant to the digging of a large irrigation canal. A valuable supplementary collection of fossils had been made, including a second, left premolar tooth from the lower jaw of *P.e.* Although there was nothing in this specimen to alter his conclusions, the new tooth had enhanced knowledge of the complete skeleton of the creature. Unfortunately, the excavations of 1897 were the last the Dutch Indies government intended to undertake, so no more fossils of *P.e.* were likely to be forthcoming.

When he finished his presentation, Dubois was satisfied. If he had not completely won over his audience, he felt he had stirred their interest in *P.e.* once again. They would, in time, come to understand the complex business about body size and brain size, he was convinced.

Though not everyone at the conference understood Dubois's innovative techniques or agreed with his conclusions, there was no doubt that his was among the most interesting and important of lectures. His fossils were clearly priceless as scientific objects. Word of the closure of the Trinil excavations – although further digging was just what was needed to resolve some of the debates – spread

Participants in the Fourth International Congress of Zoology in
Cambridge included (left to right, back row): Arthur Keith, Grafton
Elliot Smith, Eugène Dubois, T. H. Gurney, J. F. Gemmil; and (left to
right, front row): G. Swainson, Dr Stokvis, W.H.L. Duckworth, Judge
Peepers, K. Newstead.

from scientist to scientist. 'You know,' one man confided to a
friend, 'whatever that fossil is Dubois has found, it is dashed
important! You'd think they could spare a few coolies to keep
excavating at the most important fossil site anyone has ever found.'

In another corner of the meeting, the American Othniel Marsh
was making much the same assertion to his British colleague
Alexander Macalister. 'I like what this Dubois has done,' said
Marsh. 'A good man, I think, very clever. But what we need, to be
sure of his conclusions, is more fossils of *Pithecanthropus*. And
we've got to know exactly where they come from. It's a real shame
the colonial government has stopped the excavations. Not that I
blame Dubois for leaving the Indies; the fever nearly killed him, I
hear, and more than once! But the work ought to go on.'

'Ummm, yes, of course. Do you think,' Macalister wondered,
'that a resolution from this congress – an international resolution –
might influence the Dutch colonial government? Maybe we could
propose something tomorrow? An endorsement of Dubois's work,

or at least a statement of its extreme importance and a request that excavation be resumed.'

'Good idea!' replied Marsh, striking his hands together enthusiastically. 'Let's do it! I'll just have a quick confab with Dubois, make sure he approves. Then you draw it up and I'll second it.'

Dubois was immensely pleased at the idea. While he wasn't optimistic that more specimens of *P.e.* would be forthcoming, one never knew. Anyway, Kriele and De Winter and a team of labourers could be kept working until the fossils gave out. The next day Macalister introduced a resolution that was quickly adopted by the congress.

IVth International Congress of Zoology
Cambridge: August 28, 1898.

That, in the opinion of this Meeting of the members of the IVth International Congress of Zoology, the Dutch Indian Government, by ordering the exploration of Trinil, Java, leading to that most remarkable (among many) discovery of *Pithecanthropus erectus*, have laid the Zoological World under a most weighty obligation; and that the aforesaid members of the IVth International Congress of Zoology hereby desire to express their fervent hope that these investigations may be continued in the future with the same thoroughness as in the Past.

The above Resolution, having been adopted by the above mentioned meeting is herewith presented for signature by Members of the IVth International Congress of Zoology:

Alex. Macalister (Proposer)
O. C. Marsh (Seconder)

Amazingly, the resolution had the desired effect. In 1898, excavations in the Trinil area were resumed, and they continued until 1900. No new fossils of *Pithecanthropus* were found.

CHAPTER 43

Betrayal and Resurrection

In the new year, 1899, things grew much, much worse.

One of Dubois's handful of supporters in Germany since he had returned home with *P.e.* had been the anatomist Gustav Schwalbe, a large, bluff man with silver-white hair and beard and an enthusiastic, even boisterous, personality. It had been he who had the actor's femur with the exostosis sent to Dubois, and he who had boldly defended Dubois's ideas in print against Virchow's slashing attacks. Moved by Schwalbe's kindness, Dubois had sent Schwalbe a cast of the skullcap when very few were available, and in 1896, even allowed Schwalbe to spend some days in Haarlem, studying the original fossils.

It had proved an uncomfortable interlude. In person, Dubois had found Schwalbe made him uneasy. It was as if Schwalbe were appropriating the fossils; ownership was somehow implied in the way Schwalbe pointed out anatomical features to Dubois and lectured him upon the significance of *his* finds. Dubois had sensed a

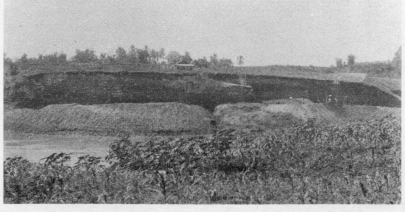

Excavations continued at Trinil throughout 1900, when Kriele took this photograph from Standpunt II (marked on map, page 157).

too-sharp ambition and a hint of ruthlessness underlying the jovial exterior. Like Haeckel, Schwalbe had seemed to be looking for something with which to combat Virchow. Dubois had the evidence, the tangible evidence of human evolution. But it was his to present, not Schwalbe's.

The days had soon passed and Schwalbe had left, but Dubois's suspicions had not died. Instead, they had grown and flourished, torturing him with visions of his prize discovery being usurped. At the end of 1897, Dubois had decided he had to write to Schwalbe, spelling out his own plans for the further publication of his fossils and making clear what possible openings would be left for other scholars after Dubois had finished his own work. Schwalbe's reply had been less than reassuring.

20 December 1897

I shall be glad to leave the femur to you for some time before publishing. Certainly we are competitors...I have almost finished a manuscript on the skull and another one on the femur...We will both have to accept the fact that one or the other of us will finish sooner.

Competitors? But the fossils are *mine*, Dubois had raged. Schwalbe had no earthly claim on them. Schwalbe had not found them, had not sacrificed eight years of his life in the gruelling search for them. He had not picked the spot for excavation or taught the men how to work; he had not lain in that wretched tent on the banks of the Bengawan Solo, sweating and close to death from fever, hoping only to live long enough to announce his finds to the world. No, I showed these fossils to Schwalbe as a professional courtesy; I never granted him the right to publish on them. He had tried to calm himself with the thought that no editor of a reputable journal would have accepted such an article from Schwalbe when Dubois's intentions to publish more lengthy studies were well known in Europe.

But between the end of 1897 and the beginning of 1899, Schwalbe had founded his own scientific journal, designed in no small measure to loosen Virchow's stranglehold on matters of anatomy and evolution in Germany. Schwalbe was editor and chief reviewer of the *Zeitschrift für Morphologie und Anthropologie* (Journal of Morphology and Anthropology), and of course he needed something extraordinary for his inaugural issue, so he opened it with an essay explaining that the purpose of the journal was to contribute to the important question of the origin of the human kind by careful comparative anatomical and developmental investigations, and to investigate the relationships between the human races, their bodily development and their higher or lower position via a purely morphological approach…

A zoology of mammals without paleontology is an extremely deficient science that can provide only highly incomplete information on the evolutionary history of the entire mammalian group with its individual members…

The apparently wide chasm which separates man and the simians can be bridged by a consideration of the fossil forms which have only recently become known. A thorough study of the fossil remains of the order of primates…is an absolute prerequisite for the foundations of zoological anthropology…

In this way, paleontology becomes the principal guide for our fascinating field of research and thus, at the end of…our investigation of the aims and methods, we arrive at Cope's dictum that 'The ancestry of man is a question to be solved by paleontology.'

That was all very well, a welcome endorsement of Dubois's own views on the importance of fossils in evolutionary studies. What followed was an absolute betrayal. Dubois could not believe his eyes: most of the *Zeitschrift*'s first issue was taken up with several hundred pages of description and analysis of *P.e.*'s skull. The sharpened blade of the weapon Schwalbe wielded was Dubois's own fossil. It was the first instalment in a series of articles in which Schwalbe measured the *P.e.* skullcap and compared it with everything: gibbons, other apes, Neanderthals, humans. He addressed Virchow's attribution of the skullcap to a gibbon in a long, meticulous discussion, pointing out detail after detail in which *P.e.* differed from a gibbon. Schwalbe emphasized and re-emphasized how the anatomy of *P.e.* revealed not only its way of life but also its phylogenetic position. He proposed a new evolutionary tree, starting from Dubois's ape-man, leading through Neanderthals to modern humans. The pathway of evolution seemed self-evident, obvious; Schwalbe's mastery of the material unquestionable. In thoroughness, complexity of analysis, and most of all in sheer length, Schwalbe's effort outshone Dubois's thirty-nine-page monograph. Somehow it did not seem to matter that Dubois's work had been written under the most difficult of circumstances during a period when he had been isolated at the ends of the earth, far from libraries, comparative collections, or colleagues.

Dubois could dispute none of Schwalbe's observations, only his overall interpretation. More than that, he was bitterly wounded. Schwalbe had stolen Dubois's fossils, as surely as if he had absconded from Haarlem with them tucked under his arm. Not one new word would he have written on *Pithecanthropus*, but for Dubois's generosity. The impact of his work did not stop there. Next, Schwalbe re-examined the Neanderthals, which he now found to be less than human and a distinct species, *Homo primigenius*. This was not a novel suggestion, but one which Schwalbe took as his battle-stance for the rest of his scientific life. It was *P.e.* that pushed Schwalbe to create a new phylogeny, to launch a new journal, to fly into the bright light of scientific celebrity like a moth to a flame.

But it was Dubois's flame in which he shone: Dubois's by right, by the sweat of his brow, by the genius of his intuitions, by the daughter he left behind in a small cemetery in Java. It was his, and Schwalbe had stolen it. Dubois would never forgive him, nor ever trust another so naively. He felt that he had been ruined, all his efforts and perseverance had been cast aside.

Although in 1899 Dubois was offered – and accepted – a position at the University of Amsterdam as Professor Extraordinarius of Crystallography, Mineralogy, Geology and Paleontology, he found no peace. His rate of publication had been slowing since 1896 and continued to drop off sharply; he could find little more to say about *P.e.* that he had not already said repeatedly. He had told his colleagues, and shown them, and argued with them. His fossils – *his* fossils – had been discussed at enormous length by Schwalbe, not to mention the more than eighty publications by various scholars before the end of 1899. They were the most important discovery of the nineteenth century, without a doubt, but their discoverer was bored.

He was also bone-weary of the battle. He had no further patience – indeed, he had never had much – for the frivolous criticisms and alternative interpretations offered by those who did not know the fossils or who would not understand them. He had shown the fossils to everyone, everywhere, had even allowed access to one whom he clearly ought not to have trusted. Dubois had diagrammed and explained the geological setting at Trinil until even a child could understand it; he had analysed and calculated and estimated and compared until his brain was sore, and still they would not understand. And now he was repaid by Schwalbe's blatant, despicable theft.

Dubois felt like an old, old man with no physical or mental power left at all. What could await him now except death? What mattered in his life was surely finished. He could not remember feeling this bad except during attacks of malaria. What was done, was done. Schwalbe had laid claim to Dubois's ideas and Dubois's discoveries, and there was no erasing all those detailed pages of meticulous German science. The new security offered by the position at Amsterdam gave Dubois some respite from financial worry, but there was no relief from the outrage that seemed to be eating him from the inside out. For once, he had no energy, no ideas, no recourse. He wanted to hide himself and his fossils in some dark corner where no one would ever find them again.

Ironically, just when he wanted to withdraw he was invited into the spotlight. The government wished him to supply the fossils of *P.e.*, or good casts of them, for the Exposition Universelle, to be held in Paris in 1900. Along with exhibits from many nations, the Dutch were planning a special display in the Pavillon des Indes Néerlandaises, devoted to objects from the Dutch East Indies. It was to be a celebration of national pride. National pride! Dubois, beleaguered and wounded, could not imagine that the general public would have any interest in the bones of his missing link. After all, the scientific community still could not understand the most basic truths about *P.e.*, so how could the uneducated public make sense of her? He was too drained even to write his refusal. The official letter sat for weeks, unattended-to and gathering dust, on his desk. For weeks Dubois did no work.

And then he had an idea, a crazy, brilliant idea. He would produce a sculpture of *P.e.* as she looked in the flesh – or rather, he would do a life-sized statue of a male *Pithecanthropus*, a hide draped around its waist for decency. Even the public would appreciate this, the image of a male *Pithecanthropus* as he might have looked in the jungles of Java so many years ago.

Dubois was an excellent artist with pen and pencil, and skilled with his hands; he had no doubts that he could produce a credible sculpture. He found a disused attic, in an old two-storey building, where he could set up his model, his clay, and the metal frame to support the sculpture. He would need to work without interruption. His plan was to make a clay figure that could be cast in plaster and painted in lifelike colours, with brown skin and orang-utan-red hair. He needed, urgently, a suitable model. It was an awkward thing, to approach a man of his acquaintance and ask him to pose naked in an unheated attic in winter for a statue of a primitive ape-man. He turned the problem over in his mind for some days, until at a crucial moment, his elder son, Jean, came in from a day of skating. Flushed, dishevelled, and bright-eyed from cold and exertion, Jean at eleven seemed the image of a little savage, a primitive man. 'My son,' Dubois said, addressing his offspring with unusual fondness, 'you'll do. You'll do very nicely.' The boy looked up, confused. Do? Do what? he thought. Seeing his puzzled expression, Dubois explained: 'You'll make a nice ape-man. You are to pose for me.'

For the rest of his winter holidays, Jean posed, miserably naked, cold, and cramped, while his father sculpted. Dubois had a precise posture in mind. He directed the boy to stand very still, and just so: his knees a little bent, feet spread apart and pointed slightly inward, eyes fixed on a deer antler that he held in his right hand. The antler, like the many fossilized antlers found at Trinil, was to provide just a suggestion of possible tool use, which Dubois found plausible but unprovable. The boy's other hand, his left, was to be just in front on his thigh, palm forward and fingers slightly open.

Jean soon found that holding still in the bitter cold was intensely difficult. He begged for frequent breaks, to warm himself in a blanket and relax his cramped muscles, and these were granted. Jean obeyed his father, in this as in nearly everything else, for Dubois was a stern paterfamilias and his word was not to be contradicted. The statue proceeded quite rapidly, given that the sculptor was a novice and the model a restless eleven-year-old boy who would rather have been reading or skating or playing ball with his brother. When it was completed, Jean was quite impressed and bragged to his fellows at school about his modelling job. 'Only my body was being used,' he added quickly, to forestall the teasing he could see coming, 'not my face!' Because of P.e.'s transitional status, Dubois gave the statue elongated apelike fingers and toes, not to mention a big toe that diverged from the others on the foot.

Before being shipped to Paris, the finished statue – nicknamed Piet, for Pithecanthropus – went on exhibit in the front hall of the Colonial Building of the Industrial Arts Museum in Haarlem. Dubois took his entire family along for the opening, to observe the public's reaction. Jean was both embarrassed and proud to see his likeness displayed in public and attracting such attention. There was no doubt that Piet caught the eye, he was so large and naked and odd-looking.

Jean reluctantly posed for this sculpture of *Pithecanthropus*,
nicknamed Piet, for the Paris Exhibition of 1900.

Jean stood near his statue for a long time, watching as people
approached and studied it. His attention was drawn to an elderly,
countrified couple who walked in, so busily gazing around themselves that they came quite close to the statue before they seemed to
see it. They halted, bewildered expressions on their faces, in front
of Piet.

'And who,' the woman asked her husband, querulously, 'is that?'

Before the man had a chance to reply, Jean took a step toward
them and blurted out proudly, 'That is my father!' He meant, of
course, that it was his father who had found the being and reproduced it as a sculpture. The couple looked at him, confused, and
then hastily moved away.

Later, in private, Jean confessed his outburst to his father.
Dubois broke into a low chuckle and smiled at the boy, patting his

shoulder warmly. Jean was confused, but grateful. It was perhaps the only time in Jean's short life that he had been so irreverent about his father and not been punished for it.

CHAPTER 44

Family

During those first five trying years back in Holland, Dubois found no solace in his family. His father was dead; his mother was not proud of him; his brother misunderstood and chastised him. Nor could he warm himself with his children's affection or his wife's sympathy, for these were sadly strained by the abrupt and disturbing changes in their world. His children had been in urgent need of his attention when they had returned to Holland in 1895, Eugenie eight, Jean seven, and Victor four. Far from the casual, languorous Indies, the children's shortcomings in manner and habit had become all too evident to their father. They had run wild in the Indies, playing only with native children and half-castes, exploring the jungle, chasing after birds and butterflies and anything that moved. They had not learnt to sit and read, or even to listen or think carefully. Their *babu* had spoiled them – *babu*s always did – but their mother had not exercised any counterbalancing influence. Anna was hopeless, Dubois realized when he compared her with the wives of his colleagues in Europe. In company, she knew how to mask her weaknesses for a short time. But she always liked to join in the conversation, and her empty-headedness was soon apparent. She was no longer a decorative companion at a banquet, nor a good housekeeper, nor even a firm mother. And Dubois's mother had only encouraged the children's harum-scarum ways since they had returned. This would not do.

Dubois decided that he could yet inculcate his values into the boys, mould their personalities. He could make the boys into sons that he could be proud of, uproot that Indies indolence and inject some Dutch vigour. Eugenie did not worry him; she would never have to earn a living and she was her father's daughter, strong-willed and intelligent. He resolved to exercise much more control over the boys' daily lives and characters, before it was too late. As his discouragement and weariness weaned him from an intensive scientific schedule, Dubois started to play a larger role in the boys' upbringing.

He established a firm routine and schedule for the boys. He made

Dubois tried to shape the characters of his children (left to right, Jean, Eugenie, Victor) but only Eugenie inherited his intelligence and drive.

sure that they rose early, well before six, and had a cold bath every morning. Before breakfast, they did fifteen minutes of exercises with an apparatus that Dubois devised himself, to build the strength in their arms and chests. He attached a pair of handgrips to the wall of the house. The handgrips were connected by thick elastic cords to a pair of adjustable cables that moved over pulleys, to give resistance. Moving rhythmically, each boy pulled against the cables in a pattern Dubois had designed to build their muscles. Sometimes he commanded them to repeat the entire set of exercises, if they were too reluctant. They went inside for breakfast (two slices of rye or wheat bread, a boiled egg, and a glass of milk) and went promptly to school. If there was extra time before school, they were sent off for a vigorous walk, regardless of the weather. 'I will not have weak sons,' Dubois told them all too frequently, 'and I will not have lazy ones.'

When the boys returned home from school, they were to wash and change. They were not to appear in front of their father dirty or dishevelled. They were expected to sit quietly through dinner, which was followed by an evening walk with their parents and Eugenie. Dubois felt the walk was a good time to instruct them in natural history, to see if they had learnt anything about the animals, birds, and plants that surrounded them. He tried desperately to teach them to observe and think. He might say suddenly, 'Jean, what bird is that calling now? Yes, very good, it is the magpie. And what does it look like? Yes, black and white, with a long tail. Does it migrate, or does it stay here through the winter? Hmm, don't know? You'd better refresh your memory when we get back.' And a little later, 'Now, Victor, do you see the nest up in that tree? You must learn to look with your eyes, to see what is around you. There it is, there! Hurry up, boy, climb up and look in the nest. Come on! Don't touch it, just tell me: are there any eggs in it? How many? What do they look like? Whose nest do you think this is?'

After the walk, the boys did their homework. There was no playing or reading for enjoyment until their work was done. They also often looked up information about the questions that their father posed during the family's walks. There was no point in hoping that he would forget to ask them the very same question the next day. Failing to answer the same question twice was the cause of considerable paternal disapproval and wrath; they had never dared to find out what failing to answer three times would provoke. Dubois quizzed them weekly on the subjects they were taught in school, to make sure that they were learning and that the teachers were not filling their minds with rubbish. At first, their ignorance was appalling, but with Dubois's daily intervention, their memories and habits improved. Finally, under his guidance, they learned to study diligently, to conduct themselves properly in the house, to be seen and not heard.

These boys bore Dubois's name, a proud name, and he was determined that they would also bear his character, if it could be instilled into them. Even when he was working hard in his study, Dubois listened for their return from school, to see if they slammed the door and thumped up the stairs or if they remembered to walk quietly like civilized people. Slowly, they began to behave with dignity and calm, as befitted their father's sons. But even after months of his tutelage, he was saddened to receive complaints about their conduct at school, where, so their teachers said, the boys were rude, noisy, and sometimes insolent. They interrupted classes, did poorly on tests, and befriended the very worst students. It was as if they had only so many hours of good behaviour in them, which were expended at home. He tried to teach them, by example and explanation, the importance of truthfulness, hard work, and discipline. In this family, a detected lie – and Dubois always knew when the children were lying – merited a much sterner punishment than an admitted wrongdoing.

After some years of this regimen, Dubois realized he could not alter their basic natures further. Despite all his efforts to be a diligent father, Jean and Victor did not do well in school and did not qualify to go to university. They were not intelligent enough to do well without working, and they were not hardworking enough to do well without being clever. It was a bitter disappointment. All his sons wanted to do was return to the Indies, to the land of sunshine and freedom, where they had been indulged and petted. They talked of it as a paradise lost.

Surprisingly, Jean and Victor had no trouble obtaining jobs once they left school. They took the chance to fulfil their dreams and travel. In 1906, when the boys left for the colonies for the first time, the entire family had been for a few days at De Bedelaar, an estate in Limburg that Dubois had bought as a country retreat. He already had plans to make it into a sort of nature park, to restore the ancient habitat and vegetation to this peaceful corner of Holland. He was already busy inventorying the plants, studying the two fens on the property, and learning what animals and birds dwelt there.

When Jean and Victor were ready to go to the station, Dubois was swimming naked in the lake. He had tried not to cast shadows over their bright plans, not to make his scepticism about their futures discouragingly plain. As so often before, he took refuge in fierce physical activity to quiet his mind. He could not even bear to get out of the lake and dress to accompany them to the station, for fear of sending them off with his disapproval ringing in their ears, as his own father had done so many years before. Better to let their mother take them, for she would send them off with a bright smile and a dream in their heads. If, as he believed, their disgrace was impending, there was little to be gained from saying so now.

The situation was a poignant replay of his own father's despair when Dubois had quit his job at the university and left for the Indies. He understood now how his father had felt – though of course, his father had been wrong, while he, in this instance, was right. He had gone off with a purpose, a holy mission of science, and he had succeeded. His sons left with no education, no purpose, no real skills: not as he had. They went off to play in the warm sunshine, like children. Their guileless, smiling faces were young, so young. They probably thought that the flowers were always in bloom in the tropics and the girls always beautiful; they dreamt they would be rich and happy in a few years' time. Jean headed for Dutch Guiana, to work as a planter for several years; he ended up in Java, using his knowledge of Malay to manage plantations, first rubber and coffee, then tea. Victor followed a similarly wandering track through the Dutch colonies.

They dreamt of wealth, but Dubois knew better. Statistically, they were more likely to be dead than rich after a few years in the colonies. And he knew they would find the Indies a different world now that they were adults; things were not so easy when there was work to be done and responsibilities to fulfil. The tropical climate was hotter than they remembered, and it required more fortitude to get real work done. His sons didn't understand that the natives had to be taught everything, and reminded and watched all the time to see that they did the work carefully, or at all. Failure always lurked just around the corner on plantations; disease and death were the constant companions of Europeans in the tropics. At every turn, they would have to guard against slacking and cheating and lying and fever. It would be a big change for them, to be, for once, the ones who had to maintain standards and hold others to them. He said goodbye to his sons, shook their hands, and then plunged back into the cold lake water as soon as they had left, as if to drown his feelings.

For several years after their departure, Jean and Victor earned a good living in the colonies. They did well enough managing their workers, better than most young men newly out from Holland. Their employers seemed happy with them, for one of the plagues of plantations was the problem of constantly firing men – or having them simply wander off – and then having to take on untrained newcomers; Jean and Victor had the knack of keeping the workforce stable and happy. They wrote home from time to time, bright and cheerful letters mostly addressed to Anna, who missed them keenly. To their father, they wrote only of crop yields and profit, with occasional anecdotes about unusual animals they had seen or shot. They sent home the skulls and notes on the body weights of unusual animals they had killed, for his studies of cephalization and body weight. This pleased him. But when Jean wrote home dramatically describing how he had killed a Sumatran royal tiger with a single shot, his father had no praise for his son's prowess. His only question was, 'Did you save the skull?'

CHAPTER 45

The New Century

With the beginning of the new century, things changed for Dubois. It was as if the dawning of the long-forecast future had brought a change of heart – or, more accurately, a petrification of heart. Dubois was beaten and bruised from his years on the lecture circuit, fighting, always fighting, with words and principles and theories and new techniques. Nothing ever brought him victory.

Worse yet (he hardly dared admit it), he was restless. He had studied, analysed, compared, and reconstructed *P.e.* until he had nothing more to say. Now that I have found the answer for myself, he thought, I have no more interest. There was no more to do with those few, wonderful fossils, and he knew from bitter experience that if he allowed someone else to study them, that man would attempt to steal his glory. That would not happen again, he vowed: never. He put the bones away in their special cases and locked them away in their own special cabinet at the Teyler Museum. He rarely took them out, only sometimes in the afternoons if he was feeling melancholy. Then he extracted them and held them up to the light and he was once again filled with wonder at the remarkable objects he had found.

What days those had been, in Java! What dreadful conditions, nearly fatal: fever and heat, in a country where even the vegetation and the rivers seemed to be determined to kill him; lazy, ignorant coolies who couldn't be bothered to understand the work; and mountains so steep a man's legs ached for days. What obstacles he had overcome during those long lonely weeks of anguish when only Prentice had understood him, when only Prentice's faith in his find and his intellect had kept him going. And here was the proof, his *P.e.*, his missing link. Whatever they said, those sceptical scientists of Europe, they could not change the truth. He was the man who had found the missing link.

From time to time, he got an idea about the bones and carried them home to work on. As matter-of-factly as he closed and locked the door to the street, Dubois rearranged the china in one of the glass-fronted cabinets in the dining room, placed the bones within on a bed of fabric, and carefully pasted newspaper over the glass in case a fellow scientist should call. In the end, inspiration always failed him and eventually he took the fossils back to the Teyler, to live once again in their special case. He had found his missing link; he knew the truth; and it was done. He had nothing more to say.

He published nothing on *P.e.* in 1900 save a brief pamphlet to be given out at the exhibition in Paris, explaining how the statue 'Piet' had been made. The rest – the other five publications that year – focused on geology, the age of the earth, the circulation of carbonate of lime. He was, after all, a professor of crystallography, mineralogy, and geology as well as of paleontology. In a few years, the university added geography to his purview as well, as if he did not have enough to do. He paid little attention to the thousands of mammalian fossils he had collected and brought back so painstakingly from Java, Sumatra, and India. They were his capital, his investments in his future, and yet he had not been able to obtain suitable quarters for storing and working on such a vast collection. Frankly, his interest in them, too, had waned. He knew enough of those fossils anyway; he had seen enough of them back in the days when every crate sent by Kriele and De Winter had been a treasure-trove eagerly explored.

By 1902, Dubois was focusing on discovering the biological laws that govern the relationship of brain size to body size in mammals.

The years rolled by, 1901, 1902, 1903, and no papers appeared on the fossils from Trinil even though Dubois continued to draw a salary as curator of the Dubois Collection. His friends grew anxious. Karl Martin, the geologist who had first described Raden Saleh's fossils from Java, started to take more interest in Dubois's neglected collection. There was a move afoot – was it Martin's scheme? – to turn the entire Dubois Collection over to the Geological Museum in Leiden, where it would come under Martin's control. Dubois fought off this proposal, claiming that most of the specimens had not yet been individually labelled and he was the only person capable of overseeing the basic labelling and registration. He led the Ministry of the Colonies to believe that one-third of the text of a larger description of the fossils was already at the printers, with many plates published, but the work never appeared. Dubois's friends began to worry that he would lose control of his collection to Martin. Jan Lorié, the geologist, wrote,

30 April 1903

How is the situation yet, with the Indonesian bones? Have you totally forgotten them? Do be careful with the Colonies and our 'mutual friend' of Leiden! I fear for a small catastrophe.

Dubois did not want to hear these fears, and buried himself in research on groundwater and geology. But Lorié persisted, warning him more explicitly a few days later,

4 May 1903

... You yourself informed me how much Martin preyed upon the Indonesian bones, which I think is very understandable. Further I know, from cases with Wichmann and Molengraaf, that he does not shrink from tricks and prevarications to gain control over what attracts him ... It is difficult for you not to attract attention with your lectures about the water supply of Amsterdam. But by now, people must find it strange that you, properly called a paleontologist, lose yourself successively in $CaCO_3$, $NaCl$, H_2O, ... while it is generally known that you receive a salary from the Colonial Office especially to work on the bones, and yet you do nothing about them, so people think. It is very obvious that the Colonial Office ultimately want to have value for their money and it appears entirely likely to me that Martin, who often comes to the ministry, will use this to grab your bones ... Therefore, I offer you a friendly warning. If I have everything wrong or exaggerated, then good, but I do not believe that.

Lorié's forecast of doom echoed in Dubois's ears, accompanied by an ominous announcement from the Dutch Minister of the Interior that the final description and publication of the fossils *would* be completed within three years. Did that mean his curatorial salary would be stopped in three years' time? What would happen to the bones themselves?

Dubois brooded, but still he did not publish anything about the Trinil fossils. The Dutch East Indies government continued excavation in the Trinil area in 1900 and then ceased. Now Dubois had no longer any hope of receiving a crate with additional fossils of *P.e.* in it, one that might have moved him to new insights and energy. In 1905, Dubois was appalled to be recalled to active duty as an army surgeon. He was almost fifty years old and still suffered from occasional bouts of fever! It was an absurd idea. He could not find out who was behind this plot, but he knew it could not be a coincidence. He suspected Martin, carrying out some devious plan to get the fossils away from him, but he could not work out how Martin had managed to influence the army. In any case, Dubois called for an immediate medical examination and was promptly declared unfit for service, with an honourable discharge.

The vultures were moving in. Where he had once worried only about Martin, Dubois soon came under attack from another source. For some years, Emil Selenka, a German zoologist especially interested in apes, had been laying plans to reopen Dubois's excavations at Trinil. Now Selenka had actually won the financial support of the Prussian Academy of Science. Would that I had been so blessed, thought Dubois when he read of this miraculous news. Through Dubois – who could not refuse, for the request came through government channels – Selenka even contacted Kriele and De Winter and obtained Dubois's old site plans. Disheartened, bored, and unwilling to return and risk his own life again, Dubois cooperated, albeit grudgingly. Steal my site, steal my men, Dubois thought bitterly. Go ahead! See what you find. I wish you well of it!

Before the expedition could be mounted, both Selenka and Kriele died. Dubois thought this nightmare was over, but he was wrong. Selenka's ambitious widow, Margarethe Lenore, decided to head up the expedition, though she had no particular academic qualifications. She put the German geologist Dr Johannes Elbert in charge of geological survey; the Dutch mining engineer Fritz Oppenoorth would handle the technical side of the excavation. She was undaunted, insufferable. Reviving the organization and raising additional money took time, so it was not until 1907 that Oppenoorth left for Java, to be followed shortly by the others.

Dubois knew all about this expedition, of course. His reaction to it was to start publishing on the Trinil fauna; the first paper appeared in 1907 and opened with the following remarks:

The excavations which at present will be carried out at Trinil, under the auspices of the Prussian Academy of Science and the widowed Frau Selenka, with the support of the Dutch government, have once again called attention to the extinct mammalian world of Java, known as the Kendeng or Trinil fauna, from which one form, the much-discussed *Pithecanthropus erectus*, has become generally renowned. It is this species, *Pithecanthropus*, in particular that has given rise to the German expedition.

There was little about *P.e.* in this article – he did not write anything new of any length about *P.e.* until many years later – only the reaffirmation of belief by a bitter, tired man: 'In short, I consider *Pithecanthropus* to be a descendant of less-specialized (less long-armed) ancestors of the Gibbons ... a descendant which has assumed the erect posture.'

Although the mere existence of Frau Selenka's expedition offended Dubois, he had no fear that they would find what his nine seasons of excavation at Trinil had failed to: more evidence of *P.e.* Still, he did not want her expedition to claim priority for describing the various new species of mammals that he had already retrieved at such cost. A second article on the fauna followed in 1908. These established his priority, so his names for the new mammalian species he had discovered at Trinil would endure.

The new expedition was an open insult to Dubois. How could his work be superseded by that of a woman! And such a woman, too! The sheer naivety, the simpering and the idiocy of her answers to a newspaper interviewer in Batavia – of course, she was seeking fame and glory before she had accomplished a single thing! – provoked his ire.

April 25, 1907

BATAVIAASCH NIEUWSBLAD: And do you not shrink from the loneliness and isolation at Trinil?

WIDOW SELENKA: Oh, that problem is so very small in comparison with those I have already overcome.

Dubois placed a large exclamation point next to this answer. Oh

THE NEW CENTURY 371

yes, survival at Trinil was only a matter of facing the loneliness, a trivial thing, he fumed. She knew nothing of what she faced, nothing. As he read further, he lost his temper completely.

BATAVIAASCH NIEUWSBLAD: We ask again, is the purpose of your excavation exclusively to trace the fossil remains of *Pithecanthropus erectus*?

WIDOW SELENKA: What else?

BATAVIAASCH NIEUWSBLAD: For all that, the main thing will be also, if possible, to establish the age of the geological strata in which the skeletal remains are found, in which Dubois made his find?

WIDOW SELENKA: Oh, yes, certainly, but the one issue encompasses the other. Certainly the age of those strata is a very important point...

BATAVIAASCH NIEUWSBLAD: And how are you disposed with regard to the outcome of your investigations? Do you think you will find what you are looking for?

WIDOW SELENKA: It is surely possible, isn't it?

Ja, ja, Dubois muttered to himself. No doubt you, the Widow Selenka, will succeed where my excavations have yielded only a few teeth, one skullcap, and a femur. *Ja,* it was so simple to establish the geology and antiquity of those beds, if only I had been more observant during the long years I worked there. Pah! I wish you luck, you black widow, I wish you luck.

By 1908, the Widow Selenka was triumphantly showing around Europe a few teeth she had found. She believed them to belong to *Pithecanthropus,* of course. Dubois was scathing about her finds, in print.

From the two teeth, which the Widow Selenka showed me as her most important finds, one was quite whole, white-looking and recent: a human lower molar to the rootless underside of which was stuck sand similar to that from Trinil, although it was 'not found at Trinil'. The other tooth, which really was excavated at Trinil, is the upper premolar of a pig.

Selenka responded vigorously to this accusation of 'forgery', as she termed it. On 9 February 1909, she rushed into print with an article on the fauna from Trinil, including expert opinions about the tooth from Dr Schlosser and Professor Dr Walkhoff. Schlosser asserted that the tooth was 'much darker than [is the case] among recent human teeth, indicating real fossilization' and pointed out that the dentine had been completely removed by natural geological processes, a characteristic of some fossils. Walkhoff asserted that the tooth could not be a forgery, for he had studied it with x-rays and microphotography.

Sensing a lively debate, the journal invited Dubois's immediate reply. He agreed that the removal of the dentine was natural, but not that it was a sign of fossilization, and that the colour and condition of the tooth were completely incompatible with the colour of the sand stuck to it. As for the question of forgery, Dubois denied he had ever suggested this was not a genuine human tooth, only that it 'imitated' something it was not. Dubois's considered opinion was that the tooth was subfossil – too modern to be fully fossilized – and might originate perhaps from a relatively recent grave dug into the sediments near to Trinil at Sondé, where the tooth had been found. It was nothing to do with *P.e.*

In the end, despite the flag-flying and trumpet-blowing in the newspapers, Selenka's two-year expedition came to naught. She and her colleagues confirmed the antiquity of the fossil-bearing strata – no surprise to Dubois there – and found mammalian fossils, lots of them, as Dubois had known that they would. What they did not find was *P.e.* He was more than a little smug about this. They could not find *P.e.* because he had already found her. She was not there, waiting for some silly woman to mount an expedition. *P.e.* was his, his idea, his find, his life.

During the years of Selenka's expedition and afterward, Dubois was not silent in the scientific world. He wrote prolifically. In addition to the three paltry articles about *P.e.* and the Trinil fauna, between 1901 and 1910, he published sixty-eight papers about other things: climate, geology, groundwater, drinking water supplies, paleoglaciers, minerals. Although in time even his friends felt he had become reclusive, Dubois could not be accused of being unproductive. What he could be – and was – faulted for was abandoning his *P.e.*, leaving her alone in the cupboard. None of the numerous topics he wrote about in these years ever engaged his heart, only his cold, crystalline intellect.

Though Dubois was effectively absent, much happened in the study of human origins in the early years of the new century. More Neanderthal remains were found, most spectacularly burials at Le Moustier and La Chapelle-aux-Saints in France, another at La Quina, and a mixed, broken collection of many Neanderthals' skeletons from Krapina in Croatia. Some important monographs appeared, too. Gustav Schwalbe, propelled perhaps by his underhanded analysis of *P.e.*, produced yet another detailed re-examination of all known Neanderthal remains and declared them to be a separate species, *Homo primigenius*. In 1906, a Croatian scientist, Dragutin Gorjanović-Kramberger, described the new Neanderthal fossils from Krapina that he had discovered. Gorjanović's work remained obscure, despite being published in German, for the French and English scientists were reluctant to read German even if they could. Gorjanović also prejudiced his case by making a sensational claim: that there was evidence of cannibalism in the smashed, charred bones at Krapina. Still, however sensational, Gorjanović's was a lengthy and thorough treatment, 218 pages long with fourteen plates of photographs. Dubois, who read German effortlessly, could not help comparing Gorjanović's impressive monograph to his own poor effort of thirty-nine pages. He despaired once again, overlooking the fact that Gorjanović had had access to all the libraries and museums of Europe in writing his work.

Even more stunning was the main scientific event of 1911: the publication of the first instalment of a massive monograph on the La Chapelle-aux-Saints Neanderthal skeleton by Marcellin Boule. Although Boule had headed the laboratory of paleontology at the Muséum National d'Histoire Naturelle in Paris since 1902, this work was a venture into new territory. His predecessor and mentor, Albert Gaudry, had deliberately avoided writing about or working on human evolution, for it had been a dangerously controversial subject in his day. Boule's ambition was to use this monograph to establish human paleontology as a respectable discipline in France, and himself as the leader of it. The subject was good, for the fossil was splendid: a remarkably complete skeleton of an aged male Neanderthal, intentionally buried in a cave, discovered with the remains of an animal's leg and a collection of stone tools, dressed flints, and flakes. Boule's thoroughly scientific analysis of these remains was designed to demonstrate how systematic and scientific the study of human fossil remains could be. In this intention, his ideas accorded well with those of Manouvrier, Dubois's great friend at the École d'Anthropologie. Where the two Frenchmen parted company violently was over the subject of phylogeny. Manouvrier, the scientific liberal, firmly defended the idea that *Pithecanthropus* was the ancestor of Neanderthals, who were in turn ancestral to modern humans, while Boule's work was underpinned by a conservative conviction that no such savage and apelike creature as a Neanderthal – much less *P.e.* – could lie anywhere in the direct ancestry of modern man.

Dubois was ignorant of the politics of French science and could not make himself care about such matters. All he saw when he read the full 279 pages of Boule's work was the deficiencies of his own monograph. He forgot that his had been the first, the ground-breaking monograph on an early human ancestor, the article whose shortcomings saved later authors, such as Gorjanović and Boule, the same painful treatment Dubois had experienced. All he could do was reproach himself for not producing such a lengthy, detailed monograph. He did not like to admit it, but once he had lifted the corner of the mystery of *P.e.* and seen what lay underneath, that had been enough. He was an impatient man with a fertile, restless mind, ill-suited to prolonged, meticulous work. He knew *P.e.* now, knew her inside and out. He could not understand why, after all he had done, others did not believe him, and he could not bear any longer their academic jibes and idiotic theories. They had doubted him and accused him of lying or foolishness: the wounds were too deep to heal. The only thing was to closet *P.e.* away, where she – and he – would be safe from further torture.

CHAPTER 46

Diversions

If he was to do no more with *P.e.*, Dubois had to find something else to occupy his brain. Boredom was agony; he could not endure it, he would not sit mentally idle. In August, work started on a large, comfortable house to be built at De Bedelaar, his country retreat in Haelen. He inventoried the plants and trees and wildlife on the thirty-eight-hectare property, intending to attempt to restore the late Pliocene habitat of the region, which was known as the Tegelen Clays after a nearby fossil site that preserved abundant plant and seed remains. He occupied his mind for months with schemes to lower the water level in the fens at De Bedelaar. This was but the first step in creating a sort of prehistoric nature park, where plants and animals surviving from the past could live at liberty. The next step would be to fertilize the water and soil so that he could carry out a massive planting scheme to restore the original forest vegetation. He planted tulip trees and Chinese rubber trees, sequoias and swamp cypress, nine species of oaks, and numerous conifers; he reintroduced tench, rudd, and other fish to the fens and constructed thickets to attract nesting birds. After a few years, he erected bat towers of wood and brick in hopes of encouraging a colony to roost there and control the mosquitoes.

Dubois's vision of recreating a natural past habitat was an extraordinary one that few understood. Locals generally thought him demented and made jokes about this Amsterdam professor who wanted to bring the past back to life. Maybe he wanted to provide a home for his missing link? Their scepticism disturbed him only a little; he was used to pursuing, through sheer strength of will and intellect, goals that others did not understand. Still, he treasured the support he found among the members of the newly established Netherlands Society for Nature Conservancy. In 1912, he was appointed a member of its board and of the board of the international society to which it was affiliated.

De Bedelaar was a welcome outlet for Dubois's energy and intellect. As soon as the house was finished, he found it a peaceful retreat from Amsterdam and the university. He spent more and more time there, as much as his teaching duties would permit. He realized, too, that De Bedelaar provided him with an acceptable way to get away from Anna. There was no longer any overlap between their interests. The countryside was boring and cold, Limburg too foreign for Anna's tastes. She preferred Amsterdam comforts and society, was utterly indifferent to Dubois's plans for a prehistoric nature-park, and could not muster any curiosity about fens or drainage or fertilizers or trees. The whole idea struck her as just another one of her husband's expensive and inconvenient dreams. When they were together, he lectured and commanded, she took refuge in misunderstanding: 'This is all too much for me, Eugène; I am not educated and clever like you!' When she was feeling greatly frustrated, she slyly undermined him. She no longer had any faith in his obsessions; she no longer thought him a great man, only demanding, irritable, and invariably stubborn, while he found her more trivial and thoughtless than ever.

But De Bedelaar was not enough to keep Dubois busy. Nature was a slow companion and Dubois was impatient. He decided to fill his time by resurrecting the Wadjak fossils from his collections, to set about cleaning and reconstructing them properly, as he had never before found time to do. It proved more interesting than he had expected. Now that he looked at them again, cleaned up, he saw that the two partial skulls – the one sent him by C. P. Sluiter so many years ago and the other found when Dubois first started work on Java – had considerably more to tell him. In a state of high excitement, he settled down to write to Sluiter.

17 December 1910

And it is now evident that everything is so important that I feel the need to share this information with you, without delay. If I had thought twice, soon after writing you in 1889, I would have realized that I am not dealing with a Papuan type but with an Australian type. I learn now, on closer acquaintance with the jaws, in particular, that this type is of a very primitive nature and in many ways links up with the Neanderthals.

Actually it is good that the task has lain fallow for so long, because in the meantime the Australians and also the Neanderthals have become better known, and because our early Javanese is in that line of descent, which on the basis of that knowledge is believed to continue further back into the past.

Typically, Dubois's interest in the Wadjak skulls waned after some months and he soon set aside the unfinished manuscript on their anatomy and significance.

The numerous fossil discoveries of recent years fostered enormous public interest in the evolution of Man. In 1910, Alfred Haddon of Cambridge published the first-ever history of anthropology, expending an entire chapter on 'The Unfolding of the Antiquity of Man'. In it, Haddon summarized the various fossil finds thought to pertain to human evolution, starting with the famous *Homo diluvii testis*, found in 1726 and now under Dubois's care in the Teyler Museum. In reality, this specimen was a fossilized skeleton of giant salamander that had been mistakenly hailed at its first discovery as 'Man, witness of the Flood', a 'rare relic of the accursed race of the primitive world', and the 'melancholy skeleton of an old sinner'. Haddon then surveyed the rest of the known fossils, but they 'fade into relative insignificance compared with the sensation caused by the discovery made by Dr Dubois in Java in 1891'.

A most satisfactory assessment, Dubois thought, reading Haddon's words. Alas for Dubois's temper, Haddon alluded to every nuance of the debates, challenges, and arguments that had ensued over *P.e.*, its dating, and the association of its parts into a single individual. Haddon wrote,

Dubois published his account in Java in 1894, and since that date a vast amount of literature has accumulated round the subject, representing three antagonistic points of view. Some, like Virchow, Krause, Waldeyer, Ranke, Bümuller, Hamann, and Ten Kate, claim a simian origin for the remains; Turner, Cunningham, Keith, Lydekker, Rudolf Martin, and Topinard believed them to be human; while Dubois, Manouvrier, Marsh, Haeckel, Nehring, Verneau, Schwalbe, Klaatsch and Duckworth ascribe them to an intermediate form. The last-mentioned sums up the evidence in these words: 'I believe that in *Pithecanthropus erectus* we possess the nearest likeness yet found of a human ancestor, at a stage immediately antecedent to the definitely human phase, and yet at the same time in advance of the simian stage.'

The English, as Dr. Dubois somewhat slyly noted, claimed the remains as human; while the Germans declared them to be simian; he himself as a Dutchman, assigned them to a mixture of both...

The discovery of these human remains has had a very noticeable effect on anthropometry. Most of them are imperfect, some very much so; as in the cases, for example, of the partial calvaria of *Pithecanthropus* and of the Neanderthal specimen. The remains are of such intense interest that they stimulated anatomists to a more careful analysis and comparison with other human skulls and with those of anthropoids... New ways of looking at problems suggested themselves, which led to the employment of more elaborate methods of measurement or description.

Very fine, Dubois nodded to himself. Haddon understands what I have done, how I have changed evolutionary studies for ever.

Though he did not travel to examine the new fossil specimens that seemed to be announced every few months, Dubois kept careful track of them. Neanderthals and more modern skeletons seemed to be unearthed in every cave in France; other types were discovered in England, Italy, and Austria; in Germany, a massively built fossil jaw from Heidelberg (*Homo heidelbergensis*, some called it) was found that belonged to a skull somewhat like *P.e.*'s. Each new fossil produced a new round of inquiries about Dubois's specimens, both from up-and-coming young scholars and from the old giants to whom he had showed *P.e.* back in those early years.

In 1911, Dubois's old ally Arthur Keith followed Haddon's lead and published a little book, *Ancient Types of Man*, summarizing the most current information on human evolution. Now curator of the Hunterian Museum at the Royal College of Surgeons in London, Keith had decided to mount an exhibition on early Man in England to attract attention. At forty-five, Keith was settled in a relatively unimportant post that he found unsatisfactory. He was a tense, anxious-eyed man with fair, frizzled hair and a pronounced Scots accent that reminded Dubois a little of his old friends Prentice and Boyd. Keith and Dubois had first met years ago, when Dubois had spoken to the Anthropological Institute of Great Britain and Ireland in 1896. On that first occasion, Keith had been one of the few who rose to defend Dubois's ideas. They had renewed their acquaintance two years later at the zoological congress in Cambridge. Dubois was interested to see what Keith had to say about *P.e.* in his new book.

Keith filled a complete ten-page chapter with an account of the discovery and interpretation of *P.e.*, Dubois was pleased to see. But when he read the chapter, his pleasure turned to exasperation. Dubois himself was described as 'now Professor of Geology in the University of Amsterdam... trained under that veteran Dutch zoologist, Max Weber.' Weber! Trained by his colleague, Weber! Dubois was appalled. What of Fürbringer, the great anatomist who had taught him so much? Keith is a little sloppy with his facts, he thought; I would not have thought him so careless. I hope he is better about the fossils. But as Dubois read on, the text became worse. 'Went out to Java in 1889 as a military surgeon. At the request of the Governor-General of Java, he explored the fossil bed of Trinil, a native hamlet in the Province of Madiun, near the centre of Java.'

Eighteen eighty-nine? What about the years he had spent on Sumatra? Dubois could not help fuming; he hurled the small red-backed book across the room in disgust. So, I only carried out orders from the governor, eh? What about all the working and writing to convince my superiors to relieve me of medical duties so I might look for fossils? What of the publication in the *Tijdschrift*? As for the Governor-General... well, *ja*, the man was helpful, very helpful at a time when few others would offer their support, but going to Trinil was hardly the governor's suggestion. It was mine, my insight, my genius to look for open-air sites along riverbanks, and the governor had nothing to do with it!

After a minute of indulging his temper, he got up from his chair and stumped across the room to fetch the book. He might as well know the worst. But the remainder of the chapter was not so bad. There was a reasonably accurate account of the locality and its stratigraphy, and, although Keith wanted to call the fossil *Homo javanensis*, he admitted that Dubois's name was 'justified'. The most important thing was that Keith supported Dubois's interpretation of the significance of the fossil specimens' shapes.

Whatever the exact date may be... the characters of the femur leave no doubt, in spite of minor peculiar features, that the fossil man of Java was as completely adapted for erect posture and erect progression as the man of to-day. There are no features in it which suggest the slouching gait of Neanderthal man... The modern human posture was attained long before the human brain reached its modern size...

The brain is the characteristic organ of man. Dubois estimated that of the fossil man of Java at 855 cc., but it is highly probable that the estimate is somewhat under the truth... If we accept the Java specimen as representative of late Pliocene man, then we must admit that the human brain was then in its more primitive stages of development...

An analysis of the dimensions and form of the Trinil skull cap reveals all the characters of the Neanderthal type in a nascent or rudimentary form.

The next year, another Englishman Dubois remembered from international conferences, W. L. H. Duckworth of Cambridge, followed Keith's lead and published a little book of his own called *Prehistoric Man*. Dubois was surprised; these books seemed to be popping up everywhere, one after another, like tulips in spring. It was as if everyone found time to take stock of the evidence and compile a synthesis of what was known about human evolution. At least Duckworth seemed to have listened carefully to Dubois's arguments about *P.e.* at the zoological congress in Cambridge in 1898:

Here we find a creature of Pliocene age, presenting a form so extraordinary as hardly to be considered human, placed so it seems between the human and simian tribes. It is Caliban, a missing link, – in fact a *Pithecanthropus*.

With the erect attitude and a stature surpassing that of many modern men were combined the heavy brows and narrow forehead of a flattened skull, containing little more than half of the weight of brain possessed by an average Englishman...

The arguments founded upon the joint consideration of the length of the thigh-bone and the capacity of the skull are of the highest interest... The body-weight is asserted to be about 70 kg... and the brain-weight about 750 gm, and the ratio of the two weights is approximately 1/94. The corresponding ratios for a large anthropoid ape (Orang-utan) and for man are given in the table following, thus:

Orang-utan	1/183
Pithecanthropus erectus	1/94
Man	1/51

The intermediate position of the Javanese fossil is clearly revealed.

Dubois found the attention satisfying, especially as his colleagues seemed to be coming around to his point of view. Late in 1912, only a week before Christmas, Arthur Smith Woodward, a fish paleontologist at the British Museum, announced an extraordinary new skull at a meeting of the Geological Society of London. Some credit was given to a solicitor, Charles Dawson, but it was quite clear that he was only the amateur antiquarian who had stumbled upon the thing. Dubois did not know Dawson, but Smith Woodward he remembered well. Calling their new find *Eoanthropus dawsoni* (Dawson's dawn-man), Dawson and Smith Woodward exhibited the back of a skull and a partial jaw with only a few teeth in place, excavated from a gravel pit near

Piltdown, Sussex. Moreover, they confidently reconstructed its gently curving forehead, a surprisingly modern face, and a complete and somewhat apelike dentition. It was a large-brained, ape-toothed wonder.

Dubois watched from the sidelines with some glee while debate ensued. Clearly the braincase of *Eoanthropus* was large, but exactly how large, and how it was to be reconstructed, became points of heated contention. It was like a replay of Dubois's trials. The face was generally agreed to be nearly vertical, quite modern in shape, with no trace of the heavy browridges that typified Neanderthals and *P.e.* But what puzzled the scientific community was the unexpected combination of a large brain and modern face with an apelike jaw. Grafton Elliot Smith seized upon the fossil as proof of his theory that the growth of the brain had come first in human evolution, but the shape of this fossil did not chime well with the evidence of *P.e.* and Neanderthals. *Pithecanthropus* and Neanderthals clearly had humanlike teeth and ape-sized brains; Piltdown showed the opposite. Some paleontologists and anatomists questioned whether the bones came from one individual: mostly Americans took this approach, Dubois noticed. It is just like what happened to me with *P.e.*, he thought. Surprise them, and they say your evidence is faulty. Besides, each scientist wanted to voice his own opinion, whether or not he had examined the fossils firsthand. An anthropologist at the Smithsonian with an unpronounceable Bohemian name, Aleš Hrdlička, even suggested the jaw came from an ancient chimpanzee while the cranium was from an intrusive, modern burial. Hrdlička alone persisted in saying plainly that this new Piltdown specimen could not be right if all the bones of Neanderthals and *P.e.* were also right. The finding of an additional tooth, a canine, after further excavation seemed to quiet the dissent, but murmurs of protest persisted.

Keith now moved to the fore with a new reconstruction of Piltdown, challenging the work of Smith Woodward. Both parties churned out criticisms and corrections and reassessments of the course of human evolution in the light of this new find. The controversy was so compelling that the debates soon enabled Keith to establish himself as a major expert in human evolution. He formed a canny alliance with Marcellin Boule, the French paleontologist who had tried to prove, in his monograph, that Neanderthals were not ancestral to man but belonged on some primitive sidebranch of the human evolutionary tree.

Very interesting. Dubois read and observed all this activity, but was not tempted back to his own fossils. He would not jump into another flaming fray like the one he had barely survived over *P.e.* Indeed, he could not understand why colleagues who had seen his specimens before – even Manouvrier and Haeckel – now wrote, asking to come and examine *P.e.* once again. Dubois was annoyed; his fossils had not changed, after all, and he disliked having colleagues visit and interrupt his routine. Besides he had never forgotten Schwalbe's perfidy; he would prefer that only the utterly trustworthy examine his fossils, and he could not think of anyone he trusted so deeply. He received letters and telegrams, as well, from some to whom he had more tenuous ties, such as Hrdlička. Even though he and Dubois had in common a warm friendship with Manouvrier, who had trained Hrdička at the École d'Anthropologie, Dubois would not make an exception.

Dubois's hesitancy notwithstanding, Hrdlička had determined to spend 1912 on a grand tour of Europe, examining all the ancient human fossils. Perhaps, he hoped, Dubois would change his mind. In Paris, Manouvrier warned him that Dubois had become something of a recluse in recent years. 'I don't know,' he said regretfully, 'if my old friend will allow you to see his precious fossils. He has

The anthropologist Aleš Hrdlička was furious when he was not allowed to see Dubois's fossils in 1912.

withdrawn from discussions of human evolution entirely. I no longer seem to have any influence with him.'

Hrdlička resolved to try to see Dubois's fossils anyway. His determination was fuelled by stories he heard in Liège, from Charles Fraipont, the son of the anatomist Julien Fraipont who had described the Spy Neanderthals. Fraipont said that Dubois had become very strange indeed, his strongly held convictions turning and twisting inside his head into grotesque shapes. In fact, Fraipont feared Dubois might be going mad and might have destroyed the fossils. Hrdlička heard other wild speculations during his trip: that Dubois had been pressured by the Roman Catholic Church to put an end to 'all this talk of descent from apes'; that Dubois had returned to Catholicism and was hiding away his own evidence because it challenged the biblical view of creation. 'His sister,' one scientist said slyly to Hrdlička, with raised eyebrows, 'is a nun.'

Hrdlička did not believe half of what he was told, but even the remaining stories were alarming. It was terribly important that these fossils be saved and exhibited for study. He wrote to Dubois begging for permission to see them. He arrived in Amsterdam on 20 June 1912, and called at the medical school of the university. Professor Dubois was not there, for he was a professor of geology, not anatomy. There was no point going around to geology, however, for Dubois was not at the university that day at all. He could be found at home, perhaps, in Haarlem. Hrdlička explained pleadingly that he had travelled all the way from America to see Dubois's fossils.

'I'll give you his address, ja,' his informant said, 'but do not be angered if he will not see you. He is not in the habit of receiving visitors these days, especially those who want to see his fossils.'

Hrdlička went anyway, unable to believe that Dubois would turn a true colleague away. He found the address, Zijlweg 77, Haarlem, without difficulty and rang the bell. When the maid, a rather young and pretty girl in a uniform, opened the door, she held out a small silver plate for Hrdlička's calling card.

'Dr Hrdlička to see Dr Dubois,' Hrdlička said with dignity.

Without even looking at his card, the maid replied immediately, as if by rote, 'Dr Dubois is not at home.'

'I am a fellow scientist,' Hrdlička responded, with what he hoped was a reassuring smile. 'I have come from America to see the professor and his famous fossils. I have written him of my plans to visit. Perhaps you would tell him I am here? I hope he will agree to see me.'

'The doctor,' repeated the maid more loudly, turning stony-faced, 'is not at home.' In an instant, her attitude had changed from friendly to dismissive. She stared at Hrdlička haughtily and he stared back, waiting. 'Would you kindly remove yourself from the premises?' She flushed in embarrassment and then closed the door in Hrdlička's face.

At that very instant, Hrdlička's eye was drawn by a lacy white curtain twitching suddenly closed over the window on the floor above. Someone had been watching him. Hdlička could now see a small round mirror there, carefully positioned so as to show a watcher on the first floor who was at the door. He was convinced that Dubois himself had observed the entire exchange. The arrangement, the deliberateness of mounting a mirror in such a place so that visitors could be turned away, staggered Hrdlička. Dubois must be mad indeed, he thought. This was something out of a cheap novel! Unfamiliar as he was with the Netherlands, Hrdlička did not know that such mirrors were a common feature there. Rather than having a servant go 'to see if the master or mistress is in', as was done elsewhere, the Dutch in Haarlem simply watched their own front doors and instructed the servants in advance.

Hrdlička did not know what to do. He stayed for three hours, drinking coffee in a small café near the house that contained the man and the fossils he had come so far to see. He felt as if he was being watched, and it was true. From time to time, Dubois glanced at him through the curtain to see what he was up to. Hrdlička stood and paced back and forth irritably on the pavement. From time to time, he stared hard at the very window behind which Dubois sat, concealed. It was as if Hrdlička was challenging Dubois, without words: 'You know I am here; well, I know you are there, too.'

So, Dubois thought, so. This was Hrdlička, the physical anthropologist at the Smithsonian, the man with the big, dark moustache, who questioned the Piltdown fossils. What was he doing? Did he not understand the message the maid had given him? Dubois would not see him: that had to be plain. Why did he remain?

For his part, Hrdlička was engaged in an active internal debate. He knew Dubois must be in the house: he was almost sure Dubois was watching from the upstairs window. Should he ring again? Perhaps it would be too rude, too open a contradiction of the not-so-polite fiction that the doctor was not at home. But he had written in advance, politely, respectfully, telling Dubois he would come today. How could he refuse to see him? Had the maid actually told Dubois that Dr Hrdlička was here? Perhaps it was a misunderstanding; perhaps he had been mistaken for someone else. Perhaps if he rang again, this time he would be admitted. Was Dubois testing his sincerity, his interest?

Frustrated, tired, and not a little annoyed, Hrdlička rang the bell again late in the afternoon. This time, it was answered by another woman, better-dressed, nice-looking, with dark hair streaked here and there with grey. It was Anna herself. 'Ja?' she said neutrally, looking carefully at the stranger.

Hrdlička bowed and removed his hat. 'Do I have the honour of addressing Madame Dubois?' he asked hopefully. She nodded uncertainly. He presented his card once again, holding it out to her. Before she could dismiss him, he declared in a rush, his words tumbling over one another, 'I am Dr Aleš Hrdlička, of the Smithsonian Institution in Washington, DC, in America. I made an appointment with your husband, Dr Dubois, to call today to see his famous *Pithecanthropus* fossils. I went first to the university, but they told me he was at home, so I came here. Your maid told me earlier that the doctor was out. Perhaps he will be able to see me now? I have come so far, and his specimens are so important.'

'Ja, that may be so,' conceded Anna with a small smile, 'but my husband is not in a position to receive foreign visitors today.'

'But—' Hrdlička interjected, desperately, pleadingly.

'Perhaps you come again tomorrow? Maybe he can see you then,' Anna offered hesitantly, softening a little.

'Alas, no, I cannot. I must travel to Berlin tomorrow. I would be most grateful if the doctor could spare me a little time, I know he is a busy and important man. If he would just grant me an hour or so to examine the fossils…' Hrdlička replied earnestly.

'No, Dr…Urdluck?' answered Anna, looking at the card and mangling the Bohemian name. 'No, I am sorry. The doctor cannot see you.'

Hrdlička's temper flared. He was hungry and weary and offended. Really, he thought, I am being treated like a tradesman with inferior goods to sell. He retrieved his calling card from Anna's hand and scribbled a note on the back, hurriedly: 'The anthropologists of the world owe you a great deal, but it is a damned shame that it is not possible for scientific purposes to even glance at the specimens! Y.T., A.H.'

He handed it back to Anna with the words, 'Here, then. Please give this to Dr Dubois, with my compliments!' Turning on his heel, he jammed his hat angrily back into place and strode off.

Anna, shamefaced, closed the door. She carried the card up to Dubois and handed it to him without a word, embarrassed at the role she had been forced to play in all this. Dubois looked at the card, turned it over and read the back, and then roared with laughter. 'Ah, Anna, Anna!' he choked out through the laughter. 'Anna, look at this!'

'Ja,' she replied quietly. 'I know. I read it. He was angry, very angry.'

'Anna, you understand nothing, nothing,' Dubois chastised her, his laughter dying away. 'The man has passion, he has spirit. I like that. He cares about the fossils and not so much about himself.'

'Then why not admit him and let him see the fossils?' asked Anna, sourly.

'I cannot, I cannot. But oh! I could like that man very much,' Dubois replied regretfully. Anna left the room. Her husband's behaviour made no sense to her and she no longer tried very hard to divine what was in his mind.

Had Hrdlička known of Dubois's response, it might have defused his anger. As it was, he was so furious at his treatment that he repeated the story over and over until it reached the ears of a reporter at *Algemeen Indisch Handelsblad,* a newspaper widely read in the Dutch Indies. Hrdlička had been treated scandalously over the matter of the Indies fossils, and he was pleased to tell the story to the newspaper. It would serve old Dubois right, Hrdlička thought, if his behaviour got him in trouble. The printed story was flamboyantly critical of Dubois, part of whose salary was still paid by the Ministry of the Colonies.

Hrdlička was still indignant as he wrote his monograph *The Most Ancient Skeletal Remains of Man,* which was published in 1914. He had seen nearly every fossil representative of an ancient human or human ancestor, except *Pithecanthropus.* All he could say of it was this:

On account of the peculiar circumstances an attempt to describe first hand the important pieces under consideration met with serious difficulties. It would surely seem proper and desirable that specimens of such value to science should be freely accessible to well qualified investigators and that accurate casts be made available to scientific institutions, particularly after twenty years have elapsed since the discovery of the originals. Regrettably, however, all that has thus far been furnished to the scientific world is a cast of the skull-cap, the commercial replicas of which yield measurements different from those reported taken off the original, and several not thoroughly satisfactory illustrations; no reproductions can be had of the femur and the teeth, and not only the study but even a view of the originals, which are still in the care of their discoverer, are denied to scientific men.

Dubois read this passage in Hrdlička's book, chuckled a little at the display of temper, then clucked his tongue and dismissed the incident from his mind. Ah, that Hrdlička was too excitable, he thought, and he had been unlucky. All these people reproached me for not showing *Pithecanthropus* to everyone. Dubois shook his head wearily at the thought. Well, of course I did not run after people to show it to them. I had already had enough misery from those bones, when I carried them all over Europe.

That this was not quite the truth, Dubois did not care to remember. Like a man with scalded skin, he was hypersensitive, and it seemed to him that the criticisms were gaining strength and volume. He did not have to hear the stories and the gossip firsthand to know what was being said.

They wanted his fossils; they all did, but they should not have them.

CHAPTER 47

Tragedy

Despite his feeling of impending doom, Dubois could not stir himself into action. His Indies fossils sat, unstudied, undescribed, gathering dust first in this basement, then in that warehouse, never in a place where scientific study was easy. Besides, his fascination had played itself out. Most of the fossils were neither numbered nor registered; there was no master list of specimens. While that tedious but essential task remained undone, he felt they were safe from the grasping hands of others. He hoarded the fossils like gold bullion, but he did not involve himself with them.

As ever, his attention and brilliance were focused elsewhere. Some papers by the Frenchman Lapicque reawakened Dubois's interest in the question of brain size and body size. Dubois knew that something important was at stake, that some universal law or mathematical principle governed this aspect of mammalian anatomy. It was big enough to interest him, but too big to grasp yet. He knew it would bear on *P.e.* and her intermediate status, if indirectly. He began gathering information with the same fervour as he had once applied to searching for fossils. He scoured the literature, wrote endless letters, begged specimens and information from museums, colleagues, acquaintances, and complete strangers around the world. Birds, reptiles, fishes, and mammals: he pursued their body weights and brain sizes like one possessed. He had to know more, still more, before the grand pattern would come clear.

By 1914, he was ready to publish a significant article, one that revealed the grandeur of his vision. In it, he articulated the principle that became known as Dubois's Law:

> *In species of Vertebrates that are equal in organization (systematically), in their modus of living and in shape, the weights of the brains are proportional to the ⅕ power of the weights of the bodies.*

It was a breathtakingly elegant proposition, a biological law that applied across all the vertebrate animals. If one compared animals of equal stages of evolutionary development – cats to tigers, for example – then there was an absolutely predictable mathematical relationship between brain size and body size. It was a magnificent, sweeping observation.

Within a species, the story was somewhat different. Dubois's masses of data suggested that the variability between individuals of one species obeyed another law, based on an exponent of ⅔ of the body weight. But this, too, was fixed and predictable. It was a stunning concept: Nature worked by laws, mathematical principles. There was reason behind the obvious diversity of animals in shape and size. The next question was, for Dubois, Why? Why should brain weight and body weight scale together in a regular fashion, both within and between species? What biological fact dictated that this be true?

He addressed this question in the second section of his paper. His idea was that this law, this regular relationship, actually reflected the number of 'sensory-motor units' in the body. By 'sensory-motor unit' he meant a part of the body consisting of the sensory nerve fibres that perceived the outside world and the muscle or motor nerves that then prompted action. A sensory-motor unit was thus a single functional entity for perceiving and reacting to the outside world. While no one could possibly count the number of sensory-motor units in a body – the sheer task of dissection would have required a microscopic precision far beyond what was possible – Dubois could measure something that he believed was closely related: the diameter of the eye. His logic went like this. The eye was a sensory organ first and foremost; it was a supreme organ of perception that directed muscular or bodily responses to what was seen. The size of the eye thus reflected the size of the optic nerve that gathered and processed visual information. Dubois's insight was that the size of the eye also reflected the extent of the eye's perceptual and responsive power, and yet it could be conveniently measured.

As an animal increased in length (he used the symbol 'L' for this), its muscle mass had to increase not by length but according to the cross-sectional area of those muscles (L^2) for everyone knew that a more powerful muscle might be longer or thicker or both. And, as the animal grew longer, its mass or weight had also to increase – not in two dimensions (length times breadth) as an individual muscle did, but in three dimensions, symbolized by L^3. The longer an animal was, the greater its muscle mass and the greater its surface area, which meant it had to have more innervation and more sensory-motor units. More sensory-motor units meant more brain, to process information and direct movement. How much more? Across species, as body size increased by length L, its brain size increased by $L^{3/5}$. The chain of reasoning was intricate and complex, but also stunningly simple.

The third significant observation had to do with cephalization, the relative braininess of various species. In some species, brain size increased exactly as predicted by Dubois's law. In others, there was an extra dollop of brain for their body size, a factor which Dubois called a cephalization quotient or coefficient. Why? Because some types of species had specializations and adaptations that required more brain per unit of body size. As examples, he presented the highly sensitive trunk of the elephant; the prehensile tail of South American monkeys; or the unusually sharp hearing and large ears of hares. These specializations caused the elephant, the monkey, and the hare to have larger brains than would otherwise be expected. The elephant's trunk and the monkey's grasping tail were almost like extra limbs; these structures required more sensory-motor units to function – and hence more brain. The hare's sharper hearing, shown by its enlarged ears and quick reaction time, also required a bigger brain.

Dubois was very proud of this remarkable new synthesis of ideas and information, but the reaction to the article was less enthusiastic than he had hoped. Those scientists already intrigued by the possible relationship between brain size and body size noticed and responded favourably, but few others seemed to appreciate the magnitude of the problem or the beauty of the answer. Through all his calculations and computations, Dubois could glimpse the vague shape of something compelling, something terribly fundamental and important. No one else seemed to care. Never mind, he consoled himself. Some day they will understand; some day they will all share my vision.

He carried out more research, collected more measurements, recalculated and rethought. More and more articles came out, fully twenty-seven between 1911 and 1920, and over half of these concerned brain size and body size. It was work he could do in the library or museum, despite the war that absorbed the attention of most of Europe between 1914 and 1918; though the Netherlands had declared itself a neutral country, the war raged all around it. Tired of his own battles, Dubois published almost nothing on human evolution in those years. Others were far more interested in

Dubois's fossils, and far more concerned at his lack of visible research on them, than he was himself. The fossils were like a nagging injury, a dull ache that never quite went away but that could not be alleviated by any remedy he could imagine. He should do something; he could not be bothered to do something; he could not see what there was of real interest left to do.

His sense of uselessness was accentuated further when Eugenie, the one child of whom he was really proud, announced her intention to marry a man twenty years her senior, Carel Hooijer. Dubois had met Hooijer and did not think him worthy of his clever, beautiful Eugenie. Anna was concerned about the difference in their ages and perhaps suspected that her daughter was in some way trying to marry her own father. Their disapproval did not sway their daughter. When Anna and Dubois threatened to fail to attend the wedding, Eugenie picked a day on which there was likely to be little newspaper coverage of the event so she could avoid public embarrassment. Eugenie and Carel Hooijer married quietly on 11 March 1915, but there was no lasting happiness. Before many years had passed, Eugenie decided that her parents were right and Carel was not clever enough or energetic enough. Rather than divorce, she simply ignored Carel whenever possible for the rest of his life.

Events arising from the 1914 meeting of the British Association for the Advancement of Science in Sydney, Australia, eventually revived Dubois's interest in anthropology. Dubois himself was not present; few European-based scientists were, the notable exception being Grafton Elliot Smith, a native-born Australian and then President of the Anthropological Section of the British Association for the Advancement of Science. Like the other participants, Smith was startled by the presentation of a virtually complete (if somewhat crushed) human skull of Pleistocene age, which had been found in Talgai, Queensland, as long ago as 1884. It was surely the oldest evidence of the existence of man on the Australian continent, so why had no one heard of this specimen? Questions abounded, answers were scarce. The newspapers picked up on the story and, before the meeting was over, the Talgai skull was famous worldwide. Smith's brother, Dr Stewart Arthur Smith, was appointed to describe, investigate, and analyse the specimen. His monograph on the oldest Australian was published in 1918, the year the Great War ended. Smith found the Talgai skull to be large and robust, like those of living Australian Aborigines. It had heavy brow ridges, a prognathous, forward-thrust face, and a broad palate with rather large canine teeth for a human, though the canines were more modest than was typical of even female apes. Despite its primitive facial features, the cranial capacity of the Talgai skull was estimated at 1300 cc, notably larger than the average for modern Aborigines. Smith concluded that the skull represented an ancestor of the Australian Aborigines, showing a surprising decrease or deterioration in brain size in Aborigines over time.

Smith's publication on the Talgai skull gave Dubois something to say, for his Wadjak skulls were also primitive Australian types, according to his reappraisal of some ten years earlier. Convinced that the Wadjak skulls made better ancestors to Aborigines than this Talgai fossil, Dubois re-entered the anthropological realm to say so. He was back, once again touting one of his fossils as the most primitive. Before the end of 1920, Dubois gave a series of four presentations to the Royal Academy of Science in Amsterdam (published in both Dutch and English) on the Wadjak fossils and their significance. There was some irony in this entire chain of events, for the Wadjak skulls had been undescribed for nearly as long as the Talgai skull. Now Dubois gave his skulls a new name, *Homo wadjakensis*, and declared this type ancestral to both modern Tasmanians and modern Australian Aborigines.

As for the Talgai skull, in Dubois's view it was no closer to the common ancestor of modern mankind than Australian Aborigines of the present time. Talgai was simply a somewhat old and primitive Aborigine, and Aborigines were the most primitive and lowest race of man known. Even Wadjak was not 'a distinctly lower type than the Australian of the present time', Dubois wrote, 'for this ancestor had reached the same stage in the evolutionary scale as the living race, at least almost'. What, then, accounted for the anatomical differences between the modern skulls and those from Wadjak? Dubois proposed a new and interesting hypothesis.

The differences may nearly all be attributed to the more vigorous development and GREATER PERFECTION OF THE TYPE, in surroundings more favourable than those in which the Australian native finds, and has found for a long time, a scanty subsistence. *Homo wadjakensis* was an optimal form. In the present race the type is evidently in a state of decadence, as also *Homo neanderthalensis* is the less vigorous and less perfect descendant of *Homo heidelbergensis*.

In other words, the skulls of Wadjak and modern Aborigines differed because they lived (or had lived) in different habitats. Like other creatures, he argued, humans evolved and adapted to their environments. He extended this hypothesis to account for the shape of Neanderthal skulls as well. Wadjak men had survived by hunting and fishing, giving their jaws and teeth almost carnivorelike features, while Neanderthals had eaten tough vegetable food that they ground up with powerful teeth and jaws more like those of a gorilla than a carnivore. The resemblance to apes in Neanderthal skulls could only be explained as a functional analogy, Dubois suggested.

Talgai had re-engaged Dubois with the fossil record of human evolution. He published on Neanderthals, more on Wadjak, and more on *P.e.* He was rejuvenated, alive again and full of ideas. He was ready to apply his brain-weight and body-size work to *P.e.*, to show she was the missing link he had always claimed.

He was distracted from this ambition, though, by bad news from the Indies. The plantations where Jean and Victor had been working in the Indies had gone bankrupt, and the owners were ruined. Was the cause his sons' mismanagement? Dubois never knew. A lot of plantations closed down at that time, for prices were very low and the world economy was depressed. Anna hoped that now her sons would return to Holland, settle down, marry and produce grandchildren that she could visit and indulge. The 'boys' – boys no longer, but grown men – decided to return to Holland via America to follow some other crazy dream. They were young and charming; they met two American girls and married. They settled down and began to succeed modestly at this and that in the new country.

Jean initially worked managing an export company in San Francisco. By the time a few years had passed, however, he was billing himself as a photographer of big game, a naturalist and an explorer, giving lectures and entertaining talks in various cities around the States. Dubois was amazed that anyone would listen to him. What did Jean know of animals, natural history? He could not tell a magpie from a mockingbird; he could not remember the name of a plant from one day to the next. His father was disgusted with Jean, and even a little bitter. He had tried so hard to teach his sons about natural history and they had resisted at every turn. And now, now Jean thought he was some kind of expert. It was nonsense.

Victor's choice of profession was even worse. Victor, the son who would never listen to his father, who had never studied a bone in his life, who had never learnt an ounce of geology, had the audacity to give lectures about the missing link. Dubois was scandalized. Some of those foolish people who paid to hear Victor might even think that this was the discoverer of *P.e.* But Victor had been only a few months old when the tooth and the skullcap had been found, not yet two years old when the femur had come to light. He could not possibly remember anything about that time and place, or even the scientific principles by which his father had interpreted the fossils. He could not even remember the campaign his father had waged, travelling all over Europe, to win scientific opinion to his side. It pained Dubois that his son traded on his good name and hard-won accomplishments this way. Why did he do it? All he could conclude was that Victor had no moral character.

Even in adulthood, Victor was the one whom Anna loved the best, the younger son still closest to her heart. She had thought she could forgive him anything, but she found to her sorrow it was not so. What she could not forgive him was his thoughtlessness in dying young. In 1922, at thirty-one years old, Victor died of tuberculosis, far away from home, in America.

Though she had recovered from some hard blows in her life, Anna's heart and mind were shattered irreparably by Victor's death, like a vase knocked to the marble floor by a boy's careless elbow. Even that bad, bad business in Java in 1893 had not been so bad as this. Anna was confused, bewildered, furious. She even accused Dubois of killing his son, of sending him off once more to the colonies to die. 'You never loved that boy as you ought to,' she said bitterly. 'No wonder he ran away from you, to his death. He tried so hard to please you, but no one ever can. No one is good enough for you: not me, your son, your students, or your colleagues. You never loved him because he wasn't clever enough for you.' Tears poured down her face and she could not speak any longer, only sat, sobbing, in a chair by the window.

Dubois was at a loss. Maybe it was true, he thought guiltily. Maybe I should have loved more, expected less. Did I drive Victor away, and Jean? I don't know. I suppose now Jean will never come home again, not now that he has married an American and settled there. But could I let my sons – *my sons* – live by lax standards? Could I let them float aimlessly through life, without any passion, any sense of conviction? It was my duty to try to instil some character into them, some backbone. *Recte et fortiter*, that was our family motto. Was I wrong? He did not know.

Anna had found her voice again, and the accusations continued to flow. 'You only use other people, you never value them. Everything must give way to you and your precious Science, even me, even the children. You have driven my children away and now you humiliate me with that hussy, that so-called housemaid from Limburg you have installed here.' She looked up at him, her face filled with anger and grief. 'I have seen how you look at Claartje, you dirty old man! I have seen it. Oh, yes, she is young and pretty and knows nothing except that you are the rich professor who employs her. Well, don't think you can carry on like some Indies colonial with a little *nyai* to keep his bed warm. I won't stand for it!'

Dubois was completely taken aback. He had admired the new housemaid's firm young figure and glossy hair, and he liked to hear the Limburg accent in her voice. He had always appreciated a lovely woman. It was true, he had entertained thoughts, from time to time ... but he had done little, just a pat on her bottom from time to time, a simple touch. He had not seen his behaviour as being like that of their Indisch friends, with their native concubines and half-caste children. Was Anna right? Did she see the sin in his soul, the sin he had been concealing even from himself? He could make no reply to her and he could not examine his soul in front of her. He was too proud to defend himself, too honest to maintain his innocence. He left the room abruptly, without a word. Henceforth, they inhabited the house in chilly silence. No more than was necessary was said between them, barely enough to maintain a veil of civility, when he was in the Haarlem house. They had been on distant terms for years, but this was the end of everything. Whenever possible, he retreated to De Bedelaar.

He still had ideas, research to do, plans and dreams, but Victor's death made him feel his age. He was no longer as quick as he had once been, nor had he the stomach for the cruel scientific infighting of the past. He did not have so many brilliant ideas any more, either. On damp days, when his body ached and creaked, Dubois mourned his lost youth, his lost family, his lost dreams. It was a sad business, this marrying and having children. They broke your heart; they always broke your heart. He would have been better off if he had stuck to science and never married, gone to the Indies alone. Dubois, the stern paterfamilias, the man who always knew where he was going, was wounded beyond all expectations. He felt weakened, as if the foundation had been swept out from beneath his feet. This was impossible, unbearable: a son dying before his father was surely against all the laws of nature. Yet the laws of nature were what Dubois clung to, as a drowning man hugged a life-preserver. He had done so all his life. It was only the laws of nature that gave him any chance of making sense of the vast, chaotic world. Now, in one wretched instant, those laws had been broken and violated. He did not know what to do, so he did nothing.

CHAPTER 48

Dangerous Times

As Dubois had always feared, forces were gathering against him. The powerful men who would wrench *P.e.* from his grasp chose this moment to strike, sensing the time was right and he – now an old warrior – was weakened.

The attack was orchestrated by Henry Fairfield Osborn, an American vertebrate paleontologist who was about to assume leadership of one of the great museums of the world, the American Museum of Natural History in New York. In 1915, Osborn published his own definitive account of human evolution, a nearly six-hundred-page tome entitled *Men of the Old Stone Age*. Osborn was somewhat critical of Dubois, referring to the 'scattered and scanty materials collected [by Dubois]' and emphasizing the resem-

Henry Fairfield Osborn, of the American Museum of Natural History, mounted an international protest against Dubois for sequestering the *P.e.* fossils.

blance of *P.e.* to a Neanderthal – a view with which Dubois disagreed completely. Osborn also used the book to propagate his pet theory, that the origin of man and of many other mammalian species lay in Asia. For Osborn, 'Asia is the mother of all continents.' He garnered support from Marcellin Boule, among others, for Boule was ever anxious to banish the brutish Neanderthals from direct human ancestry. They expected a bigger-brained, more human sort of ancestor had evolved in the East and would be found there. Osborn declared boldly,

It is possible that within the next decade one or more of the Tertiary ancestors of man may be discovered in northern India among the foothills known as the Siwaliks. Such discoveries have been heralded, but none thus far been actually made. Yet Asia will probably prove to be the center of the human race. We have now discovered in southern Asia primitive representatives of relatives of the four existing types of anthropoid apes...and since the extinct Indian types are related to those of Africa and of Europe, it appears probable that southern Asia is near the center of the evolution of the higher primates and that we may look there for the ancestors not only of prehuman stages like the Trinil race but of the higher and truly human types.

This argument differed only slightly in logic and evidence from the one Dubois had published back in 1888, when he had first argued that the Indies were the most likely home of the missing link. But Osborn dismissed *P.e.* as too apelike for his purposes. Osborn longed to find the first man, not an ape-man.

Determined to put his theory to the test, Osborn persuaded the American Museum of Natural History to mount the Central Asiatic Expedition starting in February 1921. The leader of the explorations was the dashing zoologist Roy Chapman Andrews, who with his handsome face and aristocratic pince-nez became a celebrity almost overnight. Dubbed the 'Missing Link Expedition' by the press, this adventure was funded by donations from the public that poured into the museum. It was nothing like Dubois's save in intent. Dubois had marched on foot, with a few horses, two civil engineers, and fifty convict labourers or coolies. Chapman had modern vehicles (five Dodge cars and two one-ton trucks), plus spare parts, gallons of gasoline and oil, and trained mechanics; he had the latest equipment for photography, surveying, and mapping, as well as eighteen tons of food, tents, sleeping bags, cooking gear, and camp furniture, which were carried by seventy-five camels. The admitted cost of the expedition for five years was $250,000, not counting donations in kind; in the end, the bill was more nearly $600,000.

In 1922, at the start of the expedition, Dubois and Osborn exchanged letters. The first concerned a privately printed paper on Pleistocene elephants by a Dr Hay, which Dubois arranged to have sent to Osborn because of Osborn's interest in proboscideans. Osborn ungraciously returned the work to its author, on the grounds that it was not properly published. He explained to Dubois, haughtily,

1 August 1922

A privately printed and distributed list [of species] is an innovation which, if imitated in other countries and in other languages, or in other localities in this country, will arrest the progress of Palaeontology at the present time and make the science absolutely impossible in the future.

American palaeontologists are now in a position of leadership wherein they must set an example in all matters of authorship and of procedure.

It was an arrogant, self-righteous response and Dubois was embarrassed on Hay's behalf. Dubois had no inkling that he was about to suffer still worse insults, triggered by an incident concerning J. H. McGregor, a former student of Osborn's, who had written to Dubois in the summer of 1921, asking if he might come to Amsterdam to see the *Pithecanthropus* and Wadjak fossils. McGregor had also wanted to obtain casts of *Pithecanthropus* for the forthcoming Age of Man Hall to be erected in the American Museum of Natural History. Dubois had declined, saying that the time proposed for the visit was not convenient. Now, a year later, Osborn wrote another time, asking again whether McGregor might come to Holland to study and make casts of *P.e.*, and Dubois refused once again. Osborn waited a few months and wrote a third time, explaining that McGregor had already completed a series of sculptures of *P.e.* for him for his book and longed to do something more accurate based on a first-hand inspection of the fossils.

Dubois was seriously offended. First of all, the work had already been done, by him, for 'Piet' had been sculpted for the Paris Exhibition twenty-two years ago. Second, he had already refused access and it was rude to press him. Letting another anatomist make casts of his material was the same as giving the fossils away!

How could any professional have asked such a thing? Besides, Dubois was hard at work on the fossils now himself. Surely he had the God-given right to first access to his own fossils. Besides, he had no assistant or technician who might make casts for distribution to other scholars, even if he were so inclined. Further, Osborn had embarrassed Dubois by enlisting the aid of Professor Antoon Lorentz, a Dutch Nobel-laureate, to plead his case. Dubois telegraphed Osborn baldly, 'As Professor Lorentz on your request wrote to you October in my name, remains of *Pithecanthropus* which I am now describing inaccessible in Haarlem. Please wire your intention.'

Osborn took the refusal very badly. He considered it insufferable pigheadedness on Dubois's part. The man had had those fossils out of the ground for over twenty years! How long did he think he could sequester them away? Something had to be done. As President of the vast American Museum of Natural History, Osborn understood about politics and power. The way to influence this stubborn Dutchman was to bring pressure to bear from his source of support. Osborn found it simple to rally international opinion, for Hrdička's well-known and similar story had already done some of the work for him.

Osborn addressed a letter to Dr Louis Bolk, the Secretary of the Royal Academy of Science of the Netherlands, not knowing that Bolk and Dubois had been at odds for years.

2 December 1922

We address your honourable Academy on behalf of the naturalists, and especially the anthropologists, of America, to express a universal desire that the specimens *Pithecanthropus* found by Doctor Eugène Dubois be placed in some institution in Holland where they may be examined and studied by properly qualified experts and students in anthropology and in anatomy. These priceless objects are of world-wide interest. According to an immemorial custom of both investigators and learned societies, such objects are placed where they may be examined with all possible precautions for their protection and preservation.

We write after having addressed Doctor Dubois himself on this subject and after having communicated with the Minister of the Legation. We have also had the pleasure of discussing this important matter with a distinguished visitor from the Netherlands to the United States, Professor Lorentz.

We trust that in considering this matter the Royal Academy of Sciences will take into consideration the fact that the American Museum of Natural History is extending to anthropologists and anatomists from all parts of the world the opportunity of examining and studying its unrivaled collections in anthropology, anatomy and vertebrate paleontology. We regard these precious objects preserved by nature as the natural property of the scientific world, to be easily accessible to all investigators.

The first, flamboyant signature on this letter was that of its instigator, Henry Fairfield Osborn. His name was followed by those of as many colleagues as he could induce to cosign the letter.

The letter from Osborn to Bolk started a conflagration within Dutch science. On 3 January, Bolk wrote sternly to Dubois, like a headmaster calling a naughty student into his study. As the Secretary of the Royal Academy of Sciences, and a member of the board, Bolk would like to talk to Dubois about this matter before it was brought up formally at the next meeting. He would call on Dubois at the university. At the appointed time, Bolk clumped stiffly into Dubois's office, using two canes. In 1918, he had lost his right leg to cancer and his prosthesis had never been entirely

Dubois's old enemy Louis Bolk reprimanded Dubois for his uncollegial behaviour.

satisfactory. Walking and standing were painful for Bolk now, so he had perfected the art of dignified slowness. He had dressed with especial care, wearing his royal decoration in his lapel just to remind Dubois of the august body he represented. He found Dubois not humble but already resentful at being treated like a child. Worst of all, it was happening in front of his staff and students.

'Miss Schreuder.' Dubois addressed his assistant formally. She did not immediately answer, for her eyes were big with curiosity at the sudden appearance of the Secretary of the Royal Academy of Sciences. He addressed her a trifle more sharply the second time. 'Miss Schreuder!'

'Ja, Professor Dubois?'

'Would you and the others kindly leave us? I must speak with Dr Bolk privately on matters of some importance.'

'Oh, ja, Professor, of course,' she said hurriedly, herding the others out of the room like a mother hen chasing her chicks. As the door closed behind them, Dubois could hear one of the students ask earnestly – he did not know who spoke – 'Antje, what is going on? Why is Bolk here? Is the professor in some sort of trouble?'

Dubois went rigid with anger when he heard this. His students and underlings were gossiping about him! He turned to Bolk, determined to fight for his honour.

Bolk's air of righteous superiority was infuriating. He felt Dubois had altogether too high an opinion of himself, just because he had found a few old bones, and his time had come. 'Professor Dr Dubois,' he said to open the discussion, planting himself heavily in the most comfortable chair, the one behind Dubois's massive desk. He could not stand comfortably for long. 'Let us behave like gentlemen. I am forced to call on you like this because I have had a disturbing complaint about your behaviour from scientific colleagues abroad.'

'Ja?' queried Dubois, as innocently as he could with his jaw clenched. By sitting in Dubois's chair, Bolk had transformed Dubois into a visitor, a mere transient in his own office. 'And what is that, Dr Bolk?'

Bolk pulled a thick envelope from his inner pocket and tapped it meaningfully with his spectacles. 'They say,' he replied, 'that you are refusing colleagues access to the *P.e.* fossils.'

'Who makes these charges?' challenged Dubois, reaching out his hand for the envelope. 'May I see that letter, then?'

'No,' answered Bolk, hastily moving it out of reach and looking as if he might want to slap Dubois's hand. 'No, you may not. I do not think that is necessary.'

Dubois was indignant. He might not see the charges against him? 'But if the letter concerns me,' he spluttered, 'I think I have a right, Dr Bolk ...'

Bolk cut him off firmly: 'You have no right to see my correspondence.' He replaced the envelope carefully in the inner pocket of his jacket and patted his chest as if to settle the document into place. 'None at all. And you know we have heard this complaint before; there was that incident with that fellow from the Smithsonian some years ago.'

'Hrdlička,' supplied Dubois, widening his eyes, which had turned a dangerously cold icy shade.

'Ja, that is the name. His complaint about your behaviour was in *Algemeen Indische Handelsblad* for all the world to read. So this' – Bolk patted his jacket pocket irritatingly – 'this is not the first time.'

'Dr Bolk, what you have heard is exaggerated,' replied Dubois proudly, straightening his broad, muscular shoulders and spreading his strong hands apart in a gesture of innocence. 'Hrdlička was simply unlucky. I know he made a lot of noise about things, but it was only that he went to Amsterdam while I was in Haarlem. They sent word to me he was in Amsterdam, so I left Haarlem, but he left Amsterdam to come to Haarlem, so we missed each other.'

'Such goings-on give Dutch science a bad name,' scolded Bolk. 'Something must be done.' He leaned forward and stared directly into Dubois's eyes, daring him to make an apology or offer a solution.

But Dubois had other ideas. 'Dr Bolk, who discovered these fossils?' Dubois framed the question sharply.

'You did,' Bolk conceded.

'Ja, that is right. And who realized that the missing link had to be in the Indies in the first place?' demanded Dubois. Bolk opened his mouth to answer, but Dubois continued relentlessly without waiting for a reply. 'And who risked his life and his health to recover these fossils?' Bolk nodded in Dubois's direction but, again, Dubois left him no room to speak. Dubois's voice was growing stronger and his eyes were piercing. Now he rose from his chair, standing above Bolk and staring down at him. 'Who found *Pithecanthropus*? Who found four hundred and fourteen crates of mammalian fossils that weighed nearly thirty-seven thousand kilograms? Ja, Dr Bolk, that is right. It was I.' Dubois placed his hand over his heart. 'All of it was my work, mine alone. So now you tell me, sir, Mr Secretary of the Royal Academy of Sciences, who do you suppose has the right to the fossils of the Dubois Collection?'

Bolk was speechless, flattened by the hammer of Dubois's anger and indignation. He could think of no reply to make in the face of Dubois's emotion.

'Then that is settled,' concluded Dubois, dismissively. He turned on his heel to exit the room. Stopping at the doorway, he asked one last question: 'But tell me this: why should I give my fossils away to men who did nothing for them?' And then he was gone.

Bolk stared after the silhouette of Dubois, who walked swiftly out of the door and down the corridor. The Secretary's fury grew larger by the second. The arrogance of the man was astounding. Why, Dubois had walked out on him! Somehow this interview had got totally out of control. Bolk had intended to reprimand Dubois firmly, to make him see that he must behave better, more professionally. Instead, Bolk felt as if he had been ground to dust beneath Dubois's sturdy heel, like some insect. Now he had to struggle to his feet and make his slow way past the gawking students to leave the building. It was a sensation he did not care for.

A few days later, at the Academy's regularly scheduled meeting, Bolk circulated copies of Osborn's letter and raised insidious questions about it. 'There are four issues in this matter which I think we must consider,' he intoned magisterially.

First: Is the Academy competent to take note of this request officially and to deal with this matter? Second: Is the Academy the proper organization to bring this matter to a favourable conclusion, or must the petitioners be referred to the Dutch government? Third: Is the request of the petitioners considered to be reasonable? Fourth: In the case of an affirmative answer to the third question, how can a satisfactory answer be given to their request?

After brief discussion, the members of the board of the Academy were unanimous on the first three issues. They were the highest representatives of the scientific life of the Netherlands, so of course they were the competent and proper body to take action on this matter, which concerned the entire scientific world. Clearly the Dutch government technically owned the Dubois Collection, having paid Dubois and having financed the shipping home of the 414 crates of fossils and their storage since 1895. Still, the Academy could see no need to refer the petitioners who had signed this letter directly to the government, which would only engender hostility. They already knew Dubois was possessive about his fossils, rather too much so; but publicly humiliating him would not help matters. They chose to remind him of his duty and hope for his sensible cooperation.

The unwinding of this tangled affair is made easier by the fact that Mr. Dubois, under whose care the objects in question are to be found, is a member of our Academy and there is no need to invoke a government censure, which would be contrary to the notion of collegiality. The Board is grateful for Mr. Dubois's membership in our Academy and feels that a satisfactory resolution to the problem may be brought about with the cooperation of Mr. Dubois and the advice of this Board.

There was to be no threat to Dubois's position as curator, so he had escaped the worst. However, the board had to be satisfied that Dubois would make the fossils and casts of them accessible to fellow scientists within a reasonable period of time.

The day after he received the report of the meeting, Dubois sent a reply to Bolk.

I ask the Board to clarify when the casts are to be placed at the disposal of scientists. It is my explicit wish that the casts not be made available to interested parties until I have had the opportunity to publish in the Academy's journal the description and complete figures of the fossils in question. I have promised to make as much haste as possible in writing these descriptions, so that the first part (dealing with the skullcap, the endocranium or inside of the skull, and maybe the teeth) may be presented at the May meeting of the Academy. The casts of those parts can be made available immediately after this description appears. I will undertake to present the description of the remaining objects (the femur and the teeth, if not dealt with before) before the end of the year, with the casts likewise being made available after the description appears.

True to his word, Dubois began to work like one possessed. During 1923, he published more detailed works on the skull, brain, and teeth of *P.e.*, as well as the fragmentary jaw found at Kedoeng Broebus which he now felt was also *Pithecanthropus*. His works were not long monographs, heavily illustrated, but they were something. He was able to write to the Royal Academy on 29 June that the cast of the outside of the skull of *P.e.* was made and now drying, so that it – along with the endocranial cast of the brain impressions on the inside of the skull – could be reproduced and distributed. Dubois was not easily satisfied, so many casts were destroyed, until shards of plaster littered his workroom, which was now in a house formerly occupied by a section of the Ethnographical Museum. He would not let anything less than perfect out of his hands and into those of another scientist. Casts were duly made and sent to the Smithsonian and the American Museum of Natural History.

To pacify the Royal Academy, Dubois invited Hrdlička and a group of his students who were in Europe to inspect the original *P.e.* fossils. It was perhaps a sort of apology to Hrdlička, who had increasingly come to support Dubois's position on *P.e.* In a lecture at the American University in Washington, DC, in 1920, Hrdlička had described *Pithecanthropus* as 'a creature that stood on the threshold of humanity'. He went even further, saying:

If science was to construct an advanced precursor of man it could hardly do better than what nature has given us in this specimen…Its femur, though primitive in some important respects, indicates a perfect biped posture, and a fair human-like stature…the two molar teeth show primitive human or subhuman characters. The skullcap is in nearly every respect about midway between such a skull as that of a chimpanzee and a human. The brain, as seen from the cast of the cranial cavity, is in size intermediary between that of a high ape and human, but in conformation of the frontal lobes and some other parts approaches closer to the human…Taking everything into consideration, the *Pithecanthropus* is just about what its name indicates, namely an ape-man.

In 1923, Hrdlička and the students came to Haarlem, to the Teyler Museum, where Dubois himself opened the special safe he had just persuaded the trustees to buy and extracted the precious remains for his visitors. He spent a full hour explaining and exhibiting the fossils to his fascinated audience. It was the first time Dubois had permitted anyone to examine the originals in twenty years. Hrdlička was not insensible of the honour and he and Dubois liked each other on this meeting. Having so widely spread the story of Dubois's refusal to see him in 1912, Hrdlička deliberately set out to make amends. He spoke to the American newspapers, which published statements like this: '*Pithecanthropus erectus*, the Java ape-man, the world's most famous prehistoric creature, has come out of retirement.' More to the point, in Hrdlička's next book, *The Skeletal Remains of Early Man*, he included a gracious passage about Dubois and his fossils.

We found Professor Dubois a big-bodied, big-hearted man who received us with cordial simplicity. He had all the specimens in his possession brought out from the strong boxes in which they are kept and demonstrated them to us personally and then permitted me to handle them to my satisfaction...The examination was in many ways a revelation. When Dr. Dubois publishes his detailed study, which he tells me to expect before the end of the year, *Pithecanthropus erectus* will assume an even weightier place in science than it has held up till now. None of the published illustrations or the casts now in various institutions are accurate. Especially this is true of the teeth and the thigh bone. The new braincast is very close to human. The femur is without question human.

The next to visit was J. H. McGregor, Osborn's former student. Dubois was cordial but did not like the man much, for he was full of questions and challenges. Dubois answered them easily, of course, for he had been thinking about *P.e.* for years upon years; there was nothing McGregor could come up with that he had not considered thoroughly, as quickly became evident. McGregor's attitude toward Dubois grew hourly more deferential as he realized how badly rumour had slandered this brilliant man. But Dubois never warmed to McGregor, for he could not help but hold the younger man partially responsible for Osborn's move against him.

In 1924, Dubois published more about *P.e.* in both Dutch and in English, with superb illustrations of the fossils from all views, as well as complex, dense papers about brain size and body size in mammals. Unfortunately, it was not long before he heard from Osborn once again:

I am awaiting with great impatience the publication of your promised account of *Pithecanthropus* and the receipt of additional casts, etc., which you have so kindly offered to send us. Your *Pithecanthropus* has been given an entire case of honor in our great HALL OF THE AGE OF MAN which is nearing completion after ten years of assembling of materials from all parts of the world. There is intense interest in this subject at present in the United States and thousands of people are visiting our AGE OF MAN HALL. I am therefore daily awaiting a copy of your Memoir so that the Memoir itself can be placed in the case with the casts when they arrive.

As requested, Dubois painstakingly made casts of the *Pithecan-thropus* fossils for Osborn's exhibit and resentfully delivered them to the Royal Academy, that they might certify he had complied with Osborn's request. Soon Dubois received a copy of a letter Osborn had sent to Bolk.

I am very glad indeed to inform you, in reply to your letter of February thirteenth, which I have just received, that a week ago the precious casts given by Dr. Eugène Dubois arrived here in excellent condition, accompanied by the cards which Dr. Dubois has so kindly inscribed...

I have never had a moment's doubt that the delay was not either on your part or on that of Dr. Dubois. Now that the specimens have safely arrived I trust we may both forget as soon as possible this regrettable incident...

In acknowledgment of this gift from Dr. Dubois and of the courteous manner in which it has been made, as well as in recognition of the great importance of his scientific discovery, I shall propose to our Trustees at the coming meeting in the month of May that his name be placed in the roll of Honorary Fellows of this institution, the highest scientific honor in our power to bestow.

Will you be good enough to ascertain from Dr. Dubois if we may feel at liberty to use his materials for our own scientific description, for comparisons with other materials in our large collection of duplicates? Also, if one may purchase from him another set of these casts, very carefully colored after the originals at our expense by an artist working under Dr. Dubois's direction. This colored set will conform with all our other duplicates received from various parts of the Old World which are colored after the originals.

Dubois could not believe his eyes. Not satisfied with a single set of the casts, now Osborn wanted a second one, hand-painted to resemble the originals. Where did Osborn suppose Dubois would find the time and money to engage and supervise an artist to paint them? Obviously, the promise of an honorary fellowship was meant to soften the request, but Dubois had no illusions that this was anything but a spoonful of sugar to sweeten the sour taste of yet another command from the great Henry Fairfield Osborn. Acting upon advice from Grafton Elliot Smith, Dubois arranged for Messrs R. F. Damon & Company in London to make and sell both plain and accurately coloured casts of *Pithecanthropus*, in return for a royalty on each sale. Perhaps this would deflect these incessant requests for casts from Osborn. Thus Dubois was able to reply to Osborn in the most cooperative of tones.

You may make all the use you like of the materials for scientific description and comparison. I only request that publications on the femur should be deferred until 1926.

Having transferred the right to reproduce and sell casts of the *Pithecanthropus* fossils to Messrs R. F. Damon & Co., 26, Conclurry Street, London, I cannot directly supply the coloured casts you desire, but I have made arrangements that you may obtain a set, very carefully coloured after the originals by an artist working under my directions.

There, thought Dubois, signing the letter with a flourish that nonetheless left his signature only half the size of Osborn's. He smiled to himself, not in the least displeased that he would doubt-less become an Honorary Fellow of the American Museum of Natural History.

CHAPTER 49

A New Skull

Now that the nasty business with Osborn was behind him, Dubois's interest and energy revived until his research chugged along like a well-stoked steam engine. He published on glaciers and the 'paleothermal problem' and its bearing on stellar evolution; he wrote about brain size in specialized mammalian genera; he described and produced new illustrations of the brain, skull, teeth, and femur of *Pithecanthropus* and reassessed her place in evolutionary history; he described a new pangolin, *Manis palaejavanica*, from Trinil. In this new frenzy of research and writing, he was too preoccupied in late 1925 to supervise yet another move of the Dubois Collection, this time to the unheated attic of a not-yet-completed university hospital. In his absence, the entire affair was rushed and disorganized. Labels and specimens were misplaced or transferred from box to box, and some specimens were broken.

On 27 September 1926, the Batavia news agency ANETA sent messages throughout the world announcing that a new and complete skull of *Pithecanthropus erectus* had been found near Trinil by Dr C. E. J. Heberlein, district government physician at Soerabaja. Reporters from all over Europe contacted Dubois, asking for his opinion of the sensational new find, but he was in the embarrassing position of knowing no more about it than they. On 2 October Heberlein issued a second statement amending the first: 'It is not correct to speak of a complete *Pithecanthropus* skull, but only of the front part of a human skullcap, from the apex to the line of the orbital arches, which projects slightly more than in an ordinary human skull. Of the bone matter, only a thin layer has been preserved on the spongious rock mass of volcanic origin.' Apparently, in ancient times, volcanic ash or tuff had filled the empty cranial vault, adhering to the remaining bone of the skull, which had then become fossilized.

That same day, Dubois cabled Heberlein directly: 'Accept my grateful homage and will you send me some tentative measurements and photographs from frontal, lateral, vertical and basal skull-aspect for Academy meeting of October 30?' Dubois's old friend Max Weber wrote, and Grafton Elliot Smith from London, and, of course, the ever-troublesome Osborn, who said,

> The newspaper notices concerning the new cranium said to belong to *Pithecanthropus* naturally inspire the hope that the new form may be specifically identical with your original specimens and that it will definitely settle the problem of the form of the face.
>
> I trust we can count on your cooperation to secure us a cast of the new skull at the earliest possible date.

Dubois was as amused as he was annoyed upon receipt of this letter. He had not even set eyes on this new find, much less confirmed that it was what Heberlein had announced it to be, and already Osborn was pestering him for casts! On 7 October, Dubois gave a statement to *Het Algemeen Handelsblad* and sent a copy to the *Illustrated London News*.

According to the ANETA telegram from Batavia … we cannot yet speak of a new skull of *Pithecanthropus*. It is clear to me that the object found by Dr. Heberlein, government district physician at Soerabaja, is a mass of volcanic tuff, consolidated by calcareous impregnation and partially covered with calcareous concretions, which petrous mass fills and envelops a small remnant of a skull or of another fossil resembling a human skull more than a small rock. Probably the petrous mass was picked up from the ground. It could not be obtained by excavation for this cannot be done without the permission of the Dutch East Indies government, 'Trinil' being a nature reserve.

… With such a strong impregnation and encrusting as that of the 'new *Pithecanthropus* skull', the elimination of the rock from the bone is a difficult and subtle work, which can only be done by the trained hand of an expert. It is to be hoped that this object found by Dr. Heberlein, which is in any case important, can soon be expected in Europe. Only then will we know exactly what is the nature of the object.

He was vague because he could deduce little from Heberlein's description of the object. The Minister of Instruction, Arts, and Sciences formally asked that the new skull be forwarded to Leiden for complete study, where it would come into Dubois's hands.

Heberlein telegraphed Dubois on 16 October, thanking him and promising to send photographs and to place the skull at the disposal of the Dutch government. He did not venture to give measurements of the skull, as it was deformed. Dubois was dancing with curiosity and anticipation; this new specimen was almost within his grasp. He telegraphed Heberlein urgently on 2 November: 'Thanks can you inform me when Government the Netherlands can expect skull which they will place in my hands. Not yet received photographs.'

Heberlein replied on 7 November with a full account.

I found the *Pithecanthropus* skullcap on 1 August last, at Trinil, when I made an excursion there with a few other gentlemen just to see the classic place. Since before I studied medicine I was a geologist (more especially a paleontologist), it interested me highly, but in my 23 years of service in Indonesia I had not, until then, been able to pay the place a visit, because in the main (until 1922) I was an officer of health, almost always in the territories of the Dutch government outside Java and Madura. Now I was able at last to go to Trinil, it was an enormous stroke of luck to find something interesting immediately...

We found ourselves on the dry banks of the Bengawan River a couple of bones, when I saw a skull fragment in the hands of one of the native boys who poke about there daily, which I immediately asked for. Thus the piece was found by this boy and the place where it was found lies at the right bank, practically directly beneath the *Pithecanthropus* monument. It was not found *in situ* in the strata, but grubbed loose and lying between the gravels or shingle.

First, I spent two months studying the find a little by myself, but I had decided from the beginning that this find should be preserved for the Dutch Indies or the Netherlands. (I am German by birth.)

The skull is a curved piece like the hull of a ship. The occiput is missing, likewise the left temporal and the largest part of the left parietal bone. Moreover, it is only a skullCAP, although the upper margin of the orbits is preserved. The actual fossil bone substance is reduced to a paper-thin lamella (probably by the action of sulfuric acid). I have the impression that the skull is also a little squashed by some force pushing from back to front, as is evident from the relatively large breadth and an isolated piece of the surface that sticks out, dislocated, at the back of the porous, lava-like rock... Thus, you will understand that under these circumstances I, not being a professional anthropologist, could not give you measurements.

Moreover, so far as I can judge, I have the pretty clear impression that this skull-fragment is not from a *Pithecanthropus*, but from a definite hominid or manlike form. I see this as increasing the interest of the case, given where it was found. I leave the rest with pleasure to those who are better qualified, in the first place, to you.

Dubois was puzzled over some of Heberlein's points. There was no true shingle at Trinil, so Heberlein must have been thinking of some of the rubble from old excavations, particularly Selenka's. If the find was seriously distorted, then Heberlein was probably not correct in thinking that this skull was more advanced and manlike than *Pithecanthropus*. Moreover, the mode of preservation, with the bone thinned to a paperlike width and an infilling of porous tuffaceous rock, seemed very odd. Finally, on 6 December, an envelope arrived from Java with photographs, which Dubois inspected immediately.

Oho! So that's what all the susa is about? The Malay word, *susa*, for a fuss or bother, flowed into his mind as easily as if he were still in the Indies, so evocative was the look of the envelope. It was a terrible disappointment, but Heberlein had got it quite, quite wrong. The paper-thin bone that he had taken for the cranial vault itself was nothing more or less than the layer of articular bone of the rounded joint of some enormous species. What Heberlein had thought was an infilling of the 'skull' was actually the spongy, porous bone that typically underlies the articular surface on such joints. The object was almost certainly the head of the humerus, or upper-arm bone, of a *Stegodon*, a common elephant from Trinil. Yes, there was something evocative about the shape, something hauntingly skull-like, but it was not a skull at all. If Heberlein had been better educated, he would have recognized that immediately.

Dubois wrote to Weber immediately.

But for me this is not only a great disappointment (for, although I reasoned that I should not get my expectations up, I could not yet keep down a fearful hope), but also a painful one. My own careful consideration of the photographic images, and comparison of the object with what I saw like it in my collection, taught me that I cannot at all confirm Dr. Heberlein's opinion about the nature of the object.

For me there is no doubt: the object is neither a fragment of a skull of a human form, nor of a *Pithecanthropus*, it is not even at all a skull fragment, but the largest part of a right head of a humerus of an elephant (probably *Stegodon*, which is common at Trinil).

Weber replied,

What a sad story that is. First of all because of the enormous disappointment in what the object really is. But it is especially an unpleasant and annoying story because of the great mistake made by Dr. Heberlein. Autosuggestion – wanting to see something and so, seeing it – is understandable, but what is unforgivable is this hurried and completely premature announcement which has, unfortunately, gone worldwide.

It is a bad affair for Dr. H., but it is, as you rightly remark also embarrassing for our country, and also for the high colonial officials here and in the Indies. For that reason, it is best that you, a Dutchman, correct the record, as quickly as possible... You can do it softly, pointing out the difficulties for someone who is not expert in such matters and who is not familiar with the special material from this particular site, and more of the like.

Where the newspapers have already published so much about this case, and have consulted you about this matter, like the *Rotterdamsche Courant*, I should advise you to offer an article immediately. In it you

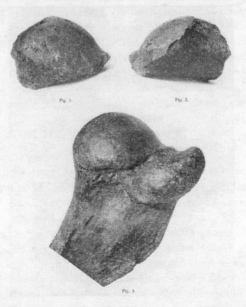

In 1926, the physician C. E. J. Heberlein mistakenly reported that he had found a new *Pithecanthropus* skull at Trinil. Top: Two views of the 'new skull'. Bottom: A humerus or foreleg bone of a fossil elephant, with a dotted line indicating the placement of the 'skull'.

may announce, without mentioning Dr. H., that the recently received photographs of the object lead you to conclude that there has been a mistake, understandable under the circumstances, etc. etc., and after that announce your conclusion.

Dubois heeded Weber's advice. He was desperately concerned to quash any further rumours or stories about this false skull, lest the taint of mistaken identity spread to his own specimens or judgements. He sent a statement to several Dutch newspapers, giving his diagnosis of the 'new *Pithecanthropus* find' based on his inspection of the photographs kindly supplied by the discoverer. 'It is not even a skull,' *Het Algemeen Handelsblad* quoted Dubois as saying, 'but beyond doubt the greater part of the articular head of a humerus, the right humerus, of an elephant – probably *Stegodon*, of which genus many bones have been found at Trinil.' Slyly, *Het Algemeen Handelsblad* also expressed an anonymous opinion that Dubois's rapid dismissal of the find might have been influenced by professional jealousy. ANETA cabled word of Dubois's diagnosis to the Indies, where his opinion appeared in the press on 9 December. To resolve the disagreement, the fossil would be entrusted to two scientists in Java, Professor W. A. Mijsberg and Dr H. J. T. Bijlmer, for study before it was sent to Amsterdam.

Dubois cabled Smith and Osborn, advising them of the identity of the new 'skull'. Next he undertook the delicate task of writing to Heberlein. It took him several tries before he felt the letter was right.

Since I first heard the news of your Trinil find, it has – the matter speaks for itself – not been out of my mind. December 6, when I received from you the long-awaited photographs and letter, was an important day for me. I heartily acknowledge my gratitude for that and for the information you sent earlier by telegraph to me. I am also indebted to you for your enthusiastic interest in the important *Pithecanthropus* problem, that caused you to preserve the object that you rightly thought resembled *Pithecanthropus* or a human form, for science and the Netherlands.

...The diagnosis I must announce to you here is: the object is not a skull, but indubitably the largest part of a caput humeri (of the right side) of an elephant and probably of the genus *Stegodon*, from which many bones have been found at Trinil...Of course, the object itself, as direct evidence, must still be studied; I hope that we may receive it here soon.

I know you must feel a great disappointment in this diagnosis as I do. It may be a comfort to you to realize that it needs a lot of experience to recognize such fragmented remains of mammals and that I, and others, are nonetheless grateful to you for taking care to preserve the supposed remains of a *Pithecanthropus*.

This difficult letter written, Dubois set about preparing a presentation for the meeting of the Royal Academy of Sciences on 18 December, 'The So-called New *Pithecanthropus* Skull'. He recounted the history of the find and its news-making progress. He showed the photographs sent by Heberlein, in conjunction with the humerus of a *Stegodon* for comparison, and no one in the audience had any doubt that his diagnosis was correct. Dubois made a point of being gracious to Heberlein, lest the physician feel publicly humiliated.

On a photograph shown me by Professor BOLK, on which the spot at which the 'skull' was found was accurately indicated, I saw clearly the rubble of an excavation, a sight so well known to me. For the rest, according to my experience obtained during five years, nowhere in that area are bones to be found that have naturally come forth out of their layer. Obviously the find that has created such a sensation is nothing but a fragment left behind as worthless by...recent excavators. There are more such fragments to be found there. They are sought by native boys loitering around, and exchanged for some money with the visitors at Trinil.

Mijsberg and Bijlmer in Java confirmed Dubois's opinion of the specimen in a written report to the Royal Academy, but unfortunately neglected to credit Dubois with making the first correct identification. Nonetheless, he felt the situation had proceeded fairly satisfactorily, until he submitted the written version of his 18 December Royal Academy presentation to Secretary Bolk for publication.

Bolk could not resist needling Dubois. 'Well, Dubois,' he remarked with feigned innocence, 'I really don't know about publishing your contribution. The report by Mijsberg and Bijlmer says much the same thing and was written three days before your lecture, on December the fifteenth. Surely they have priority.'

'But,' protested Dubois, 'my opinion was widely reported in the newspapers, on the eighth and ninth of December, and they knew of it.'

'What the newspapers report, Dr Dubois,' replied Bolk smugly, looking over the top of his glasses, 'is hardly scientific presentation and rarely accurate. Gossiping to reporters cannot give you priority.'

Dubois's broad, handsome face turned choleric. 'You are certainly correct about that, Dr Bolk,' he answered, 'as we both know. However, the contribution from Drs Mijsberg and Bijlmer was received at the Royal Academy weeks after my formal lecture was presented to that learned body of scholars. It is not, after all, when one composes a manuscript or conceives of an idea, but when it reaches a scientific audience that counts.'

'Ummm,' replied Bolk maddeningly, continuing to peruse Dubois's manuscript idly. 'I suppose so ...' He looked up slowly, a faint smile on his face. 'If you really insist, Dubois,' he added carelessly, 'I suppose we shall take it.' He had no real intention of forestalling Dubois's publication, only of twisting the knife in his side. He knew, everyone knew, that there was no surer way to infuriate Dubois than to play on his fear of having his research discoveries usurped by others.

'I do insist, Bolk,' declared Dubois firmly. 'I do.'

CHAPTER 50

Rumours and Isolation

Dubois's paper was not all that was published in 1927. Late that year, another popular book came out called *Evolution*, which repeated one of those rumours about Dubois and *P.e.* that never seemed to die: 'Their discoverer, Dr Dubois, after exhibiting them at the International Zoological Congress of 1898, withdrew into retirement in Holland, and under the influence, it is stated, of the Roman Catholic Church, refused to allow the fossils to be examined by any other scientific man.'

Dubois remained unaware of this accusation until well into the new year, which began auspiciously. On 28 January 1928, he reached his seventieth birthday. The university held a special gathering to honour him. The Rector Magnificus, Professor H. Burger, presented Dubois with a fine portrait of himself painted by the artist Frans David Oerder. Dubois also received a barrage of letters of congratulations and best wishes from his many friends and admirers worldwide, organized by Antje Schreuder. She was deeply loyal to her esteemed professor, although over the years she had suffered a too-close acquaintance with his difficult character. Shortly after this celebration, the Dutch government awarded Dubois the Order of the Knights of the Netherlands Lion, in recognition of the international importance of his work.

Retirement was normally mandatory at age seventy, and Dubois was looking forward to severing his connection with the university and its incessant demands. Now at last he could get on with studying his long-neglected Dubois Collection, which he had managed to keep intact and under his control for all these years, without ever completing even the most basic tasks of labelling, identifying, and registering all the fossils. Still, he agreed reluctantly to remain at the university for one more term, until a replacement could be arranged.

The honours he had received proved no shield against criticism. Not long after the birthday celebration, a colleague in London sent Dubois a copy of a letter to the editor of *The Tablet*, written by a Catholic priest in England.

and leave her in peace. A small house up the street in Haarlem was vacant, so Dubois rented it and moved in with his books and his specimens. He was a solitary man, alone with himself and his science. He thought that now, at last, he could organize his household to suit only himself. It would be a pleasure. He had, of course, to have servants to look after him, so he placed an advertisement in the newspaper in Limburg: 'Wanted a servant-girl, not older than 25 years, for a gentleman living on his own.' This advertisement did not attract the wholly respectable. He chose the prettier applicants, especially if they seemed to indicate by their look or their manner that they would not be averse to a little romance. Now that he was separated from Anna, he thought, it was not so wrong to seek his comforts elsewhere. After all, he brought the girls from Limburg to the big city, Amsterdam, which was what they desired, and he gave them a comfortable home and a decent wage. Was it so terrible that they wish to show their gratitude? He knew he was no longer young, but he still thought himself attractive: he was powerful, knowledgeable, and still handsome.

It was a débâcle. One after another his housemaids cheated and robbed him, playing on his weaknesses to get higher wages, fewer duties, or gifts, and then they quit. His servants changed so frequently, and were so good-looking and lazy, that the neighbours began to talk behind his back. No wonder his wife refused to live with him any longer! Finally, he begged Antje Schreuder to help him find an honest housekeeper, which she did. Schreuder's embarrassment was acute when, after only a few weeks, the woman came to her saying she had to leave the post with Dr Dubois. 'It seems,' the woman said, holding herself very upright and stiff, 'that you do not know him very well.'

'Whatever do you mean?' asked Schreuder. 'I have worked with Professor Dubois for many years, as a close colleague and assistant. He is a brilliant scientist, a genius. Of course, sometimes his mind is preoccupied with higher things, so he is thoughtless, or even irritable, but he is a man of impeccable character and honesty.'

'Perhaps at the university,' conceded the woman grudgingly, 'perhaps that is how he behaves. But not at home. I cannot stay with such a person.' She would say nothing more specific, but suddenly Schreuder knew exactly what the problem had been. With a hollow feeling in her stomach, she recalled all the rumours about Dubois's appreciation of pretty women, rumours that she had dismissed as untrue. Now she saw that his moral rectitude was nothing but a hypocritical sham. And what had everyone thought of her, his 'protégée'? She burned with shame, at her naivety, at what others might have thought of her. She had admired Dubois for a long time, forgiving his irritable temper and his selfishness as adjuncts to his greatness. She had been happy to pick up the tedious work he left undone – supervising students in the crystallography laboratory, teaching them how to use the polarizing microscope, preparing maps or slides for his lectures – because, she thought, he was too busy constructing lofty ideas. But she could never look at him the same way again now.

Schreuder withdrew from Dubois emotionally and in turn fell out of his favour. Something about this wounded Dubois deeply, though he did not realize why Schreuder had changed. He remembered, too, the look of horror on the face of the last servant before Antje's find, the country girl with the lovely fair hair. One day he had given her a little squeeze and she had recoiled in disgust. In one awful, stomach-churning moment, he had realized that she saw him as old and decrepit, an ageing lecher rather than a vigorous, still virile man. All he longed for was to be indulged and made comfortable in his own home. Of course he preferred to have a pretty girl around; who would not? If he had stayed in the Indies, he would have had a beautiful gentle *nyai* who would have cared for him lovingly as he aged. But not here, not these girls.

He realized as painfully as if he had been struck with a rock that his best days, the days of his youth and courage and great discoveries, were over. In his mind, the long string of incidents began to fuse together, into an awful mélange of indignation, condemnation, and repulsion. He was not what he once had been, what he had thought himself still to be; he was far, far less.

CHAPTER 51

Brain Work

Dubois turned to his science for comfort, concentrating once again on his brain researches. He gathered more and more data and struggled with ideas about how brain size increased as species evolved. Learned article followed learned article, until he felt he had proved his point thoroughly. The brain evolved by a doubling of the neurons during the embryonic period, through a process of cell division. Thus, mice had $\frac{1}{32}$ as many neurons as humans had, and the next level of evolutionary organization, represented by rabbits, had $\frac{1}{16}$ as many as humans, twice as many as mice. Then the group of species on the next step upward, among them monkeys, herbivores and carnivores, had again twice as many neurons ($\frac{1}{8}$ as many as humans had). The species closest to man, apes, had $\frac{1}{4}$ as many brain cells as humans. It was a geometric progression based on an extra division of the brain cells during embryonic life. What was missing from the series was any species that occupied the level of $\frac{1}{2}$ as many brain cells as humans. That level was occupied by *Pithecanthropus*, in this as in other ways a perfect transition between apes and man.

The *pattern* of evolution in this series differed from the gradual accumulation of small changes Darwin had envisioned. Here was the answer to the problem of missing links – the 'absence of evidence of continuous development', Dubois had called it. Darwin had attributed these gaps to the imperfection of the geological record and the paucity of fossils, but Dubois saw something far greater, far more interesting at work. Dubois saw evolution *per saltum*, by leaps. Ah, Dubois thought, I am not dead yet. My mind still works, still sees what others miss. This is one of my most brilliant endeavours!

He delivered his ideas first as a lecture to the Royal Academy, then as a published paper in his sometimes tortured English. He started with some commonplace observations, but ended with an extraordinary conclusion.

Clearly paleontology bears evidence of the growth of life on earth...

The minutest transitions between the members of the many parts of lines of descent with which we became acquainted, were so regularly absent, that this absence can no longer be attributed to the 'imperfection of the geological record'. Every member of a sequence is stepwise distinguished from the preceding and the following one. Again and again we find the pillars of the expected bridges, never arches...

The members of these sequences are intermediate forms, no 'transitional forms', no 'links'. Indeed, repeatedly paleontology has removed from the hypothetical stock line its at first much made of transitional forms, referring them to side branches in the genealogical tree.

Strictly speaking gradual transition is a priori impossible, because every species living as an independent creature, being adapted to particular circumstances of life, must be specialized in its peculiar way...

That we again and again meet only with pieces of these ties, and that gradual transition between creatures living independently as different species is a priori impossible, leads to the conclusion that the real transitions, the missing pieces of the ties of the relationship, the arches of the bridges connecting the species, took place *in the embryonal period of the individual life*, before the independent existence of the individual.

Of this paleontology could not furnish any documents, because they never existed.

At this point his audience was confused. What could old Dubois be talking about? Transitional species were a priori impossible? Weren't transitional forms just what Darwin had predicted? Wasn't that what Dubois had always said *Pithecanthropus* was?

His point, however, was that evolution proceeded by a cellular process. Yes, a series could be constructed that reflected the course of evolution, with $\frac{1}{32}$, then $\frac{1}{16}$, then $\frac{1}{8}$, then $\frac{1}{4}$ the brain size of humans, each level being occupied by a different sort of animal. But the series proceeded by jumps, by doubling rather than by gradual increments. There was no $\frac{1}{30}$ level, no $\frac{1}{25}$ level, nor any at $\frac{1}{12}$, $\frac{1}{10}$, or $\frac{1}{3}$. Among species at a common level, there were gradual transitions, adaptations, specializations: all the diversity and variation that Darwin had observed. But the 'real evolution', as Dubois called it, the 'progress of the degree of organization', depended on the multiplication of the units of the brain, via cell division. There was thus only abrupt change in form and structure at this level of evolution, not gradual evolution. Phylogenetic progress in the brain, in terms of the size of the cerebrum and the complexity of its function – what Dubois called the *psychoencephalon* – was determined by internal, autonomous factors, not external natural selection, as Darwin had proposed. He continued:

Besides in the case of the psychoencephalon, phylogenetic growth means at the same time perfection of the organ, continual phylogenetic progress of its functions, for the higher [level of] organization is here immediately attained by the increase of the number of cells, which at once leads to more multiple combination, greater functional complexity, direct enlargement of the animal's outer world.

Here is a law of evolution come forth out of the nature of the living being itself, not imposed by the surroundings...it appears that there actually does exist...a law of phylogenesis, and that [law operates] with progression, with perfecting.

It is self-evident that this perfecting, this steady progression cannot have been caused by factors outside the animal, to which darwinism ascribed phylogenesis. External factors can only have effected diversity of the animal forms and functions, by adaptation. It is inconceivable that they should have acted continually in one definite direction, that of perfection.

Dubois was proposing a cellular mechanism behind large-scale evolution. Darwin's ideas of adaptation and survival of the fittest accounted perfectly well for speciation, for events like the gradual transformation and specialization of the cat family into diverse forms like the slender, swift, running cheetah and the massively powerful lion. But Dubois's mechanism accounted for the creation of whole new types of animal through the simple and well-known process of cell division. This synthesis of developmental and evolutionary ideas was so radical that decades would pass after Dubois's death before his approach was widely understood and embraced.

Dubois finally retired in 1929 to work on the Trinil fossils. How little he had accomplished since he shipped them home from Java! That he had done too little, either on them or on *P.e.*, had caused him much grief and trouble. But his temperament was ill-suited to the mindless tasks of labelling, sorting, cleaning, and registering fossils; even now he sought every excuse to turn to more interesting work.

In December of 1929, he found the perfect reason, when the newspapers announced that Davidson Black, a young Canadian anatomist working at the Peking Union Medical College, had found the fossilized skull of early man in China. Dubois knew of

Black, a former student of his old friend Grafton Elliot Smith in London, and he recalled hearing that in 1919 Black had accepted a position in China in hopes of finding human ancestors. Though Black had soon found that his sponsors did not approve of fossil-hunting, he had persisted despite repeated warnings to stop this foolishness and attend to matters anatomical and medical.

Black's early years in China had yielded few fossils of merit. In 1926, he had successfully argued during a visit by the Swedish Crown Prince that two humanlike fossil teeth, found by Swedish geologists, were 'striking confirmation' of the hypothesis that China would yield a 'new Tertiary man or ancient Pleistocene man'. Calling these teeth 'one more link in the already strong chain of evidence supporting the hypothesis of the central Asiatic origin of the Hominidae', the zoological family to which mankind belongs, Black had persuaded the Crown Prince to offer funding and support for further excavations. This in turn had swayed the opinion of Black's sponsors, the Rockefeller Foundation, who in 1927 allowed him to begin systematic excavations at a cave site near Peking known as Chou Kou Tien, or Dragon Bone Hill. By the end of the first field season, Black's expedition had found an additional tooth, which he celebrated with a new name: *Sinanthropus pekinensis*, 'the Chinese man from Peking'. Dubois, like Black's other scientific colleagues, found this rather scanty evidence on which to name a new genus and species. I was criticized for *P.e.* when I had a skullcap, a femur, *and* a tooth, after all, Dubois thought. But Black had made a canny move, which led to a three-year leave of absence from his teaching duties and to more funding. The shape of Black's story was so intimately familiar to Dubois; it might as well have been his own early career in the Indies.

And now, after two years of hard work at Chou Kou Tien, Black's ambitions paid off. On 2 December the Chinese geologist W. C. Pei was in charge of the field operations. Digging deep in the Chou Kou Tien cave, by candlelight, Pei spied a large rounded fossil, a skullcap. By 4 December, Pei's telegram reached Black's hands: 'Found skullcap – perfect – look [*sic*] like man's.' On 6 December, the skull, carefully encased in glue-soaked gauze and plaster, with two thick cotton quilts and two blankets for padding, arrived in Black's hands. Pei's field identification was correct; the fossil was a largely complete skull of a primitive hominid or human ancestor. Black called a press conference in Peking on 28 December and the news was telegraphed around the world.

Dubois, like most of his colleagues, learned of the find first through newspaper accounts. He clipped a lengthy article, 'The Peking Man – An Undamaged Skull', from the 30 December 1929 edition of the *Manchester Guardian*, and perused it for details.

A new chapter in human pre-history opened with the discovery of 'Peking Man' (*Sinanthropus pekinensis*). The fossil remains most recently unearthed are of the highest significance ... The Peking ape-man shows a striking mixture of anthropoid and hominid features ...

The skull has been prepared down to its eye-sockets. The lower face is apparently missing, but the ear-hole and the back of the skull are present. Looking from below, one can see the massive jaw-socket, which suggests a biter of no mean power. The brain capacity is clearly larger (by perhaps one-quarter) than that of *Pithecanthropus*, the Java ape-man. At the same time it is still a skull of small type, definitely inferior in size to that of Neanderthal man – in fact, taken as a whole, the skull-cap very strongly suggests a very primitive Neanderthal type. The skull is that of a young adult. It bears out strikingly the 'intermediate' characteristics shown by the teeth, and jaws, the teeth being definitely of human type, the jaw being ape-like.

Before long, Dubois received a copy of the first publication on the find from Black himself, as a kind of tribute. *Sinanthropus* would surely be compared with *Pithecanthropus* and Black hoped to make a friend and colleague of Dubois. Dubois was delighted and honoured, and wrote Black to say so.

11 February 1930

It is with much pleasure that I received a copy of your 'Preliminary Note on additional *Sinanthropus* Material Discovered in Chou Kou Tien during 1928'. ... Please accept my cordial thanks for your kindness of sending this very important and interesting paper to me.

Your discovery of *Sinanthropus* I regard as a great one, possibly the greatest one ever made in paleoanthropology. Indeed this new human form strongly compels us, in my opinion, completely to review the current conceptions on human evolution.

It is with keen and joyful anticipation that we look forward to your full description of the splendid material obtained.

The reply arrived nearly two months later.

3 April 1930

Thank you ever so much for your kind letters of last February which reached me two weeks ago. I cannot tell you how much I appreciate your cordial good wishes and it is indeed a pleasure to be able to send you in this letter copies of the first photographs to be made of the new *Sinanthropus* skull after its exterior has been freed from travertine ... The report itself together with reproductions of these six photographs is now in press. I am also sending you under separate cover three reprints of preliminary papers on the Chou Kou Tien region and on *Sinanthropus*. From the latter you will see that now there can be no question of the geological age of the deposit. It will be two or three months yet before my final report on the skull can be prepared since its whole interior must be freed from travertine before the bones of the vault can be replaced in their exact natural relations. The more I study this specimen the more clearly it becomes evident that here we have a form sufficiently generalized in character to be not far removed from the type from which Neanderthal and modern types were both derived.

Dubois underlined Black's final sentence about the position of *Sinanthropus*. If his *Sinanthropus* was the ancestor of both Neanderthals and modern humans, where did Black place *Pithecanthropus* in all this? It sounded as if he followed that old theory of Schwalbe's that *Pithecanthropus* was ancestral to Neanderthals. If so, then Black would draw a letter 'Y', with

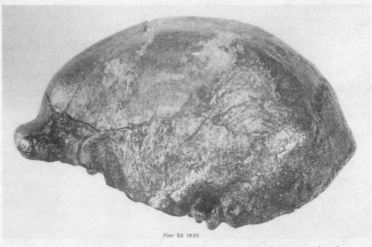

Davidson Black believed that *Sinanthropus pekinensis* was closely allied with *Pithecanthropus*. This fossil skull was found in 1929.

Pithecanthropus at the foot of the stem, *Sinanthropus* at the fork, and Neanderthals and man at the ends of the branches. Interesting... Then he turned to the second page of the letter and saw a postscript.

> Boule pointed out long ago that the morphology of the tympanic element in the La Chapelle skull recalls in certain respects the conditions obtaining in that region in the chimpanzee, presenting characters somewhat intermediate in type between the latter form and *Homo*. The relations of these parts in the *Sinanthropus* specimen may thus with propriety be termed pre-Neanderthaloid, representing an evolutionary stage preceding the Neanderthal-like types. The morphological evidence so far available with respect to the position of *Sinanthropus* in the hominid scale would thus place the latter form not far removed from the type from which evolved both the extinct Neanderthaler and the modern *Homo sapiens*.

Hmmm, Dubois hummed slightly to himself, reading. 'Boule pointed out long ago...' Yes, I suppose it was long ago, for a young man like Black, and Boule's monograph was published fifteen years after mine. My monograph was the one that started it all, that first compared a fossil form to living apes and man. Black clearly found *Sinanthropus* a man, not an ape-man and not an ape. A pre-Neanderthaloid, more advanced than *Pithecanthropus*: yes. So my *P.e.* is still the true ape-man, the missing link.

Then he turned to the photographs Black had sent. What a glorious creature was there portrayed! The skullcap was more complete than *P.e.* and included a large part of the base of the skull. A pity that most of the face was missing. Yes, there was a certain resemblance to *P.e.*, especially in side view, but also differences. What did Black say?

> Since my last report before the Society, work has progressed on the *Sinanthropus* skull specimen till now its whole external surface has been freed from travertine, with which however the interior is still filled...
>
> The preliminary photographs show in unmistakable fashion certain of the major characters which serve sharply to distinguish *Sinanthropus* from other hominid types ancient or modern.'

The next part, the technical description, Dubois followed closely, with one finger on the photographs. Black made an important point about the shape of the skull in vertical cross-section, a section to which Dubois had never paid much attention because *P.e.* was missing the lower part of the skull and its base. In *Sinanthropus*, Black said that the maximum breadth of the skull lay just above the ear holes, even though parietal eminences – the 'corners' where the walls of the skull angled into a roof – were well developed. Was this also true of *P.e.*? Hmmm, hard to tell…

The bones of the cranial vault in *Sinanthropus* varied in their thickness. They were reportedly thicker than in *Pithecanthropus* and, on the whole, much thicker than in a modern skull, especially low down at the back. There were some peculiar, primitive features about the bony ear as well – a region completely unknown in *P.e.* – where *Sinanthropus* appeared more apelike even than Neanderthals, Black said. Black suggested, because of its delicate modelling, that this specimen of *Sinanthropus* came from an adolescent female.

22 June 1930

Accept again my cordial thanks for your great kindness of sending me…copies of the first photographs to be made of the new *Sinanthropus* skull after its exterior has been freed from travertine, and of your interim report at the Annual Meeting of the Geological Society of China. Those documents concerning your great discovery and the reprints of preliminary papers on the Chou Kou Tien region and on *Sinanthropus* are indeed precious possessions to me.

Now I take the liberty of writing you again, having studied with great care the photographs with your description, comparing them with Neanderthal Man, *Homo sapiens* and *Pithecanthropus*. The result is I quite agree with you in considering *Sinanthropus* a pre-Neanderthaloid form. I may now repeat my opinion that this is the most important discovery in human paleontology.

As to the supposed nearer relations with *Pithecanthropus*, I must avow not to find them. *Sinanthropus* is a very 'primitive' type of man, but still a man, whereas *Pithecanthropus* is no man at all, in my opinion…

Please oblige me once more by communicating to me any data you should obtain on the size of the body of *Sinanthropus*, and on the cranial capacity.

The relationship between Dubois and Black continued on entirely friendly lines. Black always sent Dubois information, publications, and casts before anyone else; Dubois reciprocated. The finding of *Sinanthropus* seemed to validate Dubois's claims for his

Javan apeman; the more abundant Chinese fossils eased the ultimate acceptance of *Pithecanthropus* as a very early human ancestor, even though Dubois always believed that his find was more primitive and older than Black's.

Despite the parallels in their lives, Black's pathway to success was much smoother than Dubois's. In 1932, with the sponsorship of his former adviser, Grafton Elliot Smith, Black was elected a Fellow of the Royal Society in England, even though his monograph on *Sinanthropus* had not yet been published. In 1933, Dubois initiated a move to heap yet another honour on the younger man:

28 March 1933

Perhaps you do not know that this year again a Prix Hollandais is to be awarded by the Institut International d'Anthropologie, for the most prominent achievement in Anthropology, on which the author submits his works to the judgement of an international jury from the Institut.

Being a member of that jury, may it be permitted to me to ask you to send your works on the *Sinanthropus* to the Secretary of the Institut International d'Anthropologie? ... In my opinion yours is the most important achievement in Anthropology during the last cycle of the Prix Hollandais.

The award of the Prix Hollandais to Black was the last occasion upon which his path and Dubois's were to cross. Early one morning in 1934, Black died at his desk, working on his beloved *Sinanthropus* fossils. He was only forty-nine years old.

CHAPTER 52

The Diligent Assistant

While the *Sinanthropus* fossils were new, Dubois spent all of his time poring over Black's letters, publications, and photographs, and none on the Trinil collection. The trustees of Leiden University began to fear that Dubois would die before the collection was properly organized. Should this have occurred, most of the locality data, contained in Dubois's memory and semilegible notes, would have been lost. This would be catastrophic, for it would make the vast fossil collection nearly useless. To make sure this important work was done, they decided to appoint an assistant in November 1930.

Their choice was a curious one: Dr J. J. A. Bernsen, a Jesuit priest who had received a doctoral degree after studying the rhinoceroses from the Tegelen Clay deposits in Holland, working under Dubois himself. Dubois had mixed feelings about working so closely with a Roman Catholic priest, especially in the light of the rumours that

Father J. J. A. Bernsen undertook the enormous task of labelling, cataloguing, and ordering the Dubois Collection, but his relationship with Dubois was tortured.

had circulated for years. Still, Bernsen was his three days a week, and Dubois surely needed assistance. Bernsen entered into the tedious work with enthusiasm. Constant exposure to one another led to a growing intimacy. Bernsen and Dubois often fell into conversation as they worked. Bernsen treasured these times, when Dubois seemed to be confiding in him or at least speaking his true mind. Could the old man be lonely? Bernsen thought it unlikely, though he knew Dubois had separated from his wife, for surely such a great man, a renowned scientist, had many friends and colleagues to spend time with. On 10 November, Bernsen began to keep careful track of these conversations in his diary, writing down what he could remember of Dubois's words each day.

November 10, 1930. The conversation comes around to belief and science. Dubois thinks that the naturalist has to keep belief and science absolutely separated...Dubois tells me that he gets up in the morning at 5:30 and goes immediately to his study to think and read about evolutionary problems. 'So,' he says literally, 'I think to best serve God.'

In the course of the conversation, Dubois said that many researchers are looking for their own glory. Dubois is only looking for the truth. In an earlier conversation in October he said to me, 'If they prove to me that Pithecanthropus has been a donkey, I will be happy at last to know the truth. I am proud that I am still flexible enough to be able to change my opinion.'

Sometimes Dubois spoke to Bernsen of his frustrations.

November 12, 1930. Dubois realizes that the study of the Dubois Collection should actually have been his life-work. But it was not so. Other researches took up all his attention...He said to me, 'These days, with the moving of the collection, I have read once more what I said in 1894 about P.e. Now I am ashamed of it. I am happy that I waited until 1926 to write the definitive description of the "Pitheek" remains. At that early time, my thoughts were not well considered. Some thought that I hid "Pitheek" intentionally, because of religious considerations. That is not true. Experience can also become a disadvantage. One can get fixed in one's own experience and become insensible to new impressions.'

Having something meaty to discuss made the tedious work go more rapidly, for Bernsen's first major task was to supervise the moving of the collection one more time. Once again, the thousands and thousands of specimens were to be transferred, this time from the unheated attic room of the new university hospital to the building that had once housed the pathological laboratory in the old plague hospital. The removal started on 3 November 1930, proceeded through the bitterly cold winter, and was completed only on 15 February 1931. Then the boxes had to be unpacked and the real work began.

Once again, in the move, some specimens were damaged and some labels lost. This was inevitable, for neither Dubois nor Bernsen could possibly supervise every moment of the transfer; besides, Bernsen had never before seen the entire collection, so he was unfamiliar with the eccentric and sometimes haphazard way it was organized after so many moves. Yet Dubois was impatient with the confusion and breakage, unforgiving, and instructed Bernsen that he had to do better. 'Protecting this collection is everything,' he declared coldly. 'It will outlast us both. It must outlast us both. You will have to sacrifice more time and care in looking after it. These fossils are more important than you are.'

It was such a ferocious dressing-down that Bernsen was cowed and depressed. During his studies on rhinoceroses, Dubois had been impatient with Bernsen's slowness, with his methodical nature, but never had he lost his temper like this. On 23 November, after less than three weeks of working with Dubois, Bernsen worriedly wrote in his diary:

> I am very nervous. Feel myself overstrained. Worry about the distrust and small difficulties with Dubois. Can I never please him? He is a difficult man; his standards are so high.
>
> Dubois says he has always gone through life honestly, not being diplomatic. Perhaps this is a sort of apology for his temper. 'You are also not a diplomat,' he says to me... But he believes that diplomacy is incompatible with science. If you are a diplomat in life, avoiding the truth, then you are also one in science...
>
> He says that in the past he has been disturbed by the dishonesty of others and surprised that something like that could occur among scientists. He said this to Place, his teacher, and Place asked him how old he was.
>
> Dubois answered, 'Thirty-eight years.'
>
> Place replied, 'Do you still have to learn that even learned people have the ordinary human shortcomings?'

Some weeks later, Dubois returned to the subject of science and religion. Bernsen could not but wonder how much the presence of a man of the cloth disturbed Dubois, raising questions he had long ago put aside. Bernsen heard in Dubois's voice the anxiety of one who still struggled with faith. 'I myself speak in publications about brains, exclusively about brains – never about the psyche, let alone about the soul,' Dubois declared defensively. 'In the latter subjects I do not even want to lose myself, because I know that I cannot come any further toward the truth and because one blunders so easily on those subjects.'

Bernsen was becoming a little obsessed with Dubois. Dubois was charismatic, brilliant, quick, impatient, brutally unkind, and in instantaneous reversal, breathtakingly considerate. Bernsen did not know what to make of him. He was learning much more about Dubois's mind and personality than he ever had as a student, when he had been left largely on his own. In April, Dubois's former assistant Antje Schreuder came to pay a visit. Dubois was visibly uneasy in her presence and made an excuse to go off and do something else. Unperturbed, Schreuder stayed and talked with Bernsen, asking how the work was going and explaining some of the procedures she had used during her fourteen years as Dubois's assistant. She praised Bernsen for getting much more accomplished than she ever had, for she had had great difficulty getting the professor to sit down and tell her what she had needed to know about the specimens.

She asked how Bernsen found working with Dubois, and Bernsen hardly knew what to say. His thoughts of Dubois were intense and yet confused. 'You know that Dubois is difficult, a demanding taskmaster,' Bernsen confessed hesitantly. 'But what an intellect! It is a privilege to work with him, truly.' This confidence provoked a flood of words from Schreuder, one that both surprised and embarrassed Bernsen. Afterwards, he recorded his impressions of the afternoon in his diary.

April 23, 1931. Miss Dr. Schreuder from Amsterdam paid a visit... Speaking about Professor Dr. Dubois, she said, 'He is an intellect who rises miles and miles above the twelve or thirteen other professors we know in our field. Professor Ihle, de Beaufort, Boschma, etc. are very good people, but as professors just middling. Professor Dubois is someone who would bring honour to any university. But psychically he is a monster. His egotism knows no limits and he has brutal sensibilities.' After this she told me, among other things, about his affair with Claartje, his personal maid. She feels his wife was right to run away from him because of his affair with Claartje, a servant girl from Limburg... Miss Schreuder has a very critical mind. She can no longer stand Dubois as a human being, but judges him highly as a genius among scientists.

The very next day the man who had been Dubois's assistant before Schreuder, Professor Escher, came to visit. Bernsen wondered at the coincidence. Were Dubois's former assistants trying to tell him something? He could not decide. Escher actively avoided meeting Dubois, lest Dubois 'suspect that something is behind' his visit, in the way that he always did. Escher, too, was eager to discuss Dubois with Bernsen. 'He suffers from nerves,' Escher confided, to Bernsen's surprise. Bernsen had not considered Dubois's behaviour in this light before. Nerves? But the man was supremely self-confident, a man who could stand alone when no one else agreed with his point of view. And yet, Bernsen thought, yes, there was a nervousness, the sign of an oversensitive temperament. He had that extreme touchiness, almost as if he expected betrayal. 'He is always afraid,' Escher continued, 'that someone else will scoop up his honour and steal it.'

But no one could steal the honour of an honourable man, Bernsen thought. A priest's stock-in-trade was guilt, sin, and honour. So what was the real source of that fear? What was the guilt that made Dubois look for punishment?

True to his nature, Dubois was deeply suspicious of these visits. It was not long before he denigrated Schreuder to Bernsen: 'You mustn't believe the things she says, for she is always getting her facts wrong. It is typical of her; she is very confused.'

'But I thought her thesis was a very good piece of work,' replied Bernsen mildly. 'Didn't you praise it quite highly for its precision?'

'Ja, ja,' Dubois shook his head. 'I have said it was an important work, although I am sorry not to have told the exact truth. For I think it was not a significant work at all. It was real female work. Females have no aptitude for science. That is reserved for males. I was wrong to encourage her and now she is angry, for she sees that I do not really respect her work.'

He sounded to Bernsen like a man full of regrets, unable to face his own faults and consequently so unforgiving of others'. Perhaps this was why he was so fearful that his place in science would be transient: in his heart, he did not believe he deserved honour and glory. It was curious to find signs of deep terror in a man so brilliant, Bernsen thought. I am only now beginning to understand this man, with whom I have worked for so long. No wonder his other assistants have been so bitter and frustrated.

One day Dubois admitted to a peculiar quirk, a dislike of walking alone to the train station at the end of the day. Bernsen was puzzled. Did Dubois fear that people would think he had no friends, if he walked alone? Did he care so much how random strangers might judge him? Out of kindness, Bernsen fell into the habit of walking with Dubois to the station every day. The walk provided another occasion to listen to Dubois's confidences and stories. One day Dubois offered an assessment of his life that seemed almost to deny his professed agnosticism. 'Yet I have never written about Pithecanthropus as Haeckel did, tendentiously out of an aversion to faith. Never have I spoken about Pithecanthropus on these lines. Rightly, I have spoken about the missing link. But what yet is there against this view [that there is a missing link]? The loftiness, the greatness of life makes me believe in God.'

Sensing a confessional mood, Bernsen remained silent, simply listening. Dubois's words poured from his mouth and his soul. 'I believe that I, in leaving the Catholic Church, have done more for the Catholics, and in general for the Christian cause, than many advocates in the Catholic Church. Ah, you raise your eyebrows, Bernsen? You ask, "How can that be?" I'll tell you. I have surely demonstrated the untenableness of Darwin's ideas of gradual evolution and survival of the fittest. My researches have clashed directly with social Darwinism, too. And I am convinced that Marx would never have written his book had Darwinism not preceded it.'

It is a strange and despondent summary of a lifetime's work, Bernsen thought. Did this man have no idea of his real contributions, his real worth? Working closely with Bernsen, trying to get his own fossils in shape to be studied, Dubois seemed weighed down by a deep melancholy, brought on by confronting the many years in which he had done no work on this vast collection. 'You know, Bernsen,' Dubois confided one day, 'I never had the time to work on this material carefully, in all those years. The professorship in Amsterdam took up too much of my time; a professor must do research himself in the areas in which he is teaching, so I was drawn into those geological studies. And preparing all the lectures took so much time. You understand why I have done little on the collection, although I have always regretted it.' Dubois sighed heavily as he thought back.

'The difficulties that I have experienced spoiled my life,' he added. 'Oh, maybe you don't think so, but the Trinil collection too caused me great difficulties. In the first place, in order to search in the Indies, I gave up the promise of a professorship in the near future. Also in the Indies I had many difficulties – at first, I had no opportunity to go fossil-hunting. Later, after I had done all the work, Martin wanted to bring the collection under his control.' He shook his head at the perfidy, clucking his tongue. 'After all I had done...' His voice trailed off and he stared out of the window for a few minutes. Then he continued, 'Also Pithecanthropus caused me a lot of trouble. With the believers, the find caused conflict because of religious considerations; from nonbelievers, I received partly approval, for political reasons (I gave them an argument against faith), and partly condemnation, because they were jealous... Now, finally, I am able to work on the collection, but my resilience is gone. If I meet with further difficulties, I will have to give up entirely. Not because I dislike debate, but because I cannot bear it any longer.'

Dubois's depression lasted for weeks, as the two men toiled over the boring but necessary tasks that faced them. Unoccupied with scientific problems, Dubois turned to reflection and regret. 'What a misery I have had from those fossils,' he complained to Bernsen once, pushing aside a box full of specimens that he had been sorting and classifying. He stood up, stretched to relieve his aching back, and walked around the room as he spoke. 'Sometimes I cannot sleep at night because of it. Now that I am old, I want to correct the omission, to get the work done. I hope to live long enough, until the collection is all right.'

On another day, he continued the theme: 'I get the impression sometimes that the others here at the museum regard my work as the making of my last will and testament. It is highly unpleasant for me, that they always look at me to see if I am dead yet.' And death, thought Bernsen, is when you will confront your Maker and his judgement on your life. Is that what really haunts you, the final accounting yet to come? Bernsen did not voice his thoughts; there would have been no point. But he recognized the anguish of the lapsed Catholic in his colleague.

In the spring of 1931, Dubois was pulled out of his grey mood by receiving Black's monograph on the Chou Kou Tien remains. There were some haunting photographs of a new specimen, found on 30 July 1931. It was another spectacular find: a second *Sinanthropus* skull, somewhat fragmentary, from a young adult male. This time the base was missing, and so was the face. It was almost a perfect match in preservation for *P.e.* Once again, Dubois had new fossils to think about, and he was full of ideas and energy. The Chou Kou Tien remains once again distracted him from the mundane work on the collection, but Bernsen soldiered on, his frustration growing. And Dubois couldn't resist showing the photographs and monograph to Bernsen and talking with him about them, even though Bernsen's expertise (as Dubois well knew) lay in quite another area.

'From Black, I have received new photographs,' he remarked to Bernsen, displaying them in his hand. 'Every day I study them. In the open air, under the trees, I can think best about something like this.'

'May I see the photos, Professor?' Bernsen asked tentatively, stretching out his hand.

'Oh, ja, ja,' replied Dubois, continuing to look at them himself, oblivious to Bernsen's waiting hand. He mused, 'You know, I admire Black because of his bright mind, his excellent book. Now, you must know that, the longer I think about it, I see some resemblances to Pithecanthropus, although there are some differences as well.' He still did not relinquish the photos. Bernsen eventually gave up and withdrew his hand, knowing how reluctant Dubois was to share the photos and the information they held. Dubois gestured, displaying the pictures but never quite handing them over, pointing out features to Bernsen as if the priest were as intimately familiar with the morphology of *P.e.* as he was himself.

'For example, here, the higher frontal bone, steeper than in *P.e.*, and the shape of the skull in horizontal section. Do you see? The *Sinanthropus* skull forms a long oval, like a Neanderthal or like many human skulls. But in *P.e.*' – Dubois put down the photographs to gesture with two hands – 'that outline is distinctly pear-shaped, narrow in the front and broad in the occiput.' Bernsen nodded in agreement, wishing he could remember the shape of the *P.e.* skullcap more clearly. For all his time working with Dubois, he had never been given opportunity or permission to examine *P.e.* at any length. He picked up the photos, hoping Dubois had relinquished them at last.

Dubois lectured on, unaware. 'Yet, despite the resemblances, I feel that they do not belong to the same species.' Bernsen nodded again, not from personal conviction but from ignorance, scanning the photos greedily and trying to take in as much information as possible before Dubois reclaimed them. Dubois continued, 'Black gives a pleasant solution to this problem in his book. According to him, *Sinanthropus* is a general form – it has something of a human or Neanderthal, something of Pithecanthropus, but also very much something of monkeys – while Pithecanthropus is a very specialized form.'

There was in Dubois's voice an uncharacteristic uncertainty, as if he was struggling with conflicting ideas. Did Dubois believe Black's pleasant solution? Bernsen could not tell and, indeed, Dubois was himself unsure. Dubois wondered, in his heart, whether the differences between *Sinanthropus* and *P.e.* were too trivial for the weight they had to carry. Were they enough to make these specimens truly separate genera and species? He would never express such doubts openly, not in front of a mere assistant and former student, in any case.

The distinction or lack of distinction between *P.e.* and *Sinanthropus* was a question upon which other anthropologists and anatomists were quick to publish their opinions. Smith immediately offered his support for Black's view that *Sinanthropus* was something entirely new. In Germany, Franz Weidenreich and Hans Weinert argued that *Sinanthropus* and *Pithecanthropus* were members of one group, which should be called *Pithecanthropus*. Weinert even declared the name *Sinanthropus* to be superfluous. Boule, in France, sided with the Germans, while Hrdlička in America felt Neanderthals were also somehow involved. All this debate echoed his own early trials and made Dubois uncomfortable. He felt he had to state his opinion and be prepared to defend it, but he knew what acrimonious exchanges might follow. He had little stomach for academic brawls. Besides, he could not quite make up his own mind, for the evidence was maddeningly ambiguous. Some days he thought one thing, another day, another. It was a most distasteful situation.

Dubois started the conversation up with Bernsen about *P.e.* and *Sinanthropus* a week or so later, when the two scientists were once again working side by side, gluing the Trinil fossils back together and writing labels for them. 'You know, Bernsen, the more I look at the smaller skull of Sinanthropus (of course, I mean of the photograph), the more he starts to resemble Pithecanthropus. I should say almost alarmingly...I cannot make up my mind. I want to make a new reconstruction of the Pithecanthropus skull, to be able to compare it to the Sinanthropus remains, where they also have mandibles. When I told [a colleague] about this, he asked how I could do that, with so much missing. He asked me, "But from the mandible, the jaw, you do not have so much, ja?" and I had to admit I do not. I have only that specimen from Kedoeng Broebus, the part of the symphysis at the front of the jaw up to and including the second premolar. Thus, it is not a small piece, but not so much as Black has.'

Eagerly, Bernsen offered to assist Dubois with this proposed reconstruction, but Dubois brushed the offer away. 'No, no, thank you, Father, but I can do it myself. It is better that you carry on with sorting and registering the Trinil bones. Only sometimes I like to talk these things over with another, you know?' Bernsen was growing a little resentful at being relegated to only the most tedious and mechanical of tasks, never being included in the research on new materials or new ideas. He hoped fervently that in time Dubois might trust him with more interesting work. Sometimes Dubois spoke of giving Bernsen whole groups of fossil mammals to work up and describe, while he, Dubois, would take others. That would have been a wonderful opportunity for Bernsen, a challenging and exciting task. On other days, Dubois suggested they should work on them all together. As Bernsen came to know Dubois better, he could interpret this suggestion more accurately: he, Bernsen, would probably do the routine work while Dubois polished the ideas and interpretations. That, he would not have liked so much. But he had to bide his time, work energetically, and show himself to be trustworthy. He knew well that Dubois was touchy and suspicious of other scientists, so he took great care not to overstep the bounds of his assignment.

Two days later, still clearly troubled, Dubois stopped to talk with Bernsen again. 'I have been looking at those photographs of Sinanthropus again, Father,' he offered. 'The more I look at the pictures, the more differences I see.'

Bernsen thought to himself, a little tartly, that Dubois had changed his mind about the photos more times than there were specimens. He was too wise to put this negative thought into speech. 'What differences are those, Professor?' he asked, trying to infuse his query with respectful tones.

'Here, Father.' Dubois held out a photograph of the endocranial cast of the brain of *Sinanthropus*, next to one of *P.e.*'s brain cast.

'Look, see? The cerebrum of Pithecanthropus is more gibbonlike than humanlike, while that of Sinanthropus is humanlike.' Bernsen nodded dutifully, hoping Dubois would ask for his opinion, but it did not happen, then or ever. Dubois left the room, and the endless task of registration and organization, going back to more interesting dilemmas.

On their now-ritual walk to the station, Dubois raised the subject again. 'I am still working on the problem of Sinanthropus,' he confided to his assistant. 'Although it certainly resembles Pithecanthropus in many respects, it is, nevertheless, something entirely different. At home, I have compared the Sinanthropus skull to all sorts of gibbon skulls and among the gibbon skulls there are all sorts of great differences and variations.'

Why don't you ask me? Bernsen cried silently. Don't you think that I have learnt anything in all these years of work? But Dubois did not think about Bernsen and his state of knowledge at all. He wrote, instead, to Black.

15 June 1931

It was a great joy for me to receive, a few weeks ago, your splendid description of the adolescent skull of *Sinanthropus pekinensis*. It is indeed a joy for ever to one interested in phylogeny to possess such a work...

It is a source of particular satisfaction to me, that your conception of the relation existing between *Sinanthropus* and *Pithecanthropus* nearly agrees with the one that I have formed by the study of your preliminary descriptions and photographs. In recent weeks, at the behest of your perfect *Sinanthropus*, I thoroughly studied again *Pithecanthropus*, and I find the importance of the latter increased indeed in the way of 'archaic specializations', as you express it.

But I badly miss the principal data on the endocranial anatomy of *Sinanthropus*, which I consider to be of the greatest importance in this respect, and probably gave you conclusive proof of the different character of *Sinanthropus* and *Pithecanthropus*.

May we expect these data in the near future? You would highly oblige me once more, of course also with the complete casts.

Regardless of his stated willingness to alter his ideas in the light of new evidence, Dubois responded angrily any time Bernsen suggested a different viewpoint. This was a problem when, from time to time, he felt Dubois had made an error in his provisional identifications. The corrections should be made now, while formal registration was under way, but Bernsen could find no suitably tactful way to bring up the issue. One day, he committed a fatal error by suggesting in passing that a single, isolated tooth from the Tegelen Clays that Dubois had identified as belonging to a hippopotamus might actually be a pig's. Bernsen requested permission to examine the specimen, and Dubois became very agitated.

First of all, Bernsen was not employed to rummage among the Tegelen Clay fossils any further. Second, he, Dubois, had always been a little uncertain about this identification. He had always meant to double-check it. Bernsen knew Dubois too well to point out that twenty-five years had passed since the original identification, which had been repeated in scores of publications, and no such checking had yet occurred. For days afterward, Dubois hammered on the subject of his humiliation at Bernsen's hands, as if this small matter of misidentification had been broadcast to newspapers worldwide. From that day onward, Dubois's suspicions of interference by the Roman Catholic Church, in the person of J. J. A. Bernsen, were always active. All the resentment and regret Dubois had accumulated throughout his entire life bubbled to the surface like hot lava rising in a volcano.

'I have not published enough. How little I have done about Pithecanthropus,' Dubois mourned miserably one day early in March 1931, forgetting he had published a monograph and nearly forty papers on the subject so far. 'I have too little ambition and was satisfied as soon as I knew it for myself. After finding the truth, my interest was gone.'

Yet, Bernsen countered silently, you would not allow others to work on it, not even me, nor can I correct you in the smallest detail.

'Only after 1923 did I start to work on Pithecanthropus in earnest and to publish the results,' Dubois continued morosely. 'That will be of little account, that the discoverer says so little and so late about a famous find. And then Osborn was pressuring me through the Royal Academy that I should get the work finished and the publication done, so they will say I would never have done it without him and he will get the credit, not me. It has not been enough, what I have said about it. I should have written thick books, like the others who made famous discoveries. My work will be forgotten, overlooked.'

When Dubois resumed this self-pitying monologue the next morning, 3 March 1932, Bernsen could remain quiet no longer. The frustrations that had built up over the months of working with this demanding and hypersensitive man exploded into words. 'You will be forgotten, Professor? You? And what about my work? What about the months and months of time I have put in on your collection? This will always be the Dubois Collection, and a few years from now, who will remember the priest, Father Bernsen, who brought order to the collection? I am allowed only to do the boring tasks, the tedious ones, and for that I get no thanks or recognition.'

Dubois stared at Bernsen for a moment, as if he had suddenly sprouted tusks or wings. And then he understood, in an instant. 'Oh, Father Bernsen, you must forgive me. I am too absorbed in my own work. I have too rarely taken the time to thank you for your labour on this long task, the sort of thing I do not have the temperament to do myself. It must seem to you as if I have never taken any interest in your progress, never appreciated the many long hours you have put in on my collection.' Bernsen was not mollified, though he was glad to see Dubois felt some guilt. 'You know, Father,' Dubois said ingenuously, 'if I have seemed uncaring, it is only because I know in what good hands my collection has been put. I never thought I needed to check up on your work or encourage you, but of course it is discouraging to work without any praise or recognition.'

'It is indeed,' replied Bernsen, tight-lipped.

'Ah, I understand the need for due recognition,' Dubois answered soothingly. Bernsen nodded, almost in acceptance of the tacit apology. 'And perhaps now that we have cleared the air, we should speak of a more important thing. May I ask you a question? You may answer freely, with a clear conscience, but of course you don't have to answer at all. How do you imagine your future? Do you have aspirations for your career?' Dubois looked at him quizzically.

Bernsen was immediately suspicious. Why was Dubois asking him this? Was he going to hold out the prospect of describing various mammalian groups yet again, only to withdraw the offer the next day? He answered carefully, choosing his words with thought: 'I aspire not after a particular post, Professor, but after time ... time to carry out scientific work. Why do you ask me this?'

Dubois nodded, furrowing his brow as if concentrating. 'Ja, Father, ja. I see,' he answered. 'This is awkward. Initially I had you in mind for my successor at this museum. I have even spoken to you about it, ja? You remember, when we were talking about the saving of Pithecanthropus...But I must return to the subject at hand. Although I myself find you quite unprejudiced in your scientific work, the outside world should find it very strange indeed, if you, a Catholic priest, were appointed the guardian of Pithecanthropus. What would the Americans say, who have complained so much about access to the fossils? What about those who spread the false rumours that I was hiding them because of the dictates of the Catholic Church? They would surely see in your appointment a confirmation of those rumours. You can see the difficulty. So I think that while you might be in charge of the Dubois Collection, you can never be in custody of *P.e.*' He finished strongly, but was unable to look Bernsen in the eye for some seconds.

Bernsen was stunned. So he was to carry out the saving of the collection but was not to touch its jewel. He raised his head and spoke clearly. 'I must thank you, Professor, for speaking so frankly from the heart.' Dubois still would not look at him. Bernsen knew, by this action, that his cause was completely and utterly lost. 'I do not wish to criticize you,' he continued evenly, 'but I think perhaps it would have been fairer if you had said all this earlier. Now, after eighteen months, the collection is almost safe and the dull work is nearly completed. If that is all you think me suited for, then I shall finish up the registration and organization and then resign my post just as soon as the catalogue of specimens is completed.' He would leave with dignity, if Dubois forced the issue.

'Do you mean this?' asked Dubois with transparent delight, raising his eyes once more to Bernsen's.

'Oh, ja, Professor, ja, I will resign once everything is in order.' He could not mistake the look on Dubois's face; the man for whom he had worked so hard was gleeful at the prospect of his resignation. That evening Bernsen drafted his letter of resignation and the next morning, submitted it to the trustees of Leiden University who, after all, were technically his employers. Dubois had never personally had the power to hire or fire him.

Two days later, when Dubois next came to Leiden to work on the collection, the situation was tense. He and Bernsen exchanged only a few words, and Dubois left earlier than his accustomed hour. That night, Bernsen wrote in his diary:

March 5, 1932. No word of regret from Dubois about the sharpening of the case. On the contrary, my suspicion is confirmed by the letter I saw, saying that he (Dubois) is happy about the announcement of my resignation. Only I, the victim, must laugh sweetly as I am killed and be silent, that the outside world shall know nothing of my sacrifice.

Unnerved by the hostility emanating from Dubois, Bernsen asked for a week of study leave. He did not even wish to speak to Dubois without witnesses present, for he feared that anything he said would be distorted and misinterpreted if it could be used against him. He wished it to be known that he had done a good, thorough, and responsible job, working with the most difficult of taskmasters. Now he understood the import of those visits from Antje Schreuder and Professor Escher, who had resigned their positions after similar quarrels. They had been trying to tell him that Dubois would never share the credit for the work, that he used his assistants and then cast them aside.

After a week of thinking about little else, Bernsen decided to go directly to the burgomaster, the man officially in charge of the Dubois Collection and of its director and his assistants. But when Bernsen arrived in his office to unburden himself of the awful tale of jealousy and quarrel, the burgomaster informed him that Dubois had already been there, complaining about Bernsen.

'What? Dubois has been here, telling you that I am difficult?' Bernsen was astonished. He had not suspected Dubois of dishonesty, only of selfishness.

'Ja, Father,' the burgomaster answered curtly, watching Bernsen's reaction. The priest seemed unsettled, but not guilty, so the burgomaster continued. 'Professor Dubois came to me several days ago, telling me how difficult things were with the collection. He spoke for nearly an hour about his troubles. But I must tell you, I watched his eyes as he spoke and thought to myself, "Man, you have lying eyes." I do not believe he tells the strict truth.'

'But—' Bernsen tried to break in, but the burgomaster carried on without pause.

'There is more, Father. As Dubois was getting up to leave, he told me that you, Father, are to be fired and that Dr Van der Klaauw shall be the future director of the collection. So only at the end did he state the real purpose of his visit. Until then, he only beat around the bush. It made a very unfavourable impression on me at the time,' concluded the burgomaster seriously.

'What I am to do?' asked Bernsen.

'Leave the matter with me,' replied the burgomaster. 'But on no account should you resign your position voluntarily. I shall speak with Professor Dubois again.'

The open enmity between Dubois and Bernsen was the talk of the museum. Bernsen hated the gossip; although his colleagues mostly offered encouraging words, he was embarrassed at the looks he got from some. It was all so tragic, so avoidable, he thought. If only Dubois could have treated me fairly, could have given me the slightest room to breathe...Even Van der Klaauw, Dubois's proposed successor, urged him to stand firm and not to quit. 'You have earned the directorship,' Van der Klaauw told him. 'You now know the collection as well as anyone, except maybe Dubois himself, and he cannot live for ever.'

A week after Bernsen's interview with the burgomaster, Dubois came again to work on the collection. Bernsen had thought hard about what attitude he would take toward this man, once so respected, now so feared. 'Let us behave in a civilized fashion, Professor,' Bernsen suggested. 'We are professionals and we will carry out our work in a businesslike manner.'

'Ja,' answered Dubois sourly. 'That is easy for you to say, for you have not had a scolding from the burgomaster, as I have.'

Bernsen made no answer but continued silently to sort and classify and register the bones. He was now dealing with very fragmentary remains, so it took some concentration to see what each might represent and check it against more complete specimens. Again and again, Dubois attempted to open a conversation about their disagreements, but Bernsen was determined not to start down the road to catastrophe.

'No, Professor,' he answered. 'We have agreed to be silent about it. It is the best way, or it will all start once again. I do not wish to argue with you, only to complete the work that needs to be done. Now, this specimen' – he changed the subject as he handed a fossil to Dubois – 'do you think this is more likely to be a broken metatarsal or a metacarpal?' They discussed the fossil briefly, made a determination, started upon another one.

The day went on, neither man comfortable, both painfully aware of the harsh words that had passed between them. Each felt put upon, unfairly beleaguered by the other. When Dubois rose to go, he turned to Bernsen and asked, 'And shall you walk with me to the station, as usual?'

'No, Professor.' Bernsen shook his head, sadly. 'I think it is perhaps better that I do not accompany you any longer.' Dubois looked so grey and old and lonely as he walked down the street that Bernsen was tempted to run after him. No, he told himself, it will not do. Dubois has chosen to cast me aside and he will have to live with the consequences of his unfair action.

Months passed, but the tension remained high, their interactions stilted. In May, their quarrel erupted again, for Dubois could not leave the subject alone. He worried it like a terrier with a rat. 'You know, Bernsen, we must talk once more about our relationship. This is all your fault, from the beginning. There is something hostile in you toward me, I have always noticed it. You have repeatedly humiliated me, corrected me, pointed out every error, criticized and questioned my judgements. Even as a small boy I was always treated with special respect. But no, not you, Father, you cannot respect me. You must humiliate me and bring me down out of jealousy at my high position. In recent months I have gone through so much sorrow. It has aged me. I have even wished for the release of death to end this misery. Oh, not that I would commit suicide,' he added quickly, knowing suicide to be among the worst sins a Catholic could commit, 'for suicide is cowardly.'

Bernsen could not contain himself, he was so indignant at being accused of torturing Dubois with his criticisms. 'Is not the most important thing that the collection be correct? Have you not said this, Professor? Now I see that you are hard and that everything must give way to your interests. I personally mean nothing to you, although for two years I have done the tedious work for the collection, day in and day out. Now I see you differently and my sympathy for you has cooled.'

There was no denying the truth of the accusation. Dubois hung his head for a moment, like a schoolboy. 'Ja, Father, it is true. I am hard in that respect. I have always felt that everything must give way for the goal, everything must be arranged to serve the ends of science. So perhaps I have driven you too hard and given you only criticism, but it is for the collection, for science. I have driven myself as hard, sacrificed as much. Personally, I have always had compassion for you in this tedious work; I find you a good fellow, you know, Father.' Dubois looked up hopefully, to see if these words had appeased Bernsen. But even this admission of his selfishness – the confession of his single-minded pursuit of scientific truth – was not enough to make peace between them. Bernsen thought bitterly that surely science could be served without savaging others.

The weeks stretched on, full of barely contained ill-feeling. Soon the collection would be properly organized and registered; awareness of this fact heightened the anxiety. Both men knew that something had to be decided soon about the future of the collection and of Father Bernsen. The better specimens were all completed and registered by now; what remained were fragments, small, random bits and pieces many of which could be classified in only the most general way, by size and body part. Bernsen was scrupulous to the end, however, determined to make no mistakes or omissions for which he could be castigated. If leave he must, it would be with pride in a job well done, professionally done, even if it was unappreciated by the one whose opinion weighed most heavily.

Working systematically through some boxes of assorted rib fragments, Bernsen pulled out one that struck him as particularly odd and troubled him. Both ends were broken off and it was rather thick. True, ribs of large animals (such as elephants, buffalo, and giant deer) were just this thick; but the shape...the shape was wrong. He set it aside to show to Dubois, as he did everything that struck him as peculiar or as misidentified. Going through these oddities was always a trial, an occasion for possible explosions, but Bernsen would not neglect a single fossil. On 1 June 1932, he brought the specimen to Dubois's attention.

'Professor,' he opened the conversation carefully, holding out the fossil for Dubois to see, 'have you time to took at this specimen? It comes from the box of rib fragments that I have been sorting through. I think it is peculiar, not like the others. Perhaps it is something important.'

'Umm? Oh, ja, ja, I will take the time. Now, what is this? I see the problem, ja. It is different from the others.' He wandered off with the specimen in hand, examining it inch by inch, opening drawers or boxes now and again to make comparisons. After about half an hour, he came back to Bernsen with a smug look on his face.

'Father, you have indeed found something. After a great deal of inspection and many comparisons with other fossils, I think it is another piece of a femur of *P.e.* Imagine! After all these years, to find another piece...This will be most important if it is true. You must look very carefully for the other broken parts. I'm sure there will be some additional pieces that glue on to this, that will make it more complete. I want you to set aside all other work, and get the technician Van der Steen to help you, too, until you have gone through every single fragment that might be part of this same bone.'

Bernsen doubted that this fragment was a piece of

Pithecanthropus's femur, but he did as Dubois asked. Over the next hours, he and Van der Steen turned up two more similar pieces out of the thousands of fragments. They brought these additional pieces to Dubois as they found them, noticing that the older man grew more – not less – dissatisfied, as if he had hoped for failure. Before the end of the day, he and Bernsen once again had harsh words over Bernsen's cruel enjoyment (so Dubois thought) in catching Dubois out and finding him wrong.

The next day, all three men arrived early to continue the search. Dubois announced, 'After a close comparison with the original femur, I have arrived at the firm conclusion that the long bone you pointed out yesterday is indeed a part of the shaft of the femur of Pithecanthropus. You and Van der Steen must continue to search diligently among the boxes containing fossils from that same area, where this fragment was found.'

Some hours later, elated, Bernsen came again to Dubois, finding him lost in rapt inspection of the new femur. 'Professor,' he burst out, 'I have found it! I think I have found a piece that fits on to the one I found yesterday. May I try it, please?' And the two men, forgetting their disagreements, stared in wonder as the two pieces fitted together so neatly that there was almost an audible click.

'There,' Bernsen commented. 'It is clear. You are completely correct, Professor, it is the femur of Pithecanthropus.'

'Ja,' said Dubois heavily. 'It is. Another left femur of Pithecanthropus.' He sat silently staring at the fossils for a moment. Bernsen was jubilant but Dubois smelled only disgrace. 'This is a solemn moment,' Dubois proclaimed. 'Until now, I stood alone. But now I have a second individual of Pithecanthropus, for this is surely a left femur just like the one we found in the first place. How they will look up and take notice in Berlin!'

Suddenly Bernsen realized the implications of the find: not only had Dubois missed a bone belonging to *Pithecanthropus*, but now there were two individuals. The argument that the original skullcap, femur, and tooth had to come from one individual, because there was no other primate in the vast collection, dissolved into nothingness. The harsh accusations and disbelief that had been thrown at Dubois in those early years flooded into both men's minds, especially Virchow's stormy insistence that Dubois had created a chimera out of several individuals and probably out of several different animals. What of all the years and years of publications on brain weight and body size, based on that one skullcap and one femur? Were they, too, all swept away, drowned at sea? Yes, they had to be, if the femur and the skullcap were not from the same individual. Two left legs: there could hardly have been a more damning find. Bernsen could hardly look at Dubois's face, so clearly was the tragedy of this new scientific truth written there. Dubois's whole life's work was cruelly threatened.

'Still,' Dubois remarked, trying to save the situation, 'these pieces must certainly have come from the excavations of 1898 and 1900, after I had left the Indies. Otherwise I would have gone through the boxes more carefully and spotted these bones at the time. It is only that material that I have not examined thoroughly.'

'In the box,' pointed out Bernsen, 'there was a note lying near these pieces that said B.120.' They both knew that this was the standard code for the 120th box of the second, or B, shipment. That made the specimen one excavated during Dubois's time in Java, not later. After a moment, Bernsen added, kindly. 'Of course, we both know that many of the notes were mislaid and mixed up during the moves. And it was you yourself who said to me, Professor, "Pay careful attention to the small fragments, to see if there is not something yet of Pithecanthropus in there." Of course, we know that to find a large piece of Pithecanthropus now is impossible, for those fragments you have checked very well.'

Dubois did not answer, only sat staring at this new piece of left femur. Then he said with a sigh, 'We must carry on. I shall soak the pieces in thin glue, to strengthen them, and then glue them together. You must continue to search for more pieces.'

Although he was sympathetic to Dubois's dark mood, Bernsen could scarcely contain his exuberance as he walked out of the room, back to where Van der Steen was working. 'We've got it!' he cried. 'It fits!' Van der Steen was excited, but no more so than Bernsen himself. Bernsen felt as if his months of patient work had been vindicated, for he, too, had made a great discovery. More pieces were found, until there was a total of eight new fragments. Yet Bernsen worried over the long-term effects of these finds on his fragile and troubled relationship with Dubois.

June 4, 1932. Dubois will surely find it unpleasant that I shall have a share in the discovery. If I had not taken out the first piece that was with the rib fragments, as a piece that struck me as peculiar (as I usually do, for I always show him such pieces), then it would have been maybe not for years, or ever, that someone would have turned to look at it. I am convinced that this will not soften his determination, restated only yesterday, to apply for my discharge. Even after the finding of the *Pithecanthropus* material, he was actually already speaking with others about how much longer it would take me to finish the work.

It proved to take much less time than either of them expected. Hours after writing these words, Bernsen fell seriously ill. The next day, despite all the doctor could do, he died of internal haemorrhaging, perhaps from a bleeding ulcer. No one had suspected the toll the incessant hostility had been taking on Bernsen's health.

On 25 June, Dubois presented the new material to a meeting of the Royal Academy of Sciences. The story he told was compelling but not entirely honest. Dubois felt himself so vulnerable that he could not bear to tell the whole truth. The only other man who knew the truth, Bernsen, was dead, after registering 10,411 fossils from Trinil.

Forty years ago the two principal skeletal remains, the skullcap and the femur, of *Pithecanthropus erectus* were excavated at Trinil, Java. It was then supposed by the author of this species that both were remains of the same organism, species, or even individual. The skullcap indeed so closely resembles that part of the body in the anthropoid apes, especially the gibbons, on one hand, and in Man, on the other, that the name *Pithecanthropus*, for the genus, is fully appropriate. The name *erectus* was given to the species on account of the strikingly humanlike essential features of the femur, which imply erect attitude and gait. Together with those features, however, the Trinil femur, in the opinion of the author of the species, presented important differentiating characters, so that he found it possible, at least, to regard the skull and the femur as having been parts of one organism...

The prevailing view on the Trinil femur, however, at present as well as in the past, is to consider it absolutely... human...

It thus appears clearly that we have to regard the femur of the *Pithecanthropus* species as the true key bone to his frame, a key admitting us to the knowledge of its organization. Now, as to know a species well one single individual is insufficient, what we have wanted, for forty years, are thigh bones of other individuals of the described species, to ascertain if the particular features seen in the femur of 1892 are essential characters of the species... or mere individual differences...

In these forty years, no remains of another 'pithecanthrope' came to light... till the first days of this month other overlooked pieces appeared three [partial, additional] thigh bones of the described species.

On that day, at Leiden, in my Java collection some dissimilar fragments, not belonging to ribs, were separated from a lot of inconsiderable fragments of ribs from various Trinil mammals, which I was minutely examining. Amongst them was a bone a foot long, still partially covered with rock which my diligent assistant in the arranging of the Collection, Dr. BERNSEN, whose loss we now deplore, had put aside for my inspection, because he regarded it as a dubitable piece of deer's horn. To my great joy, I soon recognized it as the shaft of another *Pithecanthropus* thigh bone. It presented some of the same characteristics which differentiate the Trinil femur of 1892 from a human femur. Then, searching further through the rib fragments for similar pieces, that might possibly fit, I found the defective upper extremity to that thigh bone shaft, which was broken off beneath the small trochanter, and six other pieces of different sizes, which enabled me to compose two more shafts of *Pithecanthropus* thigh bones.

None of the three is comparable with the splendidly conserved femur of 1892, but they all unquestionably belong to the described species.

In 1932, Bernsen discovered the first of eight new fragments of *Pithecanthropus* femur among the unlabelled fragments from Trinil. These finds disproved Dubois's long-held assertion that the original *Pithecanthropus* femur (right) must come from the same individual as the molar and skullcap.

Dubois attributed the new specimens to the excavations carried out under Kriele's direction in 1900, so that (although the exact site of the find had not been noted at the time, as Kriele had not seen their importance) they must have lain within sixteen and forty-eight metres of the skullcap, much farther apart than the original femur and the skullcap. For this reason, and because the new bones were much more heavily corroded than the original finds, Dubois argued that the new bones were from other individuals, now represented by two new but incomplete left femurs and two new but also incomplete right femurs. More to the point, all betrayed the very same features that had initially convinced Dubois that the femur of *P.e.* was distinctly different from that of Man. These anatomical differences, he hypothesized, were due to a more tree-climbing habit in *P.e.*, although its primary means of movement was walking upright on the ground.

He concluded his lecture with a characteristically strong statement:

The morphological evidence acquired proves beyond a doubt that the skull and the femur that were excavated in 1891–1892 can have been associated in one and the same organism, a distinct species...

I still believe, now more firmly than ever, that the *Pithecanthropus* of Trinil is the real 'missing link'.

The only mention of Bernsen's role in the entire discovery was the parenthetical remark about the 'diligent assistant... whose loss we now deplore'. Bernsen was replaced by Miss M. Sanders, who between 1 October and 31 December 1932, registered another 569 specimens. Dubois took care that she never developed professional aspirations about the collection. Sanders was followed by her future husband, the herpetologist L. D. Brongersma, who brought the total number of registered specimens up to 11,284. Before long, Bernsen's heroic work on the collection was all but forgotten by most. An exception was, of course, Dubois himself, who could never seem to get the priest out of his mind.

CHAPTER 53

New Skulls from Java

The importance of the new fragments of the femur of *Pithecanthropus* was overshadowed by other Javanese discoveries.

In August 1931, the Geological Survey of Java had sent C. ter Haar to draw an accurate map of the Kendeng Hills in central Java. Ter Haar had set up his camp in the village of Ngandong on the Bengawan Solo some six miles north of Trinil. On 27 August, he had noticed a series of three layers of gravel and sand that must be old river terraces, about sixty feet above the present bed of the river. One of them was full of fossils. Among the first specimens he had pulled out was the remarkable skull of a giant water buffalo with a horn span of some seven feet.

When Ter Haar had sent word back to the survey headquarters in Bandung, the acting director, W. F. F. Oppenoorth, sent a team of trained Javanese to work systematically at Ngandong. Ever since participating in the Selenka expedition to Trinil in 1907, Oppenoorth had believed as an article of faith that there were great fossil discoveries yet to be made in central Java, but in his most ambitious dreams, he had not anticipated what was to come. Routinely, the men numbered all good specimens recovered from excavation at Ngandong. Number 29, found on 15 September, was a large part of a fossilized human skull, although the Javanese collectors did not recognize this and labelled it a tiger skull. Another strange object – an 'ape skull' – was found on 30 September. In Bandung, Oppenoorth was startled to realize that both were archaic human skulls. He reached Ngandong on 21 October to discover that yet another fragment of human skull had been recovered eight days earlier. Oppenoorth brought along a young German paleontologist employed by the Geological Survey of Java to help: G. H. R. von Koenigswald, known as Ralph.

Oppenoorth and Von Koenigswald were stunned to find that their men had found an unprecedented three fossil hominid skulls. They instituted a second numbering system, using Roman numerals, for the hominid skulls, which continued to be found over the subsequent months and years of work. It was a paleontological treasure trove. After the three finds in 1931, Skull IV was found on 25 January 1932; Skull V on 17 March; Skull VI on 13 June. The skull numbered VII was found on 24 May, but not recognized until later. Then there was a lull; no more were found until the last week in August of 1933 (Skull VIII). Skulls IX and X were excavated on 27 September and the final skull, XI, was located on 8 November 1933. None of the eleven was complete; their faces were missing and the bases of the skulls were broken away. There were also thousands of animal bones.

Oppenoorth started to write up the hominid skulls immediately, without waiting for the good luck to run out. Tactfully, he sent a copy of his first article on the new specimens to Dubois with a personal letter dated 11 May 1932, although they had not met before. Still, one aspect of the importance of the Ngandong skulls was that they had been found so close to Trinil, the home of *Pithecanthropus*, and *Pithecanthropus* was Dubois's fossil. What Oppenoorth had written was a 'provisional description', based on Skull I, nothing more. He compared the new skull to *Pithecanthropus*, *Sinanthropus*, various Neanderthals, the Wadjak skulls, and what he called the 'average' Australian Aborigine. He found the new material unmatched by any previously found fossils and so proposed a new name *Homo (Javanthropus) soloensis*. Dubois was fascinated and flattered by receiving this preliminary report. It was the beginning of a long correspondence, for Dubois wrote to Oppenoorth with many questions about the brain size and endocast of the new skull. He was gratified to receive a prompt reply from Oppenoorth:

31 May 1932

I have already received from Professor Black three casts of the *Sinanthropus* material for comparison. Of your *Pithecanthropus* I have personally paid for a cast by Kranz in Bonn... but the *Pithecanthropus* cast is very bad. I hear that there are at present new casts of it, on which one can see the inside of the skull. If you are able to help our museum obtain such a cast, possibly also one of Wadjak man, then it will be certainly a pleasure for us to send you in due time also a cast of the Ngandong skull.

The new skulls are, according to me, certainly not identical with the Wadjak type, but point to a more primitive human, something like the Neanderthal type. When you have seen my provisional description you will probably agree with me.

I believe that with this I have answered all your questions, and I would like to make a few requests, namely if you can still help me to get reprints of your description in the Academy of the *Pithecanthropus* and *Homo wadjakensis* (the description of 1894 I already own). You would greatly oblige me further by sending a few photographs of the Wadjak skulls.

As you will perhaps remember, 25 years ago I went with the Selenka expedition, *con amore*, to Indonesia to continue your work at Trinil. After I went into government service, there was no longer any opportunity for such work, until some years ago when I became the leader of the newly established Geological Survey of Java, and with it came the possibility of bringing my earlier experience into play again.

Now, after 25 years, my first activities are crowned with success, and all those years I have had an interest in, and have kept myself apprised of further finds. You will understand that this completely unexpected find is for me a great satisfaction, and you will certainly understand that I am not inclined to let the work on the fossils out of my hands without protest. I write this to you because I received a proposal to entrust the fossils to others, which came from Professor Mijsberg in Batavia, who used your name. [Mijsberg was one of the scientists to assess Heberlein's 'skull' find.] Hence, it is for me a great pleasure to hear from you personally on the matter. Of course I am completely willing to work together, and there are themes, as for instance the endocranial anatomy, on which I will not venture myself.

Soon after receiving Oppenoorth's communication, Dubois published a brief letter to the editor in the scientific journal *Nature* on the subject of the new skulls. He endorsed Oppenoorth's view that the new skull was a representative of a primitive human race, though it was less primitive than Wadjak man in Dubois's view. Oppenoorth's error, Dubois suggested, sprang from the fact that the second, more fragmentary Wadjak skull had not yet been fully described and was therefore less known to Oppenoorth. It was this second skull that more closely approached the new Ngandong skull, so he suggested that they were 'one identical type', a 'proto-Australian'. He reiterated this view in a supportive yet tactful letter to Oppenoorth.

15 June 1932

I completely agree with you, that the fossil man of Ngandong is nothing to do with the Neanderthal, but that it stands nearer the

Australian type ... But your description leaves little doubt in my mind, that Ngandong is a type identical to the Wadjak-man. The second (fragmentary) skull from Wadjak that I have mentioned, but not further described, is closer to the Ngandong skull than the other ... In my provisional opinion, that is the greatest significance of this find. It is in any case a scientifically valuable object.

Soon afterwards, Oppenoorth described Ngandong IV and V in a June 1932 issue of *De Mijningingenieur* (The Mining Engineer). Skull V was the most complete, missing only the lower part of the face and the base of the skull. While all the skulls had remarkably thick vault bones and large browridges, Skull V was gigantic. Oppenoorth estimated its cranial capacity at 1300 cc, as large as many modern Europeans and larger than, for example, the skulls of most Australian Aborigines.

Oppenoorth raised an interesting new issue as he tried to make some sense of the distribution through time and space of the various types of hominids that were now known from their skulls. In his eyes, the easiest way to align the fossils into ancestor-descendant sequences was to create two parallel but separate lineages, but how was this to be done? Initially, Oppenoorth had proposed a geographic separation, making a European sequence (in which *Palaeanthropus heidelbergensis* → *Homo neanderthalensis* → *Homo sapiens fossilis*) and an Asian lineage (*Pithecanthropus* → *Sinanthropus* → *Homo soloensis* → *Homo wadjakensis*). Now he saw it was possible that the key factor was climate. Perhaps in temperate China and Europe *Sinanthropus* evolved into *Palaeanthropus heidelbergensis*, which evolved into *Homo neanderthalensis* and then into *Homo sapiens fossilis*, while in the tropics *Pithecanthropus* evolved into *Homo soloensis* and then into *Homo wadjakensis*. Dubois made no response to Oppenoorth's suggestion, but the two men continued a cordial correspondence and Oppenoorth was welcomed by Dubois at the Teyler Museum where he examined *P.e.* and the Wadjak skulls, leaving a brain cast of the Ngandong I skull for Dubois's use. Thus, when the brain casts of the two *Sinanthropus* skulls arrived from China on 8 February 1933, Dubois could compare them with those from both Trinil and Ngandong. To Dubois, the differences were clear. *Sinanthropus* was apelike, though not so apelike as *Pithecanthropus*; *Homo soloensis* from Ngandong was simply a primitive human. The greater importance of the Chinese fossils was doubtless why

Dubois nominated Black, not Oppenoorth, for the Prix Hollandais in 1934.

Dubois's next task was to prepare a detailed comparison of the brains of *Sinanthropus* and *Pithecanthropus*, research which he presented at the 29 April 1933 meeting of the Royal Academy. Because *Sinanthropus* and *Pithecanthropus*, were much more apelike and much older (*P.e.* being the oldest) than the more humanlike Wadjak and Ngandong remains, it was the former skulls that recorded the earliest chapters of the evolution of the human brain. Ever the sceptic, Dubois took the precaution of checking the external measurements of the endocast against those in Black's publications, to make sure the casts were accurate (which he concluded they were).

His first substantive assessment of the brains of *Sinanthropus* and *P.e.* startled the listeners at the Royal Academy: 'There is obviously little difference in size between the two brains; in shape, however, they are surprisingly unalike.' Black's preliminary reports had suggested that the brain of *Sinanthropus* was bigger than that of *P.e.*, by perhaps twenty-five per cent. Was there, then, 'little difference in size' as Dubois asserted?

The issue was that the most recently found *Sinanthropus* skull was smaller than the first. Dubois adjudged the new *Sinanthropus* braincase to be approximately 918 cc in volume, close to that of *P.e.* Although the new Chinese skull was of an adolescent, that fact could not explain its unusually small brain.

Such a volume…is certainly a very low one for a human skull, as this *Sinanthropus* undoubtedly is. For at the age of this early adolescent human individual the volume of the brain is almost equal to that of the adult…The shape and the major features of the *Sinanthropus* skull, on the contrary, are those of a full-grown male Neanderthaler…We meet here with a contradiction between cranial form and cranial capacity, a contradiction emphasized by the other *Sinanthropus* skull, attributed by DAVIDSON BLACK to an adult woman. In contradistinction to the adolescent skull it, indeed, exhibits true female features. It is difficult to estimate the capacity of this very incomplete cranium; however, 1150 cc will probably not be too high an estimate. In proportion to such a female capacity a normal adult male of the same race should have about 1300 cc capacity. However the adolescent *Sinanthropus* exhibits adult morphology in combination with a brain volume very much smaller than the normal one of his age.

This is a contrast which is perfectly unconceivable [sic] if we consider this *Sinanthropus* youth as a normal individual...I may express my opinion that the adolescent *Sinanthropus* is a human male, belonging to the Neanderthal group of mankind...with an individually imperfect and hence abnormally small brain.

Ironically, Dubois found himself falling back upon Virchow's favourite excuse of old for any anatomical variation in ancient skulls: pathology. Later, when additional *Sinanthropus* skulls were found, this excuse had to be abandoned, for even adults of *Sinanthropus* had brains close in size to that of *Pithecanthropus*. Black's original estimates of brain size had been too high.

Dubois also emphasized the difference in shape between the two endocasts, illustrating this point with a pair of photographs. Taken from the top and right side, these images unfortunately made the endocasts look remarkably similar to the untrained eye, notwithstanding Dubois's conclusion to the contrary. To Dubois's expert eye, the differences were evident and attested to these being related but quite different species, but his argument was unconvincing to most. The greatest differences in shape appeared in side or lateral view, but the *P.e.* endocast was so much less complete than the *Sinanthropus* endocast that the comparison was difficult to make. However, Dubois was certain of his conclusions; he described the 'oblong and narrow' brain form of *Sinanthropus*, contrasting it with 'the more rounded, broad form of *Pithecanthropus*'.

This was the beginning of a new trend in Dubois's research. The similarities between *Pithecanthropus* and *Sinanthropus* were beginning to trouble him, for his *P.e.* was losing some of her uniqueness. He tried steadfastly to maintain her 'missing link' position, emphasizing the primitive, even apelike features of her anatomy. In 1935, Dubois published a paper entitled 'On the Gibbonlike Appearance of *Pithecanthropus erectus*', an astonishing move for the man who had so vehemently fought Virchow's early suggestion that *P.e.* was naught but a big gibbon. But now things were different and he needed to emphasize the gibbonoid features of *P.e.* to make sure that *P.e.* remained distinct from *Sinanthropus*. His fossil was apelike; Black's was humanlike. He added his morphological observations to the results of his research into the proportions of brain weight and body weight, observing that *Pithecanthropus* occupied a position in cephalization that was perfectly intermediate between the apes and man.

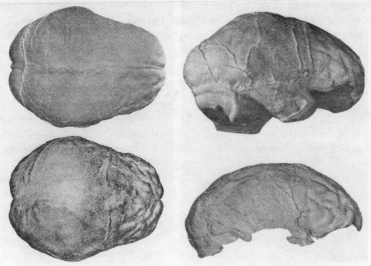

Dubois compared the brain casts of *Sinanthropus* (top) and *Pithecanthropus* (bottom), intending to highlight their differences but inadvertently emphasizing their resemblances.

In lateral view, the brain casts of *Sinanthropus* (top) and *Pithecanthropus* (bottom) differ moderately in shape.

It is therefore possible to arrange all the groups of mammals existing at present in a geometrical series of progressive ... cephalization, in which series there are no gaps (even when fossil groups are not taken into account), with one sole exception ...

The only real void space in the series is between man and the anthropomorphous apes (including gibbons). This void marks the placement of *Pithecanthropus* ...

The strongest evidence of the gibbonlike appearance of *Pithecanthropus*, however, is that provided by the volume of the psychoencephalon, exactly doubled in relation to the body weight computed from the gibbonlike chief dimensions of the femur.

Once again, the calculations reinforced Dubois's main conviction: *Pithecanthropus* was an apeman, *Sinanthropus* was an early man, and Oppenoorth's *Homo soloensis* was modern *Homo sapiens*, part of a ring species that encircled the globe, varying somewhat from location to location. However, Dubois agreed with Oppenoorth that *Homo soloensis* was no Neanderthal, since the Ngandong tibias did not show the distinctive Neanderthal morphology.

Unfortunately, the harmony between Dubois and Oppenoorth did not carry over to Oppenoorth's successor at the Geological Survey, young Ralph von Koenigswald.

CHAPTER 54

A Worthy Opponent

Von Koenigswald was a German, not tall but beefy of build, with somewhat coarse features and a blunt manner. He was also very clever, hardworking, and acutely ambitious to make his scientific mark in the Indies. His career at the Geological Survey of Java had begun back in 1931, when he had been charged with establishing the stratigraphic and chronological framework of the island, using mammalian species as markers for deposits of different ages. Only eight months after his arrival in Java, he had travelled to Ngandong with Ter Haar, to witness the excavation of Skull VI departing from Bandung on 18 June 1932. From the rural station of Paron, they had ridden in a two-wheeled horse cart to Ngawi and then walked the rest of the way through the steaming teak forests. When they had finally arrived at Ngandong, Von Koenigswald had been staggered by the scene that met his eyes.

Our excavation site lay a few hundred yards from the village houses. Our workmen had dug a pit 10 feet deep, the floor of which consisted of marly rock – a sign that the terrace gravel went down no deeper. One gravel bank had been only half dug away, and a few palm fronds stuck in the sand marked the spot where the skull lay buried. We removed the fronds and Ter Haar began to dig carefully with his hands, while I took photographs. Unfortunately, I was so excited that most of the shots were underexposed After only a few minutes we came upon a large round object: this must be the skull. It proved to be the underside of a human skull; the cranium itself was still embedded in the gravel. In the case of every previous skull the underside had been in fragments; here at last it was intact. The foramen magnum was undamaged, but the place where the cranium had been knocked in was rather more to the front. In spite of a prolonged search we could find no trace of the facial section or the jaws. The skull itself was in an excellent state of preservation and undoubtedly the most perfect specimen discovered at Ngandong. We cleaned it as well as we could on the site and packed it carefully, for the final preparation could only be carried out at Bandung. This was the first skull at whose disinterment I had personally assisted.

Von Koenigswald returned to the site twice more, witnessing the recovery of Skull VIII and Skull XI, but he longed to discover a new site, where more and more important fossil skulls would be found under his direction.

He began prospecting in the Sangiran region, north-east of the central Javanese city of Solo, in 1934, near where Raden Saleh's fossils had been found. The region's fertile soils were now prized by local farmers, who planted rice, maize, peanuts, pawpaws, and coconut palms. Von Koenigswald arrived with his native collector Atma, announcing to the local populace that he was interested in fossils. They obligingly produced fossil bones, teeth, and shells that they had found in the fields; Von Koenigswald paid small amounts of money for good specimens. Soon most of the local villagers were an avid collecting and excavating force. After some weeks, Von Koenigswald returned to Bandung, leaving Atma in charge of purchasing further finds.

Though he believed firmly that he had found an important site, perhaps as old as Dubois's Trinil site, Von Koenigswald's enthusiasm could not counteract the realities of global forces. A disastrous economic crash, begun in 1929, had continued unchecked and the value of the Indies' main exports (rubber, sugar, tea, coffee, and tobacco) had fallen to a fraction of its former worth. Plantations failed and closed monthly, their former workers returning to their villages and dire poverty. Furthermore, the first groundswell of a movement for native independence began. The colonial government responded decisively, disbanding native political parties and arresting their leaders. Salaries for government workers were slashed and all nonessential government employees – including Von Koenigswald – were fired.

Von Koenigswald asked Atma to stay at Sangiran and keep an eye out for good fossils. In 1935, Von Koenigswald and his family survived on his part-time work at the Geological Survey and his wife's salary as a teacher of German language and literature. Nonetheless, Von Koenigswald invited a French colleague to visit and inspect the Javanese fossils. Father Pierre Teilhard de Chardin was a perfect choice for colleague and possibly saviour. He was an unusual character, a tall, thin, hawk-nosed Jesuit priest with a passionate interest in paleontology and archaeology. He had worked at Piltdown in England with Charles Dawson, in China with Davidson Black, and in India with the geologist Helmut de Terra. He was a well-known and internationally respected authority in the mammalian paleontology of Asia.

In 1936, a Javanese collector employed by G. H. R. von Koenigswald
found this fossil child's skull at Modjokerto. When Von Koenigswald
identified it as *Pithecanthropus*, he started a feud with Dubois.

When Teilhard arrived in Batavia in January 1936, things were
grim indeed. Von Koenigswald was still out of work and his wife,
Luitgarde, had been stricken with typhoid. Despite the terrible
strain, Von Koenigswald was eager to show Teilhard the fossils
and discuss their interpretation. The two men left for central Java
so that Teilhard could inspect the localities himself; they forged a
firm friendship during days of walking and nights of camping in
tiny kampongs.

Teilhard left Java convinced of two things. One was the great
importance of the material Von Koenigswald was finding; the other
was the urgent need for institutional support for Von Koenigswald's
work. He recommended that Von Koenigswald write to John C.
Merriam of the Carnegie Institution in Philadelphia, and the
younger man complied, contrasting his complete lack of financial
support with the bright promise of spectacular fossil finds. 'I have

found a new fossil locality here in Java,' he wrote to Merriam. 'If *Pithecanthropus* is to be found anywhere, it will be here.'

Von Koenigswald's fortunes began to change. In late February 1936, one of his collectors, Andojo, found a fossilized child's skull in the village of Modjokerto in East Java. Along with fossils of other species, the skull was sent to the Geological Survey in Bandung, where Von Koenigswald gleefully recognized its importance. Here was the find he had been searching for. He announced it in a newspaper article, '*Pithecanthropus* Child's Skull', in *Het Algemeen Indische Dagblad* on 28 March, 1936.

> During the stratigraphic survey of the region SOERABAJA by the Geological Survey of Java, to determine the stratigraphy and age of the different strata, we also systematically searched for fossils. Only a few weeks ago was found a humanlike skull. It is a small skull, not more than 14 cm long! Consequently, this is absolutely the smallest skull found of a human up to this time. Unfortunately, it was found on the surface and is pretty well weathered. On the left side is mainly the skullcap with the upper rim of the orbits and the bone surrounding the left orbit...
>
> Although [the skull is] more than 4 cm shorter than the skullcap found by Dubois, the height of the skull (measured perpendicular to the greatest length) is nonetheless the same in the two cases. This is one of the reasons I consider this small skull to be *Pithecanthropus*...
>
> Geologically it is very important that our find from Modjokerto comes from a layer which, to judge by the fossil fauna in it, must be older than the layer in which the well-known fossils of Trinil are found. In Trinil, there is underneath the fossiliferous layer a volcanic breccia, which also contains bones but fewer than in the younger stratum above. This breccia is as old as the layer in which our new find has been made. It seems possible that the *Pithecanthropus* find from Trinil also originates from this lower level and that the place where it was found was a secondary berth, meaning that *Pithecanthropus* is older than we have supposed. Unfortunately Dubois has never published accurate statements about his sites; at the same time, we know next to nothing about the fossils in his very extensive collection.

Von Koenigswald sent a copy of the article directly to Dubois, who received it on 15 April. Perhaps Von Koenigswald hoped for support from Dubois; what he provoked instead was outrage.

Who was this upstart Von Koenigswald to criticize Dubois's work and suggest his geology was wrong? What had Von

Koenigswald ever discovered? It was certainly Von Koenigswald who was wrong, not Dubois. Dubois's rebuttal appeared in two Dutch newspapers on 18 April 1936.

On April 15 I got, as a cutting from De Preangerbode, the article ... by Dr. G. H. R. von Koenigswald in which appeared pictures of the new skullcap of the 'young *Pithecanthropus*' from right and top view ... It is immediately clear to me that we are not dealing with the skull of a *Pithecanthropus* but of a REAL HUMAN CHILD, apparently of the Wadjak race ...

That this 'new *Pithecanthropus*' is a human, Dr. von Koenigswald might have known if he had noticed an article in the Proceedings of the Royal Academy of Science in Amsterdam, vol. 36, (1933), titled 'The shape and the size of the brain in *Sinanthropus* and *Pithecanthropus*', and another article, in the same journal, 'On the gibbonlike appearance of *Pithecanthropus erectus*' (vol. 38, 1935).

The complete humanity of the 'new *Pithecanthropus*' cannot be doubted and it is entirely probable that this child skull did not come from the geologic formations in the region, north-east of Modjokerto, that contain 'the remains of the fossil vertebrates'. The collectors must have mixed up specimens collected on the surface and those deeply buried, as may also have happened at Ngandong ...

Science requires urgently that research on such fossils not remain in the hands of the very few scientists present in Java, but instead be carried out in Europe.

To this it may be added that it is absolutely untrue what Von Koenigswald says, that 'the original skull of *Pithecanthropus* was found by an overseer and sent to Dubois, so we do not know firmly that it came from the Trinil horizon; it was probably washed in from the older Djetis stratum, after which it was found by the overseer'.

Both the Modjokerto skull and the Trinil skullcap had been found by natives. If Javanese testimony about the location and manner of the find was not to be trusted, then the *in situ* placement of the Trinil fossil was more credibly documented by the notes of Kriele and De Winter.

On 5 and 7 May, Von Koenigswald replied hotly to the implication that he had made a geological as well as a paleontological error. If Dubois were right, then Von Koenigswald was unforgivably wrong, so the younger man counterattacked. It was the first skirmish in a long and bitter battle.

It is inconceivable how Professor Dubois from Holland, based on my first short publication in a newspaper, dares to condemn an entire case. I must repeat it once more: there exists no doubt that we deal here with a real fossil skull.

With regard to the circumstances of the find, Dr. J. Duyfjes, who surveyed this area, says, 'I can give Professor Dubois the positive assurance that a confusion over the finding of the new skull can be absolutely excluded. It was excavated by our collector Andojo from a pit 1 metre deep in a hard conglomerate sandstone, which certainly belongs to the fossil-bone layer of Modjokerto.

There is no change in my opinion of the identity of the skull, and before long I will publish on the subject copiously in a scientific periodical.

Professor Dubois's Wadjak man is a real primitive fossil of *Homo sapiens*, according to a recent publication … and has nothing to do with either this new find nor with the Neanderthals of Ngandong. I can assure Professor Dubois that the eleven skulls from Ngandong are real fossils and belong to the Pleistocene fauna with which they have been found …

The publications Professor Dubois cites are known to me but have no direct bearing on this find.

So now it is clear how the matter stands with Professor Dubois. Wouldn't it be better for this scientist to withhold his judgement on the skills of paleontologists working in Indonesia, with respect to working on important finds made in this country, until the appearance of the definitive publication?

In the midst of this vigorous defence, Von Koenigswald slipped an important change into his account. He had initially said that the Modjokerto child's skull had been found on the surface; now it was an excavated fossil, found in a one-metre-deep pit. Had he originally been careless in questioning the collector Andojo about the circumstances of the find, or was Von Koenigswald recasting the truth for convenience? No one would ever know, except Andojo. Years later, scholars tried to unravel the truth of the conflicting stories by asking Andojo to take them to the find-spot. Unfortunately, Andojo was by then elderly and somewhat confused about events long past. On different days, he took different scholars to different places where, he always asserted, he had found the Modjokerto skull.

Despite their vitriolic exchanges, Von Koenigswald sent Dubois additional pictures of the new skull, which Dubois acknowledged in a series of articles published in the Dutch newspaper *Nieuwe Rotterdamsche Courant* though he did not change his mind about the human identity of the skull.

Before long, Von Koenigswald began to modify his position, dropping the idea that this skull was *Pithecanthropus* and calling it *Homo modjokertensis*. A newspaper report of a lecture in late August said,

Concerning the new find, the speaker thinks it is probable, but not proven, that this is a skull of a young *Pithecanthropus*, especially now that stone tools found in Java indicate that we must expect to find a more developed human type. The speaker thus thinks it is better to give the find a new name, *Homo modjokertensis*, since it will only be possible to decide whether this is a child of *Pithecanthropus* or a somewhat higher fossil human once new finds have been made.

A temporary truce was established between Von Koenigswald and Dubois, though the former maintained steadfastly that the child's skull had not been a surface find. The identification of the child's skull with *Pithecanthropus* became 'a POSSIBILITY... although its appearance is also really different from the calvaria of Trinil'. Years later, Von Koenigswald attributed this change of name to a desire to be courteous to the ageing Dubois. At the time, it looked like a sign of uncertainty.

CHAPTER 55

To the Battlefront

The campaign against Dubois was soon joined by Pieter Vincent van Stein Callenfels. A striking and notorious individual, Stein was fully six feet tall and weighed over three hundred pounds, with an enormous beard and a thundering voice to match his size. He was an old Indies hand, having been a planter, an administrative officer, and an inspector for the Dutch Indies Archaeological Service. The newspaper *Handelsblad* referred to his 'glorious disdain for all hierarchical traditions of the official world to which he belongs' and his 'almost inconceivable influence on the Javanese'. Stein imbibed enough for a family of drunkards and ate prodigiously. He was known to the Indonesians as Tuan Setan (Lord Satan) or Tuan Raksasa, after a giant of Hindu mythology with great canine teeth and a fearsome appearance. Stein was simply a force of nature, one of those eccentrics who sometimes flourished in colonial situations, learning multiple languages and dialects and memorizing innumerable local legends, folk tales, and myths. He was also the undisputed world's expert on the archaeology of South-East Asia.

In 1936, at a conference in Oslo, he moved beyond his studies of stones, artefacts, and temples to challenge Dubois's view of human evolution in Java. Stein declared Von Koenigswald's Modjokerto skull to be *Pithecanthropus*, while denigrating the original *Pithecanthropus* as a human–ape chimera comprising a femur from one stratum and a skull from a much older level. It was a battle Dubois had thought won long ago. He suspected that Von Koenigswald and Stein were colluding against him. His anxiety increased when he learned that Stein would lecture on the prehistory of the Indies to the Mijnbouwkundige vereeniging te Delft (Mining Society of Delft) on 28 October 1936. Dubois dispatched his latest assistant, L. D. Brongersma, to the lecture to listen to Stein and report on his remarks.

Stein opened by announcing, disarmingly, that he had no understanding of paleontology, geology, and anthropology, but only about archaeology and the objects made by man. Thus the opinions he gave, Stein said, would be based on information given to him by experts, not on his own knowledge. (This was a clever way of denying responsibility if Stein was later proved wrong, Dubois thought.) 'In former times,' Stein boomed, 'it was thought that the complete fossil vertebrate fauna of Java belonged to one single faunal complex of similar age. The researches of Von Koenigswald have demonstrated convincingly that this is incorrect. One can split the fauna in three (in comparison with the British Indies):

I. Young Pliocene
II. Middle Pleistocene
III. Young Pleistocene/Holocene.'

The most recent period, he said, was adjudged to range from 50,000 to 30,000 years ago and contained *Homo soloensis* from Ngandong; the next, about 300,000 years old, contained *Pithecanthropus erectus* from Trinil; and the most ancient, about 750,000 years old, included the child's skull from Modjokerto. The dates on these periods were not exact, for no precise means of dating ancient rocks had yet been developed. (Indeed, after such methods were perfected many years later, the dates Stein had given proved to be wrong.) '*If*,' Stein added slyly, '*Pithecanthropus* is something, then it is middle Pleistocene.'

Next Stein accused Dubois of documenting the finding of *Pithecanthropus* poorly.

The Chief of Mining, Zwierzycki, searched all existing reports of the excavations for data about the finding of *P.e.* Then it turned out that the reports of the two noncommissioned officers who supervised the excavations at Trinil were missing. Even if these reports are ever found, one cannot rely much on them, because these noncommissioned officers are not scientifically trained. One cannot doubt the place that the femur was found because Dubois himself was present when it was found... Dubois was not present when the skullcap was found, and about that we have only the communications of the noncommissioned officers which, as the speaker has already said, are of no value. It is not impossible that the femur and skullcap do not belong to the same species. Since the faunas of the Middle and Young Pleistocene are very similar, it is also possible that *Homo soloensis* could be found in the Middle Pleistocene and that the femur belongs to *Homo soloensis*. The skullcap, of which the origin is yet unknown, could perhaps be connected with the child skull from Modjokerto, found in the older Pleistocene strata.

Dubois was angered by these words. Kriele and De Winter, though noncommissioned officers, had written him frequent reports and had not been such fools as Stein made them out to be. They were civil engineers, fully trained, and well accustomed to dealing with geology and the placement of objects within the ground. Most unfortunately, Dubois had not been present when any of the *P.e.* fossils were found, despite his dutiful monthly visits to the excavations.

Stein implied that Dubois had been negligent or careless, yet Dubois knew full well that nearly all excavations – including, probably, Stein's own – were carried out by unskilled workmen. The professional men who conceived of such work, analysed the finds, and wrote up the results did not shovel earth themselves, day after day. That lowly task required little more than a dull mind and a strong back. No, the proper role for a paleontologist or archaeologist in such work was to select the excavation site and make sure the men understood how to work carefully. Then one appointed field supervisors and charged them with taking detailed information about important finds made between visits from the professional leader. This was how Dubois had worked, and Davidson Black in China, and Von Koenigswald, too, in Java. Besides, if Dubois had spent all his time at Trinil he would surely have died of malaria long before anything of significance had been found. Stein talked like one unacquainted with the realities of such work in the tropics, but as he was not, his motive was surely malicious. Finally, Stein asserted that he did not believe the missing link existed at all. The only solution, Stein announced boldly, was to fund Von Koenigswald to continue his researches.

While Stein spoke out on his behalf in Europe, Von Koenigswald and his wife had determined to leave Java. They sailed on the SS *Baloeran* on 18 November, planning to visit Berlin, Paris, London, and Leiden to study fossils, visit colleagues, and try to secure a professional position for Von Koenigswald. Everywhere Von Koenigswald went, he talked up the controversy about *P.e.* and the Modjokerto child's skull. It was the only find of great significance that he had made, the only way to demonstrate the importance of his work. He hoped the Modjokerto skull would earn him an academic appointment, and the more people talked about it, the better.

Von Koenigswald delayed calling on Dubois at his Haarlem home until 17 February 1937, though this was one of the most crucial of his planned visits. Von Koenigswald later described the visit to Dubois:

He was stated to be ill and unable to see anyone; but, when I gave my name I was allowed in since I came fresh from Java. Dubois was sitting quietly in his living-room, a big, broad-shouldered, imposing man with a stereotyped, almost embarrassed smile round his mouth. When I cautiously made my request to be allowed to see his original finds (which had been deposited for some years in the Leiden Museum, where they were safer than at Haarlem), I received permission only after he had assured himself in an open telephone conversation with his assistant that I had not already tried to force my way into the sacred halls at Leiden behind his back.

The following day, in Leiden, the double safe was opened for me, and I was allowed to take the finds themselves in my hands. The fragments were dark brown in colour, weighty, and heavily fossilized. The smooth, round skullcap was deeply corroded by acid ground-water... The convolutions of the brain were clearly imprinted on the inside of the skull-cap. Holding the hollow, fragile object in one's hand – during casting it is always filled – one is particularly conscious of its fragmentary nature...

That morning in Leiden was decisive for me in many respects. I was in great difficulties at the time... But that morning it became clear to me that I must return to Java.

This meeting might have been an opportunity to establish a more friendly relationship, but Dubois admitted no correct opinion on matters Javanese except his own. To succeed, Von Koenigswald had to overturn Dubois's work on human evolution in Java; he was determined to bring the old man down. Though Dubois was nearly eighty years old, and weary from a lifetime of conflict, he would never allow his scientific work to be supplanted without a fight. He was an ageing bear, but not yet a dead one.

Youth and energy favoured Von Koenigswald, as did the fact that he had new fossils, the ultimate currency of paleoanthropology. Nonetheless, Von Koenigswald was fearful of the damage that Dubois's fierce opposition might do to his reputation. The showdown would come at a symposium on Early Man to be held at the Academy of Natural Sciences in Philadelphia on 17–20 March 1937. As a relative unknown, Von Koenigswald had been invited at the request of the sponsor of the symposium, John Merriam, who wanted to look over this young friend of Teilhard's. Von Koenigswald prepared with great care.

Dubois was, of course, also invited to the conference. However, the transatlantic trip was long, his health was poor, and he had attended enough scientific conferences to last a lifetime, he thought, never realizing the advantage he was ceding to Von Koenigswald. Dubois preferred to stay at home, with his books and the familiar comforts of De Bedelaar, though he sent a manuscript as a contribution for the conference proceedings. Oppenoorth likewise stayed in Holland. Thus it transpired that Von Koenigswald was the only expert on Indies fossils to attend. He could present the situation, explain his ideas, and secure his reputation without challenges from other authorities.

On the opening day of the conference, Von Koenigswald spoke first. He began his talk innocuously.

In 1890, Professor Eugène Dubois discovered in Trinil, in Central Java, the remains of the famous *Pithecanthropus*, also called Java Man. Since then, Java has become of special interest to scientists working on the problems of fossil man. This short address will give only a review of the latest results on the stratigraphy of the Pleistocene of Java, and its relations to early man.

Professor Dubois was the first to start excavations for fossil mammals in Java (1889–91).

That having been said, Von Koenigswald moved swiftly to attack Dubois's work.

All the remains which he collected belong, in his opinion, to one and the same stratigraphic zone, to which he gave the name 'Kendeng or Trinil zone', and of 'Pleistocene' age, according to his first publications. He later changed his opinion and called this fauna 'Pliocene'. In 1909–10 a German expedition under the leadership of Mrs. Selenka undertook new excavations in Trinil. They confirmed the Pleistocene age of Trinil. The fauna found by this expedition was, however, not as rich as that listed by Dubois.

Painting his own work as far more meticulous, Von Koenigswald revealed a new stratigraphic sequence of *seven* superimposed faunal zones, each recognizable by its typical constellation of mammalian species, where Dubois had only seen one. The Trinil zone, near the middle of the sequence, was the one in which the Modjokerto child's skull was found. Von Koenigswald glossed over the confusion about the place and manner of finding the

Modjokerto skull, although these were key issues if this skull was to be the basis of a revision of Dubois's stratigraphy.

The skull … is perfectly fossilized, and we are certain that it was found *in situ*, because the bone is so thin that it would have been destroyed by any movement or rewashing … [I]t was found in a stratum older than that near Trinil, where *Pithecanthropus* was found.

We also use the name Trinil zone, but in a sense different from that of Dubois. Our Trinil fauna is exactly the same as that described by the Selenka expedition, for the animals of the Dubois list, which are missing here, belong really to an older level, namely the Djetis zone which Dubois did not recognize.

Von Koenigswald then offered an abbreviated, unflattering, and rather inaccurate review of Dubois's assessment of *P.e.*

The first suggestion Dubois made after the find of the skullcap was, that it belonged to a kind of chimpanzee ('*Anthropopithecus*'). Later, when he found the first femur, he chose the name *Pithecanthropus erectus*, which he regarded as a primitive human. He changed his mind a few years ago and now considers it as belonging to a giant gibbon … But since *Sinanthropus* was found in China, which is quite definitely to be considered as a human being, and closely related to *Pithecanthropus*, we are sure about the hominid character of the latter.

Few present at the symposium remembered Dubois as the strong, brilliant young paleontologist of forty years ago, the man who had returned from Java with stunning fossils that turned ideas about human evolution upside-down. All they saw in their minds' eyes was the picture Von Koenigswald painted of the elderly Dubois: old-fashioned, dictatorial, unscientific.

In closing, Von Koenigswald suggested that the *Pithecanthropus* skullcap was simply that of a primitive human, but even *less* primitive than the Chinese *Sinanthropus*. In fact, the *Pithecanthropus* skullcap might even be nothing but a female of the same type of human as the Ngandong Neanderthalers, while the femur derived from another creature entirely.

Dubois was not there to object in person, nor was his paper ever read in its entirety to the conference. His abstract was read aloud on the last day, along with the titles of the papers of other absentees, but by then the damage had been done. Von Koenigswald was in the ascendancy and Dubois had been largely dismissed as an out-of-date scholar – a lucky physician, really. Much the same fate awaited Oppenoorth, whose cogent arguments against Von Koenigswald's grouping of the Ngandong skulls with Neanderthals went unheard.

Merriam and the Carnegie Foundation promised Von Koenigswald financial support, so Von Koenigswald wrote to his chief collector 'in my best Malay', enclosing a cheque to finance the purchase of more fossils at Sangiran.

The Letter

Dubois's perspective on these events was very different. When Von Koenigswald had come to Haarlem, Dubois had made a special trip from De Bedelaar and he did not feel he was being uncooperative or suspicious. Indeed, when Von Koenigswald visited in the early spring of 1937, Dubois was in an unusually mellow frame of mind. On 11 February, he had received an unexpected letter from his old, dear friend, Adam Prentice.

Prentice was the best man Dubois had ever known, the one person who had never failed him, never betrayed him, never worked against him. That business – that silly suspicion – about Anna and Prentice was completely discredited, long forgotten. The light of memory bathed Prentice and those days in Java in a golden glow of youth, of opportunity, of resonant companionship and deep understanding. To hear from Prentice again was like being transported back to those days. Dubois was lost in his fond memories of those times for weeks to come. Though he had always been suspicious of others' ambitions, Dubois was for a time blind to Von Koenigswald's dark intent.

Prentice's letter came to him through the hand of a fellow countryman, C. van den Koppel.

9 February 1937

By sending you the enclosed letter from Mr. Adam Prentice in Kediri, I fulfil a promise given to Mr. Prentice, one that I should have fulfilled earlier. Mr. Prentice asked me to bring the letter to you personally, but although I am almost ½ year in the country, I have not found the opportunity to do so, and I send it now by post to avoid further delay.

As you can see the letter is written almost a year ago. I met Mr. P. at the end of 1935, while travelling from Java to the west coast of Australia, and during this journey of 14 days I became acquainted with him, so that we, notwithstanding the great difference in age, became good friends. Actually he escaped the Indian tax for a year, by being in Scotland and British India, and, because the year was not yet completely expended, he made a trip to and from Singapore to West Australia to use up the rest of the time. He told me a lot about you, and asked me to say hello to you, when I returned to Holland.

Later he wrote to me, however, that he preferred to send you a letter, and sent me this one. Because I travelled via New Zealand, the Philippines, China and Japan, and America, I did not receive his letter until my arrival in Holland in August 1936.

I offer you my apologies, that I did not see to it that the letter reached its destination sooner.

I believe that Mr. Prentice will appreciate it very much when you write him back. He speaks Dutch very well. During the journey I made with him, he was still very healthy, a stately upright figure, who does not look his age. His address is: Mr. Adam Prentice, Kediri, Java.

For weeks, Dubois did not think of conferences, or scientific papers, or academic rivals. He did not think of *P.e.* He only thought of himself young and strong, and of the true companion of his Java days, Adam Prentice, and of his letter.

Kediri, 7 February 1936

An echo of the Past!
'Dost thou recall?'
My dear doctor,

You will hardly expect a letter from *me*! It is long, so very long since last we saw each other …

Dost thou recall from the quietness of your peaceful study in the homeland the days now long, long flown which we passed together in the peaceful atmosphere of dear old Mr. Boyd's Koffeeland Mringin, – the good old man's dwelling Ngrodjo, Willisea the block house he put up for you at Jonojang, my own quiet abode at remote Tempoersarie?

Do you remember the many pleasant meetings we had at Ngrodjo when the old gentleman & I listened with so much interest to your enlightening & informative conversation? Indeed we learned *much* from you and our minds ever reverted with satisfaction to the many agreeable meetings we three had together. Do you recall our excursion to Trinil the scene of your labours (where the famous *Pithecanthropus erectus* was found), when contrary to your wont you regaled us at dinner in the evening with a *bottle of wine* saying it 'aided digestion'.

Do you remember our bathing the next day in the river, our pleasant walk in the afternoon to the station along the country road where a snake swallowed a frog and you at once ran to the rescue forcing the snake to disgorge the frog which, still quite alive, first looked *to the right & to the left*, and then lightheartedly plunged into the stream by the roadside? Do you remember the beautiful flowers at the station which we looked at while waiting for the train? One had a delicate blue tint and you said *that* was well nigh your *favourite* colour!

Do you remember the long walks you & I had through the widespread coffee gardens at Mringin? Do you remember the Nekkie, the big man at Toeloeng Agoeng; the worldly Regent who got a decoration from Batavia but sordidly thought a *sum of money* instead would have been something more useful?

Do you remember the two corporals of the engineers who looked after your team of convicts, at the excavation work? Their mode of life ever amused you – terribly grand, living like kings, at the *beginning* of each month when money was plentiful, and ever on *very* short rations towards the *end* of the month when the money was *all spent*! Through your favourable report they got promoted in time to the rank of Sergeant. Then you photographed them & noticed how they were manoeuvring to bring full into the picture their arm shewing the new sergeant's *stripes*! ... And Mr. Mulder, P. T. Sanvraar, & Mr. Turner, controller, at Toeloeng Agoeng. Do you remember our age – you, Mr. Mulder & I – was 34 years. Ah, yes, the golden days of youth! Perhaps we had our troubles, too, but we had *youth, health, home* and *length of days* before us! Dost thou recall?

As oft as I look back, the recollection of that happy time is a green spot in my memory, and will endure as long as life lasts!

Good old Mr. Boyd died in 1902 at Kediri under Van Buren's care from *cancer of the throat*, aged 74, & was buried at Toeloeng Agoeng. We were all present, and the Asst. Resident, Regent & etc & etc attended also. It may be the kind old man smoked too heavily?

While he still lived we often spoke of you after your departure from Java, very, very, often, & always with esteem & affection. Yes, we both loved you, and never could forget you! Like a sun that had come into our orbit you brought us light and happiness – it was just a chance in life never likely to recur, for *when* does it happen that a man of learning ever comes to live on a coffee estate *for any length of time*? ...

Dubois was now an old man lost in time. The fire in his heart that had once propelled him up mountain slopes and down river-banks was banked and barely smouldering, the light of his intellect that had once burned his path through the academic centres of Europe was dimmed. The memories brought a glow to his once-sharp Garuda eyes, eyes that could see the truth in a glance and that were now faded and rimmed with wrinkles of soft, almost translucent skin. He mused for many months before he composed an answer to his friend. He had to write from the heart, not a simple letter of news or fact, but one of love and remembrance. Oh, yes, he remembered Prentice.

CHAPTER 57

Pretender to the Throne

Dubois was saved from immediate apoplexy but not from harm by his ignorance of Von Koenigswald's actions. Von Koenigswald sent letters full of flattery and praise to the older man, never hinting at the harsh criticisms he had levelled at Dubois.

12 July 1937

Now I am again back in Java, after a very stimulating study journey, and like to thank you heartily once more for the collegial and friendly reception you have given me. Even when I cannot share your scientific opinion on all points, I wish to assure you, esteemed Professor, that I feel for you the greatest personal respect...

Further I have an additional message which you, honoured Professor, will find more interesting than anyone else: I have discovered a mandible fragment of *Pithecanthropus*! That piece was found by my collector, who searches for stone tools and fossils on my behalf in Middle Java. It comes certainly from the Trinil layer...

In fact, the mandible was in the very first basket of fossils from Sangiran that Von Koenigswald examined upon his return. Dubois was in poor health when he received Von Koenigswald's letter, but he responded quickly to the exciting news.

26 August 1937

It gave me a great deal of pleasure to learn that you have had a rewarding and fruitful study journey in America and China – and especially that your return to Java was met with such a find as a mandible fragment of *Pithecanthropus*! From your indication of its geological placement and your short description, I cannot doubt that this is really another piece of the mandible of *Pithecanthropus*. The ramus, the large molars, the small canine...completely agree with that which I found on the fragment from Kedoeng Broebus and also the premolar from Trinil. Your discovery is for me really a great pleasure. I look forward greatly to receiving the photographs which you kindly promise to send me.

Yet something in Von Koenigswald's letter disturbed Dubois. His intuition alerted him to some intangible problem between them. Perhaps he should have offered to be a sort of elder brother to the younger man, guiding him through his scientific work. Von Koenigswald had a very different relationship in mind: Dubois had to recant his ancient ideas and clear the way for the young. The next day, Dubois wrote to Von Koenigswald again:

> This is a continuation of my letter of yesterday...Because of an unexpected disturbance it was written hastily and remained incomplete. I omitted, namely, to say something about the difference in our scientific opinions 'on several points' that you mentioned and to express the hope, which I have long cherished, that we will come to agree, perhaps soon. Allow me to mention something of my own scientific evolution. For many years, I was hindered by my teaching duties (which are now carried out by four men). Under these circumstances my ideas about bioevolution, especially with regard to *Pithecanthropus*, could develop or come to expression only slowly. Actually these ideas started to deviate from the current opinion in 1895 (the year of my return to Europe), because at the time I was firmly convinced that the 'Trinil femur' is not completely human. Facts that I have established during my cephalization research (since 1897), and by the new biology, which considers each organism to be an indivisible whole or entity...have made me realize that *Pithecanthropus* cannot be reckoned to be among the hominids but belongs between the hominids and the most generalized anthropoids, the gibbons. As late as 1923, I did not yet see this. Descent must certainly be accepted from the origin of humans, but not gradual development. Now I hope wholeheartedly that your new discovery will lead to agreement between us about evolution and that we will work together, which in my earnest conviction will be beneficial to science.

It was not a likely outcome.
Von Koenigswald replied:

3 September 1937

My heartfelt thanks for the friendly lines you wrote me and the trust that you expressed in me and my identification. I believe that I have meanwhile succeeded in proving that the mandible fragment belongs to *Pithecanthropus*: a few days ago, from the same layer and totally unexpectedly, there came to light also a skullcap, which completely agrees with your find from Trinil!

... So much for today. The skull is not yet completely prepared so I cannot yet measure my find, but I wanted to inform you personally of it at once, knowing how much it interests you. I really hope that the new find may contribute more clearly to the recognition of the peculiar nature and the systematic position of your *Pithecanthropus*.

Von Koenigswald had first heard of the new skullcap when his collector Atmowidjojo had written saying that they had not found additional orang-utan fossils, but enclosed a part of a human skull. Von Koenigswald left for Sangiran by the night train, anxious to be on the scene and to collect additional pieces of this skull.

Arriving at Sangiran, Von Koenigswald showed the piece around, promising ten cents for every additional piece of skull and one-half or one cent for a tooth. This strategy backfired.

We had to keep the price so low because we were compelled to pay cash for every find; for when a Javanese has found three teeth he just won't collect any more until these three teeth have been sold. Consequently we were forced to buy an enormous mass of broken and worthless dental remains and throw them away in Bandung – if we had left them at Sangiran they would have been offered to us for sale again and again! In spite of the low price, we used to pay several hundred guilders a month for fossils.

Cautiously we began to hunt through the hill-side foot by foot, and soon the first fragments of skull did really come to light. Unfortunately, they were extremely small: too late I realized that my opportunist brown friends were breaking up the largest pieces behind my back in order to get a bigger bonus. I had the good luck to find part of the frontal bone with the eyebrow ridge myself. We hunted on into the afternoon and found in all forty fragments. It was already perfectly clear that we had discovered a new *Pithecanthropus* skull...

Now, the region round the ear is decisive in answering the question, Man or ape?... This find, therefore, proved at last that *Pithecanthropus* was human.

After the skull had been reconstituted I immediately sent a preliminary photograph to old Dubois. I thought he would share my joy that the problem had finally been solved, even hoped he would declare that his first impression of *Pithecanthropus* had been right after all. I was very much mistaken, however.

This account, written twenty years after the fact, was not wholly accurate, for Dubois's response to Von Koenigswald's letter was generous.

In 1937, Von Koenigswald (in pith helmet at right, holding skull fragment) and his workers found many pieces of a skull of *Pithecanthropus* at Sangiran.

14 September 1937

You will understand how great my joy is about this skull find, which, with the mandible you have lately discovered, I am convinced will certainly contribute to the clearer recognition of the peculiar nature and systematic position of *Pithecanthropus*...I am very desirous to be allowed to learn more of your most important finds...

Von Koenigswald replied,

3 October 1937

The preparation of the *Pithecanthropus* skull is now nearly finished It is no longer possible to doubt that one really deals here with a primitive hominid, one which stands at an even lower step than *Sinanthropus*. I will, when there is a chance, report further to you in more detail.

The next month, Von Koenigswald wrote,

12 November 1937

The reconstruction of the new *Pithecanthropus* skull is now complete. I was astonished at how closely the profile of the frontal region resembled your skullcap from Trinil...

Following your suggestion, I have compared the skull once again accurately with a skull of a gibbon, and must unfortunately confess that I cannot confirm your opinion. The hominid character of the new skull can no longer be doubted, for it shows in addition to primitive characters, the following:

– the ear is positioned *under* the root of the cheekbone,

– the jaw joint has a marked articular tubercle, which traits monkeys do not possess and which appear only in humans. The affinity of *Pithecanthropus* with *Sinanthropus* appears even more clearly in the...new skull.

Von Koenigswald prepared a paper on the new jaw, calling it *Pithecanthropus*, which was published in the *Proceedings Koninklijke Akademie van Wetenschappen* (Proceedings of the Royal Academy of Science) on 27 November 1937. Dubois could not accept this identification, he warned Von Koenigswald, so he prepared an opposing paper, which he would present at the Royal Academy meeting on 29 January 1938.

12 January 1938

Now that I have looked closely at the photographic illustration you published and have studied attentively your description in the *Proceedings Koninklijke Akademie van Wetenschappen* of November 27, 1937, I must agree completely with you, that this is the mandible of a human, and in my opinion highly probably of a *Homo soloensis*.

With this important discovery, I wholeheartedly wish you luck. I regret, however, that you have given the owner of this jaw the name *Pithecanthropus*.

Had you sent me the photograph, which you promised me in your letter of July 12, and which I asked for urgently in my letter of October 20...there would be no need for me to offer a communication at the next meeting of the Academy, in which I will demonstrate the inaccuracy of the name you have assigned this jaw.

Von Koenigswald preempted Dubois's January presentation with yet another find. Shortly before the Royal Academy meeting was to take place, Von Koenigswald announced the new skullcap to a meeting of the Natuurwetenschappelijke Raad van Nederlandsch-Indië (Natural Science Council of the Dutch East Indies). As was widely reported in the press, he proclaimed this specimen to be so similar to the Trinil skullcap that the human identity of *Pithecanthropus* was indisputable. Dubois was disheartened and infuriated. Try as he might, he could not seem to publish or speak fast enough to keep up with Von Koenigswald's furious stream of announcements and publications. As Dubois reached his eightieth birthday on 28 January 1938, he was unhappy. Even a cheerful letter from his beloved daughter, Eugenie, and telegrams and cards from dozens of well-wishers around the world (including Von Koenigswald himself) could not console him. No matter what anyone said, Dubois sensed he was being overtaken and thrust aside by a younger man. He hated the sensation.

He lectured on Von Koenigswald's jaw to the Royal Academy on 29 January in an attempt to reestablish the correctness of his own opinions. He quoted extensively from Von Koenigswald's paper on the jaw, contrasting the younger man's views with his own. He pointed out every minute anatomical detail in which Von Koenigswald's new jaw differed from *P.e.* The area of the jaw where the digastric muscle attached, the chin region, and the form of the premolar tooth were 'entirely different'. Throughout the article, he emphasized how gibbonlike the Kedoeng Broebus jaw was and how humanlike Von Koenigswald's jaw from Sangiran was. Dubois also fervently denied the charge Von Koenigswald had made at the Philadelphia conference, that Dubois now considered *P.e.* to be a giant gibbon.

I never imagined *Pithecanthropus* as a 'giant *Hylobates*', only as a giant descendant from a 'generalized' form, which had inherited from its ancestor, the 'gibbonlike appearance', but had…doubled [its] cephalization…Probably, an essential change of diet caused the canine teeth to reduce and the forepart of the mandible and maxilla to shorten and resemble [the] human appearance.

His words made little impact on the listeners, for at that very meeting, Von Koenigswald's description of his new skullcap was read. Dubois sounded like a jealous old man, carping about details, while Von Koenigswald was obviously the up-and-coming expert on Javan paleontology.

On 26 March 1938, Dubois battled back again at a Royal Academy meeting, complaining about Von Koenigswald's reconstruction of the new skullcap. He based his remarks on Von Koenigswald's own words (in letters to Dubois, dated 3 September and 12 November 1937, an article about the find in the *Illustrated London News* of 11 December 1937, Von Koenigswald's communication to the Royal Academy in January 1938), and on Von Koenigswald's photographs of the specimen in various stages of preparation. In particular, Dubois drew attention to three photographs of the new skullcap. Two of these, from the *Illustrated London News*, showed the specimen in pieces, as it had been recovered, and at an early stage of preparation. The third was one Von Koenigswald had sent to Dubois in November, which showed the 'preparated' skullcap. All three photographs revealed the 'great

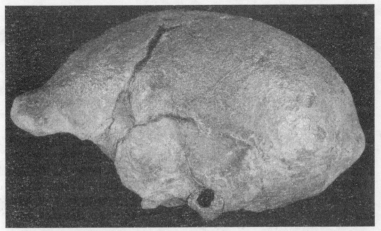

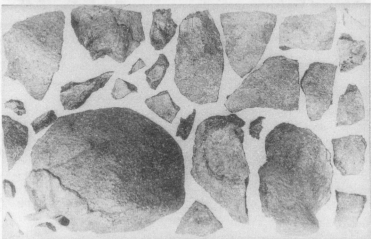

Dubois charged that Von Koenigswald made serious errors in reconstructing the skull of Sangiran II (top) from the many fragments that were found (bottom).

thickness of the skullcap', which distinguished this new skull from
P.e. 'For the general thickness of the cranial bones of *Pithecanthropus*
is only moderate, as is clearly visible and, indirectly, measurable on
the exact photographs, natural size, in my description of 1924.'

Then Dubois homed in on the reconstruction of the skullcap.
He denied the great similarity in shape of the midline profiles of
P.e. and the new skullcap (a similarity of which Von Koenigswald
had written), because the resemblance was false, caused by the 'too
abundant substitution' of plasticine for 'bone substance' that was
'deficient' at the front of the new skull. The extra plasticine eliminated the 'distinct and broad furrow' that had originally separated
the browridge from the forehead in the new skullcap, making the
reconstituted skull resemble *P.e.* in lacking this furrow. However, a
similar furrow was characteristic of more humanlike forms such as
Sinanthropus and *Javanthropus*, Dubois observed. In short, Von
Koenigswald's reconstruction had artificially altered the shape of
the new skull, producing a false resemblance to *Pithecanthropus*
and minimizing features that allied it with *Sinanthropus* or
Javanthropus. 'The real fossil,' Dubois remarked acidly, 'got lost in
the reconstruction.'

There was more. Dubois compared the size of the pieces of the
fragmentary skullcap with that of the 'preparated' skullcap, as
shown in Von Koenigswald's own photographs. Enlarged to
natural size, these images revealed startling changes in the fossil.
Dubois found, for example, that the height of the skull above the
ear hole was 112.5 mm on the fragments but only 102.5 mm on the
reconstructed skull. In another area, Dubois detected a difference
of as much as 18 mm between the pieces and the reconstructed
whole. The net effect of these inaccuracies and distortions, Dubois
concluded, was to transform the shape of the skull 'artificially,
from that of an immature individual into that of a quite adult one.'
He showed Von Koenigswald no mercy: 'Even if this reconstructed
skull were not so obviously artificial, to a large extent, its importance would not be overwhelming, considering that this is not the
only human skullcap which resembles that of *Pithecanthropus*.
This was the case already with the first *Sinanthropus* skull…
[found by] PEI and DAVIDSON BLACK…*Sinanthropus* in
every case is distinguished from *Pithecanthropus* by…significant
characters of the brain.'

Dubois's charge was a serious one, provoking a furious response
from Von Koenigswald.

5 May 1938

Our difference of opinion comes first of all from the fact that you see in *Pithecanthropus* an ape. As I wrote you already, very honoured Professor, the new find does not confirm your opinion...

Unfortunately, I have to remind you, as I said in my original letter, that my letters to you, as well as the photographs, are only meant for your personal information and not for publication.

Dubois replied on June 3.

I may remind you that on November 12, 1937, you literally wrote to me: 'To give you directly an impression of the new find, I send for your personal information a photograph that I made just a few days ago.'

The same photograph, given by you to Professor Weinert, was published already in *Die Umschau* of January 23, 1938...The photograph in your 'A new *Pithecanthropus* skull', only slightly differently oriented, was announced by you on January 29 and appeared in print towards the end of February.

The implication was clear: the photographs had already been published, by both Weinert and Von Koenigswald, when Dubois had included them in his paper. Von Koenigswald wrote to the Royal Academy, arguing that Dubois had accused him of fakery without evidence, since photographs taken at different angles may distort linear measurements. Although Von Koenigswald's reply was not published, Dubois was asked to apologize. He conceded that he did not think Von Koenigswald had *deliberately* altered the form of the skull.

The correspondence between the men was ended, but the fierce struggle between them was not. In April, Von Koenigswald was visited again in Bandung by Teilhard de Chardin, now head of the Laboratoire Palaeontologique of the Sorbonne in Paris. Teilhard was among the first to see Von Koenigswald's newest find from Sangiran, another fragmentary skull that would come to be known as *Pithecanthropus II*. On his side, Dubois tried to enlist Franz Weidenreich, the distinguished German anatomist, who now supervised research and the excavation of *Sinanthropus* remains at Chou Kou Tien. He invited Weidenreich to Haarlem on 8 August 1938, although 'unfortunately I cannot then show you the fossil remains of *Pithecanthropus*'. Weidenreich and Dubois enjoyed their meeting, each recognizing the superb anatomist in the other. After the visit, Dubois wrote to Weidenreich,

In 1938, Dubois (second from left) tried in vain to persuade Franz
Weidenreich (left) that the *Sinanthropus* fossils now in his charge were
distinctly different from both *Pithecanthropus* and Von Koenigswald's
new finds. (Third from left: H. Boschma; right, L. D. Brongersma.)

9 August 1938

I cannot let this day end without sending a heartfelt greeting to you in
Basel, with sincere thanks for what I...know now, for certain, that
we both work in harmony on the greatest scientific question that
there is for us humans. Then, I am now completely convinced of it:
that *Sinanthropus* is the most primitive human, from which
descended all later humans.

Pithecanthropus was, to him, the ape-man ancestor of
Sinanthropus. A few weeks later, after further cordial correspondence with Weidenreich, Dubois wrote happily to Eugenie:

23 August 1938

The meeting with Professor Weidenreich, in which he made it evident
that he inclines toward my view in many points, could make a union
between us possible if he had not tied himself to the position that
Pithecanthropus = *Sinanthropus*, like that. Also therefore he would
not be willing to disown Von Koenigswald, although Weidenreich
has already deviated from him concerning some published points.

Dubois felt he had perhaps found a powerful ally against Von

Koenigswald. In September, he wrote again to Eugenie: 'Weidenreich wrote that he is willing with great delight to work together ... The opponents have become partisans, fighting on the same side. That makes me hopeful.'

Though alliances were being forged in the scientific world, the political world turned ever darker and more divisive. Adolf Hitler controlled Germany, where Jews like Franz Weidenreich were no longer welcome however great their learning. Everyone in Europe, Dubois included, kept a wary eye on the military actions of their aggressive German neighbours.

CHAPTER 58

Old Friends

Dubois paused in his research to write several long overdue letters to Prentice. For the first time in many years, he felt at ease. As in the old days, it was a relief to spell out to Prentice all his concerns and thoughts, his trials and his battles. Prentice, loyal as ever, replied late in November.

Kediri, 28 November 1938

My dear old Friend,

Your letters of 15th and 19th August reached me safely and I was ever so pleased to know you still remembered me kindly notwithstanding the passing of so many long years since we sojourned at Mringin & enjoyed daily converse, often too in the company of our dear friend and wellwisher good old Mr. Boyd, but for whom we might never have met.

Very much has happened since those days yet my thoughts ofttimes revert to you, and I ever hoped all would be well with you & yours through the years that intervened.

Yes, in quiet moments the past returns fondly to mind:–

'Oft in the stilly night
When other thoughts have found me,
Fond memory brings the light
Of other days around me.'

As one advances in years one oft looks back on sweet days that are gone & on the sunny friendships of radiant youth. When you resided in Java we were in the bloom of early manhood physically fit for any task we set ourselves. We knew no pain or ache and were able to walk for hours without fatigue & could climb mountains! I ascended the Ardjoeno above Lalie Djuvo once. You climbed it too, & wrote your name on the rock beside my name. Can you recollect? It was long long ago.

Do you remember the visit to Trinil when Mr. Boyd & I came to pass a day with you at the place you made famous; of our bathing next day in the river; and our long pleasant walk in the afternoon (the three of us) from Trinil to the railway station? It was such a pleasant leisurely walk that afternoon through the peaceful countryside engaged in agreeable and interesting conversation all the way. We arrived at the railway in ample time. Outside the halte [station] there were flowers growing. The blossoms were of a delicate blue, & you told me that was a favourite colour of yours. The recollection of our visit to Trinil & the happiness you made us feel when there can never be forgotten. As often as I see the name Trinil mentioned I think of you and your labours, & of the happy day spent with you there. You had been some days busy at Trinil when, by appointment, Mr. Boyd & I called over, eager to see the place so often mentioned. And it was pleasant the three of us returning together in a happy frame of mind to Toeloeng Agoeng, no one left behind solitary & alone. Ah those delightful days!

Good Mr. Boyd passed away in 1902 of cancer of the throat aged 74 years. His two younger sons Alex & Robert, both engaged in coffee, died some years ago aged 60 & 70. The eldest son William Boyd my oldest remaining friend in Java after being long sick died 6 weeks ago over 81 years of age. His memory had gone, yet revived at intervals. Sometimes he didn't know even his own children & asked who they were, yet he always knew ME when I called. His decline arose largely I fear from the worry of straitened circumstances. When too old to work in coffee he became Secretary of the Kediri Planters Association. When his memory failed later on, the Association gave him a small pension of F75 a month, not much, but better than nothing at all in these hard times. The world crisis that struck Java in 1930, & is still with us, half ruined Java, & Wm. Boyd like ALL OF US suffered heavily! All values are 50 to 80% down here today. Hardly anyone can make any money now. People – Europeans & Native alike – are just able to live by practising economy. What money Wm. Boyd made – it wasn't much – went into houses, & house property here is down 75% & 80% in value. This no doubt preyed upon my friend's mind for he had a mortgage on his house property & sale today would hardly cover the mortgage, while leaving nothing to his heirs. Well William Boyd was the last of my old planting friends. That generation has now all but passed away!

We are all getting older. You are now in your 81st year, and like Newton still deeply engaged in scientific work. I am very glad indeed of THAT, for I know full well that to YOU study and research are labours of love without which life would lose its chief interest! I earnestly hope you will yet long be spared in good health to continue your researches and that you will see your views adopted by all whose opinion you value!

The luminous dissertation in your last letter to me re *Pithecan-thropus* I have read and reread with deep interest, & must read & reread it again. Assuredly you have the gift of clear exposition! And as I read your convincing statement of the points at issue I could not help thinking of old Mr. Boyd & the pleasure he always felt when you dropped in upon him of an afternoon or evening at Ngrodjo. He delighted in your discourse & appreciated so much the clear way in which you would explain questions he asked concerning matters on which he yearned for more light. Your stay at Mringin was most agreeable to him, & ever afterwards he spoke of you in terms of sympathy & sincere good will. We felt that a dear friend had left us and we might perchance meet him no more, but he would never fade from our mind & heart!

Returning to your disquisition I see that there are three groups among the learned –

(a) those who consider *P.e.* to be a missing link
(b) those who consider him a man ape
(c) those who regard him as the most primitive of all types of man.

You hold the first view (group a) still, just as you did before. I am glad of that. I remember at Mringin you gave me as your opinion that *P.e.* was really a missing link, there would be a series, not one link only (yet no other has been found). Of course I am speaking from memory here, for I find I have preserved nothing in writing.

Well, not long ago, it might be in January of this year, I read in a newspaper that you had altered your view, & now considered *P.e.* to be a ... GIBBON. Somehow I felt sad on reading that, but felt: – Well, if my friend has really ultimately changed his view it will only have been after yet deeper study on the subject. For the seeker after truth must ever keep an open mind, willing to suppress all predilections and weigh honestly any further evidence adduced even should it lead him to modifying beliefs long & fondly held. I knew YOUR mind would ever be open to the truth & give new facts & evidence an impartial hearing.

By post I send you the newspaper article in question where I read of your 'change' of view. It is the *Soerabaja Handelsblad* (I think of January this year but unfortunately the date is NOT printed above). It is written by G. H. R. von Koenigswald. Thinking of you, I put the paper aside for reference ...

In your own long long strenuous study of the subject endless questions and suggestions will have presented themselves to your mind & each been sifted & weighed as it arose.

When the learned are at variance it would be a mere presumption for an outsider like ME to speak positively. But looking at the question broadly I think the great majority of those who reflect on the matter will accept YOUR views. For, as far as scientific training & mental endowment are concerned, you are as fully qualified as any man living to arrive at the truth of the matter. And with qualifications equal to the most learned, YOU have made a profounder, more continuous study of the subject from month to month & year to year during half a century. So you have DEEPER knowledge & a FIRMER GRASP of all the intricacies of the case, and are consequently MORE ABLE to speak WITH AUTHORITY than any man. Were it for a court of law to judge, your evidence would win the case. But it is here no question for law courts but for the considered verdict of the scientist after due study & full & searching examination.

The German mission which came to Java in 1907 went to Trinil & worked there but found nothing. They averred however that at the time *Pithecanthropus erectus* lived in Java, MAN had already appeared ELSEWHERE on the globe. Here too I am speaking from MEMORY. Their assertion gives rise to much thought but I won't go farther in the matter as my letter is long enough already & I would not weary you with the musings of an outsider.

I also send a newspaper 23 Aug 1938 with a startling article entitled:– 'Revolution in Science'.

It is too deep for ME! It is also written in such an iconoclastic spirit that I would rather form no opinion at all but wait for the learned to deal with the matter.

Well, I must now close with every good wish from your old friend who remains

Very Sincerely Yours,
Adam Prentice

P.S. I am sending my letter by the ordinary mail so that it allows of the newspapers reaching you AT THE SAME TIME, & not leave you in any doubt as to what the newspaper article said about changed views (which are not changed at all). If I sent my letter by air mail & the newspapers by steamer mail you would be puzzled & be filled with uncertainty FOR WEEKS before the newspapers came to hand.

The letter from Prentice brought Dubois peace at the closing of the year. The world was in turmoil, the scientific world was being turned upside-down by young hotheads like Von Koenigswald who did not know of what they wrote, but Prentice was still Prentice: loyal, supportive, sound and true. Dubois passed a cold but contented Christmas at De Bedelaar, his mind filled with thoughts of warmer climes and golden friendships. It was the last communication between the two men, Prentice and Dubois, who had meant so much to each other through the years.

CHAPTER 59

The Final Conflict

Dubois's hoped-for alliance with Weidenreich against Von Koenigswald did not materialize. Weidenreich left Dubois to meet with Von Koenigswald in Java and study his new finds. Weidenreich was swayed by the young man's marvellous fossils, his charm, and his knowledge. Besides, Dubois's denial that any of the new fossils from Java or China were the same as *P.e.* was simply irrational. Before leaving, Weidenreich invited Von Koenigswald and his wife to bring the Sangiran fossils to Peking, so that the Chinese and Javan materials might be compared side by side. The two Germans, each far from home, became frequent collaborators and co-authors. The planned visit to Peking, described later by Von Koenigswald, occurred early in 1939.

We laid out our finds on the large table in Weidenreich's modern laboratory: on the one side the Chinese, on the other the Javanese skulls. The former were bright yellow and not nearly so strongly fossilized as our Javanese material; this is no doubt partly owing to the fact that they were much better protected in their cave than the *Pithecanthropus* finds, which had been embedded in sandstone and tufa. Every detail of the originals was compared: in every respect they showed a considerable degree of correspondence ... The two fossil men are undoubtedly closely allied, and Davidson Black's original conjecture that *Sinanthropus* and *Pithecanthropus* are related forms – against which Dubois threw the whole weight of his authority – was fully confirmed by our detailed comparison.

Convinced that they had resolved the matter at last, Von Koenigswald and Weidenreich wrote an article for *Nature* which they called 'The relationship between *Pithecanthropus* and *Sinanthropus*'. Their conclusion was straightforward and clear: 'Considered from the general point of view of human evolution, *Pithecanthropus* and *Sinanthropus*, the two representatives of the Prehominid stage, are related to each other in the same way as two different races of present mankind, which may also display certain variations in the degree of their advancement.'

But they could not convince Dubois, although scientific opinion was now in their favour and remained so.

For Dubois, only *P.e.* was a transitional ape-man; only *P.e.* occupied that precious ancestral position in human evolution. He would never relinquish this view. Weary, saddened, and frightened by recent political events, Dubois worked slowly on his response to Von Koenigswald's and Weidenreich's paper. Remembering his own times of trial, Dubois decided to take up the weapon of public pressure against Von Koenigswald as it had once been used against him. He tried to organize an international protest from the scientific community to the Royal Academy of Sciences, asking that the new Javan fossils be sent to Holland where they might be accessible for study. It was a failure. Some of his friends and colleagues sent letters urging the government to send the fossils back to Europe. Others declined to write on the grounds that Von Koenigswald was making quick work of publishing the remains and ought to be allowed to complete his studies, as a reward for his energy in finding them.

By the time Von Koenigswald's and Weidenreich's paper equating *Pithecanthropus* with *Sinanthropus* was published, other matters had assumed greater importance than controversies over human evolution. On 1 September 1939, Germany invaded Poland, and the world was at war. Dubois remained at De Bedelaar, deep in the country and far away from major military targets and cities. Soon Anna, her sister, and some of her sister's children also sought refuge there, for they feared correctly that it would not be long before Germany invaded the Netherlands, too. At least in the country there was simple food and some rural safety, away from the horrors of bombs and tanks and troops. Dubois worked slowly on yet another attack on Von Koenigswald; Anna and her sister tried to stock up on food and provisions to get them through the winter, with the help of a girl from the village. Dubois was still hale for a man his age, but there was a great deal of wood to be chopped for fuel and cooking and he had to seek help from younger neighbours. He still walked through his grounds and swam when the air was warm enough, but he was not the vigorous man he once had been. Just before his eighty-second birthday, he wrote to Eugenie, who would yet herself flee to De Bedelaar as the war progressed:

In his last years, Dubois lived at De Bedelaar, where Anna and her sister also sought refuge after the Germans' invasion of the Netherlands. This photograph was taken December 19, 1939.

3 January 1940

I am here, indeed, ailing, working in this much too confined space, now I still have so much to do and must do. For all that, I cannot let what I have achieved AS BY A WONDER come to nothing, by the blindness (and worse) of SOME others. Unfortunately difficulties put in the way from that quarter become continually bigger. It also becomes clearer to me, the longer this goes on, that from that quarter it is not about the TRUTH, but about the fight for what they see as hostile for mankind, for on that side they think completely wrongly about me ... I have explained to them that my researches have delivered certain evidence for the animal descent and definite descent of humans, not by gradual transformation (as according to Darwinism) but by two big leaps, leaps that have taken place everywhere in the animal kingdom – which the religious believers can and will consider to be creation. My opponents do not understand that, or rather refuse to understand it, and ascribe to me other motives than the search after the objective truth.

In March, Dubois's paper against Von Koenigswald – the first of three parts – was read before the Royal Academy of Science. It stated Dubois's objections clearly.

The child skull of Modjokerto, the mandible and the skull of Sangiran, all of them undoubtedly human, I was convinced in my own mind were morphologically distinct from *Pithecanthropus* and belonged at the same time to the proto-Australian fossil man of Java, well known under the name of *Homo soloensis* ...

Nevertheless, this '*Pithecanthropus IV*' skull was formerly, at the time that it was complete, uncrushed, and unweathered, viz., during life, as it appears to me, an exact Wadjak-man, or Solo-man, skull ...

Needless to repeat that *Sinanthropus pekinensis* is another member of the same proto-Australian group ...

Dubois could not help but see the parallels between his scientific struggles and world politics. There was strife on all sides: political, scientific, and personal. So strong was his faith in science that he hoped that a correct and accurate view of the unity of man's ancestry, and the primitiveness that had been left behind, might do much to help. He wrote again to Eugenie of these thoughts in April 1940.

3 April 1940

The circumstances are now such that nobody knows what the present situation will become, but we all feel that this, in many ways, will become SOMETHING BETTER than the recent past, because ALL nations will be compelled to reconsider themselves, and us all, in our former conceptions. Many already feel some favourable effects from that reconsideration, concerning the merits of acquiescence and intention to do their best.

On 10 May 1940, German troops invaded the Netherlands. Three days later, the Dutch government fled to exile in London and the Netherlands became occupied territory. Events were so grim and shocking that scholarly issues seemed insignificant. In June, the second part of Dubois's paper was presented, in which he spoke of the way ideas about the evolutionary process distorted assessments of the fossils themselves.

Now twenty-two years after Stewart Arthur Smith's publication [on the fossil human skulls of Talgai, Queensland], we observe, in a strikingly similar case, Von Koenigswald and Weidenreich led astray to the same mistake, by the same belief in evolution from Ape to Man through gradual transformation of parts of the body. This belief, in matters of evolution, results from almost exclusive morphological consideration of the organisms. Hence the apparent ... inconsiderate [ill-considered] supposition of those investigators, that the large, bestial canines of the apes are mainly organs of defence, and became gradually smaller and less apelike in the course of man's phylogenetic development ... Such a gradual transformation from Ape to Man is hardly conceivable ...

Apparently, Von Koenigswald, in his opinion about the nature of his finds ... [relies] more on (insufficient) stratigraphical data than on unprejudiced examination of the fossil remains themselves. No wonder that his implicit belief in human evolution from Ape to Man, by gradual transformation of parts of the body, would lead him astray about the true nature of his finds, and wrongly guide the hand which made the restorations ...

No one really listened to Dubois any more. International congresses attended by all the scientists of Europe and America were a thing of the past. Weidenreich fled China for America, getting out shortly before the Japanese invasion, but he was unable to save the *Sinanthropus* fossils. They were seized by Japanese troops and disappeared for ever, leaving only the casts, photographs, x-rays, and measurements Weidenreich had compiled. Communications with Java were so difficult after the Japanese invaded that it was years before anyone knew whether Von Koenigswald was alive. He survived internment in a prisoner-of-war camp and eventually joined Weidenreich in New York, at the American Museum of Natural History. The Sangiran and Modjokerto fossils had been safely hidden by neutral Swedish and Swiss friends, while Von Koenigswald's indomitable wife, Luitgarde, had kept the one she had deemed most important in her apron pocket throughout the war.

Events in the Netherlands were also grim. Month by month, week by week, Dutch Jews were deprived of all ordinary rights. The abundant food produced by the rich Dutch countryside was seized and shipped to the German troops, leaving little for the populace. Resistance to the German occupation grew, covertly, as German treatment of the Dutch worsened.

Dubois tried to reassure Eugenie, but the news was never good.

4 October 1940

Also in these surroundings it is not at all restful, although De Bedelaar remains untouched. We saw MANY Very lights, for months, and many bombs exploded in the environs. For cooking and heat we have mainly wood. Food is not plentiful, but sufficient. Certainly there are 'indeed worse things than to suffer from cold and to be hungry' and the 'worse things' are bearable through moral strength. The world will, IN THE END, for mankind in general, become better. What is nature, the sun, the plants and animals, but an encouragement and the more one can study nature, the better one can appreciate her magnitude and beauty. Then, one understands even the present world as a natural phenomenon, too, and perceives all horror as such.

He wrote again in a few weeks.

28 October 1940

Now I suffer from cold, in my study (second storey) with the small base-burner, which stood in times gone by in the reception room, bell floor, in Haarlem...I have still so much urgent work to do, that becomes clearer every day to me from what is published around me...because on these subjects (especially anthropological ones), the ideological principles of the present world war rest.

When the German patrols came through De Bedelaar, they saw only an aged man, his elderly wife, and her sister. No one ever guessed that this nondescript old man had shaped the course of modern paleoanthropology. Indeed, once Eugenie was at De Bedelaar, the apparent reality was even more deceptive. With the courage and independence that she had inherited from her father, Eugenie – seemingly an ordinary, middle-aged woman – set up an escape line for downed Allied flyers. She housed them in the cellars of De Bedelaar and hid their weapons under the apples stored for the winter.

In November, the last of Dubois's trilogy of protests against Von Koenigswald was read at the meeting of the Royal Academy. Attendance was very poor, as was expected. Even now, Dubois could not shake his bone-deep certainty of the importance of *P.e.* for understanding both the process of evolution and the origin of the human species. He could not abandon *P.e.*, though she was imprisoned where he could not reach her, at the Natural History Museum in Leiden. Still, he could not let her be slandered or forgotten. *P.e.* had been his life, his great discovery, his tribute to

Science and Truth, in pursuit of which he had expended his life and energies. He had to persevere.

Dubois's arguments were familiar by now, having been reiterated and elaborated in many venues. *Pithecanthropus* was the only true missing link; *Sinanthropus* and *Homo soloensis* and the new Sangiran fossils were merely early humans. Dubois's closing words were poignant:

It is most regrettable, that for the interpretation of the important discoveries of human fossils in China and Java, WEIDENREICH, VON KOENIGSWALD and WEINERT were thus guided by preconceived opinions, and consequently did not contribute to (on the contrary they impeded) the advance of knowledge of man's place in nature, what is commonly called human phylogenetic evolution. Real advance appears to depend on obtaining material data in an unbiased way...

There, Dubois thought as he wrote the last lines, I have said it. I have stated my credo, my opinions, and it remains for the world to judge who is right. But it is I who will be remembered as the man who found the missing link, and it is I who have defended and understood her better than anyone.

As the bitterly cold winter closed in, Dubois spent more and more time thinking of days gone by, living in his mind in a warm place, where the sun shone so brightly and the mountains were cloaked in shadowy green forests. Prentice was always by his side, young and handsome and fit. He remembered sitting with Prentice at the top of Ardjoeno, tired from the climb and yet too young and healthy to really notice the exertion. There they had sat, back to back, looking at the world spread at their feet. There they had carved their names in the rock, side by side to show they were companions, not one the leader and the other the follower. There their names rested still, hardly softened by the ravages of time or the hurtling downpour of tropical monsoon, he supposed. That was something which would last: that, and *P.e.*

He supposed Prentice was dead by now, and he felt he probably would not survive the winter himself. He ached with the cold and the deprivation and the misery of the German occupation, for every freedom or right that the Dutch once took for granted was now denied them. Science was still there, true and brave and difficult, but he had no heart to pursue her any longer. He was very tired: tired of trying so hard, tired of fighting, tired of being alone and misunderstood, tired of seeing the hellish downward spiral the

Dubois died on 16 December, 1940, and was buried in an
unconsecrated corner of the cemetery at Venlo, under a special
tombstone.

world had taken. To continue to hope and believe in the face of all
this took more courage than he could muster on most days.

On, 16 December 1940, Dubois died in his bed of a heart attack.
He was buried in the cemetery at nearby Venlo. His grave lay in an
unconsecrated corner, for Eugenie knew he would not rest easy
among the graves of fervent Catholics and Protestants. Besides, it
would have been an abomination to deny his convictions now. She
ordered a special tombstone.

Prof. Dr. Eug. Dubois

28–1–1858   16–12–1940

Above these words was a carving of a skull and crossbones, the
universal symbol of poison. In this case, the bones were recogniz-
ably those of *P.e.*

An Underestimated Man

In the years that have passed since his death, Eugène Dubois has not been forgotten in scientific circles. His discovery of *Pithecanthropus erectus*, the first specimen of a species that anthropologists now call *Homo erectus*, would be sufficient to ensure his fame, even without the extraordinary story of his deliberate decision to search for the missing link and his courage in doing so.

Despite the significance of his finds and an excellent appraisal of his scientific work by Theunissen, Dubois has been an underestimated man. Few anthropologists – and fewer still among the general public – have credited him with focusing the attention of the scientific community on human origins. The record clearly shows that his research and his perseverance made human evolution a controversial and exciting topic of general interest. The importance of his monograph is largely overlooked, yet it showed the missing link to be a transitional form between humans and apes, rather than a primitive human race. Perhaps the brevity of his monograph worked against Dubois, for later scholars produced monographs that dwarfed his in length and thoroughness. Surely, too, the harsh criticism meted out to Dubois – the very criticism that established the standard format for such monographs – slighted its true quality. It must not be forgotten that Dubois, sitting in a remote area of Java, singlehandedly created the conceptual framework now used in the analysis of all fossil hominid remains. It was groundbreaking work.

So, too, was his research on body-size and brain-size ratios, work that was the forerunner of the enormous field of allometric studies in biology. Dubois's contributions to cephalization studies were strongly criticized for their lack of statistics in the 1930s and 1940s, and, sadly, fell into disrepute for decades. Not until his innovative work was rediscovered and defended by scholars such as Harry Jerison, in his 1973 book *The Evolution of the Brain and Intelligence*, did the study of the allometry of the brain become once again a central issue in evolutionary biology.

Tragically, Dubois's strong personality and irascible disposition harmed his reputation. Whatever Dubois did, it was with such focused intensity that he drew criticism as a lightning rod draws electricity. He challenged, argued, insisted, persevered; he stretched the minds of his friends and enemies alike; he demanded of those around him an ever higher standard of thinking and performance. No one ever forgot Dubois; no one who ever knew him was the same afterwards. Though inadvertently, this paranoid, brilliant and stubborn man truly cast his own fate.

When and how Dubois's steadfast friend, Adam Prentice, died is unknown. His death is not recorded in the archives at the Centraal Bureau voor Genealogie. I could not find his grave in Java, nor was his son Gerardus Prentice-MacLennan listed in the Malang, Solo, or Jakarta phone books. If Prentice was still alive when the Japanese invaded Java in 1942, he surely died during the occupation, when many Europeans were interned and even those at liberty suffered harsh conditions. However, in 1973, Adam Boyd – the son of William Boyd (the Old Warrior's son) and of Prentice's daughter by his *nyai* – chanced to see the photograph of Robert Boyd and the tiger cub at Mringin in a book on human evolution. Because the same photo had hung in his father's office in Java, Boyd recognized it. Eventually he contacted Jean M. Dubois, Eugène's grandson, who gave Boyd a duplicate photo and put him in touch with Eugenie and Carel Hooijer. The correspondence between these descendants of Prentice and Dubois provides all I know of the fate of Adam Prentice.

Dubois's last battle, against Von Koenigswald, was particularly unfortunate. His position was scientifically indefensible, for Von Koenigswald's finds were surely the same species as the Trinil fossils (as were Davidson Black's *Sinanthropus* fossils from China). Worse yet, his feud with Von Koenigswald was politically unwise. Even in his lifetime, Dubois was portrayed as a lunatic who hid the fossils away; in his latter years, he was accused of having recanted and assigned his precious *P.e.* to some species of fossil gibbon. Neither of these is true; he was neither a madman nor a fool. He was simply a man of singular vision, a man who longed for but did not need affirmation of his ideas in order to act. When he died he left behind many enemies, younger scientists who were all too ready to believe the worst of him. His story became notorious, told and mistold many times, until it reached mythic proportions. It is time now for the truth, and I have told it.

Notes

Nearly all primary sources can be found in the Dubois Archives at the Naturalis, Leiden, The Netherlands. Letters held in the archives are referred to by sender, recipient, and date. In this context, 'Dubois' refers to Eugène Dubois only; other members of his family (Anna, Victor, Eugenie) are referred to by their first names only. The exceptions are Jean M. Dubois, the living grandson of Eugène, and his father Jean M. F. Dubois, the eldest son of Eugène. Other major sources are Dubois's pocket agendas (a sort of daily calendar); his journals, diaries, and notes; newspaper clippings he saved on scientific issues; his photographs, negatives, and glass slides; drafts of manuscripts and lectures; and various drafts of brief autobiographies, which are also kept in the Archives. I relied as well on the diaries of J. J. A. Bernsen, OFM, Dubois's assistant from 1930 to 1932, in which many conversations with Dubois are recorded apparently verbatim. His diary entries are cited as 'Bernsen diary', followed by the date of the entry. They are quoted with permission of the Dutch Franciscans. I have also used unpublished manuscripts and information about Dubois compiled by the late L. D. Brongersma, Dubois's last assistant, stored in the Dubois Archives in Leiden.

ABBREVIATIONS:

BRP   Bloys van Treslong Prins, P.C., 1993. *Bronnenpublikaties van de Indische Genealogische Vereniging*, vol. 5: *Grafschriften van Europeanen in Nederlandsch-Indië*. 's Gravenhage: E. J. C. Boutong de Katzmann.

BS   B.S. Name-List/Address-book of the Dutch Indies 1822–1923

GHG   Bloys van Treslong Prins, P.C., *Genealogische en Heraldische Gedenkwaardigheden betreffende Europeanen op Java*, vol. 1–4. 1934–1959. Batavia: Drukkerij Albrecht.

INN   Anonymous, 'Uitgegeven de Indische Genealogische Vereniging' vols. 1–10. *De Indische Navorscher*, 1988–1999. 's Gravenhage.

JAI   *Journal of the Anthropological Institute of Ireland and Great Britain*
NT   *Natuurkundig Tijdschrift voor Nederlandsch-Indië*
PKAW   *Proceedings Koninklijke Akademie van Wetenschappen*
TAG   *Tijdschrift van het Koninklijk Nederlandsch Aardrijkskundig Genootschap*
Verslag *Verslag van de gewone vergaderingen der wis- en natuurkundige afdeeling der Koninklijke Akademie van Wetenschappen te Amsterdam.* After 1925, this journal was continued as *Verslag van de gewone vergaderingen der afdeeling natuurkunde, Koninklijke Akademie van Wetenschappen te Amsterdam.*
VM   *Verslag van het Mijnwezen. Extra bijvoegel der Javasche courant*

CHAPTER 1. AN ECHO OF THE PAST

2 'My dear doctor': letter, Prentice to Dubois, February 7, 1936.
5 He'd had a beautiful nyai: letter, Adam Boyd to Jean M. Dubois, 5 November 1973; letter, C. R. Hooijer to Jean M. Dubois, 11 December 1974.

CHAPTER 2. THE BEGINNING

10 Dubois had been born on 28 January: Basic information about Dubois's life is summarized in Dubois's autobiographical notes in the Dubois Archives; Anonymous, 'Professor Dr. Eug. Dubois', *Vierde-Blad Avondblad*, 27 January 1933; Anonymous, 'Prof. Dubois blikt over zijn leven terug', *De Telegraaf*, 27 January 1938; L. D. Brongersma, 'Eugène Dubois', *Natuurhistorich maandblad*, 1973, vol. 62: 107–109; L. D. Brongersma, '*Pithecanthropus*: Echt en Pseudo' *Verslag*, 1982, vol. 91: pp. 34–36; L. D. Brongersma, 'Professor dr. Eug. Dubois', *Nieuwe Rotterdamsche Courant*, 28 January 1938; P. Tesch and L. D. Brongersma, 'Eugène Dubois'. *Geologie en Mijnbouw*, 1941, vol. 3, no. 2: pp. 29–33; B. Theunissen, *Eugène Dubois and the Ape-man from Java*, 1989, Dordrecht: Kluwer Academic Publishers; B. Theunissen and J. de Vos, 'Eugène Dubois, ontdekker can de rechtopgaande aapmens,' *Natuurhistorisch maandblad* 1982, vol. 71, nos. 6–7: pp. 107–114; C. D. W. Vrijland, 'Nóg herinnering aan Professor Dubois', *Teylers magazijn*, 1993, voorjaar, p. 14; A. van der Welff, 'Herinneringen

een merkwaardige geleerde: Eugène Dubois', *Teylers magazijn* 1992, najaar, pp. 6–7.

16 There, sitting on that bench: Description based on author's visit to house in Eijsden and information from the current owners, Mr and Mrs Hovens.

17 'do apes have churches?': Karl Vogt's lecture and this specific question are described in Anonymous, 'Prof. Dubois blikt', *De Telegraaf*, 1938; Dubois's autobiographical notes in the Dubois Archives; and Brongersma, 'Eugène Dubois', 1973.

20 By the end of his first year: Bernsen diary, 25 September 1931; letter, Dubois to Boeke, 3 March 1932.

20 'I always knew': Bernsen diary, 13 February 1931, last two sentences of quotation added.

21 Roermond was a good place: Dubois's autobiographical notes; Anonymous, 'Prof. Dubois blikt', *De Telegraaf*, 1938.

21 'As a consequence': E. Haeckel, *The History of Creation*, 1892, fourth English edition, London: Kegan Paul, Trench, Trubner & Co., pp. 7–9. Dubois's copy was the German version, *Natürliche Schöpfungsgeschichte*, 1868, Berlin.

CHAPTER 3. THE GAME

24 'The Ape-like men': Haeckel, *History*, 1892, p. 398.

24 'Those process of development': ibid., pp. 405–6.

24 Haeckel even hypothesized: ibid., p. 406.

25 Marie – his favourite sister: That Marie became an Ursuline sister is documented in Brongersma, 'Eugène Dubois', *Natuurhistorisch maandblad*, 1973. The impact of her decision upon Dubois is unknown.

CHAPTER 4. AMBITION

30 It was Friday: Bernsen diary, 19 November 1931, and 13 February 1931.

31 Now that he could organize things: Bernsen diary, 19 November 1930.

33 Dubois would have preferred: Bernsen diary, 17 December 1930.

33 Why had Fürbringer: Bernsen diary, 17 December 1930, and 29 January 1931.

34 If he became the man who understood the larynx: Dubois's autobiographical notes.

Chapter 5. Lightning Rod

35 Dubois called on Mia Cuypers: Bernsen diary, 19 November 1930; also Theunissen, *Eugène Dubois*, 1989, p. 48.

39 the Honourable Mr F. G. Taen-Err-Toung: Mia Cuypers's love affair with Taen-Err-Toung and marriage to him was a notorious scandal later used by her cousin, Lodewijk Van Deyssel, as the basis for his 1892 novel, *Blank en geel* (White and Yellow) according to Theunissen, *Eugène Dubois*, 1989, p. 48.

42 'I have been told': Bernsen diary, 19 November 1931.

Chapter 6. Love and Conflict

45 Anna Geertruida Lojenga: The meeting and courtship of Anna and Dubois are described in Jean M. F. Dubois, 'Trinil: A Biography of Prof. Dr. Eugène Dubois the Discoverer of *Pithecanthropus erectus*,' 1957, unpublished ms. in Dubois Archives, pp. 20ff, and Bernsen diary, 25 September 1931. Engagement announcement and wedding invitation in the Dubois Archives, Naturalis.

46 Anna's parents insisted: J. M. F. Dubois, 'Trinil', 1957, p. 20ff.

50 Was he trying to claim credit: Bernsen diary, 29 January 1931.

51 intellectually she stood not so high: Bernsen diary, 4 May 1931.

51 out of a kind of romantic chivalry: ibid.

51 They were wed: Dates of the marriage and of the Dubois children's births are recorded in the family tree and genealogical quarters compiled by Dubois and stored in the Dubois Archives, along with the wedding invitation.

52 Teaching was for Dubois a nightmare: Theunissen, *Eugène Dubois*, 1989, pp. 27, 49, based on a personal communication from one of Dubois's students, F. H. van der Marel.

52 'So the question arises': letter, Fürbringer to Dubois, 2 October 1886.

52 A colleague, Max Weber: F. Pieters and J. de Visser, 'The scientific career of the zoologist Max Wilhelm Carl Weber (1852–1937)', *Bijdragen tot de Dierkunde*, 1993, vol. 62, no. 4, pp. 193–214.

Chapter 7. Turning Point

60 Max Lohest…Marcel de Puydt: Anonymous, 'Prof. Dubois blikt', *De Telegraaf*, 1938.

61 Johannes Fuhlrott [and] Hermann Schaaffhausen: H. Schaaffhausen, 'On the crania of the most ancient races of man', *Natural History Review*, 1 April 1861, no. 2, pp. 155–80. Tr. by George Busk from

H. Schaaffhausen, 'Zur Kentniss der ältesten Rassenschädel', *Archiv für Anatomie, Physiologie und wissenschaftliche Medicin*, 1858, vol. 2, pp. 453–88.

61 a powerful and formidable opponent: An account of the debates over the original Neanderthal fossils is given in E. Trinkaus and P. Shipman, *The Neandertals*, 1992, New York: Alfred A. Knopf.

61 Virchow had once boasted: Quoted in S. Nuland, *Doctors: The Biography of Medicine*, 1988, New York: Vintage Books, p. 336.

62 'The supposition of Virchow': Newspaper clipping in Dubois's notebook marked 'Nota Palaeontolog. etc.'; no indication of source.

63 These new finds: Anonymous, 'Prof. Dubois blikt', *De Telegraaf*, 1938.

63 In 1877, when Darwin had gone to Cambridge: H. Litchfield, ed., *Emma Darwin: A Century of Family Letters*, 1915, London: Murray, vol. 2, p. 230.

CHAPTER 8. TO FIND THE MISSING LINK

65 He began to work out his reasoning: E. Dubois, 'Over de wenschelijkheid van een onderzoek naar de diluviale fauna van Ned. Indië in het bijzonder van Sumatra', *NT*, 1888, vol. 48, pp. 48–165; also manuscript versions of Dubois's final lecture at the University of Amsterdam in the Dubois Archives.

66 After perusing some reports from … Richard Lydekker: R. Lydekker, 'Notices of Siwalik Mammals', *Records of the Geological Survey of India*, 1879, vol. 12, pp. 33–52; R. Lydekker, 'Siwalik Mammalia', Memoirs of the Geol. Survey of India, *Palaeontologica India*, 1886, s. 10, *Indian Tertiary and Post-Tertiary Vertebrata*, vol. 4, pt. 1, pp. 1–18.

67 Finally his ideas began: Dubois's arguments are loosely summarized from Dubois, 'Over de wenschelijkheid', 1888.

68 some new and crucial reports about the Indies fossils: K. Martin, 'Ueberreste vorweltlicher Proboscidier auf Java und Banka', *Sammlungen des Geologischen Reichs-Museums in Leiden*, 1884–1889, vol. 4: 1–24; K. Martin, 'Fossile Säugethierreste von Java und Japan', *Sammlungen des Geologischen Reichs-Museums in Leiden*, 1884–1889, vol. 4, pp. 25–69.

69 Alfred Russel Wallace's great ideas: A. Wallace, *The Geographical Distribution of Animals*, 1876. London: Macmillan.

71 'Don't throw away': Dubois's autobiographical notes, Dubois Archives, Naturalis.

72 'For all that' [and subsequent exchanges]: Bernsen diary, 10 December 1930.

CHAPTER 9. LOGISTICS

74 'that crazy book of Darwin's': Anonymous, 'Prof. Dubois blikt', *De Telegraaf*, 1938.

76 'After thinking more about your plans': letter, Weber to Dubois, undated, probably 1887.

76 he wrote inquiring: This can be deduced from letter, De Referendaris, chief of Military Affairs, Colonial Department, to Dubois, 4 August 1887. Copies of the contracts of enlistment are preserved in the Dubois Archives.

79 Dubois's father, adamantly opposed: Bernsen diary, March 1931.

82 'I advise against this': ibid., 10 December 1931.

83 He offered to edit: letters, Fürbringer to Dubois, 15 October 1887, and 26 October 1887.

83 the steamship SS *Prinses Amalia*: Dates of departure and arrival from letter, Dubois to Stoomvaartmaatschappij, Nederlands, 3 March 1931.

CHAPTER 10. PADANG

93 Captain Hendrik Krull: A note in the Dubois Archives mentions that H. Krull of the Dutch Indies Army collected Dubois and his family upon arrival in Padang. His Christian name was confirmed by searching the enlistment records of the Koninklijk Nederlandsch-Indisch Leger, the Royal Dutch East Indies Army.

94 a *totok*, a newly arrived European: During the late nineteenth and early twentieth century, colonists in the Indies had an elaborate system of classifying people according to their ethnic origin. I have used the terms of that era as I understand them. 'Pures' was the common term for those of full European ancestry. 'Totoks' were Pures who had only recently come to the Indies; the term implied a naivety about Indies ways. 'Indos', now considered offensive in some circles, was used to describe those with a mixture of European and Indonesian ancestry. 'Natives' were those of unadulterated Indonesian ancestry; manual labourers were routinely referred to as 'coolies'. 'Indische' refers to families that were longtime residents of the Indies; such families very often intermarried with Indonesians.

99 "walking dictionary": For a recent consideration of interracial sexual attitudes and behaviour in the colonial Indies, see E. Locher-Schloten, 'So Close and Yet So Far', pp. 131–153, and P. Pattynama, 'Secrets and Danger', pp. 84–107, both in J. Clancy-Smith and F. Gouda, eds., *Domesticating the Empire*, 1998, Charlottesville: University Press of Virginia. For a turn-of-the-century perspective, see L. Couperus, *The Hidden Force*, 1990, Amherst: University of Massachusetts Press (originally *De Stille Kracht*, 1900); E. Breton de Nijs, *Faded Portraits*, 1982, Amherst: University of Massachusetts Press (originally *Vergeelde portretten uit een Indisch familiealbum*, 1954); and Multatulti (Edward Douwes Dekker) *Max Havelaar*, 1982, Amherst: University of Massachusetts Press (originally 1860, Amsterdam: Van Oorschot).

102 Dubois offered to lecture: Dubois's lecture notes, Dubois Archives, Naturalis.

104 'It is obvious that scholars': Dubois, 'Over de wenschelijkheid', 1888, p. 165.

CHAPTER 11. PAJAKOMBO

105 Kroesen was a thoughtful man: letter, Kroesen to Dubois, 8 September 1888.

106 Anna gave birth: J. M. F. Dubois, 'Trinil', 1957, pp. 35–36.

107 In September, another physician arrived: ibid., p. 31ff; Bernsen diary, 13 February 1931; L. D. Brongersma, 'The Vicissitudes of the Dubois Collection', unpublished manuscript, n.d., Dubois Archives, Naturalis, p. 5.

CHAPTER 12. FOSSILS

112 'We are really going to look forward': letter, Kroesen to Dubois, 8 September 1888.

115 a provisional report of his finds: E. Dubois, 'Voorloopig verslag over palaeontologische nasporingen in grotten bij Pajakombo (Padangsche Bovenlanden)'. Unpublished report in Dubois Archives, Naturalis.

116 'REGISTER OF RESOLUTIONS': Copy of document (in Dutch) in Dubois Archives.

CHAPTER 13. GARUDA

118 They came to a large cave: J. M. F. Dubois, 'Trinil', 1957, p. 33ff; Bernsen diary, 13 February 1931.

CHAPTER 14. FEVERS AND SPELLS

125 A slight noise: J. M. F. Dubois, 'Trinil', 1957, p. 34; Bernsen diary, 13 February 1931.

128 'Everything here has gone against me': letter, Dubois to Jentink, 17 October 1888.

130 Anthonie de Winter and Gerardus Kriele: dates of their starting to work for Dubois are recorded in his daily agenda for 1889; first names confirmed by searching the enlistment records of the Koninklijk Nederlandsch-Indisch Leger, the Royal Dutch East Indies Army.

CHAPTER 15. TO JAVA

131 He wrote for advice: letter, Dubois to Verbeek, 17 October 1889; letters, Verbeek to Dubois, 22 November 1888, 8 March 1889, and 9 March 1889.

131 'I received your letter': letter, Sluiter to Dubois, 21 December 1888; B. D. van Rietschoten, 'Uit een schrijven van den heer van Rietschoten te Blitar', NT, 1889, vol. 48, pp. 346–47, based on a letter, Van Rietschoten to Sluiter, 13 October 1888.

132 'In every respect': letter, Dubois to Sluiter, (no date) 1889, basis of E. Dubois, 'Uit een schrijven van den heer Dubois te Pajakombo naar aanleiding van den aan dien heer toegezonden schedel, door den heer Van Rietschoten in zijn marmergroeven in het Kedirische opgegraven', NT, 1890, vol. 49, pp. 209–10.

135 Permission was duly granted: copy of resolution in Dubois Archives, Naturalis.

137 the house formerly occupied by the Dutch Assistant Resident: J. M. F. Dubois, 'Trinil', 1957, pp. 36–38; photographs in the Dubois archives; details of similar houses from descriptions and photographs of Indies houses in Breton de Nijs, Faded Portraits, 1982, and R. Wassing and R. Wassing-Visser, Adoeh, Indië! Het beste van Hein Buitenweg, 1992, Atrium: The Hague.

140 a marabou stork: J. M. F. Dubois, 'Trinil', 1957, p. 38.

CHAPTER 16. JAVA FOSSILS

142 As he explained to Groeneveldt: E. Dubois, monthly report for November 1890, unpublished manuscript in Dubois Archives, Naturalis.

144 Soon the fossils usurped: photographs, Dubois Archives, Naturalis.

145 'Amidst the remains': E. Dubois, 'Palaeontologische onderzoekingen op Java': *VM*, 4th quarterly report, 1890, p. 14.

CHAPTER 17. COOLIES

147 'Will you also be so kind': letter, De Winter to Anna, 28 June 1890.

147 'All the forced labourers': letter, De Winter to Dubois, 11 July 1890.

147 'Now I have here': letter, Kriele to Dubois, 11 July 1890.

147 'So it is also very hard': letter, De Winter to Dubois, undated but between 29 September 1890 and 30 December 1890.

148 on 16 January 1891, Victor Marie Dubois: birth recorded, *BS*.

148 Sluiter replied cheerfully: letter, Sluiter to Dubois, 29 December 1890.

148 'I really would like to send you back the books': letter, Sluiter to Dubois, 6 January 1891.

148 'Why are you so disconsolate': letter, Sluiter to Dubois, 23 January 1891.

149 De Winter, working in the north: letter, De Winter to Dubois, 29 March 1891.

150 Even Dubois's own workers: Bernsen diary, 18 March 1931.

152 In contrast, Kriele and De Winter: J. M. F. Dubois, 'Trinil', 1957, p. 48ff.

CHAPTER 18. DISCOVERIES AT TRINIL

154 Dubois's uncanny ability [and much of paragraph]: Bernsen diary, 13 February 1931.

155 'The most important find': E. Dubois, 'Palaeontologische onderzoekingen op Java', *VM*, 3rd Quarterly Report, 1891, pp. 12–14.

159 'Near the place on the left bank': E. Dubois, 'Palaeontologische onderzoekingen op Java', *VM*, 4th Quarterly Report, 1891, p. 13.

159 'Besides, the most important fact': ibid.

159 'all that we possessed': Dubois, 'Palaeontologische onderzoekingen op Java', *VM*, 4th Quarterly Report, 1891, pp. 14–15.

160 'The creature': letter, Dubois to Kroesen, 30 December 1891.

Chapter 19. Gathering Resources

161 Early in 1892: letters from Weber to Dubois, 4 April 1892, and 21 October 1892.

161 The older man was Robert Boyd: Information on Robert Boyd and his family, their marriages, and their children is derived from *BRP*, *BS*, *GHG*, *INN*, and the dossier Boyd at the Centraal Bureau voor Genealogie, The Hague.

164 Their wedding … 16 January 1890: *BS*.

164 By the evening of the twenty-first: The birth of the child is recorded in *BS*.

166 'Jane de Clonie MacLennan': The death of Jane de Clonie MacLennan-Prentice and her epitaph are recorded *GHG*. The birth date of Gerard Alexander Prentice MacLennan is recorded in the same source and mentioned in a letter, Prentice to Dubois, 13 July 1893.

169 Bishop Samuel Wilberforce being bested in debate: L. Huxley, ed., *Life and Letters of Thomas Huxley*, 1900, New York: Appleton, p. 199; see also F. Darwin, ed., *Life and Letters of Charles Darwin*, 1887, London: John Murray, pp. 114–16.

Chapter 20. Friendship

175 They romped with a … tiger cub: letter, Adam Boyd to Jean M. Dubois, 23 November 1974.

Chapter 21. Trinil

178 'A few cool windy days': E. Dubois, notes, 28 July 1892, Dubois Archives, Naturalis.

179 'De Winter told me': letter, Kriele to Dubois, 7 September 1892.

182 small tin soap dish: item preserved in the Dubois Archives, Naturalis.

Chapter 22. The Birth of *Pithecanthropus*

185 'The most important find': E. Dubois, 'Palaeontologische onder-zoekingen op Java', *VM*, 3rd Quarterly Report, 23 November 1892, p. 10.

185 'This being was in no way equipped': ibid., pp. 12–13.

186 'Because of this find': ibid., pp. 11, 14.

187 'In calculating the relative volume': letter, Dubois to Groeneveldt, 4 December 1892.

187 'I have made a terrible mistake': There is no documentary evidence of this letter whatsoever.

188 'I received your letter': letter, Dubois to Weber, 19 December 1892.

190 In the very act of writing: letter, Dubois to Groeneveldt, 28 December 1892, complete with 'A' overwritten by 'P'.

191 'I have, Your Excellency': letter, Dubois to Groeneveldt, 28 December 1892.

Chapter 23. 1893

195 Its editor and publisher, P. A. Daum: Information about Daum from E. Beekman, 'Introduction', 1987, pp. 1–2, in P. A. Daum, *Ups and Downs of Life in the Indies*, translated by Elsje Qualm Sturtevant and Donald W. Sturtevant, Amherst: University of Massachusetts Press. (Originally published as P. A. Daum, *Ups en downs in het Indische leven*, 1890, Batavia: feuilleton.)

196 'IN PURSUANCE': Anonymous, 'Homo Erectus', 'Palaeontologische onderzoekingen op Java', *Bataviaasch Nieuwsblad*, 6 February 1893, no. 57. Almost certainly, this piece was written by P. A. Daum, the editor of the newspaper.

201 'rather hastily': J. A. C. A. Timmerman, 'Belangrijke palaeontologische vondsten op Java', *TAG*, 1893, s. 2, vol. 10, pp. 310–12, 312.

Chapter 24. Disaster

204 'Ngrodjo, Saturday morning': letter, Prentice to Dubois, no date but certainly early May of 1893 as Dubois starts for Lalie Djuvo on 4 May according to his daily agenda.

206 And there he carved his name: This incident is mentioned in a letter, Prentice to Dubois, 28 November 1938. The date of their climb up Gunung Ardjoena is recorded in Dubois's 1893 daily agenda, as is the date of their departure from Lalie Djuvo.

Chapter 25. Letters from a Friend

208 'Mringin, 9 July 1893': letter, Prentice to Dubois, 9 July 1893.

210 'Tempoersarie, 13 July 1893': letter, Prentice to Dubois, 13 July 1893, a few Dutch words translated into English for clarity.

212 'Tempoersarie, 16 July 1893': letter, Prentice to Dubois, 16 July

1893. Prentice refers to Dubois's site as Ngawi, the nearest sizeable town, but I have substituted 'Trinil', for clarity.

213 'Shall we take a photograph': letter, Prentice to Dubois, February 7, 1938.

CHAPTER 26. AFTERMATH

218 'Anna abortus': Dubois's daily agenda has a handwritten entry that says simply 'Anna abortus', crossed out and then rewritten, on 30 August 1893. This is the only documentation of this event.

219 He practised science: Bernsen diary, October (no date, but before 7 October) 1931.

CHAPTER 27. PERSEVERANCE

221 'Trinil, 8 August 1893': letter, Kriele to Dubois, 8 August 1893.

221 'The Resident from Solo': letter, De Winter to Dubois, 25 August 1893.

222 'Regarding the free people': letter, De Winter to Dubois, 3 September 1893. 'Free people' refers to workers who are not forced labourers.

222 Last year, in 1892: E. Dubois, 'Naschrift op "De Klimaten der Voorwereld en de Geschiedenis der Zon"'. *NT*, 1892, vol. 51, pt. 1, pp. 93–100.

223 'Geboegan, Oenerang, 27 September 1893': letter, Prentice to Dubois, 27 September 1893. 'Trinil' substituted for 'Ngawi' for clarity.

224 He decided to erect a monument: The monument still stands at the site museum at Trinil in East Java.

CHAPTER 28. THE MONOGRAPH

226 'It would be foolish to doubt': E. Dubois, *Pithecanthropus erectus. Eine Menschenaehnliche Uebergangsform aus Java*, 1894, Batavia: Landsdrukkerij, p. 2.

227 Adjusting his calculations for *P.e.* accordingly: ibid, pp. 10–11.

228 In his monograph, Dubois remarked: ibid., p. 6.

229 Moreover, the general gracility: ibid., pp. 10–13.

229 Prentice had called at Toeloeng Agoeng: letter, Prentice to Dubois, 31 October 1893.

230 Anna Grace: The marriage of Anna Grace Boyd to M. G. de Witte,

an employee of a sugar company, on 11 October 1893, is recorded in *BS*.

230 'Oenarang, 31 October 1893': letter, Prentice to Dubois, 31 October 1893.

CHAPTER 29. WRITING UP

232 *P.e.* must have walked like a man: Dubois, *Pithecanthropus erectus*, 1894, p. 23.

232 'The points suffice': ibid., p. 23.

233 'pillar, girder and siphon': ibid., pp. 26–27.

233 *P.e.* must have stood perhaps 1.7 metres: ibid.

234 'An Anthropopithekos has become': Dubois, *Pithecanthropus erectus*, 1894, p. 31.

235 Evolution, Dubois became convinced: ibid., p. 37.

235 'forerunner of the gibbon *Hylobates*': ibid., pp. 37–39.

235 'Although already quite advanced': ibid., p. 31.

CHAPTER 30. SEPARATION AND LOSS

237 'Do not listen to pontianaks': This incident is based on a similar one in Couperus, *Hidden Force*, 1985, p. 176ff.

239 'The *djongas* Nassi': photograph of Nassi, labelled by Dubois, in Dubois Archives.

CHAPTER 31. INTERMISSION

246 'Geboegan, Oenarang, 30 June 1894': letter, Prentice to Dubois, 30 June 1894.

248 'Mringin, 20 October 1894': letter, Prentice to Dubois, 20 October 1894. 'Trinil', substituted for 'Ngawi'.

249 'Toeloeng Agoeng, 3 November 1894': letter, Prentice to Dubois, 3 November 1894.

250 'Toeloeng Agoeng, 7 November 1894': letter, Prentice to Dubois, 7 November 1894.

CHAPTER 32. TO INDIA

251 'Mringin, 21 December 1894': letter, Prentice to Dubois, 21 December 1894. Also letters, Prentice to Galloway and Prentice to Lyon, 21 December 1894.

252 'December 29, 1894': Dubois's India journal, dates given.

254 'January 10, 1895': ibid., date given.

CHAPTER 33. CALCUTTA

256 'January 22, 1895': ibid., date given.

257 'January 23, 1895. Alcock is': ibid., date given.

258 'January 23, 1895. Yesterday I studied in the museum': ibid.

258 'The significant name': Anonymous, 'Notes', *Nature*, 3 January 1895, vol. 51, p. 230.

259 'January 27, 1895': Dubois's India journal, date given.

259 a group of natives: Ethnographic exhibits and showcases displaying 'exotic' indigenous people were common from 1870 to about 1930. For an analysis, see R. Corbey, 'Ethnographic Showcases', *Cultural Anthropology*, 1993, vol. 8, no. 3, pp. 338–69.

259 'February 2, 1895': Dubois's India journal, date given.

259 'February 3, 1895': ibid., date given.

260 He was far better off: Dates, times, and stations for Dubois's outward journey in India given in C. L. Griesbach's written advice, 1895, in the Dubois Archives, Naturalis.

264 'Indian Museum, 9 February 1895': letter, Alcock to Dubois, 9 February 1895. Phrases in German translated into English for clarity; 'armoire' substituted for 'almirah' for clarity.

265 'Monday. Call on Deputy Commissioner': Griesbach, advice, 1895.

266 'For horse get about': ibid.

267 'The Punjab Government has been informed': ibid.

268 'Let me know when you': ibid.

268 Dubois wrote a suitably officious letter: letter, Dubois to Collector and Magistrate of Saharapur, 13 February 1895.

270 'Sir, Please explain': There is no direct evidence of the contents or intended recipient of the telegram, although the existence of a telegram which Alcock refuses to send is apparent from a letter, Alcock to Dubois, 17 February 1895. Dubois's later accusation that Prentice had an affair with Anna while Dubois was in India is shown by Prentice's denial in a letter, Prentice to Dubois, 23 June 1895.

CHAPTER 34. SIRMOOR STATE

272 He had set up a school: The existence of this school is mentioned in an undated letter, M. M. Carliton to Sukh Chain Sinha, which was sent to Dubois by Sukh Chain Sinha on 3 April 1895.

273 'younger brothers': The metaphor of the Dutch ruler in the East Indies as the elder brother of the native regent or prince was a common one reflected in an official directive from the Dutch government in 1820. This policy figures prominently in such Dutch colonial literature as Multatuli, *Max Havelaar*, 1982, and Couperus, *Hidden Force*, 1985.

274 he received a letter from the Collector: letter and *purwana*, Collector and Magistrate of Saharanpur to Dubois, 15 February 1895.

274 Letters were written and notes filed: telegrams, Griesbach to Punjab Government, 18 February 1895.

274 'Indian Museum, 17 February 1895': letter, Alcock to Dubois, 17 February 1895.

CHAPTER 35. SIWALIK ADVENTURES

278 His itinerary sounded like: Brongersma, notes on India trip, Dubois Archives, Naturalis.

278 Dubois sent another telegram…A reassuring reply: telegram, Dubois to Maharajah of Sirmoor, 25 February 1895; telegram, Maharajah of Sirmoor to Dubois, 26 February 1895.

278 'Obstruction by Rajah Nahan': telegram, Foreign Department to Government of the Punjab Revenue and Agricultural Departments, 1 March 1895.

279 'Indian Museum, 3 March 1895' letter, Alcock to Dubois, 3 March 1895.

279 a copy of an article: P. Matschie, 'Noch einmal *Pithecanthropus erectus*', *Naturwissenschaftliche Wochenschrift*, 1895, vol. 10, pp. 122–23.

280 Dubois had already written Gamble: The existence of this letter is mentioned in a letter, Gamble to Dubois, 15 March 1895.

280 He sent yet another letter…His letter of 4 March: letter, Dubois to Maharajah of Sirmoor, 4 March 1895: letter, Maharajah of Sirmoor to Dubois, 4 March 1895.

280 Dubois replied immediately: second letter, Dubois to Maharajah of Sirmoor, 4 March 1895.

280 By letter the next morning: letter, Maharajah of Sirmoor to Dubois, 5 March 1895.

280 The guide was Sukh Chain Sinha: letter, Sukh Chain Sinha to Dubois, 3 April 1895, and included letters of reference.

281 'some 5 fossil bones': letter, Maharajah of Sirmoor to Dubois, 10 March 1895.

282 'Toeloeng Agoeng, 7 March 1895': letter, Prentice to Dubois, 7 March 1895.

283 'The case of my missing link': Brongersma, notes taken on a letter, Dubois to Anna, 16 March 1895. Original letter not in archives.

283 'I hope you will succeed': letter, Gamble to Dubois, 15 March 1895.

283 'Did you read Lydekker's critique': letter, Griesbach to Dubois, 18 March 1895.

284 'Griesbach writes about the critique': Brongersma, notes on letter, Dubois to Anna, 28 March 1895. Original letter not in archives.

284 he sent a desperate telegram: telegram, Dubois to Griesbach, 29 March 1895.

CHAPTER 36. LEAVING INDIA

286 'Review of Dubois's *Pithecanthropus erectus*': All quotations from the review come from R. Lydekker, 'Review of Dubois *Pithecanthropus erectus*: Eine menschenaehnliche Uebergangsform aus Java', *Nature*, 1895, vol. 51, p. 291.

287 It contained a begging letter: letter, Sukh Chain Sinha to Dubois, 3 April 1895.

288 "It is only justice": O. Marsh, 'On the *Pithecanthropus erectus*, from the Tertiary of Java', *American Journal of Science*, 1896, s. 4, vol. 1, pp. 475–82.

289 'Marsh sent me a reprint': Brongersma, notes on letter, Dubois to Anna, 9 April 1895. Original letter not in archives.

290 '14 April 1895': Brongersma, notes on letter, Dubois to Anna, 14 April 1895. Original letter not in archives.

CHAPTER 37. TOELOENG AGOENG

295 'You have been seducing my wife': That Dubois made this accusation is plain in a letter, Prentice to Dubois, 23 June 1895.

CHAPTER 38. DEPARTURE

300 'The Dutch anthropologist': H. ten Kate, 'Review of Dubois's *Pithecanthropus erectus*, eine menschenaehnliche Uebergangsform aus Java', *Nederlandsch koloniaal centraalblad*, 1894–1895, vol. 1, pp. 127–29.

300 And Rudolf Martin: R. Martin, 'Kritisch Bedenken gegen den

Pithecanthropus erectus Dubois', *Globus*, 1895, vol. 67, pp. 213–17.

300 The next was Daniel Cunningham: D. J. Cunningham, 'Dr. Dubois's So-called Missing Link', *Nature*, 1894–5, vol. 51, pp. 428–29; D. J. Cunningham, 'A Paper on *Pithecanthropus erectus*, the Man-Like Transitional Form of Dr. Eug. Dubois', *Journal of Anatomy and Physiology*, 1895, vol. 29, n.s. 8: xviii–xix.

300 'By a series of easy'…'The fossil cranium': Cunningham, 'Dr. Dubois's So-called Missing Link', 1895, pp. 428–9.

301 Accompanied by Janet Boyd: She accompanied the Dubois family on this voyage 'to keep some order among the 3 young children' and then entered school in the Netherlands, according to a letter, C. R. Hooijer, to Jean M. Dubois, 11 December 1974. Hooijer describes Janet as a 'half-sister' to Adam Boyd; Adam Boyd was the son of William Boyd and Samila, who was in turn the daughter of Adam Prentice and his *nyai*. Janet is probably one of the two children, 'Errol and Janet', of William Boyd and his first Javanese wife, mentioned in a letter, Adam Boyd to Jean M. Dubois, 5 November; Janet's birth is not recorded in *BS* (not an uncommon circumstance for a female child of mixed race at the time).

302 'Mringin, 23 June 1895': letter, Prentice to Dubois, 23 June 1895.

CHAPTER 39. EUROPE

304 a ferocious storm: The storm and the exchange between Dubois and Anna are described in Jean M. F. Dubois, 'Trinil', 1957, p. 190ff.

308 'Look at that skull!': This incident is described ibid., p. 191.

308 'It is the ape-man!': The homecoming is remembered in a letter, Ant Spitzen to Brongersma, 9 September 1941.

310 'But, boy…what use is it?': Bernsen diary, March (no date) 1931.

CHAPTER 40. THE BATTLEFIELD

312 the Ministry for the Colonies: Brongersma, 'Vicissitudes', p. 24.

312 Third International Congress of Zoology: Programme preserved in the Dubois Archives, Naturalis.

313 Virchow was his fiercest opponent: see P. Shipman, *The Evolution of Racism*, 1994, New York: Simon & Schuster, for a recounting of the battles between Virchow and Haeckel over evolution.

313 'Here the fantasy': R. Virchow, 'Commentary on Krause's discussion

of Dubois's *Pithecanthropus erectus, eine menschenaehnliche Uebergangsform aus Java'*, *Zeitschrift für Ethnologie*, 1895, vol. 27, pp. 81–88; also, Virchow, 'Die Frage von dem *Pithecanthropus erectus'*, *Zeitschrift für Ethnologie*, 1895, vol. 27, pp. 435–42.

314 Now, for the first time: E. Dubois, '*Pithecanthropus erectus*, eine menschenaehnliche Uebergangsform', *Compte-rendu des séances du Troisième Congrès International de Zoologie, Leyde, 11–16 septembre 1895*, 1896, Leiden, pp. 251–71.

318 the American Marsh came forward: O. C. Marsh, 'A Commentary on Dubois's "*Pithecanthropus erectus*, eine menschenaehnliche Uebergangsform"' *Compte-rendu des séances du Troisième Congrès International de Zoologie, Leyde, 11–16 septembre 1895*, 1896, Leiden, p. 272.

318 Although some believed: See J. F. van Bemmelen, 'Het Leidsche internationale zoölogencongres: Dubois's aapmensch voor de vierschaar der wetenschap', *Java-bode*, November 1895, vol. 16.

318 Van Bemmelen's findings: J. M. van Bemmelen, 'Der Gehalt an Fluorcalcium eines fossilen Elephantenknochen aus der Tertiärzeit,' *Zeitschrift für anorganische Chemie*, 1897, vol. 15, pp. 84–122.

319 'September 17, 1895 / Professor Virchow': postcard, Jentink to Dubois, 17 September 1895.

319 'September 17, 1895 / Judging from': letter, Dubois to Jentink, 17 September 1895.

320 the abandoned suitcase: J. M. F. Dubois, 'Trinil', 1957, p. 78ff; also A. Hrdlička, *The Skeletal Remains of Early Man*, 1930, Washington, DC: Smithsonian Miscellaneous Collections, vol. 83, p. 38.

322 Sir William Turner: W. Turner, 'On M. Dubois's Description of Remains Recently Found in Java, Named by Him *Pithecanthropus erectus*. With Remarks on So-called Transitional Forms between Apes and Man', *Journal of Anatomy and Physiology*, 1896, vol. 29, no. 9, pp. 424–45.

322 'Of course, not being a special anatomist': letter, Munro to Dubois, 23 December 1896.

322 'the most important hitherto recorded': W. Turner, 'Discussion of Dubois's "On *Pithecanthropus erectus*: A Transitional Form between Man and the Ape"', *JAI*, 1896, vol. 25, p. 250ff. The discussion followed Dubois's presentation to the Royal Dublin Society on 20 November 1895.

323 'After the erect position': letter, Munro to Dubois, 26 November 1895.

323 'lowest human cranium': D. J. Cunningham, 'A paper on *Pithecanthropus erectus*, the Man-like Transitional Form of Dr. Eug. Dubois', *Journal of Anatomy and Physiology*, 1895, vol. 29, n.s. 9, pp. 18–19.

323 'Professors Sir W. Turner': Quotations in this paragraph come from E. Dubois, 'On *Pithecanthropus erectus*: A Transitional Form between Man and Apes', *JAI*, 1896, vol. 25, pp. 240–55, 244.

324 'It is unfortunate': W. H. Flower, 'Discussion of Dubois's "On *Pithecanthropus erectus*, A Transitional Form between Man and the Ape"', *JAI*, 1896, vol. 25, p. 248.

324 'The opportunity which Dr. Dubois': Turner, 'Discussion', *JAI*, 1896, p. 249–51.

325 'I have studied': J. Garson, 'Discussion of Dubois's "On *Pithecanthropus erectus*, A Transitional Form between Man and the Apes"', 1896, *JAI*, vol. 25, p. 251–52.

325 'The femur is extremely': ibid.

326 'What strikes me most forcibly': J. A. Thomson, 'Discussion of Dubois's "On *Pithecanthropus erectus*, A Transitional Form between Man and the Apes"', *JAI*, 1896, vol. 25, p. 253–54.

326 'As to whether or no': ibid., p. 254.

326 'The chief question': A. Keith, 'Discussion of Dubois's "On *Pithecanthropus erectus*, A Transitional Form between Man and the Ape"', *JAI*, 1896, vol. 25, p. 253.

327 'To my mind': ibid.

328 'Saturday November 23, 1895': O'Mulligan, 'Bones of Contention', the *Evening Telegraph* (Dublin), 23 November 1895.

329 'According to all the rules of classification': R. Virchow, 'Commentary on Dubois's *Pithecanthropus erectus*, betrachtet als eine wirkliche Uebergangsform und als Stammform des Menschen', *Zeitschrift für Ethnologie*, 1895, vol. 27, pp. 744–47, 744.

329 the most satisfactory bit: J. M. F. Dubois, 'Trinil', 1957, p. 81.

330 'I am well aware': E. Dubois, '*Pithecanthropus erectus* betrachtet als eine wirkliche Uebergangsform und als Stammform des Menschen', *Zeitschrift für Ethnologie*, 1895, vol. 27, p. 723–38, 737.

330 Wilhelm Branco and William Dames: Theunissen, *Eugène Dubois*, 1989, p. 109.

Chapter 41. More Skirmishes

332 In February: letter, Dubois to Haeckel, 22 February 1896.

332 '12 May 1896': letter, Schwalbe to Dubois, 12 May 1896.

333 the Prix Broca: certificate in Dubois Archives, Naturalis.

334 On 8 January 1897: Brongersma, 'Vicissitudes', p. 19.

334 On 5 February: letter, Place to Dubois, 5 February 1897.

335 'Among the students': letter, Schrijnen to Dubois, 10 February 1897.

335 '18 February 1897': letter, Dubois to Place, 18 February 1897.

335 But if Seydel was rejected: letter, Place to Dubois, 19 February 1897.

336 'Dr. Victor Dubois, Venlo': telegram, Dubois to Victor, 20 February 1897.

336 'I believe': letter, Victor to Dubois, 21 February 1898.

337 '22 February 1898': letter, Dubois to Victor, 22 February 1898.

339 'Toeloeng Agoeng, 15 April 1896': letter, Prentice to Dubois, 15 April 1896.

CHAPTER 42. USING HIS BRAINS

341 the Fourth International Congress of Zoology: Programme preserved in the Dubois Archives, Naturalis.

342 'The next question': E. Haeckel, 'On our present knowledge of the origin of Man', *Annual Report of the Board of Regents of the Smithsonian Institution for the year ending June 30, 1898*, 1899, pp. 461–80, p. 468–70. Translation of a discourse given at the Fourth International Congress of Zoologists at Cambridge, England, 26 August, 1898.

343 'To this momentous interpretation': ibid. p. 471.

344 'Virchow further asserted': ibid., pp. 471–72.

347 'It is actually...the size': E. Dubois, 'De verhouding van het gewicht der hersenen tot de grootte van het lichaam bij de zoogdieren', *PKAW*, 1897, s. 2, vol. 5, no. 10, pp. 1–41, 10.

349 'From all these considerations': E. Dubois, 'Remarks upon the Brain-Cast of *Pithecanthropus*', *Proceedings of the Fourth International Congress of Zoology, Cambridge 22–27 August 1898*, 1899, London, pp. 78–96, 96.

351 'IVth International Congress of Zoology': Copy of resolution in Dubois Archives, Naturalis.

CHAPTER 43. BETRAYAL AND RESURRECTION

353 '20 December 1897': letter, Schwalbe to Dubois, 20 December 1897.

354 'to contribute to the important question': G. Schwalbe, 'Ziele und Wege einer vergleichenden physischen Anthropologie', *Zeitschrift für Morphologie und Anthropologie*, 1899, vol. 1, pp. 1–15, 2.

354 'The apparently wide chasm': ibid., p. 5.

354 'In this way, paleontology': ibid., p. 15.

355 Although in 1899 Dubois was offered: Brongersma, 'Vicissitudes', p. 19; Theunissen, *Eugène Dubois*, 1989, p. 3.

355 more than eighty publications: Theunissen, *Eugène Dubois*, 1989, pp. 80, 122.

357 'You'll do very nicely': J. M. F. Dubois, 'Trinil', 1957, p. 192ff.

357 '*not* my face!': ibid., p. 195.

358 'That is my father!': ibid., p. 196.

CHAPTER 44. FAMILY

360 In company, she knew how: Bernsen diary, 4 May 1931.

360 Eugenie did not worry him: author's interview with Victor E. Dubois and Nelleke Hooijer.

360 He established a firm routine: J. M. F. Dubois, 'Trinil', 1957, p. 207.

363 Jean and Victor did not do well: Bernsen diary, 2 March 1931.

363 When Jean and Victor were ready: Bernsen diary, 2 March 1931.

365 'Did you save the skull?': J. M. F. Dubois, 'Trinil', 1957, p. 203.

CHAPTER 45. THE NEW CENTURY

366 Now that I have found: Bernsen diary, 2 March 1931.

368 There was a move afoot: Brongersma, 'Vicissitudes', p. 20.

368 He led the Ministry of the Colonies: ibid.

368 '30 April 1903': Postcard, Lorié to Dubois, 30 April 1903.

368 '4 May 1903': letter, Lorié to Dubois, 4 May 1903.

369 recalled to active duty: Brongersma, 'Vicissitudes', p. 20.

369 Emil Selenka, a German zoologist: Theunissen, Eugène Dubois, 1989, p. 118.

370 'The excavations which at present': E. Dubois, 'Eenige van Nederlandschen kant verkregen uitkomsten met betrekking tot de kennis der Kendeng-fauna (fauna van Trinil)', *TAG*, 1907, s. 2, vol. 24, pp. 449–58, 449.

370 'In short, I consider': ibid., quoted by E. Dubois, 'The fossil human remains discovered in Java by Dr. G. H. R. von Koenigswald and attributed by him to *Pithecanthropus erectus*, in reality remains of

Homo sapiens soloensis (conclusion)', *PKAW*, 1940, vol. 43, pp. 1268–75, 1271.

370 'April 25, 1907 / *Bataviaasch Nieuwsblad*': Anonymous, interview with Mme Selenka, *Bataviaasch Nieuwsblad*, 25 April 1907.

371 'From the two teeth': E. Dubois, 'Das geologische Alter der Kendeng-oder Trinil-fauna', *TAG*, 1908, s. 2, vol. 25, pt. 6, pp. 1235–70, 1252.

371 On 9 February 1909: M. Selenka, 'Die fossile Zähne von Trinil', *TAG*, 1909, s. 2, vol. 26, pp. 398–9. Following Selenka's article are contributions from Schlosser, pp. 398–9, Walkhoff, p. 399, and Dubois, pp. 400–401.

373 Dragutin Gorjanovič-Kramberger: D. Gorjanovič-Kramberger, 'Der diluviale Mensch von Krapina in Kroatien: ein Beitrag zur Paläoanthropologie,' 1906, in O. Walkoff, ed., *Studien über die Entwicklungsmechanik des Primateskelletes*, Kreidel, Wiesbaden, pp. 59–277.

373 A massive monograph on the La Chapelle-aux-Saints Neanderthal: M. Boule, 'L'homme fossile de La Chapelle-aux-Saints', *Annales de Paleontologie*, 1911–1913, Paris.

373 Boule's work was underpinned: See also discussion of Boule's perspective in Trinkaus and Shipman, *Neandertals*, 1993.

374 he had lifted the corner: Paraphrased from P. J. van der Feen and W. S. S. van Bentham-Jutting, 'Antje Schreuder, Amsterdam, 15 november 1887–Amsterdam, 2 februari 1952', *Geologie en mijnbouw*, 1952, vol. 14, pp. 121–25, 122.

CHAPTER 46. DIVERSIONS

375 In August, work started: M. Gijsbers, pers. comm. to P. Storm.

375 a sort of prehistoric nature park: Leakey and Slikkerveer, *Man-ape*, 1993, p. 155.

376 '17 December 1910': letter, Dubois to Sluiter, 17 December 1910.

377 'Man, witness of the Flood'; 'rare relic'; 'melancholy skeleton': A. C. Haddon, *History of Anthropology*, 1910, London: Watts & Co., p. 70.

377 'fade into relative insignificance': ibid., p. 76.

377 'Dubois published his account': Haddon, *History*, 1910, pp. 77–78.

377 "I believe that in *Pithecanthropus erectus*": Haddon, ibid., p. 77, was quoting W. H. L. Duckworth, *Morphology and Anthropology*, 1904, p. 520.

378 'Dubois's old ally': Information about Keith from A. Keith, *An Autobiography*, 1950, London: Watts.

378 'now Professor of Geology': A. Keith, *Ancient Types of Man*, 1911, New York and London: Harper and Bros., p. 131.

379 'Went out to Java': ibid.

379 'Whatever the exact date may be': ibid., p. 134.

380 'Here we find a creature': W. H. L. Duckworth, *Prehistoric Man*, 1912, Cambridge, UK: Cambridge University Press, pp. 2–3.

380 Calling their new find: A thorough account of the Piltdown affair can be found in F. Spencer, *Piltdown, A Scientific Forgery*, and F. Spencer, *The Piltdown Papers*, both 1990, both New York: Oxford University Press.

383 In fact, Fraipont feared: F. Spencer, *Aleš Hrdlička, M.D., 1869–1943: A Chronicle of the Life and Work of an American Physical Anthroplogist*, 1979, Ph.D. dissertation, University of Michigan. Ann Arbor: University Microfilms, p. 425, citing letter, Hrdlička to Holmes, 22 June 1912.

383 'all this talk of descent': ibid., p. 418, citing letter, Hrdlička to Strickler, 22 June 1912.

385 'The anthropologists of the world': A general account of this incident is given in Spencer, *Hrdlička*, 1979; visiting card preserved in Dubois Archives, Naturalis.

386 'On account of the peculiar circumstances': A. Hrdlička, *The Most Ancient Skeletal Remains of Man*, 1914, Annual Report, Smithsonian Institution, p. 498.

387 he had been unlucky: Bernsen diary, 2 March 1931, with minor paraphrasing for clarity.

CHAPTER 47. TRAGEDY

388 '*In species of Vertebrates*': E. Dubois, 'On the Relation between the Quantity of Brain and the Size of the Body in Vertebrates', *PKAW*, 1914, vol. 16, pp. 647–68, 655.

391 Eugenie…announced her intentions: author's interview with Victor E. Dubois and Nelleke Hooijer; Dubois family genealogy, Dubois Archives.

391 the Talgai skull was famous: A. Keith, *Antiquity of Man*, 1925, London: Williams and Northgate: pp. 440–41, 448.

392 'A distinctly lower type'…'The differences may nearly all be attributed': E. Dubois, 'The Proto-Australian Fossil Man of Wadjak, Java', *PKAW*, 1922, vol. 23, pp. 1013–1051, 1030.

393 they met two American girls: author's interview with Jean M. Dubois.

393 billing himself as a photographer: Poster for a lecture by Jean M. F.
   Dubois is reproduced in Leakey and Slikkerveer, *Man-Ape*, 1993,
   p. 145.
394 In 1922, at thirty-one years old: Obituary notices for Jean M. F.
   Dubois preserved in Dubois Archives, Naturalis.
394 Anna's heart and mind: Bernsen diary, 4 May 1931.
395 'I have seen how you look at Claartje': Antje Schreuder's account
   of the story of Dubois's affair with Claartje is recorded ibid., 23
   April 1931.

CHAPTER 48. DANGEROUS TIMES

397 'scattered and scanty materials': H. F. Osborn, *Men of the Old
   Stone Age*, 1915, New York: Scribner's, p. 81.
398 'Asia is the mother': H. F. Osborn, 'Foreword', in R. C. Andrews,
   On the Trail of Ancient Man, 1926, New York: G. P. Putnam's
   Sons, p. vii.
398 'It is possible': Osborn, *Men of the Old Stone Age*, 1915, p. 511.
398 Chapman had modern vehicles: Expedition details from Andrews,
   On the Trail, 1926, pp. 3–23.
398 '1 August 1922': letter, Osborn to Dubois, 1 August 1922.
399 McGregor had also wanted: letter, McGregor to Dubois, 2 June
   1921.
400 'As Professor Lorentz': telegram, Dubois to Osborn, undated.
400 '2 December 1922': letter, Osborn to Bolk, 2 December 1922.
401 Bolk wrote sternly to Dubois: letter, Bolk to Dubois, 3 January
   1923.
401 Bolk clumped stiffly: Amputation of Bolk's right leg in 1918 is
   attested to by Dr. Robert Baljet, pers. comm. to author.
403 'I know he made a lot of noise': Bernsen diary, 2 March 1931.
404 'First: is the Academy competent': Report of the meeting of the
   Koninklijke Nederlandsche Akademie van Wetenschappen, Dubois
   Archives, Naturalis.
405 'The unwinding of this tangled affair': ibid.
405 'I ask the Board to clarify': letter, Dubois to Bolk, 14 February
   1923, language slightly modified for clarity.
405 He was able to write: letter, Dubois to Bolk, 29 June 1923.
406 'a creature that stood at the threshold'; 'If science was to construct':
   Hrdlička, lecture given at the American University in 1920, quoted
   in Spencer, *Aleš Hrdlička*, 1979, p. 503.
407 'We found Professor Dubois': A. Hrdlička, *The Skeletal Remains of*

Early Man, 1930, Washington, DC: Smithsonian Miscellaneous Collections 83.

407 'I am awaiting with great impatience': letter, Osborn to Dubois, 2 April 1924.

408 'I am very glad indeed to inform you': letter, Osborn to Bolk, 28 February 1925.

409 'You may make': letter, Dubois to Osborn, 25 March 1924.

409 an Honorary Fellow: certificate preserved in the Dubois Archives, Naturalis.

CHAPTER 49. A NEW SKULL

410 a new and complete skull: letter, Heberlein to Dubois, 7 November 1926; E. Dubois, 'The so-called new *Pithecanthropus* skull', *PKAW*, 1927, vol. 30, no. 1. Read at the meeting of 2 December 1926.

410 'Accept my grateful homage': telegram, Dubois to Heberlein, 2 October 1926.

411 'The newspaper notices': letter, Osborn to Dubois, 6 October 1926.

411 'According to the ANETA telegram': copy of press release in Dubois Archives dated 7 October 1926.

411 Heberlein telegraphed Dubois: telegram, Heberlein to Dubois, 16 October 1926.

412 'Thanks can you inform me': telegram, Dubois to Heberlein, 2 November 1926.

412 'I found the *Pithecanthropus* skullcap': letter, Heberlein to Dubois, 7 November 1926.

413 'But for me': letter, Dubois to Weber, 7 December 1926.

413 'What a *sad* story that is': letter, Weber to Dubois, 7 December 1926.

415 'It is not even a skull': E. Dubois, '*Pithecanthropus erectus*. De "nieuwe *Pithecanthropus* vondst"', *Algemeen Handelsblad*, 8 December 1926.

415 Dubois cabled Elliot Smith: telegram, Dubois to Elliot Smith, 8 December 1926; letter, Elliot Smith to Dubois, 8 December 1926.

415 'Since I first heard': letter, Dubois to Heberlein, 10 December 1926.

416 'On a photograph': Dubois, 'The So-Called Skull', 1927, p. 137.

416 'Mijsberg and Bijlmer': This incident is described in Brongersma, 'Vicissitudes', pp. 41–42.

CHAPTER 50. RUMOURS AND ISOLATION

418 'Their discoverer, Dr Dubois': F. W. MacBride, *Evolution*, 1928, London: Sixpenny Library Series, p. 75.

418 On 28 January 1928: Numerous letters of congratulations and a book signed by many of the attendees at the celebration are preserved in the Dubois Archives, Naturalis.

419 '11 February 1928': letter, F. A. B. J. Vroom S. J. to *The Tablet*, 11 February 1928.

421 'Wanted a servant-girl': Bernsen diary, 23 April 1931.

421 'It was a débâcle': ibid.

421 'It seems': ibid.

CHAPTER 51. BRAIN WORK

423 'absence of evidence of continuous development': E. Dubois, 'The law of the necessary phylogenetic perfection of the Psychoencephalon', *PKAW*, 1928, vol. 31, pt. 3, p. 304.

424 'Clearly paleontology bears evidence': ibid., pp. 304–305.

425 'Besides in the case of the psychoencephalon': ibid., pp. 313–14.

425 That he had done too little: Bernsen diary, 14 January 1931, 2 March 1931, and 12 November 1931.

426 'striking confirmation'; 'New Tertiary man'; 'one more link': Quotes and account from J. Lanpo and H. Weiwen, *The Story Of Peking Man from Archaeology to Mystery*, 1990, Beijing: Foreign Languages Press, pp. 26–7.

426 a new name: *Sinanthropus pekinensis*: D. Black, 'On a Lower Molar from the Chou Kou Tien Deposits', *Paleontologica Sinica*, 1927, ser. C, vol. 7, fasc. I.

426 On 2 December, the Chinese geologist: Account and telegram from Lanpo and Weiwen, *The Story*, 1990, p. 65.

427 'A new chapter': G. Balchior, 'The Peking Man – An Undamaged Skull', *Manchester Guardian*, 30 December 1929.

427 '11 February 1930': letter, Dubois to Black, 11 February 1930.

427 '3 April 1930': letter, Black to Dubois, 3 April 1930.

429 'Boule pointed out long ago': ibid.

429 'Since my last report before the Society': D. Black, 'Interim Report on the Skull of *Sinanthropus*', 29 March 1930, Annual Meeting of the Geological Society of China, preserved in Dubois Archives.

430 '22 June 1930': letter, Dubois to Black, 22 June 1930.

431 '28 March 1933': letter, Dubois to Black, 28 March 1933.

CHAPTER 52. THE DILIGENT ASSISTANT

432 Their choice was a curious one: Brongersma, 'Vicissitudes', p. 23ff.

433 'The conversation comes around': Bernsen diary, 10 November 1930.

433 'Dubois realizes that the study': ibid., 12 November 1930.

434 'I am very nervous': ibid., 23 November 1930.

435 'I myself speak': ibid., 13 December 1930.

435 'Miss Dr. Schreuder from Amsterdam': ibid., 23 April 1931.

436 'He suffers from nerves': ibid., 24 April 1931.

436 'He is always afraid': ibid.

436 'I have said': ibid., 10 June 1931; last sentence of paragraph added.

437 One day Dubois admitted: ibid., 19 February 1932.

437 'Yet I have never written': ibid., 19 January 1931.

437 'I believe': ibid., 29 May 1931; sentences beginning 'Ah, you ask', 'You ask', and 'I'll tell' added.

437 'I never had the time': ibid., 14 January 1931.

438 'The difficulties that I have experienced': ibid., 10 December 1930.

438 'Also *Pithecanthropus* caused me a lot of trouble': ibid.

438 'What a misery I have had': ibid., 2 March 1931.

438 'I get the impression': ibid., 29 April 1931.

439 'Every day I study them': ibid., 29 May 1931.

439 'You know, I admire Black': ibid.

440 'Black gives a pleasant solution': ibid.

440 'the more I look at the smaller skull': ibid., 8 June 1931.

441 Sometimes Dubois spoke of giving Bernsen: Brongersma, 'Vicissitudes', p. 24.

441 'The more I look at the pictures': Bernsen diary, 10 June 1931.

442 'Although it certainly resembles': ibid., 15 June 1931.

442 '15 June 1931': letter, Dubois to Black, 15 June 1931.

443 One day, he committed: Brongersma, 'Vicissitudes', p. 24.

443 'I have not published enough': Bernsen diary, 2 March 1932.

443 'After finding the truth': ibid.

443 'Only after 1923': ibid., with minor additions for clarity.

443 Bernsen could remain quiet: Incident and dialogue, with minor additions for clarity, from ibid., 3 March 1932.

445 'No word of regret': ibid., 5 March 1932.

446 the burgomaster informed him: Incident and dialogue from ibid., 9 March 1932.

447 Even Van der Klaauw: ibid., 12 March 1932.

447 'That is easy for you to say': ibid., 16 March 1932.

447 'And shall you walk': ibid., 16 March 1932.

448 'There is something hostile in you': Bernsen diary, 12 May 1932.

448 'Now I see you are hard': ibid.

448 'I have always felt': ibid.

449 Working systematically: ibid., 2 June 1932.

449 'After a great deal of inspection': paraphrased slightly from ibid.

450 'After a close comparison': ibid., 1 June 1932.

450 'This is a solemn moment': ibid.

451 'these pieces must certainly have come': ibid.

451 'In the box': ibid.

451 'Dubois will surely find it unpleasant': ibid., 4 June 1932.

452 he died of internal haemorrhaging: Brongersma, 'Vicissitudes', p. 27.

452 'Forty years ago': E. Dubois, 'The distinct organization of *Pithecanthropus* of which the femur bears evidence, now confirmed from other individuals of the described species', *PKAW*, 1932, vol. 35, no. 6, pp. 716–22, 716–18.

454 'The morphological evidence acquired': ibid., pp. 721–2.

454 Bernsen was replaced: Brongersma, 'Vicissitudes', p. 31.

CHAPTER 53. NEW SKULLS FROM JAVA

455 In August 1931, the Geological Survey of Java: The account of the discovery comes from G. H. R. von Koenigswald, *Meeting Prehistoric Man*, 1956, London: Thames & Hudson, p. 65ff.

456 After the three finds in 1931: Dates from F. Weidenreich, 'Morphology of Solo Man', *Anthropological Papers of the American Museum of Natural History*, NY, 1951, vol. 43, part 3, p. 217.

456 'provisional description': W. F. F. Oppenoorth, '*Homo (Javanthropus) soloensis*, een pleistocene mensch van Java', *Wetenschappelijke mededeelingen Dienst van den Mijnbouw in Nederlandsch-Indië*, 1932, vol. 20, pp. 49–63.

456 '31 May 1932': letter, Oppenoorth to Dubois, 31 May 1932.

457 Dubois published a brief letter: E. Dubois, 'Early man in Java', *Nature*, 1932, vol. 130, p. 20.

457 'One identical type'; 'proto-Australian': ibid.

457 '15 June 1932': letter, Dubois to Oppenoorth, 15 June 1932.

458 Oppenoorth described Ngandong IV and V: W. W. F. Oppenoorth, 'De vondst van palaeolitische menschelijke schedels op Java', *De Mijningingenieur*, 1932, June.

458 Oppenoorth had proposed a geographic separation: ibid., p. 114.

459 Dubois's next task: E. Dubois, 'The Shape and the Size of the Brain in *Sinanthropus* and *Pithecanthropus*', *PKAW*, 1933, vol. 36, no. 4, pp. 415–23.

459 'There is obviously little difference': ibid., p. 419.

459 'Such a volume': ibid., pp. 422–3.

460 'oblong and narrow': ibid.

461 'It is therefore possible': E. Dubois, 'On the Gibbonlike Appearance of *Pithecanthropus erectus*', *PKAW*, 1935, vol. 38, pp. 578–585, 580 and 585.

CHAPTER 54. A WORTHY OPPONENT

463 'Our excavation site': For quotations and general account of Von Koenigswald's experiences in Java see Von Koenigswald, *Meeting Prehistoric*, 1956, p. 74.

464 all nonessential government employees: M. C. Ricklefs, *A History of Modern Indonesia since c. 1300*, 1993, Stanford: Stanford University Press, p. 186ff.

465 When Teilhard arrived: Information about Teilhard de Chardin's visit comes from P. V. T. Tobias, 'Life and Work of Professor Dr. G. H. R. von Koenigswald', in *Auf den Spuren des* Pithecanthropus, 1984, Frankfurt: Waldemar Kramer: pp. 25–95; letter, Teilhard de Chardin to Mlle. Teilhard-Chamdon, 24 January 1936, quoted in P. Teilhard de Chardin, *Letters from a Traveller*, 1962, London: Collins, p. 380.

466 'If *Pithecanthropus* is to be found anywhere': quoted in Von Koenigswald, *Meeting Prehistoric*, 1956, p. 92, and Tobias, 'Life and Work', 1984, p. 39.

466 'During the stratigraphic survey': G. H. R. von Koenigswald, 'Een nieuwe *Pithecanthropus* ondekt', *Algemeen Indische Dagblad*, 28 March 1936.

467 'On April 15 I got': E. Dubois, 'Nieuwe *Pithecanthropus* ondekt?' *Algemeen Handelsblad*, 18 April 1936; E. Dubois, 'Ecn nieuwe *Pithecanthropus* ondekt?' *Het Vaderland*, 18 April 1936.

468 'It is inconceivable': G. H. R. von Koenigswald, '*Pithecanthropus erectus*, Antwoord dr. Von Koenigswald', *Algemeen Handelsblad*, 7 May 1936.

468 Unfortunately, Andojo was by then elderly: J. de Vos, '*Homo modjokertensis* – vindplaats, ouderdom en fauna', 1994, *Cranium*, vol. 11, no. 2, pp. 103–107.

469 a series of articles: E. Dubois, 'Fossil humans and *Pithecanthropus*.

The youngest find in Java no *Pithecanthropus*', *Nieuwe Rotterdamsche Courant*, 2 August 1936.

469 'Concerning the new find': Anonymous, '*Homo modjokertensis*: Lecture of Dr. Von Koenigswald', *Handelsblad*, 29 August 1936.

469 'a POSSIBILITY': G. H. R. von Koenigswald, 'Erste Mitteilung über einen fossilen Hominiden aus den Altpleistocän Ostjavas', *PKAW*, 1936, vol. 39, no. 8, pp. 1000–1009. Communicated at the meeting of 26 September 1936.

469 a desire to be courteous: Von Koenigswald, *Meeting Prehistoric*, 1956, p. 82.

469 a sign of uncertainty: letter, Oppenoorth to Dubois, 28 October 1936.

CHAPTER 55. TO THE BATTLEFRONT

470 'glorious disdain'; 'almost inconceivable influence': Anonymous, 'Dr. Van Stein Callenfels', *Handelsblad*, 22 October 1936.

470 Tuan Setan: Anonymous, *Handelsblad*, 24 July 1936.

470 Stein declared Von Koenigswald's: Anonymous, 'Prehistoric Congress in Oslo, lecture of Dr. Van Stein Callenfels', *De Telegraaf*, 8 August 1936.

471 'In former times': Information and quotations below on this lecture taken from L. D. Brongersma, report on lecture of Van Stein Callenfels, Delft, 28 October 1936, and Anonymous, 'Praehistorische vondsten op Java; Voordracht Dr. Van Stein Callenfels', *Handelsblad*, 29 October 1936.

471 'The Chief of Mining': Brongersma, report, 1936.

472 They sailed on the SS *Baloeran*: Anonymous, 'Dr. Von Königswald, Studiereis naar Europa', *Handelsblad*, 7 November 1936; Von Koenigswald, *Meeting Prehistoric*, 1956, p. 33.

472 Von Koenigswald delayed: Dubois gives 17 February 1937 as the date of this visit in E. Dubois, 'On the fossil human skull recently described and attributed to *Pithecanthropus erectus* by G. H. R. von Koenigswald', *PKAW*, 1938, vol. 41, pp. 380–386, though Von Koenigswald, *Meeting Prehistoric*, 1956, pp. 32–3, suggests the visit occurred in October 1936. The October date is contradicted by the report in the newspaper *Handelsblad*, (see previous note) of the departure of the Von Koenigswalds from the Indies on 18 November 1936, so I have accepted Dubois's date.

473 'He was stated to be ill': Von Koenigswald, *Meeting Prehistoric*, 1956, pp. 32–3.

473 Nonetheless, Von Koenigswald was fearful: In a letter, Von Koenigswald to Smit, 6 May 1982, written more than forty years after Dubois's death, Von Koenigswald still remembers his deep concern over Dubois's opposition.

474 'In 1890, Professor Eugène Dubois': G. H. R. von Koenigswald, 'A review of the stratigraphy of Java and its relations to early man', in G. G. MacCurdy, ed., *Early man*, 1937, Philadelphia: J. B. Lippincott & Co., pp. 23–32, 23.

474 'All the remains': ibid., pp. 25–6, 27.

475 'The skull ... is perfectly fossilized': ibid., p. 28.

475 'The first suggestion': ibid.

475 His abstract was read aloud: E. Dubois, 'Early Man in Java and *Pithecanthropus erectus*', in G. G. MacCurdy, ed., *Early Man*, 1937, pp. 315–22, 315.

476 'in my best Malay': Von Koenigswald, *Meeting Prehistoric*, 1956, p. 93.

CHAPTER 56. THE LETTER

477 'February 9, 1937': letter, Van den Koppel to Dubois, February 9, 1937.

478 'Kediri February 7, 1936' letter, Prentice to Dubois, February 7, 1936.

CHAPTER 57. PRETENDER TO THE THRONE

481 '12 July 1937': letter, Von Koenigswald to Dubois, 12 July 1937.

481 '26 August 1937': letter, Dubois to Von Koenigswald, 26 August 1937.

482 'This is a continuation': letter, Dubois to Von Koenigswald, 27 August 1937.

482 '3 September 1937': letter, Von Koenigswald to Dubois, 3 September 1937.

483 'We had to keep the price so low': Von Koenigswald, *Meeting Prehistoric*, 1956, pp. 97–8.

484 '14 September 1937': letter, Dubois to Von Koenigswald, 14 September 1937.

484 '3 October 1937': letter, Von Koenigswald to Dubois, 3 October 1937.

484 '12 November 1937': letter, Von Koenigswald to Dubois, 12 November 1937.

485 Von Koenigswald prepared a paper: G. H. R. von Koenigswald, 'Ein Unterkieferfragment des *Pithecanthropus* aus den Trinilschichten Mittenjavas', *PKAW*, 1937, vol. 40, pp. 883–93.

485 '12 January 1938': letter, Dubois to Von Koenigswald, 12 January 1938.

485 As was widely reported: Anonymous, 'De Fossiele Mensch van Java; De Weg der Evolutie; De beroemdste is nog altijd de *Pithecanthropus*', *Handelsblad*, 18 January 1938.

486 Even a cheerful letter: letter, Eugenie to Dubois, 27 January 1938.

486 'entirely different': E. Dubois, 'The mandible recently described by G. H. R. von Koenigswald, compared with the mandible of *Pithecanthropus erectus* described in 1924 by Eug. Dubois', *PKAW*, 1938, vol. 41, pp. 139–47, 146–47.

486 'I never imagined': ibid., pp. 145–46.

486 an article about the find: G. H. R. von Koenigswald, '*Pithecanthropus* received into human family', *Illustrated London News*, 11 December 1937; G. H. R. von Koenigswald, 'Ein neuer *Pithecanthropus*-Schädel', *PKAW*, 1938, vol. 41, pp. 185–92.

487 'preparated': E. Dubois, 'On the fossil human skull recently described and attributed to *Pithecanthropus erectus* by G. H. R. von Koenigswald', *PKAW*, 1938, vol. 41, pp. 380–86, 380.

487 'great thickness of the skull-cap': The quotations in this paragraph are from Dubois, 'On the fossil human skull', 1938, pp. 382–3.

488 'The real fossil ... got lost': ibid., p. 384.

488 'artificially from that of an immature individual': ibid., p. 385.

488 'Even if this reconstructed skull': ibid.

489 '5 May 1938': letter, Von Koenigswald to Dubois, 5 May 1938.

489 'I may remind you': letter, Dubois to Von Koenigswald, 3 June 1938.

489 Von Koenigswald wrote: Von Koenigswald, *Meeting Prehistoric*, 1956, p. 99.

489 'unfortunately I cannot': letter, Dubois to Weidenreich, 23 July 1938.

490 '9 August 1938': letter, Dubois to Weidenreich, 9 August 1938.

490 '23 August 1938': letter, Dubois to Eugenie, 23 August 1938.

491 'Weidenreich ... wrote': letter, Dubois to Eugenie, 2 September 1938.

CHAPTER 58. OLD FRIENDS

492 'Kediri, 28 November 1938': letter, Prentice to Dubois, 28 November 1938.

CHAPTER 59. THE FINAL CONFLICT

497 'We laid out our finds': Von Koenigswald, *Meeting Prehistoric*, 1956, p. 101.

497 'Considered from the general': G. H. R. von Koenigswald and F. Weidenreich, 'The relationship between *Pithecanthropus* and *Sinanthropus*', *Nature*, 1939, vol. 144, pp. 926–29, 928.

499 '3 January 1940': letter, Dubois to Eugenie, 3 January 1940.

500 'The child skull of Modjokerto': E. Dubois, 'The fossil human remains discovered in Java by Dr. G. H. R. von Koenigswald and attributed by him to *Pithecanthropus erectus*, in reality remains of *Homo wadjakensis* (syn. *Homo soloensis*)', *PKAW*, 1940, vol. 43, pp. 494–96, 494. Read at the meeting of 30 March 1940.

500 '3 April 1940': letter, Dubois to Eugenie, 3 April 1940.

500 'Now twenty-two years': E. Dubois, 'The fossil human remains discovered in Java by G. H. R. von Koenigswald and attributed by him to *Pithecanthropus erectus*, in reality remains of *Homo soloensis*. Continuation', *PKAW*, 1940, vol. 43, pp. 842–52, 843–44.

501 They were seized: The best accounts of the loss of the *Sinanthropus* fossils are given in: H. Shapiro, *Peking Man*, 1974, New York: Simon & Schuster, and J. Lanpo and H. Weiwen, *The Story*, 1990. A more lively but possibly less accurate recounting is C. Janus and W. Brashler, *The Search for Peking Man*, 1975, New York: Macmillan.

501 Von Koenigswald's indomitable wife: Tobias, 'Life and Work', 1984, pp. 60–63.

502 '4 October 1940': letter, Dubois to Eugenie, 4 October 1940.

502 '28 October 1940': letter, Dubois to Eugenie, 28 October 1940.

502 'an escape-line for downed Allied flyers': author's interviews with Jean M. Dubois, Victor E. Dubois, and Nelleke Hooijer.

503 'It is most regrettable': E. Dubois, 'The fossil human remains discovered in Java by G. H. R. von Koenigswald and attributed by him to *Pithecanthropus erectus*, in reality remains of *Homo sapiens soloensis*. Conclusion', *PKAW*, 1940, vol. 43, pp. 1268–75, 1275. Punctuation changed slightly for clarity.

504 'Prof. Dr. Eug. Dubois': Dubois's tombstone, as described, can be seen in the cemetery at Venlo.

EPILOGUE. AN UNDERESTIMATED MAN

505 an excellent appraisal: Theunissen, *Eugène Dubois*, 1989.

505 allometry of the brain: H. Jerison, *Evolution of the Brain and Intelligence*, 1973, New York: Academic Press.

Glossary

Note: Spellings and usages are nineteenth- and early twentieth-century, not modern.

adik (Indies) – boy or younger brother; form of address for younger native man

ado (Indies) – an expression of disbelief and astonishment

ajo (Indies) – an exclamation of encouragement, like 'let's go!' or 'OK!'

alang-alang (Indies) – species of tall, coarse, wild grass with sharp edges

anak mas (Indies) – literally, a golden child; a native child adopted by a European family

Ardjoena (Indies) – Prince Ardjoena, a heroic figure from the Hindu Ramayana myths; also, the name of a volcano in Java

babu (Indies) – nursemaid or ladies' maid

barang-barang (Indies) – carried items or luggage

bhisti (Raj) – native water-bearer

bok'n (Indies) – no, not

cepat (Indies) – hurry

chit (Raj) – small official receipt

chuprassi (Raj) – office servant or messenger

delman (Indies) – type of horse-drawn carriage

desa (Indies) – village

diam (Indies) – quiet; be quiet

djati (Indies) – teak

djongas (Indies) – houseboy or butler; the head male servant of the household

dokar (Indies) – small horse-drawn cart

dukun (Indies) – medicine man or traditional healer

durian (Indies) – a fruit with an extremely pungent odour

fabriek (Dutch) – a plantation or manufacturing plant

gamelan (Indies) – traditional Javanese or Balinese orchestra consisting of gongs, xylophones, and other percussion instruments

Garuda (Indies) – mythological eagle who carried the god Vishnu on his back

gunung (Indies) – mountain

hati-hati (Indies) – take care; beware

head-jaksa (Indies) – native magistrate

Indische (Indies) – a European or part-European who has lived a long time in the Indies

Indo (Indies) – native of the Indies, now considered a derogatory usage

ja (Dutch, Indies) – yes

kampong (Indies) – village or neighbourhood

kassian (Indies) – common expression of sympathy, meaning 'Take pity' or 'It's a pity!'

kebaya (Indies) – loose, hip-length overblouse trimmed in lace, originally Chinese but worn by many European women in the Indies

khitmagar (Raj) – native foreman, 'head boy', or overseer

kokkie (Indies) – cook

maidan (Raj) – large parade ground or public space

mandi (Indies) – the bathing room. Water for bathing is stored in a huge pottery jug and ladled over the body.

mandur (Indies) – foreman

mejuffrouw (Dutch) – Miss; respectful term of address for an unmarried well-to-do woman

melati (Indies) – jasmine

mevrouw (Dutch) – Mrs or Madame; respectful term of address for a well-to-do married woman

mijnheer (Dutch) – sir; respectful term of address for a well-to-do man

mungkin, mungkin tidak (Indies) – maybe, maybe not

nasi goreng (Indies) – the common fried rice dish of the Indies

ngrodjo (Indies) – headquarters; also, the name given to Boyd's house

njonja (Indies) – madame; a respectful term of address for a married European woman

nyai (Indies) – native mistress of a European; a concubine *obat* (Indies) – medicine

orang belanda (Indies) – person of Dutch ancestry; generally, a European

orang djager (Indies) – hunter

panjang kursi (Indies) – long chair or chaise, often made of rattan with wooden leg rests that swivel out from the arms

patjol (Indies) – short-handled hoe used by Indies native farmers

picol (Indies) – a unit of measure equivalent to 61.76 kilograms or about 135 pounds

pontianak (Indies) – female spirit or demon

poodle-faker (Raj) – womanizer or ladies' man

prahu (Indies) – native boat or outrigger

Pure (Indies) – person of European ancestry

purwana (Raj) – permit to work in a region, in the form of an open letter to the populace asking that assistance be rendered as needed to the holder of the *purwana*

rijstafel (Indies) – literally, 'rice table', a dish consisting of rice accompanied by many small dishes of spicy stews and condiments

roro (Indies) – princess or maiden of noble birth

sadhu (Raj) – holy man

sahib (Raj) – sir or lord; similar to Indies *tuan*, a respectful form of address used by natives speaking to a European male

sarong (Indies) – piece of cloth wrapped like an ankle-length skirt and worn by both sexes. The pattern on the sarong may indicate place of origin within the Indies, and status.

sedaka (Indies) – ceremonial offering

sinjo (Indies) – a boy, of either European or Eurasian parentage

songket (Indies) – an intricately patterned cloth with gold or silver threads, made in Sumatra

susa (Indies) – fuss, nuisance, or bother

syce (Raj and Indies) – native groom, one in charge of the horses

tehsildar (Raj) – local tax collector

tempo doeloe (Indies) – times gone by; an expression of nostalgia for the colonial past in the Indies

tiffin (Raj) – luncheon; the midday meal

tjempaka (Indies) – type of magnolia

toeloeng (Indies) – Help!

totok (Indies) – European recently arrived in the Indies; newcomer

tuan (Indies) – lord or master; respectful form of address used by natives speaking to male Europeans

tukang kebun (Indies) – gardener

tunggu (Indies) – Wait!

tutup (Indies) – literally 'closed'; slang for a common garment of the Indies, a lightweight, high-collared man's jacket that buttons up the front

Very lights (European) – signal flares used at night by the military, named after their inventor E. W. Very

VOC (Dutch) – Vereenigde Oostindische Compagnie, the Dutch East Indies Company, which controlled trade in the Indies from the late 1500s until the early 1800s

wallah (Raj) – man; when hyphenated, slang for a specialist in some particular trade or task, as in a 'punkah-wallah', who pulls a string that moves a large fan or punkah

waringin (Indies) – banyan tree

warung (Indies) – small native shop or stall

Bibliography

The first section of the bibliography is a listing of the publications of Eugène Dubois, derived from an unpublished bibliography in the Dubois Archives that was compiled in 1979 by L. D. Brongersma, with additions or corrections based on Theunissen, 1989. Entries in this part are organized by year of publication. I do not list as publications the printing of the title only, prior to the publication of the text, nor do I consider reprints of articles with separate pagination to be publications. The second section gives literature cited in the notes or text, which is organized alphabetically by first author. All publications by Dubois have been omitted in this section. Abbreviations are as for the notes.

PART I. PUBLICATIONS OF EUGÈNE DUBOIS

1884
Dubois, Eugène, 'Over Anatomie in hare betrekking tot de Beeldende Kunst. I'. *Maanblad gewijd aan de belangen van het teekenonderwijs en kunstnijverheid in Nederland*, no. 1, 1 June 1884, pp. 2–4.

1885
——, 'Over Anatomie in hare betrekking tot de Beeldende Kunst. II'. *Maandag gewijd aan de belangen van het teekenonderwijs en kunstnijverheid in Nederland*, no. 8, 1 January 1885, pp. 65–9.

1886
——, 'Ueber den Larynx'. In Max Weber, *Studien über Säugethiere, ein Beitrag zur Frage nach dem Ursprung der Cetaceen*. 1886. Jena: Gustav Fischer. Pp. 88–111.
——, 'Zur Morphologie des Larynx'. *Anatomische Anzeiger*, vol. 1, no. 7, pp. 178–86; no. 9, pp. 225–31.

1888
——, 'Over de wenschelijkheid van een onderzoek naar de diluviale fauna van Nederlandsch Indië, in het bijzonder van Sumatra'. *NT*, vol. 48, pp. 148–65.

1889

——, 'Uittreksel van een schrijven van den Heer Dubois te Pajacombo naar aanleiding van den aan dien Heer toegezonden schedel, door den Heer van Rietschoten in zijn marmergroeven in het Kedirische opgegraven'. *NT*, vol. 49, pp. 209–10.

1890

——, 'Beschrijving van een bloeienden *Amorphophallus titanum*, Beccari, aangetroffen te Boea bij de grot der Batang Pangian, den 24sten November 1889'. *Teysmannia*, vol. 1, pp. 89–91.

1891

——, '*Anoa santeng* Dubois'. In F. A. Jentink, 'On *Lepus netscheri* Schlegel, *Felis megalotis* Müller and *Anoa santeng* Dubois'. *Notes Leyden Museum*, vol. 13, pp. 217–22.

——, 'De Klimaten der Voorwereld en de Geschiedenis der Zon'. *NT*, vol. 51, pt. 1, pp. 37–92.

——, 'Palaeontologische onderzoekingen op Java: 3rd quarter 1890'. *VM*, pp. 12–15.

——, 'Palaeontologische onderzoekingen op Java: 4th quarter 1890'. *VM*, pp. 14–18.

——, 'Voorloopig Bericht omtrent het Onderzoek naar de Pleistocene en Tertiare Vertebraten-Fauna van Sumatra en Java, gedurende het jaar 1890'. *NT*, vol. 51, pt. 1, pp. 93–100.

——, 'Palaeontologische onderzoekingen op Java: 1st quarter 1891'. *VM*, pp. 12–13.

——, 'Palaeontologische onderzoekingen op Java: 2nd quarter 1891'. *VM*, pp. 11–12.

1892

——, 'Palaeontologische onderzoekingen op Java: 3rd quarter 1891'. *VM*, pp. 12–14.

——, 'Palaeontologische onderzoekingen op Java: 4th quarter 1891'. *VM*, pp. 12–15.

——, 'Palaeontologische onderzoekingen op Java: 2nd quarter 1892'. *VM*, pp. 14–18.

——, 'Naschrift op "De Klimaten der Voorwereld en de Geschiedenis der Zon."' *NT*, vol. 51, ser. 8, vol. 12, pp. 270–74.

1893

——, 'Palaeontologische onderzoekingen op Java: 3rd quarter 1892'. *VM*, pp. 10–14.

——, 'Palaeontologische onderzoekingen op Java: 4th quarter 1892'. *VM*, pp. 11–12.
——, 'Die Klimate der Geologischen Vergangenheit und ihre Beziehung zur Entwicklungsgeschichte der Sonne'. Nijmegen: H. C. A. Thieme, and Leipzig: Max Spohr.

1894
——, 'Palaeontologische onderzoekingen op Java: 3rd quarter 1893'. *VM*, pp. 15–17.
——, 'Palaeontologische onderzoekingen op Java: 4th quarter 1893'. *VM*, pp. 12–15.
——, *Pithecanthropus erectus. Eine Menschenaehnliche Uebergangsform aus Java*. Batavia: Landsdrukkerij.

1895
——, '*Pithecanthropus erectus*. Eine Menschenaehnliche Uebergangsform aus Java'. *Jaarboek van het Mijnwezen Nederlandsch-Oost-Indië*, vol. 24, pp. 1–77.
——, *The Climates of the Geological Past and their Relation to the Evolution of the Sun*. London: Swan, Sonnenschein & Co.

1896
——, 'The Place of "*Pithecanthropus*" in the Genealogical Tree'. *Nature*, vol. 53, no. 1368, pp. 245, 247.
——, '*Pithecanthropus erectus*, eine Stammform des Menschen'. *Anatomische Anzeiger*, vol. 12, no. 1, pp. 1–22.
——, '*Pithecanthropus erectus*, eine menschenaehnliche Uebergangsform'. *Compte-rendu des séances du Troisième Congrès International de Zoologie, Leyde, 11–16 septembre 1895*, pp. 251–71.
——, '*Pithecanthropus erectus*, betrachtet als eine wirkliche Uebergangsform und als Stammform des Menschen'. *Verhandlungen Berliner Gesellschaft für Anthropologie, Ethnologie, und Urgeschichte*, 14 December 1895, pp. 723–38. (Reprinted in *Zeitschrift für Ethnologie*, vol. 27, pp. 723–38.)
——, 'Résumé d'une communication de M. le Dr. Eug. Dubois sur le *Pithécanthropus erectus du pliocène de Java'. *Bullétin de la Société Belge Géologique, Paléontologique, et Hydrologique*, vol. 9, Procès-Verbaux, pp. 151–60.
——, 'Näheres über den *Pithecanthropus erectus* als menschenähnliche Uebergangsform'. *Internationale Monatschrift Anatomie und Physiologie*, vol. 13, pt. 1, pp. 1–26.
——, 'On *Pithecanthropus erectus*: a Transitional Form between Man

and the Apes'. *Transactions of the Royal Dublin Society*, ser. 2, vol. 6, pp. 1–18.

——, 'On *Pithecanthropus erectus*: a Transitional Form between Man and the Apes (Abstract)'. *JAI*, no. 96, February, pp. 240–48.

——, 'De thans bekende soorten van fossielen Menschaapen'. *Tijdschrift der Nederlandsche Dierkundige Verslagen*, ser. 2, vol. v, pt. 2, pp. 70–74.

——, 'On the occurrence of *Crocodilus porosus* far above the tideway in a Sumatran river'. *Notes Leyden Museum*, vol. 18, p. 134.

——, 'Le "*Pithécanthropus erectus*" et l'origine de l'homme'. *Bullétin de la Société d'Anthropologie de Paris*, ser. 4, vol. 7, pt. 5, pp. 460–67.

1897
——, 'Ueber drei ausgestorbene Menschaffen'. *Neues Jahrbuch für Mineralogie, Geologie, und Paleontologie*, vol. 1, pp. 83–104.

——, 'De Verhouding van het Gewicht der Hersenen tot de Grootte van het Lichaam bij de Zoogdieren'. *PKAW*, vol. 5, no. 10, pp. 1–41.

——, 'Sur le Rapport du Poids de l'Encéphale avec la Grandeur du Corps chez les Mammifères'. *Bullétin de la Société d'Anthropologie de Paris*, sér. 4, vol. 8, pt. 4, pp. 337–76.

1898
——, 'Ueber die Abhängigkeit des Hirngewichtes von der Körpergrösse bei den Säugethieren'. *Archiv für Anthropologie*, vol. 25, pts. 1–2, pp. 1–28.

——, 'Ueber die Abhängigkeit des Hirngewichtes von der Körpergrösse beim Menschen'. *Archiv für Anthropologie*, vol. 25, pt. 4, pp. 423–41.

1899
——, 'The Brain-cast of *Pithecanthropus erectus*'. *Proceedings of the Fourth International Congress of Zoology, Cambridge, 1898, 22–27 August 1898*, pp. 78–95.

——, 'Over den Kringloop der Stof op Aarde'. Rede uitgesproken bij de aanvaarding van het ambt van buitengewoon hoogleraar aan de Universiteit van Amsterdam, 20 February 1899. Leiden: E. J. Brill.

1900
——, 'Données justificatives sur l'essai de reconstruction plastique du *Pithécanthropus erectus*'. Leaflet distributed at the International Exhibition of Paris.

——, 'Données justificatives sur l'essai de reconstruction plastique du *Pithécanthropus erectus*'. *Petrus Camper, Nederlandsche bijdragen tot de anatomie*, vol. 1, pt. 2.

——, '*Pithecanthropus erectus*: A form from the Ancestral Stock of Mankind'. *Report of the Smithsonian Institution for 1898*, pp. 445–49.

——, 'Over den Ouderdom der Aarde'. *TAG*, ser. 2, vol. 17, pp. 697–734.

——, 'De grootte van den kringloop der koolzure kalk en de ouderdom der aarde. I'. *Verslag*, vol. 9, pp. 12–28.

——, 'De grootte van den kringloop der koolzure kalk en de ouderdom der aarde. II'. *Verslag*, vol. 9, pp. 99–115.

——, 'The Amount of the Circulation of the Carbonate of Lime and the Age of the Earth. I'. *PKAW*, vol. 3, pp. 43–62.

——, 'The Amount of the Circulation of the Carbonate of Lime and the Age of the Earth. II'. *PKAW*, vol. 3, pp. 116–30.

1901
——, 'Paradoxe klimatische toestanden in het Palaeozoïsche tijdvak, beschouwd in verband met den vroegeren aard der zonnestraling'. *Handelingen 8ste Nederlandsch Natuur- en Geneeskundig Congres, Rotterdam 11–14 April 1901*, pp. 311–26.

——, 'Zur systematischen Stellung der ausgestorbeben Menschaffen'. *Zoologische Anzeiger*, vol. 24, no. 652, pp. 556–60.

——, 'Les causes probables du Phénomène paléoglaciaire permo-carboniférien dans les basses latitudes'. *Archives Musée Teyler*, ser. 2, vol. 7, pt. 4, pp. 311–60.

——, 'Notes et Corrections'. Ibid., pp. 361–2.

1902
——, 'Over den toevoer van natrium en chloor door de rivieren aan de zee'. *Verslag*, vol. 10, pp. 493–504.

——, 'On the Supply of Sodium and Chlorine by the Rivers to the Sea'. *PKAW*, vol. 4, pt. 7, pp. 388–99.

——, 'De geologische samenstelling en de wijze van ontstaan van den Hondsrug in Drenthe'. *Verslag*, vol. 11, pp. 43–50.

——, 'De geologische samenstelling en de wijze van ontstaan van den Hondsrug in Drenthe'. *Verslag*, vol. 11, pp. 150–52.

——, 'The geological structure of the Hondsrug in Drenthe and the origins of that ridge'. *PKAW*, vol. 5, pt. 2, pp. 93–101.

——, Idem, 'Second communication'. Ibid., pp. 101–103.

——, 'Staring en het Steenkolenvraagstuk in Zuid-Limburg'. *TAG*, ser. 2, vol. 19, pp. 869–70.

——, 'Les causes probables du Phénomène paléoglaciaire permo-carboniférien dans les basses latitudes (deuxième étude)'. *Archives Musée Teyler*, ser. 2, vol. 8, pp. 73–91.

——, 'Notes sur les conditions locales dans lesquelles se sont formés les dépôts paléoglaciaires permo-carbonifériens dans l'Afrique australe, l'Inde et l'Australie'. *Archives Musée Teyler*, ser. 2, vol. 8, pt. 1, pp. 157–63.

——, 'La structure géologique et l'origine du Hondsrug dans la Province Drenthe'. *Archives Néerlandaises Sciences exactes et naturelles*, ser. 2, vol. 7, pt. 4/5, pp. 484–96.

1903

——, 'De geologische gesteldheid van onzen bodem en drinkwater voor Amsterdam'. *Algemeen Handelsblad*, 3 February 1903, Avondblad, 2de blad.

——, 'De drinkwaterquaestie'. *Algemeen Handelsblad*, 9 February 1903, Ochtendblad.

——, 'Nog eens het drinkwater'. *Algemeen Handelsblad*, 11 February 1903, Ochtendblad.

——, 'De Water-quaestie'. *Algemeen Handelsblad*, 12 February 1903, Ochtendblad, 1ste blad.

——, 'De Watervraag'. *Algemeen Handelsblad*, 12 February 1903, Avonblad, 2de blad, p. 5.

——, 'De Waterquaestie'. *Algemeen Handelsblad*, 13 February 1903, Ochtendblad, 1ste blad, p. 2.

——, 'Toch overvloed van zoetwater uit het duin te halen'. *Algemeen Handelsblad*, 9 March 1903, Avondblad.

——, 'Diep gelegen keinenleem van een jongeren ijstijd in den bodem van Noord-Holland'. *Verslag*, vol. 12, pp. 17–22.

——, 'Feiten ter opsporing van de bewegingsrichting en den oorsprong van het grondwater onzer zeeprovinciën'. *Verslag*, vol. 12, pp. 187–212.

——, 'Over de herkomst van het zoete water in den ondergrond van eenige minder diepe polders'. *Verslag*, vol. 12, pp. 593–603.

——, 'Deep Boulder-Clay beds of a latter glacial Period in North-Holland'. *PKAW*, vol. 6, pt. 4, pp. 340–45.

1904

——, 'Over de herkomst van eenige chemische bestanddeelen van het grondwater in ons laagland'. *Pharmaceutisch Weekblad*, vol. 41, no. 3, pp. 46–51.

——, 'Niet-biologische vorming van limoniet'. *Pharmaceutisch Weekblad*, vol. 41, no. 7, pp. 137–39.

——, 'Facts leading to trace out the motion and the origin of the underground water in our sea-provinces'. *PKAW*, vol. 6, pt. 10, pp. 738–60.

——, 'Richting en uitgangspunt der diluviale ijsbeweging over ons land'. *Verslag*, vol. 13, pp. 44–5.

——, 'Klei van Tegelen, Teyler lezing'. Newspaper clipping, 23 November 1904.

——, 'On the direction and the starting point of diluvial ice motion over the Netherlands'. *PKAW*, vol. 7, pt. 1, pp. 40–44.

——, 'On the Origin of the Fresh-water in the Subsoil of a few shallow polders'. *PKAW*, vol. 7, pt. 1, pp. 53–63.

——, 'Over een equivalent van het Cromer Forest-Bed in Nederland'. *Verslag* , vol. 13, pp. 243–51.

——, 'On an Equivalent of the Cromer Forest-Bed in the Netherlands'. *PKAW*, vol. 7, pt. 3, pp. 214–22.

——, 'Corrigenda en Addenda bij de mededeeling van den Heer Eugène Dubois "Over een equivalent van het Cromer Forest-Bed in Nederland"'. *Verslag*, vol. 13, pp. 453–54.

——, 'Corrigenda et Addenda to the paper "On an Equivalent of the Cromer Forest-Bed in the Netherlands"'. *PKAW*, vol. 7, pt. 5, pp. 382–83.

——, 'Etudes sur les eaux souterraines des Pays Bas. I. L'eau douce de sous-sol des Dunes et des Polders'. *Archives Musée Teyler*, ser. 2, vol. 9, pt. 1, pp. 1–96.

1905
——, 'Sur en équivalent du Forest-Bed de Cromer dans le Pays-Bas (Traduction avec une note additionelle par M. O. van Ertborn)'. *Bullétin de la Société Belge Géologique, Paléontologique, et Hydrologique*, vol. 18, pp. 240–52.

——, 'Note sur un espèce de Cerf d'Age Icenien (Pliocène Supérieur). *Cervus falconeri* Dawk., trouvée dans les argiles de la Campin'. *Bullétin de la Société Belge Géologique, Paléontologique, et Hydrologique*, vol. 10, Mémoires, pp. 121–24.

——, 'De geographische en geologische beteekenis van den Hondsrug en het onderzoek der zwertsteenen in ons noordsch diluvium'. *Verslag*, vol. 14, pp. 360–68.

——, 'The geographical and geological signification of the Hondsrug, and the examination of the erratics in the Northern Diluvium of Holland'. *Verslag*, vol. 8, pt. 5, pp. 427–36.

——, 'L'âge de l'argile de Tégelen et les Espèces de Cervidés qu'elle con-teint'. *Archives Musée Teyler*, ser. 2, vol. 9, pt. 4, pp. 605–15.

——, 'De Voorziening van Amsterdam met Drinkwater uit de Duinen'. *Nederlandsch Tijdschrift van Geneeskunde*, 2de helft, no. 20, pp. 1346–65.

——, 'Bestaat er gevaar voor verzouting eener goed aangelegde prise d'eau in de duinen?' *Nederlandsch Tijdschrift van Geneeskunde*, 2de helft, no. 25, pp. 1707–1708.

——, 'L'âge des différentes assizes englobées dans la Série du "Forest-Bed" ou le Cromerian'. *Archives Musée Teyler*, ser. 2, vol. 10, pt. 1, pp. 59–74. Also published in *Société Belge Géologique, Paléontologique, et Hydrologique*.

1906

——, 'Ueber Facettengeschiebe im niederländischen Diluvium'. *Centraalblad für Mineralogie, Geologie, Palaeontologie*, 1906, pt. 1, p. 15.

——, 'Etudes sur les eaux souterraines des Pays-Bas. II. L'eau salée peut-elle envahir une prise d'eau dans les dunes?' *Archives Musée Teyler*, ser. 2, vol. 10, pt. 2, pp. 75–84.

——, 'La Pluralité des Périodes Glaciaires dans les dépôts pleistocènes et pliocènes des Pays-Bas. I'. *Archives Musée Teyler*, ser. 2, vol. 10, pt. 2, pp. 163–79.

1907

——, 'Note sur une nouvelle espèce de Cerf des argiles de la Campine *Cervus ertbornii*, n. sp'. *Taxandria, Gedenkschriften der Geschieden Oudheidkundigen Kring der Kempen, Turnhout*, vol. 4, pp. 80–74.

——, 'Eenige van Nederlandschen kant verkregen uitkomsten met betrekking tot de kennis der Kendeng-fauna (Fauna van Trinil)'. *TAG*, ser. 2, vol. 24, pt. 3, p. 449–58.

——, 'Sur quelle échelle s'accomplit le phénomène du transport atmo-sphérique de sel marin?' *Archives Musée Teyler*, ser. 2, vol. 10, pt. 4, pp. 461–71.

1908

——, 'Heeft Roodharigheid de Beteekenis van atavitische Varieteit?' *Nederlandsch Tijdschrift van Geneeskunde*, 1ste helft, no. 7, pp. 553–56.

——, 'Het zoutgehalte van zeewater'. *Oprechte Haarlemsche Courant*, Stadseditie, 8 May 1908.

——, 'On the Correlation of the Black and the Orange Coloured pigments and its Bearing on the Interpretation of Redhairedness'. *Man*, vol. viii, pt. 6, art. no. 46, pp. 87–89.

——, 'Das geologische Alter der Kendeng-Oder Trinil-Fauna'. *TAG*, ser. 2, vol. 25, pt. 6, pp. 1235–70.

——, 'Een Duitsch opstel in een Nederlandsch wetenschappelijk tijdschrift'. *Nieuwe Rotterdamsche Courant*, 15 December 1908, 2de blad A.

1909

——, 'Over een veeljarige schommeling van den grondwaterstand in de Hollandsche duinen'. *Verslag*, vol. 17, pp. 782–90.

——, 'On a long-period Variation in the Height of the Groundwater in the Dunes of Holland'. *PKAW*, vol. 11, pt. 3, pp. 674–81.

——, 'Fossiele tand van Sondé'. *Nieuwe Rotterdamsche Courant*, 25 March 1909, Ochtendblad B.

——, 'Die Fossilie Zähne von Trinil'. *TAG*, ser. 2, vol. 26, pt. 3, pp. 399–401. Response to a note by Margarethe Selenka.

——, 'Een "Raadsel", dat geen Raadsel is'. *Album der Natuur*, no indication of volume, p. 283.

——, 'Een en ander over Geologie en Hydrologie onzer duinen'. *Verslag van den Elfde Algemeene Vergadering van de Vereeniging voor Waterleidingsbelangen in Nederland, Nijmegen 17–18 September 1909*, pp. 81–98, 100, 101.

——, 'Over het Ontstaan van de Vlakten in het Duin'. *TAG*, ser. 2, vol. 26, pt. 6, pp. 896–910.

——, 'De Prise d'eau der Haarlemsche Waterleiding'. *Rapport uitgebracht aan Burgemeester en Wethouders van Bloemendaal*, 53pp.

1910

——, 'Geen "artiesisch" drinkwater voor Amsterdam'. *De Amsterdammer*, no. 1700, 23 January 1910, p. 2.

——, 'Over Duinvalleien, den vorm der Nederlandsche Kustlijn en het ontstaan van laagveen in verband met bodembewegingen'. *TAG*, ser. 2, vol. 27, pt. 3, pp. 395–402.

——, 'De Haarlemsche Waterleiding. Over Dr. Pareau's Twijfel aan de aanzienlijke daling van het grondwaterpeil door de Haarlemsche Waterleiding nabij hare prise d'eau teweeggebracht en nog wat'. *Haarlem's Dagblad*, 28 February 1910, 2de blad.

1911

——, 'De Beteekenis der palaeontologische gegevens voor de ouderdomsbepaling der Klei van Tegelen'. *TAG*, ser. 2, vol. 28, pt. 2, pp. 234–46.

——, 'De Hollandsche Duinen, Grondwater en Bodemdaling'. *TAG*, ser. 2, vol. 28, pt. 3, pp. 395–413.

——, 'Over den Vorm van het Grondwatervlak in het Duin'. *TAG*, ser. 2, vol. 28, pt. 6, pp. 895–902.

——, 'Berekening van een grondwaterstroom'. *De Ingenieur*, vol. 26, no. 50, p. 1074.

1912

——, 'Over de Plaats van *Pithecanthropus* in het Zöologisch Systeem'. *Archives Musée Teyler*, ser. 3, vol. 1, pp. 142–49.

1913

——, 'De betrekking tusschen hersenmassa en lichaamsgrootte bij de gewervelde dieren'. *Verslag*, vol. 22, pp. 593–614.

1914

——, 'On the Relation between the Quantity of Brain and the Size of the Body in Vertebrates'. *PKAW*, vol. 16, pt. 2, nos. 1–5, pp. 647–68.

——, 'Die Gesetzmässige Beziehung von Gehirnmasse zu Körpergrösse bei den Wirbeltieren'. *Zeitschrift für Morphologie und Anthropologie*, vol. 18, pp. 323–50.

——, 'Evenwichten in den Kringloop der Stof op de Aarde'. *Archives Musée Teyler*, ser. 3, vol. 2, pp. 61–75.

——, 'Van Oude tot Nieuwe Levenswerelden'. *Archives Musée Teyler*, ser. 3, vol. 2, pp. 103–21.

——, 'Het Liedsche Duinwater, Ein Hydrologische Studie'. Printed for the Water Company at Leiden, 31 pp.

1915

——, 'De natuurlijke grens van Nederland beschouwd in verband met de daling van den bodem'. *Handelsblad 15de Natuur- en Geneeskundig Congres, Amsterdam 8–10 April, 1915*, pp. 435–43.

1916

——, 'Hollands Duin als natuurlijke Zeewering en de tijd'. *TAG*, ser. 2, vol. 33, pt. 3a, pp. 395–415.

1917

——, 'De Maat der Hersenen'. *Archives Musée Teyler*, ser. 3, vol. 3, pp. 282–94.

——, 'Hoe ontstonden de vennen bij Oisterwijk'. *Verslag Algemeen Vergaderingen 1913–1917*, pp. 81–91.

1918

——, 'De Betrekking der hoeveelheden van de Hersenen, het neuron en zijn deelen tot de lichaamsgrootte'. *Verslag*, vol. 26, pp. 1416–25.

——, 'On the Relation between the Quantities of the Brain, the Neurone and its Parts, and the Size of the Body'. *PKAW*, vol. 20, pts 9/10, pp. 1328–37.

1919

——, 'De beteekenis der grootte van het neuron en zijn deelen'. *Verslag*, vol. 27, pt. 4, pp. 503–20.

——, 'The Significance of the Size of the Neuron and its Parts'. *PKAW*, vol. 21, pt. 5, pp. 711–29.

——, 'Vergelijking van het hersengewicht, in functie van het lichaams-gewicht, tusschen de twee seksen'. *Verslag*, vol. 27, pp. 713–32.

——, 'Comparison of the Brain Weight in Function of the Body Weight, between the Two Sexes'. *PKAW*, vol. 21, pts. 6/7, pp. 850–69.

——, 'Over het ontstaan en de Geologische Geschiedenis van Vennen, Venen en Zeeduinen'. *Archives Musée Teyler*, ser. 3, vol. 4, pp. 266–93.

1920

——, 'De Hoeveelheidsbetrekking van de Hersenen tot het Lichaam der Gewervelde Diersooten en hare Beteekenis'. *Vakblad voor Biologie*, vol. 1, pt. 6, pp. 83–9.

——, 'De hoeveelheidsbetrekking van het zenuwstelsel bepaald door het mechanisme van het neuron'. *Verslag*, vol. 28, pt. 6, pp. 623–38.

——, 'The Quantitative Relations of the Nervous System determined by the Mechanism of the Neurone'. *PKAW*, vol. 22, pts. 7–8, pp. 665–80.

——, 'De proto-Australische fossiele Mensch van Wadjak, Java, I'. *Verslag*, vol. 29, pt. 1, pp. 88–105.

1921

——, 'De proto-Australische fossiele Mensch van Wadjak, Java, II'. *Verslag*, vol. 29, pt. 6, pp. 866–87.

——, 'De beteekenis der groote schedelcapaciteit van *Homo neandertalensis*'. *Verslag*, vol. 29, pt. 7, pp. 987–1004.

——, 'Over beweging van grondwater bij vorst en dooiweder.' *Verslag*, vol. 29, pt. 7, pp. 1021–22.

Molengraaf, G. A. F., en Eug. Dubois, 'Praeadvies over de Vraag van den Minister van Arbeid waaraan de aanwezigheid van artesisch grondwater in de duingronden te danken is'. *Algemeen Handelsblad*, 30 October and 10 November 1921. Reprinted in *Verslag*, vol. 30, pts. 4–5, pp. 208–13.

1922
Dubois, Eugène, 'Over den schedelvorm van *Homo neandertalensis* en van *Pithecanthropus erectus*, bepaald door mechanisme factoren'. *Verslag*, vol. 30, pt. 7, pp. 391–411.

——, 'The Proto-Australian Fossil Man of Wadjak, Java'. *PKAW*, vol. 23, pt. 7, pp. 1031–51.

——, 'On the Significance of the Large Cranial Capacity of *Homo neandertalensis*'. *PKAW*, vol. 23, pt. 8, pp. 1271–88.

——, 'On the Motion of Ground Water in Frost and Thawing Weather'. *PKAW*, vol. 24, pts. 6/7, pp. 313–32.

——, 'On the Cranial Form of *Homo neandertalensis* and *Pithecanthropus erectus*, Determined by Mechanical Factors'. *PKAW*, vol. 24, pts. 6/7, pp. 307–32.

——, 'Phylogenetische en Ontogenetische toeneming van het volumen der hersenen bij de Gewervelde Dieren'. *Verslag*, vol. 31, pt. 6, pp. 307–32.

——, 'Hat sich das Gehirn beim Haushunde, im Vergleich mit Wildhuntarten, vergrössert oder verkleinert?' *Bijdragen tot de Dierkunde*, pt. 22, pp. 315–20.

1923
——, 'Phylogenetic and Ontogenetic Increase of the Volume of the Brain in Vertebrata'. *PKAW*, vol. 25, pts. 7–8, pp. 230–55.

——, 'Limburg's bodem als getuige van klimaatsveranderingen'. *Handelingen 19de Nederlandsch Natuur- en Geneeskundig Congres, Maastricht 5–7 April 1923*, pp. 50–68.

——, 'De voornaamste eigenschappen van den schedel en de hersenen van *Pithecanthropus erectus*'. *Algemeen Handelsblad*, 27 May 1923, Ochtendblad.

——, 'Over de onderkaak en het gebit van *Pithecanthropus erectus*'. *Algemeen Handelsblad*, 25 November 1923, Ochtendblad.

1924

——, 'Over de voornaamste eigenschappen van den schedel en de hersenen, de onderkaak en het gebit van *Pithecanthropus erectus*'. *Verslag*,
vol. 32, pt. 9, pp. 135–48.

——, 'On the Principal Characters of the Cranium and Brain, the
Mandible and the Teeth of *Pithecanthropus erectus*'. *PKAW*, vol. 27,
pts. 3–4, pp. 265–78.

——, 'Over de hersenhoeveelheid van gespecialiseerde zoogdierges-
lachten'. *Verslag*, vol. 33, pt. 4, pp. 319–26.

——, 'On the Brain Quantity of Specialized Genera of Mammals'.
PKAW, vol. 27, pts. 5–6, pp. 430–37.

——, 'Figures of the Calvarium and Endocranial Cast, a Fragment of
the Mandible and Three Teeth of *Pithecanthropus erectus*'. *PKAW*,
vol. 27, pts. 5/6, pp. 459–64.

1925

——, 'Geologische aanvulling van de mededeeling aan den heer Bolk:
over het bestaan van een langhoofdig Gorillaras'. *Verslag*, vol. 34, pt.
3, p. 285.

——, 'Het palaeothermale probleem en de evolutie der Zon'. *Algemeen
Handelsblad*, 7 March 1925, Avondblad.

——, 'Het palaeothermale probleem in het licht van de reus- en dwerg-
theorie der stellaire evolutie'. *Algemeen Handelsblad*, 31 May 1925,
Ochtendblad. Also published in *Verslag*, vol. 34, pt. 6, pp. 539–56.

——, 'The Paleothermal Problem in Light of the Giant and Dwarf
Theory of Stellar Evolution'. *PKAW*, vol. 28, pt. 6, pp. 587–604.

——, 'Over de Plaats van den *Pithecanthropus* onder de Primaten en
zijn genealogische Betrekkingen, naar de Beschouwingen van Boule'.
Vakblad voor Biologen, vol. 7, no. 1, pp. 1–5.

1926

——, 'Het palaeothermale probleem, poolverplaatsing en de evolutie
der zon'. *Verslag Geologische Sectie Geologie-Mijnbouw Generale
Nederlandsch Kolonie*, vol. 3, pt. 5, pp. 123–31.

——, 'Over de voornaamste onderscheidende eigenschappen van het
femur van *Pithecanthropus erectus*'. *Verslag*, vol. 35, pt. 3, pp.
443–55.

——, 'On the Principal Characters of the Femur of *Pithecanthropus
erectus*'. *PKAW*, vol. 29, pt. 5, pp. 730–43.

——, 'Over brokken van glaciaal geslepen en geschramde rotsbodems
als zwerfsteenen in ons Diluvium'. *Verslag Geologische Sectie*

Geologie-Mijnbouw Generale Nederlandsch Kolonie, vol. 3, pt. 5, pp. 144–45.

——, '*Manis palaejavanica*, het reuzenschubdier der Kendeng-fauna'. *Algemeen Handelsblad*, 31 October 1926, Ochtendblad.

——, '*Manis palaejavanica*, het reuzenschubdier der Kendeng-fauna'. *Verslag*, vol. 35, pt. 8, pp. 949–58.

——, '*Pithecanthropus erectus*. De "nieuwe *Pithecanthropus*-vondst"'. *Nieuwe Rotterdamsche Courant*, 8 December 1926, Avondblad.

——, 'De zoogenaamde "*Pithecanthropus*"-vondst'. *Nieuwe Rotterdamsche Courant*, 8 December 1926, Avondblad C.

——, 'De zoogenaamde nieuwe *Pithecanthropus*-vondst'. *Algemeen Handelsblad*, 18/19 December 1926, Avondblad/Ochtendblad.

——, '*Manis palaejavanica*, the Giant Pangolin of the Kendeng Fauna'. *PKAW*, vol. 29, pt. 9, pp. 1233–43.

——, 'Figures of the femur of *Pithecanthropus erectus*'. *PKAW*, vol. 29, pt. 9, pp. 1275–77.

1927
——, 'De zoogenaamde nieuwe *Pithecanthropus*-vondst'. *Verslag*, vol. 36, pt. 1, pp. 62–6.

——, 'The So-Called New *Pithecanthropus* Skull'. *PKAW*, vol. 30, pt. 1, pp. 134–37.

——, 'Über die Hauptmerkmale des Femur von *Pithecanthropus erectus*'. *Anthropologische Anzeiger*, vol. 4, pt. 2, pp. 131–46.

——, 'Opmerkingen over eenige uitkomsten der Palaeontologie met betrekking tot de evolutie der dierenwereld'. *Handelingen 21ste Nederlandsch Natuur- en Geneeskundig Congres, Amsterdam 19–21 April 1927*, pp. 150–51.

Dubois, Eugène, en L. M. R. Rutten, 'Verslag omtrent het verzoek van het Natuurhistorisch Genootschap in Limburg, gericht tot den Minister van Onderwijs, Kunsten, en Wetenschappen, om een jaarlijksch subsidie groot f. 1000.– etc'. *Verslag*, vol. 36, pt. 9, pp. 252–59.

Dubois, Eugène, 'De *Pithecanthropus*'. *Haarlem's Dagblad*, 30 September 1927.

1928
——. 'De Wet der noodwendige phylogenetische volmaking van het Psychoencephalon'. *Verslag*, vol. 37, pt. 3, pp. 252–59.

——, 'The Law of the Necessary Phylogenetic Perfection of the Psychoencephalon'. *PKAW*, vol. 31, pt. 3, pp. 304–14.

1930

——, 'De Aapmensch'. Catalogus van de Afdeeling Wetenschap in het Nederlandsch Paviljoen der Internationale Tentoonstelling te Luik. Leiden: S. C. van Doesburgh, pp. 118–20, 122.

——, 'L'homme singe'. Catalogue de la Section des Sciences dans le Pavillon Néerlandais de l'Exposition Internationale à Liège. Leiden: S. C. Doesburgh, pp. 119, 121, 123.

——, 'Die phylogenetische Grosshirnzunahme autonome Vervollkommnung der animalen Funktionen'. Biologica Generalis, vol. 6, pt. 2, pp. 247–92.

——, 'Corrections and additions "Die phylogenetische Grosshirnzunahme…"' Biologica Generalis, vol. 6, unknown page.

——, 'Phyloblastese het beginsel en de grondvoorwaarde der aanpassingsbetrekkingen'. Algemeen Handelsblad, 28 September 1930.

1931

——, 'Over de afneming van het zoetwaterlichaam in Holland's duinen door menschelijk ingrijpen'. Handelingen 23ste Nederlandsch Natuur- en Geneeskundig Congres, Delft 7–9 April, 1931, pp. 251–53.

1932

——, 'The distinct organization of Pithecanthropus of which the femur bears evidence, now confirmed from other individuals of the described species'. PKAW, vol. 35, pt. 6, pp. 716–22.

——, 'Praehistorische Vondsten'. Algemeen Handelsblad, 12 May 1932, Ochtendblad.

——, 'Schakelvorm tusschen Mensch en Dier'. Algemeen Handelsblad, 10 June 1932, Avonblad.

——, 'Early Man in Java'. Nature, vol. 130, no. 3270, p. 20.

——, 'De afzonderlijke organisatie van Pithecanthropus, waarvan het femur getuigt, thans bevestigd door andere individuen van de beschreven soort'. Verslag, vol. 41, pt. 6, pp. 76–77.

1933

——, 'De schijnbare en de werkelijke cephalisatie van den Australischen inboorling'. Algemeen Handelsblad, 29 January 1933, Ochtendblad.

——, 'De schijnbare en de werkelijke cephalisatie van den Australischen inboorling'. Verslag, vol. 42, pt. 1, p. 10.

——, 'The seeming and real cephalization of the Australian aborigine'. PKAW, vol. 36, pt. 2, pp. 2–13.

——, 'Corrigendum to "The seeming and real cephalization of the Australian aborigine"'. PKAW, vol. 36, pt. 2, p. 240.

——, 'De vorm der Hersenen bij *Sinanthropus* en bij *Pithecanthropus*'. *Algemeen Handelsblad*, 26 March 1933, Ochtendblad.

——, 'De vorm en de grootte der hersenen bij *Sinanthropus* en bij *Pithecanthropus*'. *Verslag*, vol. 42, pt. 3, pp. 40–42.

——, 'Corrigenda'. *Verslag*, vol. 42, pt. 4, p. 53.

——, 'The Shape and Size of the Brain in *Sinanthropus* and in *Pithecanthropus*'. *PKAW*, vol. 36, pt. 4, pp. 415–23.

——, 'Repliek'. *TAG*, vol. 50, p. 785.

1934

——, 'New Evidence of the Distinct Organization of *Pithecanthropus*'. *PKAW*, vol. 37, pt. 3, pp. 139–45.

——, 'Bespreking van "The Age of *Pithecanthropus*" door L. J. C. van Es'. *Mensch en Maatschappij*, vol. 10, pt. 3, 6 pages.

——, 'Phylogenetic Cerebral Growth'. *Congrès Internationale de Sciences Anthropologiques et Ethnologiques*, Comptes rendus de la première session, Londres 1934, pp. 71–5.

——, 'Über die Gleichheit der Cephalisationsstufe aller Menschen-gruppen bei verschiedenem spezifischen Gehirnvolumen'. *Biologica Generalis*, vol. 10, pt. 1, pp. 185–93.

1935

——, 'On the Gibbonlike appearance of *Pithecanthropus erectus*'. *PKAW*, vol. 38, pt. 6, pp. 578–85.

——, '*Pithecanthropus erectus* als organisme'. *Handelingen 25ste Nederlandsch Natuur- en Geneeskundig Congres, Leiden 23–25 April 1935*, pp. 147–59.

——, 'The sixth (fifth new) femur of *Pithecanthropus erectus*'. *PKAW*, vol. 38, pt. 8, pp. 850–53.

1936

——, 'Nieuwe *Pithecanthropus* ontdekt?' *Algemeen Handelsblad*, 18 April 1936, Avondblad, 5de blad, p. 10.

——, 'Een nieuwe *Pithecanthropus* ontdekt?' *Het Vaderland*, 18 April 1936, Avondblad 13.

——, 'Strijd om een Schedel'. *De Telegraaf*, 19 April 1936, 5de blad, p. 11.

——, 'Brief aan Prof. Dr. J. P. Kleiweg de Zwaan, Voorzitter van het Nederlandsch Nationaal Bureau voor Anthropologie, te Amsterdam'. *Mensch en Maatschappij*, vol. 12, pt. 4, pp. 303–304.

——, 'Over fossiele Menschen en den *Pithecanthropus*'. *Nieuwe Rotterdamsche Courant*, 26 July 1936, Ochtendblad 13.

——, 'Fossiele Menschen en *Pithecanthropus*. De jongste vondst op Java geen *Pithecanthropus*. II'. *Nieuwe Rotterdamsche Courant*, 2 August 1936, Ochtendblad 13, p. 2.

——, 'Fossiele Menschen en *Pithecanthropus*. *Pithecanthropus* geen mensch. III'. *Nieuwe Rotterdamsche Courant*, 12 August 1936, Avondblad E, p. 2.

——, 'Fossiele Menschen en *Pithecanthropus*. Rectificatie'. *Nieuwe Rotterdamsche Courant*, 22 August 1936, Avondblad 13, p. 3.

——, 'Fossiele Menschen en *Pithecanthropus*'. *Nieuwe Rotterdamsche Courant*, August 1936. (Reprint of four publications immediately above with corrections and an additional figure.)

——, 'Racial Identity of *Homo soloensis* Oppenoorth (including *Homo modjokertensis* von Koenigswald) and *Sinanthropus pekinensis* Davidson Black'. *PKAW*, vol. 39, pt. 10, pp. 1180–85.

1937
——, 'On the Fossil Human Skulls recently discovered in Java and *Pithecanthropus erectus*'. *Man*, vol. 37, art. no. 1, pp. 1–7.

——, 'The osteone arrangement of the thigh-bone compacta of Man identical with that first found of *Pithecanthropus*'. *PKAW*, vol. 40, pt. 10, pp. 864–70.

——, 'Early Man in Java and *Pithecanthropus erectus*'. In G. G. MacCurdy, ed., *Early Man*, Philadelphia: J. B. Lippincott Company, pp. 315–22.

1938
——, 'Prof. Dr. Eug. Dubois over den *Pithecanthropus erectus* (verslag van een lezing, gemaakt door Dr. E. M. Krutzer)'. *Natuurhistorisch maandblad*, vol. 27, pt. 9, pp. 92–5.

——, 'The mandible recently described and attributed to the *Pithecanthropus* by G. H. R. von Koenigswald, compared with the mandible of *Pithecanthropus erectus* described in 1924 by Eug. Dubois'. *PKAW*, vol. 41, pt. 2, pp. 139–47.

——, 'On the fossil human skull recently described and attributed to *Pithecanthropus erectus* by G. H. R. von Koenigswald'. *PKAW*, vol. 41, pt. 4, pp. 380–86.

——, 'Over de spronggrootte van den phylogenetischen en ontogenetischen Hersengroei'. *Vakblad voor Biologen*, vol. 20, pt. 3, pp. 37–46.

1939
——, 'Explanatory Statement concerning the communication of Eug. Dubois in Proceedings K.N.A.W., vol. 41, no. 4, 1938; On the fossil

human skull recently described and attributed to *Pithecanthropus erectus* by G. H. R. von Koenigswald'. *PKAW*, vol. 42, pt. 1, p. 53.

——, 'On insignificance of cranial vault-height in phylogenetic brain-growth'. *PKAW*, vol. 42, pt. 2, pp. 125–26.

1940

——, 'The fossil human remains discovered in Java by Dr. G. H. R. von Koenigswald and attributed by him to *Pithecanthropus erectus*, in reality remains of *Homo wadjakensis* (syn. *Homo soloensis*)'. *PKAW*, vol. 43, pt. 4, pp. 494–96.

——, 'The fossil human remains discovered in Java by Dr. G. H. R. von Koenigswald and attributed by him to *Pithecanthropus erectus*, in reality remains of *Homo soloensis*'. *PKAW*, vol. 43, pt. 5, p. 653. (This is an announcement of a change of title.)

——, 'The fossil human remains discovered in Java by Dr. G. H. R. von Koenigswald and attributed by him to *Pithecanthropus erectus*, in reality remains of *Homo soloensis*. Continuation'. *PKAW*, vol. 43, pt. 7, pp. 842–51.

——, Idem., *PKAW*, vol. 43, pt. 9, p. 1142. (Corrigenda to above.)

——, 'The fossil human remains discovered in Java by Dr. G. H. R. von Koenigswald and attributed by him to *Pithecanthropus erectus*, in reality remains of *Homo sapiens soloensis*. Conclusion'. *PKAW*, vol. 43, no. 10, pp. 1268–75.

PART II. LITERATURE CITED

Andrews, R. C., *On the Trail of Ancient Man*. 1926. New York: G. P. Putnam's Sons.

Anonymous, *B.S. Name-List/Address-Book of the Dutch Indies 1822–1923*.

Anonymous, ('Homo Erectus'), 'Palaeontologische onderzoekingen op Java'. *Bataviaasch Nieuwsblad*, 6 February 1893, no. 57.

Anonymous, 'Notes', *Nature*, 3 January 1895, vol. 51, p. 230.

Anonymous, 'Interview with Madame Selenka'. *Bataviaasch Nieuwsblad*, 25 April 1907.

Anonymous, 'Report of views of Dr. Van Stein Callenfels'. *Handelsblad*, 24 July 1936.

Anonymous, 'Prehistoric Congress in Oslo, lecture of Dr. Van Stein Callenfels'. *De Telegraaf*, 8 August 1936.

Anonymous, '*Homo modjokertensis*: Lecture of Dr. Von Koenigswald'. *Handelsblad*, 29 August 1936.

Anonymous, 'Lecture of Dr. Van Stein Callenfels'. *Handelsblad*, 22 October 1936.

Anonymous, 'Praehistorische vondsten op Java; Voordracht Dr. Van Stein Callenfels'. *Handelsblad*, 29 October 1936.

Anonymous, 'Dr Von Königswald, Studiereis naar Europa'. *Handelsblad*, 7 November 1936.

Anonymous, 'De Fossiele Mensch van Java; De Weg der Evolutie; De beroemdste is nog altijd de *Pithecanthropus*'. *Handelsblad*, 18 January 1938.

Anonymous, 'Prof. Dubois blikt over zijn leven terug'. *De Telegraaf*, 27 January 1938.

Anonymous, 'Uitgegeven door de Indische Genealogische Vereniging'. *INN*, 1988–1997.

Balchior, G., 'The Peking Man – An Undamaged Skull'. *Manchester Guardian*, 30 December 1929.

Beekman, E. M., 'Introduction'. In P. A. Daum, *Ups and Downs of Life in the Indies*. 1987, Amherst: University of Massachusetts Press, pp. 1–49.

Bemmelen, J. F. van, 'Het Leidsche internationale zoölogencongres: Dubois's aapmensch voor de vierschaar der wetenschaap'. *Java-bode*, November 1895, vol. 16.

Bemmelen, J. M. van, 'Der Gehalt an Fluorcalcium eines fossilen Elephantenknochen aus der Tertiärzeit.' *Zeitschrift für anorganische Chemie*, 1897, vol. 15: pp. 84–122.

Black, D., 'On a Lower Molar from the Chou Kou Tien Deposits'. *Paleontologica Sinica*, 1927, ser. C, vol. 7, fasc. I.

Black D., 'Interim Report on the Skull of *Sinanthropus*'. *Annual Meeting of the Geological Society of China*, 29 March 1930.

Bloys van Treslong Prins, P. C., *GHG*, 1934–1939, vol. 1–4. Batavia: Drukeerij Albrecht.

——, *BRP*, 1993, vol. 5. 's Gravenhage: J. C. Boutong de Katzmann.

Boule, M., 'L'homme fossile de La Chapelle-aux-Saints'. *Annales de Paléontologie*. 1911–1913, Paris.

Brongersma, L. D., 'Professor Dr. Eug. Dubois'. *Nieuwe Rotterdamsche Courant*. 28 January 1938.

——, 'Eugène Dubois'. *Natuurhistorich maandblad*, 1973, vol. 62: pp. 107–109.

——, '*Pithecanthropus*: Echt en "Pseudo"'. *Verslag*, 1982, vol. 91: 34–36.

——, 'The Vicissitudes of the Dubois Collection'. Unpublished manuscript, n.d., Dubois Archives, Naturalis.

Corbey, R., 'Ethnographic Showcases, 1870–1930'. *Cultural Anthropology*, 1993, vol. 8, no. 3, pp. 338–96.

Couperus, L., *The Hidden Force*. 1985. Translated by A. Teixeira de Mattos. Amherst: University of Massachusetts Press. Originally published as *De Stille Kracht*. 1900, Amsterdam: L. J. Veen.

Cunningham, D. J., 'Dr. Dubois's So-called Missing Link'. *Nature*, 1894–5, vol. 51, pp. 428–29.

——, 'A Paper on *Pithecanthropus erectus*, the Man-Like Transitional Form of Dr. Eug. Dubois'. *Journal of Anatomy and Physiology*, 1895, vol. 29, n.s. 8, pp. 18–19.

Daum, P. A., *Ups and Down of Life in the Indies*. 1987, Amherst: University of Massachusetts Press. Translated by Elsje and Donald Sturtevant. Originally published as *Ups en downs in het Indische leven*. 1890. Batavia: Feuilleton.

Dekker, E. D. (pseudonym Multatulti), *Max Havelaar*. 1982, Amherst: University of Massachusetts Press. Translated by Roy Edwards. Originally published 1860. Amsterdam: Van Oorschot.

Deyssel, L. van, *Blank en Geel*. 1979. Amsterdam. (Originally published 1892.)

Dubois, J. M. F., 'Trinil: A Biography of Prof. Dr. Eugène Dubois the Discoverer of *Pithecanthropus erectus*'. 1957. Unpublished ms. in Dubois Archives.

Duckworth, W. H. L., *Prehistoric Man*. 1912. Cambridge, UK: Cambridge University Press.

Feen, P. J. van der, and W. S. S. van Bentham-Jutting, 'Antje Schreuder, Amsterdam, 15 november 1887–Amsterdam, 2 februari 1952'. *Geologie en mijnbouw*, 1952, vol. 14, pp. 121–25.

Flower, W. H., 'Discussion of Dubois's "On *Pithecanthropus erectus*, A Transitional Form between Man and the Apes"'. *JAI*, 1896, vol. 25, p. 248.

Garson, J., 'Discussion of Dubois's "On *Pithecanthropus erectus*, A Transitional Form between Man and the Apes"'. *JAI*, 1896, vol. 25, pp. 251–52.

Gorjanovič-Kramberger, D., 'Der diluviale Mensch von Krapina in Kroatien: ein Beitrag zur Paläoanthropologie'. 1906. In O. Walkoff, ed., *Studien über die Entwicklungsmechanik des Primatenskelletes*. Kriedel, Wiesbaden, pp. 59–277.

Haddon, A. C., *History of Anthropology*. 1910. London: Watts and Co.

Haeckel, E., *The History of Creation*. Fourth English, 1892. London: Kegan Paul, Trench, Trubner & Co., Ltd.

——, 'On our present knowledge of the origin of Man'. *Annual Report of the Board of Regents of the Smithsonian Institution for the year ending June 30, 1898*. 1899. Pp. 461–80. Translation of a discourse given at the Fourth International Congress of Zoologists at Cambridge, England, 26 August 1898.

Hrdlička, A., 'The Most Ancient Skeletal Remains of Man'. 1914, *Annual Report of the Smithsonian Institution*, 1914, pp. 491–552.

——, *The Skeletal Remains of Early Man*. 1930. Washington, DC: Smithsonian Miscellaneous Collections, vol. 83.

Janus, C., and W. Brashler, *The Search for Peking Man*. 1975. New York: Macmillan.

Jerison, H., *Evolution of the Brain and Intelligence*. 1973. New York: Academic Press.

Kate, H. ten, 'Review of Dubois's *Pithecanthropus erectus*, eine menschenaehnliche Uebergangsform aus Java'. *Nederlandsch koloniaal centraalblad*, 1894–95, vol. 1, pp. 127–29.

Keith, A., 'Discussion of Dubois's "On *Pithecanthropus erectus*, A Transitional Form between Man and the Apes"'. *JAI*, 1896, vol. 25, p. 253.

——, *Ancient Types of Man*. 1911. New York and London: Harper & Bros.

——, *Antiquity of Man*. 1925. London: Williams and Northgate.

——, *An Autobiography*. 1950. London: Watts.

Koenigswald, G. H. R. von, '*Pithecanthropus erectus*, Antwoord Dr. Von Koenigswald'. *Algemeen Handelsblad*, 7 May 1936.

——, 'Een nieuwe *Pithecanthropus* ondekt'. *Algemeen Indische Dagblad*, 28 March 1936.

——, 'Erste Mitteilung über einen fossilen Hominiden aus den Altpleistocän Ostjavas'. *PKAW*, 1936, vol. 39, no. 8, pp. 1000–1009. Communicated at the meeting of 26 September 1936.

——, 'Ein Unterkieferfragment des *Pithecanthropus* aus den Trinilschichten Mittenjavas'. *PKAW*, 1937, vol. 40, pp. 883–93.

——, 'A review of the stratigraphy of Java and its relations to early man'. In G. G. MacCurdy, ed., *Early Man*. 1937. Philadelphia: J. B. Lippincott and Co., pp. 23–32.

——, '*Pithecanthropus* received into human family'. *Illustrated London News*, 11 December 1937.

——, 'Ein neuer *Pithecanthropus*-Schädel'. *PKAW*, 1938, vol. 41, pp. 185–92.

——, *Meeting Prehistoric Man*. 1956. London: Thames & Hudson.

Koenigswald, G. H. R. von, and F. Weidenreich, 'The relationship between *Pithecanthropus* and *Sinanthropus*'. *Nature*, 1939, vol. 144, pp. 926–29.

Lanpo, J., and H. Weiwen, *The Story of Peking Man from Archaeology to Mystery.* 1990. Translated by Yin Zhinqui. Beijing: Foreign Languages Press.

Leakey, R. E., and J. Slikkerveer, *Man-ape, Ape-man.* 1993. Leiden: Netherlands Foundation for Kenya Wildlife Service.

Litchfield, H., ed., *Emma Darwin: A Century of Family Letters.* 1915. London: Murray.

Locher-Schloten, E., 'So Close and Yet So Far'. In J. Clancy-Smith and F. Gouda, eds., *Domesticating the Empire.* 1998. Charlottesville: University Press of Virginia, pp. 131–53.

Lydekker, R., 'Notices of Siwalik Mammals'. *Records of the Geological Survey of India,* 1879, vol. 12, pp. 33–52.

——, 'Siwalik Mammalia'. Memoirs of the Geological Survey of India. *Palaeontologica India,* 1886, s. 10, *Indian Tertiary and Post-Tertiary Vertebrata,* vol. 4, pt. 1, pp. 1–18.

——, 'Review of Dubois's *Pithecanthropus erectus.* Eine menschenaehnliche Uebergangsform aus Java'. *Nature,* 1895, vol. 51, p. 291.

MacBride, F. W., *Evolution.* 1928, London: Sixpenny Library Series.

Marsh, O., 'On the *Pithecanthropus erectus,* from the Tertiary of Java'. *American Journal of Science,* 1895, s.4, vol. 1. pp. 475–82.

——, 'A Commentary on Dubois's "*Pithecanthropus erectus,* eine menschenaehnliche Uebergangsform"'. *Compte-rendu des séances du Troisième Congrès International de Zoologie, Leyde, 11–16 September 1895.* 1896. Leiden, p. 272.

Martin, K., 'Ueberreste vorweltlicher Proboscidier auf Java und Banka'. *Sammlungen des Geologischen Reichs-Museums in Leiden,* 1884–89, vol. 4, pp. 1–24.

——, 'Fossile Säugethierreste von Java und Japan.' *Sammlungen des Geologischen Reichs-Museums in Leiden,* 1884-89, vol. 4, pp. 25–69.

——, 'Kritische Bedenken gegen den *Pithecanthropus erectus* Dubois'. *Globus,* 1895, vol. 67, pp. 213–17.

Matschie, P., 'Noch einmal *Pithecanthropus erectus'. Naturwissenschaftliche Wochenschrift,* 1895, vol. 10, pp. 122–23.

Nuland, S., *Doctors: The Biography of Medicine.* 1988. New York: Vintage Books.

O'Mulligan, unknown first name, 'Bones of Contention'. *The Evening Telegraph,* (Dublin), 23 November 1895.

Oppenoorth, W. F. F., '*Homo (Javanthropus) soloensis.* Een pleistocene mensch van Java'. *Wetenschappelijke mededelingen Dienst van den Mijnbouw in Nederlandsch-Indië,* 1932, vol. 20, pp. 49–63.

——, 'De vondst van palaeolitische menschelijke schedels op Java'. *De Mijningingenieur,* June 1932.

Osborn, H. F., *Men of the Old Stone Age*. 1915, New York: Scribner's.

——, 'Foreword'. In R. C. Andrews, *On the Trail of Ancient Man*. 1926. New York: G. P. Putnam's Sons.

Pattynama, P., 'Secrets and Danger'. In J. Clancy-Smith and F. Gouda, eds., *Domesticating the Empire*. 1998. Charlottesville: University Press of Virginia, pp. 84–107.

Pieters, F., and J. de Visser, 'The scientific career of the zoologist Max Wilhelm Carl Weber (1852–1937)'. *Bijdragen tot de Dierkunde*, 1993, vol. 62, no. 4, pp. 193–214.

Ricklefs, M. C., *A History of Modern Indonesia Since c. 1300*. 1993. Stanford: Stanford University Press.

Rietschoten, B. D. van, 'Uit een schrijven van den heer Van Rietschoten te Blitar'. *NT*, 1889, vol. 48, pp. 346–47.

Schaaffhausen, H., 'On the crania of the most ancient races of man'. *Natural History Review*, 1 April 1861, no. 2, pp. 155–80. Translated by G. Busk from H. Schaaffhausen, 'Zur Kentniss der ältesten Rassenschädel'. *Archiv für Anatomie, Physiologie und wissenschaftliche Medicin*, 1858, vol. 2, pp. 453–88.

Schwalbe, G., 'Ziele und Wege einer vergleichenden physischen Anthropologie'. *Zeitschrift für Morphologie und Anthropologie*, 1899, vol. 1, pp. 1–15.

Selenka, M., 'Die fossile Zähne von Trinil'. *TAG*, 1909, s. 2, vol. 26, pp. 398–99. (Includes comments from Schlosser, Walkoff, and Dubois.)

Shapiro, H., *Peking Man*. 1974. New York: Simon & Schuster.

Shipman, P., *The Evolution of Racism*. 1994. New York: Simon & Schuster.

Spencer, F., *Piltdown, A Scientific Forgery*. 1990. New York: Oxford University Press.

——, *The Piltdown Papers*. 1990. New York: Oxford University Press.

——, *Aleš Hrdlička, M.D., 1896–1943: A Chronicle of the Life and Work of an American Physical Anthropologist*. 1979. Ph.D. dissertation, University of Michigan. Ann Arbor: University Microfilms.

Teilhard de Chardin, P., *Letters from a Traveller*. 1962. London: Collins.

Tesch, P., and L. D. Brongersma, 'Eugène Dubois'. *Geologie en Mijnbouw*, 1941, vol. 3, no. 2, pp. 29–33.

Theunissen, B., *Eugène Dubois and the Ape-man from Java*. 1989. Dordrecht: Kluwer Academic Publishers.

——, and J. de Vos, 'Eugène Dubois, ontdekker can de rechtopgaande aapmens'. *Natuurhistorisch maandblad*, 1982, vol. 71, nos. 6–7, pp. 107–114.

Thomson, J. A., 'Discussion of Dubois's "On *Pithecanthropus erectus*, A Transitional Form between Man and the Apes"'. *JAI*, 1896, vol. 25, pp. 253–54.

Timmerman, J. A. C. A., 'Belangrijke palaeontologische vondsten op Java'. *TAG*, 1893, s. 2, vol. 10, pp. 310–12.

Tobias, P. V. T., 'Life and Work of Professor Dr. G. H. R. von Koenigswald'. In *Auf den Spuren des Pithecanthropus*. 1984. Frankfurt: Waldemar Kramer, pp. 25–95.

Trinkaus, E., and P. Shipman, *The Neandertals*. 1992. New York: Knopf.

Turner, W., 'On M. Dubois's Description of Remains Recently Found in Java, Named by Him *Pithecanthropus erectus*. With Remarks on So-Called Transitional Forms between Apes and Man'. *Journal of Anatomy and Physiology*, 1896, vol. 29, n.s. 9, pp. 424–45.

——, 'Discussion of Dubois's "On *Pithecanthropus erectus*: A Transitional Form between Man and the Apes"'. *JAI*, 1896, vol. 25, p. 249.

Virchow, R., 'Commentary on Krause's discussion of Dubois's "*Pithecanthropus erectus, eine menschenaehnliche Uebergangsform aus Java*"'. *Zeitschrift für Ethnologie*, 1895, vol. 27, pp. 81–88.

——, 'Die Frage von dem *Pithecanthropus erectus*'. *Zeitschrift für Ethnologie*, 1895, vol. 27, pp. 435–42.

——, 'Commentary on Dubois's "*Pithecanthropus erectus*, betrachtet als eine wirkliche Uebergangsform und als Stammform des Menschen"'. *Zeitschrift für Ethnologie*, 1895, vol. 27, pp. 744–47.

Vos, J. de, '*Homo modjokertensis* – vindplaats, ouderdom en fauna'. 1994, *Cranium*, vol. 11, no. 2, pp. 103–107.

Wallace, A. R., *The Geographical Distribution of Animals*. 1876. London: Macmillan.

Wassing, R., and R. Wassing-Visser, *Adoeh, Indië!* 1992. Atrium: The Hague.

Weidenreich, F., 'Morphology of Solo Man'. *Anthropological Papers of the American Museum of Natural History*, NY, 1951, vol. 43, pt. 3.

Acknowledgements

Some ten or so years ago, John de Vos of the Naturalis asked if I would be interested in 'doing something' with the underutilized Dubois Archives, of which he had become the curator. The twinkle in his eye should have warned me that he was inviting me to acquire an obsession, but even had I understood – and I did not – I would not have passed up the opportunity. John has been endlessly patient, knowledgeable, and helpful. At an early stage in this work, he put me in touch with a potential assistant, Paul Storm, then a graduate student studying the Wadjak fossils. Over the years, Paul earned his own Ph.D. and then worked part-time for me translating nearly all of the Dutch and German documents used in this work and tirelessly researching obscure bits of information in response to my queries. Paul has been an invaluable colleague, and this book would not have happened without his efforts. Additional translations from the Dutch were made by Marcel van Tuinen, to whom I am grateful. Ans Molenkamp and Caroline Pepermans of the Naturalis were wonderfully helpful with illustrations, some of which were printed from the original glass negatives by Hans de Herder of the Nationaal Fotografie Restoratie Atelier. My first forays into the Dubois Archives, Paul's participation (and my travel costs) were funded by a grant to me from the Wenner-Gren Foundation.

Marijke Gijsbers kindly provided information about De Bedelaar. Living descendants of Eugène and Victor Dubois – Jean M. Dubois in California, and Victor Dubois, Nelleke Hooijer, and A. Hooijer-Ruben in Holland – trusted me with family documents and photographs, told me family stories, and gave me permission to quote from Jean M. F. Dubois's unpublished book, 'Trinil'. Joost P. M. van Heijst, Secretary of the Dutch Franciscans, gave permission for the quotations from Bernsen's diary. Christine Hertler kindly shared information with me, as did Bert Theunissen. The Hovens family showed me through Dubois's childhood home in Eijsden.

The adventure of my first trip to Java would not have been nearly so much fun without my travelling companion and friend, Sally

McCutcheon. Our drivers, Anto Sanyoto (kindly recommended to me by Heri Harjono) and Dodif Hendro Susilo helped me find places where Dubois had lived or worked and showed me traces of Dutch colonial life in Java. The amazingly efficient and charming Yodha Susanti, of the Hotel Tugu in Malang, understood my unusual quest and arranged many things for me, including a visit to a coffee plantation in Wlingi, which serves as my model for Mringin. In Jakarta, Veronica Grasman and Cynthia Mackie willingly gave time to help a friend of a friend. The people of Java themselves were astonishingly kind to a blonde, blue-eyed foreigner who came looking for the past in their country.

The BBC paid my way to Java for my second visit, and the film crew – Charlie Smith, Philip Martin, Alicky Lockhart, Steve Robinson, Mike Carling, Fraser Barber, and, from the Discovery Channel, Alex Mittendorf – made for a marvellous, productive, and laughter-filled trip. Without them, I would never have been paddled down the Solo River in a prahu or sprained my ankle and covered myself in mud slipping down the banks of the Solo.

At home, the mainstay of my life, my first reader, and my best friend is my husband, Alan Walker, who only rarely complained about my obsession with a man dead nearly sixty years. Alan provided several astonishing insights into Dubois's character. My cat, Amelia, assisted in much of the typing and my horse, Wigston Magna, did his best to give me perspective. My editorial colleagues at Penn State – Barbara Kennedy, Nancy Marie Brown, and Gigi Marino – read parts of the manuscript, giggled over my Indonesian adventures, and generally served as stalwart friends. Cheryl Glenn, Bill Earnshaw, Chris Dean, and Claire Van Vliet encouraged me to take on this strange and unusual book. Claire, bookmaker and printer extraordinaire, even offered to design it for me. Marla Caplan gave me the courage to go to Java, without which I could not have understood Dubois's life. At Simon & Schuster, Denise Roy had faith in my ability to write such a book and provided intelligent, gentle editing and occasional cheerleading.

Thank you all, so much. It has been great fun.

PICTURE CREDITS

Naturalis, the Nationaal Natuurhistorisch Museum (copyright Nationaal Natuurhistorich Museum, Leiden, the Netherlands): pages ii, 12, 46, 84, 121, 129, 133, 141, 144, 146, 154, 156, 157, 158, 162,

181, 196, 214, 224, 229, 240, 246, 257, 281, 309, 314, 331, 333, 347, 350, 352, 358, 361, 367, 414, 419, 428, 432, 453, 461, 490, 504; A. Hooijer-Ruben and Nelleke Hooijer: pages 78, 499; Jean M. Dubois: page 175; by permission of the Société d'Anthropologie de Paris: page 316; Anatomische les; G. J. Rooij/Universiteitmuseum De Agnietenkapel, Amsterdam: pages 49, 53, 401; Natur-Museum Senckenberg: pages 465, 484, 487; Smithsonian Institution Archives, Record Unit 9521, Oral History interviews with Thomas Dale Stewart, 1975, 1986 (negative number 4816): page 382; Neg./Transparency number 36106, courtesy of the Library, American Museum of Natural History: page 397; Förderverein Ernst-Hackel-Hause V: page 314; La Famille Lohest: page 61; pages 11, 68, 90, 261 drawn by Jeff Mathison expressly for this publication.

Index